Along the Trail with
LEWIS AND CLARK

SECOND EDITION

by **BARBARA FIFER** *and* **VICKY SODERBERG**
with maps by **JOSEPH MUSSULMAN**

MONTANA MAGAZINE

FARCOUNTRY PRESS

Acknowledgments

Many thanks to the advisers, all members of the Lewis and Clark Trail Heritage Foundation, who advised us and tried to protect us from our own mistakes: Robert N. Bergantino, Dave Borlaug, Charles V. Campbell, Tom Davis, Larry D. Epstein, Jim Fazio, Carolyn Gilman, Karen M. Goering, Jane Sale Henley, Mrs. Michael M. Howard, Kat Imhoff, Mimi Jackson, Barbara Kubik, Ron Loge, Robert Moore, Frank Muhly, Donald F. Nell, James M. Peterson, Chuck Raddon, Wilmer Rigby, Sheila Robinson, Steve Russell, Jane Schmoyer-Weber, Ernest W. Smith, Gene Swanzey, John E. Taylor, Richard N. Williams, the Lewis and Clark Bicentennial Council; and Washington State Governor's Lewis and Clark Trail Committee members Martin Plamondon II, Ralph H. Rudeen, Carole Simon-Smolinski; and Bill Hanson.

Front cover, top: Overlooking the Missouri River between Nebraska and Missouri. *Photo by Chuck Haney*
The **compass** is a replica of the one used by Meriwether Lewis, which is at the Smithsonian Institution. *Photo courtesy VIAs, Inc.*
Portraits of William Clark (at left) and Meriwether Lewis by Charles Willson Peale (1741-1847). *Courtesy Independence National Historic Park, Philadelphia*

ISBN 1-56037-188-9

© 2001 Montana Magazine

CONTENTS

How To Use This Book

The Maps

Based on USGS 1:100,000 quads

Reading the Maps. North is always up on the page, south is down, west is to your left, east to your right. To trace the expedition's westbound journey, read the chapters in consecutive order, and read the maps from right to left. To follow their eastbound return, read the chapters in reverse order, and read the maps from left to right.

Numerals in flags on the maps link to bracketed numerals ([1], [2], etc.) at the text describing them. Within each chapter, numerals were assigned in priority for that area—with [1] representing the most informative Lewis and Clark interpretation—and are not related to the Corps' movement through that area.

These maps are intended to be used with current state highway maps.

- No attempt has been made to show distinctions between paved and unpaved surfaces, since roads and highways are continually under construction or reconstruction.
- Some secondary state or county roads may be gravel surfaced, and during some seasons of the year are not suitable for certain types and sizes of vehicles.
- A warning symbol will be found next to a few roads, notably in Montana and Idaho. These indicate that some severe limitations prevail, such as steep grades, tight curves, surfaces impassable when wet, or absence of services.
- Small towns, villages, and settlements have not been differentiated with regard to size, but have been included primarily for reference, and may not all have tourist amenities or services.
- The scale is 1/8 inch to the mile (1 inch = 8 miles) in nearly all of the maps. In chapters 1, 2, 11, 14, and 22, refer to the graphic mileage scales.

The "Trail." The route of the Lewis and Clark Expedition is not a "trail" in any modern sense. The Corps traveled by various types of watercraft up and down six major western rivers, the Missouri, Jefferson, Beaverhead, Clearwater, Snake, and Columbia. When compelled to travel by land they often followed Indian "roads."

Therefore, the green federal and state highway identification symbols on the maps, corresponding to the familiar shapes of roadside signs, indicate only that a given road is more or less near to the actual water or land route of the expedition. It is difficult in general, and impossible in many instances, to follow the trail exactly as it was in 1804. Some of the places where one can actually retrace a portion of the trail are discussed in the "Touring Today" section of each chapter.

Parts or all of the party traveled by land, on foot or horseback:

- Westbound, from the headwaters of the Beaverhead River over the Rocky Mountains to the middle Clearwater River;
- Eastbound, in Washington, from the mouth of the Walla Walla River to the mouth of the Clearwater;
- Eastbound, Meriwether Lewis's party from Travelers' Rest to the vicinity of Fort Benton, Montana;
- Eastbound, William Clark's party from Travelers' Rest to Park City, 22 miles west of Billings, Montana.

The captains sometimes scouted ahead of the party, sometimes by intervals of several days, and a distance of many miles. Meanwhile, the expedition's hunters routinely ranged far on either side of the rivers and the land trails.

Lewis and Clark Expedition Campsites. Locations of the expedition's campsites, including Camp DuBois, Fort Mandan and Fort Clatsop, are only approximate. In fact, of the 600 different campsites the Corps of Discovery occupied between May 1804 and September 23, 1806, no one knows the exact location of a single one of them. In any case, many of the possible sites have long since been washed away by nearly 200 annual spring floods, or covered up by the waters of reservoirs on the Missouri, Snake and Columbia rivers. Many areas where they might have camped are now on private land. A few possible sites are on public land, such as Fort Clatsop.

Cautions:

- When traveling on Indian lands, be aware that certain locations may be sacred and should not be encroached upon. Do not explore or camp off the beaten path, and inquire locally if signs are absent or unclear.
- Respect the rights of property owners. In rural areas, property owners may be hard to find. If you can't get permission from the owner, stay off the land.
- Do not take artifacts from any place, either public or private land. The removal of historic artifacts from either public or private property is prohibited by state and/or federal laws. The removal of any object whatsoever, either natural or otherwise, from any national park, is prohibited.

Excerpts from the Journals. On the maps, excerpts from the westward journey are bordered in red; those from the homeward-bound journey are bordered in green. The journalists' original spelling, punctuation, and capitalization have been retained. Sergeant Gass's journals were edited and published in 1805; the original version was lost long ago. All excerpts have been selected from *The Journals of the Lewis and Clark Expedition*, edited by Gary Moulton (12 volumes, 1983–1999), and are reproduced by permission of the University of Nebraska Press, Lincoln, Nebraska.

HISTORY OVERVIEWS

We hope the historical overviews in this book will whet your appetite to learn more about the Corps of Discovery. Many, many books interpreting the whole expedition or specific facets are available; see "For Further Exploration" at the back of the book. Here you also will find organizations of people who continue to research, learn about, and savor this American story.

Quotations in the text from the journals are taken from The Journals of the Lewis and Clark Expedition, edited by Gary Moulton (12 volumes, 1983–1998), and are reproduced by permission of the University of Nebraska Press, Lincoln, Nebraska.

We've used spellings and punctuation from the Moulton edition exactly. Spelling the same word the same way every time was a relatively new idea in 1803. Noah Webster (1758-1843) spent his lifetime crusading to convince Amer-

icans to use American spellings and to adopt standardized spelling. And he had published his first "Blue-Backed Speller" just twenty years before Lewis began preparing for the expedition. The orthographically challenged can only envy the freedom the expedition's journalists enjoyed.

When a series of quotations comes from one journal writer, he is not re-identified at each passage. When a different writer is first quoted, his name is then given.

TOURING TODAY

Tracing Lewis and Clark's route today is still an adventure—how much of an adventure and how close to the realities encountered by the Corps is up to you.

Dramatic changes have occurred in the topography and development along the trail, but one factor has remained constant: diverse climates still exist. The same challenges of temperature extremes and snow (even in the summer), torrential rains, high winds and scorching heat face today's explorers.

Along the trail you'll encounter everything from interstate highways to unsurfaced roads but don't take this access for granted. Road conditions change quickly, making it critical to check with local authorities before traveling in unfamiliar areas. Snow closures, gumbo-mud roads, and flooding occur without warning and are common in many places throughout the year.

Access across rivers is limited; be sure you know which side of the river you need to be on to visit the sites on your list. Since most of the trail follows a river, careful planning may be necessary to avoid backtracking.

Museums and public properties rely heavily on donations to exist. If you've enjoyed your visit, please consider a contribution as your way of saying thank you.

General Tips—Top off your gas tank when you can, particularly in Iowa, the Dakotas, Montana and Idaho. Towns and services can be very far apart, or may close at 6 p.m. and on Sundays.

Carry plenty of water for the car and its passengers.

Don't rely on a cellular phone. It might not work in many mountainous and rural areas.

Call ahead to confirm hours for sites in

smaller towns. Schedules are often based on the availability of volunteers.

Wildlife viewing opportunities are abundant but keep in mind that despite their beauty, these are wild birds and animals—unpredictable and deadly. No photo is worth risking your life.

Along the Expedition's Path—Because of the extensive forest fires in Idaho and western Montana during the summer and fall of 2000, access to some areas may be restricted. Be sure to check with the forest Service for current information.

The significant attractions, interpretive sites and campgrounds along the trail are listed here. They appear in chronological order for the westbound journey. The remainder of related sites are listed under the town in which they're located. Expedition-related sites are designated with the following symbols: ★ ●

The listing of towns, attractions, accommodations and food service in this book is by no means exhaustive. Inclusion is not an endorsement, but an indication of the variety available.

Around the Area—Towns are listed alphabetically and include things to see and do, camping, lodging and restaurant options. The geography and proximity of locations in this section varies between chapters. Check your state highway map for mileage information. When traveling along secondary and unpaved roads, allow plenty of time to reach your destination.

Accommodations—Listed alphabetically starting with campgrounds, then hotels, followed by bed and breakfasts. A variety of accommodations is included with emphasis on those offering reasonable rates and amenities for the area.

Campgrounds—Each listing indicates the facilities available. The word "modern" indicates flush toilets and running water. "Primitive" means pit toilets or outhouses and, usually, the lack of running water. If the campground is designated as "primitive" there are no designated sites and often no water or other facilities. "30' limit" indicates maximum trailer length of 30 feet.

Hotels/Bed and Breakfasts—Lodging price codes represent the average cost of a double room. K-plus-numeral at the end of a listing indicates the age under which kids stay free in the same room with an adult: $ under $45; $$ $45-$75; $$$ $76-$125; $$$+ over $125.

Restaurants—Information about restaurants is designed to show the breadth and variety of offerings. Keep in mind that fast food options are plentiful in urban areas, and that restaurants change owners, menus and pricing often.

Restaurant price code is based on average cost of a dinner: $ indicates under $7; $$ is $8-$15; $$$ is over $15.

Special Needs Facilities—Because public buildings generally have handicapped accessibility, we have not included the ♿ symbol in listings for museums, restaurants, and so on. The symbol alerts readers to descriptions of designated rooms in lodgings, campground toilets, especially friendly trails and parks, and attractions designed for the hearing- and sight-impaired as well as the mobility-impaired.

State tourism offices are listed in "For Further Exploration" at the back of the book.

CHAPTER 1

To December 5, 1803

BEGINNINGS

❧ The Plan, the Crew, and How They Changed ❧

Captain Meriwether Lewis wrote on May 20, 1804, that he was on his way *to join my friend companion and fellow labourer Capt. William Clark...with the party destined for the discovery of the interior of the continent of North America.*

That party expected to travel up the Missouri River until its tributaries stopped at the Rocky Mountains, cross a ridge, and go down the waters of the Columbia River to the Pacific Ocean.

About forty men and a big dog were going to leave the United States, most of them for parts of three years. The larger group would travel about 8,000 miles by boat, on foot, and sometimes on horseback. On a few really good days going home down the Missouri, they might travel sixty or more miles—but heading upriver, outward bound, they made as few as four miles progress in a day. They left the "U' States" informed with the contemporary misconception of the biggest land barrier ahead, the Rockies. They hoped to make friends with people native to the "interior," but didn't know their languages. Any item they needed had to be carried along, crafted, or harvested.

As they traveled, they were instructed to:
- collect and describe plants and animals new to science;
- accurately record latitude and longitude of the rivers, mountains, and other features;
- note the land's economic potential—its farming lands, climate, water supply, timber, wildlife, and mineral resources;
- follow the Missouri to its headwaters and then locate rivers flowing down the west side of the Rockies to the Columbia and into the Pacific;
- write about the Indian nations, how they lived, what they believed, their languages;
- convince those nations that the new government had good intentions and wanted to be a trading partner, and that they should make peace with their neighbors.

All they learned they'd record, in duplicate, in daily journal entries. Their faithful attention gives us a rich record, but one with tantalizing holes and sometimes an overly terse style.

They would be completely out of communication with home. For months at a time they would see no one like themselves.

No doctor traveled with them, and the era's best medical supplies were not as beneficial as a modern first-aid kit.

They carried some plain preserved foods and had to learn to eat whatever was available: bison, salmon, roots, dogs, horses.

When their clothing wore out they had to make more from the only material around—leather. "Cold weather gear" in ten feet of snow meant having more layers to add.

Entertainment? They had a violin and some jaw harps in their trade goods, plus their own voices.

Despite the physical sufferings, they experienced moments of joyous awe. In the chapters ahead, just read their reactions to the first views of the Rocky Mountains, the Pacific Ocean, and other sights. Only one enlisted man deserted; he was captured, tried, and sent back to the U' States in the return party.

Most of the expedition's members unified, and took pride in learning how to manage the Missouri River. After they'd been on their way for two months, Captain Lewis first referred to his band as "the corps of volunteers for North Western Discovery."

Thomas Jefferson, as much scientist as politician, truly was interested in adding to human knowledge. In that part of their assignment, he thought, it shouldn't matter whether

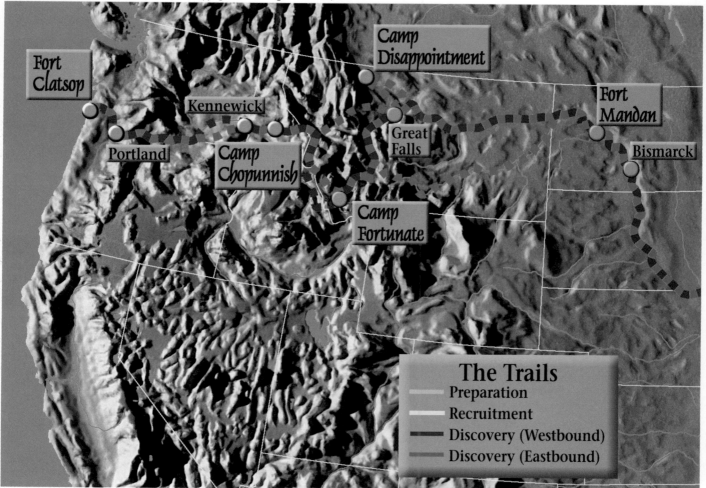

The Trails
Preparation
Recruitment
Discovery (Westbound)
Discovery (Eastbound)

the Corps traveled into lands beyond their country's boundaries. Purely scientific exploration would benefit all the world's nations. (Accordingly, both France and Britain issued passports for the expedition to enter their lands.)

But as much as Jefferson loved knowledge for its own sake, he also didn't want the new United States—twenty-seven years old in 1803—to share its continent with other nations. Early in 1803, United States diplomats sent to France to buy the port of New Orleans were offered a bigger deal: the right to claim the land between the Mississippi and the Missouri River's headwaters. France very recently had obtained what was called Louisiana from Spain; in fact the little fort at St. Louis would still have a Spanish commandant when Lewis arrived there.

Even though the Louisiana Purchase was

vast, from the time the Corps of Discovery left behind the Rocky Mountains in fall 1805 until they recrossed in the following spring, the Corps were beyond the purchase's borders.

For years, Thomas Jefferson had wanted his nation to make such an exploration. When he became President, Jefferson hired a personal secretary: Meriwether Lewis, whose family home of Locust Hill was about ten miles west of Jefferson's **[1]** Monticello outside Charlottesville, Virginia. Thus employed, Lewis lived in the "President's House" (not yet called the White House) in **[2]** Washington, District of Columbia, and had his office in its East Room. Jefferson knew that Lewis had a keen eye for and interest in scientific observation. No doubt the two discussed the president's pet military operation from time to time.

When Jefferson could make the expedition a reality, it was as a military expedition that

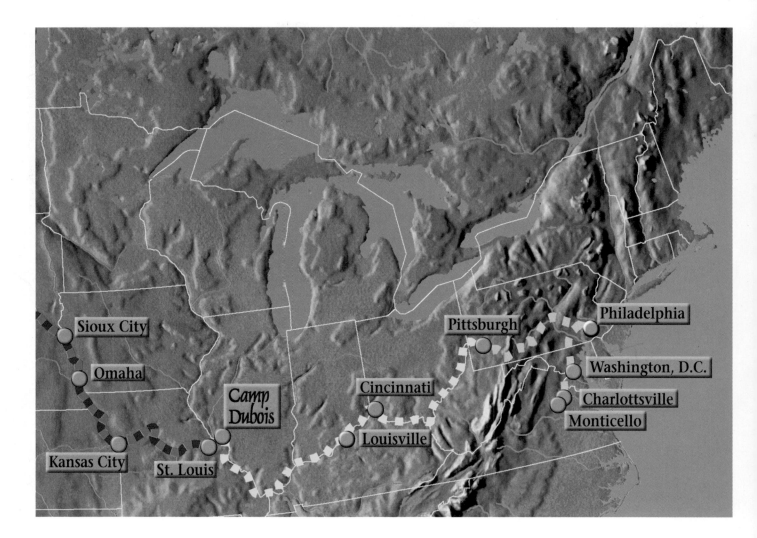

included a few hired civilians. The President named Lewis (a captain on detached army duty) to head the command. Lewis selected as co-leader a man who once had been his own army commander, William Clark, and together they chose the expedition's other members.

According to Secretary of War Henry Dearborn, dealing with peacetime military reductions, Lewis must be captain and Clark his lieutenant. Although Lewis objected strenuously, Dearborn could do no differently. So Lewis apologized to Clark and went right on calling him captain. In all their writings, the leaders called themselves co-captains; in all their actions they were equals.

The Corps included three sergeants, and the rest of the enlisted men were privates. Before embarking, they hired another civilian interpreter (a couple of other interpreters had enlisted in the army for the trip). Clark took

along his personal servant, the black slave York who had been raised with him. After the first winter, two more hired interpreters who knew some (but not all) local Indian tongues traveled along. One of them was a teenaged mother who carried her newborn baby. Lewis took along his own Newfoundland retriever, Seaman.

As the men set out from Camp Dubois, Illinois Territory, in spring 1804, Lewis was nearly thirty years old and Clark four years older. The Corps' youngest enlisted man was nineteen and the oldest thirty-five. The men came from the states of Connecticut, Kentucky, Massachusetts, Maryland, New Hampshire, North Carolina, Pennsylvania, Tennessee, and Virginia; and Missouri, which was not yet even a territory.

The plan, as it evolved during the trip, was for the expedition to leave St. Louis in the spring of 1804 and take their boats up the Mis-

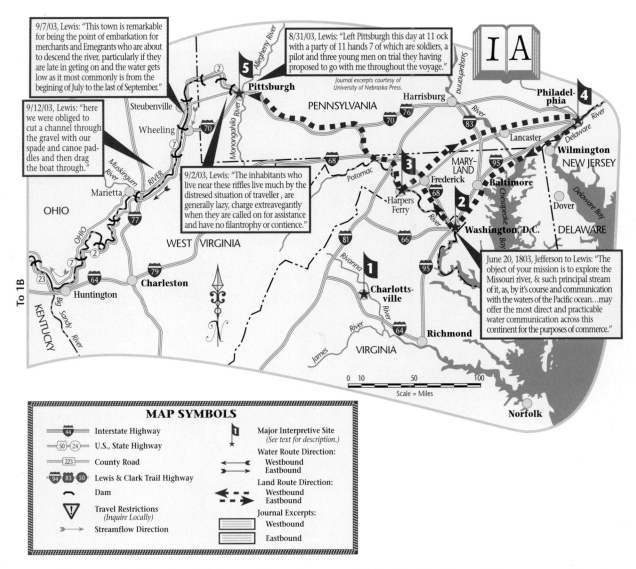

9/7/03, Lewis: "This town is remarkable for being the point of embarkation for merchants and Emegrants who are about to descend the river, particularly if they are late in geting on and the water gets low as it most commonly is from the begining of July to the last of September."

9/12/03, Lewis: "here we were obliged to cut a channel through the gravel with our spade and canoe paddles and then drag the boat through."

9/2/03, Lewis: "The inhabitants who live near these riffles live much by the distresed situation of traveller, are generally lazy, charge extraveganly when they are called on for assistance and have no filantrophy or contience."

8/31/03, Lewis: "Left Pittsburgh this day at 11 ock with a party of 11 hands 7 of which are soldiers, a pilot and three young men on trial they having proposed to go with me throughout the voyage."

Journal excerpts courtesy of University of Nebraska Press.

June 20, 1803, Jefferson to Lewis: "The object of your mission is to explore the Missouri river, & such principal stream of it, as, by it's course and communication with the waters of the Pacific ocean…may offer the most direct and practicable water communication across this continent for the purposes of commerce."

To 1B

MAP SYMBOLS

Interstate Highway	
U.S., State Highway	
County Road	
Lewis & Clark Trail Highway	
Dam	
Travel Restrictions *(Inquire Locally)*	
Streamflow Direction	

Major Interpretive Site *(See text for description.)*

Water Route Direction:
Westbound
Eastbound

Land Route Direction:
Westbound
Eastbound

Journal Excerpts:
Westbound
Eastbound

0 10 50 100
Scale = Miles

souri River to the Mandan–Hidatsa villages in today's North Dakota, the last stop on the Upper Missouri for white traders at the time. There they'd spend the winter of 1804-1805. In the spring, the keelboat would return to St. Louis, carrying specimens of plants and animals new to science, plus the captains' journals and maps of the trip so far. Just in case they didn't return.

The rest of the men, called the permanent party, would spend 1805 pushing up the Missouri in the two pirogues (plus canoes built during the winter). As they went farther upstream, waterways would get ever smaller. The men would end up having to store boats to retrieve on the return trip, and eventually they'd be on foot. They hoped to trade with local Indians for horses to carry them and their gear over the mountain barrier.

While the Northwest Passage—an all-water route to the Pacific Ocean—was only a hope, scientists theorized that the Continental Divide existed. The Missouri flowed generally from the northwest into the Mississippi, which flowed south into the Gulf of Mexico on the Atlantic Ocean. But British, American, and Spanish explorers along the Pacific had seen that rivers flowed into the ocean from the east, and in 1792 an American had named the Columbia River and explored its mouth on the Pacific. So, somewhere in between, a high mountain barrier divided the continent's water flows.

Geographers thought that the barrier, the Rocky Mountains, was a "height of land," and so the captains expected a brief portage over the barrier and down the west side, where they'd float downstream to the Pacific.

Having reached the ocean in the summer of

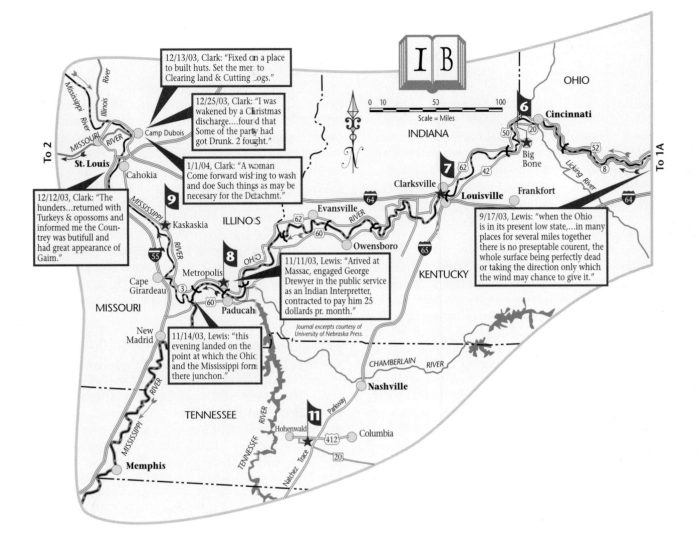

12/13/03, Clark: "Fixed on a place to built huts. Set the men to Clearing land & Cutting Logs."

12/25/03, Clark: "I was wakened by a Christmas discharge....found that Some of the party had got Drunk. 2 fought."

1/1/04, Clark: "A woman Come forward wishing to wash and doe Such things as may be necesary for the Detachmt."

12/12/03, Clark: "The hunders...returned with Turkeys & opossoms and informed me the Countrey was butifull and had great appearance of Gaim."

11/11/03, Lewis: "Arived at Massac, engaged George Drewyer in the public service as an Indian Interpretter, contracted to pay him 25 dollards pr. month."

11/14/03, Lewis: "this evening landed on the point at which the Ohio and the Mississippi form there junchon."

9/17/03, Lewis: "when the Ohio is in its present low state,...in many places for several miles together there is no preseptable courent, the whole surface being perfectly dead or taking the direction only which the wind may chance to give it."

Journal excerpts courtesy of University of Nebraska Press.

1805, they'd return home at once, about a year and a half total travel time. If, on the coast, they met a trading ship, some of the men (and journals and specimens) could go home by sea and perhaps arrive before the land travelers. Only perhaps, because weather conditions and other ports of call ruled the schedules of ocean voyages around Cape Horn, the tip of South America.

It was a reasonable plan given the state of knowledge before the expedition set out. But surprises along the way would call for changes. The captains' flexibility was one of the expedition's greatest strengths.

The biggest surprise would be that the Rocky Mountains were many mountain chains, one after another for 250 miles east to west. Before the mountains, an unexpected series of falls on the Missouri would use up a month of portaging. Another surprise would come when the

Corps met some Indian nations who were hostile to them. Because the expedition had to return through these nations' lands, the captains decided they needed every man to return overland. Just as well, for they met no trading ships all that winter on the Pacific. And they didn't even reach the actual coast until mid-November of 1805, far too late to return by land that year.

When the Corps arrived at St. Louis after more than two years of being out of communication with the nation, people were surprised that they had survived.

All but two members of the permanent party returned. One had chosen to stay in the Rockies, with his partners' and the captains' consent, and one had died of an illness the best doctors in the world couldn't have treated at the time.

For Meriwether Lewis, the expedition began in the spring of 1803. Jefferson sent him to train with the best scientists in the nation, friends of the knowledge-loving president. Starting in mid-April, Lewis studied celestial navigation for three weeks with Andrew Ellicott, astronomer and mathematician, at Ellicott's home in Lancaster, Pennsylvania. Being able to determine longitude and latitude by reading the heavens was crucial to mapping accurately lands the expedition would visit.

From Ellicott's, Lewis went on to [4] Philadelphia for further navigational training by mathematician Robert Patterson. Spending about a month in the city, Lewis also studied natural history and botany with Benjamin Smith Barton, anatomy and fossils with Caspar Wistar, and medicine with the preeminent American physician of the time, Benjamin Rush.

Rush limited his training to the types of injuries and illnesses he thought most likely for men traveling in the wilderness. As an army officer, Lewis already had had to know basics like how to set broken bones, fix dislocated joints, and drain off "bad blood." His mother, Lucy Meriwether Lewis Marks, was an esteemed herb doctor back home, and her son knew quite a bit about using plants as medicine. (Meriwether was a boy when his father died and his mother married John Marks.) Besides offering training, Rush also compounded medications for the expedition to carry in their valued medicine chest. These were based on medical principles of the day: treat an ailing body by bleeding it and/or purging it.

All of these scientists, and others that Jefferson knew, had been invited by the president to suggest questions for the captains to ask each Native American nation they met. Some were about diet and commerce and some about beliefs, and there was a vocabulary list that they hoped would show which tribes were related to each other. Clark usually carried out this duty, carefully interviewing hosts and recording their answers.

During his time in Philadelphia, Lewis energetically shopped for needed supplies. From local merchants and from the three-year-old federal Schuylkill Arsenal in a western suburb, he obtained food, useful tools including loud "blowing-trumpets" to hail people at a distance, and other necessities. He found "portable soup" and metal cargo boxes, and bought powder to make ink (not waterproof, so their journals were in great danger all those months in splashing rivers); beads, fishhooks, flags, glass lenses for fire-starting, and other items to give to Indians, or trade for food; "kittles" and other cooking utensils; thermometers, knives and axes; candles (plus molds and wicks for making more, which they'd use). In June, Lewis dispatched more than a ton and a half of supplies, by horse-drawn wagon, to Pittsburgh via Harpers Ferry, then in Virginia.

Back in March and early April, before going to Pennsylvania, Lewis had spent a month at the new [3] Harpers Ferry federal arsenal. The Corps was issued at least fifteen of the newest-style rifle, the first one designed just for the U.S. Army (but the captains, York, and some others preferred their personal longer-barreled "Kentucky" rifles). Rifles needed gunpowder and lead balls, and the powder had to be kept dry, but the men were traveling by water. At Philadelphia, Lewis bought lead canisters to hold the powder supply. When a canister was opened, its powder was divided among the men, who then were responsible for keeping their own powder dry. When emptied, the waterproof containers were melted and their lead molded into bullets.

At Harpers Ferry, Lewis also had supervised the building and testing of a 176-pound iron boat frame; when covered with animal hides and caulked with pine tar out in the field, it would carry a great amount of freight. Or so the theory went.

After further supply purchases in the St. Louis area over the following winter, Lewis had collected tons of food, medicine, trade goods, and other supplies, for the party of fewer than forty men to transport; modern estimates range from ten tons upward. Even so, the Corps ran out of trade goods, and were reduced to offering brass and pewter buttons cut from the men's uniforms. But they did not run out of powder or bullets.

TOURING TODAY

✧ LEWIS PREPARES ✧

ALONG THE EXPEDITION'S PATH

Lewis & Clark & Sacagawea Memorial (Charlottesville, VA)—Statue honoring the trio sits in Midway Park. Always open. Ridge & Main Sts.

[1] ★ Monticello (Charlottesville, VA)—Thomas Jefferson's mountaintop estate where he lived from 1770 until his death in 1826. Includes his home and a plantation community where archaeological excavation continues. Tours of the house include several principal rooms containing personal items detailing his eclectic interests and inventions. Items from the Expedition are displayed. The extensive garden was planned by Jefferson and horticulture remained a serious hobby throughout his lifetime. Garden and community tours are also offered (Apr-Oct). Daily 8 to 5 (Mar-Oct), 9 to 4:30 (rest of year); admission fee. I-64 exit 121, 0.5 miles S on VA 20, 1.5 miles E on VA 53. 804/984-9822, 804/984-9800.

Monticello Visitor Center (Charlottesville, VA)—Exhibits and film shown here are offered in conjunction with the estate and focus on items recovered during excavations. Gift shop. Daily 9 to 5:30 (Mar-Oct), 9 to 5 (rest of year); free. I-64 exit 121, S on VA 20. 804/977-1783.

[2] Thomas Jefferson Memorial (Washington, D.C.)—Beneath a circular dome stands a 19-foot bronze statue of Jefferson by Rudolph Evans. Surrounding it are panels etched with some of his most powerful and provocative writings. Tours upon request. Daily 8 to midnight; free. S.E. side of Tidal Basin. 202/426-6821.

U.S. Capitol (Washington, D.C.)—Visit the chamber where Congress approved funding for the Expedition. This vast complex is best traversed with map and guidebook in hand. Guided tours are popular but often crowded in the summer. Gallery passes are available from your senators or representative but should be requested several months in advance. Daily 9 to 8 (Mar-Aug), 9 to 4:30 (rest of year); free. Capitol Hill. 202/225-6827.

[2] White House (Washington, D.C.)—Although the room where Lewis stayed is not on the tour, visitors see several of the public rooms, some furnished with items from Jefferson's time. Tickets are required for the self-guided tours that take place from 10 to noon Tue-Sat. A limited number are distributed each day (beginning at 7:30) at the visitor center at 15th and E Sts. Tickets may also be available from your senators or representative with advance notice. Entertainment is provided in the outdoor waiting area during the summer. Tours begin at the SE gate near E St. 202/456-7041.

March 16, 1803–April 18, 1803
[3] ★ Harpers Ferry National Historic Park (Harpers Ferry, WV)—Although the focus here is on John Brown and his abolitionist raid in 1859, several hiking trails and exhibits interpret how the area touched American history. Additional trails link to the Appalachian Trail, Maryland Heights, and Virginius Island. The armory visited by Lewis, where he obtained weapons and where mechanics created his iron-boat frame, was destroyed in 1861 by Confederate forces and never rebuilt. Additional Expedition interpretation is planned. Daily 8 to 5; admission fee. Along US 340 in town. 304/535-6223.

April 19–May 10, 1803
● **Sehner-Ellicott-von Hess House** (Lancaster, PA)—It was here, in 1803, that Andrew Ellicott tutored Lewis in mapmaking and surveying skills. No longer a private residence, it now houses offices for the Historic Preservation Trust of Lancaster County. 123 N. Prince.

May 10–June, 1803
[4] ★ Academy of Natural Sciences (Philadelphia, PA)—Housed here is the Lewis & Clark Herbarium, a collection of more than 200 specimens collected by the Corps. Other science exhibits include a dinosaur hall and live animal shows. Daily 10 to 4:30; admission fee. 19th and Benjamin Franklin Pkwy. 215/299-1000.

[4] American Philosophical Society (Philadelphia, PA)—Research library affiliated with group that provided significant support to the Expedition. Although access to the library and research collection is limited to researchers (by appointment), on-line rotating exhibits focus on books, manuscripts, photos, and artwork from the Society's collection at www.amphilsoc.org/library/exhibits. Weekdays 9 to 4:45; free. 105 S. Fifth St. 215/440-3400.

Around the Area

Charlottesville, Virginia

Charlottesville-Albemarle Chamber of Commerce—Fifth & E. Market Ave. 804/295-3141.

Ash Lawn–Highland—Restored 550-acre estate and home of President James Monroe with living history and special events. Guided tours. Daily 9 to 6 (Mar-Dec), 10 to 5 (rest of year); admission fee. I-64 exit 121, 0.5 miles S on VA 20, 3 miles E on VA 53, 5 miles S on CR 795. 804/293-9539.

Michie Tavern—Circa 1784 homestead that provided lodging and meals to travelers for decades. Tours include interactive living history interpretation. Lunch available. Daily 9 to 5; admission fee. I-64 exit 121, 0.5 miles S on VA 20, 1 mile E on VA 53. 804/977-1234.

Montpelier (Orange, VA)—Lifelong home of President James Madison. 2700-acre estate contains formal gardens, forested hiking trails, archaeological excavations of plantation housing. House and garden tours focus on Madison, his wife Dolley, and continuing research and preservation process. Daily 9:30 to 5:30 (Apr-Nov), 9:30 to 4:30 (rest of year); admission fee. 4 miles SW of Orange on VA 20. 540/672-2728.

University of Virginia—Designed by Thomas Jefferson and opened in 1825, the Rotunda here was modeled after the Pantheon. Tours outlining the history of the Rotunda and surrounding area are conducted daily. Tours at 10, 11, 2, 3, and 4; free. US 29 (Bus.) and US 250 (Bus.). 804/924-7969.

Virginia Discovery Museum—Children's museum with hands-on and multimedia exhibits encourage kids to explore the world around them. Tue-Sat 10 to 5, Sun noon to 5; admission fee. Historic Downtown Mall. 804/977-1025.

▲ Charlottesville KOA—70 sites (57 w/hookups); fee; water; modern/&; showers; open Mar-Oct; grills/fire rings; tables. Pools, store, and cabins. Closest campground to Monticello. I-64 exit 121, S on VA 20 to CO 708, 1.5 W on CO 708. 804/296-9881.

▲ Misty Mountain Camp Resort—110 sites (94 w/hookups); fee; water; modern/&; showers; open all year; grills/fire rings; tables. Dump station; groceries; coin laundry. Recreation center; pool; fishing; basketball; playground; hiking. I-64 exit 107, 1 mile W on US 250. 888/647-8900.

Lancaster, Pennsylvania

Pennsylvania Dutch Convention and Visitors Bureau—US30 & Greenfield Rd. 717/299-8901, 800/723-8824. **Walking Tours** start here; costumed guides meet groups for 90-minute strolls through history. Daily at 1 (Sept-Oct); admission fee. Queen and Vine Sts. 717/392-1776.

Discover Lancaster County History Museum—Multimedia and hands-on exhibits explore area history from the 1700s to the present with an emphasis on Amish heritage. Daily 9 to 8 (summer), 9 to 5 (rest of year); admission fee. 2249 Lincoln Hwy. E. 717/393-3679.

Heritage Center Museum—Displays of decorative and folk arts include quilts, furnishings, and textiles. Tue-Sat 10 to 5 (Apr-Dec); donations. Penn Square. 717/299-6440.

Historic Rock Ford Plantation—Tours of well-preserved 18th century home of Revolutionary War officer. Tue-Fri 10 to 4, Sun noon to 4 (Apr-Oct); admission fee. 881 Rock Ford Rd. in Lancaster County Park. 717/392-7223.

Landis Valley Museum—Extensive living history site dedicated to interpretation of rural life among Pennsylvania's German population from 1750 to WWII. Mon-Sat 9 to 5, Sun noon to 5 (closed Jan-Feb); admission fee. 2.5 miles N on PA 272 (Oregon Pike). 717/569-0401.

Wheatland—Restored mansion of President James Buchanan. Tours given by costumed guides who provide delightful insights into Buchanan's life here and in Washington. Daily 10 to 4 (Apr-Nov); admission fee. 1120 Marietta Ave. 717/392-8721.

▲ Old Mill Stream Camping Manor—240 sites; fee; water; modern/&; showers; open all year; grills/fire rings; tables. Paddleboats; playground; recreation center; basketball. Dump station; rental cars; cable hookup; groceries; propane. 5 miles E on US 30. 717/299-2314.

⊞ Best Western Eden Resort Inn—274 rooms; indoor and outdoor pools; fitness room; tennis court; ⊗ restaurant; pets. US 30 & PA 272. 717/569-6444. $$ K18

⊞ Ramada Inn—160-room restored historic hotel, outdoor pool, restaurant. 0.4 miles S of US 30 on PA 501. 717/393-0771. $$$ K12

⊞ Your Place Country Inn—125 rooms, outdoor pool, ⊗ restaurant. 4.5 miles E on US 30. 717/393-3413. $$ K17

⊯ King's Cottage—9 rooms in restored Spanish mansion, full breakfast. 1.5 miles E on US 462. 717/397-1017. $$$+

Lynchburg, Virginia

Poplar Forest—Built by Jefferson in 1806 as a personal retreat. Archaeological excavation continues on the grounds; the octagonal house is being restored. Guided tours. Daily 10 to 4 (Apr-Nov); admission fee. From VA 460, N on VA 811, E on VA 661. 804/525-1806.

Philadelphia, Pennsylvania

Philadelphia Visitor Center—Open daily 9 to 5. 16th St. & JFK Blvd. 205/636-1666, 800/537-7676. Another visitor center is at **Independence National Historic Park** (see below), 3rd St. & Chestnut. 215/597-8974.

Fairmount Park

Situated along both shores of the Schuylkill (SKOO-kuhl) River, was the site of the 1876 Centennial Exposition and is now home to a multitude of museums as well as an extensive biking and hiking trail system. Several historic homes lining the riverfront are also open to visitors. Fairmount Park includes:

Horticulture Center—Reflecting pool anchors well-landscaped arboretum with indoor and outdoor displays. The

Japanese House and Garden regularly host tea ceremonies. Daily 9 to 3; donations. Belmont Horticulture Dr. 215/685-0096.

Mann Center for the Performing Arts—Outdoor amphitheater with a summer schedule that includes the Philadelphia Orchestra. 52nd & Parkside. 215/878-7707.

Philadelphia Museum of Art—A collection that spans 2,000 years of paintings, sculpture, drawings, furnishings, and glass. Don't forget to take the "Rocky" run up the front steps. Guided tours offer both general information and specialized looks at periods and individual artists. Tues-Sun 10 to 5; admission fee. Benjamin Franklin Parkway at 26th St. 215/763-8100.

Philadelphia Zoo—Spend hours here communing with the animals. Special primate reserve is home to 11 species and the children's zoo is hands-on. Daily 9:30 to 4:45 (Mar-Nov), 10 to 4 (rest of year); admission fee. 3400 W. Girard Ave. 215/243-1100.

Rodin Museum—Collection of over 100 originals and casts is the largest outside Paris. Formal garden is a pleasant place to relax. Tues-Sun 10 to 5; donations. Benjamin Franklin Pkwy at 22nd St. 215/763-8100.

Franklin Institute Science Museum—Sprawling complex is the national memorial to Franklin and his curiosity and inventiveness. Interactive exhibits cover scientific investigation, mathematics and communication, and include a historical perspective. **Fels Planetarium** offers daily shows with laser shows on weekends. **Mandell Center** brings everything into the 21st century and beyond and **Omniverse Theater** shows films on a 4-story, 79-foot wide dome. Daily 9:30 to 4; admission fee (combination tickets are available). Benjamin Franklin Pkwy & 20th St. 215/448-1200.

Independence National Historic Park

A collection of several historic sites maintained by the National Park Service. The **visitor center** at Chestnut & 3rd is the best place to start with a half-hour introductory film, walking tour maps, and daily activity schedules. 215/597-8974. Park highlights include:

Congress Hall—Congress called this home from 1790 to 1800, and Washington and Adams were inaugurated here. Chestnut & 6th Sts.

Declaration House—A reconstruction of the house where Jefferson drafted the Declaration of Independence in June 1776. 7th & Market Sts.

Independence Hall—Both the Declaration of Independence and the Constitution were signed here. The Assembly Room has been restored to its 1775-87 look, as have other rooms. Guided tours run regularly and are the only means of admission: On Independence Square, Chestnut St. between 5th & 6th. Daily 9 to 5; free.

Liberty Bell Pavilion—Glass building is permanent home of the bell, and rangers bring its history to life. Daily 9 to 5; free. 5th, 6th, Chestnut & Market Sts.

New Hall Military Museum—Honors early Army, Navy, and Marine Corps (1775-1805) in a reconstructed 1790s building. Chestnut between 3rd & 4th Sts.

Mummers Museum—Covers the history and heritage of the uniquely American Mummers and their annual New Year's Day parade in interactive and multimedia displays. String band concerts are held on Tuesday nights in the summer. Tue-Sat 9:30 to 5, Sun noon to 5 (June-Sept); Tue-Sat 9:30 to 5 (rest of year); admission fee. 1100 S. 2nd St. 215/336-3050.

Please Touch Museum—A feast for the senses in an atmosphere where visitors are encouraged to use more than eyes and ears to experience artworks, science concepts, and historical and cultural objects. Daily 9 to 6 (Jul-Aug); 9 to 4:30 (rest of year); admission fee. 210 N. 21st St. 215/963-0667.

Washington, D.C.

Visitor Information Center—Open Mon-Sat 8 to 6, Sun noon to 5. Ronald Reagan Bldg., 1300 Pennsylvania Ave. N.W. 202/328-4748.

DumbartonHouse—Historic house filled with domestic arts exhibits, children's exhibits, and a variety of historical papers from Washington, Jefferson, and the Madisons. Tue-Sat 10 to 12:15; admission fee. 2715 Q St. N.W. 202/337-2288.

Explorers Hall National Geographic Society—Hands-on, multimedia displays describing a variety of expeditions sponsored by the Society. Natural phenomena and anthropology are also interpreted. Mon-Sat 9 to 5, Sun 10 to 5; free. 17th & M St. NW. 202/857-7588.

Library of Congress—After the original collection was destroyed during the War of 1812, several thousand volumes of Thomas Jefferson's personal collection became the basis for the current holdings, which exceed 100 million items. Permanent American Treasures exhibit and rotating exhibits. Reading rooms, exhibit halls, and visitor center are spreading through the three-building complex. Guided tours; regularly scheduled special events. Most areas are open Mon-Sat 8:30 to 5:30; free. 1st & Independence Ave. S.E. 202/707-8000.

National Gallery of Art—Highlights of the vast collection are Western European holdings dating from the 13th century, and over 3 centuries of American works. Guided tours focus on broad topics and periods as well as individual artists. Concerts and other events take place year-round. Mon-Sat 10 to 5, Sun 11 to 6; free. Constitution Ave. between 3rd and 7th Sts. N.W. 202/737-4215.

★ **National Museum of American History**—Diverse collection tells the country's story through exhibits on virtually every aspect of American life. A few items related to the Lewis and Clark Expedition will be on tour during 2003-2006. Daily 10 to 5:30; free. Constitution Ave. between 12th and 14 Sts. N.W. 202/357-2700.

Following the months in Lancaster and Philadelphia, Captain Lewis returned to the President's House for a couple of weeks. Here he received Jefferson's formal instructions for the trip, and sent a farewell letter to his mother at Locust Hill. He assured Lucy Marks that he'd be back in a year and a half, after traveling among Indian nations who were friendly to the United States, and that he would be in no more danger than "were I to remain at home for the same length of time." Lewis traveled to Harpers Ferry to arrange for the weapons, tools, and iron boat frame to be transported by a second wagon, also to meet him in **[5]** Pittsburgh. Reaching that riverboat building center in mid-July, the captain ordered a keelboat suitable for navigating down the Ohio River (which forms there), then up the Mississippi, and up the Missouri to the Mandan-Hidatsa villages.

Lewis learned that the Ohio was running shallower than usual this summer of 1803. Then the boatbuilder turned out to be irresponsible, according to Lewis, getting drunk and berating his employees who then quit and left the yard short-handed until new hires were made. The wagons from Harpers Ferry arrived at Pittsburgh six days after Lewis did, and the very next day Lewis received a copy of the Louisiana Purchase treaty forwarded by Jefferson. It had been signed, in France, on May 2. Everything was ready except the keelboat, whose building dragged on week after week—clear until the end of August.

In Pittsburgh, or sometime after leaving Washington, Lewis purchased with his own money the Newfoundland retriever he called Seaman. Bred for ocean-going rescues, the dog cost $20—half a month's pay for an army cap-tain. Man and dog boarded the keelboat along with seven soldiers assigned to get it to the Illinois country, and Lewis hired three young men to make the trip as a trial for joining the expedition. One he soon dismissed; modern historians think the other two may have been privates George Shannon and John Colter, later chosen for the permanent party.

Escaping northwestward from Pittsburgh in the brand-new keelboat was far from the end of Lewis's troubles. The Ohio River's extreme shallowness (now worsened by lateness in the year) forced him to buy a pirogue—a large open boat—only five days later, to lighten the keelboat's load. From there to the Falls of the Ohio, Lewis had to hire men with horses along the way to pull his boats over shoals, and he complained about what these river vultures charged. At Wheeling (now West Virginia) two days later, Lewis bought a second pirogue to spread out the cargo further.

Then the captain did what he would more times on the big journey: he stopped keeping his journal for a couple of months, which is how long it took to reach Fort Massac at today's Metropolis, Illinois.

From letters he wrote to Jefferson and to Clark in the interim, we know the Ohio River trek's difficulties, and that men and boats needed two weeks (until September 28) to reach Cincinnati from Pittsburgh. There the group rested for about a week, and Lewis crossed the Ohio River to visit **[6]** Big Bone Lick in Kentucky and inspect mammoth fossils found there a few months earlier. He wrote Jefferson in great detail about them, just the sort of informed observation that the president had hoped for, and forwarded specimens.

TOURING TODAY

꒰ LEWIS ON THE OHIO RIVER ꒱

[ ] **Bracketed numbers key sites to maps**	♿ Special-needs accessible	⊨ Bed & breakfast
★ L&C in-depth interpretation, unchanged landform	⊗ Restaurant	▲ Camping, RV park
• L&C interpreted site	⊞ Motel, hotel, cabin	

Bridges across the Ohio River: Newell, WV to East Liverpool, OH (toll bridge); Costonia, OH to Weirton, WV; US 22 Weirton, WV to Steubenville, OH; I-70 and I-470 Ohio to Wheeling, WV; Bellaire, OH to Benwood, WV; Moundsville, WV to Ohio; at Hannibal Dam near New Martinsville, WV; St. Mary's, WV to Newport, OH; I-77 at Marietta, OH; Belpre, OH to Parkersburg, WV (toll bridge); US 50 at Parkersburg, WV; Ravenswood, WV; US 33 at Pomeroy, OH; US 35 at Point Pleasant, WV; US 52 at Huntington, WV; US 60 at Ashland, WV; between Russell, WV and Ironton, OH; KY 10 and OH 253; US 23 at Portsmouth, OH; US 68 between Maysville, KY and Aberdeen, OH; I-275E, I-275W, I-71 at Cincinnati and Covington.

Ferries across the Ohio River: Sistersville, WV to Fly, OH auto/passenger service (Mon-Fri 7 to 5; Sat 8 to 5, Sun 9 to 5, fee); Anderson Ferry—west of Cincinnati on US 50 (daily auto/passenger service upon signal, fee) 606/485-9210.

Along the Expedition's Path

July 15-August 31, 1803
[5] Point State Park (Pittsburgh, PA)—At the head of the Ohio River, the blockhouse of British Fort Pitt, established 1758, still stands. A museum provides additional exhibits and interpretation of the area's early history. Also within the park is an enormous fountain (Apr-Nov). Park open daily dawn-dusk; free. Blockhouse open Wed-Sat 9:30 to 4, Sun noon to 4; free. Museum open Wed-Sat 10 to 4:30, Sun noon to 4:30; admission fee. 101 Commonwealth Pl. Park 412/471-0235, blockhouse 412/471-1764, museum 412/281-9284.

August 31, 1803
Harmony Museum (Harmony, PA)—Established in 1804, Harmony was the first attempt by George Rapp to create a communal society. Artifacts are housed in several period buildings. Guided tours are available. Tue-Sun 1 to 4; admission fee. 724/452-7341, 888/821-4822.
Old Economy Village (Ambridge, PA)—Town built 1824-1830 by George Rapp and the Harmony

Society (after they left Harmony and spent 10 years in New Harmony, IN) in their quest to for the perfect community. Original buildings still occupy much of the town and may be toured. Tue-Sat 9 to 4, Sun noon to 4; admission fee. 724/266-4500.

September 3, 1803
△ Tomlinson Run State Park (New Manchester, WV)—Over 6 miles of hiking and biking trails. 50 sites (10 w/hookups); fee; water; modern/&; showers; open 5/1-10/15; grills/fire rings; tables. Fishing; pool; mini golf; playground; boat rental. Dump station. WV2 north to WV 8. 304/564-3651.

September 6, 1803
Old Fort Steuben (Steubenville, OH)—Opened in 1787 to facilitate surveying of the Ohio River. Eight of the 10 original buildings have been restored. Ongoing archaeological digs, re-enactments, tours. Daily 10 to 5 (May-Oct); admission fee. 100 South St. 740/264-6304.

September 7, 1803
● Patrick Gass Grave Site (Wellsburg, WV)—Sgt. Gass is buried alongside his wife atop a hill near the top of the cemetery. Brooke Cemetery. Pleasant St.

September 8, 1803
Wheeling Heritage Trail (Wheeling, WV)—Fourteen miles of trail along the Ohio River have been paved for hiking and biking. The trail currently runs from downtown to the Pike Island Locks and Dam and additional development is planned. The downtown section is below street level, hugs the riverbank, and is lit at night. Stairways provide access to Main Street businesses. A riverfront memorial to the Corps is planned.

September 9, 1803
Grave Creek Mound State Park (Moundsville, WV)—Prehistoric burial mound was originally surrounded by a moat. On-site museum houses relics from 1000 BC. Mon-Sat 10 to 4:30, Sun 1 to 5; admission fee. 801 Jefferson Ave. 304/843-1410.

September 12, 1803
Leith Run Recreation Area (Marietta, OH)—Part of the Wayne National Forest, this multi-use park has a wildlife viewing area and a wetland trail, Ohio River overlooks, volleyball and horseshoe pits, picnic areas, and playground. △ 18 sites (all w/full hookups); fee; water; modern/&; showers; fire rings/grills; picnic tables. Dump station. Fishing; hunting; boating on the Ohio River. 18 miles N on OH 7. 740/473-2871.

September 13, 1803
● Historic Harmar Village (Marietta, OH)—A historic district in the area of Fort Harmar, which was visited by the Corps on this date. The actual fort, built in 1785, was at the end of Market St. near the river confluence. In the village are shops, museums, and historic homes. Open daily (most shops closed on Mondays); some admission fees. 100 block of Maple St.
Ohio River Islands National Wildlife Refuge (Parkersburg, WV)—Series of 20 islands along almost 400 miles of the river. Wide variety of birds and mammals are present as are freshwater mussels. Camping is not permitted, but hiking, picnics, fishing, photography, and wildlife watching are. Middle Island is accessible by bridge and has a designated auto tour route. This is also the only island where bikes are allowed. Other islands are accessible only by private boats that may be landed on the beaches. Hunting is allowed in season. Daily dawn to dusk; free. Office is at 3004 7th St. in Parkersburg, but access to Middle Island bridge is off I-77 exit 179) 20 miles N on WV 2 to St. Marys, turn left on George St. 304/422-0752.

September 14, 1803
Blennerhassett Island Historical State Park (Parkersburg, WV)—Harman Blennerhassett's home was well established when Lewis passed this Ohio River island. There is no evidence that Lewis stopped, although Blennerhassett was deeply involved in American politics, hosting George Rogers Clark and others. He was eventually tried for treason with Aaron Burr in 1806. The man-

sion burned in 1811 and the island later served as part of the Underground Railroad. Reconstruction of the mansion was based on archaeological excavations, and a crafts village was built. ⊗ Restaurants, bike rentals, and picnic areas. A museum detailing the excavation and reconstruction process is located in Point Park. Tue-Sun 10 to 5:30 (May-Sept), Thur-Sat 10 to 4:30, Sun noon to 4:30 (Sept-Oct); admission fee. Access by sternwheeler from Point Park at 2nd & Ann Sts. (fee) 304/420-4800, 800/225-5982.

September 15, 1803
▲ Forked Run State Park (Reedsville, OH)—198 sites; fee; water; primitive/&; showers; open all year; grills/fire rings; tables. Lake fishing, swimming, and boating; hiking and nature trails; boat rental; picnic area; playground. Boat access to Ohio River. Dump station; groceries; coin laundry. 3 miles SW on OH 124. 740/378-6206.

Sept 16, 1803
Buffington Island State Monument (Portland, OH)—The monument commemorates a Civil War battle, but the island was here when Lewis came by. Picnic area. Daily dawn to dusk; free. OH 124 and the river. 614/297-2630.

Between September 18 & 24, 1803
▲ Wolford's Landing (Sciotoville, OH)—Grassy location along the riverfront. 83 sites (all w/hookups); fee; water; modern/&; showers; open all year; grills/fire rings; tables. Dump station; fishing; bike rentals; playground. Can be noisy due to nearby train tracks. US 52 to OH 140, turn S to river. 740/776-9956.

September 26, 1803
Rankin House State Memorial (Ripley, OH)—Home of one of Ohio's abolitionist leaders. Between 1825 and 1864, records indicate, 2,000 slaves found refuge at this stop on the Underground Railroad. Home has been restored. Wed-Sun noon to 5 (summer); admission fee. N off US 52. 937/392-1627.

September 27, 1803
Ulysses S. Grant Birthplace (Point Pleasant, WV)—Restored 3-room cabin where the 18th president was born on April 27, 1822. Wed-Sat 9:30 to 5, Sun noon to 5; donations. OH 232 & US 52. 937/378-4222.

October 6, 1803
[6] ★ Big Bone Lick State Park (Covington, KY)—Site of 1803 mammoth bone discovery that Lewis visited in order to record his observations and take specimens for Jefferson. Today, a museum interprets the finds and their significance. Outside, the & fully-accessible **Discovery Trail** is a re-creation of conditions leading to the original bog (represented by a life-size diorama). Park open daily dawn-dusk, museum open daily 8 to 7 (summer), Wed-Sun noon to 5 (rest of year); admission fee for museum. ▲ 62 sites (all w/hookups); fee; water; modern/&; showers; open all year; grills/fire rings; tables. Coin laundry; recreation program; fishing; mini golf. 22 miles SW on KY 338. 3380 Beaver Rd. 859/384-3522.

Between October 7 & 13, 1803
Point Park (Carrollton, KY)—City park located at the confluence of the Kentucky and Ohio rivers. Boat dock/ramp, playground, picnic area. Daily dawn to dusk; free. 2nd and Main Sts.
General Butler State Park—High use park dedicated to one of Kentucky's most prominent military families. **Butler-Turpin Home** is the restored 1859 family home and archaeological exhibits detail excavation of the original 1790 cabin (daily 10 to 3, Feb-Dec). Recreation is also plentiful with hiking trails, a 9-hole golf course, mini-golf, boat dock and rentals on the lake, playground and picnic areas. ⊞ 53-room lodge with ⊗ restaurant, 23 cabins, ▲ 111 sites (all w/hookups); fee; water; modern/&; showers; open year round; grills/fire rings; tables. 1 mile S on US 227. 502/732-4384, 800/325-0078.
Clifty Falls State Park (Madison, IN)—A deep, boulder-filled canyon and several waterfalls provide ex-

cellent hiking terrain at this popular park. Views from the south end of the park encompass the town of Madison and expanses of Ohio River bluffs. A ⊞ 63-room inn with ⊗ restaurant adjoins the indoor pool. A nature center and tennis courts are nearby, as is an observation tower. Picnic areas with shelters, an outdoor pool and a large amphitheater provide additional options. ▲ 165 sites (106 w/hookups); fee; water; modern/&; showers; open all year; grills/ fire rings; tables. W of town with entrances off IN 56 and IN 62. 1501 Green Road. 812/265-1331 (park); 812/265-4135 (inn).

AROUND THE AREA

TOWNS LISTED ALPHABETICALLY

Cincinnati, Ohio
Cincinnati Convention and Visitors Bureau—Open weekdays 9 to 5. 300 W. 6th St. 513/621-2142, 800/246-2987. There is also an information booth at Fountain Square, open daily 10 to 5:30.
Cincinnati Zoo and Botanical Garden—This zoo prides itself on its roster of rare species, including white Bengal tigers. There is an underwater viewing area for the polar bears, an African plains area, and camel rides in the summer. Animal shows abound. A train and tram wind through the luxuriously planted grounds. Daily 9 to 6 (summer); 9 to 5 (rest of year); admission fee. I-75 exit 6. 513/281-4700, 800/944-4776.
Harriett Beecher Stowe House—The author grew up and penned *Uncle Tom's Cabin* here. Exhibits on her life and the history of slavery and abolition. Guided tours. Tue-Thurs 10 to 4; donations. 2950 Gilbert Ave. 513/632-5120.
Kings Island—Full-scale amusement park with over 300 rides and attractions including a wooden looping rollercoaster, water park with surfing pool, and plenty of live entertainment. Opens at 9 with varied closing times (summer); admission fee. I-71 exit 25A. 513/754-5700, 800/288-0808.
The Museum Center at Union

Terminal—Art Deco station with extensive mosaic murals is now home to a **children's museum**, the **Cincinnati History Museum** complete with a re-creation of the 1850s boat landing, the **Museum of Natural History and Science** with its limestone cave and waterfalls, and an Omnimax theater, along with ⊗ several restaurants. Museums open Mon-Sat 10 to 5, Sun 11 to 6; individual admission fees, combination ticket available. I-75 exit 1H (Ezzard Charles Dr.) 513/287-7000, 800/733-2077.

William Howard Taft National Historic Site—Birthplace and childhood home of the man who served as a chief justice of the Supreme Court and the 27th president. Daily 10 to 5; free. 2038 Auburn. 513/684-3262.

Covington, Kentucky

Northern Kentucky Visitor Center—605 Philadelphia. 859/655-4159, 800/447-8489.

Cathedral Basilica of the Assumption—Modeled after Notre Dame Cathedral in Paris, the 82 stained-glass windows here are spectacular, one supposedly the largest church window in the world. Tours are given with advance notice. Weekdays 10:30 to 3:30, Sat 10 to 3:30, Sun 11 to 5; donations. Madison at 12th St. 859/431-2060.

Mimosa Mansion Museum—Tours of this 1850s home, the largest in the area, take visitors through 22 rooms filled with original furnishings. Weekends 1 to 6; admission fee. 412 E. 2nd St. 606/261-9000.

⊞ **Hampton Inn Riverfront**—151 rooms, outdoor pool, fitness center, ⊗ restaurant. I-71/75 exit 192. 859/581-7800. $$$ K18

⊞ **Holiday Inn Riverfront**—156 rooms, outdoor pool, ⊗ restaurant. I-71/75 exit 192. 859/291-4300. $$$ K18

⊨ **The Sandford House**—5 rooms in French Empire Mansion, full breakfast. 1026 Russel St. 859/291-9133.

Gallipolis, Ohio

Our House Museum—Restored 1819 river inn. Also includes a museum of early American history. Tue-Sat 10 to 4, Sun 1 to 4 (summer), Sat 10 to 4, Sun 1 to 4 (May, Sept, Oct); admission fee. 432 1st Ave. 740/446-0586.

Ironton, Ohio

Lawrence County Historical Museum—Restored Victorian that served as an Underground Railroad stop. Historic clothing collection. Fri-Sun 1 to 5 (Apr-Dec); admission fee. 506 S. 6th St. 740/532-1222.

Marietta, Ohio

Marietta/Washington County Convention and Visitors Bureau — Maps and touring suggestions are provided here. 316 3rd St. 740/373-5178, 800/288-2577. **Campus Martius: Museum of the Northwest Territory**—A reconstruction of early Marietta as the first white settlement in the Northwest Territory. Within the museum is Putnam House, the only remaining original building. Exhibits highlight the history of local Indians as well. Mon-Sat 9:30 to 5, Sun noon to 5 (summer), closed Mon & Tue (rest of the year); admission fee. 2nd & Washington Sts. 740/373-3750, 800/860-0145.

Indian Mounds—Several are located throughout the city: Quadranaou Mound at 4th and Warren Sts.; Capitolium Mound, 615 5th St.; Mound Cemetery 400 5th St.; and Sacred Via (a prehistoric sacred walled walkway) running from the 700 block of 3rd St. to the Muskingum River.

Ohio River Museum—The history of life on the river is told through riverboat models, memorabilia, and a video. An historic sternwheeler is moored here as well. Mon-Sat 9:30 to 5, Sun noon to 5, closed Mon & Tue (rest of year), sternwheeler open Apr-Oct (river level permitting); admission fee. Washington & Front Sts. 740/373-3750, 800/860-0145.

⊼ **Camp Civitan**—42 sites (all w/hookups); fee; water; modern/ ♿; showers; open 4/1-11/1; grills/ fire rings; tables. Playground; putting green; boat ramp. Dump station. I-77 exit 1, at the county fairgrounds, 922 Front St. 740/373-7937.

Maysville, Kentucky

Maysville Tourism Commission—216 Bridge St. 606/564-9411 **Mason County Museum**—Charming local museum dedicated to pioneer settlement, regional history, genealogy, and promoting local artisans. Mon to Sat 10 to 4 (reduced hours Jan-Feb); admission fee. 215 Sutton. 606/564-5865.

Old Washington—1785 village listed on the National Register was a way station for those traveling the Buffalo Trace. Visitor center, shops, and a full schedule of events. Interpretive tours available. Mon-Sat 10 to 4:30, Sun 1 to 4:30; fee for tours. S of town on US 68. 606/759-7411.

Underground Railroad Museum & Visitor Center—Museum relates the area's importance as a link on the covert escape route for slaves in the 1800s. Mon-Sat 10 to 4, Sun 1 to 4; free. 115 E. 3rd. 606/564-9411.

⊞ **Best Western Maysville**—54 rooms, indoor pool, spa, continental breakfast. US 68 & KY 9. 606/759-5696. $$$ K12

Pittsburgh, Pennsylvania

The Greater Pittsburgh Convention & Visitors Bureau—Open weekdays 9 to 5. 4 Gateway Center. 412/281-7711, 800/359-0758. *The Carnegie* Cultural complex that sponsors several performing arts series along with summer concerts in the sculpture court, has a museum dedicated to Andy Warhol and houses the city's own Carnegie Library. 4400 Forbes Ave. 412/622-3131 Other highlights include:

Carnegie Museum of Art—Emphasis is on Impressionists, post-Impressionists and 19th and 20th century American works. The architectural center combines drawings, models, and photographs that document building in America. Guided tours are offered on a variety of topics. Tues-Sat 10 to 5, Sun 1 to 5, also open Mon. in the summer; admission fee. 412/622-3131.

Carnegie Museum of Natural History—Ten complete skeletons fill Dinosaur Hall, and there are interactive exhibits on Egypt and the Polar regions. Geology,

gems, and minerals are a large portion of the collection, and animal mounts are plentiful. A discovery room for kids adds more hands-on activities. Tues-Sat 10 to 5, Sun 1 to 5, also open Mon. in the summer; admission fee. 412/622-3131.
Carnegie Science Center—A fully interactive science experience offering a wind tunnel, tornadoes, earthquakes, and a finely-detailed, animated miniature railroad and village. Omnimax theater and planetarium. Docked on the riverfront is the USS *Requin,* a WWII submarine where tours are given by former crew. Daily 10 to 5; admission fee (separate fee for sub tours, planetarium, and Omnimax theater). Next to Three Rivers Stadium. 412/237-3400, submarine 412/237-1550.
Cathedral of Learning—A 42-story gothic tower on the University of Pittsburgh campus. Inside are 23 classrooms decorated in a variety of national styles to celebrate the city's ethnic heritage. December is magical when each sports traditional holiday decor. Weekdays 9 to 3; Sat 9:30 to 3; Sun 11 to 3; admission fee. On the Quad at 5th and Forbes Aves. 412/624-6000.
The Frick Art & Historical Center—Anchored by Henry Clay Frick's restored 19th century home (the only mansion remaining along Millionaire's Row), this complex also contains a greenhouse, children's playhouse, museum filled with classic autos and carriages, and a museum showcasing artworks from the Renaissance through the 18th century. Tue-Sat 10 to 5:30, Sun noon to 6; admission to the grounds is free, donations are accepted at the museums, and there is a fee for house tours. 7227 Reynolds St. 412/371-0606.

Pomeroy, Ohio
Meigs County Museum—Museum of local history with extensive genealogical and photographic archives. Tue-Fri 1 to 4:30, donations. 144 Butternut Ave. 740/992-3810.

Portsmouth, Ohio
1810 House—Living history pioneer homestead. Hands-on experiences. Weekends 2 to 4 (May-Nov); admission fee. Sunrise Ave. at 20th St. 740/354-3760.
Southern Ohio Museum Center—Rotating exhibits of art and local and regional history. Performing arts calendar. Tue-Fri 10 to 5, Sat/Sun 1 to 5; admission fee. 825 Galla St. 740/354-5629.

Vevay, Indiana
Switzerland County Museum—Local and river history including steamboat models. Guided tours relate interesting trivia. Daily noon to 4 (Apr-Oct); admission fee. 210 E. Market St. 812/427-3560.

Wheeling, West Virginia
Wheeling Convention and Visitors Bureau—1401 Main St. 304/233-7709, 800/828-9097.
Kruger Street Toy & Train Museum—A restored Victorian schoolhouse harbors this charming collection that delights kids of all ages. Wed-Mon 10 to 6 (June-Dec), Fri-Sun 10 to 6 (rest of year); admission fee. 144 Kruger St. 304/252-8133, 877/242-8133.
Oglebay Park—Popular 1500-acre park with a glass museum where craftsmen provide demonstrations, the summer mansion of the park's namesake, and a zoo with hands-on exhibits, 1863 train, and planetarium. 4 miles of hiking and biking trails, picnic and sports areas, swimming, fishing, boating, par-3 and miniature golf course, and horse rentals are available. Hours vary at each location, park open 24 hours; admission fee includes pool, mansion, golf, zoo, tennis, and fishing. ⊞ 212 rooms, indoor and outdoor pools, spa, fitness center, ⊗ restaurant, cabins. $$$ K18 2 miles N of junction of US 40 and I-70. 304/243-4000.
West Virginia Independence Hall—This was a busy place during the Civil War when pro-Union West Virginia declared independence from Virginia. An exquisite period restoration project with guided and self-guided tours. Daily 10-4 (Mar-Dec), closed on Sun (rest of year); admission fee. 16th & Market Sts. 304/238-1300.

↢ Lewis and Clark ↣

Upon reaching Cincinnati near the end of September 1803, Meriwether Lewis had found a letter from William Clark awaiting him. Earlier that year, Lewis had written Clark to recruit some backwoodsmen—good hunters and trackers—from around his homes at **[7]** Clarksville, Indiana, and Louisville, Kentucky, across the Ohio River at the Falls. Lewis had warned him not to choose "young gentlemen" for a trip like this. In the Cincinnati letter, Lewis liked how his co-captain had replied, and promptly wrote back that Clark's ideas about the "judicious selection of our party perfectly comport with my own."

Clark, his slave York, and seven other recruits awaited the keelboat at Clarksville.

Lewis arrived in mid-October and indeed agreed with Clark's selection of men for the corps. Along with the two privates already on board, the seven later were accepted for the permanent party, and are popularly called "the nine young men from Kentucky." They were Charles Floyd, his cousin Nathaniel Pryor, Reubin Field and his brother Joseph (whom Clark had enlisted in August), John Shields, George Gibson, and William Bratton. After the new men were sworn into the army, the enlarged group set off on October 26, 1803.

During the rest at Clarksville, Lewis had stayed with his co-captain in the brand-new home William Clark was sharing with his older brother, George Rogers Clark. In the Revolutionary War, the elder Clark had conquered Illinois Territory for the United States by taking the British fort at Kaskaskia. For their service, he and his men were given land in future Indiana, and George Rogers Clark had donated acreage for the Clarksville townsite.

Arriving at [8] Fort Massac on November 11, the Corps stopped for two days. They added Private John Newman to the company, and made their most important civilian hire: George Drouillard. With a French-Canadian father, a Shawnee mother, and a surname that the captains could only spell phonetically (usually as Drewyer), he could "speak" Plains Indian sign language as well as Shawnee, French, and English. He was also a great wilderness scout and hunter; the captains would choose him more often than any other man for special assignments.

The first came right away, in fact. Eight soldiers assigned to the Corps from a Tennessee army camp should have been awaiting Lewis and Clark here at Massac, but were not. Lewis sent Drouillard to locate them and catch up with the Corps at St. Louis.

The keelboat and pirogues reached the Ohio's mouth on the Mississippi on November 14; more than thirty years later the city of Cairo, Illinois, would be founded there. After taking celestial observations for latitude and longitude, and exploring the area by boat and on foot, the Corps turned up the Mississippi on the 20th. Clark, an experienced surveyor, would have been an apt pupil as Lewis shared the lessons received in Pennsylvania.

Their third day of travel on the Mississippi ended at Cape Girardeau, a settlement of over a thousand souls (about the size of St. Louis at the time). November 28 brought them to [9] Fort Kaskaskia, on the Illinois bank opposite Old Ste. Genevieve, three miles south of Ste. Genevieve proper. (The fort's actual site was covered by the Mississippi in the late 1800s.) At Kaskaskia, eight army men joined the expedition, although their formal enlistment dates would vary: Sergeant John Ordway and privates John Boley, John Collins, John Dame, Patrick Gass, Francois Labiche, Peter M. Weiser, and Joseph Whitehouse. The following spring, Dame would be named to the return party, and the others to the permanent party.

By now the captains had given up the idea of starting up the Missouri this year. They would winter in the St. Louis area, the last trading place to obtain supplies, and a place where they could meet men who had been up the Missouri and learn more about what to expect. Lewis assigned Clark responsibility for the boats and their men, and all but Lewis headed upstream on December 3.

On the 5th, Lewis set out overland, by horseback, to present his credentials at St. Louis. He welcomed the offer of Kaskaskia postmaster John Hay and fur trader Nicholas Jarrot, both "well acquainted with the English & French Languages," to go along as translators. Lewis had learned that the fort's commandant spoke French and Spanish but not English, and Lewis spoke no Spanish.

TOURING TODAY

⫷ LEWIS AND CLARK, 1803 ⫸

[ ]	Bracketed numbers key sites to maps	♿	Special-needs accessible	⊨	Bed & breakfast
★	L&C in-depth interpretation, unchanged landform	⊗	Restaurant	⛺	Camping, RV park
•	L&C interpreted site	⊞	Motel, hotel, cabin		

Bridges across the Ohio River: I-65 between Jeffersonville, IN and Louisville, KY; I-64 between Louisville, KY and New Albany, IN; IN 135/KY 228 between Mauckport, IN and Brandenburg, KY; US 231 at Owensboro, KY; US 41 between Evansville, IN and Henderson, KY; US 45 at Paducah, KY; I-24 at Paducah, KY; US51/US60 at Cairo, IL.

Bridges across the Mississippi River: I-57 at Cairo, IL; IL 146/MO 34/74 at Cape Girardeau, MO; I-255 south of St. Louis.

Ferries across the Ohio River: Higginsport, OH to Augusta, KY daily auto/passenger service (daily 8 to 8, fee) 606/756-2464; KY 91 (11 miles NW of Marion, KY) to Cave-In-Rock, IL (daily 6 am to 10 pm on signal; free).

ALONG THE EXPEDITION'S PATH

October 14-26, 1803

[7] ★ Clark's Point (Clarksville, IN)—On this ground within Falls of the Ohio State Park, George Rogers Clark built his cabin in 1803 and, a few months later, Lewis met William Clark here to begin their journey together. Archaeological excavations have established the probable cabin site, and a reconstruction is planned with interpretation about the Expedition. A trail to the interpretive center is also planned. Tue-Sat 9 to 5, Sun 1 to 5; free. Harrison and Bailey. 812/280-9970.

[7] Falls of the Ohio State Park (Clarksville, IN)—Within the 375-million-year-old Devonian fossil beds found here, over 600 species have been identified (most for the first time). The limestone outcroppings provide excellent viewing opportunities for the 220 acres of beds, particularly in late summer and early fall when the river is at its lowest. Fishing, hiking, and picnics are also popular. An interpretive center's multimedia exhibits complement the full-size mammoth skeleton in the lobby. Time-line displays and interactive activities bring the concepts alive. The center is adjacent to Clark's Point. Park open dawn to dusk (free); center open Mon-Sat 9 to 5, Sun noon to 5; admission fee. I-65 exit 0. 812/280-9970.

[7] ★ Filson Club Historical Society (Louisville, KY)—Founded in 1884, this group has gathered an exceptional collection of documents and photographs related to all aspects of the state's history. Expedition-related original documents and artifacts. Exhibits showcase only a small portion of holdings at any one time. Only the genealogy library charges a fee. Weekdays 9 to 5. 1900 Ferguson Mansion, 1310 S. Third. 502/635-5083.

[7] ★ Locust Grove Historic Home (St. Matthews, KY)—1790 Georgian mansion built by Clark's sister Lucy and her husband, William Croghan. Both Lewis and Clark stayed here in 1806 on their way back to Washington. George Rogers Clark moved here in 1809. Several plantation buildings and gardens have also been restored. Dozens of important people of the time stayed here and the visitor center exhibitions details the property's illustrious history. Guided tours are provided and children have a special area where reproduction clothing and a Revolutionary War soldier's trunk and equipment are ripe for exploration. Mon-Sat 10 to 4:30, Sun 1:30 to 4:30; admission fee. I-264 exit 22, 0.5 miles W on US 42. 561 Blankenbaker Ln. 502/897-9845.

Between October 26 & November 10, 1803

Fort Knox (Fort Knox, KY)—A military base since 1918, training Army and Marine Corps. The Gold Vault is here, but not open to the public. Tours are offered of the Patton Museum where the history of armored and cavalry troops is told. Two-mile **Heritage Walking Trail** is a self-guided trip through a natural area, unchanged since the mid-1800s. (800/334-7540). Museum open daily 10 to 4:30; free. 502/624-3812.

Otter Creek Park (just W of Fort Knox, KY)—Wilderness area along the Ohio River cliffs, with scenic overlooks and 15 miles of hiking trails. Rappelling, climbing, and spelunking opportunities. Nature center, pool, boating, canoeing, and fishing. ⊞ Lodge with ⊗ restaurant, cabins. ▲ 202 sites (136 w/hookups); fee; water; modern/&; showers; open all year; grills/fire rings; tables. Groceries; dump station; pavilion. On KY 1638, 3 miles W of US 31. 502/942-3641.

Angel Mounds State Historic Site (Evansville, IN)—Site of a prehistoric Moundbuilders' village that was occupied from 1100 to 1450. An interpretive center supplements reconstructed dwellings and sacred places. Trails through the area include nature interpretation. Tue-Sat 9 to 5, Sun 1 to 5; admission fee. I-164, Covert Ave. exit. 8215 Pollack Ave. 812/853-3956.

John James Audubon State Park (Henderson, KY)—Established as a memorial to the naturalist who lived here for 9 years, this park contains nature center and a natural area with trails containing over 150 varieties of wildflowers. At the museum, the story of Audubon's life is told through his artwork and memorabilia. A gallery containing paintings and original prints from his publications is particularly popular. The Discovery Center provides hands-on activities for children of all ages. Extensive recreation facilities include a 9-hole golf course, swimming, boat dock and rentals, fishing, and a recreation program. ▲ 64 sites (54 w/hookups); fee; water; modern/&; showers; open all year; grills/fire rings; tables. Dump station; coin laundry; playground. N on US 41. 270/826-2247.

Cave-in-Rock State Park (Cave-in-Rock, IL)—Discovered in 1729, this 55-foot-wide cave, carved by water, now sits atop the Ohio River bluffs and has harbored a variety of robbers, murderers, and other ne'er-do-wells. Hiking trails climb the bluffs and are a bit strenuous. Several picnic areas dot the area and fishing and boating on the Ohio are popular. ⊞ Cabins and a ⊗ restaurant (618/289-4545) supplement ▲ 59 sites (34 w/hookups); fee; water; primitive/&; no showers; open all year; grills/fire rings; tables. Dump station. Off IL 1 on the river. 618/289-4325.

▲ Tower Rock Recreation Area (Cave-in-Rock, IL)—35 sites (no hookups); fee; water; primitive/ &; no showers; open 5/1-12/15; grills/fire rings; tables. Boat ramp on the Ohio; fishing; hiking trails. Follow signs 4 miles W on county road, 7 miles S on FR 101. 618/287-2201.

▲ Steamboat Hill/Ohio River Recreation Area (Golconda, IL)—17 primitive sites; fee; water; primitive; no showers; open 4/1-12/15; grills/fire rings; tables. 1 mile N on IL 146, 0.5 miles E on FR 411. 618/658-2111.

November 11, 1803

[8] ★ Fort Massac State Park (Metropolis, IL)—A reconstruction of the fort visited by George Rogers Clark in 1778 and by the Corps in 1803 is part of this 1470-acre park. It is alleged that Capt.

Daniel Bissell, commander from 1801 to 1808, was involved with Aaron Burr's plot to conquer the southwest. Museum provides exhibits on 18th century life, and a re-enactors encampment is held each fall. ▲ 58 sites; fee; water; modern/primitive/&; showers; open all year; grills/fire rings; tables. Boat ramp; playground; nature trails; fishing. Dump station. E of town off US 45. 1308 E. 5th St. 618/524-9321.

November 20, 1803
Trail of Tears State Park (Cape Girardeau, MO)—Memorializes the route used by the Cherokees on their forced march to Oklahoma. Marked trails follow their path taken in 1838-39. Abundant wildlife viewing. ▲ 53 sites (18 w/hookups); fee; water; modern/&; showers; open all year; grills/fire rings; tables. Dump station; coin laundry; boating; fishing; swimming; playground. 10 miles N on MO 177. 573/334-1711.

November 27, 1803
[9] ★ Fort Kaskaskia State Historic Site (Ellis Grove, IL)—The original fort, built by French residents of the area, had been destroyed by its creators in 1766 to prevent its capture by the British in the French and Indian War. Later, the U.S. Army created its own facilities that the Corps visited.
Bolduc House (Ste. Genevieve, MO)—Restored 1785 home of wealthy merchant filled with period French Canadian furnishings. Mon-Sat 10 to 4, Sun 11 to 5 (Apr-Nov); admission fee. 125 S. Main 573/883-3105.

AROUND THE AREA

TOWNS LISTED ALPHABETICALLY

Aurora, Indiana
Hillforest—Restored 1852 Italian Renaissance estate of a wealthy industrialist. Tours provide an intimate glimpse into his elaborate lifestyle. Tue-Sun 1 to 5 (Apr-Dec); admission fee. 213 5th St. 812/926-0087.

Boonville, Indiana
Warrick County Museum—Located in a 1901 schoolhouse, local and regional history exhibits are supplemented by state and national traveling exhibits. Tours and special programs. Mon-Thur 11 to 2, Sun 1 to 4; donations. 217 S. 1st St. 812/897-3100.

Cairo, Illinois
Cairo Chamber of Commerce—220 8th St. 618/734-2737.
Custom House Museum—An eclectic collection of local, Civil War, and Indian artifacts. Model turn-of-the-century post office and extensive photography collection. Weekdays 10 to 3; donations. 1400 Washington Ave. 618/734-1019.
Magnolia Manor—Victorian home with original furnishings, graceful curving staircase, and well-preserved architectural features. Guided tours. Mon-Sat 9 to 5, Sun 1 to 5; admission fee. 2700 Washington Ave. 618/734-0201.

Cape Girardeau, Missouri
Cape Girardeau Cape River Heritage Museum—Exhibits detailing area heritage and history, including Mississippi River transportation. Wed, Fri, Sat 11 to 4; admission fee. 538 Independence St. 573/334-0405.

Evansville, Indiana
Evansville Convention and Visitors Bureau—401 SE Riverside Dr. 812/421-2200, 800/433-3025.
Evansville Museum of Arts & Science—Complex of several areas dedicated to the history of art, experiential exhibits of science and technology, and a planetarium. A 19th-century river town has been recreated, and the transportation center relates the history of man's inventions. Tue-Sat 10 to 5, Sun noon to 5; admission fee. 411 SE Riverside Dr. 812/425-2406.
Reitz Home Museum—French Second Empire 1871 mansion of a lumber magnate has been restored and contains many original furnishings highlighted by ornate architectural motifs. Guided tours bring the time to life. Tue-Sat 11 to 3:30, Sun 1 to 3:30; admission fee. 124 SE First St. 812/426-1871.

Jeffersonville, Indiana
Howard Steamboat Museum—Housed in an 1890s Romanesque Revival mansion built by the founder of the local shipyards. Restoration has been completed, and the original furniture and collection of ship-related items are to be seen. Tours given Tue-Sat 10 to 4, Sun 1 to 4; admission fee. 1101 E. Market. 812/283-3728.

Louisville, Kentucky
Louisville Visitors Information Center—Open Mon-Fri 8:30 to 5, Sat 9 to 4, Sun 11 to 4. 400 S. 1st St. 502/582-3732.
Actors Theatre—Award-winning company with international reputation. Hosts annual festival for new plays in the spring. Season from Sept through June; admission fee. 316 W. Main. 502/584-1205.
Churchill Downs/Kentucky Derby Museum—Monument to the heart of Kentucky with three floors of exhibits and hands-on displays exploring all aspects of thoroughbreds and their importance to the state. A simulation of Derby Day is popular. Tours of Churchill Downs are given, weather permitted. Mon-Sat 9 to 5, Sun noon to 5; admission fee. 704 Central Ave. 502/637-1111.
Louisville Science Center—An 1800s warehouse has been transformed into a sleek, high-tech home for hundreds of hands-on exhibits exploring science and math from a variety of perspectives. Special area for kids under 8. IMAX theatre brings in films that broaden the imagination. Mon-Thur 10 to 5, Fri-Sat 10 to 9, Sun noon to 5; admission fee, combination tickets available. 727 W. Main. 502/561-6100.
Louisville Slugger Museum—The 120-foot, 68,000-pound metal baseball bat at the entrance sets the stage for the treasures within. Visiting fans explore the history of America's sport through memorabilia in a recreated locker room and dugout before touring the manufacturing area. Mon-Sat 9 to 5; admission fee. 800 W. Main. 502/588-7228.
Portland Museum—At the Falls of the Ohio, this museum includes multimedia exhibits recounting

200 years of river heritage. Highlighted are films of the 1937 flood. Displays also located in adjacent antebellum mansion. Tue-Fri 10 to 4:30; admission fee. 2308 Portland Ave. 502/776-7678

Six Flags Kentucky Kingdom—Amusement park with over 100 rides highlighted by the world's longest stand-up roller coaster, a 15-story free-fall ride, water park, and special area for children under 49 inches tall. Sun-Thur 10 to 9, Fri-Sat 10 to 10 (summer) open weekends only (Apr, May, Sept, Oct); admission fee. I-65 Fair Center exit. 502/366-2231, 800/727-3267.

Metropolis, Illinois

Super Museum—Superman's hometown celebrates their hero with a museum dedicated to the comic strip, TV shows, and movies. Daily 9 to 5; admission fee. 517 Market St. 618/524-5518.

New Albany, Indiana

Southern Indiana Chamber of Commerce—4100 Charleston Rd. 812/945-0266.

Carnegie Center for Art & History—Home to a hand-carved, animated diorama portraying pioneer life, this museum also has an impressive art collection, innovative historical exhibits, and hosts a variety of traveling exhibits. Tue-Sat 10 to 5:30; admission fee. 201 E. Spring St. 812/944-7336.

Culbertson Mansion State Historic Site—Philanthropist William Culbertson's exquisite French Second Empire mansion cost $120,000 in 1867 and is filled with marble fireplaces, a towering 3-story staircase, frescoed ceilings,

period antiques, and charming tour guides. Tue-Sat 9 to 5, Sun 1 to 5 (Mar-Dec); donations. 914 E. Main St. 812/944-9600.

New Harmony, Indiana

Atheneum—Dramatic, contemporary visitor center for Historic New Harmony provides a film about the town's communal history and contributions to scientific inquiry. Exhibit about the founders and diorama of its past. Walking tours are conducted among surviving buildings, the roofless church, and outdoor sculptures. Daily 9 to 5 (Apr-Oct), 9 to 4 (Mar, Nov, Dec); admission fee for film and walking tours. North & Arthur Sts. 812/682-4474, 800/231-2168.

▲ Harmonie State Park—200 sites (all w/hookups); fee; water; modern/&; showers; open all year; grills/fire rings; tables. Dump station; outdoor pool; hiking trails; picnic area; playground; summer recreation programs; bike rentals. 4 miles S on IN 69. 812/682-4821.

Owensboro, Kentucky

Owensboro-Daviess County Chamber of Commerce—335 Frederica St. 270/926-1860.

Owensboro Museum of Science and History—Exhibits cover the spectrum with scientific fields including archaeology and anthropology. Local and regional history displays and a hands-on area for children. Tue-Sat 10 to 5, Sun 1 to 4; free. 220 Davis St. 270/687-2732.

Paducah, Kentucky

Paducah-McCracken County Convention and Visitors Bureau—128 Broadway. 270/443-8783, 800/723-8224.

Market House Museum—Turn-of-the-20th-century building houses an 1877 drugstore and local and regional history displays. Art center hosts revolving exhibitions and theater hosts a full schedule of events. Museum open Mon-Sat noon to 4 (Mar-Dec); admission fee. 121 Market House Sq 502/443-7759.

Museum of the American Quilters Society—The stories of individual pieces, as well as history of the craft, are told in engaging style. Mon-Sat 10 to 5, Sun 1 to 5 (Apr-Oct), closed Sun (rest of year); admission fee. 215 Jefferson. 270/442-8856.

Ste. Genevieve, Missouri

Great River Road Interpretive Center—66 S. Main St. 573/883-7097, 800/373-7007.

Felix Valle Home State Historic Site—Stone Federal-style 1818 house used as both home and office is furnished in period style. Mon-Sat 10 to 4, Sun noon to 5; admission fee. 2nd & Merchant Sts. 573/883-7102.

Ste. Genevieve Museum—Interpretation of the city's role throughout history, including the Civil War. Audubon bird mounts and Indian exhibits. Daily 9 to 4 (Apr-Oct), noon to 4 (rest of year): admission fee. 3rd & Merchant Sts. 573/883-3461.

Vevay, Indiana

Switzerland County Museum—Local and river history including steamboat models. Guided tours relate interesting trivia. Daily noon to 4 (Apr-Oct); admission fee. 210 E. Market St. 812/427-3560.

CHAPTER 2

December 5, 1803 to May 13, 1804
CAMP DUBOIS

Captain Meriwether Lewis had been in Pittsburgh when Jefferson's letter reached him on July 22, 1803, confirming that the United States had signed the treaty purchasing "Louisiana," lands that were drained by the Mississippi and Missouri rivers. The government of "Upper Louisiana" was based in the village of St. Louis, which had developed near the Missouri River's mouth on the west side of the Mississippi. By 1803, the forty-year-old French settlement was home to somewhat more than 1,000 residents, of whom 268 were slaves and 56 were free blacks. Lewis, with local men John Hay and Nicholas Jarrot as interpreters, arrived there on December 8 by his account, after spending the night at Cahokia on the Illinois side.

As soon as Lewis presented himself to the the lieutenant governor of Upper Louisiana, Carlos Dehault Delassus, he learned that the transfer of Louisiana from Spain to France had not yet occurred. Because Lewis carried only a French and British passports for the expedition, Colonel Delassus politely required time to contact his superior in New Orleans about allowing these Americans into Spanish territory. He told Lewis that December was not the time to start up the Missouri (which the captains knew), and so expedition members could winter on the east—American—side of the Mississippi. By spring, Delassus would have a reply and, he said, could no doubt allow them passage.

Lewis just as politely agreed that he was sure by spring there would be no obstacle to their traveling into Upper Louisiana. Lewis spent the evening visiting with Delassus and returned to Cahokia the next day. Writing to Jefferson about the encounter, Lewis used such terms as "friendly," "much politeness," and "as a friend." He also explained the necessity of a winter encampment.

While Lewis stayed at Cahokia to "acquire information of the Countrey," Captain William Clark and the rest of the command made their way up the Mississippi. On the Illinois side on December 4, they saw the ruins of Fort de Chartres, once the French capital of Upper Louisiana. After the British had captured the fort, the wandering Mississippi began stealing its land from the conqueror, so the British had abandoned the site three decades earlier.

At mid-afternoon on a cold, rainy, violently windy December 7, the boats put in at Cahokia, Illinois's oldest town, and three days later set out up the Mississippi for the mouth of Wood River. Trader Jarrot owned 400 acres there, and offered it to the expedition; the site had plentiful game, and timber for logs and fuel, and would serve well for their winter stay. The boats arrived at Wood River on December 12 in wind, hail and snow. Because the Missouri has since shifted its course to the east, the exact site now is thought to be in Missouri.

The next day they began building a camp that Sergeant John Ordway called "Camp River Dubois" and we now refer to as Camp Dubois [1]. (Wood River had been named Rivière à Dubois after a French surname, and Americans wrongly translated the phrase to Wood River instead of Wood's River.) The wooden or log buildings may have had a palisade around them. During the winter, the soldiers received some rations and supplies from an Illinois military commissary, and had the services of an army doctor.

Lewis, based at Cahokia, traveled back and forth to St. Louis, corresponded regularly with Clark and sent information to Jefferson, bought more supplies including all-important mosquito netting, and interviewed anyone he met who knew about the people and the land up the Missouri River. On December 16, Private George Drouillard arrived at Cahokia from Tennessee with the eight army men sent for the expedition. Four of them lacked skills that

Lewis thought needed for the journey, and were immediately released, but he accepted privates Hugh Hall, Thomas P. Howard, and John Potts. Corporal Richard Warfington was also kept, and later agreed to spend the winter of 1804-1805 at Fort Mandan—even though his enlistment ended in August 1804—to command the keelboat and its return party.

Clark, after overseeing the camp's construction, worked out how to refit the keelboat for carrying more freight and serving, if needed, as a floating fort. He dealt with drunken soldiers and fighting soldiers and thieving soldiers, and created shooting and athletic contests to help keep the men's minds occupied. He assessed their hunting and other skills and how they got along in close quarters, and kept notes on strengths and weaknesses—looking to the months ahead, and to selection of the permanent party. He faithfully recorded weather conditions, and practiced celestial observations. He answered letters from family, dolefully telling his sister's
husband in mid-January: "I have not been from Camp to any house since my arrival here." By the time Lewis arrived, Clark had been ill for a while, but he took a six-mile horseback ride the next day. Clark got his turn to visit St. Louis for at least three weeks in February, and two or three more weeks in March.

When both captains were gone from camp, according to Lewis's Detachment Orders of February 20, 1804, Sergeant Ordway was in charge of "good poliece and order..." Some men didn't obey Ordway the first time, and were confined to camp for ten days. On March 3, Lewis again sent orders to the camp, "mortified and disappointed" about the behavior of men who later turned out to be excellent expedition members, Reubin Field and John Shields, the blacksmith and gunsmith. Now was the time to establish military discipline.

In the spring, Clark wrote this genial summary:

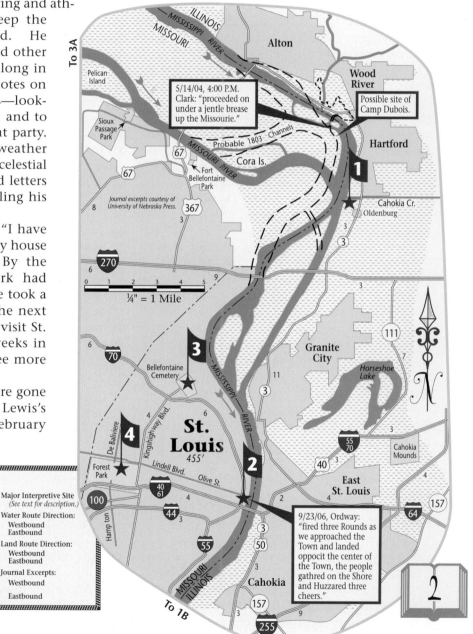

5/14/04, 4:00 P.M. Clark: "proceeded on under a jentle brease up the Missourie."

Possible site of Camp Dubois.

9/23/06, Ordway: "fired three Rounds as we approached the Town and landed oppocit the center of the Town, the people gathred on the Shore and Huzzared three cheers."

¼" = 1 Mile

MAP SYMBOLS

Interstate Highway	
U.S., State Highway	
County Road	
Lewis & Clark Trail Highway	
Bottom Lands *(Roads may be impassable during certain seasons.)*	
Travel Restrictions *(Inquire Locally)*	
Streamflow Direction	

Major Interpretive Site *(See text for description.)*

Water Route Direction:
Westbound
Eastbound

Land Route Direction:
Westbound
Eastbound

Journal Excerpts:
Westbound
Eastbound

Capts. Lewis & Clark wintered at the enterance of a Small river opposite the Mouth of Missouri Called Wood River, where they formed their party, Composed of robust helthy hardy young men, recomended.

As it turned out, the captains chose well, and few discipline problems occurred, notably only in the expedition's earliest days, when disobedience was punished promptly and firmly.

At Camp Dubois, the men awoke Clark on Christmas morning with a round of gunfire—a Southern tradition. Their feast included deer and turkey, and cheese and fresh butter. New Year's Eve and Day brought more complaints in Clark's journal about drunkenness, which was the way many Americans then celebrated both days. On New Year's Day, Clark put up a dollar prize for a shooting contest as a diversion. Private George Gibson won.

When the temperature reached 10° below in January 1804, the men built sleds to haul enough firewood. They had to watch for frostbite when their boots froze to their skin.

Late in February, John Shields and Alexander Willard crafted metal articles for the trip.

Other men boiled maple sap to supplement purchased sugar (to the delight of Indians they would meet, including Sacagawea), and parched corn to carry dry.

In ceremonies held March 10 and 11, 1804, at St. Louis, Spain transferred Upper Louisiana to France, which then conveyed it to military representatives of the United States. Lewis and Clark must have attended the event, but neither recorded it. Perhaps to them the formality was old news.

The captains then began drafting speeches to deliver to native peoples. In April they issued "Knives Tomahawkes &c. &c. to men…" These tools couldn't be replaced during the trip, and men who misplaced theirs along the way were sent back—regardless of weather or other conditions—to retrieve them.

On May 8, the men loaded their keelboat and one of two dugouts, and tested the keelboat on the Mississippi. On the 11th Drouillard brought in seven French boatmen, who were hired for the trip's first leg. Two days later, Clark sent a messenger to Lewis in St. Louis saying that men and boats were "in health and readiness to Set out."

TOURING TODAY

～ CAMP DUBOIS AREA ～

[ ]	**Bracketed numbers key sites to maps**	♿ Special-needs accessible	⊨ Bed & breakfast
★	L&C in-depth interpretation, unchanged landform	⊗ Restaurant	⋀ Camping, RV park
•	L&C interpreted site	⊞ Motel, hotel, cabin	

Bridges on main highways over the Mississippi River in this area are Clark Bridge, the only cable-stay bridge in the world, Alton, IL (US 67); St. Louis, MO (I-270, I-55/70, I-255/US 50). Bridge over the Missouri River is on US 67.

Ferries—Free ferries will float you and your vehicle across the Mississippi at Brussels, IL and Kampsville, IL. These ferries operate 24 hours, 7 days a week. Golden Eagle (near St. Charles, MO, 618/883-2217) and Winfield (in Batchtown, MO 618/396-2408) ferries both charge a fee and run 5am to 8pm. (Sun starting at 8am.)

ALONG THE EXPEDITION'S PATH

Winter 1803 to May 13, 1804 (Return Sept. 23, 1806)

[1] Lewis and Clark State Historic Site (Hartford, IL)—Camp Dubois and the expedition are memorialized in a rotunda supported by 11 concrete columns, each representing a state through which the group travelled. Informational plaques summarize their adventures. A reconstruction of the camp and an interpretive center are scheduled to open by 2003.

Daily; free. IL 3, 3.5 miles N of I-270. 618/344-5268.

★ Camp Dubois—Originally on the Mississippi's eastern shore, the exact site is now thought to be in Missouri because of two centuries of flooding and erosion that shifted the river's course. While here, both Lewis and Clark travelled repeatedly to Cahokia and St. Louis, gathering information and provisions.

[2] ★ Jefferson National Expansion Memorial (St. Louis, MO)—90-acre complex located on the site of the original St. Louis settlement honoring Thomas Jefferson, Louisiana Purchase, and westward exploration and expansion. After the expedition, both Lewis and Clark lived on sites now contained in the park. 8am to 10pm (summer), 9 to 6 (winter); free. 11 N. 4th St., at the Arch. 314/655-1700.

Gateway Arch (St. Louis, MO)—Ride a tram to the top of this 630-foot stainless steel arch for a dramatic view of the area. Documentary film; historical overview along the ride. Get tickets early in the day. 8am to 10pm (summer), 9 to 6 (winter); admission fee. 877/982-1410.

Museum of Westward Expansion (St. Louis, MO)—Early explorers and pioneers in life-size exhibits; large collection of Indian Peace medals, including a large Jefferson medal of the type the Corps distributed. Football-field–length exhibit of David Muench landscape photographs shows ecological zones through which the Corps passed. 8am to 10pm (summer), 9 to 6 (winter); free. 314/655-1700.

Old Courthouse (St. Louis, MO)—Built in 1839; nine years later, it saw the beginning of the Dred Scott case. Scott, a slave in Missouri, sued for freedom after his master had taken him to live in two free states and then returned with him to Missouri. Film presentation of St. Louis history, including the Corps of Discovery, trial reenactments. Guided tours involve several flights of stairs. Daily 8 to 4:30; free. 314/655-1600.

[3] ★ Bellefontaine Cemetery (St. Louis, MO)—Final resting place of Captain William Clark and other historical figures. Monument was dedicated during the 1904 expedition centennial. Daily 8 to 5; free. 4947 W. Florissant Ave. 314/381-0750.

[4] ★ Missouri History Museum (St. Louis, MO)—Four floors of exhibits document Indian cultures, Louisiana Purchase, Lewis and Clark Expedition (with a national bicentennial exhibit opening in 2003), westward expansion, 1904 World's Fair, the Gilded Age, and more. Computers put you in the center of the past. Wed-Sun 10 to 6; Tue to 8; free. Jefferson Memorial Building, Forest Park. 314/746-4599.

AROUND THE AREA

Meeting of the Great Rivers National Scenic Byway—Begins in Alton at the Melvin Price Locks and Dam and continues along the river to Kampsville. Views of the bluffs, countryside and historic stone houses in a relatively unspoiled area. 800/258-6645.

Alton, Illinois

Alton Convention & Visitors Bureau—Alton takes pride in its potential stature as "the most haunted town in America," coined by those who study ghostly appearances. Local tours highlight this unusual heritage. 200 Piasa, 800-258-6645.

Alton Cemetery—Mobs destroyed three of abolitionist editor Elijah Lovejoy's presses in 1836, and a year later he was killed by another pro-slavery mob. 90-foot monument commemorates his life. Daily; free. 2 blocks N of E. Broadway on 5th St. and Monument Ave.

Alton Museum of History and Art—Visit Lovejoy's print shop, explore river town life. Exhibits about Underground Railroad, and Robert Wadlow, world's tallest man. Fri-Sun 1 to 4; admission fee. 2809 College, in Loomis Hall. 618/462-2763.

National Great Rivers Museum—Under construction at the Melvin Price Locks and Dam for a 2001 opening, this museum provides an intimate, interactive look at the Mississippi (and other rivers) and their significance throughout American history. At Melvin Price Locks & Dam. 888-899-2602.

Penitentiary Monument—Partial stone wall is a remnant of the state's first prison, denounced by reformist Dorothea Dix. It was used as a Civil War prison camp, and interpretive signs relate the Civil War's impact on the area. Always open; free. Broadway and William Sts.

Sam Vadalabene Bike Trail—A 14.5-mile paved trail along the Great River Road from Alton, IL to Pere Marquette State Park. Incredible scenery, including the recently refurbished Piasa Bird Native American bluff painting. The **Mark**

Twain National Wildlife Refuge parallels the trail from Pere Marquette State Park to the Brussels Ferry. Bike rentals. 618/465-6676.

⊞ **Comfort Inn**—62 rooms, indoor pool, exercise room, hot tub, pets, continental breakfast. &. 11 Crossroads Cr. 618/465-9999, 800/228-5150. $$ K18

⊞ **Holiday Inn Alton**—137 rooms, indoor pool, ⊗ restaurant, hot tub, exercise room, pets. &. 3800 Homer Adams Pkwy. 618/462-1220. $$$ K18

⊨ **Beall Mansion**—5 rooms in elegant, historic brick mansion, full breakfast. 407 E. 12th. 618/474-9100. $$$+

Ballwin, Missouri

Castlewood State Park—Towering bluffs along the Meramec River make this park popular for fishing, canoeing, hiking, and picnics. Bike and horse trails. Daily 7am to 10pm; free. East on Kiefer Creek Road, off New Ballwin Road from MO 100. 636/227-4433.

Cahokia, Illinois

Cahokia Courthouse State Historic Site—Built in 1737 as a residence, it served as a courthouse from 1793 until 1814 and was often visited by Lewis. Interactive exhibits detail early French impact on the area. Tue-Sat 9 to 5; donations. Off I-55/70 at IL 3. 618/332-1782.

▲ **Cahokia RV Parque**—116 sites (111 w/hookups); fee; water; modern/&; showers; open all year; grills/fire rings; tables. Pool; playground. Dump station; coin laundry. 2 miles W of I-255 exit 13 on IL 157. 1st & Elm Sts. 618/332-7700.

Collinsville, Illinois

Cahokia Mounds State Historic Site—The largest Indian mound north of Mexico, Monks Mound (100 feet high with a 14-acre base), is part of an archaeological complex dating from 700 A.D. Flourishing as the hub of a trading nation between 900 and 1500, the town grew to nearly 20,000 in population. A United Nations World Heritage Site. Picnic area and guided tours daily 8 to dusk. Interpretive Center daily 9 to 5; donations. I-55/70, exit 6, on IL 111. 618/346-5160.

⊞ Days Inn—60 rooms, pool, ⊗ restaurant, pets. ᕱ. Hilltop location with scenic views. I-55/70, exit 11. 618/345-8100. $$ K16

⊞ Holiday Inn Collinsville/St. Louis, 231 rooms, indoor pool, ⊗ restaurant, hot tub, exercise room. I-70, exit 11, 1000 Eastport Plaza Dr. 618/345-2800. $$$ K18

Elsah, Illinois

Village of Elsah Museum—With the entire town on the Historic Register, this is the starting point for walking tours. Free. 51 Mill St. 618/374-1059.

⊨ **Green Tree Inn**—6 rooms in historic mansion, private entrances, full breakfast. 15 Mill St. 618/374-2821, 800/701-8003. $$$

⊗ **Elsah Landing Restaurant**—Old-fashioned bakery and restaurant in historic setting, renowned fare, ᕱ. Daily 11 to 7:30, smoke-free. 11 miles W of Alton on IL 100, N on Elsah Rd. 18 LaSalle St. 618/786-7687. $

Grafton, Illinois

Pere Marquette State Park—A 7,895-acre preservation and recreation area dedicated to Father Jacques Marquette, a French missionary and explorer with a 1673 group seeking the Mississippi/Illinois confluence. ▲ Many options for RVs, tents and organized group camps. Deluxe rooms and ⊗ meals are available at the ⊞ stone lodge and 22 cabins constructed in the 1930s by the Civilian Conservation Corps. Don't miss the scrumptious Sunday brunch. 15 miles of hiking trails for varying abilities wind along the river. 12 miles of equestrian trails; horses available for rent. Picnic areas along the river and atop the bluffs. Visitor center and interpretive programs tell of people on this land over the centuries. ▲ 115 sites (80 w/hookups); fee; water; modern/ ᕱ; showers; open all year/full operation Apr-Oct; grills/fire rings; tables; 15-day limit. Fishing; boating; boat ramp/dock. Dump station. 25 miles W of US 67 on IL 100. 618/786-3323.

Sam Vadalabene Bike Trail is 14.5 miles from Alton, IL to Pere Marquette State Park. See description above under Alton, Illinois.

⊞ **Ruebel Hotel**—22 rooms in historic hotel, 10 secluded cottages and 4 rooms in lodge on river bluff. ⊗ Restaurant. 217 E. Main. 618/786-2315. $$

Granite City, Illinois

Horseshoe Lake State Park—Indians resided in the area from 8000 B.C., and artifacts from the Woodland Period, 1000 B.C. to 1000 A.D., have been found. Now a 2,854-acre park where visitors can picnic, boat, and fish. 3.5 miles of trails for hiking. **Walkers Island Birdwalk** is a self-guided 4-mile trail for all seasons. Daily 7am to 10pm; free. ▲ 48 sites; fee; water; primitive; open all year/full operation Apr-Oct; grills/fire rings; tables; 15-day limit. Dump station. 4 miles S of I-270 on IL 111. 618/931-0270.

▲ **KOA-St. Louis Area**—74 sites (67 w/hookups); fee; water; modern/ᕱ; showers; open Mar-Oct; grills/fire rings; tables. Pool; playground; ⊞ cabins. Dump station; coin laundry; groceries. I-270 exit 3A, 0.25 mile S on IL 3, 0.5 mile E on Chain of Rocks Road. 800/562-5861.

Kampsville, Illinois

Center for American Archeology—Exhibits of artifacts and interactive displays demonstrating dig and research methods. Tour and programs at local dig sites. Open June to mid-Nov, Mon-Sat 10 to 5, Sun noon to 5; admission fee. Broadway & Marquette. 618/653-4316.

Kimmswick, Missouri

Mastodon State Historic Site—When an American mastodon was found here the area became a site for Ice Age study. Museum exhibits a replica skeleton and prehistoric articles discovered in the park. 425-acre park; interpretive and hiking trails. Daily 9 to 4:30, Sun noon to 4:30; free, admission fee for museum. 20 miles S of St. Louis on I-55, take Exit 186. 636/464-2976.

Robertsville, Missouri

Robertsville State Park—Along the Meramec River and Calvey Creek, this wetland area attracts waterfowl. Hiking, picnic area, and boat ramp. ▲ 27 sites (15 w/hookups); fee; water; modern/ᕱ; showers; open all year/full operation Apr-Oct; grills/fire rings; tables; 15-day limit. Dump station; coin laundry; firewood. 5 miles S of I-44 on Highway O. 636/257-3788; 800/334-6946.

St. Louis, Missouri Area

St. Louis Convention and Visitors Bureau, One Metropolitan Square, Suite 1100, 63102. 314/421-1023; 800/916-0092.

Metrolink—Light rail service between Lambert Field and downtown area. 314/231-2345.

Field House and Toy Museum—Restored childhood home of poet Eugene Field, also owned by Dred Scott attorney Roswell Field. Museum of antique toys and dolls. Wed-Sat 10 to 4, Sun noon to 4; admission fee. 634 S. Broadway. 314/421-4689.

Forest Park

Site of the 1904 World's Fair and one of the largest urban parks in the U.S. Variety of delightful museums, cultural sites and a zoo. You can fish, picnic, golf on 3 courses, rent a canoe or paddleboat, ice skate or roller skate depending upon the season, or bike a 7-mile trail. Shuttle Bug provides transportation. Bounded by I-64, Kingshighway Blvd., Lindell and Skinker. 314/289-5300. Park includes;

The Jewel Box and Rose Garden—Floral and plant displays for every season. Daily 9 to 5; admission fee. Free on Mon and Tues mornings. 314/531-0080.

Missouri History Museum—See **[4]** under Along the Expedition's Path in this chapter.

The Muny—Outdoor theatre and music amid the trees. June to August; fees vary. 314/361-1900.

St. Louis Art Museum—Housed in the 1904 World's Fair Palace of Fine Arts is a collection that spans centuries, including pre-Columbian, Native American, Impressionist, Oriental and German Expressionist works. Tours available. Tue 1:30 to 8:30, Wed-Sun 10 to 5; free. 314/721-0072.

St. Louis Science Center—Dinosaurs, planetarium, and laser show combine with over 600 interactive exhibits on technology, environment, society and outer space. A new gallery, Cyberville, has 45 activities for all ages.

Daily 9 to 5, Fri to 9; museum free, admission fee for some areas and special exhibits. 5050 Oakland Ave. 800/456-7572.

St. Louis Zoo—Ride the railroad for an overview of more than 6,000 animals. Watch the sea lions romp and perform, or catch a movie of the residents. Experience the interactive Insectarium with its Butterfly Dome, and walk the 10-acre River's Edge exhibit to see large animals from around the world in natural habitats. Daily 9 to 5, until 8 on Tues during the summer; free. 314/781-0900.

Ulysses S. Grant National Historic Site—Visitor center and restored home of Ulysses and Julia Grant bring the mid-1800s to life. The original Spanish land grant was to James Mackay, a trader to the Mandan villages who met with Lewis and drew him a map. Daily 9 to 5; free. 7400 Grant Rd. 314/842-3298.

Grant's Farm—Once owned by Ulysses S. Grant. A day here includes the Budweiser Clydesdales, animal shows, petting zoo, tours of Grant's cabin and visit to a wildlife preserve. Apr-Oct; free, fee for parking. 10501 Gravois. 314/843-1700.

Holocaust Museum—Multimedia exhibits detail Jewish life in Europe from the 1930s to the Holocaust and beyond. Weekdays 9:30 to 4, Sun 10 to 4; donations. 12 Millstone Campus Dr. 314/432-0020, ext. 3711.

Jefferson Barracks Historic County Park—Established in 1826, this Army post remained active for 120 years. Generals Robert E. Lee and Ulysses S. Grant both served here. Exhibits and restored buildings. Tue-Fri 10-4:30, weekends noon to 4:30; free. At end of S. Broadway, 533 Grant Rd. 314/544-5714.

Scott Joplin House State Historic Site—Ragtime composer Joplin and his wife lived here in 1902 when eight of his compositions, including "The Entertainer," were published. Along with exhibits on his life and work, the apartment is restored to its former appearance. Tue-Fri 10 to 4, Sat-Sun 12 to 5. Daily guided tours; admission fee. 2658A Delmar Blvd. 314/340-2790.

Laumeier Sculpture Park &

Museum—Outdoor collection of sculpture from around the world. Picnic, walk the trails, relax. Free concerts on summer Sunday nights. Park open daily 7am to a half-hour past sunset, museum open Tue-Sat 10 to 5, Sun noon to 5; free. 12580 Rott Rd. at Geyer Rd. 314/821-1209.

Magic House/St. Louis Children's Museum—Explore science and communications using computers, a walk-through maze and a gigantic circular slide. Special areas for those under 7. Tue-Thur noon to 5:30, Fri noon to 9; Sat 9:30 to 5:30, Sun 11 to 5:30; admission fee. 516 S. Kirkwood Rd. 314/822-8900.

Missouri Botanical Garden—Walk or take a tram ride through 79 acres of lush landscape. Japanese and English woodland gardens, tropical rainforest. Tours of Victorian country home. Home and Garden tours daily 9 to 5 (home closed Jan.), summer until 8; admission fee. Tower Grove Ave. and Shaw Blvd. 800/642-8842, 314/577-9400.

Riverboat Cruises—Board the *Becky Thatcher* or *Tom Sawyer* for a narrated one-hour cruise. Daily 10 to 10; admission fee. At the levee below the Arch. 800/878-7411.

St. Louis Ambush—Professional indoor soccer (NPSL). Oct to April. Kiel Center. 314/962-4625

St. Louis Blues—Professional hockey (NHL). Oct to April. Kiel Center, 1401 Clark. 314/622-2500.

St. Louis Cardinals—Professional baseball (NL). April to Sept. Hall of Fame Museum is located across the street, and stadium tours are conducted daily. Busch Stadium. 314/421-3060.

St. Louis Rams—Professional football (NFL). Aug to Dec. Trans World Dome. 314/425-8830.

St. Louis Walk of Fame—Follow the sidewalk stars honoring the achievements of hometown folks. Open 24 hours; free. 6504 Delmar. 314/727-7827.

Taille de Noyer—A 17-room mansion which began as a two-room log fur trading post and cabin. Sun 1 to 4 (Feb-Dec); admission fee. 1896 S. Florissant Rd. 314/524-1100

Vaughn Cultural Center—Storytelling and exhibits document African-American culture and history. Mon-Fri 10 to 5; free. 3701

Grandel Square. 314/615-3600.

▲ **Jellystone Park**—110 shaded sites (82 w/hookups); fee; water; modern/&; showers; open Mar-Oct; grills/fire rings; tables. ⊞ Cabins; swimming; groceries; coin laundry; dump station; firewood; rec hall; playground; & sites. I-44/270 exit 261 (Six Flags), 0.5 mile W on Fox Creek Rd. 636/938-5925.

▲ **KOA St. Louis West at Six Flags**—154 wooded sites in hilly area (89 w/hookups); fee; water; modern/&; showers; open Mar-Nov; grills/fire rings; tables. ⊞ Cabins; pool; groceries; coin laundry, dump station; firewood; rec hall; playground; & sites. I-44/270 exit 261, W on Bus 44. 636/257-3018

▲ **KOA St. Louis South**—I-55 exit 185 to W Outer Rd., 2.5 miles S. 138 sites (88 w/hookups); fee; water; modern/&; showers; open all year; grills/fire rings; tables. Pool; groceries; coin laundry; dump station; firewood; rec hall; playground; & sites. 800/562-3049, 636/479-4449

▲ **Pin Oak Creek RV Park & Campground**—141 shaded sites on a lake (120 w/hookups); fee; water; modern; showers; open Apr-Oct; grills/fire rings; tables. Pool; lake fishing; groceries; coin laundry; dump station; firewood; rec hall; playground. I-44 exit 247, 1 mile E on County AT. 636/451-5656

⊞ **Adam's Mark Hotel**—910 rooms, indoor/outdoor pools, ⊗ restaurant. Special packages. W. 4th & Chestnut. 314/241-7400, 800/444-2326. $$$+ K18

⊞ **Drury Inn**—123 rooms, indoor pool, continental breakfast, pets, hot tub. &. I-55/70, exit 11. 618/345-5700. $$ K18

⊞ **Fairfield Inn**—135 rooms, continental breakfast, pool. &. I-270 exit 25. 314/731-7700. $$ K12

⊞ **Huckleberry Finn Youth Hostel**—1904-08 S. 12th St Soulard. 314/241-0076. $

⊞ **The Mayfair Grand Heritage Hotel and Suites**—170 rooms, restaurant. Weekend and off-season rates. 806 St. Charles. 314/421-2500, 800/757-8483. $$$+ K18

⊞ **Washington University Housing**—Pool, ⊗ restaurant, coin laundry. 6515 Wydown. 314/935-5050. $

⚑ **Fleur-de-Lys Inn Mansion at the Park**—4 luxurious rooms in restored 1913 mansion, full breakfast. Smoke-free. 3500 Russell Blvd. 314/773-3500, 888/969-3500. $$$+

⚑ **Lafayette House**—5 rooms and suite, full breakfast. 1876 mansion overlooking Lafayette Park. Smoke-free. 2156 Lafayette Ave. 314/772-4429. $$$

⚑ **Lehmann House**—4 rooms, full breakfast, TV. 1893 mansion. 10 Benton Place. 314/231-6724. $$

⚑ **Larimore Plantation House**—Full breakfast, pets, hot tub, TV, secluded spot near the Mississippi River. 11475 Lilac Ave. 314/868-8009. $$

⚑ **Napoleon's Retreat**—4 rooms, full breakfast, TV. 1870 mansion. 1815 Lafayette. 314/772-6979. $$

⊗ **Blueberry Hill**—The country's largest jukebox collection surrounded by rock and roll memorabilia. L & D daily, Sun brunch. 3504 Delmar (Washington University area). 314/727-0080. $

⊗ **Hunan Manor Chinese Restaurant**—Inexpensive lunch buffet. L & D daily. 606 Pine St (downtown). 314/231-2867. $$

⊗ **J's on the Landing**—Italian, ♿. L Mon-Fri, D Sat-Sun. 220 Biddle (Laclede Landing). 314/241-5000. $

⊗ **Kennedy's Second Street Co.**—Family oriented, ♿. L & D daily, Sun brunch. 612 N. Second (Laclede Landing). 314/421-3655. $$

⊗ **McDonald's Riverboat**—Try this Golden Arches aboard a refurbished, floating riverboat, ♿. 322 S. Leonor K. Sullivan Blvd (Laclede Landing). 314/231-6725. $

⊗ **Skeeter's Eatery**—The Everglades on the Mississippi, ♿. L & D daily. 727 N. First St (Laclede Landing). 314/241-2220. $$

⊗ **Tony's**—Award-winning Italian cuisine in an elegant atmosphere. ♿. Smoke-free. D Mon-Sat. 410 Market St 314/231-7007. $$$

St. Louis County, Missouri

Powder Valley Conservation Nature Center—Extensive indoor exhibits and viewing area. 112 forested acres with three trails, ♿ one with mobility-impaired access. No picnic area, trails for hiking only. Some facilities ♿. Center Mon-Sun 8 to 5, trails until 8; free. I-44 exit Watson Rd E, N on Geyer Rd to Cragwold. 314/301-1500.

Stanton, Missouri

Antique Toy Museum—Over 3,000 antique cars, trucks, trains and dolls. Daily 9 to 5 (May-Oct); admission fee. 2426 S. Outer Rd. 573/927-5555.

Jesse James Wax Museum—The theory: James wasn't killed in 1882, but lived under the name of J. Frank Dalton until he died in 1950 at 103. Antiques and personal belongings of Jesse and other gang members alongside documents supporting the theory. Daily 10 to 5; admission fee. I-44 exit 230. 573/927-5233.

Meramec Caverns—Discovered in 1716, this 5-story cave complex was busy during the 1800s: Underground Railroad station, Civil War munitions depot, James gang hideout. A constant 60°, paved walkways and electric lights enhance tours that include the 1500-seat ballroom with "Stage Curtain" formation. Riverboat cruises, canoe rentals, ⊗ restaurant and gift shop. Tours daily 9 to 7 (May-Aug), 9 to 5 rest of year; admission fee. ♿. ⊞ 40-unit motel open Apr-Oct, $ K12. ▲ Campground has 40 sites (all w/hookups); fee; water; modern/♿; showers; open Apr-Oct; grills/fire rings; tables. Cafe; groceries; firewood; boating; canoeing; fishing; swimming; playground. I-44 exit 230, 3 miles S through La Jolla Park. Campground 573/468-3166; motel 573/451-5400; caverns 573/468-3166.

▲ **KOA Stanton**—43 open/shaded sites (30 w/hookups); fee; water; modern/♿; showers; open Mar-Dec; grills/fire rings; tables. Swimming; coin laundry; dump station; groceries; firewood; ⊞ cabins; pool; boating; canoeing; canoe rentals; bike rentals; float trips; playground; ⊗ restaurant. I-44 exit 230, one block S on County W. 573/927-5215.

Sullivan, Missouri

Meramec Conservation Area—Over 4,000 acres along the Meramec River for fishing and hiking. 9.5 miles of hiking trails, 12 miles of equestrian trails. Restrooms/♿. Daily to sunset; free. S of Stanton on MO 185. 573/468-3335.

Meramec State Park—Miles of riverbank to explore on foot or by boat. Deeper within the 6,785 acres are 30 caves and many springs. Carry your own lantern on a guided tour of Fisher Cave. ⊞ Motel and ⊗ dining lodge, general store and cabins. Picnic areas with shelters and play areas. ▲ 208 sites (76 w/hookups); fee; water; modern/♿; showers; open all year/full operation Apr-Oct; grills/fire rings; tables; 15-day limit. Canoe rentals; fishing. Dump station; coin laundry; firewood. 3 miles E of Sullivan on MO 185. 573-468-6072.

▲ **KOA—Sullivan/Meramec**—46 wooded sites (30 w/hookups); fee; water; modern/♿; showers; open all year; grills/fire rings; tables. ⊞ Cabins; dump station; coin laundry; groceries; firewood; pool; playground. I-44 exit 226, 0.25 mile S on MO 185, 1.25 miles NE. 573/468-8750.

⊞ **Best Western Inn**—48 rooms, pool, continental breakfast, coin laundry, pets. ♿. I-44 exit 225. 573/468-3136. $$ K18

⊞ **Family Motor Inn**—63 rooms, pool, continental breakfast, coin laundry, pets, hot tub. ♿. Some efficiencies and a playground. I-44 exit 225. 573/468-4119. $$ K12

Sunset Hills, Missouri

Watson Trails Park—Terrific for kids. Playground, fishing lake and duck pond. Several hiking trails; all lead back to the lake or playground. Daily until sunset; free. 12450 W. Watson. 314/842-7265.

West Alton, Missouri

★ **Riverlands Environmental Demonstration Area**—Restored wetlands and native prairie adjacent to the **Melvin Price Locks and Dam**. Habitat for peregrine falcons and bald eagles with Teal Pond fisheries habitat. Hiking trails and interpretation. Daily; free. Along both sides of the Missouri access road to Melvin Price Locks. 314/355-6585.

CHAPTER 3

May 14 to June 6, 1804

SETTING OFF

Late on a rainy spring afternoon, the Lewis and Clark expedition left Camp Dubois, heading upstream—west—on the Missouri. Sergeant John Ordway began his journal that day:

Monday May the 14th 1804. Showery day. Capt Clark Set out at 3 oClock P.M. for the western expedition. one Gun fired. a nomber of Citizens see us Start. the party consisted of 3 Sergeants & 38 Good hands…we Sailed up the Missouri 6 miles & encamped…

opposite the mouth of Coldwater Creek, close to Fort Bellefontaine. The army fort for which this suburb and park are named would be built in 1805, and see service until 1826.

They needed to get the feel of the Missouri River, and test how the boats carried their loads. For the first part of the trip, until winter, they used a keelboat and two pirogues. The keelboat was 55 feet long and 8 feet wide, had 22 oars and also a mast so the men could hoist a sail when the wind was right.

Where the river was shallow, the men had to "pole" the boat, each one pushing a wooden pole against the river bottom while he walked from bow to stern along the deck. Even slower and more wearying was "cordelling," when the river bottom was too soft to pole, or too shallow for the boat. The men walked ashore if there was a bank—or in the rocky shallows—pulling the boat by long towlines. After their tow ropes wore out, they twisted new cords of elk hide.

Surrounding the deck, storage chests were attached to the gunwales; their lids could be lifted to make a fort-like wall in case of attack. Supplies for the men and gifts for Indians filled these chests. But the goods had to be unloaded

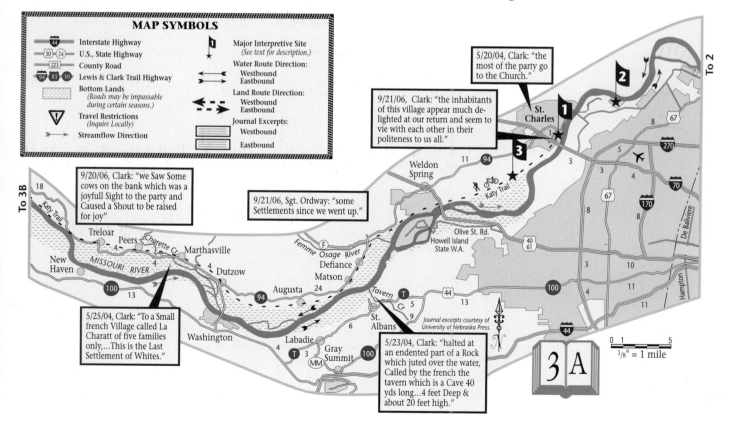

MAP SYMBOLS

Interstate Highway
U.S., State Highway
County Road
Lewis & Clark Trail Highway
Bottom Lands
(Roads may be impassable during certain seasons.)
Travel Restrictions
(Inquire Locally)
Streamflow Direction

Major Interpretive Site
(See text for description.)
Water Route Direction:
Westbound
Eastbound
Land Route Direction:
Westbound
Eastbound
Journal Excerpts:
Westbound
Eastbound

5/20/04, Clark: "the most of the party go to the Church."

9/21/06, Clark: "the inhabitants of this village appear much delighted at our return and seem to vie with each other in their politeness to us all."

St. Charles

9/20/06, Clark: "we Saw Some cows on the bank which was a joyfull Sight to the party and Caused a Shout to be raised for joy"

9/21/06, Sgt. Ordway: "some Settlements since we went up."

Weldon Spring

Katy Trail

Treloar
Peers
Charette Cr.
Marthasville

New Haven

MISSOURI RIVER

Dutzow

Olive St. Rd.
Howell Island State W.A.

Femme Osage River

Defiance
Matson

Augusta

Tavern

5/25/04, Clark: "To a Small french Village called La Charatt of five families only,…This is the Last Settlement of Whites."

Washington

Labadie

Gray Summit

St. Albans

Journal excerpts courtesy of University of Nebraska Press.

5/23/04, Clark: "halted at an endented part of a Rock which juted over the water, Called by the french the tavern which is a Cave 40 yds long…4 feet Deep & about 20 feet high."

3A

0   1   5
¹/₈" = 1 mile

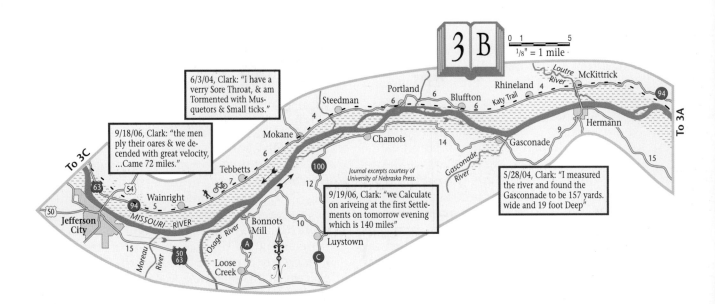

To 3C

To 3A

3 B

0 1 5
1/8" = 1 mile

6/3/04, Clark: "I have a verry Sore Throat, & am Tormented with Musquetors & Small ticks."

9/18/06, Clark: "the men ply their oares & we decended with great velocity, ...Came 72 miles."

Journal excerpts courtesy of University of Nebraska Press.

9/19/06, Clark: "we Calculate on ariveing at the first Settlements on tomorrow evening which is 140 miles"

5/28/04, Clark: "I measured the river and found the Gasconade to be 157 yards. wide and 19 foot Deep"

McKittrick
Rhineland
Loutre River
Portland
Bluffton
Katy Trail
Steedman
Hermann
Mokane
Chamois
Gasconade
Gasconade River
Tebbetts
Wainright
MISSOURI RIVER
Bonnots Mill
Osage River
Luystown
Jefferson City
Moreau River
Loose Creek

and reloaded until the keelboat was properly balanced to navigate the shallow, snag-filled Missouri.

The keelboat would go only as far as the Mandan villages (in today's North Dakota). After the winter of 1804-1805, some soldiers would take it back downriver to St. Louis, loaded with specimens of plants and animals unique to the high plains.

Pirogues are simply-designed open boats with shallow drafts. The captains had the smaller one painted white. About 39 feet long, it used six pairs of oars and held five soldiers and their leader, Corporal Richard Warfington, with cargo for a total of eight tons. The larger pirogue, 42 feet long and painted red, had seven pairs of oars and carried nine tons, including eight hired French boatmen.

No one can say how many "good hands" were in the party when it left Camp Dubois, but historian Gary E. Moulton thinks there probably were forty-two. Ordway and the other sergeants said thirty-eight in their journals, but they didn't list the names. We don't know whether Captain William Clark's slave York was counted, since he was a servant, not a soldier. French boatmen came and went.

And Captain Meriwether Lewis? When the party set out from Camp Dubois, he was still in St. Louis, making arrangements with Captain Amos Stoddard to pay anyone who arrived there with an IOU that Lewis had signed. This would include the French boatmen next spring—and anyone else the expedition might meet and hire or purchase goods from over the next two or more years. Lewis also was sending President Thomas Jefferson samples of miner-

als, some hand-drawn maps, and a horned lizard.

Clark sent Lewis a message to meet the group at [1] St. Charles, Missouri, but he wrote in his field notes: "The mouth of the River Dubois is to be considered as the point of *departure.*"

The main party arrived at St. Charles on May 16 and repacked the boats several times while waiting for Lewis. Clark thought the village's 450 French residents were "pore and extreemly kind." Francois Duquette, a prosperous grain mill owner with "a Charming wife," invited Clark to dinner.

Three of the men—William Werner, Hugh Hall, and John Collins—enjoyed the St. Charles hospitality a bit too much. They were absent without leave that first night, and Collins behaved "in an unbecomeing manner at the Ball last night...," Ordway recorded in the proceedings of their court-martial on the 17th. The jury of five sentenced Warner and Hall to 25 lashes, but urged leniency because of their otherwise good behavior. Collins was sentenced to 50 lashes on his back, and his was the only punishment carried out.

It was standard punishment for the army of the day. As commanders of a military expedition, Lewis and Clark followed army standards of good discipline. Their small group was heading into dangerous and unknown country, where they expected that some Indian nations would be hostile, and each man had to obey every order for the whole party to survive.

The camp in St. Charles was at the site of today's Frontier Park. Lewis and several prominent St. Louis residents arrived on horseback during heavy rain on May 20, and the whole expedition set off mid-afternoon the next day "under three Cheers from the gentlemen on the bank" (Clark).

At St. Charles, Lewis and Clark made two important additions to the party, both of French and Indian descent and both boatmen who had been up the Missouri before. The one-eyed Pierre Cruzatte and Francois Labiche became privates in the expedition's permanent party, as guides and interpreters.

For a few days, the expedition traveled through areas of white settlement. When they stopped at Tavern Cave near today's St. Albans on the 23rd, "maney people assembled to See us…" (Clark). Lewis climbed Tavern Rock and nearly fell from it, but somehow used his knife to stop the tumble. Earlier that day they had passed tiny Boone's Settlement, near today's Matson, founded by the ever-westering Daniel Boone. Two days later, opposite today's Washington, they came to La Charette, a village of seven French families who traded with the Indians. Clark wrote: "The people at this Village is pore, houses Small, they Sent us milk & eggs to eat." These few houses were near today's Marthasville, but the shifting Missouri has washed away the actual site.

La Charette then was the last settlement of whites on the Missouri. The day after passing it, Lewis wrote—and he and Clark signed—Detachment Orders for the expedition. They divided the permanent party into three squads, or messes, under sergeants Charles Floyd, Floyd's cousin Nathaniel Pryor, and John Ord-way. Until they reached the Mandan villages, these squads were to man the keelboat. Corporal Warfington's command of five soldiers would made up next spring's return party. Baptiste Deschamps commanded the red pirogue.

The orders described all the routine duties and restrictions, from the shifts of night guards to the requirement "to see that no cooking utensels or loos lumber…is left on the deck to obstruct the passage…" The men were to cook their rations at night and save leftovers for the next day's march, when there would be no cooking.

Although they would hunt for fresh meat as much as possible, the men carried field provisions of the day, not too varied or healthful. One day, the orders stated, parched "corn and grece will be issued…, the next day Poark and flour, and the day following indian meal and poark," and then the cycle would repeat. No salt pork would be issued when hunting parties were successful. Pushing upriver against the Missouri's current was very hard work, and each man would need up to eight *pounds* of fat meat per day. York gathered greens if he could, and when Sacagawea joined the party later,

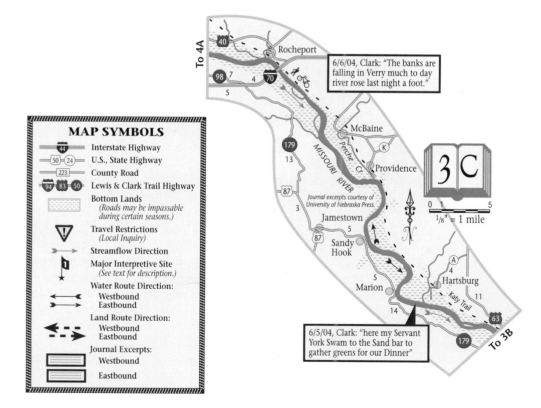

MAP SYMBOLS

Interstate Highway
U.S., State Highway
County Road
Lewis & Clark Trail Highway
Bottom Lands
  (Roads may be impassable during certain seasons.)
Travel Restrictions
  (Local Inquiry)
Streamflow Direction
Major Interpretive Site
  (See text for description.)
Water Route Direction:
  Westbound
  Eastbound
Land Route Direction:
  Westbound
  Eastbound
Journal Excerpts:
  Westbound
  Eastbound

6/6/04, Clark: "The banks are falling in Verry much to day river rose last night a foot."

Journal excerpts courtesy of University of Nebraska Press.

3C

0   1   5
⅛" = 1 mile

6/5/04, Clark: "here my Servant York Swam to the Sand bar to gather greens for our Dinner"

one of her great gifts would be collecting plants to improve the men's diet.

As the trip began in earnest, rainy weather for the first week hampered the astronomical observations that Lewis and Clark needed to make accurate maps. Mosquitoes and ticks were nuisances when there was no rain. Deer were plentiful, so the salt pork could be saved.

These first days of the great adventure, the Corps traveled only about twelve to fourteen miles a day, setting out at 6:00 a.m. and stopping later to eat breakfast. Spring runoff kept the Missouri running fast and rising. Here was some of their most difficult travel—until they reached the awesome barrier of the Rocky Mountains.

TOURING TODAY

❧ SETTING OFF ❧

[ ]	**Bracketed numbers key sites to maps**	♿	Special-needs accessible	⚑	Bed & breakfast
★	L&C in-depth interpretation, unchanged landform	⊗	Restaurant	⚠	Camping, RV park
•	L&C interpreted site	⊞	Motel, hotel, cabin		

Bridges over the Missouri River in this area are in St. Charles (I-70; MO115); Weldon Spring (US 40/61); Washington (MO 47); Hermann (MO 19); Jefferson City (US 54).

ALONG THE EXPEDITION'S PATH

To walk or bike alongside the Missouri River in this area, try the Katy Trail. More trailheads are listed in Chapter 4.

[3] ★ Katy Trail State Park (MO)—This section of the crushed limestone, 225-mile trail runs along the northern shore of the Missouri River between St. Charles and Rocheport (139 miles). It also parallels MO 94 in many places and provides access to areas where Lewis and Clark camped. The trail is open sunrise to sunset and access is limited to pedestrian and non-motorized traffic, except for ♿ motorized wheelchairs. Horses are allowed only on the section from Calhoun to Sedalia (see chap. 4) and mileage markers from the old railbed are still in use. Weather conditions often impact the trail significantly, with flooding and trail closures frequently occuring. Always obtain current trail conditions before venturing out. 800/334-6946, 573/526-4522.

Katy Trail trailheads:
St. Charles (mile 39.5)—Parking and restrooms. Phone, water, bike rentals, groceries, food, lodging and camping nearby.
Greens Bottom Rd. (mile 45.7)—Parking and restrooms. This is a less crowded eastern starting point.
Weldon Spring (mile 56.0)—Parking.
Defiance (mile 59.1)—Parking. Restrooms, phone, water, groceries, food and lodging nearby.
Matson (mile 60.6)—Parking and restrooms. Phone, water, and food nearby.
Augusta (mile 66.3)—parking and restrooms. Water, phone, bike rentals, groceries, food and lodging nearby.
Dutzow (mile 74.0)—Parking and restrooms. Phone, water, bike rentals, food and lodging nearby.
Marthasville (mile 77.7)—Parking, restrooms and water. Phone, bike rentals, camping, food and lodging nearby.
Treloar (mile 84.4)—Parking and restrooms. Phone, water and food nearby.
Mckittrick (mile 100.8)—Parking and restrooms. Across the river in Hermann, water, phone, groceries, food, lodging and camping are available.
Rhineland (mile 105.0)—Restrooms, water, and phone nearby.
Bluffton (mile 110.9)—Restrooms,

restaurant, phone, water, bike rentals, lodging and camping nearby.
Portland (mile 115.9)—Parking and restrooms. Water, phone and food nearby.
Steedman (mile 121.4)—Restrooms, water, phone, food and camping nearby.
Mokane (mile 125.0)—Parking and restrooms. Water, phone, groceries and food nearby.
Tebbetts (mile 131.2)—Parking and restrooms. Water, phone, groceries, lodging, and food nearby.
Wainwright (mile 137.6)—No services.
North Jefferson (mile 143.2)—Parking, restrooms, and water. Katy Spur Trail heads south from here to the river and auxiliary parking. Across the river in Jefferson City, phone, groceries, food, lodging and camping are available.
Claysville (mile 149.8)—No services.
Hartsburg (mile 153.6)—An area just east of here has a grade greater than 5%; another is about 3 miles west. Parking, water, restrooms and phone. Food, groceries, camping and lodging nearby.
Wilton (mile 157.4)—An area just east of here has a grade greater than 5%. Restrooms, water, groceries and camping nearby.

Easley (mile 162.5)—An area just east of here has a grade greater than 5%. Restrooms, water, groceries, food and camping nearby.

Providence (mile 165.5)—Parking and restrooms nearby.

McBaine (mile 169.5)—Just west of here is a grade greater than 5%. Parking and restrooms. Water, phone, food nearby. About a mile west is intersection with MKT trail to Columbia.

Rocheport (mile 178.3)—An area 1 mile west of here has a grade greater than 5%. Parking, restrooms, water and phone. Bike rentals, groceries, food and lodging nearby.

May 15,1804
(Return Sept. 23, 1806)
Pelican Island Natural Area (St. Louis County, MO)—2,259-acre, undeveloped site accessible by boat or by foot from Sioux Passage County Park when the river is low. Habitat similar to that encountered by the Corps. Daily 4am to 10pm; free. 6 miles W of Florissant on Douglas Road. 636/441-4554.
Sioux Passage County Park (St. Louis County, MO)—Well-developed park with picnic and recreation areas, hiking trails, river access for fishing, not boats. Daily 4am to 10pm; free. 6 miles W of Florissant on Douglas Road. 314/615-7275.

May 16-20, 1804
(Return Sept. 21, 1806)
[1] ★ The Lewis and Clark Center (St. Charles, MO)—This delightful museum lets you experience the sights and sounds as Lewis and Clark met and completed preparations. Daily 10:30 to 4:30; admission fee. 701 Riverside Drive. 636/947-3199.
[1] Frontier Park (St. Charles, MO)—Municipal park commemorating journey's beginning is located in area of actual camp. Annual Lewis and Clark festival in May. Interpretive signs. Hike where the Corps did. Nicely shaded picnic area. Fishing and boating access. Daily until dusk; free. 500 Riverside Dr. (MO 94.) 636/949-3372.
[2] St. Stanislaus Conservation Area (St. Louis County, MO)—A Jesuit seminary was established here in 1823 for missionaries to Indians. Hiking trails crisscross the park, including La Charbonniere bluff (Clark on May 16, 1804: "appears to Contain great quantytes of Coal..."). Daily 4am to 10pm; free. I-370 to Earth City Expressway, go 3.5 miles N (changes to Aubuchon Rd). 636/441-4554.

May 22, 1804
Howell Island Wildlife Area (Chesterfield, MO)—Shore- and songbirds abound along 7.5 miles of trails. Access is by boat, although foot access is possible via concrete causeway when the river is low. Daily 4am to 10pm; free. 2 miles from Chesterfield on County C and MO 109. 636/441-4554.
● **Weldon Spring Wildlife Area** (Weldon Spring, MO)—Biking and hiking trails. Boat ramp and fishing access. Parking areas along MO 94, S of MO 40/61. Daily 4am to 10pm; free. 8 miles from St. Peters on County D. 636/441-4554.

May 23, 1804
● **Tavern Cave** (St. Albans, MO)—Currently no public access, but visible from the river. Interpretive exhibits in St. Albans. Public access is planned by 2003. 8 miles from Labadie on St. Albans Road.

May 25, 1804
● **J.E. Rennick Riverfront Park/ Washington Access** (Washington, MO)—Boat and fishing access. Interpretive sign, picnic and recreation areas. Primitive restrooms/&. Scenic overlooks with benches. Always open; free. Front & Jefferson Sts. 636/390-1080.

May 26, 1804
(Return Sept. 20, 1806)
New Haven City Park (New Haven, MO)—Good place to picnic along the Missouri. Fishing, boating access. Daily 6am to 10pm; free. In town on Miller St off MO 100. 573/237-2349.
Hermann Riverfront Park (Hermann, MO)—City park with river access and good picnic spots. Hiking, pavillion, pool, lake fishing. ▲ 41 sites (all w/hookups); fee; water; modern/&; showers; open Apr-Nov; grills/fire rings; tables. In town at MO 19 & MO 100. 573/486-5400.

May 27-28, 1804
(Return Sept. 20, 1806)
Gasconade Park Access (Gasconade, MO)—River access for canoeing and fishing. ▲ Primitive camping allowed, primitive restrooms/&. Daily 4am to 10pm; free. E on Main St. to Oak St. 636/441-4554.

May 30-31, 1804
Chamois City Park (Chamois, MO)—Boating and fishing access. Hiking along the river. Daily 4am to 10pm; free. In town on MO 100. 573/763-5725.
Mokane Access (Mokane, MO)—Large boat ramp. Fishing, hiking and ▲ primitive camping. Daily 4am to 10pm; free. 1 mile W of town on MO 94 (gravel road). 573/254-3330.

June 1-2, 1804
(Return Sept. 19, 1806)
Bonnots Mill Access (Bonnots Mill, MO)—On Osage River, 1.5 miles from Missouri River. River access, canoeing, ▲ primitive camping. Scenic view area overlooking both rivers. Primitive restrooms/&. Daily 4am to 10pm; free. In town on County A. 573/368-2225.

June 4, 1804
● **Madison Street Overlook** (Jefferson City, MO)—Interpretive signs and scenic view. Picnic area. Always open; free. At bottom of Madison Street.

June 5, 1804
Hartsburg Access (Hartsburg, MO)—River access and interpretive sign. Access road is gravel. Daily 4am to 10pm; free. 17 miles S of Columbia on US 63, W on County A, 2 miles on River Rd. 573/751-4115.
Marion Access (Marion, MO)—River access, fishing, hiking, ▲ primitive camping. Daily 4am to 10pm; free. 12 miles NW of Jefferson City on MO 179. 573/751-4115.
Eagle Bluffs Conservation Area (McBaine, MO)—Wetland complex for songbirds in spring, shorebirds in summer. Hawks and egrets nest here. Good opportunity to see deer, turkey, and fox. The Katy

Trail runs alongside. Daily 4am to 10pm; free. 7 miles SW of Columbia on County K, 1 mile W on Burr Oak Rd., 2 miles S on Star School Rd. 573/445-3882.

June 6, 1804
Taylors Landing—River access, fishing and picnic area. Daily 4am to 10pm; free. 8 miles SW of Columbia on I-70. 573/751-4115.

Around the Area

TOWNS LISTED ALPHABETICALLY

Brentwood, Missouri

St. Louis Children' Aquarium—Want to pet a shark, hold a turtle, or explore a cave? This is the place. New exhibits feature humpback whales. Daily 9 to 5; admission fee. 416 Hanley Industrial Ct. 314/647-9594.

Chesterfield, Missouri

Dr. Edmund A. Babler Memorial State Park—Heavily wooded 2,439-acre park with something for everyone. Hiking trails and wide bike trails, nature programs, horse rentals and trails, tennis court, swimming pool and a nature center. ♿ The **Jacob L. Babler Outdoor Education Center** provides accommodations for campers with special needs. Picnic areas with shelters and play areas. ▲ 77 sites (24 w/hookups); fee; water; modern/♿; showers; open all year/full operation Apr-Oct; grills/fire rings; tables; 15-day limit. Dump station; coin laundry; firewood. 20 miles W of St. Louis on MO 109, between US 40 & MO 100. 636/458-3813.

Faust County Park—1800s living history village, estate of Missouri's second governor, with a 1920s carousel and the **Butterfly House**, a 3-story conservatory sheltering over 60 species. Park open daily dawn-dusk, village open weekends (June-Oct), estate and carousel Tue-Sun 10 to 4 (Feb-Dec); Butterfly House Tue-Sun 9 to 4 (until 5 in summer); admission fees for carousel, Butterfly House, and tours. 15185 Olive St. Rd. 314/532-7298.

Columbia, Missouri

Columbia Convention & Visitor Bureau—300 S. Providence Rd. 573/875-1231.

Finger Lakes State Park—1,132-acre park reclaimed from strip mines. Former pits provide for swimming, canoeing and fishing. Bike trails. Designated areas for off-road motorcycles and all-terrain vehicles with scheduled races. ▲ 36 sites (17 w/hookups); fee; water; modern/♿; showers; open all year/full operation Apr-Oct; grills/fire rings; tables; 15-day limit; 30' limit. Boat ramp; dump station; firewood. 10 miles N of Columbia on US 63. 573/443-5315.

Nifong Memorial Park/Maplewood—Restored 1877 farm home and outbuildings, fishing pond and petting zoo. Also serves as county historical museum. Sun 2 to 5; donations. 3701 Ponderosa. 573/443-8936.

Rock Bridge Memorial State Park—Spend a day investigating the geologic diversity of this 2,238-acre park. The limestone cave system, which includes **Devil's Icebox Cave**, has created a natural rock bridge and sinkholes. Interpretive signs along the hiking trails, equestrian trails and boardwalk. Over 700 acres set aside as the **Gans Creek Wild Area**. Picnic area with shelters and play areas; nature programs; fishing; day-use only. 7 miles S of Columbia on MO 163. 573/449-7402.

▲ **Rocky Fork Lakes Conservation Area**—A good basic primitive camping site. Fishing, boating and 9 miles of hiking trails on 2200 acres. Open 4am to 10pm; free. 7 miles N of Columbia on US 63. 573/751-4115.

Shelter Insurance Gardens—Charming oasis with a fern grotto, rose garden, stream, and a one-room school. ♿ Special area designed for the visually-impaired. Free summer concerts. Daily; free. 1817 W. Broadway. 573/445-8441.

University of Missouri

Botany Greenhouses and Herbarium—Plants from the jungle, tropics and desert displayed in native habitat. Herbarium showcases preserved specimens. Mon-Fri 8 to 4; free. At U of M in Tucker Hall. 573/882-6519.

Museum of Anthropology—Exhibits on the history of civilization. Mon-Fri 9 to 4; free. At U of M in Swallow Hall. 573/882-3573.

Museum of Art and Archaeology—Asian, African and pre-Columbian exhibits. American and European paintings and sculpture from 1500. Ancient Roman and Greek collection. Tues-Fri 9 to 5, Thur 6 to 9, weekends noon to 5; free. At U of M in Pickard Hall. 573/882-3591.

State Historical Society of Missouri—Changing exhibits of newspapers and books. Highlight is collection of political cartoons and paintings by Thomas Hart Benton and others. Mon-Fri 8 to 4:30, guided tours by appointment; free. At U of M in Ellis Library. 573/882-7083.

▲ **Cottonwoods RV Park**—97 sites (all w/hookups); fee; water; modern/♿; showers; open all year/full operation Mar-Dec; grills/fire rings; tables. Groceries; dump station; coin laundry; firewood; rec hall; playground; pool; whirlpool. I-70 exit 128A, 3 miles N on US 63, 0.25 mile NE on Oakland Gravel Rd. 573/474-2747.

⊞ **Budgetel Inn**—102 rooms, continental breakfast, pets, coin laundry. ♿. I-70 exit 124. 573/445-1899. $$ K18

⊞ **Drury Inn**—123 rooms, indoor pool, continental breakfast, pets, hot tub. ♿. I-70 exit 124. 573/445-1800. $$ K18

⊞ **Howard Johnson Lodge & Suites**—60 rooms, indoor pool, full breakfast, exercise room, hot tub. ♿. In-room refrigerators and microwaves. I-70 exit 128B. 573/815-0123. $$ K18

⊗ **The 63 Diner**—1950s decor, kids' menu. L & D Tue-Sat, B Sat only. US 763, 3 miles N of I-70. 573/443-2331. $

Danville, Missouri

Graham Cave State Park—Sandstone cave was home to Indians over 10,000 years ago. Carved bluffs, wooded glades and waterfalls enhance the secluded atmosphere. Interpretive exhibits recount the cave's history. Spacious picnic area with shelters and playgrounds. Hiking and biking trails. ▲ 53 sites (18 w/hookups); fee; water; modern/♿; showers; open all year/full operation Apr-Oct; grills/fire rings; tables; 15-day limit. Fishing; boat ramp; dump station; coin laundry; firewood. I-70 Danville exit, 2 miles W on County TT. 573/564-3476.

Defiance, Missouri
Daniel Boone Home & Boonesfield Village—Boone built this four-story stone house while serving as judge of the Femme Osage District from 1800 to 1804 and lived here until his death in 1820. Newly opened early 1800s living history village enhances the atmosphere. Daily 9 to 6 Mar-Oct; 11 to 4 (rest of year); admission fee. 5 miles W of Defiance on County F. 636/798-2005.

Eureka, Missouri
Six Flags St. Louis—Amusement park with over 100 rides. Monster roller-coasters; WB and DC Comics theme areas; Time Warner Studios where you can be the star; Hurrican Harbor water park; water rides and more. Daily 10am (Memorial Day to Labor Day); weekends only April, May, September, and October; admission fee. I-44 at Allenton Rd. 636/938-4800.

Fulton, Missouri
Kingdom Expo Center & Auto World Museum—Collection of vintage cars and other assorted memorabilia. Mon-Sat 11 to 5, Sun 12:30 to 5 (Mem. Day to Labor Day; 10 to 4 rest of year; admission fee. 1920 N. Bus. 54. 573/642-2080.
Winston Churchill Memorial and Library—The Church of St. Mary the Virgin, Aldermanbury, London (built in 866) was reconstructed on the Westminster College campus to commemorate Churchill's speech given here March 5, 1946. It shelters a library and museum of Churchill memorabilia, including 5 paintings by him, and other World War II artifacts. Nearby is "Breakthrough," a sculpture by his granddaughter created with sections of the Berlin Wall. Daily 10 to 4:30; admission fee. Westminster Ave. and W. 7th St. 573/592-1369.

Glencoe, Missouri
Rockwoods Reservation—Picnic areas and 13.5 miles of hiking trails. Climb the rocks, have a picnic. Conservation Education Center focuses on wildlife and forestry. Animal reserve, exhibits. Facilities and trails ♿. Daily until dusk; free. 4 miles N of I-44 on MO 109. 314/458-2236.
Wabash Frisco & Pacific Steam Railroad—Relax on a two-mile trip on a miniature steam train. Sundays 11:15 to 4:15 (May-Oct); admission fee. I-44 exit 264 at Eureka, 3 miles N on MO 109. 636/587-3538.

Gray Summit, Missouri
Purina Farms—An interactive look at pets and farm animals with a visit to the hayloft, multimedia exhibits and a petting zoo. Tue-Sun 9:30 to 3 (Memorial Day to Labor Day); Wed-Sun 9:30 to 1 (rest of year); reservations required; free. 2 blks N on MO 100, 1 mile N on County MM. 314/982-3232.
Shaw Arboretum—A refuge of water, plants and flowers maintained by Missouri Botanical Garden. 12 miles of hiking trails through a variety of ecosystems. Exhibits on conservation, 5-acre native wildflower garden. Daily 7 to dusk; admission fee. I-44 & MO 100. 636/451-3512.

Hermann, Missouri
Deutschheim State Historic Site—Absorb the lives of early German immigrants by touring the Pommer-Gentner and Strehly houses and two 19th century period gardens. An anti-slavery German newspaper, *Lichtfreund* (Friend of Light), was published from the print shop on the Strehly House ground floor. Daily 8 to 4:30. Guided tours daily; admission fee. Tours begin at 109 W. Second St. 573/486-2200.
1894 & More Museum—Extensive gun collection and area primitives. Daily 1 to 5; admission fee. 129 E. Third. 573/486-1894.
Historic Hermann Museum and Information Center—Located in the 1871 German School Building are exhibits relating to Missouri River history and the area's people. A piece of the Berlin wall ties past to present. Deutsche Schule is a separate section of the building dedicated to artisans and their crafts. Take time to watch them at work. Museum open daily 10 to 4 (April-October); admission fee. 3rd and Schiller Sts. 573/486-2017.

⊞ **Vinchester Inn**—12 rooms, continental breakfast, refrigerators, microwaves. 129 E. 3rd St. 573/486-4440. $ K12
⚑ **Hermann Hill Vineyard & Inn**—5 elegant rooms, balconies and fireplaces, full breakfast, smoke-free, ♿. 711 Wein St. 573/486-4455. $$$+
⚑ **Miss Buehler's Garden Cottage**—3 bedroom cottage sleeps 6, full breakfast, smoke-free. Whirlpool, TV, refrigerator, microwave. 573/486-2477. $$
⊗ **Vintage 1847 Restaurant**—German specialties, steak and seafood in historic building, kids' menu. L & D daily. At Stone Hill Winery, on MO 100, W of MO 19. 573/486-3479. $$

Hillsboro, Missouri
Sandy Creek Covered Bridge State Historic Site—Originally built in 1872, destroyed by floodwaters in 1886 and rebuilt. Perfect for a picnic or to run off steam. Interpretive exhibits about Missouri's covered bridges. Daily 7am to 10pm; free. 5 miles N of Hillsboro on US 21. 636/464-2976.

Jefferson City, Missouri
Jefferson City Convention & Visitor Bureau—213 Adams St. 573/634-3616; 800/769-4183.
Cole County Museum—Collection of inaugural gowns, period furnishings, and other historical artifacts. Daily 10 to 5 (Feb-Dec); admission fee. 109 Madison. 573/635-1850.
Governor's Mansion—Built on the site of the original capitol, this 1871 mansion is still used by the state's chief executive. Tours of the first floor are given Tue/Thur 10 to 3 (closed August/December); free. 100 Madison. 573/751-7929.
Jefferson Landing State Historic Site—Steamboats docked here frequently in the mid-1800s as they traveled between St. Louis and Kansas City. Three remaining buildings contain a visitor center and museum with exhibits on the Landing's history and riverboat trade. Union Hotel contains a state museum gallery. Daily 10 to 4; free. Jefferson and Water streets. 573/751-3475.
Missouri Highway Patrol Safety Education Center—Historical perspective of law enforcement. Exhibits and actual patrol cars.

Mon-Fri 8 to 5; free. 1510 E. Elm. 573/526-6149.

Missouri Veterans Memorial—Veterans Walk, a terraced waterfall, is the focal point of this monument. Daily; free. NE side of the State Capitol. 573/751-3779.

Missouri Veterinary Museum—Collection of more than 2,500 items related to the profession along with information on pet care. Wed-Sat noon to 4; donations. 2500 Country Club. 573/636-8737.

• **Missouri Capitol**—Built overlooking the Missouri River and part of the Jefferson Landing Historic Site. Contains paintings by Thomas Hart Benton, N.C. Wyeth and others portraying the legends, lore and heritage of the state. Also houses the State Museum with exhibits detailing environmental and societal development. Daily 8 to 5; tours available; free. Capitol Avenue. 573/751-4127.

Runge Conservation Nature Center—Five interpreted trails, & three of them paved. Educational programs, multi-sensory exhibits and a relaxing wildlife viewing area inside the center. Area open daily 6am to 8pm (Apr-Oct), 6am to 6pm (rest of year), center open daily 8 to 5, Sun noon to 5; free. On MO 179, 0.5 mile N of US 50. 573/526-5544.

▲ **Binder Park Campground**—53 sites (40 w/hookups)/no tent sites; fee; water; modern/&; showers; open all year; grills/fire rings; tables. Cafe; groceries; coin laundry; firewood; boating; canoeing; fishing; hiking; dump station. Extensive & accessibility. Bus. 50 W to Binder Lake Rd, N to Rainbow Dr. 573/634-6482.

▲ **Osage Campground & More**—45 sites (30 w/hookups); fee; water; modern; showers; open all year; grills/fire rings; tables. Groceries; coin laundry; firewood; boating; canoeing; fishing; swimming; playground. 8 miles E on US 50, left on river road before bridge. 573/395-4066.

▦ **Best Western Inn**—79 rooms, pool, continental breakfast, pets, ⊗ restaurant. &. US 54, Ellis Blvd exit. 573/635-4175. $$ K12

▦ **Capitol Plaza Hotel**—255 rooms, pets, indoor pool, hot tub, exercise room, coin laundry, ⊗ restaurant. 415 W. McCarty.

573/635-1234, 800/338-8088. $$$ K12

▦ **Comfort Inn**—50 rooms, pool, continental breakfast. &. US 54, Ellis Blvd exit. 573/636-2797. $$ K18

⊗ **Pizzaria Napolitana**—Italian and Greek menu, kids' menu, &. L & D Sun-Fri, D only Sat. 2336 Missouri Blvd. 573/636-5221. $

Jonesburg, Missouri

▲ **KOA-Jonesburg**—52 sites (41 w/hookups); fee; water; modern; showers; open Mar-Nov; grills/fire rings; tables. Pool; playground; pond fishing. Dump station; coin laundry; groceries; firewood. I-70 exit 183, 1 mile N on County E. 636/488-5630.

Kingdom City, Missouri

▲ **Crooked Creek Campground**—90 wooded sites (72 w/hookups); fee; water; modern; showers; open all year; grills/fire rings; tables. Fishing; swimming; playground. Coin laundry; dump station; firewood; groceries; tent rentals. I-70 exit 144, 1.75 miles S on gravel road. 573/642-4993.

▦ **Days Inn**—60 rooms, continental breakfast. &. I-70 & US 54. 573/642-0050. $$ K16

Rocheport, Missouri

⊨ **School House Bed & Breakfast**—10 rooms in a 3-story restored 1890 schoolhouse. Full breakfast, TV. Close to Katy Trail State Park. 573/698-2022. $$$

[1] St. Charles, Missouri

• **St. Charles Chamber of Commerce**, 230 S. Main. 636/946-7776, 800/366-2427.

First State Capitol State Historic Site—Legislative sessions were held here from June 4, 1821, to October 1, 1826, when the capital was moved to Jefferson City. Inspect the lawmakers' chambers, residences and a store on your own, or take a guided tour. Exhibits in visitor center provide extensive background. Daily 10 to 4; admission fee for guided tours. 200 S. Main. 636/946-9282.

Goldenrod Showboat—Presents stellar productions in dinner theater. Box office open daily. Shows Wed-Sun; admission fee. 1000 Riverside Dr. 636/946-2020.

▲ **Sundemeier RV Park**—114 paved sites in urban area (all w/hookups); fee; water; modern; showers; open all year; grills/fire rings; tables. Cafe; groceries; coin laundry; boating; canoeing; fishing; swimming; playground. I-70 exit 229, follow signs. 636/940-0111, 800/929-0832.

▦ **Budgetel Inn**—142 rooms, indoor pool, continental breakfast, ⊗ restaurant, coin laundry, pets. &. 1425 S. Fifth St., 0.25 mile W of bridge on I-70. 636/949-6936. $$ K18

▦ **Econolodge**—52 rooms, indoor pool, continental breakfast, coin laundry, hot tub. &. I-70 exit 227. 636/946-9992. $$ K18

▦ **Hampton Inn**—122 rooms, pool, continental breakfast, exercise room. &. I-70 exit 225. 636/947-6800. $$ K18

⊨ **Boone's Lick Trail Inn**—5 rooms, full breakfast, smoke-free, &, TV. Along the river and adjacent to Katy Trail. 636/947-7000. $$$+

⊨ **Lady B's Bed & Breakfast**—Themed rooms, full breakfast, smoke-free, TV. Kitchenette and homemade breads. 636/947-3421. $$

⊗ **Vintage House Restaurant and Wine Garden**—German food and fresh seafood in historic winery and garden, kids' menu. D daily, Sunday brunch. 1219 S. Main. 636/946-7155. $$

Weldon Spring, Missouri

A.A. Busch Wildlife Area—Fish in one of 32 lakes, explore numerous hiking and biking trails. An auto trail provides wildlife viewing. Reservations required for free interpretive programs. Open daily until dusk; free. MO 94 & County D. 636/441-4554.

Wentzville, Missouri

Wentzville Historical Society & Museum—Emphasis on area's tobacco growing heritage including 1885 factory. Area history and memorabilia. Daily 10 to 5 (summer); free. 506 S. Linn. 636/332-9821.

▦ **Ramada Limited West**—82 rooms, pool, continental breakfast, coin laundry. &. 1400 Continental Dr. 636/327-5515. $$ K16

CHAPTER 4

June 7 to 28, 1804

TO THE KANSAS RIVER

Although the Corps of Discovery had left towns behind, they would not be the only European/American men on the Missouri River for the rest of this year. On June 8 and again on June 12, 1804, they met trappers coming downriver. The first party had been trapping for one year and were in a hurry to get on and sell their furs: they "were out of Provesions and out of [gun]Powder" (Clark).

The second party brought a pleasant—and useful—surprise. Among these men was Pierre Dorion, Sr., a French Canadian trader in his mid-50s who knew Captain William Clark's older brother, George Rogers Clark, a hero of the Revo-

lutionary War on the "western frontier" of Kentucky, Ohio, Indiana and Illinois. Dorion had married into the Yankton Sioux and lived with the Yanktons for more than 20 years.

The captains "questioned him untill it was too late to Go further and Concluded to Camp for the night" near today's Brunswick, Missouri. They didn't learn much that was new from Dorion and his party, but invited "old" Dorion (his son, Pierre, Jr., was "young" Dorion) to travel with them to the Yanktons and act as interpreter. Being able to have clear conversations with the Sioux, the Indians they most feared, would be a great help.

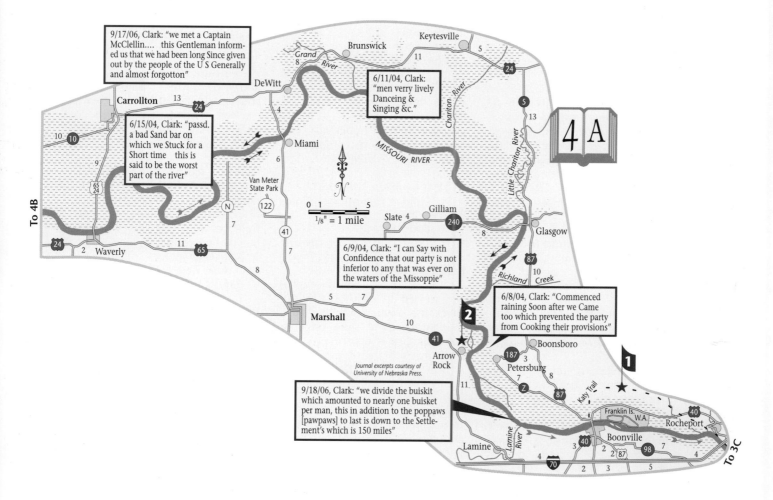

9/17/06, Clark: "we met a Captain McClellin.... this Gentleman informed us that we had been long Since given out by the people of the U S Generally and almost forgotton"

6/11/04, Clark: "men verry lively Danceing & Singing &c."

6/15/04, Clark: "passd. a bad Sand bar on which we Stuck for a Short time   this is said to be the worst part of the river"

6/9/04, Clark: "I can Say with Confidence that our party is not inferior to any that was ever on the waters of the Missoppie"

6/8/04, Clark: "Commenced raining Soon after we Came too which prevented the party from Cooking their provisions"

Journal excerpts courtesy of University of Nebraska Press.

9/18/06, Clark: "we divide the buiskit which amounted to nearly one buisket per man, this in addition to the poppaws [pawpaws] to last is down to the Settlement's which is 150 miles"

1/8" = 1 mile

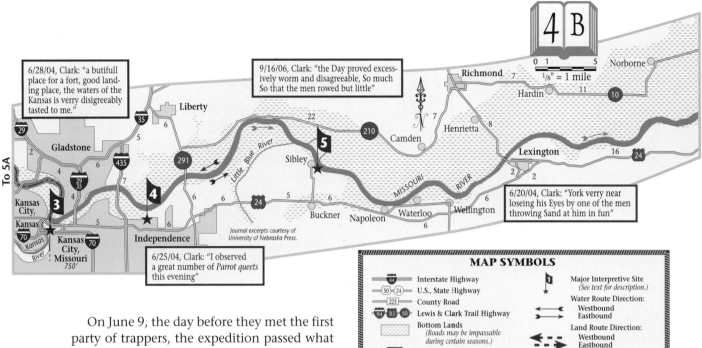

6/28/04, Clark: "a butifull place for a fort, good landing place, the waters of the Kansas is verry disigreeably tasted to me."

9/16/06, Clark: "the Day proved excessively worm and disagreeable, So much So that the men rowed but little"

6/25/04, Clark: "I observed a great number of *Parrot queets* this evening"

6/20/04, Clark: "York verry near loseing his Eyes by one of the men throwing Sand at him in fun"

MAP SYMBOLS

44	Interstate Highway
50 24	U.S., State Highway
223	County Road
94 83 50	Lewis & Clark Trail Highway
	Bottom Lands (Roads may be impassable during certain seasons.)
⬇	Travel Restrictions (Inquire Locally)
	Streamflow Direction

Major Interpretive Site (See text for description.)

Water Route Direction:
Westbound
Eastbound

Land Route Direction:
Westbound
Eastbound

Journal Excerpts:
Westbound
Eastbound

On June 9, the day before they met the first party of trappers, the expedition passed what is now **[2]** Arrow Rock State Historic Site. They knew it as "Prairie of Arrows." Indian people had named Arrow Rock and taught that name to French visitors nearly a century before.

A little way upstream, in strong current, the keelboat got into a "disagreeable and Dangerous Situation, particularly as immense large trees were Drifting down and we lay imediately in their Course." The boat struck a snag and was turned sideways against the current. Some of the men swam ashore with ropes attached to the boat and in just "a fiew minits" turned it around. Clark was apparently reassured, noting that "our party is not inferior to any" group of rivermen.

With the strong current and the river still rising, their progress through this area was slow, often only nine or ten miles in a long day. But the men were "in high Spirits," and on the night of the 11th "verry lively Danceing & Singing &c." That day the wind had blown so hard that the Corps stayed put, resting and drying out wet items (a constant problem) and cleaning their guns. Hunters killed two deer and two bears, whose meat was "jerked" (dried) to preserve it.

Day after day, Clark called this country "butifull" and noted how "troublesome" the mosquitoes were. Many of the men had dysentery and several kinds of skin infections, all caused by the Missouri's water; Clark thought

the water caused only the dysentery. The men were eating almost nothing but meat, and it probably was slightly spoiled most of the time. They didn't know that could be part of the problem, because—as historian Gary E. Moulton points out—science would not begin to understand bacteria and germs for another fifty years.

An example of the self-sufficiency this trip required came on June 17 and 18, when the Corps stopped opposite present Waverly, Missouri to cut ash wood to make new oars, "which we were very much in want of." Sergeant John Ordway recorded that they made twenty oars here. They also made cord for a tow rope; when the keelboat could not even be poled upriver (see Chapter 3), the men had to "cordelle," or walk onshore pulling it against the water.

Another example of self-sufficiency came a few days later, near today's Sibley, Missouri. Clark decided to walk ahead of the boats on June 23 and let the party catch up with him. But after he set out, the wind was too strong and Captain Meriwether Lewis decided to halt the party and spend the day drying and cleaning gear. Clark wrote:

I Killed a Deer & made a fire expecting the

boat would Come up in the evening. the wind
continueing to blow prevented their moveing,
as the distance by land was too great for me to
return by night I concluded to Camp, Peeled Some
bark to lay on, and geathered wood to make fires
to Keep off the musquitors & Knats.

The island where Lewis and company spent the day might be today's Fishing River Island, but changes in the river's flow, and the shifting of shore and islands, make it difficult to be sure.

In 1808, William Clark would build what became **[5]** Fort Osage at this site, naming it for George C. Sibley, a government Indian trader. Clark negotiated a treaty with the Osage Indians for half of today's state of Missouri and much of Arkansas. In return, the Osage could settle around the new fort and enjoy its protection.

Summer was in full bloom by the time the Corps of Discovery reached the mouth of the Kansas River in today's **[3]** Kansas City, Kansas,

on June 26. Clark found the area "a butifull place for a fort" but he thought that Kansas River water tasted disagreeable. They stopped here for a break, drying out wet clothing and gear, and repacking supplies. Hunters killed several deer and the men dressed skins for later use.

The last night at this camp, June 28-29, privates John Collins and Hugh Hall broke into the expedition's whiskey keg while on guard duty. For the second time in less than five weeks, they stood court-martial. Collins was sentenced to 100 lashes on his bare back for getting drunk and for allowing Hall also to steal whiskey, and Hall received a sentence of 50 lashes. This time, Hall did not get off with a suspended sentence.

After their punishment, the captains held a parade inspection of the whole company, once again emphasizing that this was a military expedition and that discipline would be maintained.

TOURING TODAY

ஜ TO THE KANSAS RIVER ஜ

[ ] Bracketed numbers key sites to maps	♿	Special-needs accessible	⊨ Bed & breakfast
★ L&C in-depth interpretation, unchanged landform	⊗	Restaurant	▲ Camping, RV park
● L&C interpreted site	⊞	Motel, hotel, cabin	

Bridges over the Missouri River in this area are in Boonville (MO 5); Glasgow (MO 240); Miami (MO 41); Waverly (US 65/24); Lexington (MO 13); Independence (MO 291); Kansas City (I-71, I-69, I-435).

ALONG THE EXPEDITION'S PATH

[1] ★ **Katy Trail State Park** (MO)—This 86-mile section of the 225-mile trail runs between Rocheport and Boonville. The trail is open during daylight hours only. Access is limited to pedestrian and non-motorized traffic, except for ♿ motorized wheelchairs. Horses are allowed only on the section from Calhoun to Sedalia and mileage markers from the old railbed are still in use.

Weather conditions often impact the trail significantly, with flooding and trail closures frequently occurring. Always obtain current trail conditions before venturing out. (More Katy Trail trailheads are listed in Chapter 3.) 800/334-6946, 573/526-4522.
Katy Trail trailheads:
Rocheport (mile 178.3)—An area 1 mile west of here has a greater than 5% grade. Parking, restrooms, water and phone. Bike rentals, groceries, food and lodging nearby.
New Franklin (mile 188.2)—An area just east of here has a greater than 5% grade. Parking and restrooms. Phone, water, bike rentals, groceries, food and lodging nearby.
Franklin (mile 189.0)—Restrooms, water and food nearby.

Boonville (mile 191.8)—Parking. Restrooms, phone, water, bike rentals, groceries, food and lodging nearby.
Pilot Grove (mile 203.2)—Parking, water, and restrooms. Phone, groceries, food, camping, lodging nearby.
Clifton City (mile 215.4)—Parking and restrooms. Phone, water and groceries nearby.
Sedalia (mile 229)—Parking and water. Phone, restrooms, groceries, food, camping and lodging nearby.
Green Ridge (mile 239.2)—Parking, water and restrooms. Phone, groceries, and food nearby.
Windsor (mile 248)—Parking and restrooms. Phone, water, groceries, food, camping and lodging nearby.

Calhoun (mile 255.5)—Parking and restrooms. Phone nearby.
Clinton (mile 264.6)—Parking and restrooms. Phone, water, groceries, food, camping, and lodging nearby.

June 7, 1804
Franklin Island Wildlife Area (New Franklin, MO)—River access, hunting, fishing and wildlife refuge. Primitive restrooms. Access road is rough gravel. Seasonal flooding. Daily 4am to 10pm; free. 2 miles E of Boonville on US 40. 573/884-6861.

June 8, 1804
(Return Sept. 18, 1806)
DeBourgmount River Access (Lamine, MO)—Boating and fishing access on the Lamine River, 2 miles to the Missouri. 1.5 miles N of I-70 on MO 41. 816/530-5500.

June 9, 1804
[2] ★ Arrow Rock State Park/ Historic Site (Arrow Rock, MO)—Historic village brings 19th-century Missouri to life. The old courthouse, an 1875 gunsmith's shop, and artist George Caleb Bingham's home are among the buildings. ⊗ The Old Tavern (1834) has been restored and is open for meals daily. Summer theater productions are held Wed-Sun in the Lyceum, a renovated 1872 church. Guided tours daily (Memorial Day to Labor Day); admission fee for historic site and tours. Hike to the river overlook and have a picnic. ▲ 45 sites (23 w/hookups); fee; water; modern; showers; open all year/full operation Apr-Oct; grills/fire rings; tables; 30' limit; 15-day limit. Fishing; dump station; playground; groceries; fire wood. Museum located in the Old Tavern is open daily 10 to 4, Sun 12 to 5; free. In town at 4th & Van Buren. 660/837-3330.

June 10-11, 1804
Stump Island Park (Glasgow, MO)—City park on spot where the Corps camped. Fishing, boating, ▲ primitive camping. Daily; free. In town on MO 5. 816/338-2377.

June 12, 1804
Brunswick Access (Brunswick, MO)—On the Grand River, 3 miles above the Missouri. Fishing, boating, ▲ primitive camping. Daily 4am to 10pm; free. In town, US 24 & Polk. 660/751-4115.

June 14, 1804
Miami Riverfront Park (Miami, MO)—Small museum, fishing, boating, ▲ primitive camping. Daily; free. In town on MO 41, S of bridge. 660/852-3370.

June 15, 1804
Grand Pass Wildlife Area (Saline County, MO)—The Corps of Discovery camped here. Hiking and birding are the big attractions, ▲ primitive camping is available. Fishing and river access. 8 miles W of Marshall on US 65, 5 miles N on County N. 660/595-2444.

June 26-28, 1804
(Return Sept. 15, 1806)
[3] ★ Clark's Point (Kansas City, MO)—located in a rejuvenated city park where a statue of Lewis, Clark, Sacagawea, York and Seaman was unveiled in the summer of 2000. Overlook of the Kansas and Missouri rivers. Interpretation of Corps' camp on return trip. Always open; free. 8th & Jefferson.

AROUND THE AREA

TOWNS LISTED ALPHABETICALLY

Arrow Rock, Missouri
⊞ **Westward Trail Inn**—Suite-size room accommodates up to 5 people, full breakfast. 660/837-3335. $$

Blue Springs, Missouri
Burr Oak Woods Conservation Nature Center—Nature trails of varying lengths across 1,071 acres. Natural history exhibits in the visitor center include a 3,000-gallon aquarium. Trails open daily 8 to 8 (Apr-Oct), 8 to 5 (rest of year); center open daily 8 to 5, Sun noon to 5; free. 1 mile N of I-70 exit 20 on MO 7; 1 mile W on Park Road. 816/228-3766.
▲ **Blue Springs Lake**—57 sites (all w/hookups); fee; water; modern/ &; showers; May-Labor Day; grills/fire rings; tables. Lake swimming; boat ramp; boat rentals; fishing; playground; group activities. Dump station; firewood. I-470 exit 14, E on Bowlin Rd. 816/229-8980.
⊗ **Jose Miguel's**—Family food in a Spanish ambiance, kids' menu. L & D daily. I-70 exit 20. 816/228-6606. $$

Bonner Springs, Kansas
National Agricultural Center/ Hall of Fame—Congress created this tribute to the American farmer. Thousands of artifacts and exhibits. Mon-Sat 9 to 5, Sun 1 to 5 (Mar-Nov); admission fee. I-70 & KS 7, 630 Hall of Fame Dr. 913/721-1075.

Boonville, Missouri
Boonville Chamber of Commerce—200 Main, Suite 4 (in the County Bldg). 660/882-2721.
Boone's Lick State Historic Site—Salt-making business owned and operated by Daniel Boone's sons, Daniel and Nathan. An interpretive trail leads to the salt springs where the business began. Nice picnic area. Daily to sunset; free. 19 miles NW on MO 87 and County MM. 660/837-3330.
Kemper Military School & College—Begun in 1844, it is the oldest military school west of the Mississippi. On Sundays watch the drill on the parade grounds. Daily, free guided tours. 701 Third St. 660/882-5623.
Old Cooper County Jail & Hanging Barn—Tours of 1848 jail and museum. Weekdays, increasing to daily Memorial Day-Labor Day; admission fee. 614 E. Morgan. 660/882-7977.
⊞ **Comfort Inn**—51 rooms, coin laundry, hot tub. I-70 exit 101. 660/882-5317. $$ K12
⊩ **Morgan Street Repose**—3 suites in 1869 Victorian home, full breakfast. Near Katy Trail, bicycles, gardens. 800/248-5061, 660/882-7195. $$

Edgerton, Kansas
Lanesfield School Historic Site—Experience a one-room schoolhouse lesson on history from costumed teachers. Tue-Sun 1 to 5; free. 18745 S. Dillie Rd. 913/893-6645.

Excelsior Springs, Missouri

Watkins Woolen Mill State Historic Site—Originally part of 3,660-acre Bethany Plantation, the mill, owner's house and outbuildings have been restored. Tour the 19th-century woolen mill and house. Visitor center exhibits relate mill's history. Surrounded by Watkins Mill State Park. Daily 10 to 4, Sun 11 to 5, daily 10 to 5 (summer), Sun noon to 6 (summer); admission fee. 1 mile N of US 69 on MO 92, turn on County RA. 816/296-3357, 800/334-6946.

⊨ **Crescent Lake Manor**—4 rooms in a 3-story Georgian on a colonial estate. Walking paths, pool. 816/637-2958. $$

Fairway, Kansas

Shawnee Mission State Historic Site—This mission school for Indian children was established by Rev. Thomas Johnson in 1839. It became an important stop on the Santa Fe Trail. Guided tours available. Tue-Sat 10 to 5, Sun 1 to 5; free. 53rd & Mission Rd. 913/262-0867.

Grandview, Missouri

Truman Farm Home—Harry S. Truman spent part of his boyhood and young adult life as a farmer here. In his spare time he courted Bess Wallace and served as a soldier and postmaster. Period and original furnishings, several outbuildings. Fri-Sun 9 to 4 (May-Aug); free. I-435 S to US 71. 816/254-2720.

Higginsville, Missouri

Confederate Memorial State Historic Site—Memorial to the 40,000 Missourians who fought for the Confederacy. A chapel and cemetery, fishing lakes and picnic areas. Daily to sunset; free. 1 mile N of Higginsville on MO 13. 660/584-2853.

Hillsdale, Kansas

Hillsdale State Park—Along the east side of Hillsdale Reservoir is a combination of woodlands, meadows and bluffs for hiking, biking, boating and fishing. A nature trail along with over 20 miles of biking trails hug the shoreline. Lake swimming and beach. ▲ 194 sites (98 w/hookups); fee; water; modern/&; open all year/full operation Apr-Oct; grills/fire rings; tables. Dump station. 2 miles W on 255th St. 913/783-4507.

Independence, Missouri

Independence Department of Tourism—111 E. Maple St. 816/325-7111.

1859 Jail, Marshal's Home & Museum—See the world as Frank James and William Quantrill did. Hands-on exhibits and one-room schoolhouse. Mon-Sat 10 to 4, Sun 1 to 4 (Mar-Dec); admission fee. 217 N. Main. 816/252-1892.

Main Street Motor Museum—A 1940s car dealership is home to displays of classic, antique and rare autos. Daily 10 to 6 (Apr-Oct); admission fee. 315 N. Main. 816/833-7370.

[4] ★ National Frontier Trails Center—Restored mill where the Oregon, Santa Fe and California trails began. Housed inside are a museum, interpretive center, films and an extensive research facility devoted to westward expansion, including Lewis and Clark Expedition. Mon-Sat 9 to 4:30, Sun 12:30 to 4:30; admission fee. W. Pacific & Osage Sts. 816/325-7575.

Pioneer Spring Cabin—1850s furnished cabin. The spring on this property was a neutral meeting ground for Indians and settlers. Weekends 10 to 4 (Apr-Oct); free. Truman & Noland Rds. 816/325-7111.

Harry S. Truman Courtroom & Office—Restored courtroom of county judge Harry Truman. Multimedia presentation and exhibits recount his early life. Fri-Sat 9 to 4:30; admission fee. Main & Lexington. 816/795-8200, ext 260.

Harry S. Truman Library & Museum—The history of a common man who grew up to be president. Trace his accomplishments and see his Oval Office in the White House Gallery. Special exhibits and programs recount his leadership roles and his everyday life. Open daily 9 to 5, Thurs until 9, Sun 12 to 5; admission fee. US 24 & Delaware. 816/833-1225, 816/833-1400.

Harry S. Truman National Historic Site—Built in 1862 by Bess's grandfather. The Trumans lived here from the time they were married, and the home served as the summer White House from 1945 to 1953. Guided tours daily 9 to 4:30; admission fee (tickets available on first-come basis starting at 8:30 at the ticket center at Truman Rd. & Main St.). 219 N. Delaware. 816/254-9929.

RLDS World Headquarters Complex—Peace pavilion, Japanese meditation garden, film. Recitals on the organ at 3pm during summer. Daily 9-5; free. River & Walnut. 816/833-1000, ext. 3030.

Vaile Mansion—Exquisitely preserved 31-room Victorian mansion. Mon-Sat 10 to 4, Sun 1 to 4 (Apr-Oct); admission fee. 1500 N. Liberty. 816/325-7111.

▦ **Howard Johnson Hotel**—170 rooms, indoor and outdoor pools, pets, ⊗ restaurant, hot tub. I-70 exit 12. 816/373-8856, 800/338-3752. $$$ K18

▦ **Shoney's Inn**—114 rooms, pool, pets, ⊗ restaurant. Take advantage of the inexpensive breakfast buffet. I-70 exit 12, 816/254-0100. $$ K18

⊨ **Serendipity Bed & Breakfast**—4 rooms & suites in historic area, full breakfast, pets, TV, &. 800/203-4299. $$

⊨ **Woodstock Inn**—11 rooms, full breakfast, smoke-free, &. In historic area near Truman home and library. 800/276-5202, 816/833-2233 $$$

⊗ **Red Mule Pub & Grill**—Hearty country meals, kids' menu, &. L & D daily. 16506 E. US 40 (1.5 miles S of I-70 exit 14), 816/478-1810. $$

⊗ **Rheinland**—German food in Bavarian atmosphere, kids' menu, smoke-free, &. L & D daily. 208 N. Main, 816/461-5383. $$

Jackson County, Missouri

Longview Lake—Boating, water-skiing and fishing on 930-acre lake with full service marina. Swimming beach, boat rental, golf course, 7 miles of bike trails. ▲ 120 sites (60 w/hookups); fee; water; modern/&; showers; Apr-Sept; grills/fire rings; tables. Dump station; coin laundry; firewood; group activities; equestrian trails; boat rental; playground. Daily 7 to sunset; free. I-470 & Raytown Rd, S to Longview Rd. 816/966-8976.

Kansas City, Kansas

Kansas City Convention & Visitors Bureau—727 Minnesota Ave. 913/321-5800.

Children's Museum of Kansas City—Watch your shadow stay on the wall after you're gone, create chain reactions and be part of a salt water aquarium. Designed for kids under 12. Tue-Sun 10 to 4; admission fee. 4601 State (Indian Springs Shopping Center). 913/287-8888.

Community Nature Center Nature Trail—Small, urban wildlife preserve with hiking trails and wildlife viewing. Daily to sunset; free. 72nd & Parallel Pkwy. 913/334-1100.

Grinter Place State Historic Site—Home of Moses Grinter, who built a trading post and ran the first ferry across the Kansas River in the 1850s. Wed-Sat 10 to 5, Sun 1 to 5; donations. I-70 exit 414, 2 miles S. 913/299-0373.

Huron Cemetery—Tribal burial ground of the Wyandots from 1844 to 1855. Daily to sunset; free. In Huron Park, between 6th & 7th Sts. 913/321-5800.

River City, U.S.A.—Sightseeing cruises on the river aboard the *Missouri River Queen*, a 3-deck sternwheeler. Daily at 2 (Jun-Aug), Sat/Sun at 2 (Mar-May, Sept-Dec); admission fee. I-70 Fairfax exit. 913/281-5300, 800/373-0027.

⊞ **American Motel**—158 rooms, pool, coin laundry. I-70 exit 414. 800/905-6343, 913/299-2999. $ K12

⊞ **Best Western Inn**—113 rooms, pool, hot tub, pets, continental breakfast, coin laundry. I-35 exit 234, 1 block S on US 169. 800/368-1741, 913/677-3060. $$ K18

Kansas City, Missouri

Convention & Visitors Bureau of Greater Kansas City—City Center Square, 1100 Main, Suite 2550. 816/221-5242, 800/767-7700.

American Jazz Museum—Audio and video stroll through the history of this uniquely American music. All the great performers are here. Tue-Sat 9 to 6, Sun noon to 6; admission fee. 1616 E. 18th. 816/474-8463 (18th & Vine Historic District).

Arabia Steamboat Museum—Tons of treasure recovered from the steamboat that sank in 1856. Interactive exhibits, full-size replica of the *Arabia* with a working paddle wheel. Mon-Sat 10 to 6, Sun noon to 5; admission fee. 400 Grand. 816/471-4030.

Benjamin Ranch—A working ranch in the city (it's even near the Mall). Originally a stop along the Santa Fe Trail. Horseback riding. Daily 8 to dusk; fees vary for activities. I-435 & E. 87th St. 816/761-5055.

Thomas Hart Benton Home & Studio State Historic Site—Self-guided tours of Benton's home & studio he used from 1939 until his death in 1975. Mon-Sat 10 to 4, Sun noon to 5 (11 to 4 in the winter); admission fee. 3616 Belleview. 816/931-5722.

Black Archives of Mid-America—One of nation's largest collections of black art, paintings and sculptures. Research and exhibits on local black leaders. Mon-Fri 9 to 4:30; admission fee. 2033 Vine. 816/483-1300.

Cave Spring Interpretive Center—Exhibits on the natural and cultural history of Kansas City at one of the Santa Fe Trail stops. Bring a picnic, hike the nature trails and explore a cave, spring and wildlife habitats. Hiking trails open daily, center open Tue-Sat 10 to 5; free. 8701 Gregory at Blue Ridge Blvd. 816/358-2283.

City Hall/Observation Deck—Dramatic view of the city from the 30th floor. Mon-Fri 8:30 to 4:15; free. 414 E. 12th St. 816/274-2222.

Comedysports—Unique improvisational fun for the entire family. Teams of comedians compete on Astroturf complete with referee. 512 Delaware. 816/842-2744.

Fleming Park—Along Lake Jacomo, this county park is a haven for watersports. Fishing, boat rental, swimming beach, full-service marina. Picnic area and shelters, nature trails and native animal enclosure for bison, elk and whitetail deer. **Missouri Town 1855** on the east shore is a reconstructed living history town. Park open daily, Missouri Town 1855 open Wed-Sun 9 to 5 (weekends only late November-mid-April); admission fee for Missouri Town 1855. Park is at I-470 South exit Woods Chapel Rd., Missouri Town 1855 is at I-70 Blue Springs exit. 816/795-8200.

Hallmark Visitor Center—History of Hallmark cards, with exhibits on creativity. Mon-Fri 9 to 5, Sat 9:30 to 4:30; free. Crown Center. 816/274-5672, 816/274-3613.

Kaleidoscope—Creativity exploration for kids 5 to 12. Sensory art experiences and imagination experiences. Open Crown Center hours Mon-Sat; free. Crown Center. 816/274-8300.

Kansas City Blades—Professional hockey (IHL). Kemper Arena. 1800 Genessee. 816/842-1063.

Kansas City Chiefs—Professional football (NFL). September through December. Arrowhead Stadium, I-70 & Blue Ridge Cutoff. 816/924-9400; 800/676-5488.

Kansas City Museum—Hands-on history and science exhibits in the historic R.A. Long Mansion. Planetarium, Challenger Learning Center, National History Hall and a real soda fountain. Tue-Sat 9:30 to 4:30, Sun noon to 4:30; admission fees for both museum and planetarium, combo tickets available. 3218 Gladstone. 816/483-8300.

Kansas City Royals—Professional baseball (AL). April through September. Kauffman Stadium, I-70 & Blue Ridge Cutoff. 800/422-1969, 816/921-8000.

Kansas City Trolleys—Drivers provide a narrated tour through the city's main areas. Passengers can use this as regular transportation, fee includes 3 reboards on the same day. Daily (Mar-Dec); admission fee. 816/221-3399

Kansas City Wizards—Major league soccer. March through September. Arrowhead Stadium. 816/472-4625.

Kemper Museum of Contemporary Art—International collection of contemporary art with additional special exhibits. Sculpture garden, concerts, programs. Tue-Fri 10 to 4, Sat 10 to 5, Sun 11 to 5; free. 4420 Warwick Blvd. 816/561-3737, 816/753-5784.

Line Creek Museum of Archaeology—Life-size diorama and artifacts related history of 6 prehistoric Native American cultures. Located at a 2200-year-old Hopewell Indian site. Weekends 11 to 4; admission fee. 5940 NW Waukonis. 816/587-8822.

Loose Park—Site of Civil War Battle of Westport. Smith Municipal Rose Garden and lake. Daily, horticulture reference library open Mon-Fri 8 to 4; free. 51st & Wornall. 816/561-9710.

Alexander Majors Historical House—Home of Pony Express founder and headquarters for the largest freight company in the frontier. Outbuilding and gift shop. Sat-Sun 1-4 (Apr-Dec); admission fee. 8201 State Line Rd. 816/333-5556.

Negro Leagues Baseball Museum—Memorabilia and interactive exhibits tell the story of the Leagues' contribution to America's Sport. Open Tue-Sat 9 to 6, Sun noon to 6; admission fee. 1601 E. 18th. 816/221-1920. (18th & Vine Historic District)

Nelson-Atkins Museum of Art—Extensive collection of art from 3000 BC to present. Diverse cultures and media. Outside is **Kansas City Sculpture Park**, a haven of art and beautiful landscaping featuring works by Henry Moore. You can't miss "Shuttlecocks" by Claes Oldenburg and Cooshe van Bruggen. Tue-Thur 10 to 4, Fri 10 to 9, Sat 10 to 5, Sun 1 to 5; admission fee. 4525 Oak. 816/751-1278.

Shoal Creek Missouri—Step back into the 19th century at this living history museum. Special tours and programs available. Tue-Sat 9 to 3, Sun noon to 4; admission fee. 7000 NE Barry Rd (in Hodge Park). 816/792-2665.

Swope Park
City park is home to the Kansas City Zoo, Lakeside Nature center, golf courses, swimming, nature trails. Open daily. Swope Parkway & Meyer Blvd. 816/444-3113.

Kansas City Zoo—Dynamic facility with 95-acre African exhibit, Australian exhibit, IMAX theatre, pony and camel rides, animal presentations. Daily 9 to 5 (Apr to mid-Oct), 9 to 4 (rest of

year); admission fee, parking fee and tickets for IMAX theatre. I-435 & 63rd St. 816/871-5700.

Lakeside Nature Center—Exhibits, live animals, lectures and nature programs. Guided hikes along nature trails. Tue-Sat 9 to 5; free. 5600 E. Gregory. 816/444-4656.

Starlight Theatre—8,000-seat outdoor amphitheatre presenting concerts and Broadway musicals. Open June-Aug; admission fees vary. Meyer Blvd & Swope Parkway. 816/333-9481.

Toy & Miniature Museum of Kansas City—Excellent collection of miniatures and furnished antique dollhouses in restored 1911 mansion. Wed-Sat 10 to 4, Sun 1 to 4; admission fee. 5235 Oak. 816/333-2055.

Worlds of Fun—Amusement park with over 140 rides including several water rides and the free-fall "Detonator." Daily (Memorial Day-Labor Day), weekends spring and fall; admission fee. Adjacent to Oceans of Fun, I-435 east loop exit 54. 816/454-4545.

▲ **KOA-KC East**—88 grassy sites (72 w/hookups); fee; water; modern; showers; open Mar-Oct; grills/fire rings; tables. Pool; bike rental; recreation. Dump station; coin laundry; groceries; firewood. I-70 exit 28 & County H, follow signs. 816/690-6660.

⊞ **Best Western Country Inn-North**—44 rooms, pool. I-435 exit 54, 2633 NE 43rd St. 816/459-7222, 800/528-1234. $$ K12

⊞ **Clubhouse Inn-KCI**—138 rooms, indoor pool, full breakfast, hot tub, exercise room. Weekend specials. I-29 exit 13. 816/464-2423. $$$ K16

⊞ **Residence Inn Union Hill**—96 rooms, continental breakfast, pets, pool, hot tub, exercise room. 2975 Main St. 816/561-3000. $$$+

⊞ **Ritz-Carlton**—373 rooms, pets, pool, exercise room, ⊗ restaurant. 401 Ward Pkwy in Country Club Plaza. 816/756-1500. $$$+

⊗ **Charlie's Lodge**—Steak and seafood in a hunting lodge, kids' menu, early bird dinner. L & D daily. 7953 State Line Rd. 816/333-6363. $$

⊗ **Colony Steakhouse & Lobster Pot Seafood Feast**—Dinner

seafood buffet, kids' menu. L & D daily. I-435 exit 75B. 816/333-5500. $$

⊗ **Gates & Sons Bar-B-Q**—Kansas City tradition for over 50 years. Seven locations throughout the city. $

⊗ **Jazz: A Louisiana Kitchen**—New Orleans style Creole in a casual atmosphere. L & D daily, jazz nightly Wed-Sun. 1823 W. 39th St. 816/531-5556. $$

⊗ **Madry's Dash of Flavor**—Buffet style soul food to the sounds of jazz and gospel. L & D daily, closed Mondays. 28 E. 39th St. 816/752-3274. $$

⊗ **Streetcar Named Desire**—Burgers, sandwiches in 1964 streetcar. Crown Center, 2450 Grand Blvd. 816/472-5959. $

⊗ **Winslow's City Market Smokehouse**—Barbecue and blues. L & D daily, L only on Mondays. 20 E. 5th St. 816/471-7427. $$

Kearney, Missouri
Jesse James Birthplace & Museum—Restoration of home where outlaws Jesse and Frank were raised. Decorated with original furnishings. Museum contains personal possessions and multimedia presentations. Production of "The Life and Time of Jesse James" Fri-Sun in August. Daily 9 to 4, Sun noon to 4; admission fee. E on MO 92, follow signs 3 miles on Jesse James Farm Rd. 816/628-6065.

Lawrence, Kansas
Lawrence Convention & Visitors Bureau—734 Vermont, Suite 101. 785/865-4411, 888/529-5267.

Clinton State Park—Along the shore of 7,000-acre Lake Clinton, this park is dedicated to the enjoyment of watersports. Boating access is plentiful with 16 ramps, courtesy docks and a marina. Fishing for bass is excellent, and hunting (along with wildlife viewing) is allowed in adjacent **Clinton Wildlife Area**. Archeological excavations indicate that the first hunters were here in 8000 B.C. Interpretive programs, hiking, and swimming. ▲ 404 sites (240 w/hookups); fee; water; modern/♿; showers; open all year; grills/fire rings; tables; 15-day limit. Dump station; coin laundry. 4 miles W of

Lawrence on US 59, 2 miles S on County 13. 785/842-8462.

Lawrence Riverfront Park Trails—For casual bikers, there are several miles of level trail along the north side of the Kansas River. A rougher 8-mile loop over a dirt track is also available. Daily to sunset; free. 2nd Street Bridge. 785/832-3450.

University of Kansas

Museum of Anthropology—Prehistoric specimens and artifacts from around the world. Mon-Sat 9 to 5, Sun 1 to 5; free. 14th St & Jayhawk Blvd (Spooner Hall). 785/864-4245.

Natural History Museum and Biodiversity Research Center—Panorama of plants in natural settings, animal mounts and fossils. Live snakes and bees. Mon-Sat 10 to 5, Sun noon to 5; donations. 14th & Jayhawk Blvd (Dyche Hall). 785/864-4540.

Spencer Museum of Art—Highlights are Renaissance and baroque paintings, decorative arts, graphic arts, 19th and 20th century American works. Tue-Sat 10 to 5, Sun noon to 5; free. 1301 Mississippi. 785/864-4710.

Watkins Community Museum—Permanent exhibits include a restored 1878 playhouse, 1920 electric car, and a U.S. bicentennial quilt. Rotating exhibits in the 1888 bank building document pioneer life and the contribution of women to the area. Tue-Sat 10 to 4, Sun 1:30 to 4; donations. 1047 Massachusetts. 785/841-4109.

▲ KOA—Lawrence/Kansas City—75 grassy sites (59 w/hookups); fee; water; modern; showers; open all year; grills/fire rings; tables. Pool; dump station; coin laundry; playground; firewood; groceries. I-70 exit 204. 0.5 mile N on US 59/40, 0.33 mile E on US 24/40. 785/842-3877.

⊞ Best Western Hallmark Inn—60 rooms, pool, pets, continental breakfast. 730 Iowa St. 785/842-6500. $$ K12

⊞ Bismarck Inn—53 rooms, continental breakfast. I-70 exit 204. 785/749-4040, 800/665-7446. $ K16

⊞ Days Inn—101 rooms, pool, continental breakfast, pets, coin laundry. 2309 Iowa St. 785/843-9100. $$ K18

Lawson, Missouri

Watkins Mill State Park—Hilly wooded area surrounding Watkins Woolen Mill State Historic Site. Museum and visitor center, biking and hiking trails, lake swimming, fishing and boating. ▲ 100 sites (58 w/hookups); fee; water; modern/&; showers; open all year/full operation Apr-Oct; grills/fire rings; tables; 15-day limit. Dump station; coin laundry. 1 mile N of US 69 on MO 92, turn on County RA. 816/580-3387, 800/334-6943 (museum).

Lee's Summit, Missouri

⊞ Comfort Inn—52 rooms, indoor pool, continental breakfast, pets, hot tub. US 50 & MO 291. 816/524-8181. $$ K18

Lenexa, Kansas

Legler Barn Museum—Stone barn built along the Santa Fe Trail provides a living history experience complete with pioneer museum, trunk shows, and meals. Tue-Sat 10 to 4, Sun 1 to 4; donations. 14907 W. 87th (in **Sar-Ko-Par Trails Park**). 913/492-0038.

⊞ Guesthouse Suite Hotel—59 suites, indoor pool, exercise room. Great value. 9775 Lenexa Dr. 913/541-4000, 800/648-4994. $$ K16

Lexington, Missouri

Lexington Tourism Bureau—Maps for driving tour of historical buildings along the Santa Fe Trail through town available here. 817 Main St. 660/259-3082.

Battle of Lexington State Historic Site—Union troops were defeated here by Missouri State Guard troops who captured the port of Lexington during the battle, September 16-18, 1861. Also learn about the Battle of the Hemp Bales. Tour the Anderson-Davis House, used by both sides as a hospital during the 1861 battle. A mile-long interpretive trail takes you through the battlefield. Visitor center exhibits complete the picture. Mon-Sat 9 to 4:30, Sun 12 to 5; admission fee. On 13th St. 660/259-4654.

Lexington Historical Museum—Exhibits, artifacts and memorabilia about the Civil War Battle of Lexington and also the Pony Express. Daily 1 to 4:30 (June-Sept), weekends 1 to 4:30 (Apr-Oct); admission fee. 112 S. 13th St. 660/259-6313.

Log House Museum—1830 cabin of unusual design. Documents life of pioneers and hardships they faced. Wed-Sat 9 to 5, Sun noon to 5 (Apr-Oct); admission fee. Main & Broadway. 660/259-4960.

⊞ Lexington Inn—60 rooms, pool, pets, ⊗ restaurant, coin laundry. US 24 & MO 13. 660/259-4641. $ K5

Liberty, Missouri

Historic Liberty Jail—Mormon leader Joseph Smith was jailed here. His story is recounted through multimedia and interactive exhibits. Open daily 9 to 9; free. Main & Mississippi. 816/781-3188.

Jesse James Bank Museum—Bank with the dubious honor of "hosting" the first U.S. daylight, peacetime robbery. Original 1858 vault, ledger books and James items. Mon-Sat 9 to 4; admission fee. Historic Old Liberty Square. 816/781-4458.

⊞ Best Western Hallmark Inn—61 rooms, pets, pool, coin laundry. I-35 exit 16, E on MO 152. 816/781-8770. $$ K18

Lone Jack, Missouri

Lone Jack Civil War Museum—Site of August 16, 1862 Civil War Battle. Multimedia programs, exhibits. Battlefield diorama. Wed-Sat 9 to 5, Sun 1 to 4 (Apr-Oct), weekends rest of year; donations. MO 150 & US 50. 816/566-2272.

Marshall, Missouri

● Van Meter State Park—Remains of earthwork known as the "Old Fort" document history of inhabitation by the Missouri Indians. Abundant wildflowers invite exploration. Visitor center contains several interpretive exhibits and exhibits on Indian history. Picnic and play areas, hiking trails, fishing. ▲ 20 sites (12 w/hookups); fee; water; modern; showers; open all year/full operation Apr-Oct; grills/fire rings;

tables; 30' maximum; 15-day limit. 14 miles NW of Marshall on MO 122. 660/886-7537.

Olathe, Kansas
Olathe Area Chamber of Commerce—128 S. Chestnut. 913/764-1050.
Mahaffie Farmstead & Stagecoach Stop Historic Site—Only farm used as a Santa Fe Trail stop still in existence. Tours available year-round except January; admission fee. I-35 & KS 150, 1100 Kansas City Rd. 913/782-6972.
Ernie Miller Nature Center—Exhibits, some of them hands-on, and diorama portray the area's natural history. Nature trails open daily until dusk, center open Tue-Sat 9 to 5, Sun 1 to 5; free. 909 N. Hwy K-7. 913/764-7759.
⊞ **Best Western Hallmark Inn**—85 rooms, continental breakfast, pool. 211 N. Rawhide, 913/782-4343, 800/528-1234. $$ K18
⊗ **Kansas Machine Shed**—Old-fashioned country cooking, kids' menu. B L & D daily. I-35 exit 220. 913/780-2697. $$

Overland Park, Kansas
Overland Park Chamber of Commerce—P.O. Box 12125. 913/491-3600.
Deanna Rose Children's Farmstead—Farm for kids complete with buildings, animals. Birds of prey exhibit. Picnic area and playground. Daily 9 to 8 (summer); free. 13800 Switzer Rd. 913/897-2360.
NCAA Hall of Champions—A museum dedicated to intercollegiate athletics. Multimedia and photographic displays including areas that place you in the center of the action at kickoff, and at center court during the Final Four. Mon-Sat 10 to 5, Sun noon to 4; admission fee. Located at the NCAA headquarters, 6201 College Blvd. 913-339-0000.
Overland Park Arboretum and Botanical Gardens—Developing on 300-acre site with woodchip trails and water garden. Open all year; free. Antioch & 179th St. 913/865-3604.
⊞ **Amerisuites**—126 suites, pool, exercise room. Great value. 6801 W. 112th St., 913/451-2553, 800/833-1516. $$$ K18

⊞ **Doubletree Hotel**—357 rooms, pets, indoor pool, hot tub, restaurant, jogging trail. Weekend rates. I-435 & US 69. 913/451-6100. $$$ K18
⊞ **Drury Inn**—155 rooms, pool, continental breakfast, pets. 10951 Metcalf Ave. 913/345-1500. $$$ K18
⊞ **Fairfield Inn**—134 rooms, pool, continental breakfast. I-435 exit 77. 913/381-5700. $$ K18
⊞ **Hampton Inn**—134 rooms, pool, hot tub, continental breakfast. 10591 Metcalf Frontage Rd. 913/341-1551. $$ K18
⊗ **J. Alexander's**—Hearty, generous meals in casual/historic ambiance. L & D daily. 11471 Metcalf. 913/469-1995. $$
⊗ **Dick Clark's American Bandstand Grill**—American classic menu with enormous desserts in rock and roll memorabilia heaven, dancing to the oldies nightly. L & D daily. I-475 & Metcalf (look for the giant stack of records). 913/451-1600.
⊗ **La Mediterranee**—Elegant French cuisine. L & D Mon-Sat. I-435/US 169 exit 79, 2 miles N on US 169. 913/341-9595. $$$
⊗ **Mrs. Peter's Chicken Dinners**—Just like mom used to make, &. L & D daily, D only Sat. US 24, 3 blocks W of I-635. 913/287-7711. $$
⊗ **Trinh Villa**—Vietnamese specialties. L & D Mon-Sat. 103rd at I-69. 913/888-8820. $

Shawnee, Kansas
Shawnee Area Chamber of Commerce—10913 Johnson Dr. 913/631-6545.
Johnson County Historical Museum—Documents area's impact on national events. Children's workshops and hands-on exhibits. Tue-Sat 10 to 4:30, Sun 1 to 4:30; free. Shawnee Parkway & Lackman Rd. 913/631-6709.
Old Shawnee Town—Several 1800s structures, some relocated here, others reproductions. All furnished to the period. Tue-Sat 12 to 5; admission fee. 57th St & Cody. 913/268-8772.
Shawnee Mission Park/Mill Creek Streamway Park—Nature trails, an 8-mile paved trail, and off-road bike trails. An interpretive

center on the Pony Express, lake swimming, boat ramp and picnic areas. Daily to sunset; free. 87th St. & Barkley Dr. 913/888-4713.

Sibley, Missouri
[5] ★ **Fort Osage**—Established by William Clark in 1808, it was the first permanent U.S. fort in the Louisiana Purchase. Blockhouse, trading house, officers' quarters and soldiers' barracks have been reconstructed. Exhibits and gift shop in the visitor center. Area overlooks the Missouri River. Open Wed-Sun 9 to 4:30 (weekends only Thanksgiving to mid-April); admission fee. 1 mile N of Sibley, follow the signs. 816/795-8200 ext. 1260.

Smithville, Missouri
▲ **Camp Branch**—365 sites (36 w/hookups); fee; water; modern/&; showers; open all year/full operation Mar-Oct; grills/fire rings; tables. Lake swimming; boat ramp; canoeing; fishing; hiking; group activities. Dump station; coin laundry; firewood. N on US 169 from I-29 to MO 92, 6 miles E to County E, 3 miles N. 816/532-0803.
▲ **Crows Creek**—415 sites (193 w/hookups); fee; water; modern/&; showers; open all year/full operation Mar-Oct; grills/fire rings; tables. Lake swimming; boat ramp; canoeing; fishing; hiking; group activities. Dump station; coin laundry; firewood. 4.5 miles W on MO 92 from I-35, 3.5 miles N on County E. 816/532-0803.

Topeka, Kansas
Topeka Convention & Visitors Bureau—1275 SW Topeka Blvd. 785/234-1030, 800/235-1030.
Combat Air Museum—Examples of technology used from the Spanish-American War to the space shuttle. A recreated German POW barracks. Mon-Sat 9 to 4:30, Sun 10 to 4:30; admission fee. Forbes Field. 785/862-3303.
Dornwood Park—Several miles of connected hiking and biking trails through a wooded park on the edge of town. Open daily to sunset; free. I-70 exit 363, 1 mile S on California, E on 25th St. 785/272-5900.

Gage Park

A miniature train takes you for a tour. Then hit the swimming pool, the 1908 carousel, the picnic area or the playground. **Reinisch Memorial Rose and Rock Garden** is in bloom from early spring to late fall. Daily 6am to 11pm; admission fee for some activities. On Gage Blvd. between W. 6th & 10th Sts. Also includes:

Topeka Zoo—The Amazon Basin takes you to a tropical rain forest habitat. Large mammals entertain with their antics. Daily 9 to 6; admission fee. In Gage Park. 785/272-5821.

Kansas Museum of History—Collection of art and artifacts from prehistoric times to present. Audiovisual presentations and children's discovery room. Mon-Sat 9 to 4:30, Sun 12:30 to 4:30; free. 6425 SW 6th St. 785/272-8681.

Ward-Meade Park & House—Acres of gardens surround this 1870 Victorian. The house is open for tours. A log cabin, schoolhouse, general store and railroad depot are also located here. Gardens open daily to dusk, tours Tue-Fri at 11 and 2, Sat/Sun 1 and 2; admission fee for tours. 124 NW Fillmore St. 785/295-3888.

▲ **Lake Shawnee**—154 sites (all w/hookups); fee; water; modern; showers; open all year; grills/fire rings; tables; 40' limit. Fishing; hiking; lake swimming; boat ramp; boat rental; dump station; playground; tennis courts. Recreational facilities open to public; planned group activities; picnic area. I-70 East Topeka Tnpk exit, 0.5 mile SE on 21st St, 1.5 mile S on Croco Rd, 0.5 mile W on East Edge Rd. 785/267-1859.

▲ **KOA of Topeka**—72 grassy sites (46 w/hookups); fee; water; modern; showers; open all year/full operation Mar-Nov; grills/fire rings; tables. Hiking; pool; dump station; coin laundry; playground; ⊞ cabins; groceries. 9 miles E of US 75 on US 24, 1.25 miles N on gravel road. 758/246-3419.

⊞ **Best Western Meadow Acres**—83 rooms, indoor pool, continental breakfast. 2950 S. Topeka. 785/267-1681. $$ K12

⊞ **Clubhouse Inn**—121 rooms, pool, full breakfast, hot tub, coin laundry. Reasonable suites and weekend rates. 924 SW Henderson Rd. 785/273-8888. $$$ K16

⊞ **Days Inn**—62 rooms, indoor pool, continental breakfast, pets, hot tub. Suites are same price as double rooms and have refrigerators. 1510 SW Wanamaker Rd. 785/272-8538. $$ K12

⊞ **The Senate Luxury Suites**—52 rooms in historic hotel, hot tub, continental breakfast, coin laundry. Some efficiencies and 2-bedroom units. 900 SW Tyler, W of Capitol Bldg. 785/233-5050. $$$ K15

⊫ **Heritage House**—11 distinctive rooms, full breakfast, TV. Opposite zoo. Dinner served Mon-Sat. 785/233-3800. $$$

⊗ **Annie's Santa Fe**—Popular Mexican spot, kids' menu. L & D daily. I-740 & Wanamaker Rd. (Westridge Mall). 785/271-1060. $

⊗ **Roost Family Restaurant**—Family-oriented country meals, kids' menu, Sunday brunch. 24 hours. I-70 & Wanamaker Rd. 785/272-9573. $

CHAPTER 5

June 29 to July 21, 1804

TO THE PLATTE RIVER

After the trial and punishment of John Collins and Hugh Hall (see Chapter 4), the expedition left the Kansas River late in the afternoon and traveled another seven miles up the Missouri River. Captain William Clark estimated that they had come 366 river miles from the mouth of the Missouri.

On the morning of June 30, 1804, "a verry large wolf Came to the bank and looked at us," from near "a gange of turkeys" (Clark). On land, birds were sitting on their nests and raising young; on the river, many groups of wood ducklings swam behind their mothers.

The party camped opposite today's **[1]** Leavenworth on July 1, after a short night's sleep and 13 miles of travel. Clark wrote that one of the sentinels had spotted "either a man or Beast, which run off." All the men "prepared for action," but no danger arose.

The Fourth of July, 1804, was the United States' 28th birthday. The Corps of Discovery celebrated by firing their swivel cannon to welcome the day, then traveled 15 miles up the river. They named Independence Creek, and camped for the night at the site of today's Atchison, Kansas. Captains Meriwether Lewis and William Clark gave their men an extra ration of whiskey, and ordered the gun fired again. Poor Private Joseph Field celebrated the day by getting a snakebite, which Lewis "doctored" with a tree-bark poultice. Clark wrote this summary of the group in his journal:

Capt. Lewis my Self & York

in all 46 men July 4th   4 horses & a Dog

Sergeant John Ordway wrote that this was "one of the most beautiful places I ever Saw in my life, open and beautifully Diversified with hills & vallies all presenting themselves to the River…"

A couple of days later, several men were ill, and the captains decided poor food preparation was the cause. Lewis wrote out an order on July 8 assigning cooks "to insure a prudent and regular use of all provisions…" and to clean the cooking utensils. They were on the right track, but hadn't found the answer (see Chapter 4).

The night of July 9 showed how tense the men were about meeting the Sioux. The small hunting party traveling ashore didn't join the boaters when they camped on an island near today's Nodaway, Missouri. This wasn't unusual, so when a fire was spotted on shore, Baptiste Deschamps and other boatmen went with a pirogue to pick up the hunters. Clark wrote:

…they returned & informed, that when they approached the fire, it was put out, which caused them to return, this report causd. us to look out Supposeing a pty. of Soux going to war, firierd the bow piec [swivel cannon] to allarm & put on their guard the men on Shore everey thing in readiness for Defence.

The next morning, all set out to explore where the fire had been.

…Soon discovered that our men were at the fire, they were a Sleep early last evening, and from the Course of the Wind which blew hard, their yells were not hea[r]d by party in the perogue, a mistake altogether—.

At this tense time, and with "our men…much fatigued," Private Alexander Willard had the bad luck to fall asleep on guard duty the night of July 11. This offense could be punished by death, according to army rules, because it endangered everyone. The very next day, the captains themselves formed the court-martial, instead of naming other soldiers as before.

Willard was charged with lying down and sleeping while on guard. He pleaded guilty to lying down and not guilty to sleeping, but the captains convicted him of both. They sentenced him "to receive One hundred lashes on his bear back, at four different times in equal propation."

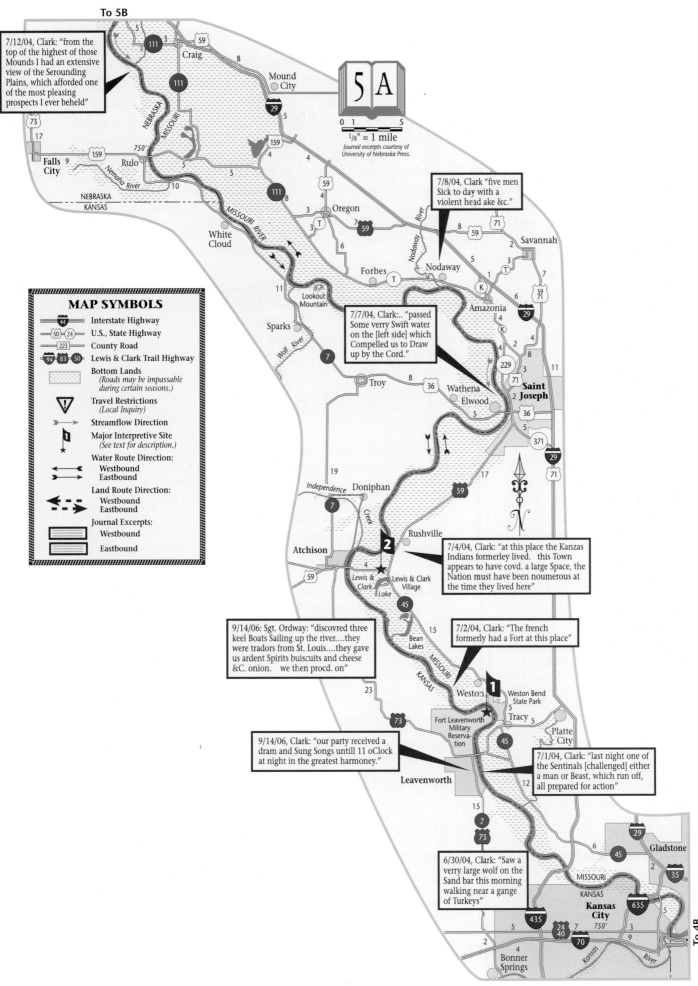

5 A

0 1 5
1/8" = 1 mile
Journal excerpts courtesy of
University of Nebraska Press.

7/12/04, Clark: "from the top of the highest of those Mounds I had an extensive view of the Serounding Plains, which afforded one of the most pleasing prospects I ever beheld"

7/8/04, Clark "five men Sick to day with a violent head ake &c."

7/7/04, Clark:.. "passed Some verry Swift water on the [left side] which Compelled us to Draw up by the Cord."

MAP SYMBOLS

44	Interstate Highway
50 24	U.S., State Highway
223	County Road
94 83 50	Lewis & Clark Trail Highway
	Bottom Lands (Roads may be impassable during certain seasons.)
!	Travel Restrictions (Local Inquiry)
→	Streamflow Direction
▶	Major Interpretive Site (See text for description.)
	Water Route Direction: Westbound Eastbound
	Land Route Direction: Westbound Eastbound
	Journal Excerpts: Westbound Eastbound

7/4/04, Clark: "at this place the Kanzas Indians formerley lived. this Town appears to have covd. a large Space, the Nation must have been noumerous at the time they lived here"

9/14/06: Sgt. Ordway: "discovered three keel Boats Sailing up the river....they were tradors from St. Louis....they gave us ardent Spirits buiscuits and cheese &C. onion. we then procd. on"

7/2/04, Clark: "The french formerly had a Fort at this place"

9/14/06, Clark: "our party received a dram and Sung Songs untill 11 oClock at night in the greatest harmoney."

7/1/04, Clark: "last night one of the Sentinals [challenged] either a man or Beast, which run off, all prepared for action"

6/30/04, Clark: "Saw a verry large wolf on the Sand bar this morning walking near a gange of Turkeys"

To 4B

Interestingly, they also "Concluded to Delay here to-day with a view of...refreshing our men who are much fatigued..." This camp was across from the mouth of the Big Nemaha River, possibly in today's Holt County, Missouri—shifts in the courses of both rivers cause uncertainty.

The next couple weeks were uneventful, with the party traveling from 9 to as many as 20 miles a day. Wind, weather and river conditions controlled their speed.

Clark noted that "The Soil of Those Praries [in today's Otoe County, Nebraska] appears rich but much Parched with the frequent fires..."

July 21 brought the expedition to the Platte River. Lewis biographer Stephen Ambrose writes: "To go past the mouth of the Platte was the Missouri riverman's equivalent of crossing the equator." That night they camped—not too comfortably—above Papillion Creek in today's Sarpy County, Nebraska, with "a great number of wolves about us all night...hard wind...cold"

TOURING TODAY

๑ TO THE PLATTE RIVER ๑

[ ] **Bracketed numbers key sites to maps**	♿ Special-needs accessible	⚑ Bed & breakfast
★ L&C in-depth interpretation, unchanged landform	⊗ Restaurant	▲ Camping, RV park
● L&C interpreted site	⊞ Motel, hotel, cabin	

Bridges over the Missouri River in this area are in Leavenworth, KS (NE 92/MO 92); Atchison, KS (US 59); St. Joseph, MO (US 36); near Big Lake State Park (US 159); Phelps City, MO (US 136); and Nebraska City, NE (US 75).

ALONG THE EXPEDITION'S PATH

July 1, 1804
(Return Sept. 14, 1806)
● **Leavenworth Landing Park** (Leavenworth, KS)—An area celebrating Leavenworth's role as a gateway to the west. Sculptures document the railroads and river transportation hub. Walking trails lead to scenic river overlooks. Open daily to sunset; free. 1913 C.W. Parker carousel. Delaware and the Missouri River. 913/651-2132.
● **Fort Leavenworth Overlook** (Fort Leavenworth, KS)—Hiking, picnic area, interpretive sign. In town on Sherman Ave. 913/684-5604.
Fort Leavenworth National Recreation Trails—Over 30 miles of trails within Fort Leavenworth

wind through the historic fort area, hills and Missouri River bottoms. Be sure to get the free trail guide from the museum since most trails aren't marked and you don't want to end up in a restricted area by mistake. Daily; free. Enter through the main gate. 913/684-3767.
Fort Leavenworth
Self-guided tour of this military post, which has been home to generals from Custer to Patton to Powell, starts at the Frontier Army Museum and passes the U.S. Disciplinary Barracks (only military maximum security prison), the 1828 Rookery, Sutler's Home, Berlin Wall monument, and other historical buildings. Don't miss the **Buffalo Soldier Monument**, a tribute to black cavalrymen in the frontier wars.
[1] ★ **Frontier Army Museum**—One hundred years of military history, westward expansion, Indian relations, including the Lewis and Clark Expedition, an army mission. Establishment and growth of the Command and General Staff College, the Army's senior tactical school. Home of Company B 1st US

Dragoons living history unit. Mon-Fri 9 to 4, Sat 10 to 4, Sun noon to 4; free. Through Fort Leavenworth main gate, on Reynolds Ave. 913/684-5604 ext. 6.

July 2, 1804
(Return Sept. 13, 1806)
Weston Bend State Park (Weston, MO)—River overlook/♿, picnic areas, fishing, hiking and biking trails. Interpretation about tobacco and its importance to local economy. ▲ 37 sites (22 w/hookups); fee; water; modern/♿; showers; open all year/full operation Apr-Oct; 15-day limit. 1 mile S of MO 273 on MO 45. 816/640-5443.

July 4, 1804
● **Independence Park** (Atchison, KS)—River access for boating and fishing. Hike where "Capt Lewis walked on shore" to view the surrounding country. Open daily to sunset; free. Downtown on the river. 913/367-5081.
[2] ★ **Lewis and Clark State Park** (Rushville, MO)—Sugar Lake (called Gosling Lake in the journals) is prime bird habitat. Interpretive exhibits on the expedition. Shaded picnic areas. Swimming,

fishing and boating in the lake. ▲ 70 sites (44 w/hookups); fee; water; modern; showers; open all year/full operation Apr-Oct; grills/fire rings; tables; 15-day limit. Lake swimming; boating; fishing; playground. Dump station; coin laundry; firewood. 3 miles S of US 59 on MO 45, 1 mile W on MO 138. 816/579-5564.

July 9, 1804
(Return Sept. 11, 1806)
Nodaway Island Access (Savannah, MO)—The captains named a Nodaway Island in this area, but two centuries of river channel changes mean we don't see what they did. Restrooms/&. River access for fishing and boating. ▲ Primitive camping. Daily 4am to 10pm; free. On County T, W of Amazonia. 573/751-4115.
Payne Landing Access (Oregon, MO)—River access for fishing and canoeing. Access road is gravel and crosses low-capacity bridge. ▲ Primitive camping. Daily 4am to 10pm; free. S of County T between Forbes and Forest City (follow signs). 573/751-4115.

July 13, 1804
Thurnau Wildlife Area (Craig, MO)—Wildlife management area in bottomland timber habitat. 2.5 miles of trails, river access for boating and fishing. ▲ Primitive camping. Daily 4am to 10pm; free. W of Craig on MO 111. 573/751-4115.

July 14, 1804
● **Indian Cave State Park** (Shubert, NE)—3 miles of river frontage along wooded bluffs are home to wildlife. Sandstone overhang with rock carvings; expedition camped here. Hike through the cave. Explore the reconstructed cabin, general store and 1-room school from St. Deroin, an 1854-1911 river community. Pioneer craft artisans on weekends. Look for wild turkey and whitetail deer as you hike over 20 miles of trails. Adirondack shelters are available for backpackers and extended primitive camping trips. ▲ 264 sites (134 w/hookups); fee; water; modern/&; showers; open all year; grills/fire rings; tables. Dump station; coin laundry; play-

ground. 5 miles E of NE 67 on NE S64E. 402/883-2575.

July 15, 1804
Langdon Bend Access (Rock Port, MO)—River access for boating and fishing. Daily 4am to 10pm; free. N of Langdon on County U. 573/751-4115.
Hoot Owl Bend Access (Rock Port, MO)—River access for fishing. Hiking in the area is good, but access is at end of 2 miles of gravel road and subject to flooding. ▲ Primitive camping. Daily 4am to 10pm; free. Gravel road from Langdon on County U. 573/751-4115.

July 16-17, 1804
[3] Missouri River Historical Museum/Brownville State Recreation Area (Brownville, NE)—Museum is in the *Captain Meriwether Lewis*, a restored sidewheeler dredge vessel docked here. River access for boating and fishing. ▲ 14 sites; water; primitive; open all year; grills/fire rings; tables. Museum open daily 10 to 6 (May-Oct); admission fee. S of Brownville bridge. 402/274-5696.

July 18-19, 1804
Watson Access (Watson, MO)—River access for fishing and canoeing in pretty area. ▲ Primitive camping. Gravel access road. Daily 4am to 10pm; free. W of I-29 on County A, N on County BB. 573/751-4115.
Waubonsie State Park (Hamburg, IA)—Hike the Ridge Trail to this river overlook; the view is a delight. Ravines and bluffs border many of the trails. Follow Sunset Ridge interpretive trail for view of the Loess Hills. ▲ 95 sites (22 w/hookups); fee; water; modern; showers; open all year/full operation Apr-Oct; grills/fire rings; tables; 35' maximum. Groceries, dump station. Jct. IA 2 & US 275, 4 miles S on US 275/IA 2, 1 mile W on IA 2, 0.5 mile S on IA 239. 712/382-2786.
Riverview Marina State Recreation Area (Nebraska City, NE)—River access for boating, fishing. ▲ 46 sites; fee; water; modern; showers; open all year; grills/fire rings; tables. US 73/75 & NE 2. 402/873-7222.

July 21, 1804
(Return Sept. 9, 1806)
Schilling Wildlife Area (Plattsmouth, NE)—Hiking, fishing, waterfowl and wildlife observation. Have a picnic. Special tours of waterfowl migration areas on Sun (Nov-Dec). Daily 8 to 4:30; free. Main St E, 1 mile E on Refuge Rd. (On the Missouri). 402/298-8041.

AROUND THE AREA

TOWNS LISTED ALPHABETICALLY

Atchison, Kansas
Atchison Chamber of Commerce—200 S. 10th St. 913/367-2427, 800/234-1854.
Atchison County Historical Museum—Exhibits on Amelia Earhart and World War I. Gun and barbed wire collections. Mon-Fri 9 to 4:30, Sat 10 to 4, Sun noon to 4; donations. 200 S. 10th St. 913/367-6238.
Amelia Earhart Birthplace—Earhart was born on July 24, 1897, in this home built by her grandfather and spent her early childhood here. Exhibits include her flying memorabilia. Mon-Sat 9 to 5, Sun noon to 4 (May-Sept), daily 1 to 4 (rest of year); admission fee. 223 N. Terrace. 913/367-4217.
International Forest of Friendship—A U.S. bicentennial gift to the United States from the city and the Ninety Nines (international organization of women pilots). Forest includes trees from 50 states and over 30 countries. A paved trail leads through the forest. Granite plates honor those who have contributed to the world of aviation. Daily to sunset; free. 2 miles SW of town on Warnock Lake. 913/367-2427.
Jackson Park—Irises line the park's roads in spring and there is a spectacular view of the Missouri valley from Guerrier Hill. Take a picnic. Daily to dusk (May-Oct); free. 1500 S. 6th St.
⊞ **Comfort Inn**—45 rooms, continental breakfast, pets. &. 509 S. 9th St. 913/367-7666. $ K16

Cameron, Missouri
★ **Wallace State Park**—Home to

Trice-Dedman Memorial Woods, a prime example of the area as Lewis and Clark saw it. Hiking trails and picnic area. ▲ 88 sites (43 w/hook-ups); fee; water; modern; showers; open all year/full operation Apr-Oct; grills/fire rings; tables. Dump station; lake swimming; canoeing; fishing; playground; firewood. 6 miles S of US 36 on US 69, 2 miles E on MO 121. 816/632-3745.

Elmwood, Nebraska
Bess Streeter Aldrich Museum—Memorabilia and history about author who wrote more than 100 short stories and 9 novels dealing with family values and pioneer history. Tours of her home at 204 East F St. are Wed/Thu/Sat/Sun 2 to 5; museum free, admission fee for house tours. 124 West D St. 402/994-4125.

Glenwood, Iowa
Mills County Historical Museum—Extensive collection of artifacts from the Earth Lodge Peoples who inhabited the area about 1,000 years ago. Restored 1881 cottage, 1-room school, 1900 barn. Antique equipment and machinery. Weekends 1:30 to 4 (Memorial Day-Labor Day); admission fee. Glenwood Park, US 34. 712/527-5038.

Hiawatha, Kansas
Davis Memorial—The saying goes, "if you don't think highly of yourself, nobody will" and John Davis was a believer. Visit his tomb, completed in 1937 at a cost of $500,000. Surrounding are 11 life-size marble statues of Davis and his wife at various times in their lives. 0.5 mile E on Iowa St. (Hope Cemetery). 785/742-7136.

⊞ **Hiawatha Inn**—40 rooms, pool, ⊗ restaurant. ♿. US 36 & US 73. 785/742-7401. $ K12

Highland, Kansas
Native American Heritage Museum State Historic Site—Exhibits of pioneer and Indian life in an 1846 Presbyterian mission and restored chapel. Wed-Sat 10 to 5, Sun 1 to 5; free. 2 miles E on old US 36, 0.25 mile N on KS 136. 785/442-3304.

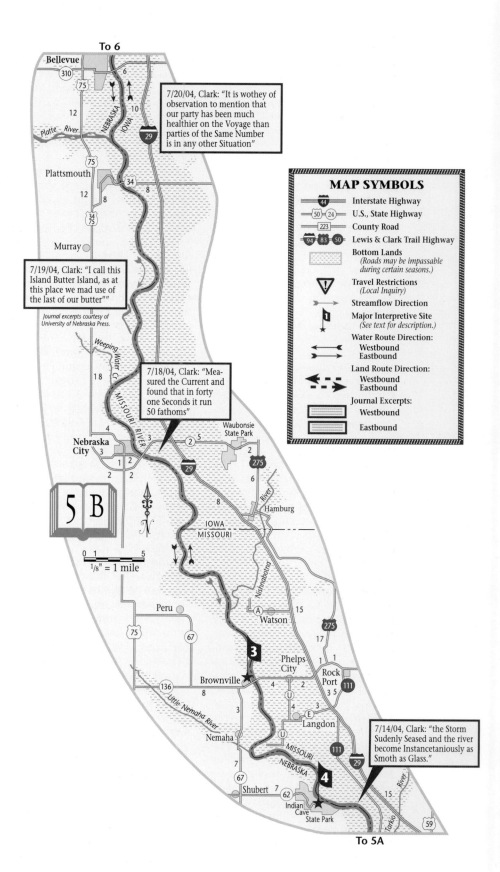

7/20/04, Clark: "It is wothey of observation to mention that our party has been much healthier on the Voyage than parties of the Same Number is in any other Situation"

7/19/04, Clark: "I call this Island Butter Island, as at this place we mad use of the last of our butter""

Journal excerpts courtesy of University of Nebraska Press.

7/18/04, Clark: "Measured the Current and found that in forty one Seconds it run 50 fathoms"

7/14/04, Clark: "the Storm Sudenly Seased and the river become Instancetaniously as Smoth as Glass."

MAP SYMBOLS

Interstate Highway
U.S., State Highway
County Road
Lewis & Clark Trail Highway
Bottom Lands
(Roads may be impassable during certain seasons.)
Travel Restrictions
(Local Inquiry)
Streamflow Direction
Major Interpretive Site
(See text for description.)
Water Route Direction:
Westbound
Eastbound
Land Route Direction:
Westbound
Eastbound
Journal Excerpts:
Westbound
Eastbound

Leavenworth, Kansas

Leavenworth–Lansing Convention & Visitor Bureau—Self-guided tour information available. 518 Shawnee. 913/682-4113, 800/844-4114.

Victorian Carroll Mansion and Museum—Intricately carved woodwork and vibrant stained glass windows abound in this 1867 home. One room dedicated to Leavenworth history. Mon-Sat 10:30 to 4:30, Sun 1 to 4:30 (May-Aug), daily 1 to 4:30 (rest of year); admission fee. 1128 5th Ave. 913/682-7759, 800/844-4114.

⊞ **Best Western Hallmark Inn**—52 rooms, pool, continental breakfast, pets. ♿ US 73 & KS 7. 913/651-6000. $$ K12

⊗ **The Historic Skyview Restaurant**—Varied menu in Victorian mansion, dress code. D only. Smokefree. 504 Grand. 913/682-2653. $$

Lincoln, Nebraska

Star City Visitor Center, 201 N. 7th St. 402/434-5348, 800/423-8212.

Star Tran provides bus transportation, regular routes/♿.

Lincoln's Children's Museum—Science, history, art and culture for kids. Special preschool area. Sun/Mon 1 to 5, Tue-Sat 10 to 5; admission fee. 13th & O Sts. 402/477-4000.

Lincoln Zoo—Exhibits scaled for kids. Petting zoo, pony rides. Over 300 animals including camels and a red panda. Ride the Iron Horse railroad. Adjacent botanical garden. Daily 10 to 5 (mid-Apr-Sept); admission fee. 27th & B Sts. 402/475-6741.

MoPac East Recreation Trail—Take a spin through the surrounding countryside. This 25-mile level trail extends east from Lincoln to Wabash. Trailheads in Lincoln at 84th St & O Street or on 33rd St near Peter Pan Park. Additional trailheads are in Walton, Eagle and Elmwood.

Museum of Nebraska History—Walk through 12,000 years of cultural history including an Indian earth lodge and pioneer sod house. Mon-Sat 9 to 4:30, Sun 1:30 to 5; donations. 15th & P Sts. 402/471-4754.

National Museum of Roller Skating—Interactive history of the competitive sport and technology. Includes Hall of Fame. Weekdays 9 to 5; free. 4730 South St. 402/483-7551.

Pioneers Park & Nature Center—Six miles of hiking trails. You'll see bison, elk and whitetail deer. Interpretive programs offered at outdoor amphitheater. 2 museums with natural history and native animal displays. Park open daily 6 am to midnight (summer), 8 to 5, Sun noon to 5 (rest of year); free. W. Van Dorn St. 402/441-7895.

Nebraska Capitol—Possibly the most ornate in the country. Bas-reliefs on the exterior walls, elaborate tile work throughout the interior. Beautiful murals. Take the elevator to the observation deck. Weekdays 8 to 5, Sat 10 to 5; free (guided tours available). 1445 K St. 402/471-0448.

University of Nebraska State Museum & Ralph Mueller Planetarium—Explore natural history in the Age of Dinosaurs gallery. Handle snakes and fossils in the Encounter Center. Laser light shows and sky shows Tue-Sun at 2 during the summer, Sat/Sun only rest of the year. Open Mon-Sat 9:30 to 4:30, Sun 1:30 to 4:30; admission fee. 14th & O Sts. 402/472-2642.

Wilderness Park—Hiking and biking trails along Salt Creek from W. Van Dorn St. south to Saltillo Rd.

⊞ **Comfort Suites**—60 suites, indoor pool, continental breakfast, pets, hot tub. ♿. 2 miles S of I-80 exit 403. 402/476-8080. $$ K18

⊞ **The Cornhusker**—290 rooms, pool. Elegant surroundings. 333 S. 13th. 402/474-7474, 800/793-7474. $$$+ K18. ⊗ The Renaissance offers continental cuisine, has dress code. L & D Mon-Sat. $$$

⊞ **Fairfield Inn**—63 rooms, indoor pool, continental breakfast, pets, hot tub. ♿. 2 miles S of I-80 exit 403. 402/476-6000. $$ K18

⊞ **Hampton Inn**—111 rooms, pool, continental breakfast. ♿. Suites have refrigerators and are the same price as doubles. 1301 W. Bond Cir. (airport area). 402/474-2080, 800/426-7866. $$$ K18

⊞ **Harvester Motel**—80 rooms, pool, ⊗ restaurant, continental breakfast, coin laundry. ♿. 1511 Center Park Rd. 402/426-3131, 800/500-1366. $$ K12

⊞ **Sleep Inn**—80 rooms, pool, coin laundry, continental breakfast. ♿. Off season rates. I-80, exit 399. 402/475-1550, 800/627-5337. $$ K18

⊗ **Harvester Restaurant**—Hearty German and Czechoslovakian menu, kids' menu, ♿. B, L & D daily. 1501 Center Park Rd. 402/420-2494. $$

⊗ **Inn Harms Way**—Seafood and continental specialties in restored railroad station. L & D Mon-Sat. 201 N. 7th St. 402/438-3033. $$

⊗ **Lazlo's Brewery & Grill**—American, hickory-smoked specialties; kids menu. L & D daily. 710 P St. 402/434-5636. $$

⊗ **Rock 'n' Roll Runza**—1950s burger joint with 3-D menus, kids' menu. L & D daily. 210 N. 14th St. 402/474-2030. $

Mound City, Missouri

● **Squaw Creek National Wildlife Refuge**—Bald eagles, geese, ducks and pelicans can be seen along the 10-mile auto tour. Hiking trails get you closer to the birds. Museum with natural history exhibits and interpretation on the area. Picnic area. Daily to 4:30; free. Adjacent to Big Lake State Park. I-29 exit 79, 2 miles W on US 159. 660/442-3187.

Nebraska City, Nebraska

Nebraska City Chamber of Commerce, 806 1st Ave. 402/873-3000, 800/514-9113.

Arbor Lodge State Historical Park—Arbor Day creator J. Sterling Morton built this 52-room mansion with a Tiffany skylight. Smell the roses in the Italian terraced garden, admire the 250 types of trees or walk through the pine grove he planted in 1891. Grounds open daily 8 to sunset, home tours daily 9 to 5 (Apr-Oct); admission fee. 2300 W. 2nd Ave. 402/873-7222.

John Brown's Cave & Historical Village—Cabin that sheltered slaves on the Underground Railroad. Enter a tunnel where they hid. Rural village recreated on adjacent village green. Daily 10 to 5 (Apr-Nov); admission fee. 1924 4th at Corso St. 402/873-3115.

Wildwood Historic Home—10-

room 1860s brick home furnished with Victorian antiques. Adjacent art barn showcases midwestern artists. Tue-Sun 11 to 5 (Apr-Oct); admission fee. Steinhart Park Rd. 402/873-6340.

⊞ **Apple Inn**—65 rooms, refrigerators, king suites with or without Jacuzzi, outdoor pool. &. 402/873-5959, 800/659-4446. $ K15

⊞ **Days Inn**—29 rooms, refrigerators. &. US 75 & NE 2. 402/873-6656. $ K12

⊞ **Lied Conference Center**—96 rooms, refrigerators, fitness center, indoor pool, sauna, Jacuzzi. &. ⊗ Restaurant. Park adjacent. I-29 exit 10. 402/873-8733, 800/546-5433 $$$ K18

⊗ **Ulbrick's Cafe**—You'll need reservations to devour delectable panfried chicken served family-style. 1513 S. 11th St. 402/873-5458. $$

Rock Port, Missouri

Big Lake State Park—Focal point is 625-acre oxbow lake carved by the Missouri River. Hiking trails take you to prime bird-watching sites and **Squaw Creek National Wildlife Refuge.** ⊞ Motel rooms and housekeeping cabins. ▲ 75 sites (60 w/hookups); fee; water; modern; showers; open all year/full operation Apr-Oct; grills/fire rings; tables; 30' maximum; 15-day limit. Pool; boat ramp; lake fishing; canoeing; playground. Dump station; coin laundry; firewood. 7 miles W on MO 118, 3 miles S on MO 111. 660/442-8770.

▲ **KOA-Rock Port**—56 grassy, shaded sites (51 w/hookups); fee; water; modern; showers; open Apr-Oct; grills/fire rings; tables. Pool; playground. Dump station; coin laundry; groceries. 0.5 mile W of I-29 on US 136. 660/744-5485, 800/KOA-5415.

⊞ **Rock Port Inn**—37 rooms, pets. &. I-29 & US 136 exit 110. 660/744-6282. $ K12

St. Joseph, Missouri

St. Joseph Convention & Visitors Bureau, 109 S. 4th St., 816/233-6688, 800/785-0360.

First Street Trolley—Travel to historic sites aboard a turn-of-the-20th-century streetcar. Ride all day for one fee. Runs daily (May-Oct); admission fee. 816/233-6700.

Jesse James Home—Home where James lived as "Mr. Howard" with his wife and two children until being gunned down on April 3, 1882, by one of his gang members. Mon-Sat 10 to 5, Sun 1 to 5 (June-Aug), Mon-Sat 10 to 4, Sun 1 to 4 (rest of year); admission fee. 12th & Penn Sts. 816/232-8206.

Knea-Von Black Archives—Travel through a simulation of the Underground Railroad to exhibits on George Washington Carver, Martin Luther King, Jr. and others. Weekdays 10 to 5; admission fee. 1901 Messanie. 816/233-6211.

Krug Park—Visit the exhibits of buffalo, deer and longhorn cattle or relax in the rose garden. Walking trails, a castle and playground will help burn off children's extra energy. Daily to sunset; free. St. Joseph Ave & Krug Park Place. 816/271-5500.

National Military History Museum—Retrospective and tribute to the armed forces from the Civil War to the present. Weekdays 10 to 5; admission fee. 701 Messanie. 816/233-4321.

Patee House—Headquarters of the Pony Express. Memorabilia and interpretive exhibits about the evolution of transportation and communication in the West. Mon-Sat 10 to 5, Sun 1 to 5 (Apr-Oct), Mon-Sat 10 to 4, Sun 1 to 4 (rest of year); admission fee. 12th & Penn Sts. 816/232-8206.

Pony Express National Memorial—Located in the old Pike's Peak Stables where the first ride began. Interpretive exhibits of the Express's development. Mon-Sat 9 to 5, Sun 1 to 5; admission fee. 914 Penn St. 816/279-5059, 800/530-5930.

● **St. Joseph Museum** (St. Joseph, MO)—Delightful museum on local history. Lewis and Clark, Civil War, Pony Express, Jesse James and Native American collections. Mon-Sat 9 to 5, Sun 1 to 5; admission fee. Charles St & 11th. 816/232-8471.

Society of Memories Doll Museum—Over 600 dolls, dollhouses and miniatures. Toys and antique clothing. Tue-Sat 10 to 4, Sun noon to 5 (June-Sept); admission fee. 1115 S. 12th St. 816/233-1420.

▲ **AOK Campground**—48 grassy, lake sites (all w/hookups); fee; water; modern; showers; open all year; grills/fire rings; tables. Pool; fishing; playground. Dump station; coin laundry; groceries; firewood. 0.25 mile N of I-29 exit 53 on US 71. 816/324-4263.

▲ **Ol' Mac Donald's Farm**—104 grassy sites (64 w/hookups); fee; water; modern; showers; open all year; grills/fire rings; tables. Horse trails and rentals; pool; boat rentals; fishing; hiking; playground. Dump station; firewood. 3 miles N of I-29 exit 53 on US 71. 816/324-6447.

⊞ **Days Inn**—100 rooms, pool, continental breakfast, ⊗ restaurant. &. 816/279-1671. $$ K12

Savannah, Missouri

● **Andrew County Museum & Historical Society**—Pioneer history. Collections of Kewpie dolls, French/German dolls and Hummels in an 1844 log house. Mon-Sat 10 to 4, Sun 1 to 4; free. In Duncan Park. 816/324-4720.

Sidney, Iowa

Fremont County Historical Museum Complex—Buildings assembled here contain everything from mastodon tusks to an 1863 drug store soda fountain. Sun 1 to 4 in summer; free. East side of square. 712/374-2719.

Thurman, Iowa

Forney Lake Wildlife Area—Excellent waterfowl viewing with peak time for geese and bald eagles in March. Take a canoe for the best spots. Daily to dusk (closed Sept-Dec); free. I-29 exit 24, 3.5 miles on County L31 (mostly gravel). 712/374-3133.

CHAPTER 6

July 22 to August 3, 1804

THE COUNCIL BLUFF

From July 22, 1804, to the morning of the 27th, the Corps of Discovery paused at a site they named Camp White Catfish after Private Silas Goodrich caught such a creature there. It was on the Iowa side of the Missouri River across from Bellevue, Nebraska. The men cut down willows and built bowers for shelter, pitched their tents, and erected a flagpole. They also unloaded the boats to dry out goods and supplies.

This stopover had several purposes: to rest, make new oars and boat poles, prepare reports to send back to Thomas Jefferson, and especially to meet with the Oto people who lived in the area, as Captain William Clark wrote, *to let them Know of the change of Government, The wishes of our Government to Cultivate friendship with them, the Objects of our journy and to present them with a flag and Some Small presents*

Interpreter George Drouillard—whose mother was Shawnee—and Private Pierre Cruzatte—son of an Omaha woman—were sent to find the Otos. In a couple of days they were back, having found the Oto village (18 miles west into Nebraska) empty. It was summer, and Plains Indians were hunting bison.

On July 27, the party set out again, able to sail 15 miles. Clark complained in his journal that the mosquitoes at that night's camp were as large as houseflies, and had been "rageing all night." This was in the area of today's Douglas Street Bridge in Omaha.

The next day, having passed the site of today's city of [1] Council Bluffs, Iowa, the party traveling on shore met a Missouri Indian who said he was with the Oto bison hunters. The Missouris and the Otos, both small tribes, lived together. After staying overnight at their camp in present Pottawattamie County, Iowa, the Missouris set off to invite the others to meet the Corps of Discovery a little way upriver. It would be the expedition's first meeting with Native Americans.

The Corps arrived at the agreed-upon site on July 30, and camped. Even though eager to meet the Otos, both Clark and Captain Meriwether Lewis followed another part of their orders that day. Each wrote in detail of an animal known in Europe but not previously in North America: the badger. Private Joseph Field had shot it, and Lewis stuffed the hide to send to President Jefferson.

Near today's [2] Fort Calhoun, Nebraska, they camped on the Missouri's shore just below a bluff (the river since has shifted away to the east). They awaited the Otos for four days, bothered by those "troublesome" mosquitoes but enjoying ripe fruits and berries. At sundown on August 2, six Oto and Missouri chiefs—along with some warriors and a French trader who lived with them—arrived. They brought a gift of fresh fruit.

The next day Lewis told the visitors that they had a new "father," his way of explaining the change of government. He distributed presents (which included officers' hats and coats, medals with Jefferson's portrait, and a U.S. flag), demonstrated the most powerful weapons, and had the men perform a drill.

The Otos and Missouris answered that they were happy to be friends with the new government. Used to trading with whites, they asked for a gift of ammunition and whiskey, which they received.

Clark carefully described their language, and his ideas on which other nations they were related to—one of the captains' scientific duties. He also quizzed the French trader about what trading routes these people used, and learned that Santa Fe, now in New Mexico, was only 25 days' travel away, and that area Pawnees were trading there right then.

The council at the site the Corps called the Council Bluff was a short one. The men headed upriver again at 4:00 p.m. that same day.

TOURING TODAY

ᕯ THE COUNCIL BLUFF ᕯ

[ ] Bracketed numbers key sites to maps ★ L&C in-depth interpretation, unchanged landform • L&C interpreted site	♿ Special-needs accessible ⊗ Restaurant ⊞ Motel, hotel, cabin	⚑ Bed & breakfast ▲ Camping, RV park

Bridges over Missouri River in this area are in Plattsmouth, NE (US 34); Bellevue, NE/toll bridge (NE 370); and several between Omaha, NE and Council Bluffs, IA.

ALONG THE EXPEDITION'S PATH

July 22-26, 1804
(Return Sept. 8, 1806)
[1] ★ **Lewis and Clark Monument Park** (Council Bluffs, IA)—Overlook above the Missouri River, picnic area. Open daily to sunset; free. I-29 & Rainbow Rd. (2 very low clearance underpasses). Alternate route: left on Jocelin, 1.5 miles to Monument Rd., cross unguarded railroad crossing, then 1 mile to access road. 712/328-4650.
★ **Western Historic Trails Center** (Council Bluffs, IA)—Has official interpretation of Camp White Catfish; reenactment on last weekend of July. Museum on 300-acre site that includes natural prairie with trails to the Missouri River bottoms. Video presentation and interactive exhibits cover experiences on trails of the West from early 1800s to today, and the native peoples whose lands were crossed. Daily 9 to 5, 9 to 6 (summer); free. From I-80 take South 24th St. interchange in Council Bluffs; turn S on S. 24th for about 0.12 mile and watch for sign on right side. 3434 Downing Ave. 712/366-4900.

July 28, 1804
•**N.P. Dodge Park** (Omaha, NE)—Highly developed park on the riverfront with hiking trails and lots to do. A place to sleep and play, not conducive to solitude. Inter-

pretive signs, pool, full-service marina. ▲ 66 sites (46 w/hookups); fee; water; modern; showers; open May-Oct; grills/fire rings; tables. Pershing Drive, N of Mormon Bridge. 402/444-4673.

July 30 to August 3, 1804
[2] ★ **Fort Atkinson State Historic Park** (Fort Calhoun, NE)—Established in 1819 to keep the peace between fur traders and Native Americans. Living history demonstrations, recreated artisan shops. Visitor center with exhibits and information. Park open daily 8 to 5, Visitor Center open daily 9 to 5 (summer), weekends only 10 to 5 (Sept & Oct); admission fee. 7th & Madison Sts. 402/468-5611.

AROUND THE AREA

TOWNS LISTED ALPHABETICALLY

Ashland, Nebraska
Mahoney State Park—Atop the Platte River bluffs, this highly developed park offers a variety of activities and accommodations. A nature conservatory and observation tower provide panoramic views. ⊞ A 40-room lodge ($$), plus 41 two-bedroom and 4 three-bedroom cabins ($$$) sit atop a bluff. Other amenities include two 200-foot water slides, miniature golf, tennis, equestrian trails, fishing bridge/♿, picnic areas, and a shuttle to nearby state parks. ▲ Primitive camping; 2 RV areas with 149 sites (all w/hookups); fee; water; modern/♿; showers; open all year; grills/fire rings; tables. I-80 exit 426. 402/944-2523.
Strategic Air Command Museum—Indoor collection of more

than 30 military aircraft and missiles. Try the flight and training simulators, the interactive children's gallery, the wind tunnel. Watch and listen to workers actually restoring aircraft. Daily 9 to 5; admission fee. I-80 exit 426. 402/944-3100, 800/358-5029.

Bellevue, Nebraska
Bellevue Tourism, 112 W. Mission Ave. 402/293-3080, 800/467-2779.
Fontenelle Forest Nature Center—Wilderness with 17 miles of trails, ♿ accessible boardwalk, ravines, loess ridges and marshes. Excellent bird watching. Visitor Center contains a butterfly garden and exhibits. Trails open until dusk, Visitor Center open daily 8 to 5; admission fee. 1111 Bellevue Blvd N. 402/731-3140.
▲ **Haworth Park**—109 sites (all w/hookups); fee; water; modern/♿; showers; open Mar-Nov; grills/fire rings; tables. Boat ramp, fishing, playground, hiking trails. NE 370 & Payne Dr (at the Missouri River). 402/293-3098.
⊞ **Best Western White House Inn**—58 rooms, coin laundry, refrigerators, hot tub. 2 miles N of NE 370 on US 75. 402/293-1600. $$ K16
♿ **Quality Inn & Suites**—127 rooms, pool, full breakfast, hot tub, coin laundry, ⊗ restaurant. 1 mile E of US 75 on NE 370. 402/292-3800. $$ K18

Council Bluffs, Iowa
Council Bluffs Convention and Visitor Bureau, 7 N. 6th St, 712/325-1000, 800/228-6878.
Lake Manawa State Park—A great place to stay when exploring the Council Bluffs/Omaha area. ▲ 73 sites (35 w/hookups); fee;

water; modern; showers; open all year/full operation Apr-Oct; grills/fire rings; tables. Lake swimming, boating and fishing. 1 mile S on IA 192. 712/366-0220.

RailsWest Railroad Museum—The railroad's impact on western expansion. Memorabilia and HO-scale exhibits. Mon-Tue, Thurs-Sat 10 to 4, Sun 1 to 5 (summer), weekends 1 to 5 (May-Dec.); admission fee. 1512 S. Main. 712/323-5182.

Pottawattamie County "Squirrel Cage" Jail—A "lazy susan" was built inside a cage in this 3-story building. When the cage was rotated, the jailers could view all the prisoners from one vantage point. Wed-Sat 10 to 4, Sun noon to 4 (Apr-Sept); admission fee. I-80 exit 3, 226 Pearl. 712/323-2509.

Wabash Trace Bike/Nature Trail—Begins behind Lewis Central School in Council Bluffs, and continues SE for 63 miles through the Loess Hills. 712/328-6836.

⊞ **Best Western Crossroads of the Bluffs**—108 rooms, pets, continental breakfast, pool, coin laundry. Special packages. I-29/80 exit 1B. 712/322-3150, 800/528-1234. $$ K18

⊞ **Fairfield Inn**—62 rooms, pool, continental breakfast, pets, hot tub. Suites are reasonably priced. Off-season rates. I-80 exit 3. 712/366-1330, 800/228-2800. $$ K18

⊞ **Heartland Inn**—89 rooms, continental breakfast, pets, hot tub. I-80 exit 5. 712/322-8400, 800/334-3277. $$ K17

⊞ **Western Inn**—51 rooms, pool, continental breakfast. I-80 & Madison Ave. 712/322-4499, 800/322-1842. $$ K11

⊨ **The Terra Jane Bed & Breakfast**—5 rooms on a working farm, full breakfast, hot tub. Mile-long nature/exercise trail. Close to Wabash Trace Bike/Nature Trail. 712/322-4200. $$$

⊗ **Tish's**—Hearty sandwiches/ ice cream parlor amid sand volleyball courts, kids' menu, ♿. L & D daily. 1207 S. 35th St. 712/323-5456. $$

Gretna, Nebraska

Ak-Sar-Ben Aquarium—Geologic exhibits, reptiles, amphibians, large aquarium tanks. Located in

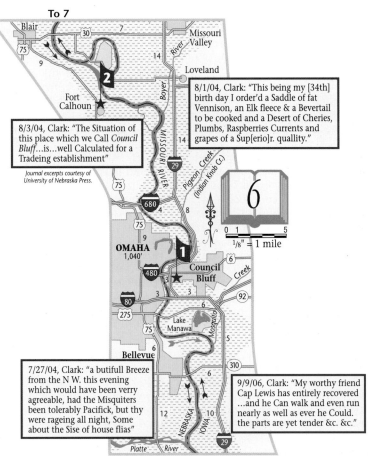

To 7

Blair

Missouri Valley

Loveland

Fort Calhoun

8/1/04, Clark: "This being my [34th] birth day I order'd a Saddle of fat Vennison, an Elk fleece & a Bevertail to be cooked and a Desert of Cheries, Plumbs, Raspberries Currents and grapes of a Sup[erio]r. quallity."

8/3/04, Clark: "The Situation of this place which we Call *Council Bluff*...is...well Calculated for a Tradeing establishment"

Journal excerpts courtesy of University of Nebraska Press.

OMAHA 1,040'

Council Bluff

$\frac{1}{8}$" = 1 mile

7/27/04, Clark: "a butifull Breeze from the N W. this evening which would have been verry agreeable, had the Misquiters been tolerably Pacifick, but thy were rageing all night, Some about the Sise of house flias"

9/9/06, Clark: "My worthy friend Cap Lewis has entirely recovered ...and he Can walk and even run nearly as well as ever he Could. the parts are yet tender &c. &c."

Platte River

Bellevue

To 5B

Schram Park State Recreation Area, a day-use park with hiking/biking trails and picnic areas. Mon-Fri 10 to 4:30, weekends 10 to 5 (summer), Wed-Sun 10 to 4:30 (rest of year); admission fee. 21502 W NE 31. 402/332-3901.

Louisville, Nebraska

Platte River State Park—Woodlands scenery along Platte River Valley. Climb the Lincoln Journal Tower to enjoy the vista. ⊗ Restaurant in lodge serves buffalo specialty items. ⊞ Lodge ($$$) open Memorial Day-Labor Day, weekends only Sept-Oct. Cabins ($$$) open May-Oct. Park open daily 6am to 10pm; admission fee. 1.5 miles S of I-80 on NE 50, 2 miles W on Spur 13E. 402/234-2217.

Neola, Iowa

▲ **Arrowhead Park**—200 sites (all w/hookups); fee; water; modern; showers; open all year/full opera-

MAP SYMBOLS

Interstate Highway
U.S., State Highway
County Road
Lewis & Clark Trail Highway
Bottom Lands *(Roads may be impassable during certain seasons.)*
Travel Restrictions *(Local Inquiry)*
Streamflow Direction
Major Interpretive Site *(See text for description.)*
Water Route Direction: Westbound Eastbound
Land Route Direction: Westbound Eastbound
Journal Excerpts: Westbound Eastbound

tion May-Oct; grills/fire rings; tables. Lake fishing, boating, boat rentals, hiking trails. I-80 exit 23, 0.5 mile S on County L55. 712/485-2295.

Omaha, Nebraska

Greater Omaha Convention & Visitor Bureau, 6800 Mercy Rd. #202, 402/444-4660, 800/332-1819.

Botanical Gardens—Relax in the arboretum, rose garden or delightful children's garden. Tue-Sat 10 to 4; free. 6th & Cedar. 402/346-4002.

Boys Town—Father Edward Joseph Flanagan's home for young people. Tours include the historic house and shrine, gardens, educational facilities, Hall of History. Tape and guided tours available. Daily 8 to 5:30 (Memorial Day-Labor Day), 8 to 4:30 (rest of year); free. 139th & W. Dodge Rd. 402/498-1140.

Durham Western Heritage Museum—A century of history inside Union Station; highlights are an awesome coin collection and old-fashioned soda fountain. Original Union Pacific Railroad advertising posters, trail layouts, memorabilia, golden spike exhibit, model of President Lincoln's funeral car. Tue-Sat 10 to 5, Sun 1 to 5; admission fee. 801 S. 10th. 402/444-5071.

Freedom Park—Museum housing U.S.S. *Hazard* and U.S.S. *Marlin*, a World War II minesweeper and submarine. Newly added is the U.S.S. LSM-45, an amphibious landing ship. Tour the ships and learn about ships in 1940s warfare. Daily 9 to 6 (Apr-Oct); admission fee. 2497 Freedom Park Rd. 402/345-1959.

General Crook House at Fort Omaha—Home of Western frontier general who defended Chief Standing Bear and worked to establish Indians' rights to constitutional protection. Mon-Fri 10 to 4, guided tours Sun 1 to 4; admission fee. 30th and Fort Sts. 402/455-9990.

Great Plains Black History Museum—African-American history interpreted through documents, wax figures, dolls, painting and other arts. Mon-Fri 10 to 2; admission fee. 2213 Lake St. 402/345-2212.

Henry Doorly Zoo—Experience the world's largest indoor rain forest, walk through the shark and octopus tank, watch the penguins. Visit the IMAX theater, open air aviary, or the coral reef. Daily 9:30 to 5; admission fee. 3701 S. 10th St. 402/733-8401.

Gerald R. Ford Birthplace—Replica of house where he was born, White House memorabilia and Betty Ford Rose Garden. Daily 7:30 to dusk; free. 32nd & Woolworth. 402/444-5955.

Heartland of America Park & Fountain—Computerized light show (at dusk) and 300' water jet in the Missouri. Take a ferry boat for a closer look. Outdoor summer concerts. Park open daily 5am to 11pm, fountain 11 to 11 (May-Sept); free. 8th & Douglas Sts. 402/444-7275.

● **Joslyn Art Museum**—Paintings of Indians and landscapes by two artists who traveled up the Missouri a few years after the Lewis and Clark Expedition, George Catlin (in 1823) and Karl Bodmer (in 1833). Extensive Impressionist collection and broad variety of 20th century American works. Tue-Sat 10 to 4, Sun noon to 4; admission fee. 2200 Dodge. 402/342-3300.

Mormon Trail Center at Winter Quarters—More than 600 Mormon pioneers died here during the winter of 1846. Interactive exhibits about their journey, a cemetery, pioneer buildings and Mormon craft exhibits. Guided tours available. Daily 9 to 9; free. 3215 State. 402/453-9372.

Neale Woods Nature Center—Woodland and prairie preserve with 9 miles of trails along the Missouri River, observatory, live animal exhibits. Daily 8 to 5; admission fee. 14323 Edith Marie Ave. 402/453-5615.

Omaha Children's Museum—Investigate the arts, humanities and sciences at this multi-sensory wonderland. Tue-Sat 10 to 5, Sun 1 to 5; admission fee. 500 S. 20th St. 402/342-6164.

⊞ **Clarion Carlisle Hotel**—138 rooms, pets, continental breakfast, pool, hot tub, ⊗ restaurant, coin laundry. I-80 exit 445, L Street E to 108th, 10909 M St. 402/331-8220, 800/526-6242. $$$ K18

⊞ **Hawthorn Suites Hotel**—88 suites with full living quarters, continental breakfast, pool, hot tub, coin laundry. Special packages and weekend specials. I-80 exit 445, E to 108th St., S to M St. 11025 M St. 402/331-0101, 800/527-1133. $$$ K12

⊞ **Holiday Inn Express-Downtown**—Pets, continental breakfast, hot tub, exercise room, coin laundry. 3001 Chicago St. 402/345-2222, 800/465-4329. $$ K18

⊞ **Quality Inn**—102 rooms, pool, bike rentals, ⊗ restaurant, continental breakfast, exercise room. 2808 S. 72nd St. 402/397-7137, 800/228-9669. $$ K12

⊞ **Savannah Suites**—34 suites, pool, continental breakfast. I-80 exit 445. 402/592-8000. $$ K12

⊗ **Chardonnay**—Cozy bistro with gourmet fare, dress code. D daily. 10220 Regency Circle (in the Marriott Hotel). 402/399-9000. $$$+

⊗ **Great American Diner**—Rock 'n' roll lives! Kids' menu, Sunday brunch. B L & D daily. 72nd St & I-80 exit 449. 402/397-2904. $$

⊗ **La Casa**—Italian dishes, specialty pizza, kids' menu. ⅃. D daily. 4432 Leavenworth. 402/556-6464. $

⊗ **V-Mertz**—Continental specialties in renovated warehouse. L & D Mon-Sat. 1022 Howard. 402/345-8980. $$$

CHAPTER 7

August 4 to 21, 1804

A DESERTION AND A DEATH

Soon after the expedition left the Council Bluff, Private Moses B. Reed announced he had left his knife behind, and went back for it. A French boatman also was missing; he had been with those who went to invite the Oto people to the council, and never returned. On August 7, nearing the area of today's Little Sioux Delta Park, Iowa, the captains sent four men downriver to look for the two deserters, especially Reed. (He was an army enlisted man, but the Frenchman was a civilian.) They had orders to kill Reed if he did not surrender peaceably.

The main party continued to discover wildlife unknown in the east. On August 5, Captain Meriwether Lewis recorded that he "Killed a serpent...[which had] No pison teeth therefore think him perfectly inocent" even though it looked like a rattlesnake. It was a bull snake.

That same day, walking on shore in today's Harrison County, Iowa, Captain William Clark made the scientific observation that the Missouri's banks were crumbling, and that in two years the river would run where he stood. To this day, the river's course changes complicate efforts to locate the expedition's exact campsites.

A wildlife discovery more exciting than a new type of snake came on August 8. Because of a severe windstorm overnight, the party got a "late" start that morning: 8:00 a.m. North of the Little Sioux River, Lewis wrote, they saw "a great number of feathers floating down the river...a very extraordinary appearance...[covering] sixty or seventy yards of the breadth of the river" for three miles. Then, having moved upstream through the feathers, "we were surprised by...a flock of Pillican" on a large sandbar, which they named Pelican Island. Lewis shot at random and killed one bird, which he dissected and wrote about in great detail. No one had expected to see pelicans on the Missouri.

August 11 brought the expedition to the site of a frequent frontier tragedy. At Blackbird Hill [4], in today's Thurston County, Nebraska, was the grave of Chief Blackbird and 400 of his Omaha Indian people, who had died four years before, of smallpox. Omahas were friendly with white traders, who had brought the disease among them.

At the time, no one yet understood this. About the Omahas, Clark wrote: "The cause or way those people took the Small Pox is uncertain, the most Probable from Some other Nation by means of a warparty[.]"

The captains paused to honor the Omahas, attaching a white flag bordered "with Blue white & read" to a flagpole at the burial mound. Sergeant John Ordway wrote that "this Black bird was a great king among his people. they carry him provision at certain times..."

Wanting to meet the surviving Omahas, the expedition set up camp on the 13th a few miles south of today's [5] Dakota City, Nebraska. They sent five men to find Tonwantonga, or Big Village, to their west, to deliver gifts and an invitation to a council. As things worked out, the Corps stayed in this camp a week. But the Omahas were out hunting bison and never met with the expedition.

However, chiefs of the Otos and Missouris arrived at the camp on August 18, hoping the Corps would help them make a peace treaty with the Omahas. (At least one of these chiefs had spoken with the captains at the Council Bluff; see Chapter 6.) Also arriving that day was the group who had captured Private Reed, although the French boatman "decived them and got away," Clark wrote.

Reed confessed to desertion and to stealing army property (his gun and ammunition). He was sentenced to run the gauntlet four times—all the party formed two lines and beat him with switches as he passed through. Reed also was dismissed from the permanent party, the group going to the Pacific. He would be allowed to winter at Fort Mandan and go back to St. Louis with the return party.

In the evening, after punishing Reed, the

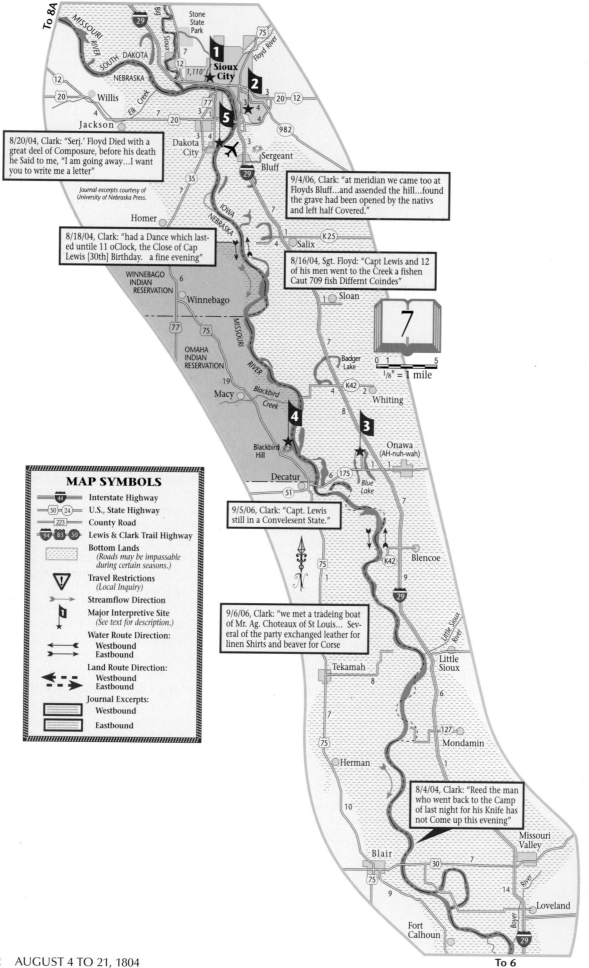

To 8A

MISSOURI RIVER

SOUTH DAKOTA

NEBRASKA

Stone State Park

1 **Sioux City** ★ 1,110'

2

Willis

5

Jackson

Dakota City

✈

Sergeant Bluff

8/20/04, Clark: "Serj.' Floyd Died with a great deel of Composure, before his death he Said to me, "I am going away…I want you to write me a letter"

Journal excerpts courtesy of University of Nebraska Press.

9/4/06, Clark: "at meridian we came too at Floyds Bluff…and assended the hill…found the grave had been opened by the nativs and left half Covered."

Homer

IOWA
NEBRASKA

8/18/04, Clark: "had a Dance which last-ed untile 11 oClock, the Close of Cap Lewis [30th] Birthday.   a fine evening"

8/16/04, Sgt. Floyd: "Capt Lewis and 12 of his men went to the Creek a fishen Caut 709 fish Differnt Coindes"

Salix   K25

WINNEBAGO INDIAN RESERVATION

Winnebago

Sloan

7

MISSOURI RIVER

OMAHA INDIAN RESERVATION

Badger Lake

0   1   5
1/8" = 1 mile

Macy   Blackbird Creek

Whiting

4   **3**

Blackbird Hill

Onawa (AH-nuh-wah)

Decatur   175

Blue Lake

9/5/06, Clark: "Capt. Lewis still in a Convelesent State."

MAP SYMBOLS

- 🛣 **44** Interstate Highway
- **50** **24** U.S., State Highway
- **223** County Road
- **94** **83** **50** Lewis & Clark Trail Highway
- ▒ Bottom Lands *(Roads may be impassable during certain seasons.)*
- ⚠ Travel Restrictions *(Local Inquiry)*
- → Streamflow Direction
- **1** Major Interpretive Site *(See text for description.)*
- ←→ Water Route Direction: Westbound Eastbound
- ←--- Land Route Direction: Westbound Eastbound
- ▦ Journal Excerpts: Westbound
- ▤ Eastbound

Blencoe

K42

9/6/06, Clark: "we met a tradeing boat of Mr. Ag. Choteaux of St Louis… Several of the party exchanged leather for linen Shirts and beaver for Corse

Tekamah

Little Sioux

Little Sioux River

Mondamin

Herman

8/4/04, Clark: "Reed the man who went back to the Camp of last night for his Knife has not Come up this evening"

Missouri Valley

Blair

Loveland

Boyer River

Fort Calhoun

Corps celebrated Captain Lewis's 30th birthday with a dance and some whiskey!

Just as the captains had no way of understanding smallpox, now they faced another illness that doctors of the time could not cure. Back on July 30, Clark had written "Serjt. [Charles] Floyd verry unwell a bad Cold &c." The next day, Sgt. Ordway noted, "Sergeant Floyd has been Sick Several days but now is Gitting Some better."

But on August 19, Clark wrote, "Sergt. Floyd was taken violently bad...and is dangerously ill we attempt in Vain to releive him...we could get nothing to Stay on his Stomach a moment...every man is attentive to him...", especially York. Historians believe that Floyd had a ruptured appendix that caused the fatal infection peritonitis. It would be two more decades before doctors even understood this illness. The accepted treatment in 1804—draining off some of Floyd's "bad blood" and dosing him with purgative—only may have made the sick man worse.

Clark stayed up most of that night with Floyd, who was as ill "as he can be to live," but even so, the party set off upriver on the 20th. They stopped at noon to "make a warm bath for Sergt. Floyd hopeing it would brace him a little..." but Floyd died before it was ready, "haveing Said to me...that he was going away..." He was 21 or 22.

Floyd died near today's town of Sergeant Bluff, Iowa, where "he was buried with the Honors of War much lamented..." The party named the bluff for him, traveled a mile or so upriver and camped at the mouth of a river they also named for Floyd. Even with the sergeant's death and burial, they traveled 13 miles that day.

By 1857, the Missouri River had eaten away at the bluff where Floyd was buried. His remains were moved to **[2]** Sioux City, Iowa, and in 1901 the tall monument to him was erected there.

For all the dangers, injuries, and illnesses the Corps of Discovery suffered from 1804 to 1806, Floyd was the only one who died on the trip.

TOURING TODAY

⤳ A DESERTION AND A DEATH ⤳

[ ] Bracketed numbers key sites to maps	♿ Special-needs accessible	⮞ Bed & breakfast
★ L&C in-depth interpretation, unchanged landform	⊗ Restaurant	▲ Camping, RV park
● L&C interpreted site	⊞ Motel, hotel, cabin	

Bridges over the Missouri River in this area in Missouri Valley, IA (US 30); Onawa, IA (IA 175/NE 51); Sioux City, IA (US 75/77, US 20).

ALONG THE EXPEDITION'S PATH

August 4, 1804
● **Wilson Island Recreation Area** (Missouri Valley, IA)—Hiking and biking trails. Connected by a road along the river to DeSoto. ▲ 132 sites (65 w/hookups); fee; water; modern; showers; open all year/ full operation Apr-Oct; grills/fire rings; tables. Fishing; boating; dump station. I-29 Loveland exit, 6 miles W on County G14. 712/642-2069.

● **DeSoto National Wildlife Refuge** (Missouri Valley, IA)— Spring and fall are prime viewing times for migrating waterfowl at this 7,800-acre site. During the winter bald eagles also make this their home. 12-mile interpreted auto trail, 4 self-guided nature trails, picnic areas. Dioramas with life-size animals take visitors back to 1804. Steamboat *Bertrand* hull recovered from the Missouri River serves as visitor center and museum for a collection of artifacts, Daily 9 to 4:30; admission fee. US 30 near the state line. 712/642-2772.

August 5, 1804
(Return Sept. 7, 1806)
● **Remington Access** (Harrison County, IA)—River access for fishing and boating. Daily, free. I-29 Exit 89, 5 miles W on gravel road.

Access limited during heavy rains or high water. 712/647-2785.

August 6, 1804
(Return Sept. 6, 1806)
● **Little Sioux Delta Park** (Little Sioux, IA)—Interpretation of Corps' meeting with traders employed by René Auguste Chouteau on the return trip (see Chapter 26). Hiking and fishing along the river. ▲ Undesignated sites; fee; water; primitive; open all year; grills/fire rings; tables. Boating access and picnic area. 1 mile W of I-29 & IA K45. 712/647-2785.

August 8, 1804
Pelican Point State Recreation Area (Tekamah, NE)—Primitive 36-acre park on the river for boating, hiking and fishing. ▲ 25 sites;

fee; water; primitive; open all year; grills/fire rings; tables. 40' limit. 4 miles E and 4 miles N from town on access roads, last few miles are gravel, 402/374-1727.

- **Huff Warner Access Area** (Blencoe, IA)—Interpretative signs, hiking and picnic areas, boating and fishing access. ▲ Undesignated sites; fee; water; primitive; open all year; grills/fire rings; tables. 2.5 miles S of I-29, exit 104, on gravel road, follow signs. 712/423-2400.

Decatur Bend Access (Onawa, IA)—Hiking and picnic areas, boating and fishing access. ▲ 6 sites; fee; water; primitive; open all year; grills/fire rings; tables. 4 miles W on IA 37, 1 miles S on access road. 712/423-2400.

(Return Sept. 5, 1806)
Beck Memorial Park (Decatur, NE)—boating/fishing access, picnic area and hiking. Daily 5am to 10pm; free. In town on NE 75. 402/349-5593.

[3] ★ **Lewis and Clark State Park** (Onawa, IA)—Replica keelboat and pirogues—as accurate as can be determined—are the focus of extensive interpretation. Annual festival 2nd weekend in June. Swimming, fishing and boating, nature and hiking trails. ▲ 81 sites (all w/hookups); fee; water; modern; showers; open all year/full operation Apr-Oct; grills/fire rings; tables; 30' limit. Dump station, groceries. I-29 & IA 175, 1 mile W on IA 175, 1 mile N on IA 324. 712/423-2829.

August 10-11, 1805
(Return Sept. 4, 1806)
- **Snyder Bend County Park** (Salix, IA)—▲ 40 sites (15 w/hookups); fee; water; modern; showers; open May-Oct; grills/fire rings; tables; 14-day limit. Boat ramp; swimming; playground; fishing. I-29 exit 134, follow signs 3 miles W. 712/946-5622.
- **Lighthouse Marina** (Whiting, IA)—▲ 50 sites (all w/hookups); fee; water; modern; showers; open all year; grills/fire rings; tables. Boat ramp/dock; fishing; coin laundry. I-29 exit 120, 2.5 miles W on Whiting Rd, 1 mile S on county road. 712/458-2066.

[4] ★ **Blackbird Hill Overview**

(Decatur, NE)—Interpreted roadside pullout for view of the vicinity of Chief Blackbird's burial ground. Daily sunrise-sunset; free. 3 miles N of Decatur on US 75, milepost 152. 402/837-5301.

August 13-19, 1804
[5] ★ **Cottonwood Cove Park** (Dakota City, NE)—Fishing and boating access at city park. Playground and picnic area. ▲ 20 sites (10 w/hookups); fee; water; modern; open all year; grills/fire rings; tables; 14-day limit. 13th & Hickory Streets. 402/987-3448.

- **Tonwantonga** (Homer, NE)—Historic Omaha Indian village. Interpretation, hiking. Always open; free. 10 miles S of Sioux City on NE 75.

August 20, 1804
(Return Sept. 4, 1806)
[1] ★ **Sergeant Floyd Riverboat Museum** (Sioux City, IA)—Exhibits detail the history of transportation on the Missouri with an emphasis on the Expedition. Scale models of steamboats and keelboats. See an accurate bust of Floyd, created from a plaster cast of his skull. Daily 8 to 6 (May-Sept), 9 to 5 rest of year; free. I-29 exit 149, 1000 S. Larson Park Rd. 712/279-0198.

[2] ★ **Sergeant Floyd Monument** (Sioux City, IA)—100' white stone monument at Floyd's final burial site. Dramatic view of the Missouri River Valley. Daily to sunset; free. I-29 exit 143, on US 75S atop Floyd's Bluff.

Scenic Park (South Sioux City, NE)—Relaxing area along the Missouri. ▲ 53 sites (all w/hookups); fee; water; modern; showers; open Apr-Sept; grills/fire rings; tables. Fishing; ramp/dock; hiking trails; playground. From US 20 & US 77, N on E. 9th, E on E. 6th, N on D St. 402/494-7531.

August 21, 1804
[1] ★ **Sioux City Riverfront Trail** (Sioux City, IA)—Hike along the river to the mouth of the Floyd River. Visitor center and interpretive exhibits are aboard the motor vessel *Sgt. Floyd*. Picnic area. Trailhead for several biking and hiking trails. Daily 6am to 10pm; free. I-29 exit 147, S toward the river. 712/279-0198.

- **Stone State Park** (Sioux City, IA)—**Dorothy Pecaut Nature Center**, natural history programs, hands-on area details the Loess Hills' rare geology, prairie and woodland trails. ▲ 31 sites (9 w/hookups); fee; water; modern; showers; open all year/full operation Apr-Oct; grills/fire rings; tables. Hiking and interpretive trails; biking trails; fishing; playground. Dump station. Center open Tue-Fri 9 to 4, weekends 1 to 4; donations. I-29 exit 151, 4 miles N on NE 112. 712/255-4698.

Around the Area

TOWNS LISTED ALPHABETICALLY

Loess Hills Scenic Byway—Auto tours of landscape unique to western Iowa and parts of China. 712/886-5441.

Bancroft, Nebraska
Bancroft Cemetery—Graves of Joseph LaFlesche, the last Omaha chief, and his daughter Susette. In the late 1800s, Susette and her white husband, Thomas Tibbles, played key roles in the passage of laws protecting Indian rights.
John G. Neihardt Center—Exhibits on the life of Nebraska's poet laureate. See his study and a Sacred Hoop Garden. Mon-Sat 9 to 5, Sun 1:30 to 5; free. Washington & Elm Sts. 402/648-3388, 888/777-4667.

Fremont, Nebraska
Dodge County Convention & Visitors Bureau, 92 W. 5th St. 402/721-2641, 800-727-8323.
Fremont & Elkhorn Valley Railroad (FEVR)—30-mile trip to Hooper and back aboard renovated cars from the 1920s and '40s. Stopover in Hooper (45 minutes) is time to stretch your legs along the Main Street historic district. Weekends 1:30 (May-Oct); admission fee, reservations required. 1835 N. Somers. 402/727-0615, 800/942-7245.
May Museum—Richly carved woodwork, delicate tile work and windows dominate this mansion. Victorian garden and gazebo. Enjoy the free summer concerts.

Thur-Sun 1:30 to 4:30 (Apr-Dec); admission fee. 1643 N. Nye. 402/721-4515.

Λ Fremont State Recreation Area—783 sites (83 w/hookups); fee; water; modern; showers; open all year; grills/fire rings; tables. Lake swimming; boating; fishing; playground; hiking. Dump station; groceries. Broad St & 23rd St, 3 miles W on 23rd. 402/727-3290.

⊞ Comfort Inn—48 rooms, pool, pets, continental breakfast, hot tub. Suites are reasonably priced and have microwaves and refrigerators. 1649 E. 23rd St. 402/721-1109, 800/228-5151. $$ K18

⊞ Holiday Lodge—99 rooms, pool, pets, exercise room. US 30 & Bus. US 275. 402/727-1110. $$

⊗ KC's Cafe—Return to the 1940s and '50s; kids' menu. L & D daily. 631 Park. 402/721-3353. $$

Homer, Nebraska

O'Connor House—1870 mansion with curving staircase, Italian fireplaces, early machinery and office equipment. Sun 2 to 4 (June-Aug); donations. 2 miles E on gravel road. 402/698-2161

Honey Creek, Iowa

Hitchcock Nature Area—Hiking trails, expansive views of Loess Hills, wilderness preserve and Missouri River. Nature room with exhibits. Daily 6:30am to 10pm; donations. 27792 Ski Hill Loop. 712/545-3659.

Missouri Valley, Iowa

Missouri Valley Chamber of Commerce, 400 E. Erie. 712/642-2553.

Harrison County Museum—Two-story log building filled with pioneer history. 10 other buildings to explore. Picnic area. Mon-Sat 9 to 5, Sun 12 to 5 (Apr-Nov); admission fee. 3.5 miles N of town on US 30. 712/642-2114.

⊨ Apple Orchard Inn—3 rooms, full breakfast, near DeSoto National Wildlife Refuge. 712/642-2418. $$$

Onawa, Iowa

Onawa Chamber of Commerce, 1009 Iowa Ave. 712/423-1801.
Kiwanis Museum Complex—Restored C & NW depot with railroad memorabilia, 1800s country school. Country church with artifacts from original Swedish settlers. Weekends 1 to 5; donations. N. 12th St. 712/423-1422.

Λ KOA Onawa/Blue Lake—120 sites (96 w/hookups); fee; water; modern; showers; open Apr-Oct; grills/fire rings; tables. Pool; boat ramp; dock; boat rental; fishing. Dump station; firewood. I-29 exit 112, 1 mile W on IA 175, 1.5 miles N on county road. 712/423-1633.

⊗ Onawa Casino Omaha—All-you-can-eat buffet is a great value; buffet for L & D daily, B on Sat/Sun. 5 miles NW of I-29 exit 112. 712/423-3700.

Salix, IA

Λ Brown's Lake/Bigelow Park—52 sites (42 w/hookups); fee; water; modern; showers; open May-Oct; grills/fire rings; tables. Hiking; biking; boating; fishing; swimming beach; playground. Dump station. 1 mile W of I-29/Salix interchange. 712/946-7114.

Sioux City, Iowa

Sioux City Visitor Bureau, 801 4th Street. 712/279-4800, 800-593-2228.
SHRA Railroad Museum—Railroad history with tours of a caboose and 1943 locomotive. Mon, Wed-Sat 11 to 5, Sun 12 to 5; donations. 2001 Leech Ave. 712/258-5267.

● Sioux City Public Museum—Exhibits in the 1890 Pierce Mansion include pioneer handcrafts from needlework to log cabins. Natural history exhibits and mounts. Tue-Sat 9 to 5, Sun 2 to 5; admission fee. 2901 Jackson. 712/279-6174.

Λ Stone State Park—Fine view of the Missouri and Big Sioux river valleys. 49 sites (14 w/hookups); fee; water; primitive; open all year/full operation Apr-Oct; grills/fire rings; tables; 30' maximum. Fishing, hiking. I-29 & 12, 5 miles N on IA 12. 712/255-4698.

Λ Sioux City North KOA—105 sites (90 w/hookups); fee; water; modern; showers; open all year; grills/fire rings; tables. ⊞ Cabins; pool; playground. Dump station; groceries; firewood. I-29 exit 4/McCook Rd. 605/232-4519, 800/562-5439.

⊞ Comfort Inn—70 rooms, indoor pool, continental breakfast, hot tub, spacious rooms. Suite may be cheaper than a double room. Off-season rates. 4202 S. Lakeport St. 712/274-1300, 800/228-5150. $$ K18

⊞ Fairfield Inn—62 rooms, indoor pool, pets, continental breakfast, hot tub. Suites are roomy and a better value than doubles. US 20 & Lakeport St. 712/276-5600, 800/445-8667. $$ K18

⊗ The First Edition Beef, Seafood & Spirits—Southwestern specialties and steaks. 🕭. L & D weekdays, D only Sat. 416 Jackson. 712/277-3200. $$

⊗ Green Gables—Casual, family soda fountain, kids' menu. L & D daily. 1800 Pierce St. 712/258-4246. $

South Sioux City, Nebraska

⊞ EconoLodge—60 rooms, continental breakfast, pets, hot tub, coin laundry. I-29 exit 144B or US 20 exit 2. 402/494-4114. $ K12

CHAPTER 8

August 22 to September 20, 1804

COUNCIL AT CALUMET BLUFF

The Corps of Discovery passed the mouth of the Big Sioux River north of today's Sioux City, Iowa, on August 21, 1804. Their campsites in this area would be in both today's Nebraska and today's South Dakota.

During this part of the trip the Corps had their first meeting with the Sioux Indians that they had feared, but the council went well. Meanwhile, Private George Shannon, youngest member of the Corps and still a teenager, was lost alone on the prairie for more than two weeks.

On August 22, near **[1]** Ponca, Nebraska, and only two days after they had buried Sgt. Charles Floyd, Captain Meriwether Lewis was testing some unknown mineral samples and came "near poisoning himself by the fumes & tast[e]" (Clark). Lewis treated himself with purgative pills Dr. Benjamin Rush had concocted back in Philadelphia—the standard medical practice of the time. Three days later, Lewis, Captain William Clark, York and eight others hiked to **[3]** Spirit Mound (eight miles north of today's Vermillion, South Dakota) on a hot day. They had heard that Indians believed dwarfish devils with giant heads and very evil spirits lived here. Clark noted with concern that Lewis became very tired and weak. Did Clark fear losing another man so soon?—his co-captain yet?

The 22nd also saw the first election by Americans west of the Mississippi, when the men voted to nominate Private Patrick Gass to replace Floyd as sergeant. Balloting was held at that night's camp, near today's **[2]** Elk Point, South Dakota; the general area is visible from **[1]** Ponca State Park. (Gass, who lived until 1870—he was nearly 100—became the last surviving member of the Corps.) Four days later, writing out the official orders, Lewis first used the term "corps of volunteers for North Western Discovery."

On August 23, Private Joseph Field was the first of the Corps to kill a bison. Lewis and 11 others went to carry the meat and hide back to the boats. From here to the Rocky Mountains, they saw more and more bison, day after day.

Near today's Yankton, South Dakota, on the 27th, interpreter Pierre Dorion, Sr., said they were entering Sioux country. The Corps set the prairie afire, the standard signal for a council. Three boys—two Sioux and one Omaha—appeared at the mouth of the James River and camped overnight with the Corps.

After a meeting place upriver was agreed upon, the Sioux boys led Sergeant Nathaniel Pryor, Dorion, and another Frenchman to their camp.

The Corps moved upstream and went into camp at a site they named Calumet Bluff from the French term for the Indians' ceremonial "peace" pipe. On the 29th, a party including 70 Yankton Sioux men (and a number of women) and trader Pierre Dorion, Jr., arrived and camped across the Missouri. Pryor reported how friendly they had been, and described his first sight of their conical bison-skin lodges: the Plains Indian tipi.

This meeting again showed how little the military captains understood the native cultures. Throughout their expedition, they insisted that each tribe met must have a main chief and subchiefs, just as their own army was organized. Plains Indian cultures didn't work that way, but perhaps native people who had already met Europeans weren't completely surprised by the whites' idea.

When the council began, Clark wrote that "we made" one man the main chief, one the secondary chief, and three the subchiefs. They gave presents and medals fitting each chief's new title, and then gave the speech like that at the Council Bluff about the "new father" (President Thomas Jefferson) and his and the nation's desire for peace and trade. They invited the Yanktons to visit Jefferson in Washington, D.C., the following spring.

After sharing "the pipe of peace," the Indian leaders asked time to talk over the proposal,

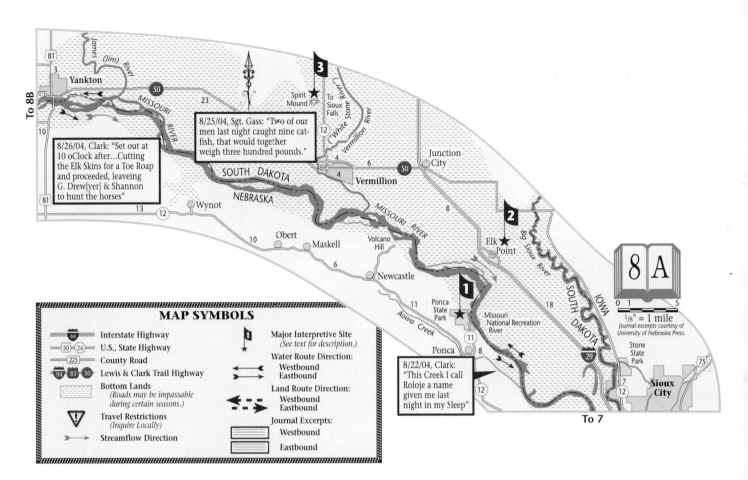

Journal excerpts courtesy of University of Nebraska Press.

MAP SYMBOLS

Interstate Highway	
U.S., State Highway	
County Road	
Lewis & Clark Trail Highway	
Bottom Lands	
(Roads may be impassable during certain seasons.)	
Travel Restrictions	
(Inquire Locally)	
Streamflow Direction	

Major Interpretive Site	
(See text for description.)	
Water Route Direction:	
Westbound	
Eastbound	
Land Route Direction:	
Westbound	
Eastbound	
Journal Excerpts:	
Westbound	
Eastbound	

8/25/04, Sgt. Gass: "Two of our men last night caught nine catfish, that would together weigh three hundred pounds."

8/26/04, Clark: "Set out at 10 oClock after...Cutting the Elk Skins for a Toe Roap and proceeded, leaving G. Drew[yer] & Shannon to hunt the horses"

8/22/04, Clark: "This Creek I call Roloje a name given me last night in my Sleep"

and withdrew to a bower, or shelter of tree branches. Lewis and Clark went off to eat dinner together "and Consult about other measures." That night, in a big circle around three fires, Sioux warriors danced and sang of battles. Dorion told men of the Corps it was good manners to honor the dancers by throwing small gifts into the circle.

The next morning, the Indians spoke. They very politely told the Americans what the whites had failed to understand. Shake Hand (the Americans' "first chief") mentioned that he had an English medal and a Spanish medal from when he had met those people. He said he'd be happy to meet "My Grand Father," but mostly wanted traders to visit the Yanktons. Clark recorded his words as "...our Women has got no Cloathes and we have no Powder & Ball..."

White Crane, the "second chief," said his father was a chief, and "you have made me a Chief," but he was a young man and too inexperienced to speak much, although he agreed with Shake Hand.

Half Man, whom they had named only a subchief, let them know that he was the son of a chief, and himself "a Chief of Some note." Of the Yankton Sioux, he said "we open our ears" to the messge of peace, but warned "I fear

those nations above will not open their ears, and you cannot I fear open them" His prediction about the Teton Sioux upriver was accurate (see Chapter 9).

The council ended with all agreeing that Pierre Dorion, Sr., would stay the winter among the Yanktons, trying to make peace between them and other nations. (His son Pierre, Jr., a trader among the Yankton, was also at this council, having come with the Sioux.) On September 1, the Corps "proceeded on" up the Missouri.

Poor George Shannon not only missed the council, but also was out wandering the prairie alone. He was eighteen or nineteen years old, and lost in vast and unfamiliar country, home of possibly hostile people.

On August 26, near today's Vermillion, South Dakota, interpreter George Drouillard and Shannon had been sent out to hunt for the expedition's horses. They were told "to follow us Keeping on the high lands." The next day, Drouillard was back, saying he had walked all night but couldn't find Shannon or the horses. Now privates Joseph Field and John Shields went out overnight, but couldn't find the younger man.

When the expedition went into camp at Calumet Bluff, they saw Shannon's tracks. In three days of rushing to catch up, he had gotten ahead of them! Clark wrote that, Shannon "not being a first rate Hunter," they sent Private John Colter after him.

On September 3 and 5, the Corps saw the tracks of Colter still following Shannon, and both men still ahead of them. On the earlier date, Shannon had two horses, but by two days later he had lost one. Colter returned to the Corps without Shannon on September 6.

Finally, on the 11th, the keelboat crew spotted Shannon on shore, waiting for a trading boat. For 16 days, he had had nothing to eat but wild grapes and one rabbit, "which he Killed by shooting a piece of hard Stick" after he had used his last bullet. Clark marveled, "thus a man had like to have Starved to death in a land of Plenty for want of Bulletes or Something to kill his meat." Bison had come within thirty yards of Shannon's camp. (Shannon recovered, made the entire trip, and later served as a state senator in Missouri.)

After the council at Calumet Bluff, the party traveled uneventfully, passing White Bear Cliff (already bearing one of the nicknames for the grizzly bear, which the Corps hadn't yet encountered) at today's **[4]** Gavins Point. As September came on, nights and mornings were cooler, the river was very low, and the animals hunters brought in were fat for winter.

The men saw several animals new to them: on September 5, in today's Bon Homme County, South Dakota, the mule deer; on the 7th Lewis and Clark explored a prairie dog town in Boyd County, Nebraska, like small boys: pouring water down a hole to flush out the creature, and sticking a pole down to see how deep the hole was. Three days after that, Clark wrote that they found a petrified fish backbone in today's Gregory County, South Dakota. On September 14, south of the White River, Clark killed a "Goat of this Countrey" that looked like an antelope or gazelle—the pronghorn—and Shields killed the first jackrabbit known to science. At night they heard "many wolves of Different Sorts howling about us"—both wolves and coyotes, actually. On September 16, one of the hunters killed a

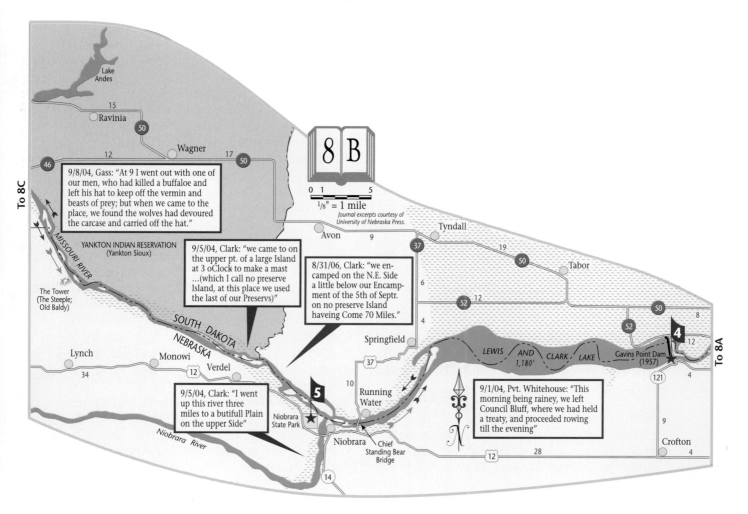

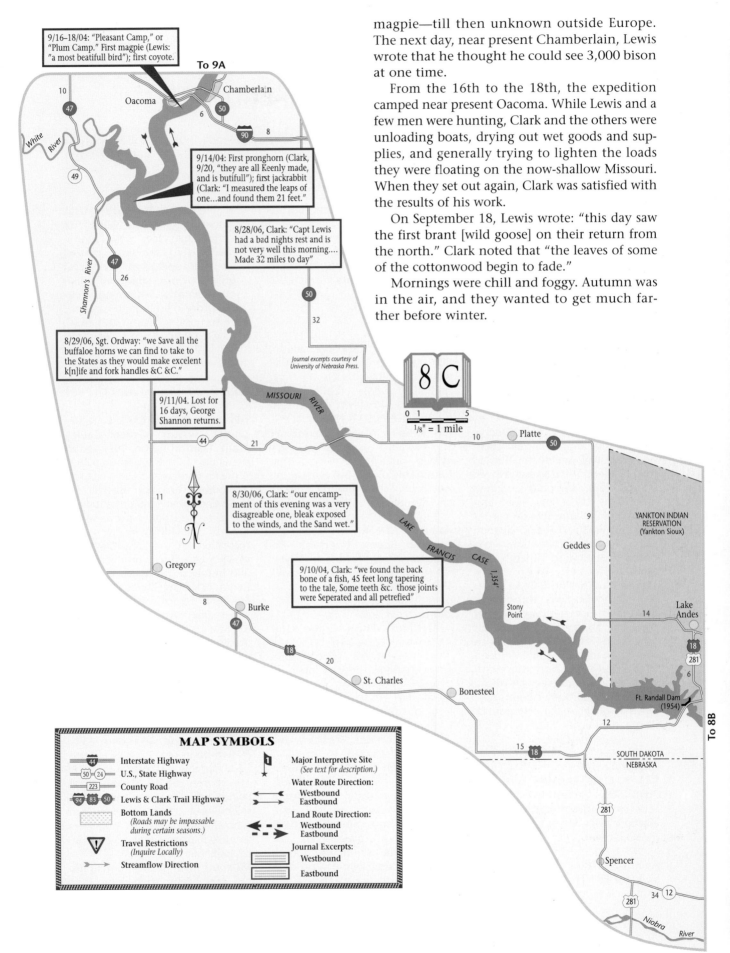

9/16–18/04: "Pleasant Camp," or "Plum Camp." First magpie (Lewis: "a most beatifull bird"); first coyote.

To 9A

9/14/04: First pronghorn (Clark, 9/20, "they are all Keenly made, and is butifull"); first jackrabbit (Clark: "I measured the leaps of one...and found them 21 feet."

8/28/06, Clark: "Capt Lewis had a bad nights rest and is not very well this morning.... Made 32 miles to day"

8/29/06, Sgt. Ordway: "we Save all the buffaloe horns we can find to take to the States as they would make excelent k[n]ife and fork handles &C &C."

9/11/04. Lost for 16 days, George Shannon returns.

8/30/06, Clark: "our encampment of this evening was a very disagreable one, bleak exposed to the winds, and the Sand wet."

9/10/04, Clark: "we found the back bone of a fish, 45 feet long tapering to the tale, Some teeth &c. those joints were Seperated and all petrefied"

Journal excerpts courtesy of University of Nebraska Press.

8 C

0 1 5
1/8" = 1 mile

Chamberlain
Oacoma
White River
Shannon's River
Missouri River
Lake Francis Case
Gregory
Burke
St. Charles
Bonesteel
Platte
Geddes
Stony Point
Lake Andes
Ft. Randall Dam (1954)
YANKTON INDIAN RESERVATION (Yankton Sioux)
SOUTH DAKOTA
NEBRASKA
Spencer
Niobra River

To 8B

MAP SYMBOLS

Interstate Highway
U.S., State Highway
County Road
Lewis & Clark Trail Highway
Bottom Lands
(Roads may be impassable during certain seasons.)
Travel Restrictions
(Inquire Locally)
Streamflow Direction

Major Interpretive Site
(See text for description.)
Water Route Direction:
Westbound
Eastbound
Land Route Direction:
Westbound
Eastbound
Journal Excerpts:
Westbound
Eastbound

magpie—till then unknown outside Europe. The next day, near present Chamberlain, Lewis wrote that he thought he could see 3,000 bison at one time.

From the 16th to the 18th, the expedition camped near present Oacoma. While Lewis and a few men were hunting, Clark and the others were unloading boats, drying out wet goods and supplies, and generally trying to lighten the loads they were floating on the now-shallow Missouri. When they set out again, Clark was satisfied with the results of his work.

On September 18, Lewis wrote: "this day saw the first brant [wild goose] on their return from the north." Clark noted that "the leaves of some of the cottonwood begin to fade."

Mornings were chill and foggy. Autumn was in the air, and they wanted to get much farther before winter.

TOURING TODAY

⁓ COUNCIL AT CALUMET BLUFF ⁓

Bridges over the Missouri River in this area are far apart (98 miles on south side, 70 miles on north side) so plan carefully. Yankton, SD (US 81); Pickstown, SD (US 18/281); west of Platte, SD (SD 44); Chamberlain, SD (I-90); Big Bend Dam (SD 47).

ALONG THE EXPEDITION'S PATH

August 21, 1804
(Return Sept. 1, 1806)
[1] ★ Ponca State Park (Ponca, NE)—Significant transition point between two levels of human management of the Missouri River. Downstream, shipping channels and dams affect the river; upstream, only dams do—except for the short Wild and Scenic Missouri segment in central Montana. From Ponca upstream to Yankton, SD, the river is pretty much as the Corps saw it. Hiking trails to several scenic overlooks throughout 859 acres. Interpretative center planned. Take a trail ride, swim or fish. ▲ 164 sites (87 w/hookups); fee; water; modern; showers; open all year/full operation May-Sept; grills/fire rings; tables; firewood. ⊞ 14 two-bedroom cabins (Apr-Nov). Pool; boating; playground. Dump station. 2 miles N on NE 9 & 12. 402/755-2284.

August 22, 1804
[2] ★ Gass Election Site (Elk Point, SD)—Interesting old cemetery with interpretation about election. River access for fishing. 1 mile S of town.

August 24, 1804
Volcano Hill Historic Site (Newcastle, NE)—Ionia Volcano is not visible from this city park, but located about 5 miles north and east. Clark seemed to be among those who thought this bluff a true volcano, which was disproved before the 20th century. Picnic area. Always open; fee. In town on NE 12. 402/355-2675.

August 25, 1804
Clay County Park (Vermillion, SD)—▲ 9 primitive sites; fee; water; primitive; open all year; grills/fire rings; tables. Boat ramp/dock. 4 miles W on the Timber Road. 605/987-2263.
[3] ★ Spirit Mound (Vermillion, SD)—Mound itself is privately owned, but can be viewed from turnout on SD 19; use caution. Always open; free. About 7 miles N of Vermillion's northern edge.

August 27, 1804
Yankton Scenic Overlook—Expansive view of the Missouri Valley. Below Gavins Point Dam on NE 1121 W. 605/665-3636.
Gavins Point Dam—Downstream Area
▲ **Chief White Crane Unit** (Yankton, SD)—116 sites (104 w/hookups); fee; water; primitive/modern; showers; open all year/full operation May-Sept; grills/fire rings; tables. Swimming; boat ramp/dock; fishing; playground. Dump station. 5 miles W on SD 52, below the dam. 402/667-7873.
▲ **Pierson Ranch Unit** (Yankton, SD)—74 sites (68 w/hookups); fee; water; primitive/modern; showers; open May-Sept; grills/fire rings; tables. 45' maximum length. Swimming; boat ramp/dock; fishing; playground; tennis court. Dump station. 5 miles W on SD 52, below the dam. 402/667-7873.

▲ **Nebraska Tailwaters Unit** (Yankton, SD)—52 sites (32 w/hookups); fee; water; primitive/modern; showers; open all year/full operation May-Sept; grills/fire rings; tables; 50' maximum length. Swimming; boat ramp/dock; fishing; playground; visitor center. Dump station. 1 mile S on US 81, 4 miles W on NE 121, below the dam. 402/667-7873.

August 28—September 3, 1804
(Return Sept. 1, 1806)
[4] ★ Lewis and Clark Lake Regional Visitor Center/Gavins Point Dam (Crofton, NE)—Interpretation of Calumet Bluff council. A prairie garden and Lewis & Clark interpretive trail are outside. Exhibits and audiovisual presentations on the construction of the dam, history of the Missouri River, and recreation on the lake. Glassed-in viewing areas focus on geographic and historical highlights. Discovery Room for children brings history to life. Daily 10 to 6 (Memorial Day-Labor Day), Mon-Fri 8 to 4:30, Sat/Sun 10 to 6 (rest of year); free. 9 miles N on NE 121, or 4 miles W of Yankton. 402/667-7873.
Lewis and Clark Lake
Lewis and Clark State Recreation Area—825 acres along the lake for fishing, hiking and just relaxing. ⊞ Resort is open Apr-Oct with lakeside lodging. 34 rooms ($$$), 3 two-bedroom units, 7 three-bedroom units, 10 cabins for up to 10 people ($$$+), beach pool, coin laundry, jogging, bike rental, microwaves and refrigerators in all rooms. Reduced rates mid-week and off-season. 5 miles W on SD 52. 605/665-2680.
Missouri River Trail—10-mile hiking and biking route runs from Yankton to Lewis and Clark Lake.

North Shore

▲ **Yankton**—82 sites (all w/hookups); fee; water; modern; showers; open all year/full operation May-Sept; grills/fire rings; tables. Swimming; boat ramp; fishing; playground; bike trails. Dump station. 5 miles W of Yankton on SD 52. 605/668-2985.

▲ **Midway**—208 sites (all w/hookups); fee; water; modern; showers; open all year/full operation May-Sept; grills/fire rings; tables. Swimming; boat ramp; fishing; playground; bike trails. 6 miles W of Yankton on SD 52. 605/668-2985.

▲ **Gavins Point**—76 sites (all w/hookups); fee; water; modern; showers; open all year/full operation May-Sept; grills/fire rings; tables. Swimming; boat ramp; fishing; playground; bike trails; hiking; horse camp/trails. 8 miles W of Yankton on SD 52. 605/668-2985.

▲ **Tabor**—10 primitive sites; fee; **no** water; primitive; open all year; fire rings. Boat ramp/dock. 6 miles S of Tabor off SD 50. 605/668-2985.

▲ **Sand Creek**—12 primitive sites; fee; water; primitive; open all year; fire rings. Boat ramp/dock; picnic shelters. 1 mile N of Springfield on SD 37, 3 miles E on access road. 605/668-2985.

▲ **Springfield**—12 sites (6 w/hookups); fee; water; modern/primitive; showers; open all year; grills/fire rings; tables. Boat ramp/dock; swimming; playground. Dump station. Edge of Springfield on SD 37. 605/668-2985.

South Shore
(all sites W of NE 121 on R54C)

▲ **South Shore**—Undesignated primitive sites; fee; water; primitive; open all year; grills/fire rings; 40' maximum length. Swimming; boat ramp; fishing. 1 mile W. 402/388-4169.

▲ **Weigand/Burbach**—149 sites (all w/hookups); fee; water; modern/primitive; showers; open all year; grills/fire rings; tables. Fishing; fish cleaning station; boating; full-service marina; beach; picnic shelters; groceries; dump station. 4 miles W. 402/388-4169.

▲ **Miller Creek**—Undesignated primitive sites; fee; water; primitive; open all year; grills/fire rings; tables. Boat ramp; fishing. 5 miles E on NE 12. 402/388-4169.

[5] ★ **Niobrara State Park** (Niobrara, NE)—Superb views of the Missouri and Niobrara rivers. Historical interpretive center traces impact of the Indians from the time of Lewis and Clark to the Mormons. Trail rides, ⊞ 12 two-bedroom and 3 three-bedroom cabins. Several blufftop hiking trails. ▲ 119 sites (69 w/hookups); fee; water; modern; showers; open all year; grills/fire rings; tables; firewood. Pool; fishing, coin laundry; playground. 1 mile W on NE 12. 402/857-3373.

September 7, 1804
Karl Mundt National Wildlife Refuge (Pickstown, SD)—Over 500 acres set aside as a winter haven for bald eagles. Although closed to the public, a viewing area is set up below the spillway at the Fort Randall Dam.

Fort Randall Dam/Historical Site (Pickstown, SD)—Sitting Bull was held prisoner here in 1882 and the remains of the fort's chapel, built in 1856, are still visible. Several hiking trails lead to Lake Francis Case. Always open; free. Just below the dam on the south side. Guided tours of the dam daily 9 to 4:30 (Memorial Day-Labor Day); free. 1 mile W on US 18/281. 605/487-7845.

September 8-17, 1804
Lake Francis Case—
East Shore

▲ **Creek Recreation Area** (Pickstown, SD)—134 sites (all w/hookups); fee; water; modern; showers; open May-Aug; grills/fire rings; tables. Boat ramp/dock; fishing; playground; hiking trails. Dump station. 1 mile W on US 18. 605/487-7847.

▲ **North Point** (Pickstown, SD)—74 sites (all w/hookups); fee; water; modern; showers; open all year; grills/fire rings; tables. Boat ramp/dock; fishing; playground. Dump station. 2 miles NW on US 118/281. 605/487-7046.

▲ **White Swan**—Undesignated primitive sites; free; **no** water; primitive; open all year; grills/fire rings; tables. Boat ramp/dock. 12 miles W of Lake Andes on SD 50. 605/487-7847.

▲ **Pease Creek**—20 primitive sites; free; water; primitive; open all year; grills/fire rings; tables. Boat ramp/dock; swimming; picnic area; dump station. 474 acres. 8 miles S of Geddes on SD 1804. 605/487-7847.

▲ **Platte Creek** (Platte, SD)—72 sites (39 w/hookups); fee; water; modern; showers; open May-Oct; grills/fire rings; tables; firewood. Swimming; boat ramp/dock; fishing. Dump station. 6 miles W on SD 44, 10 miles S on SD 1804. 605/337-2587.

▲ **Snake Creek** (Platte, SD)—96 sites (91 w/hookups); fee; water; modern; showers; open all year/full operation May-Oct; grills/fire rings; tables; firewood. Swimming; boating; fishing; hiking. Dump station. 14 miles W on SD 44. 605/337-2587.

▲ **Elm Creek**—20 primitive sites; free; **no** water; primitive; open all year; grills/fire rings; tables. Boat ramp/dock. 12.5 miles S of Pukwana on SD 50, 7 miles W. 605/734-6772.

▲ **American Creek Recreation Area**—40 sites (16 w/hookups); fee; water; modern; showers; open May-Sept; grills/fire rings; tables; 32' maximum length; firewood. Swimming; boat ramp/rental; groceries; fishing. Dump station. 2 miles N of I-90 exit 263. 605/734-6772.

▲ **Left Tailrace**—73 sites (63 w/hookups); fee; water; modern/primitive; showers; open May-Sept; grills/fire rings; tables; 14-day limit. Boat ramp; fishing; fish cleaning station; playground; amphitheater/interpretive programs. 2 miles SW on SD 47 below the dam. 605/245-2255.

▲ **Old Fort Thompson**—24 primitive sites; fee; water; modern; open all year; grills/fire rings; tables. Boat ramp/dock; playground; picnic area. 1 mile W of Fort Thompson on SD 47W. 605/245-2173.

Lake Francis Case/West Shore
▲ **South Shore**—50 primitive

sites; fee; water; primitive; open Apr-Oct; grills/fire rings; tables. Boat ramp/fishing. Above dam off US 18/281. 605/487-7847.

⚤ South Scalp—12 primitive sites; free; water; primitive; open all year; frills/fire rings; tables. Boat ramp/dock; picnic area; dump station. 10 miles N of Bonesteel on SD 1806. 605/487-7847.

⚤ Buryanek—26 primitive sites; fee; water; primitive; open all year; grills/fire rings; tables. Boat ramp/dock. Trail interpretation. 18 miles W of Platte on SD 44, 2.5 miles N. 605/337-3484.

⚤ West Chamberlain—40 primitive sites; fee; water; modern; showers; open May-Oct; grills/fire rings; tables; 32' maximum length. Boating; fishing; playground; dump station. 2 miles NW of Chamberlain on US 16, 605/337-3484.

September 18-20, 1804
(Return August 26, 1806)
Big Bend Dam (Fort Thompson, SD)—This dam creates Lake Sharpe to the north with 200 miles of shoreline. Exhibits and information in lobby. Weekdays 8 to 4, tours at 10 and 1; free. On SD 47. 605/245-2331.
Lake Sharpe/North Shore

⚤ North Shore—Primitive camping and day-use area with swimming and boating access, primitive rest rooms. 2 miles W of Big Bend on SD 47W, 1 mile N. 605/245-2491.

⚤ West Bend—126 sites (all w/hookups); fee; water; modern/primitive; showers; open all year; grills/fire rings; tables; ⊞ cabins. Boat ramp/dock; swimming; hiking trails; playground; dump station. 26 miles E, 9 miles S of Pierce on SD 34, 605/224-5605.

Around the Area

TOWNS LISTED ALPHABETICALLY

Beresford, South Dakota
Beresford Chamber of Commerce, 510 W. Oak. 605/763-5864.
Union County State Park—Good place to spend the night. **⚤** 24

sites (10 w/hookups); fee; water; modern; showers; open all year/full operation May-Oct; grills/fire rings; tables; firewood. 499 acres. Hiking and horseback riding trails. I-29 exit 38, 0.5 miles E/1 mile S on county road. 605/987-2263.

⊗ Emily's Cafe—Hearty diner fare, kids' menu. ♿. B L & D daily. I-29 & SD 46. 605/763-5300.

Chamberlain, South Dakota
Chamberlain Area Chamber of Commerce, 115 W. Lawler, 605/734-6541.
Akta Lakota Museum—Large collection of Sioux and Lakota artifacts, artwork and multimedia exhibits. Mon-Sat 8 to 6, Sun 1 to 5 (May-Sept), Mon-Fri 8 to 4:30 (Oct-Apr); free. I-90 exit 263 in St. Joseph's Indian School. 605/734-3455, 800/798-3452.
Great Plains Resource Center/ Roam Free Park—View native plants and wildlife along two walking trails, but watch for rattlesnakes. Daily dawn to dusk (Memorial Day-Labor Day); free. 2 miles N on SD 50. 605/734-6541.
Native American Loop—South Dakota Scenic Byway runs along SD 1806 between Chamberlain and Fort Pierre. Information and an audio cassette for the self-guided tour are available at 115 W. Lawler.

⊞ Alewel's Lake Shore Motel—29 rooms (4 two-bedroom units), pets. View of the lake. Open Apr-Nov, off-season rates. 1115 N. River St. 605/734-5566. $

⊞ Best Western Lee's Motor Inn—60 rooms (10 two-bedroom units), indoor pool, hot tub. Off-season rates. 220 W. King. 605/734-5575. $$ K12

⊞ Super 8—56 rooms, pool, continental breakfast, hot tub. Some rooms with view of Missouri River, off-season rates. I-90 exit 263. 605/734-6548, 800/800-8000. $$ K5

⊗ Bridges—Local specialties in western surroundings, kids' menu, outdoor dining. ♿. B L & D daily. I-90 exit 260 (in Cedar Shore Resort). 605/734-6376. $$

⊗ Casey Drug & Jewelry—Claims to serve best cheeseburger in the region, kids' menu. B L & D daily.

I-90 exit 263, in Welcome West Plaza. 605/734-6530.

Elk Point, South Dakota
⊗ Edgar's—Turn-of-the-20th-century soda fountain. In Pioneer Drug, 1 mile E of I-29 exit 15. $

Kennebec, South Dakota
⚤ KOA-Kennebec—80 sites (62 w/hookups); fee; water; modern; showers; open May-Oct; grills/fire rings; tables; firewood. Pool; mini golf; playground. Coin laundry; groceries; dump station. I-90 exit 235, 1 mile N on County 235. 800/562-6361.

⊞ Budget Host Inn—16 rooms, continental breakfast, pets, coin laundry. Off-season rates. I-90 exit 235. 605/869-2210. $

Mitchell, South Dakota
Mitchell Area Chamber of Commerce—601 N. Main. 605/996-5567, 866/273-CORN.
The Corn Palace—Intricate Moorish architecture in the midst of the plains. A new exterior mosaic is created each September from over 2,000 bushels of corns, grasses and grains. Guided tours daily 8am to 9pm (Memorial Day-Labor Day), 8 to 5 (May/Sept), Mon-Fri 8 to 5 (Oct-Apr); free. 6th and Main. 605/996-5567, 800/257-2676.
Enchanted World Doll Museum—Cross the drawbridge and enter this castle filled with thousands of dolls exhibited in fairy tale/nursery rhyme and 18th/19th century settings. Daily 8 to 8 (Memorial Day-Sept), Mon-Sat 9 to 5, Sun 1 to 5 (Apr/May/, Oct/Nov); admission fee. 615 N. Main. 605/996-9896.
Middle Border Museum of American Indian and Pioneer Life—Complex contains 2 art galleries and 4 restored 1890-1900 buildings that relate the story of life on the plains for Indians and pioneers. Artifacts date to the early 17th century. Mon-Sat 8 to 6, Sun 10 to 6 (June-Aug) Mon-Fri 9 to 5, Sat/Sun 1 to 5 (May/Sept); admission fee. 1311 S. Duff (Dakota Wesleyan University). 605/996-2122.
Oscar Howe Art Center—Collection of works by contemporary Sioux artist in Carnegie Library where he painted a dome mural for the WPA in 1940. Mon-Sat 9

to 5; donations. 119 W. Third. 605/996-4111.

Prehistoric Indian Village and Archedome Research Center—Walk through the scale model lodge constructed on the site of a 1000 A.D. pre-Mandan Indian village. A swinging bridge leads to the museum and archaeology center that contain exhibits on prehistoric life in the area/⅖. Picnic area. Daily 8 to 6 (Memorial Day-Labor Day), daily 9 to 4 (rest of year); admission fee. 1 mile N of The Corn Palace on Indian Village Rd. 605/996-5473.

Soukup and Thomas International Balloon and Airship Museum—Explore two centuries of air travel history. Artifacts, memorabilia, interactive exhibits. Daily 8 to 8 (Memorial Day-Labor Day), Mon-Sat 9 to 5, Sun 1 to 5 (Sept-May, closed Jan); admission fee. 7th and Main. 605/996-2311.

▲ **Dakota Campground**—67 sites (53 w/hookups); fee; water; modern; showers; open all year; grills/fire rings; tables. Pool; wading pool; playground; hot tub; dump station; coin laundry; groceries. I-90 exit 330, 0.25 mile S. 605/996-9432.

▲ **KOA-Riverside**—96 shady sites (86 w/hookups); fee; water; modern; showers; open May-Oct; grills/fire rings; tables. Pool; mini golf; playground. Dump station; coin laundry; groceries. I-90 exit 335, 0.5 mile N on Riverside Rd., 0.5 mile W on SD 38. 605/996-1131, 800/562-1236.

▲ **Lake Mitchell Campground**—70 sites (all w/hookups); fee; water; modern; showers; open Apr-Oct; grills/fire rings; tables; firewood. Swimming; boat dock/rentals; fishing; playground; hiking trails. Coin laundry; dump station. 1.25 miles N of Corn Palace on SD 37. 605/996-9643.

⊞ **AmericInn Motel & Suites**—53 rooms, 3 two-bedroom units, continental breakfast, coin laundry. ⅖. I-90 exit 332. 605/996-9700. $$ K12

⊞ **Anthony Motel**—34 rooms, pool, coin laundry. Efficiencies are same price as a double. Off-season rates. I-90 exit 330, 0.5 mile N, 1518 W. Havens Rd. 605/996-7518, 800/477-2235. $$ K16

⊞ **Best Western Motor Inn**—77 rooms, pool, continental breakfast, pets, coin laundry, hot tub, mini golf. Off-season rates. I-90 exit 332. 605/996-5536, 800/528-1234. $$ K16

⊞ **Comfort Inn**—60 rooms, indoor pool, continental breakfast, coin laundry, hot tub. Off-season rates. I-90 exit 332. 605/996-1333, 800/221-2222. $$ K18

⊗ **The Depot**—Restored depot with running model trains. B L & D daily. 210 S. Main. 605/996-9417. $$

⊗ **Town House Cafe**—All-you-can-eat buffet, kids' menu. B L & D daily. 103 N. Main. 605/996-4615. $$

Oacoma, South Dakota

Old West Museum—Herds of buffalo and longhorn cattle create atmosphere for an assortment of Old West and Sioux Indian relics and equipment. Daily 7:30am to 9pm (June-Aug), dawn to dusk (Apr/May/Sept/Oct); admission fee. US 16 just N of I-90 exit 260. 605/734-6157.

World Wildlife Adventures—Mounted animals from around the world exhibited in natural settings. Daily 8am to 9pm (June-Aug), 9 to 7 (May/Sept/Oct); admission fee. I-90 exit 260. 605/734-5857.

▲ **Cedar Shore Campground**—24 sites (all w/hookups); fee; water; modern; showers; open Apr-Oct; grills/fire rings; tables firewood. ⊞ Cabins. Pool; river swimming; boat ramp/dock/rental; hot tub; coin laundry; groceries; fishing; kids' program; playground. I-90 exit 260, 2 miles E on Bus 90, 1.5 miles N on River Rd. 605/734-5273.

▲ **Familyland Campground**—89 grassy sites along the river (64 w/hookups); fee; water; modern; showers; open Apr-Oct; grills/fire rings; tables. Pool; playground. Coin laundry; dump stations; groceries. I-90 exit 260. 605/734-6959, 800/675-6959.

⊞ **Cedar Shore Resort** (Lake Francis Case)—99 rooms along the Missouri River, pets, marina, beach, fishing, tennis, indoor pool, playground, coin laundry, ⊗ restaurant, lounge. Off-season rates. I-90 exit 260, 2.5 miles E on Bus. 90. 605/734-6376, 888/697-6363. $$$ K18

⊞ **Days Inn**—45 rooms, indoor pool, continental breakfast, pets, coin laundry, hot tub. Off-season rates. I-90 exit 260. 605/734-4100. $$ K12.

⊗ **Al's Oasis**—A slice of plains history with buffalo burgers and nickel cups of coffee, kids' menu. B L & D daily. I-90 exit 260. 605/734-6054. $$

Pickstown, South Dakota

⊞ **Fort Randall Inn**—17 rooms (1 two-bedroom unit), pets, coin laundry, ⊗ restaurant. Wooded setting, lake view. US 18/281. 605/487-7801 $

Platte, South Dakota

⊞ **Kings Inn** Motel—34 rooms, pets, continental breakfast. Family units. On SD 44. 605/337-3385, 800/337-7756. $$ K12

Royal, Nebraska

Ashfall Fossil Beds State Historical Park—Watch the paleontologists at work as they continue to discover complete skeletons hidden under volcanic ash for 10 million years. Documented species include camels, sabertooth deer, rhinoceroses and 3-toed horses. Open Mon-Sat 9 to 5, Sun 11 to 5 (Memorial Day-Labor Day), Wed-Sat 10 to 4. Sun 1 to 4 (May/Sept); admission fee. 6 miles N of US 20. 402/893-2000.

▲ **Grove Lake State Wildlife Area**—15 primitive sites; free; water; primitive; open all year; grills/fire rings; tables. Boat ramp; fishing; playground. 2 miles N on US 20. 402/370-3374.

Sioux Falls, South Dakota

Sioux Falls Convention and Visitors Bureau—200 N. Phillips, Suite 102. 605/336-1620, 800/333-2072.

Battleship USS South Dakota Memorial—Memorial is a full-scale outline of the WWII battleship and includes a museum and scale model. Daily 10 to 6; free. I-29 exit 79, 1 mile E. 605/367-7141.

Great Plains Zoo/Delbridge Museum of Natural History—Grizzly bears, penguins, zebras and other animals in natural habitat exhibits. In the museum are over 1,150 mounted animals in realistic exhibits. Daily 9 to 5 (Apr-Oct), 10 to 5 (rest of year); admission fee. I-29 exit, 1 mile E on SD 42, 0.25 mile S on Kiwanis Ave. 605/367-7059.

Old Courthouse Museum— Changing historical and cultural exhibits in restored courthouse. Mon-Sat 9 to 5, Sun 1 to 5; donations. 200 W. 6th. 605/367-4210.

Pettigrew Home and Museum— 1889 Queen Anne-style mansion with personal collections and Life on the Prairie exhibit on natural and cultural history. Guided tours. Tue-Fri 9 to 5 (closed noon to 1); donations. 131 N. Duluth. 605/367-7097.

Sioux Falls Recreation Trail and Greenway—13-mile paved trail along the Big Sioux River. Begins at Falls Park.

▲ Sioux Falls Camp Dakota—66 grassy-shaded sites (all w/hookups); fee; water; modern; showers; open May-Oct; grills/fire rings; table; firewood. Pool; hot tub; playground; coin laundry; dump station; groceries. I-90 exit 390. 605/528-3983.

▲ Sioux Falls KOA—126 sites (102 w/hookups); fee; water; modern; showers; open May-Oct; grills/fire rings; tables. ⊞ Cabins. Pool; mini golf; playground. Coin laundry; dump station; groceries. I-90 exit 399. 605/332-9987.

▲ Tower Campground—44 sites (43 w/hookups); fee; water; modern; showers; open Apr-Oct; grills/fire rings; tables; firewood. Pool; playground; dump station; coin laundry. I-29 exit 79. 605/336-7110.

▲ Yogi Bear of Sioux Falls—98 sites (all w/hookups); fee; water; modern; showers; open all year/full operations Apr-Oct; grills/fire rings; tables; firewood. ⊞ Cabins. Pool; mini golf; hot tub; playground. Coin laundry; dump station. I-229 & I-90. 605/332-2233.

⊞ Best Western Ramkota Inn— 227 rooms, pets, hot tub, wading pool, playground. ⊗ restaurants, coin laundry. &. I-29 exit 81. 605/336-0650. $$ K17

⊞ Best Western Town House— 44 rooms, indoor pool, continental breakfast, pets. ⊗ restaurant. Off-season rates. 400 S. Main. 605/336-2740. $$ K16

⊞ Comfort Suites—61 rooms, indoor pool, continental breakfast, pets, hot tub. I-29 exit 77. 605/362-9711. $$ K18

⊞ Country Inn & Suites—71 rooms, pool, continental breakfast, hot tub, exercise room. 200 E. 8th St. 605/373-0153. $$$ K12

⊞ Ramada Limited—67 rooms, pool, continental breakfast, exercise room, hot tub, coin laundry. Off-season rates. I-29 exit 79. 605/330-0000, 800/272-6232. $$ K18

⊗ Kristina's Cafe & Bakery—Casual bistro. B & L daily, D Thur/Fri. 12th St. & Phillips. 605/331-4860. $$

⊗ Minerva's—Continental food and great service, kids' menu. L & D Mon-Sat. 11th St. & Phillips. 605/334-0386. $$

⊗ Sioux Falls Brewery—Four brew-pubs amid blues and jazz. &. L & D daily. 431 N. Phillips. 605/332-4847. $$

Vermillion, South Dakota

Vermillion Area Chamber of Commerce—906 E. Cherry. 605/624-5571.

The Shrine to Music Museum— The history of music told through exhibits of over 6,000 instruments including a collection of rare Italian stringed instruments (1540-1793). Try to find the zither shaped like a crocodile or the South Pacific trumpet mask. Open Mon-Fri 9 to 4:30, Sat 10 to 4:30, Sun 2 to 4:30; free. Clark and Yale Sts. (USD campus). 605/677-5306.

W.H. Over State Museum—Dioramas, photos, costumes and exhibits document South Dakota's heritage. Mon-Fri 8 to 5, Sat/Sun 1 to 4:30; donations. SD 50 at Ratingen St. 605/677-5228.

⊞ Comfort Inn—46 rooms, continental breakfast, pets, hot tub. 7.5 miles W of I-29 exit 26 on SD 50. 605/624-8333. $$ K18

Yankton, South Dakota

Yankton Area Chamber of Commerce, 218 W. 4th St. 605/665-3636, 800/888-1460.

Cramer-Kenyon Heritage Home—1886 Queen Anne mansion with original furnishings and beautiful woodwork. Majestic flower and vegetable gardens. Guided tours Turs-Sat 1 to 5 (Memorial Day-Labor Day); admission fee. 509 Pine. 605/665-7470.

Dakota Territorial Museum— Guided tours of restored depot, schoolhouse and blacksmith shop. Tue-Sat 10 to 5, Sun 1 to 5 (May-Aug), Tue Sat 10 to 5 (rest of year; admission fee. 8th & Summit. 605/665-3898.

Gavins Point National Fish Hatchery and Aquarium—Learn about fisheries management. Exhibits of live fish and aquatic life native to the area. Aquarium open daily 10 to 4 (Apr-Oct), hatchery open daily 8 to 4; free. 3.5 miles W on SD 52. 605/665-3352.

⊞ Best Western Kelly Inn—124 rooms, pets, wading pool, hot tub, ⊗ restaurant. &. 1607 SD 50E. 605/665-2906. $$ K14

⊞ Broadway Inn—38 rooms, pool. 1210 Broadway (Hwy. 81). 605/665-7805.

⊞ Comfort Inn—46 rooms, continental breakfast, pets, hot tub. 1.5 miles N on US 81. 605/665-8053. $$ K18

⊞ Days Inn—45 rooms, continental breakfast, pets, hot tub. 1.75 miles N on US 81. 605/665-8717. $$ K12

⊨ Mulberry Inn Bed & Breakfast— 605/665-7116. $$

⊗ Jodean's—Friday seafood buffet, great salad and dessert bars, kids' menu, early bird specials. D daily, Sunday brunch. 2 miles N on US 81. 605/665-9884. $$

⊗ Quarry Steak House & Lounge —Steaks, seafood, fresh-baked bread. Overlooks lake area. 4 miles N on Hwy 52. 605/665-4337. $$

CHAPTER 9

September 21 to October 1, 1804

MEETING THE TETON SIOUX

At 1:00 a.m. on September 21, Corps of Discovery members were startled awake. They had pulled their boats onto an island for the night, and the Missouri's swift current was eating away the sand underneath. By moonlight, they boarded the boats and pulled away in the nick of time. Captain William Clark wrote, "we had pushed off but a few minets before the bank...gave way, which would Certainly have Sunk both Perogues, by the time we made the opsd. Shore our Camp fell in..."

Sgt. John Ordway noted the narrow escape, adding cheerily that afterward "the moon Shined pleasant all night."

At daylight they set off around the Big Bend of the Missouri, traveling 30 river miles where they could have walked only about 2,000 yards on land, Clark estimated.

On the 22nd, they passed Cedar Island and Regis Loisel's impressive cedar trading fort, a site now under Big Bend Reservoir. Clark noted the surrounding "Indian Camps in a Concel [conical] form," and Ordway was interested in the dog travois the Sioux people used. He wrote, "we are informed that the Indians tie theirs dogs to these [tipi] poles and they have to dragg them from camp to another loaded with their Baggage &.C"

At the Bad River, the Corps finally met the Teton Sioux. The visit had its tense moments for both sides, and was not helped by the language barrier. Pierre Dorion had stayed with the Yanktons, so conversation went awkwardly through Private Pierre Cruzatte's Omaha language to an Omaha prisoner of the Tetons, who translated to her captors.

These people called themselves Lakota, or "dwellers of the prairie," but French traders were using the name learned from the Chippewa—"Sioux," which meant "enemy." Today they are known as Lakota Sioux, or simply Lakota.

Two camps with a total of 140 lodges were set up in the general area of **[2]** today's Pierre.

On September 25, three chiefs—Black Buffalo, Partisan, and Buffalo Medicine—greeted the captains. After a ceremonial pipe and the giving of medals and other presents on shore, the captains rowed the chiefs to the keelboat. When Clark later took the visitors back ashore in a pirogue, three warriors seized the boat's cable and refused to allow it to rejoin the keelboat. Used to traders who arrived with many goods, they and Black Buffalo wanted more presents.

Feeling threatened by Black Buffalo's words and gestures, Clark drew his sword. Seeing this, Captain Meriwether Lewis on the keelboat ordered his men "to Stand to their arms," including the biggest weapons: a small cannon and two swiveling blunderbusses, which were oversized shotguns. Sioux warriors notched their arrows and cocked their guns.

Black Buffalo freed the pirogue's cable, and that boat rowed to the Corps' other two, returning with 12 armed men. During these moments Clark stood ashore with two interpreters, surrounded by Indians, while the three chiefs stepped aside and talked together. When they finished, Clark offered his hand in peace, but Black Buffalo and Partisan refused to take it. Clark turned and started for the pirogue.

Black Buffalo stopped Clark, wading into the Missouri. He said that what he actually wanted was for the boats to stay so that the women and children could come see them, and possibly trade—even though, he added, the Corps didn't seem like merchants, and didn't have enticing trade goods.

Clark ended the standoff by saying that his men planned to proceed upriver a little way and make camp. At the chiefs' request, he welcomed them and some warriors aboard the keelboat, where they spent that night. Clark probably was not alone when he wrote that he had had "a bad nights Sleep."

Lewis instructed Cruzatte to visit the 48 Omaha women and children that the Teton Sioux had captured two weeks before, and

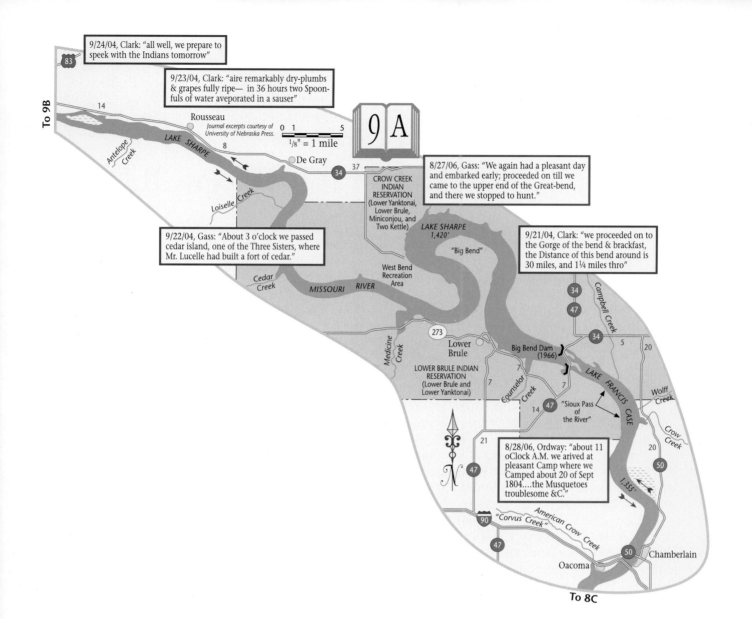

9/24/04, Clark: "all well, we prepare to speek with the Indians tomorrow"

9/23/04, Clark: "aire remarkably dry-plumbs & grapes fully ripe— in 36 hours two Spoonfuls of water aveporated in a sauser"

Rousseau
Journal excerpts courtesy of University of Nebraska Press.

0 1   5
1/8" = 1 mile

De Gray

9A

8/27/06, Gass: "We again had a pleasant day and embarked early; proceeded on till we came to the upper end of the Great-bend, and there we stopped to hunt."

CROW CREEK INDIAN RESERVATION
(Lower Yanktonai, Lower Brule, Miniconjou, and Two Kettle)

LAKE SHARPE
1,420'

"Big Bend"

9/22/04, Gass: "About 3 o'clock we passed cedar island, one of the Three Sisters, where Mr. Lucelle had built a fort of cedar."

West Bend Recreation Area

9/21/04, Clark: "we proceeded on to the Gorge of the bend & brackfast, the Distance of this bend around is 30 miles, and 1¼ miles thro"

MISSOURI   RIVER

Lower Brule

LOWER BRULE INDIAN RESERVATION
(Lower Brule and Lower Yanktonai)

Big Bend Dam (1966)

"Sioux Pass of the River"

LAKE FRANCIS CASE

Wolff Creek

8/28/06, Ordway: "about 11 oClock A.M. we arived at pleasant Camp where we Camped about 20 of Sept 1804....the Musquetoes troublesome &C."

1,355'

"Corvus Creek"

American Crow Creek

Chamberlain

Oacoma

To 9B

To 8C

learn what the Sioux planned. The Omahas stated that the Sioux planned to rob or harm the Corps. Meanwhile, the Sioux worried that these visitors were friends of the Omahas and had come for revenge.

Despite the misunderstanding, the Sioux were generous hosts. On September 26, they carried each captain to the central lodge on a bison skin, an honor accorded great chiefs; they gave the party bison meat for their journey, and served them dog meat. Clark wrote, "raw Dog Sioux think great dish—used on festivals," but Ordway noted that this meat was "cooked in a decent manner to treat our people with."

That night the men of the Corps witnessed a scalp dance. The Teton women danced, displaying Omaha scalps while the men sang the story of their battle.

The Corps stayed another day, which again ended with feasting and a scalp dance. Afterward, Clark was returning to the keelboat when his pirogue crashed into it and broke the keelboat's anchor cable. He yelled for the men on the keelboat to take its oars for control. Partisan believed this uproar signaled an Omaha attack, and summoned warriors. Seeing those men, Lewis—on shore—thought the Sioux were attacking, and had his men load their guns.

Luckily, all was cleared up without bloodshed. But the Corps spent another sleepless night on guard. Clark felt "verry unwell I think for the want of Sleep."

On the morning of September 28, they hunted unsuccessfully for the anchor in the Missouri's silt, then headed upriver even though Teton men tried to stop them by grabbing the keelboat's ropes. Buffalo Medicine flagged down the boat and came aboard, saying Partisan had ordered his men to try to stop the Corps. Buffalo Medicine rode along for two days, until the boat "was turned by accident...and rocked verry much," scaring him. He went ashore and headed home.

The next day, October 1, brought the Corps to the mouth of the Cheyenne River, opposite a trading post run by Jean Vallé. Clark quizzed the French trader about the people, game, and lands up the Cheyenne, and listened to his description of the Black Hills. These were places the Corps would not visit, so Clark eagerly collected the information.

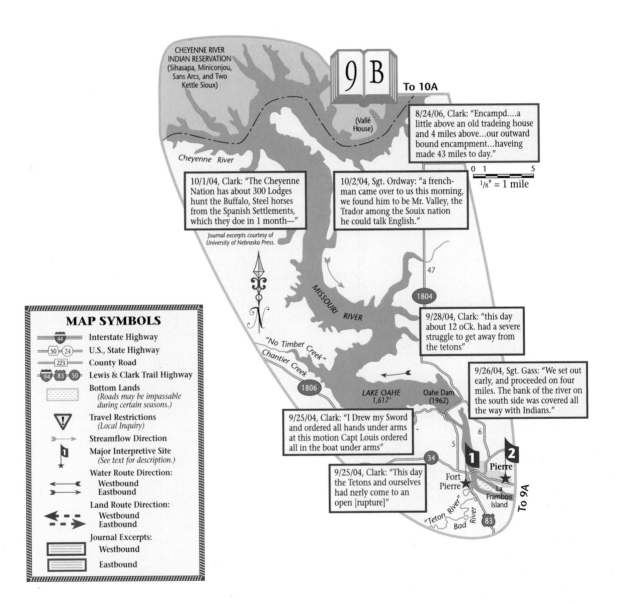

CHEYENNE RIVER INDIAN RESERVATION
(Sihasapa, Miniconjou, Sans Arcs, and Two Kettle Sioux)

9 B

To 10A

(Vallé House)

8/24/06, Clark: "Encampd....a little above an old tradeing house and 4 miles above...our outward bound encampment...haveing made 43 miles to day."

Cheyenne River

0 1 5
1/8" = 1 mile

10/1/04, Clark: "The Cheyenne Nation has about 300 Lodges hunt the Buffalo, Steel horses from the Spanish Settlements, which they doe in 1 month—"

10/2/04, Sgt. Ordway: "a frenchman came over to us this morning, we found him to be Mr. Valley, the Trador among the Souix nation he could talk English."

Journal excerpts courtesy of University of Nebraska Press.

47

1804

MISSOURI RIVER

9/28/04, Clark: "this day about 12 oCk. had a severe struggle to get away from the tetons"

"No Timber Creek"
Chantier Creek

1806

LAKE OAHE 1,617'

Oahe Dam (1962)

9/26/04, Sgt. Gass: "We set out early, and proceeded on four miles. The bank of the river on the south side was covered all the way with Indians."

9/25/04, Clark: "I Drew my Sword and ordered all hands under arms at this motion Capt Louis ordered all in the boat under arms"

6

5

34

1

2

Pierre

Fort Pierre

La Frambois Island

To 9A

9/25/04, Clark: "This day the Tetons and ourselves had nerly come to an open [rupture]"

"Teton River"
Bad River

83

MAP SYMBOLS

44	Interstate Highway
50 24	U.S., State Highway
223	County Road
94 83 50	Lewis & Clark Trail Highway
	Bottom Lands *(Roads may be impassable during certain seasons.)*
▽!	Travel Restrictions *(Local Inquiry)*
	Streamflow Direction
1	Major Interpretive Site *(See text for description.)*
	Water Route Direction:
←	Westbound
→	Eastbound
	Land Route Direction:
	Westbound
	Eastbound
	Journal Excerpts:
	Westbound
	Eastbound

TOURING TODAY

✂ MEETING THE TETON SIOUX ✂

[ ] Bracketed numbers key sites to maps	♿ Special-needs accessible ⊨ Bed & breakfast
★ L&C in-depth interpretation, unchanged landform	⊗ Restaurant ▲ Camping, RV park
● L&C interpreted site	⊞ Motel, hotel, cabin

Bridges over the Missouri River in this area are in Pierre, SD (US 14/US 83); Oahe Dam (SD 1804/1806).

ALONG THE EXPEDITION'S PATH

September 21, 1804
(Return Aug. 27, 1806)
● **West Bend State Recreation Area** (Pierre, SD)—▲ 126 sites (68 w/hookups); fee; water; modern; showers; open May-Oct; grills/fire rings; tables. Lake swimming; boat ramp/dock; fishing; playground. Dump station; firewood. 26 miles E on SD 34, 8.5 miles S. 605/224-5605.
▲ **Iron Nation** (Lower Brule, SD)—12 primitive sites; free; **no** water; primitive; open all year; grills/fire rings; tables. Boat ramp/dock; playground. 9 miles W on BIA blacktop. 605/245-2255.

September 22, 1804
● **Medicine Knoll River Overlook** (Pierre, SD)—Roadside park with shaded picnic area and magnificent view of the Missouri. Always open; free. 15 miles W on SD 34.
Cedar Island (Pierre, SD)—Viewpoint on the river to area where islands existed. Islands are now underwater. Always open; free. 23 miles W on SD 34.
DeGrey Recreation Area (Pierre, SD)—Boat ramp, fishing, ▲ primitive camping. Always open; free. 27 miles E on SD 34. 605/765-9410.

September 23, 1804
● **Farm Island State Recreation Area** (Pierre, SD)—Lake swimming; boat ramp/dock; fishing; hiking; playground; ⊞ cabins. ▲ 85 sites (55 w/hookups); fee;

water; modern; showers; open all year/full operation May-Oct; grills/fire rings; tables. Dump station; firewood. 4 miles E on SD 34. 605/224-5605.
Lake Oahe Downsteam Recreation Area, North Unit (Pierre, SD)—Swimming; boating; fishing; playground; hiking trails. ▲ 161 sites (87 w/hookups); fee; water; modern; showers; open May-Oct; grills/fire rings; tables; firewood; 32' maximum length. Dump station. 4 miles N on SD 1806. 605/224-5862.
Lake Oahe Downsteam Recreation Area, South Unit (Pierre, SD)—Swimming; boating; fishing; playground. ▲ 45 sites (29 w/hookups); fee; water; modern; open Apr-Labor Day; grills/fire rings; tables; firewood; 32' maximum length. Dump station. 4 miles N on SD 1806. 605/224-5862.
LaFramboise Island Recreation Area (Pierre, SD)—Forested island (thought to be the Teton Council Site) is home to variety of wildlife. Trailhead for several miles of hiking and biking trails is at end of causeway. Picnic area with drinking water and rest rooms. Daily sunrise to sunset; free. Access from Steamboat Park. 605/224-5862.

September 29–October 1, 1804
Oahe Dam/Lake Oahe (Pierre, SD)—Tour one of the largest rolled-earth dams. Exhibits explain how it provides power, recreation and irrigation to the area. Daily 10 to 8, tours 9 to 3:30 (Memorial Day-Labor Day); free. 8 miles N on SD 1806. 605/224-5862.
▲ **West Shore** (Pierre, SD)—Boating, fishing and swimming access. Daily sunrise to sunset. 8 miles N on SD 1806. 605/765-9410.
▲ **Cow-Spring Creek** (Pierre, SD)—31 sites (10 w/hookups);

free; water; primitive; open all year; grills/fire rings; tables; 14-day limit. Boat ramp/dock; marina; boat rental; groceries. 19 miles NW on SD 1804. 605/224-5862.
▲ **Little Bend** (Pierre, SD)—13 primitive sites; free; no water; primitive; open all year; grills/fire rings; tables. Boat ramp, dock. 24 miles N on SD 1804. 605/765-9410.
▲ **Bush's Landing Recreation Area** (Pierre, SD)—Primitive camping, boating and fishing access. 32 miles N of on SD 1804. 605/765-9410.

AROUND THE AREA

TOWNS LISTED ALPHABETICALLY

Fort Pierre, South Dakota
[1] ★ Verendrye Monument—Hike to the bluff where, in 1743, two brothers buried a lead tablet, staking claim to the land for France. Interpretation on how they set the stage for Lewis and Clark, and others. Daily 7am to 10pm; free. In town on US 83.

Pierre, South Dakota
Pierre Chamber of Commerce, 800 W. Dakota Ave. 605/224-7361, 800/962-2034.
Cowan Ranch—Trail rides along the Missouri or across the prairie. Reservations required. 605/224-5796.
[2] ★ South Dakota Cultural Heritage Center—Multimedia exhibits about the state's cultural and territorial history. Mon-Fri 9 to 4:30, Sat/Sun 1 to 4:30, admission fee for adults, free on 1st Sunday of month. 900 Governor's Dr. 605/773-3458.

South Dakota Discovery Center & Aquarium—Dozens of exhibits explore the physical sciences. Three aquariums and exhibits chronicle the life of the Missouri River. Mon-Sat 10 to 5, Sun 1 to 5 (summer), Sun-Fri 1 to 5, Sat 10 to 5 (rest of year); admission fee. 805 W. Sioux Ave. 605/224-8295.

South Dakota National Guard Museum—Military memorabilia both inside (weapons and uniforms) and out (Sherman tank and A-7D jet fighter). Mon/Wed/Fri 8 to 5; free. 301 E. Dakota St. 605/224-9991.

South Dakota Capitol—Fully restored terrazzo tile floor, marble staircases and leaded glass windows. Capitol Lake is home to Flaming Fountain Memorial and migrating waterfowl. Daily 8am to 10pm; free, guided tours. Capitol and Nicollett Aves. 605/773-3765.

⊞ **Budget Host**—36 rooms, indoor pool, pets, hot tub, 640 N. Euclid. 605/224-5896. $ K12

⊞ **Governor's Inn**—82 rooms, indoor pool, pets, continental breakfast, coin laundry, exercise room, hot tub. 700 W. Sioux Ave. 605/224-4200, 800/341-8000. $$ K18

⊞ **Kelly Inn**—47 rooms, pool, continental breakfast. 713 W. Sioux Ave. 605/224-4140. $ K16

⊗ **Cattleman's Club**—Hearty food and great river view. D only Mon-Sat. 5 miles E on US 34. 605/224-9774. $$

⊗ **KozyKorner**—Steak, seafood and soups, kids' menu. B L & D Mon-Sat. 217 E. Dakota. 605/224-9547. $

CHAPTER 10

October 2 to 24, 1804

PUSHING ON TO THE MANDANS

As autumn 1804 came on, the Corps of Discovery moved rapidly upriver and into today's North Dakota. Days grew shorter and nights colder, but the men ate well because game was plentiful and fat for winter. Overhead, birds flew south, and Captain William Clark noted "black clouds flying."

During this time, one of the men went against the captains. The Corps was now in danger-filled country, where every soldier had to obey orders without debate. Following their own orders, Clark and Captain Meriwether Lewis had to forestall mutiny. What they did, and how a visiting Arikara chief reacted, show interesting differences between the cultures.

On October 8, at the mouth of the Grand River, the Corps came to three villages of the Arikara, farmers who traded produce such as corn, beans, squash, and tobacco to the Sioux. Luckily for the Corps, trader Joseph Gravelines was there. He had lived among the Arikara for thirteen years, so the language barrier did not cause misunderstandings as it had with the Teton Sioux. Clark wrote that this visit was "all Tranquillity."

Pierre-Antoine Tabeau, a French-Canadian fur trader, also was with the Arikaras. He warned the captains that each village's chief—Lighting Crow or Crow at Rest, Hay, and Eagle's Feather—was equal to the others. The captains gave the same present to each: an American flag, a red coat and cocked hat, and a Jefferson Peace Medal. Then they named Lighting Crow the "Grand Chief."

The Arikaras used bullboats, well designed small boats of bison hide stretched over bowl-shaped willow frames. Clark marveled when, on a very windy day, he saw three women paddle safely across the river in a bullboat laden with meat, when "the waves were as high as I ever Saw them in the Missouri."

When they met together, the captains urged the Arikaras to end their wars with the Man-dans and others. The three chiefs agreed, and asked Lewis and Clark's help in making peace with the Mandans. When the boats pushed off on October 12, one of the chiefs—possibly Eagle's Feather—rode along to council with the Mandans.

The next day, Clark wrote uncomfortably that the party "passed a Camp of Sioux...those people did not Speak to us."

At the same time as that reminder of danger, the captains had had enough of Private John Newman's behavior. They arrested him for "repeated expressions of a highly criminal and mutinous nature," trying to undermine discipline and the expedition's purpose, and also trying to turn the men against their co-captains.

On October 13, a cold and rainy day, the Corps journeyed from early in the morning until noon, then halted to hold Newman's court-martial. Nine or possibly ten men made up the jury. Sgt. John Ordway, one of them, recorded that the trial lasted for two hours after Newman pleaded not guilty.

Newman was convicted, and sentenced to seventy-five lashes of the whip on his bare back. He also was "discarded from the permi-nent party engaged for North Western discov-ery." The captains agreed to this punishment, but allowed Newman to stay with the party over winter. They couldn't abandon him on the prairie without a weapon, but now he was a civilian and they couldn't give him govern-ment property. He was to do such work that winter as the captains assigned.

After the verdict, the Corps of Discovery traveled on the rest of the day in rain. Getting to the Mandan villages was that urgent.

The next day, October 14, they again trav-eled from early morning until noon, when they stopped on a sandbar to carry out Private Newman's whipping.

This form of punishment was standard in the U.S. Army, a tradition brought to these shores from Europe. But the Arikara chief traveling

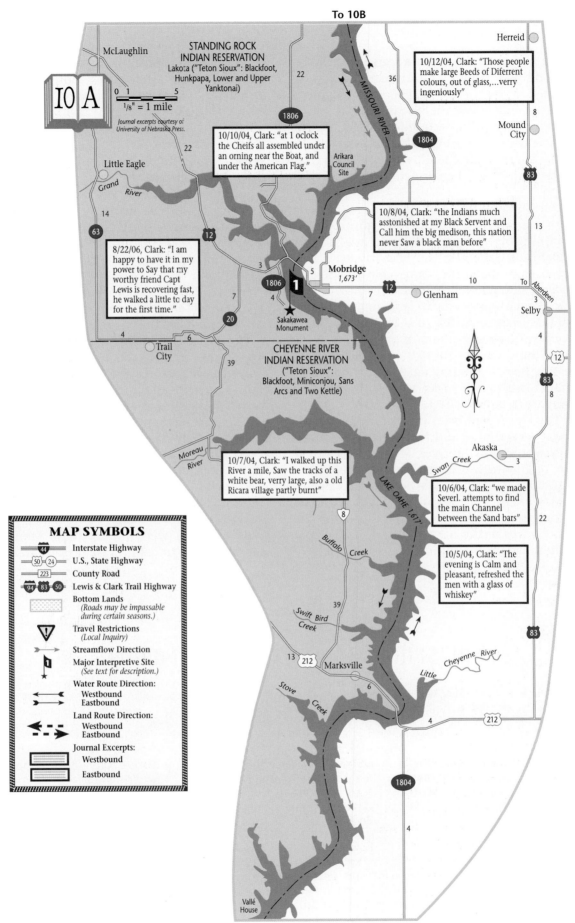

Herreid

McLaughlin

STANDING ROCK INDIAN RESERVATION
Lakota ("Teton Sioux": Blackfoot, Hunkpapa, Lower and Upper Yanktonai)

10/12/04, Clark: "Those people make large Beeds of Diferrent colours, out of glass,...verry ingeniously"

Mound City

IO A

0   1   5
1/8" = 1 mile
Journal excerpts courtesy of University of Nebraska Press.

22

1806

1804

8

10/10/04, Clark: "at 1 oclock the Cheifs all assembled under an orning near the Boat, and under the American Flag."

Little Eagle

22

Arikara Council Site

83

Grand River

14

10/8/04, Clark: "the Indians much asstonished at my Black Servent and Call him the big medison, this nation never Saw a black man before"

13

63

12

8/22/06, Clark: "I am happy to have it in my power to Say that my worthy friend Capt Lewis is recovering fast, he walked a little to day for the first time."

3

1806

5   Mobridge
1,673'

12   10   To Aberdeen

1

7

4

20

Sakakawea Monument

4

Glenham   3

Selby

Trail City

4   6

39

CHEYENNE RIVER INDIAN RESERVATION
("Teton Sioux": Blackfoot, Miniconjou, Sans Arcs and Two Kettle)

4

12

83

8

N

Akaska

3

Moreau River

Swan Creek

10/7/04, Clark: "I walked up this River a mile, Saw the tracks of a white bear, verry large, also a old Ricara village partly burnt"

10/6/04, Clark: "we made Severl. attempts to find the main Channel between the Sand bars"

22

8

LAKE OAHE 1,617'

10/5/04, Clark: "The evening is Calm and pleasant, refreshed the men with a glass of whiskey"

Buffalo Creek

MAP SYMBOLS

44	Interstate Highway
50 24	U.S., State Highway
223	County Road
94 83 50	Lewis & Clark Trail Highway
	Bottom Lands (Roads may be impassable during certain seasons.)
⚠	**Travel Restrictions** (Local Inquiry)
→	Streamflow Direction
⚑	**Major Interpretive Site** (See text for description.)
	Water Route Direction:
←→	Westbound
→→	Eastbound
	Land Route Direction:
	Westbound
	Eastbound
	Journal Excerpts:
	Westbound
	Eastbound

39

Swift Bird Creek

Cheyenne River

13   212   Marksville

Little

6

Stove

Creek

4   212

83

1804

4

Vallé House

along had never seen such a thing. Clark wrote that he was "allarmd" and "Cried aloud (or effected to Cry)" until "I explained the Cause of the punishment and the necessity..."

The chief replied, according to Clark, that he "thought examples were also necessary, & he himself had made them by Death, his nation never whiped even their Children, from their burth."

Punishment given, the men pushed on upriver a few more miles, crossing into today's North Dakota, camping that night at a site now under Lake Oahe near Langelier Bay Recreation Area. From here the Corps moved quickly upriver; dining on beavers that, Ordway noted, the French boatmen were trapping. Other wildlife was plentiful too: In today's Sioux County, Clark saw a herd of pronghorn swimming the river, the animals so numerous that Arikara boys swimming among them killed 58 animals with plain sticks. He also "counted 52 Gangues of Buffalow & 3 of Elk at one view..."

The Corps had been hearing from Indians about a very large and ferocious type of bear they would meet upriver. Its hair had a mixture of gray with black or brown, so that from a distance it could look silvery. Clark called it the "white bear" in his journals. Today, we call it the grizzly, nicknamed "silvertip" from the whitish tips of the hairs of its outer coat that seem silvery in the sunlight.

On October 20, hunting near abandoned Mandan lodges a few miles south of today's Bismarck, Private Pierre Cruzatte wounded a grizzly that escaped. Clark "Saw Several fresh tracks of that animal double the Sise of the largest track I ever Saw..." Their first grizzly—at today's Double Ditch Indian Village—was by no means their last.

As the Corps of Discovery pressed on toward their first winter's haven, Ordway's journal told the tale of the changing season:

Sunday 21st Oct. [camp at Heart River] *Some frozen rain last night   Snow this morning.... Snowed Slowly untill 12 oClock....*

Monday 22nd Oct. Some Snow last night....

Tuesday 23 Oct. a little Snow last night a cloudy morning....

The skies cleared, but the men did not dawdle.

Finally, on October 24, they met a Mandan hunting party about three miles south of today's Washburn. It was led by Chief Sheheke, whom European traders called Big White because of his heavy weight and light skin color. When the peace-seeking Arikara chief Eagle's Feather was introduced, the Mandans welcomed him and shared a peace pipe. After the Corps camped for the night, the Arikara chief visited the Mandans' camp. Later, when Eagle's Feather went home, some Mandans went with him to confirm their peace treaty.

TOURING TODAY

❧ PUSHING ON TO THE MANDANS ❧

[ ] Bracketed numbers key sites to maps	♿ Special-needs accessible	⊨ Bed & breakfast
★ L&C in-depth interpretation, unchanged landform	⊗ Restaurant	▲ Camping, RV park
• L&C interpreted site	⊞ Motel, hotel, cabin	

Bridges over the Missouri River in this area are west of Gettysburg, SD (US 212); Mobridge, SD (US 12); Mandan/Bismarck, ND (I-94).

ALONG THE EXPEDITION'S PATH

October 2-13, 1804
[1] Sakakawea Monument (Mo-

bridge, SD)—Near the probable site where the interpreter died six years after the expedition's conclusion. Interpretation about the Corps. 6 miles W on US 12, 4 miles S on SD 1806.

Lake Oahe (South Dakota)
Sutton Bay—Boating and fishing access and ▲ primitive camping, **no** water. 16 miles W of Agar on SD 1804. 605/765-9410.

Forest City—Boat ramp/dock and fishing access. ▲ Primitive camping, **no** water. 19 miles W of Gettysburg on US 212. 605/765-9410.

● **West Whitlock Area**—Replica of abandoned Arikara village and interpretive trail along river. ⊞ cabins, lake and river fishing. ▲ 103 sites (50 w/hookups); fee; water; modern; showers; open May-Oct; grills/fire rings; tables.

Ramp/dock; swimming; playground; dump station. 2 miles E on US 12, 1 mile S on paved access road. 605/845-2252.

Indian Memorial—▲ 81 sites (all w/hookups); fee; water; modern; showers; open all year; grills/fire rings; tables; 14-day limit. Swimming; ramp; playground; fishing. 3 miles W on US 12. 605/845-2252.

October 14, 1804

• **Langelier Bay Recreation Area (Linton, ND)**—Interpretive exhibit, fishing and boating access. ▲ Primitive camping. Always open; free. 32 miles from Linton on US 83.

October 15, 1804

[4] ★ **Fort Yates Historic Site** (Fort Yates, ND)—Once home to the Arikara, it is now on the Standing Rock Indian Reservation. Boating; fishing; picnic area. Always open; free. Off ND 24. 701/854-7231.

October 16, 1804
(Return Aug. 20, 1806)

• **Beaver Creek Recreation Area (Linton, ND)**—Nature trail to bluff with interpretation and overlook. ▲ 84 sites; fee; water; modern/primitive; open all year; grills/fire rings; tables. Fishing, boating, hiking, picnic area. Daily 6am to 10pm; free. 13 miles from Linton on ND 13, 2 miles SW on ND 1804. 701/255-0015.

October 19, 1804
(Return August 18, 1806)

• **Graner Park/Sugar Loaf Bottoms** (Mandan, ND)—Fishing, boating access. Hiking and interpretive signs. ▲ Primitive camping. Daily 6am to 10pm; free. 20 miles S on ND 1806. 701/667-3360

• **Kimball Bottoms** (Bismarck, ND)—Fishing and boating access. Hiking and wildlife viewing. ▲ Primitive camping. Daily 6am to 10pm; free. 7 miles S on ND 1804. 701/222-6714.

General Sibley Park (Bismarck, ND)—Shady county park with Missouri River access. Fishing; ramp; swimming; playground; nature and hiking trails. ▲ 120 sites (all w/hookups); fee; water; modern/primitive; showers; open May-

Oct; grills/fire rings; tables. 4 miles S on S. Washington St. (eastbound exit 34/westbound exit 37), 11 miles S. 701/222-1844.

October 20, 1804
(Return Aug. 18, 1806)

On-A-Slant Indian Village (Mandan, ND)—An advanced agricultural village of 1,000 in the 17th century. These earth lodges were already abandoned when Lewis and Clark passed by. Some have been reconstructed and have costumed interpreters. Artists-in-residence create traditional works, which are sold at the trading post. Located in Fort Abraham Lincoln State Park.

[2] ★ **Fort Abraham Lincoln State Park** (Mandan, ND)—Last post of Lieutenant Colonel George Custer with the 7th Cavalry. His home and other buildings have been reconstructed; costumed guides provide tours and living history interpretation. The visitor center takes you through time from days of the Mandan village here, through Lewis and Clark's visit, to the homesteading era. Nature and interpretive trails, horse trails and guided rides. Paved recreation trail runs to Bismarck/Mandan. The Fort Lincoln Trolley runs between the park and 3rd Street Station in Mandan. ▲ 97 sites (40 w/hookups); fee; water; modern; showers; open all year; grills/fire rings; tables. Hiking; playground; fishing. 5 miles S on ND 1806. 701/663-9571. Campground reservations 800/807-4723.

Oahe Wildlife Management Area (Mandan, ND)—Hardwood forest with wetlands is home to waterfowl, songbirds and deer. Hiking and ▲ primitive camping are allowed throughout the 23,500 acres. River access. Area is on both sides of the Missouri. From Mandan, 10 miles S on ND 1804. 701/224-3344.

October 21, 1804
(Return Aug. 18, 1806)

• **I-94 Mandan Scenic Overlook** (eastbound only)—Interpretative signs, picnic area.

October 22, 1804

• **Double Ditch Indian Village** (Bismarck, ND)—Earthlodge rings

still remain from the two different Indian villages erected here. A scenic overlook of the Missouri. 12 miles N on ND 1804. 701/328-2666.

AROUND THE AREA

TOWNS LISTED ALPHABETICALLY

Bismarck, North Dakota

Bismarck–Mandan Convention & Visitors Bureau, Burnt Boat Dr. and Tyler Parkway. 701/222-4308, 800/767-3555.

Camp Hancock State Historic Site—Established to protect railroad workers in the mid-1800s. Supply depot is a museum of railroad history. Grounds open dawn to dusk, museum Wed-Sun 1 to 5 (May-Sept); free. 1st & Main Streets. 701/224-2464.

Dakota Zoo—Primarily native plains animals with several exotic animal exhibits. Daily 10 to 8 (May-Sept); admission fee. Along the river, at E end of Memorial Bridge. 701/223-7543.

Former Governor's Mansion—Home to 23 chief executives since 1893. Wed-Sun 1 to 5 (May-Sept); free. 320 E Avenue B. 701/225-3819.

Highway 1804 Missouri River Auto Tour—For 30 miles this road follows the Missouri River. Designated stops at Double Ditch Indian Village, Steckel Boat Landing and Painted Woods Wildlife Management Area. Waterfowl, deer, pheasant and turkey are plentiful along the drive. Begins in Bismarck at Pioneer Park. 701/224-3344.

Lewis & Clark Riverboat—Cruise the Missouri aboard a replica 19th century paddlewheeler. Mon-Fri 2:30, Sat 2:30, 6:00, 8:30, Sun noon, 2:30, 7:00; admission fee. Under the Grant Marsh Bridge. 701/255-4233.

[3] ★ **North Dakota Heritage Center**—State historical museum exhibits span development from the state's geological beginnings, including interpretation of the Corps of Discovery. Interpreted arboretum trail. Mon-Fri 8 to 5, Sat 9 to 5, Sun 11 to 4; donations. Capitol Mall. 701/328-2666.

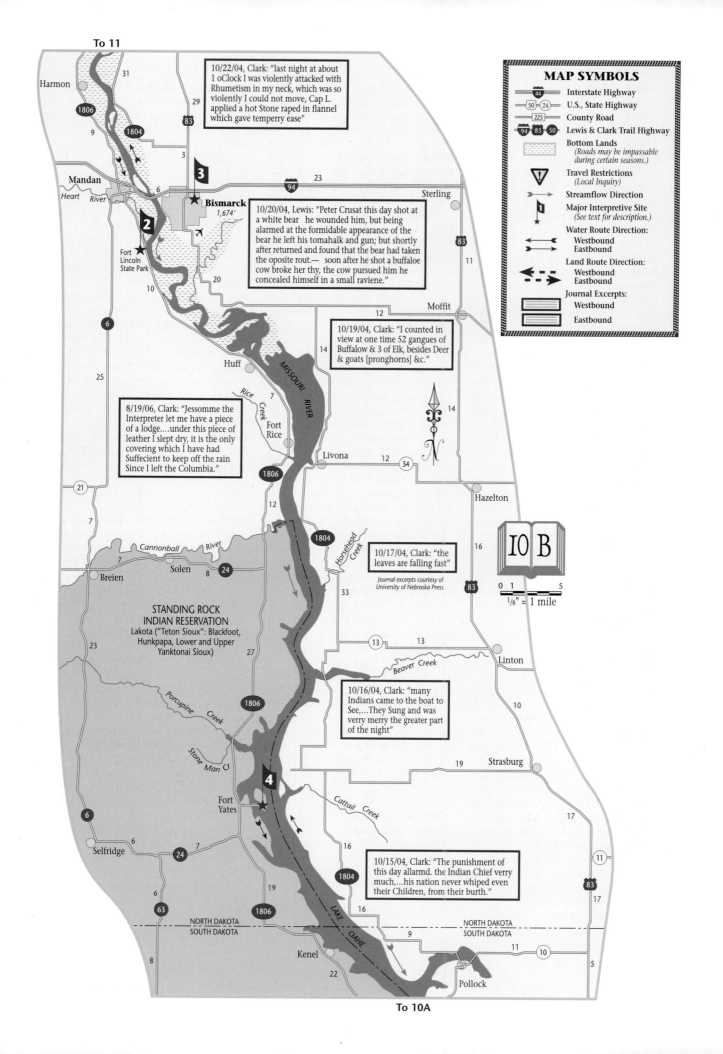

Harmon

31

29

1806

9

1804

3

10/22/04, Clark: "last night at about
1 oClock I was violently attacked with
Rhumetism in my neck, which was so
violently I could not move, Cap L.
applied a hot Stone raped in flannel
which gave temperry ease"

83

3

3

Mandan

Heart *River*

6

94   23   Sterling

★ Bismarck
1,674'

2

Fort
Lincoln
State Park ★

20

10/20/04, Lewis: "Peter Crusat this day shot at
a white bear   he wounded him, but being
alarmed at the formidable appearance of the
bear he left his tomahalk and gun; but
shortly after returned and found that the bear had taken
the oposite rout.— soon after he shot a buffaloe
cow broke her thy, the cow pursued him he
concealed himself in a small raviene."

83

11

6

10

12   Moffit

25

Huff

Rice *Creek*

7

Fort Rice

14

10/19/04, Clark: "I counted in
view at one time 52 gangues of
Buffalow & 3 of Elk, besides Deer
& goats [pronghorns] &c."

MISSOURI *RIVER*

8/19/06, Clark: "Jessomme the
Interpreter let me have a piece
of a lodge....under this piece of
leather I slept dry, it is the only
covering which I have had
Suffecient to keep off the rain
Since I left the Columbia."

14

N

Livona

12   34

21

Hazelton

16

7

12

1804

10/17/04, Clark: "the
leaves are falling fast"

Horsehead *Creek*

Journal excerpts courtesy of
University of Nebraska Press.

1806

12

Cannonball   *River*

7

Solen

8   24

Breien

33

83

**STANDING ROCK
INDIAN RESERVATION**
Lakota ("Teton Sioux": Blackfoot,
Hunkpapa, Lower and Upper
Yanktonai Sioux)

27

23

13   13

Linton

10/16/04, Clark: "many
Indians came to the boat to
See,...They Sung and was
verry merry the greater part
of the night"

Beaver *Creek*

10

Porcupine *Creek*

1806

Stone Man Cr

4

★

Fort
Yates

Cattail *Creek*

19   Strasburg

17

16

1804

10/15/04, Clark: "The punishment of
this day allarmd. the Indian Chief verry
much,...his nation never whiped even
their Children, from their burth."

11

83

17

6

Selfridge

6

24   7

16

19

6

63

1806

NORTH DAKOTA   NORTH DAKOTA
SOUTH DAKOTA   SOUTH DAKOTA

9

11   10

8

Kenel

LAKE *OAHE*

22

Pollock

5

MAP SYMBOLS

44	Interstate Highway
50 24	U.S., State Highway
223	County Road
94 83 50	Lewis & Clark Trail Highway
	Bottom Lands *(Roads may be impassable during certain seasons.)*
▽!	Travel Restrictions *(Local Inquiry)*
	Streamflow Direction
1	Major Interpretive Site *(See text for description.)*
	Water Route Direction: Westbound / Eastbound
	Land Route Direction: Westbound / Eastbound
	Journal Excerpts: Westbound / Eastbound

10 B

0   1   5
⅛" = 1 mile

North Dakota Capitol—Guided tours of the 19-story "skyscraper of the prairie." Statue of Sakakawea—the Hidatsa spelling is preferred in North Dakota—on the grounds. Mon-Fri 8 to 5, Sat 9 to 4, Sun 1 to 4 (hourly tours in summer); free. End of N. 6th St. 701/328-2480.

Ward Village Overlook—View the Missouri from the hill above Pioneer Park. Interpretation and trail through remains of 18th century Mandan village. Daily dawn to dusk (Mar-Oct); free. N. Grandview Rd. off Burnt Boat Rd.

⚠ Bismarck KOA—118 sites (84 w/hookups); fee; water; modern: showers; open Apr-Oct; grills/fire rings; tables. ⊞ Cabins; pool; playground; coin laundry; groceries. 1 mile N of I-94 exit 161. 701/222-2662.

⊞ Best Western Doublewood Inn—143 rooms, pets, pool, hot tub. ♿. I-94 exit 159. 701/258-7000, 800/554-7077. $$ K18

⊞ Expressway Inn—163 rooms, pool, pets, continental breakfast, hot tub, playground. 200 Bismarck Expressway. 701/222-2900, 800/456-6388. $ K14

⊞ Holiday Inn—215 rooms, pets, indoor pool, hot tub, exercise room, ⊗ restaurant. ♿. 605 E. Broadway. 701/255-6000. $$$ K18

⊞ Radisson Inn Bismarck—306 rooms, pool, pets, restaurant, hot tub, exercise room. 800 S. 3rd St. 701/258-7700, 800/333-3333. $$ K18

⊗ Meriwether's—On the banks of the Missouri River, Dakota-style American cuisine, including game. Kids' menu. L & D daily, Sun brunch. I-94 exit 157, 0.25 mile N on Tyler Pkwy, 0.75 mile W on Burnt Boat Rd., 0.75 mile S on N. River Rd. 701/224-0455. $$$

⊗ Caspar's East 40—American food with fireplace ambiance, kids' menu. L & D Mon.-Sat. I-94 exit 159. 701/258-7222. $$$

⊗ Peacock Alley—Turn-of-the-20th-century hotel, kids' menu. L & D Mon-Sat, Sun brunch. 422 E. Main. 701/255-7917. $$

Fort Yates, North Dakota
Standing Rock—Sacred to the Arikara and the Dakota Sioux tribes. Legend is that an Indian woman, jealous of her husband's other wives, refused to travel when the tribe left camp. A party later returned to find her and her child turned to stone. Always open; free. Opposite the Standing Rock Tribal Agency Office. 701/854-7291.

Gettysburg, South Dakota
Dakota Sunset Museum—Highlight is 20-foot Medicine Rock near the Little Cheyenne River. Legend is that the Sioux tribes held healing ceremonies around it. Daily 1 to 5 (Memorial Day to Labor Day); donations. 205 W. Commercial. 605/765-9480.

⚠ Gettysburg City Park—15 sites (5 w/hookups); fee; water; modern; showers; open May-Sept; grills/fire rings; tables. Wading pool; play ground. 5 blocks S on US 212 & Main St. 605/765-2264.

⚠ South Whitlock Resort—42 sites (40 w/hookups); fee; water; modern; showers; open Apr-Nov; grills/fire rings; tables. Boat ramp/dock/rental; fishing; coin laundry; groceries; dump station. 8 miles W on US 212. 605/765-9762.

Mandan, North Dakota
⚠ Mandan Camping Area—25 sites (6 w/hookups); fee; water; modern; showers; open May-Sept; grills/fire rings; tables. Playground; indoor pool; tennis courts. 3rd St. SE. 701/667-3280.

⊞ Seven Seas Inn—103 rooms, pets, pool, ⊗ restaurant, hot tub. I-94 exit 152. 7 01/663-7401. $$ K18

Mobridge, South Dakota
Oscar Howe Indian Murals—Created by a Lakota Sioux to portray tribal culture. Mon-Fri 8 to noon, 11 to 5; free. Scherr-Howe Arena, 212 Main. 605/845-3700.

Klein Museum—One-room school and Lakota Sioux artifacts. Weekdays 9 to 5 (closed Tue), Sat/Sun 1 to 5 (Apr-Oct); admission fee. 1.5 miles W on US 12. 605/845-7243.

Sitting Bull Burial Site—The Sioux chief died near here in 1890, and was reburied here in 1953. Panoramic view of the Missouri Valley. Always open; free. 6 miles W on US 12, 4 miles S on paved rd. 605/845-2387.

⊞ Wrangler Motor Inn—61 rooms, pets, pool, exercise room, hot tub, ⊗ restaurants. 820 W. Grand Crossing. 605/845-3641, 800/341-8000. $$ K13.

⊗ Dakota Country Cafe—Homestyle food, kids' menu. 122 W. Grand Crossing. 605/845-7495. $

⊗ The Wheel—Casual and hearty fare served overlooking Lake Oahe. B L & D daily, lunch buffet. 0.5 mile W on US 12, 605/845-7474. $

Moffit, North Dakota
Long Lake National Wildlife Refuge—Geese, gulls and sandhill cranes are among the species that migrate here. Picnic area. Stop at the headquarters (7:30 to 4) for permission to enter. Daily sunrise to sunset; free. SE from town on US83 and over dike. 701/387-4397.

New Salem, North Dakota
Salem Sue—At 38 feet tall and 50 feet long, she's touted as the world's largest cow. I-94 exit 27 S (but you can see her from the Interstate).

⚠ North Park—15 sites (3 w/hookups); free; water; modern; open all year/full operation May-Sept; grills/fire rings; tables. Golf course; tennis courts; playground. 0.25 mile S, 0.75 mile W of I-94 exit 27.

CHAPTER 11

October 26, 1804 to April 7, 1805

WINTER AT FORT MANDAN

The Corps of Discovery reached the area of their first winter's camp on October 26, 1804. Two Mandan villages sat on either side of the Missouri near the mouth of the Knife River, and **[2]** three Hidatsa villages were arranged north up the Knife (see map 11A). Smallpox in the 1790s had reduced the Mandan people from nine villages to only two, and now they lived near the Hidatsa for mutual protection.

After their troubles with the Teton Sioux, captains Meriwether Lewis and William Clark were especially cautious of the Mandans and Hidatsas. Over four days, the captains met with chiefs of the villages, presenting through interpreters the ideas of peace with the Arikara and trade with and allegiance to the "new father." The diplomacy went slowly—blowing sand made the council site uncomfortable, and not all chiefs were able to attend each day. The successful conclusion, including smoking the pipe with the visiting Arikara chief, marked the beginning of friendships between the captains and especially chiefs Black Cat and Sheheke.

On November 2, men of the Corps began building a two-winged, stockaded fort of cottonwood logs. Sergeant John Ordway noted that "our huts" were "4 Rooms 14 feet Square" on each of two walls. This rough little shelter was grandly named **[1]** Fort Mandan, "in honour of our Neighbours." Even though the fort was unfinished, the Corps moved into it only two weeks later, when the weather turned colder.

The Mandans were farmers who traded with other Indians, the French, and the English. Over the winter, many Indian and white visitors came to the villages and Fort Mandan. The captains quizzed everyone about lands up the Missouri River, carefully recording it all. When the keelboat went downriver next spring, they would send a duplicate of these notes with it.

Among other things, the Mandans said that crossing the Rocky Mountains would take only half a day by horseback up the east side.

Also over this winter, the co-captains wrote detailed observations on the plants, animals, and Native Americans met so far (including vocabularies of the languages). They copied out the daily astronomical observations to aid mapmakers, and Clark drew their maps. They prepared animal and bird skeletons and hides to send back to President Jefferson. In case the expedition did not return from the Pacific, at least some knowledge they had gathered would be preserved.

The men of the Corps spent much time hunting, then as spring neared, they built six canoes of cottonwood. A big part of the winter's diet was corn obtained from the Mandans. Someone cut up an iron stove that had burned out on the trip upriver, and the Mandans traded corn for four-inch-square metal pieces that they used to make arrowheads and bison-hide–scrapers.

In November, Toussaint Charbonneau arrived at camp and offered his services as interpreter and cook. This forty-six-year-old Frenchman spoke no English, but his two wives were Shoshones. The captains expected to trade with the Shoshones for horses to carry their gear over the Rockies, and welcomed this help. It would be slow and awkward: the captains speaking English to one of the French-and-English speakers in the Corps, who spoke French to Charbonneau, who could speak Hidatsa to his wives, who would then translate the message into their native Shoshone.

Only one of the wives went with the Corps the next spring. She was Sacagawea, then fifteen or sixteen years old. (Her name also is transliterated into English as Sacajawea and Sakakawea, and the latter spelling from Hidatsa is preferred in the Dakotas.) Early in 1804, Charbonneau married her from the Hidatsa village where she had lived for five years after being captured in future Montana. On February 11, 1805, Sacagawea gave birth to a son, Jean Baptiste Charbonneau, whom she carried to the Pacific and back on a cradleboard. During the trip, the captains nicknamed him Pomp.

Christmas 1804 began with three volleys of the men's rifles awakening their captains before dawn. Clark also allowed cannon fire at the day's flag-raising. While some hunted, others danced "untill 9 oClock P. M., when the frolick ended &c." On New Year's Day 1805, 16 of the men entertained a neighboring village, their music and dancing calming "Some little miss understanding" between whites and Indians. When York danced, it "Some what astonished them, that So large a man Should be active."

In March of 1805, as ice on the Missouri began to break up and the river level rose from melting snow, the Corps began preparing to head out. On the 18th, Clark wrote: "a cold cloudy Day...I pack up all the merchindize into 8 packs equally devided So as to have Something of every thing in each Canoe & perogue." Twelve days later, still held by weather, he noted that the men were "in high Spirits...fiew nights pass without a Dance."

The Corps of Discovery were eager to travel on toward the country that whites had never before seen.

At last, the permanent party's thirty-three people and one dog turned their two pirogues and six canoes north up the Missouri River into new lands.

Simultaneously, on April 7, with Corporal Richard Warfington in charge, the return party headed downriver in the keelboat, taking the reports, plant and animal specimens, and even a living prairie dog, prairie hen, and four magpies (of the six creatures, only one magpie made it to Washington alive).

TOURING TODAY

❧ FORT MANDAN AREA ❧

[ ] Bracketed numbers key sites to maps	♿ Special-needs accessible	⊨ Bed & breakfast	
★ L&C in-depth interpretation, unchanged landform	⊗ Restaurant	⛺ Camping, RV park	
● L&C interpreted site	⊞ Motel, hotel, cabin		

Bridge over the Missouri on Alt. 200 at Washburn.

ALONG THE EXPEDITION'S PATH

Oct. 24, 1804
Return Aug. 17, 1806
● **Cross Ranch State Park** (Washburn, ND)—Nestled along a rare, free-flowing stretch of the Missouri, this park protects cultural and natural history. Visitor center with summer interpretive programs. 15 miles of hiking trails. ⛺ 85 primitive sites; fee; water; modern/primitive; showers; open all year; grills/fire rings; tables. ⊞ Cabin. Boat ramp. Daily dawn to dusk; admission fee. 8 miles SW on ND 1806. 701/794-3731.

Cross Ranch Nature Preserve (Washburn, ND)—Self-guided trail winds through 6,000 acres of forest and prairie ecosystems. Daily dawn to dusk; free. 8 miles SW on ND 1806, across from state park. 701/794-8741.

Oct. 26, 1804 to Apr. 7, 1805
Return Aug. 17, 1806
[1] ★ **Fort Mandan** (Fort Mandan, ND)—Replica of the expedition's 1804-1805 winter fort. Interpreted tours daily in summer, expanded interpretation on weekends. Always open; free. 2.5 miles W of U S 83 on CR 17. 701/462-8535.

[2] ★ **Knife River Indian Villages National Historic Site** (Stanton, ND)—Take the history trail or the nature trail to explore excavations of earthlodge villages visited by the expedition during the winter of 1804-05. Here they met Sacagawea and Charbonneau. Guided tours of replica of furnished Mandan earthlodge at 11, 1, and 3 during the summer. Exhibits and interpretive information at the eagle-shaped visitor center recount the site's history. Daily 8 to 6 (summer), 8 to 4:30 (winter); donations. 0.5 mile N on the river. 701/745-3309.

[3] ● **Fort Clark State Historic Site** (Stanton, ND)—A fur trading post was erected here following the Corps' encampment. Smallpox wiped out those living in the fort and the adjacent Mandan village and the fort was not reopened until the 1850s. Self-guided tour of earthlodge rings and trading post foundation. Summer interpretive programs. Daily sunrise to sunset; free. 7.5 miles SE on ND 200A. 701/328-3567.

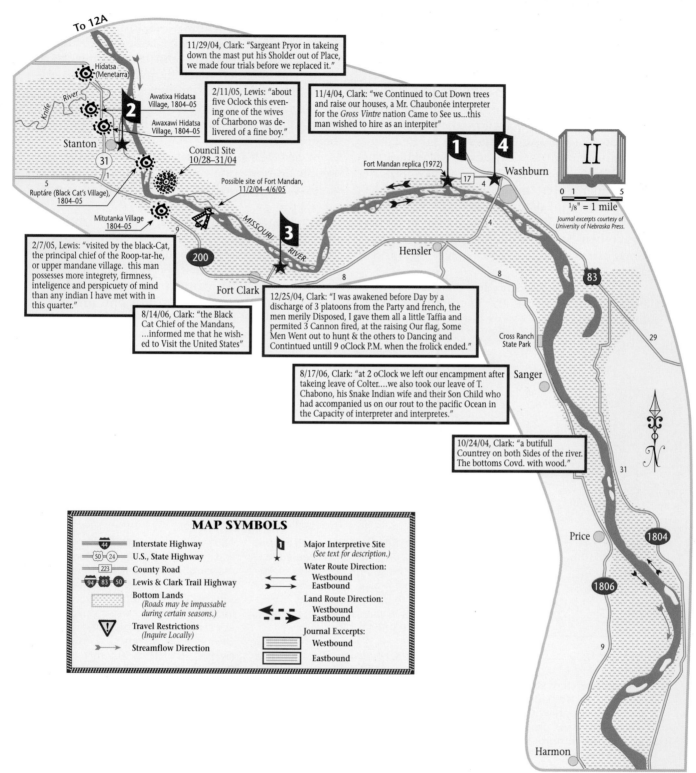

To 12A

Hidatsa (Menetarra)

Awatixa Hidatsa Village, 1804–05

Awaxawi Hidatsa Village, 1804–05

2

Knife River

Stanton

31

5 / 1

Ruptáre (Black Cat's Village), 1804–05

Mitutanka Village 1804–05

Council Site 10/28–31/04

Possible site of Fort Mandan, 11/2/04–4/6/05

MISSOURI

9

200

3

RIVER

Fort Clark

8

Fort Mandan replica (1972)

1 **4**

17

4

Washburn

4

Hensler

8

Cross Ranch State Park

Sanger

83

29

Price **1804**

1806

9

31

Harmon

To 10B

11/29/04, Clark: "Sargeant Pryor in takeing down the mast put his Sholder out of Place, we made four trials before we replaced it."

2/11/05, Lewis: "about five Oclock this evening one of the wives of Charbono was delivered of a fine boy."

11/4/04, Clark: "we Continued to Cut Down trees and raise our houses, a Mr. Chaubonée interpreter for the *Gross Vintre* nation Came to See us...this man wished to hire as an interpiter"

2/7/05, Lewis: "visited by the black-Cat, the principal chief of the Roop-tar-he, or upper mandane village. this man possesses more integrety, firmness, inteligence and perspicuety of mind than any indian I have met with in this quarter."

8/14/06, Clark: "the Black Cat Chief of the Mandans, ...informed me that he wished to Visit the United States"

12/25/04, Clark: "I was awakened before Day by a discharge of 3 platoons from the Party and french, the men merily Disposed, I gave them all a little Taffia and permited 3 Cannon fired, at the raising Our flag, Some Men Went out to hunt & the others to Dancing and Contintued untill 9 oClock P.M. when the frolick ended."

8/17/06, Clark: "at 2 oClock we left our encampment after takeing leave of Colter....we also took our leave of T. Chabono, his Snake Indian wife and their Son Child who had accompanied us on our rout to the pacific Ocean in the Capacity of interpreter and interpretes."

10/24/04, Clark: "a butifull Countrey on both Sides of the river. The bottoms Covd. with wood."

II

0 1 5
⅛" = 1 mile

Journal excerpts courtesy of University of Nebraska Press.

MAP SYMBOLS

- **44** Interstate Highway
- **50 24** U.S., State Highway
- **223** County Road
- **94 83 50** Lewis & Clark Trail Highway
- Bottom Lands *(Roads may be impassable during certain seasons.)*
- ⚠ Travel Restrictions *(Inquire Locally)*
- Streamflow Direction

- **1** Major Interpretive Site *(See text for description.)*
- Water Route Direction:
  - Westbound
  - Eastbound
- Land Route Direction:
  - Westbound
  - Eastbound
- Journal Excerpts:
  - Westbound
  - Eastbound

[4] ★ **Lewis and Clark Interpretive Center** (Washburn, ND)—Exhibits and displays provide overview of entire expedition with primary emphasis on the winter at Fort Mandan. Music enhances hands-on experiences. Interpretive programs and demonstrations throughout the summer. Bergquist Gallery features one of four exisiting complete sets of Karl Bodmer prints, including portraits made at Fort Clark in 1833. Lewis and Clark Days are held in early June each year. Gift shop. Daily 9 to 7 (Memorial Day-Labor Day), 9 to 5 (rest of year); admission fee. US 83 & ND 200A. 701/462-8535.

AROUND THE AREA

TOWNS LISTED ALPHABETICALLY

Washburn, North Dakota
McLean County Historical Museums—A 1905 courthouse and old store; Indian artifacts, military uniforms, and pioneer memorabilia. Lewis and Clark mural and expedition exhibits. Tue-Sat 1 to 5 (June-Aug); donations. 610 Main. 701/462-3526.

▦ **Scot Wood Motel**—25 rooms; pets. 1 mile S of ND 200 off US 83. 1323 Frontage Rd. 701/462-8191. $

CHAPTER 12

April 8 to 26, 1805

TO THE YELLOWSTONE RIVER

Traveling north and then west up the Missouri River, the Corps of Discovery moved rapidly across today's western North Dakota in the spring of 1805. Paddling and poling the pirogues and canoes, they moved twenty-five or more miles a day. When the wind was right, they put up sails and sped along at three miles an hour!

But high wind also could slow them down, as on April 19 when it was blowing so hard they "dared not to venture our canoes on the river" but rather stayed "in a safe harbour" (Lewis). On the 25th, the early morning wind was so cold that "the water friezed on the oars...as the men rowed."

Worse, on April 13, a squall of wind had almost overturned the white pirogue, the boat the Corps thought their "most steady and safe." Interpreter Toussaint Charbonneau, not a very good sailor, was steering when the wind came up. He turned the wrong direction and only made things worse for a few minutes. Captain

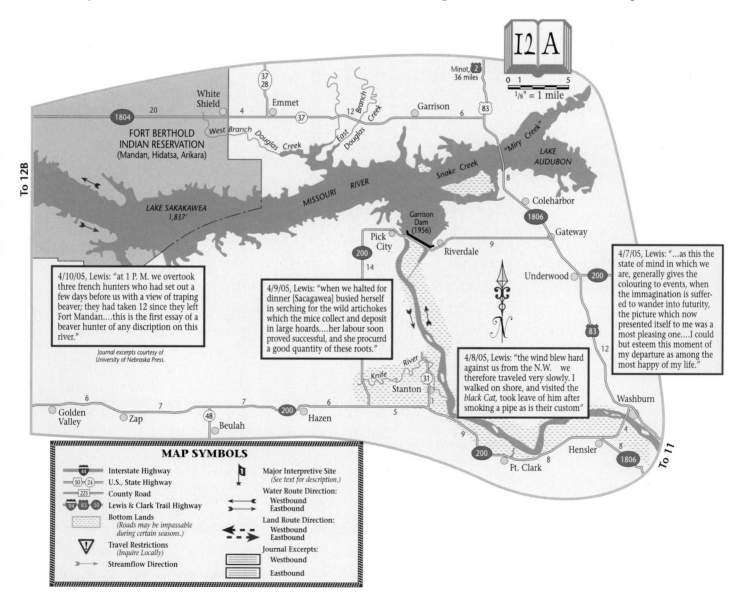

12 A

0   1   5
$1/8" = 1$ mile

4/10/05, Lewis: "at 1 P. M. we overtook three french hunters who had set out a few days before us with a view of traping beaver; they had taken 12 since they left Fort Mandan....this is the first essay of a beaver hunter of any discription on this river."

Journal excerpts courtesy of University of Nebraska Press.

4/9/05, Lewis: "when we halted for dinner [Sacagawea] busied herself in serching for the wild artichokes which the mice collect and deposit in large hoards....her labour soon proved successful, and she procurrd a good quantity of these roots."

4/8/05, Lewis: "the wind blew hard against us from the N.W.   we therefore traveled very slowly. I walked on shore, and visited the *black Cat,* took leave of him after smoking a pipe as is their custom"

4/7/05, Lewis: "...as this the state of mind in which we are, generally gives the colouring to events, when the immagination is suffered to wander into futurity, the picture which now presented itself to me was a most pleasing one....I could but esteem this moment of my departure as among the most happy of my life."

MAP SYMBOLS

- Interstate Highway
- U.S., State Highway
- County Road
- Lewis & Clark Trail Highway
- Bottom Lands
  (Roads may be impassable during certain seasons.)
- Travel Restrictions
  (Inquire Locally.)
- Streamflow Direction

- Major Interpretive Site
  (See text for description.)
- Water Route Direction:
  Westbound
  Eastbound
- Land Route Direction:
  Westbound
  Eastbound
- Journal Excerpts:
  Westbound
  Eastbound

Meriwether Lewis ordered the sails taken down quickly, and sent interpreter George Drouillard to the helm.

On board at the time were Charbonneau's wife Sacagawea and their baby boy, the two captains, three men who couldn't swim, the precious astronomical instruments, the journals and medicines, plus the best presents saved for Indians yet to be seen. The river's waves were high, and Lewis thought that if the boat had overturned, all the people "would most probably have perished." Charbonneau was to get them all into similar trouble just a month later.

Wildflowers were in bloom and wildlife was abundant. Lewis noted on April 19 that "The beaver of this part of the Missouri are larger, fatter, more abundant and better clad with fur than those of any other part of the country that I have yet seen." Mosquitoes began to be "very troublesome to us," just as they are for today's travelers. On the 22nd, Lewis and his Newfoundland dog, Seaman, were walking on the shore when he temporarily acquired another big pet: "I met with a buffaloe calf which attatched itself to me and continued to follow close at my heels untill I embarked and left it. it appeared allarmed at my dog which

was probably the cause of it's so readily attaching itself to me."

The Corps knew they were nearing the Yellowstone River, because this area had been described well by the Hidatsas, Charbonneau, and Jean Baptiste Lepage—a French trapper who had enlisted at Fort Mandan. High winds slowed down the boats; Captain William Clark wrote that "dureing those winds we eat Drink & breeth…Sand"). On April 25, Lewis took a few men and headed overland in a straight line in the direction of the Yellowstone, to gain enough time to "make the necessary observations" of its latitude and longitude without detaining all the Corps. They reached the Yellowstone two miles upstream from its mouth, where they camped. The next day they walked down the Yellowstone to the Missouri and back.

Clark and the others coming via the Missouri reached the mouth of the Yellowstone at noon the following day. Both he and Lewis thought the site on the Missouri's south side would be excellent for a trading post. Indeed, forts later were built there, but on the **[2]** Missouri's opposite shore. These were Fort Union, a fur trading post built twenty-four years later, and military Fort Buford built in 1866.

TOURING TODAY

⤳ TO THE YELLOWSTONE RIVER ⤶

[ ] Bracketed numbers key sites to maps	♿ Special-needs accessible ⊨ Bed & breakfast
★ L&C in-depth interpretation, unchanged landform	⊗ Restaurant ⋀ Camping, RV park
● L&C interpreted site	⊞ Motel, hotel, cabin

Bridges over the Missouri River in this area are at Garrison Dam (ND 200); New Town, ND (ND 23); Williston, ND (US 85); Ft. Union, ND (ND58).

ALONG THE EXPEDITION'S PATH

April 8, 1805
Garrison Dam National Fish Hatchery (Riverdale, ND)—Hatchery for northern pike, smallmouth bass, walleye, chinook salmon,

paddlefish, crappie and trout. Dioramas and aquarium. Daily 8:30 to 3:30; free. 701/654-7441.

April 9-10, 1805
● **Beulah Bay** (Beulah, ND)—⋀ 70 sites (50 w/hookups); fee; water; primitive; open Apr-Nov; grills/fire rings; tables; firewood. Boat ramp/dock; swimming; playground; hiking trails. 15 miles N of ND 200 on ND 49. 701/873-5916.

April 11-12, 1805
(Return August 13, 1806)
● **Indian Hills Recreation Area**

(Garrison, ND)—Mile long road/trail leads to hilltop interpretation point. ⋀ 47 sites (20 w/hookups); fee; water; modern/primitive; showers; open all year; grills/fire rings; tables. ⊞ Cabin rentals; boating; fishing; hiking trails. 34 miles SW of Garrison on ND 1804. 701/743-4122.
● **Fort Stevenson State Park** (Garrison, ND)—Interpretation area and exhibits on the expedition. Activities focus on Lake Sakakawea with marina/boat rentals, fishing/cleaning station and swimming beach. ⋀ 145 sites (100 w/hookups); fee;

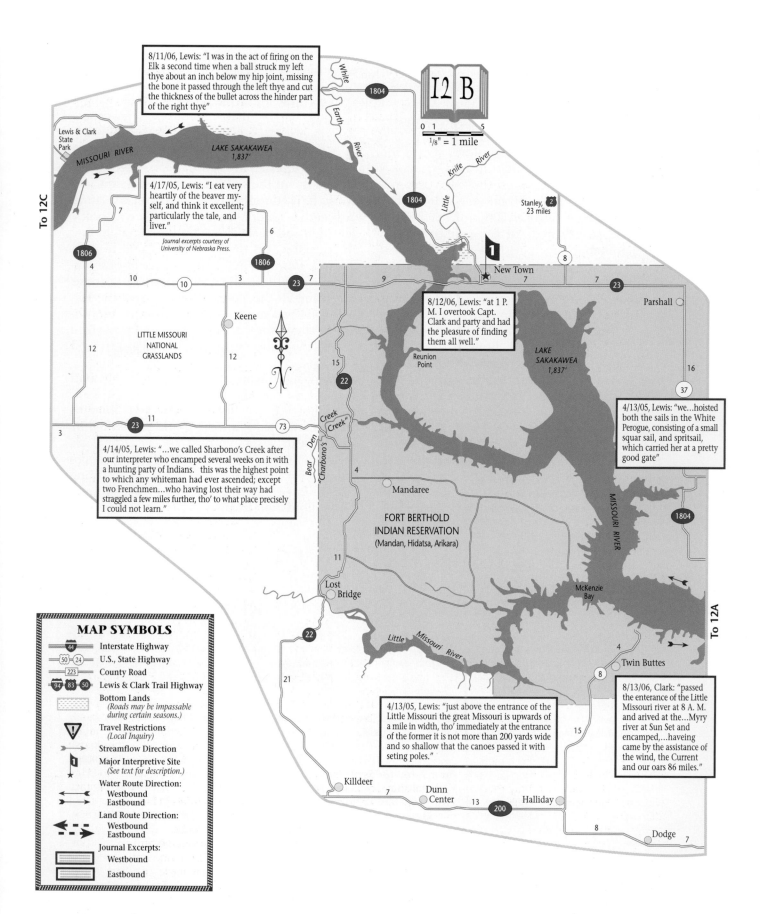

8/11/06, Lewis: "I was in the act of firing on the Elk a second time when a ball struck my left thye about an inch below my hip joint, missing the bone it passed through the left thye and cut the thickness of the bullet across the hinder part of the right thye"

4/17/05, Lewis: "I eat very heartily of the beaver my-self, and think it excellent; particularly the tale, and liver."

Journal excerpts courtesy of University of Nebraska Press.

8/12/06, Lewis: "at 1 P. M. I overtook Capt. Clark and party and had the pleasure of finding them all well."

4/13/05, Lewis: "we...hoisted both the sails in the White Perogue, consisting of a small squar sail, and spritsail, which carried her at a pretty good gate"

4/14/05, Lewis: "...we called Sharbono's Creek after our interpreter who encamped several weeks on it with a hunting party of Indians. this was the highest point to which any whiteman had ever ascended; except two Frenchmen...who having lost their way had straggled a few miles further, tho' to what place precisely I could not learn."

4/13/05, Lewis: "just above the entrance of the Little Missouri the great Missouri is upwards of a mile in width, tho' immediately at the entrance of the former it is not more than 200 yards wide and so shallow that the canoes passed it with seting poles."

8/13/06, Clark: "passed the enterance of the Little Missouri river at 8 A. M. and arived at the...Myry river at Sun Set and encamped,...haveing came by the assistance of the wind, the Current and our oars 86 miles."

MISSOURI RIVER

LAKE SAKAKAWEA 1,837'

Lewis & Clark State Park

To 12C

Keene

LITTLE MISSOURI NATIONAL GRASSLANDS

New Town

Stanley, 23 miles

Parshall

LAKE SAKAKAWEA 1,837'

Reunion Point

Mandaree

FORT BERTHOLD INDIAN RESERVATION (Mandan, Hidatsa, Arikara)

Lost Bridge

McKenzie Bay

Twin Buttes

Killdeer

Dunn Center

Halliday

Dodge

MISSOURI RIVER

Little Missouri River

Bear Den Creek

"Charbono's Creek"

MAP SYMBOLS

44	Interstate Highway
50 24	U.S., State Highway
223	County Road
94 83 50	Lewis & Clark Trail Highway
	Bottom Lands *(Roads may be impassable during certain seasons.)*
⚠	Travel Restrictions *(Local Inquiry)*
→	Streamflow Direction
★	Major Interpretive Site *(See text for description.)*

Water Route Direction:
← → Westbound
→ Eastbound

Land Route Direction:
← -- - Westbound
- - → Eastbound

Journal Excerpts:
Westbound
Eastbound

water; modern; showers; open all year/full operation May-Sept; grills/fire rings; tables; firewood. Groceries; dump station. 3 miles S on CR 15. 701/337-5576.

April 14, 1805
(Return Aug. 12, 1806)
[1] ★ **Three Tribes Museum** (New Town, ND)—History and culture of the Three Affiliated Tribes (Arikara, Mandan, Hidatsa), some expedition-related exhibits. Daily 10 to 6; admission fee. W on ND 23. 701/627-4477.

• **Crow Flies High Butte Historic Site** (New Town, ND)—In the area where Clark's party and Lewis's reunited on the return in 1806. Several exhibits provide interpretation of 1805 and 1806 campsites. Always open. 2 miles W on ND 23. 701/859-3071.

April 17, 1805
• **Lewis and Clark State Park** (Williston, ND)—Upland birds, wildlife viewing on hiking trails, spring wildflowers. Self-guided nature trail through intact native prairie. ▲ 87 sites (52 w/hookups); fee; water; modern; showers; open all year/full operation May-Sept; grills/fire rings; tables. Swimming; boating; fishing; playground; groceries; dump station. 16 miles E on ND 1804, 3 miles S on Co 15. 701/859-3071.

April 18, 1805
• **Tobacco Garden Bay** (Watford City, ND)—▲ 65 sites (all w/hookups); fee; water; modern; showers; open May-Oct; grills/fire rings; tables. Swimming; boat ramp/dock; boat rentals; fishing; playground; groceries; dump station. 26 miles N on ND 1806. 701/842-6931.

April 25-26, 1805
(Clark return Aug. 3, 1806)
[2] ★ **Fort Union Trading Post National Historic Site** (Williston, ND)—Built in 1828 for John Jacob Astor's American Fur Company, the fort was an immediate success for trade with Plains Indians. It was a melting pot of tribes and nationalities. Visitors included artists John James Audubon and George Catlin, Father Pierre DeSmet and Prince Maximilian of Wied. It was disman-

tled in the late 1860s, but you can visit the National Park Service's excellent reconstruction and the Lewis and Clark Expedition wayside exhibit. Interpretive programs, tours. Daily 8 to 8 (Memorial Day-Labor Day), 9 to 5:30 (rest of year); donations. 24 miles SW on US 2 and ND 1804. 701/572-9083.

[2] • **Fort Buford State Historic Site/Missouri-Yellowstone Confluence** (Williston, ND)—Both Sitting Bull, who surrendered here in 1881, and Chief Joseph, brought here after his 1877 surrender, were held in the guardhouse. Museum exhibits and some original buildings. Waterfowl, songbirds, deer, small mammals, owls, hawks and eagles. Fishing for paddlefish. Confluence can be seen from picnic area, and a path runs from the picnic area down to the river bottom. ▲ Primitive camping. Daily 9 to 6 (May-Sept); donations. 22 miles SW on US 2 and ND 1804. 701/572-9034.

AROUND THE AREA

TOWNS LISTED ALPHABETICALLY

Sections of Hwys 1804 and 1806—226 paved miles for hiking and biking along the Lewis and Clark National Historic Trail.

Alexander, North Dakota
• **Lewis and Clark Trail Museum**—Scale model of Fort Mandan and other exhibits on 19th century pioneer and homesteading life. Mon-Sat 9 to 5, Sun 1 to 5 (Memorial Day-Labor Day); admission fee. Downtown on US 85. 701/828-3595.

Beulah, North Dakota
Great Plains Synfuels Plant—Coal gasification plant. Tours of scale model and audiovisual presentation. Weekdays 7:30 to 4, tours at 9:30, 10:30, 1, 2; free. 8 miles N on CR 21. 701/873-6667.

Dunn Center, North Dakota
Dunn County Museum—Pioneer room and business settings. Log cabin and homestead. Daily 9 to 4:30 (May-Aug); donations. 5

blocks N, 1.5 blocks W from ND 200. 701/548-8057.
Lake Ilo National Wildlife Refuge—Haven for migrating waterfowl at impounded lake. Fishing; boating; picnic area; hiking trails. Headquarters on S side of lake, open weekdays 8 to 4:30. Refuge open daily dawn to dusk. 1 mile W off ND 200. 701/548-8110.

Epping, North Dakota
Buffalo Trails Museum—Seven buildings of regional history, dioramas, fossils. Photo gallery and dentist office. Mon-Sat 9 to 5, Sun 1:30 to 5:30 (May-Sept); admission fee. Main Street. 701/859-4361.

Garrison, North Dakota
Garrison Chamber of Commerce, P.O. Box 759. 701/463-2600.
Audubon National Wildlife Refuge—Eight-mile self-guided driving trail. Migratory waterfowl, shore and upland game birds. Headquarters, 3 miles N of Coleharbor, 1 mile E of US 83, open weekdays 8 to 4:30. Refuge open dawn to dusk. 701/442-5474.
⊞ **Garrison Motel**—30 rooms. Off-season rates. W on ND 37, off US 83. 701/463-2848. $ K12

Lake Sakakawea
▲ **Douglas Creek** (Garrison, ND)—25 sites; fee; water; primitive; open all year; grills/fire rings; tables. Boat ramp; fishing. 11 miles W on ND 37, 5 miles S, 4 miles E. 701/654-7411.
▲ **Downstream** (Riverdale, ND)—101 sites (all w/hookups); fee; water; modern; showers; open May-Sept; grills/fire rings; tables; firewood. Boating; fishing; playground; hiking trails; dump station. 1 mile W on ND 200 to Garrison Dam, 0.3 mile E to Fish Hatchery, 1.5 miles S on access road. 701/654-7411.
▲ **East Totten Trail** (Garrison, ND)—30 sites (all w/hookups); fee; water; primitive; open May-Sept; grills/fire rings; tables. Swimming; boat ramp; fishing; dump station. 5 miles S of ND 37 on US 83. 701/654-7411.
▲ **McKenzie Bay** (Watford City, ND)—36 sites, (32 w/hookups);

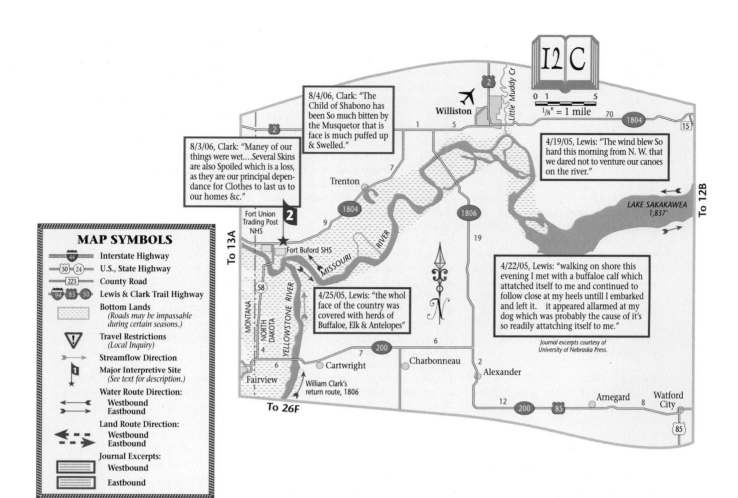

MAP SYMBOLS

44	Interstate Highway
50 24	U.S., State Highway
223	County Road
94 83 50	Lewis & Clark Trail Highway
	Bottom Lands *(Roads may be impassable during certain seasons.)*
	Travel Restrictions *(Local Inquiry)*
	Streamflow Direction
	Major Interpretive Site *(See text for description.)*
	Water Route Direction: Westbound Eastbound
	Land Route Direction: Westbound Eastbound
	Journal Excerpts: Westbound Eastbound

Map text:

8/4/06, Clark: "The Child of Shabono has been So much bitten by the Musquetor that is face is much puffed up & Swelled."

8/3/06, Clark: "Maney of our things were wet....Several Skins are also Spoiled which is a loss, as they are our principal dependance for Clothes to last us to our homes &c."

4/19/05, Lewis: "The wind blew So hard this morning from N. W. that we dared not to venture our canoes on the river."

4/25/05, Lewis: "the whol face of the country was covered with herds of Buffaloe, Elk & Antelopes"

4/22/05, Lewis: "walking on shore this evening I met with a buffaloe calf which attached itself to me and continued to follow close at my heels untill I embarked and left it. it appeared allarmed at my dog which was probably the cause of it's so readily attatching itself to me."

Journal excerpts courtesy of University of Nebraska Press.

Williston, Trenton, Fort Union Trading Post NHS, Fort Buford SHS, MISSOURI RIVER, YELLOWSTONE RIVER, MONTANA, NORTH DAKOTA, Cartwright, Fairview, William Clark's return route, 1806, Charbonneau, Alexander, Arnegard, Watford City, LAKE SAKAKAWEA 1,837', Little Muddy Cr

To 13A, To 26F, To 12B

0 1 5 ⅛" = 1 mile

---

fee; water; modern; showers; open May-Sept; tables. Boat ramp; fishing; playground; cabins; boat rental; dump station; restaurant. 53 miles E. 701/759-3366, 701/842-6508.

▲ Wolf Creek Recreation Area (Riverdale, ND)—93 sites; fee; water; primitive; open all year; grills/fire rings; tables. Boat ramp; fishing; playground. 1 mile E on ND 200, 4.5 miles N on gravel road. 701/654-7411.

Killdeer, North Dakota

Highway 22 Trail (Killdeer to New Town)—61 paved miles across the Badlands.

Little Missouri State Park—Travel on the 30 miles of trail here is easiest on horseback, but hikers are plentiful. Wildlife viewing. ▲ 30 sites (10 w/hookups); fee; water; primitive; open May-Sept; grills/fire rings; tables; firewood. 17 miles N of Killdeer on ND 22 701/328-5357.

Minot, North Dakota

Minot Convention & Visitors Bureau, 1015 S. Broadway. 701/857-8206, 800/264-2626.

Pioneer Village and Museum—10 buildings. Pioneer and regional history. Tue-Sun 10 to 6 (May-Sept); admission fee. 1.25 miles E on US 2 at the fairgrounds. 701/839-0785.

Roosevelt Park and Zoo—Ride the Magic City Express from the zoo to the pool. Zoo has Bengal tigers and a special penguin exhibit. Pool has 360' waterslide. Flower gardens and hiking trails. Daily 10 to 8 (May-Aug) 8 to 4 (Sept-Apr); admission fee. 1219 Burdick Expressway. 701/852-2751.

Upper Souris National Wildlife Refuge—Driving tour with Souris River views. Shorebirds, whitetail deer, upland game birds. Fishing; boating; picnic area. Daily 5 am to 10 pm; free. CR 6 W of US 83. 701/468-5467.

▲ Minot KOA—65 sites (50 w/hookups); fee; water; modern; showers; open Apr-Oct; grills/fire rings; tables. Playground; coin laundry; groceries; dump station. 2.5 miles E on US 52. 701/839-7400, 800/562-7421.

▲ Roughrider Campground—80 sites (66 w/hookups); fee; water; modern; showers; open May-Oct; grills/fire rings; tables. Playground; recreation area; firewood; coin laundry; groceries; dump station. 4 miles W of US 83 on US 2/52, 0.5 mile N on CR 17. 701/852-8442.

⊞ Fairfield Inn—62 rooms, pool, pets, continental breakfast, hot tub. Suites are the same prices as doubles. Off-season rates. 900 24th Ave SW. 701/838-2424, 800/228-2800. $ K18

⊞ Safari Inn—100 rooms, pets, pool, hot tub. & 1510 26th Ave. SW. 701/852-4300, 800/735-5868. $$ K18

⊗ Field and Stream—hearty fare in lodge atmosphere, kids' menu, dress code. &. Limo service from motels. D Mon-Sat. US 83N. 701/852-3663. $$$

⊗ **The Fortune Cookie**—Variety of oriental dishes from mild to hot, kids' menu. L & D daily. 1 mile S on US 83. 701/852-1471. $$

⊗ **Homesteaders**—Casual country atmosphere with home-baked pastries, kids' menu. 2501 US 2. 701/832-2274.

New Town, North Dakota

▲ **4 Bears Casino and Lodge**—85 sites (all w/hookups); fee; water; modern; showers; open Apr-Oct; grills/fire rings; tables. Casino. Swimming; boat ramp; fishing; coin laundry; groceries; dump station. ⊞ 40 rooms, pets, continental breakfast. 4 miles W on ND 23. 701/627-4018. $$ K12

⊗ **Scenic 23 Supper Club**—Locally-caught walleye served overlooking Lake Sakakawea, kids' menu, country music. D only Mon-Sat. 7 miles E on ND 23. 701/627-3949. $$

Pick City, North Dakota

▲ **Lake Sakakawea State Park**—300 sites (150 w/hookups); fee; water; modern; showers; open all year/full operation May-Sept; grills/fire rings; tables. Swimming; boat ramp; fishing; playground; hiking; groceries; dump station. 1 mile N of Pick City. 701/487-3315.

Parshall, North Dakota

Paul Broste Rock Museum—Personal collection of specimens from around the world. Mon-Sat 9 to 5, Sun noon to 5 (May-Sept); admission fee. N edge of town, 1 block W of ND 37. 701/862-3264.

Watford City, North Dakota

Pioneer Museum—Regional pioneer history through recreated room and building settings. Tue-Sun 1 to 5:30 (Memorial Day-Labor Day); admission fee. 104 Park Ave. W. 701/842-2990.

Theodore Roosevelt National Park—Badlands area to which Roosevelt came in 1883 to hunt. Antelope, deer, and numerous herds of bison roam both the North and South units, while elk are found only in the North, and bighorn sheep in the South. Prairie dogs and golden eagles are also plentiful. A 36-mile driving loop begins near the South Unit visitor center. Also in the South Unit is Roosevelt's first cabin from the **Maltese Cross Ranch and Museum**. The North Unit has a 14-mile drive to the Oxbow Overlook. Hiking trails traverse both areas, but bikers are restricted to the park roads. 701/623-4466.

▲ **Juniper/North Unit**—50 sites; fee; water; modern; open all year/full operation May-Sept; grills/fire rings; tables. Horse

and hiking trails. 15 miles S on US 85, 6 miles W on park rd. 701/842-2333.

▲ **Cottonwood/South Unit**—78 sites; fee; water; modern; open all year/full operation May-Sept; grills/fire rings; tables; 30' limit. 5 miles N on park rd. 701/623-4466.

⊞ **McKenzie Inn**—12 rooms, pets, hot tub. 120 SW 3rd St. 701/842-3980. $ K12

Williston, North Dakota

Williston Convention & Visitors Bureau, 10 Main St. 701/774-9041, 800/615-9041.

▲ **Buffalo Trails Campground**—122 sites (102 w/hookups); fee; water; modern; showers; open May-Oct; grills/fire rings; tables. Playground; coin laundry; groceries; dump station. US 2 & US 85, 2 miles N on US 2/85, 0.5 mile on frontage rd. 701/572-3206.

⊞ **Select Inn**—60 rooms, pool, pets, continental breakfast, coin laundry, hot tub. 213 35th St W. 701/572-4242, 800/641-1000. $ K12

⊞ **Super 8 Lodge**—82 rooms, pool, pets, continental breakfast, hot tub. Off-season rates. 2324 2nd Ave W. 701/572-8371, 800/800-8000. $ K12

⊗ **Trapper's Kettle**—Hearty buffet in trapper's cabin, kids' menu. 1.5 miles N on US 2 & 85. 701/774-2831.

CHAPTER 13

April 27 to June 13, 1805

THE PUZZLE OF MARIAS RIVER

From the mouth of the Yellowstone River to the mouth of the Musselshell, the Corps of Discovery traveled west up the Missouri River, in eastern Montana. They encountered no native people in this area, which to this day is sparsely settled.

Day after day, both captains marveled at the abundant wildlife around them. They saw wolf packs chasing pronghorns, and Captain Meriwether Lewis noted how the wolves took turns attacking in order to tire the fleet "antelope." On the riverbanks were carcasses of bison that had drowned, the men surmised, when they broke through the Missouri's ice; these carcasses often showed signs of being eaten by the

"white bear," or grizzly. Captain William Clark saw bighorn sheep running "for some distance with great aparent ease along the side of the river bluff where it was almost perpendicular..." (Lewis)

They often dined on beaver—the tail was preferred as a great delicacy. Sacagawea gathered and prepared foods the men didn't know of, adding variety to their diet of meat. On May 8, she picked wild licorice, and also introduced the men to breadroot, which Clark described as a "white apple" that "the Indians of the Missouri make great use of...dressed in different ways..."

Nine days before, on April 29, Lewis at last had killed a grizzly bear. Various Indians had

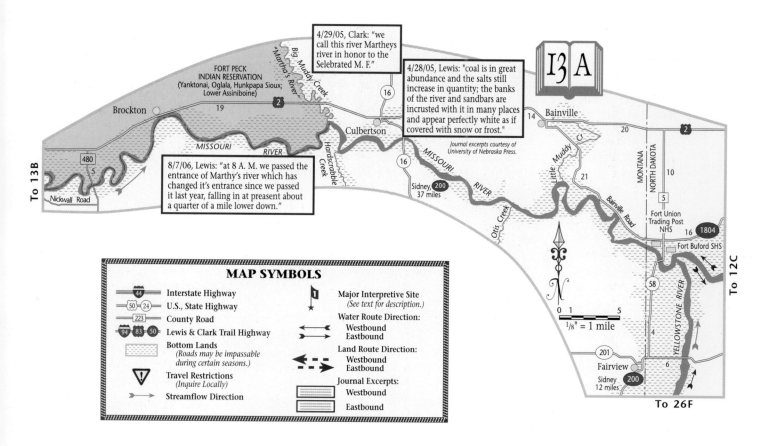

4/29/05, Clark: "we call this river Martheys river in honor to the Selebrated M. F."

4/28/05, Lewis: "coal is in great abundance and the salts still increase in quantity; the banks of the river and sandbars are incrusted with it in many places and appear perfectly white as if covered with snow or frost."

8/7/06, Lewis: "at 8 A. M. we passed the entrance of Marthy's river which has changed it's entrance since we passed it last year, falling in at present about a quarter of a mile lower down."

Journal excerpts courtesy of University of Nebraska Press.

FORT PECK INDIAN RESERVATION (Yanktonai, Oglala, Hunkpapa Sioux; Lower Assiniboine)

MAP SYMBOLS

Interstate Highway
U.S., State Highway
County Road
Lewis & Clark Trail Highway
Bottom Lands
(Roads may be impassable during certain seasons.)
Travel Restrictions
(Inquire Locally)
Streamflow Direction

Major Interpretive Site
(See text for description.)
Water Route Direction:
Westbound
Eastbound
Land Route Direction:
Westbound
Eastbound
Journal Excerpts:
Westbound
Eastbound

1/8" = 1 mile

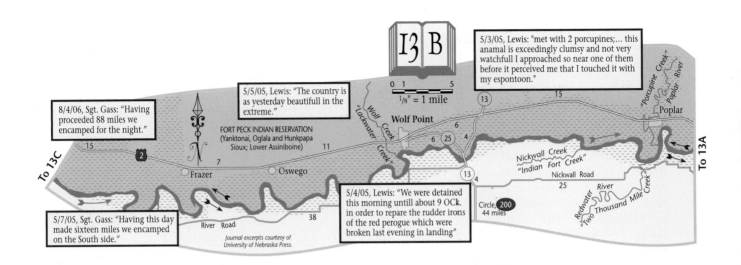

To 13C

To 13A

8/4/06, Sgt. Gass: "Having proceeded 88 miles we encamped for the night."

5/5/05, Lewis: "The country is as yesterday beautifull in the extreme."

5/3/05, Lewis: "met with 2 porcupines;... this anamal is exceedingly clumsy and not very watchfull I approached so near one of them before it perceived me that I touched it with my espontoon."

FORT PECK INDIAN RESERVATION
(Yanktonai, Oglala and Hunkpapa
Sioux; Lower Assiniboine)

Wolf Point

Poplar

$\frac{1}{8}$" = 1 mile

5/7/05, Sgt. Gass: "Having this day made sixteen miles we encamped on the South side."

5/4/05, Lewis: "We were detained this morning untill about 9 OCk. in order to repare the rudder irons of the red perogue which were broken last evening in landing"

Journal excerpts courtesy of University of Nebraska Press.

Frazer

Oswego

River Road

Nickwall Creek
"Indian Fort Creek"

Nickwall Road

Circle
44 miles

Redwater River

"Two Thousand Mile Creek"

"Lackwater Creek"

"Wolf Creek"

"Porcupine Creek"

"Poplar River"

warned the Corps about the grizzly's speed, strength, and ferocity. Although this one was estimated to weigh 300 pounds, it was not full grown. Lewis was amazed that, when wounded, the bear still charged him. Even so, Lewis continued for the time being to underestimate the grizzly. He wrote, "the Indians may well fear this anamal equiped as they generally are with their bows and arrows or indifferent fuzees [guns], but in the hands of skillfull riflemen they are by no means as formidable or dangerous as they have been represented." Future adventures would change his mind.

Hard winds hampered their travel, as did cold weather. On May 2, in today's Richland County, an inch of snow fell. Clark thought it a very extraordinary climate, where he could "behold the trees Green & flowers Spred on the plain, & Snow an inch deep."

On May 8 they passed and named the Milk River, whose color Clark thought "resembles tea with a considerable mixture of milk." They surmised, correctly, that this was the Hidatsas' "The River That Scolds At All Others."

Just west of there, Fort Peck Dam, completed in 1940, forms Fort Peck Reservoir, which backs up the Missouri past the mouth of the Musselshell River. The lake has flooded the entire river bottom where the Corps of Discovery traveled and camped on this stretch (Map 13C).

But the Missouri was still free-flowing here on May 14, 1805, when an accident happened that could have ended the expedition right then, by their estimate 2,200 river miles from St. Louis and nowhere near the Pacific.

Late that afternoon, interpreter Toussaint Charbonneau was steering the white pirogue, "unfortunately for us," Lewis wrote, because Charbonneau "cannot swim and is perhaps the most timid waterman in the world…" In the boat were the interpreter's wife Sacagawea and baby Jean Baptiste, four men including two who could not swim, and—luckily—Private Pierre Cruzatte, an excellent boatman.

Wind caught the sail and Charbonneau turned the wrong direction, so that the boat upset and waves washed in. The boat was filled within an inch of the top when it righted again. Charbonneau was hysterical. Cruzatte threatened to shoot him if he didn't "do his duty." Instantly, Cruzatte ordered two men to bail with kettles already on board, and two others to join him in rowing to shore. At the back of the boat, Sacagawea was catching articles that were beginning to float away.

These "articles" seem to have counted nearly as much as the people on board. Clark wrote: "This accident had like to have cost us deerly…" and Lewis continued:

for in this perogue were embarked our papers, Instruments, books, medicine, a great proportion of our merchandize, and in short almost every article indispensibly necessary to…insure the success of the enterprize in which, we are now launched…"

He credited the "resolution and fortitude of

Cruzatte" and "equal fortitude and resolution" of Sacagawea for saving the day.

They camped the next day above Snow Creek in present Valley County to dry out goods and assess the damage, but rain fell and halted them another day. Lewis noted without further detail that "our medicine sustained the greatest injury, several articles of which were intirely spoiled..."

Five days later, Lewis the make-do doctor had to act also as a veterinarian. After one of the men shot a beaver for food, the dog Seaman "as usual" went to retrieve. But the beaver, still alive, bit the dog's leg, severing an artery. Lewis wrote that it was difficult to stop the bleeding, and feared that the wound could prove fatal after all. But, only ten days later, Seaman proved his worth—and his strength—when a bull bison charged through the sleeping camp. "My dog saved us by causing" the bison to veer away from tents and men.

On May 20, 1805, the Corps of Discovery reached the Musselshell River, which they labelled by translating its Hidatsa name. Hunters explored five miles up the Musselshell, finding a creek the captains named Sacagawea River, perhaps to honor her quick action in the pirogue accident.

The nights were cold, and high winds hampered both travel and rest. On May 23, Lewis noted a severe frost overnight, with ice at the river's edge in the morning. As a month before, water again "freized on the oars." Wild roses were in bloom and "very abundant," but the following morning, ice appeared on the river again.

They continued to see bighorn sheep, and finally, on May 25, Clark killed one. Lewis described it in great detail, noting that native people used the horns to make shooting bows, combs, "watercups spoons and platters..." He thought "civilized man" might use the horns the same way.

Now the Corps was in the Missouri Breaks, where "The Country on either hand is high broken and rockey..." with cliffs "ju[t]ting in on both sides," and "the river bottoms are narrow and afford scarecely any timber."

On May 26, Lewis climbed 300 feet up the cliffs to walk on land after Clark told him of mountains in the distance, probably the Highwood Range northeast of today's Great Falls, Montana. He wrote:

I beheld the Rocky Mountains for the first time...covered with snow and the sun shone on it...I felt a secret pleasure in finding myself so near the head of the heretofore conceived boundless Missouri; but when I reflected on the difficulties which this snowey barrier would most probably throw in my way to the Pacific, and the sufferings and hardships of myself and party in them, it in some measure counterballanced the joy...

Even if he was wrong about how near the main-range Rockies were, Lewis was only too right in considering the sufferings and hardships waiting there.

The Corps were traveling about 20 miles a day; often towing and poling the boats up the [2] Missouri River, the men walking in cold water "even to their armpits..."

When they passed through the White Cliffs area of the [1] Missouri Breaks on the 31st, Lewis described the stone in great detail, and then recorded the cliffs' amazing appearance: *with the help of a little immagination...[the cliffs] represent eligant ranges of lofty freestone buildings, having their parapets well stocked with statuary...I should have thought that nature had attempted here to rival the human art of masonry had I not recollected that she had first began her work.*

Leaving the Breaks, the Corps of Discovery faced a major surprise—and their biggest puzzle yet. On June 2, they came to two apparently equal rivers that seemed to form the main Missouri, one flowing from the northwest and the other from the southwest. No information had prepared them for this, including a map Jefferson had supplied them, published in London just three years before, and based on exploration of the upper Missouri country by a Hudson's Bay Company surveyor.

The north "fork" was muddy like that of the Missouri already traveled, and so most of the men at once deemed it the main river. But the captains thought that a river coming down from the Rockies should be clearer so near the mountains. They thought this north fork picked up its silt by crossing many miles of flat country.

The Corps set up camp on the [3] point between the two streams, near present Loma, Montana. They would stay here for ten days, exploring and deciding which river was the Missouri. While in this camp, some of the men

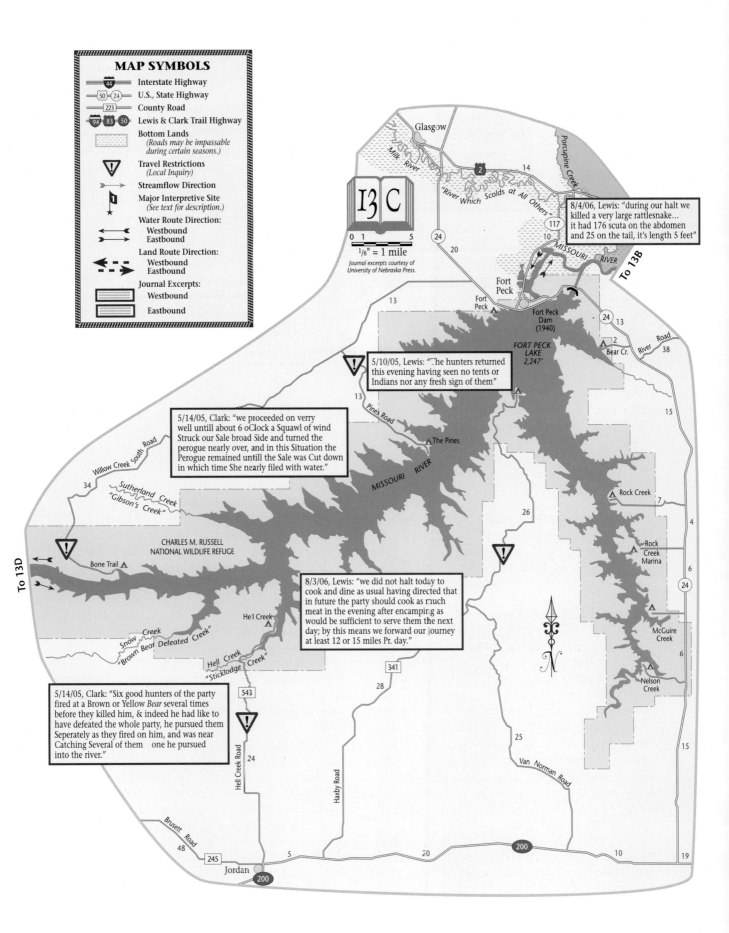

MAP SYMBOLS

- **Interstate Highway** — 44
- **U.S., State Highway** — 50 24
- **County Road** — 223
- **Lewis & Clark Trail Highway** — 94 83 50
- **Bottom Lands** *(Roads may be impassable during certain seasons.)*
- ▽! **Travel Restrictions** *(Local Inquiry)*
- **Streamflow Direction**
- **Major Interpretive Site** *(See text for description.)*
- **Water Route Direction:**
  - Westbound
  - Eastbound
- **Land Route Direction:**
  - Westbound
  - Eastbound
- **Journal Excerpts:**
  - Westbound
  - Eastbound

13 C

0 1   5
1/8" = 1 mile

Journal excerpts courtesy of University of Nebraska Press.

8/4/06, Lewis: "during our halt we killed a very large rattlesnake… it had 176 scuta on the abdomen and 25 on the tail, it's length 5 feet"

5/10/05, Lewis: "The hunters returned this evening having seen no tents or Indians nor any fresh sign of them"

5/14/05, Clark: "we proceeded on verry well untill about 6 oClock a Squawl of wind Struck our Sale broad Side and turned the perogue nearly over, and in this Situation the Perogue remained untill the Sale was Cut down in which time She nearly filed with water."

8/3/06, Lewis: "we did not halt today to cook and dine as usual having directed that in future the party should cook as much meat in the evening after encamping as would be sufficient to serve them the next day; by this means we forward our journey at least 12 or 15 miles Pr. day."

5/14/05, Clark: "Six good hunters of the party fired at a Brown or Yellow *Bear* several times before they killed him, & indeed he had like to have defeated the whole party, he pursued them Seperately as they fired on him, and was near Catching Several of them   one he pursued into the river."

Glasgow

Milk River

"River Which Scolds at All Others"

Porcupine Creek

2

14

117

24

20

10

MISSOURI RIVER

To 13B

Fort Peck

Fort Peck

Fort Peck Dam (1940)

13

24

13

2

Bear Cr.

River Road

38

FORT PECK LAKE 2,247'

13

Pines Road

The Pines

MISSOURI RIVER

15

Rock Creek

7

4

Rock Creek Marina

6

26

24

McGuire Creek

6

Nelson Creek

N

Willow Creek South Road

34

Sutherland Creek "Gibson's Creek"

CHARLES M. RUSSELL NATIONAL WILDLIFE REFUGE

Bone Trail

To 13D

Hell Creek

Snow Creek

"Brown Bear Defeated Creek"

Hell Creek "Sticklodge Creek"

543

Hell Creek Road

24

341

28

Haxby Road

25

Van Norman Road

15

Brusett Road

48

245

Jordan

200

5

20

200

10

19

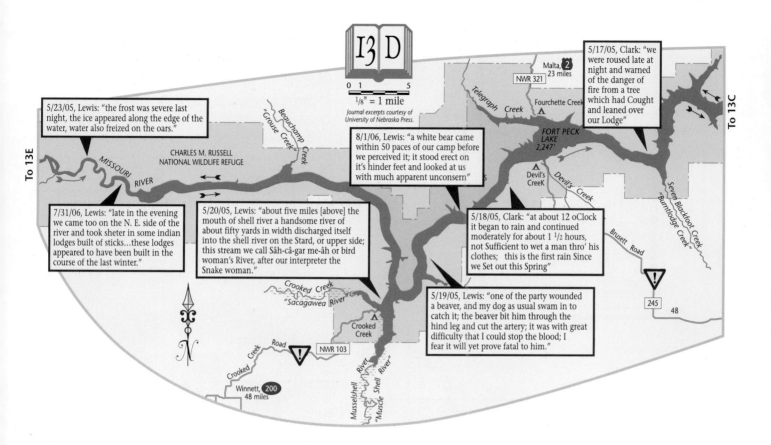

13 D

0 1 5
1/8" = 1 mile
Journal excerpts courtesy of
University of Nebraska Press.

5/23/05, Lewis: "the frost was severe last night, the ice appeared along the edge of the water, water also freized on the oars."

5/17/05, Clark: "we were roused late at night and warned of the danger of fire from a tree which had Cought and leaned over our Lodge"

8/1/06, Lewis: "a white bear came within 50 paces of our camp before we perceived it; it stood erect on it's hinder feet and looked at us with much apparent unconsern"

CHARLES M. RUSSELL
NATIONAL WILDLIFE REFUGE

MISSOURI RIVER

7/31/06, Lewis: "late in the evening we came too on the N. E. side of the river and took sheter in some indian lodges built of sticks...these lodges appeared to have been built in the course of the last winter."

5/20/05, Lewis: "about five miles [above] the mouth of shell river a handsome river of about fifty yards in width discharged itself into the shell river on the Stard, or upper side; this stream we call Sâh-câ-gar me-âh or bird woman's River, after our interpreter the Snake woman."

5/18/05, Clark: "at about 12 oClock it began to rain and continued moderately for about 1 1/2 hours, not Sufficient to wet a man thro' his clothes; this is the first rain Since we Set out this Spring"

5/19/05, Lewis: "one of the party wounded a beaver, and my dog as usual swam in to catch it; the beaver bit him through the hind leg and cut the artery; it was with great difficulty that I could stop the blood; I fear it will yet prove fatal to him."

Crooked Creek
"Sacagawea River"

Crooked Creek

Crooked Creek Road

NWR 103

Winnett, 200
48 miles

Musselshell River
"Muscle Shell River"

Malta, 2
23 miles

NWR 321

Fourchette Creek

Telegraph Creek

FORT PECK LAKE
2,247'

Devil's CreeK

Devil's Creek

Brusett Road

Seven Blackfoot Creek
"Burnlodge Creek"

245

48

To 13E

To 13C

dressed skins for clothing and healed their bruised feet.

On June 4, Lewis took six men and headed up the north fork. Clark, with five others, went up the south fork. Each party would walk upstream for at least one and a half days—longer if necessary—to determine which was the Missouri.

Making a knapsack out of a blanket, Lewis noted this was the first time he had ever carried a pack on his back, "and I am fully convinced that it will not be the last." It wasn't.

Lewis's party saw bison, pronghorns, wolves, foxes, mule deer, elk, and the biggest prairie dog town yet. By June 6, Lewis thought this river had its origins on the plains, and not in the Rockies. His party began their return, camping without shelter in a rainstorm, "an uncomfortable nights rest…" They traveled "only about 18 miles" the rainy next day, but found "an old Indian stick lodge" that was "dry and comfortable" while the rain continued all night.

They got back to the camp at the forks about 5:00 p.m. on June 6, two days later than planned, and found the others worrying about them. Lewis had traveled, he estimated, 77½ miles.

Clark and *his* party had found a stick lodge their first night on the southerly fork, June 4, and it protected them from "Some little rain & Snow.…" As they moved upriver the next day, Clark could see that the stream "Continued its width[,] debth & rapidity and the Course west of South," and he decided that "going up further would be useless." Their allotted time spent, his party therefore turned back, arriving at the base camp about 5:00 p.m. on June 8, only to await Lewis's group for two more days.

Lewis was certain that the north fork he had explored was not the Missouri, and he named it in honor of his cousin Maria Wood. (Maria's River is today's Marias River, pronounced *muh-RYE-uss*.)

Cruzatte, the experienced Missouri River man, was equally sure the Marias was really the Missouri. Since most of the men trusted his river knowledge, Lewis and Clark decided that now *Lewis* and some men would go farther up the southerly fork than Clark had gone. The Mandans had told the Corps about a great falls on the Missouri River, one that took half a day to walk around. If Lewis found the falls, his and Clark's judgment would be verified.

The Corps also decided to leave the red pirogue, and some animal specimens, tools, food, and ammunition, in what the French boatmen called a cache (pronounced *cash*) and Lewis called a cellar—a pit lined with sticks, grass and skins. They tied the red pirogue to trees on an island and covered it with branches. On their way back from the Pacific, they could retrieve the items.

Even though Lewis wasn't feeling well, he and four men set off the morning of June 11; that night he treated himself with a drink made of chokecherry bark. The main party, with Clark, stayed in camp that day. Sacagawea also was ill, so Clark bled her, and thought it helped.

On his third day out, Lewis split his small group into three, sending interpreter George Drouillard with Private George Gibson one direction, and Private Joseph Field in another, to hunt—while he and Private Silas Goodrich proceeded upriver. After only two more miles *my ears were saluted with the agreeable sound of a fall of water and advancing a little further I saw the spray arrise above the plain like a collumn of smoke…* but the men walked seven more miles before they could "gaze on this sublimely grand specticle…" of the Great Falls of the Missouri. They were only about ten miles upriver from where Clark dutifully had turned back the week before.

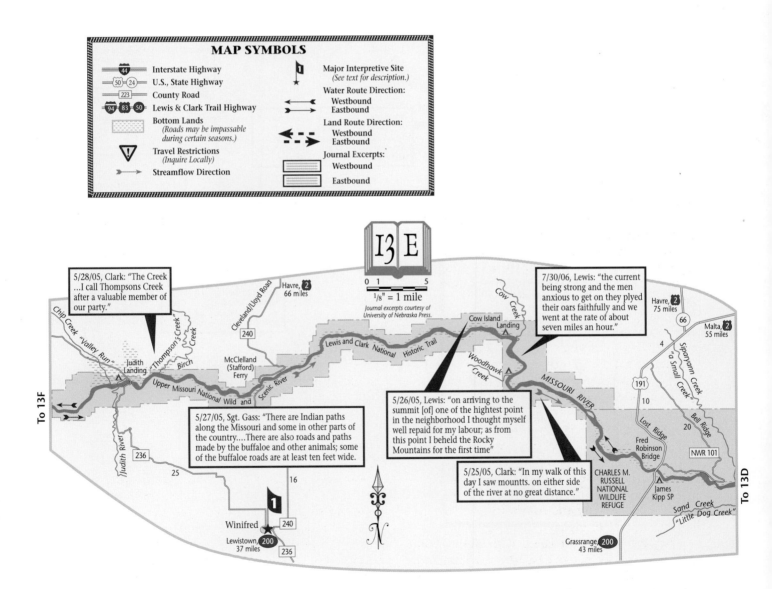

MAP SYMBOLS

Interstate Highway
U.S., State Highway
County Road
Lewis & Clark Trail Highway
Bottom Lands *(Roads may be impassable during certain seasons.)*
Travel Restrictions *(Inquire Locally)*
Streamflow Direction

Major Interpretive Site *(See text for description.)*
Water Route Direction: Westbound / Eastbound
Land Route Direction: Westbound / Eastbound
Journal Excerpts: Westbound / Eastbound

13 E

0 1 5
¹/₈" = 1 mile
Journal excerpts courtesy of University of Nebraska Press.

5/28/05, Clark: "The Creek …I call Thompsons Creek after a valuable member of our party."

7/30/06, Lewis: "the current being strong and the men anxious to get on they plyed their oars faithfully and we went at the rate of about seven miles an hour."

5/27/05, Sgt. Gass: "There are Indian paths along the Missouri and some in other parts of the country….There are also roads and paths made by the buffaloe and other animals; some of the buffaloe roads are at least ten feet wide.

5/26/05, Lewis: "on arriving to the summit [of] one of the hightest point in the neighborhood I thought myself well repaid for my labour; as from this point I beheld the Rocky Mountains for the first time"

5/25/05, Clark: "In my walk of this day I saw mountts. on either side of the river at no great distance."

Havre, 66 miles
Havre, 75 miles
Malta, 55 miles
Grassrange, 43 miles
Lewistown, 37 miles
Winifred
To 13F
To 13D

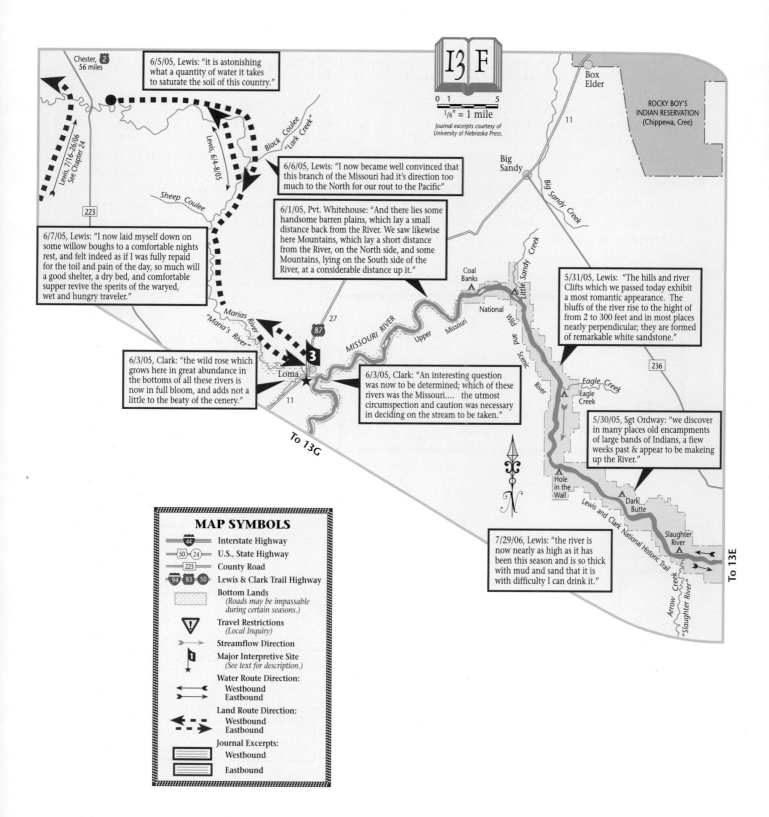

Chester, ②
56 miles

6/5/05, Lewis: "it is astonishing what a quantity of water it takes to saturate the soil of this country."

Lewis, 7/16–26/06 See Chapter 24

Lewis, 6/14–8/05

Black Coulee "Lark Creek"

Sheep Coulee

223

6/7/05, Lewis: "I now laid myself down on some willow boughs to a comfortable nights rest, and felt indeed as if I was fully repaid for the toil and pain of the day, so much will a good shelter, a dry bed, and comfortable supper revive the sperits of the waryed, wet and hungry traveler."

6/6/05, Lewis: "I now became well convinced that this branch of the Missouri had it's direction too much to the North for our rout to the Pacific"

6/1/05, Pvt. Whitehouse: "And there lies some handsome barren plains, which lay a small distance back from the River. We saw likewise here Mountains, which lay a short distance from the River, on the North side, and some Mountains, lying on the South side of the River, at a considerable distance up it."

Marias River
"Maria's River"

27

87

6/3/05, Clark: "the wild rose which grows here in great abundance in the bottoms of all these rivers is now in full bloom, and adds not a little to the beaty of the cenery."

3

Loma

11

To 13G

MISSOURI RIVER   Upper   Missouri

6/3/05, Clark: "An interesting question was now to be determined; which of these rivers was the Missouri.... the utmost circumspection and caution was necessary in deciding on the stream to be taken."

Box Elder

11

ROCKY BOY'S INDIAN RESERVATION (Chippewa, Cree)

Big Sandy

Big Sandy Creek

Little Sandy Creek

Coal Banks

National

Wild   and   Scenic   River

5/31/05, Lewis: "The hills and river Clifts which we passed today exhibit a most romantic appearance. The bluffs of the river rise to the hight of from 2 to 300 feet and in most places nearly perpendicular; they are formed of remarkable white sandstone."

236

Eagle Creek

Eagle Creek

5/30/05, Sgt Ordway: "we discover in many places old encampments of large bands of Indians, a fiew weeks past & appear to be makeing up the River."

Hole in the Wall

Lewis and Clark National Historic Trail

Dark Butte

7/29/06, Lewis: "the river is now nearly as high as it has been this season and is so thick with mud and sand that it is with difficulty I can drink it."

Slaughter River

Arrow Creek   "Slaughter River"

To 13E

13 F

0 1   5
1/8" = 1 mile

Journal excerpts courtesy of University of Nebraska Press.

MAP SYMBOLS

44	Interstate Highway
50 24	U.S., State Highway
223	County Road
94 83 50	Lewis & Clark Trail Highway

Bottom Lands
(Roads may be impassable during certain seasons.)

⚠ Travel Restrictions
(Local Inquiry)

→ Streamflow Direction

⚑ Major Interpretive Site
(See text for description.)

Water Route Direction:
→ Westbound
→ Eastbound

Land Route Direction:
◄ - - Westbound
- - ► Eastbound

Journal Excerpts:
Westbound

Eastbound

TOURING TODAY

❧ THE PUZZLE OF MARIAS RIVER ❧

Bridges over the Missouri River in this area are at Culbertson, MT (MT 16); Culbertson, MT (County 251/480); Wolf Point, MT (MT 13); Fort Peck, MT (MT 24); US 191; Loma, MT (county road); Fort Benton, MT (MT 80).

Ferries: McClelland Ferry (free, Apr-Oct); County 236; Virgelle Ferry (free, 7 to 7, Sun 9 to 5, May-Oct).

Exploring the Trail in this segment can be a challenge. The area is sparsely inhabited—much of it little changed since Lewis and Clark passed through, with few visitor services between towns. Access to the Missouri shore is primarily on gravel and dirt roads with travel speeds of as little as 15 miles per hour. A flexible schedule is required since rain quickly makes roads temporarily impassible. Carry food, fuel, blankets, and plenty of water (1 gallon a day per person), and plan ahead; gas stations and other basic services can be far apart.

ALONG THE EXPEDITION'S PATH

May 8, 1805
Downstream (Fort Peck, MT)— Shady park with extensive day-use recreational facilities. ▲ 57 sites (52 w/hookups); fee; water; modern; showers; open May-Oct; grills/fire rings; tables; 35' limit. Boat ramp/dock; fishing; playground; hiking. 0.5 miles E of town on MT 117. 406/526-3224.

May 9-10, 1805
Fort Peck Recreation Area (Fort Peck, MT)

▲ **West End**—12 sites (all w/hookups); fee; water; modern; showers; open May-Oct; grills/fire rings; tables; 35' limit. Boat ramp; fishing; swimming. 2 miles SW on MT 24. 406/526-3411.

▲ **Bear Creek Access**—Unmarked campsites; free; **no** water; primitive; open all year; fire rings. Fishing. 11 miles SE on MT 24, 7 miles W on gravel road. 406/526-3411.

▲ **Rock Creek Access**—Unmarked campsites; free; **no** water; primitive; open all year; fire rings. Fishing. 40 miles SE on MT 24, 10 miles W on Rock Creek Rd. 406/526-3411.

▲ **McGuire Creek**—Unmarked campsites; free; **no** water; primitive; open all year; fire rings. Fishing. 44 miles SE on MT 24, 7 miles W. 406/526-3411.

▲ **Nelson Creek**—Unmarked campsites; free; **no** water; primitive; open all year; fire rings.

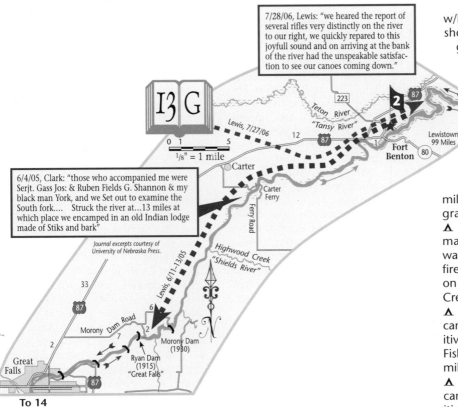

7/28/06, Lewis: "we heard the report of several rifles very distinctly on the river to our right, we quickly repared to this joyfull sound and on arriving at the bank of the river had the unspeakable satisfaction to see our canoes coming down."

6/4/05, Clark: "those who accompanied me were Serjt. Gass Jos: & Ruben Fields G. Shannon & my black man York, and we Set out to examine the South fork.... Struck the river at...13 miles at which place we encamped in an old Indian lodge made of Stiks and bark"

Journal excerpts courtesy of University of Nebraska Press.

1/8" = 1 mile

Fishing; boat ramp/dock. 49 miles SE on MT 24, 7 miles W. 406/526-3411.

May 11, 1805

▲ **The Pines** (Fort Peck, MT)—Unmarked campsites; free; water; primitive; open all year/full operation May-Sept; fire rings. Boat ramp; fishing. 7 miles W on MT 24, 12 miles SW on Willow Creek Rd, 12 miles S on Pines Rd. 406/526-3411.

May 13, 1805

Hell Creek State Park—The drive from Jordan winds through prime wildlife area. 18 miles from town, a pullout offers a spectacular view. This is fossil and dinosaur country but digging in the park is prohibited. Ask at Garfield County Museum in Jordan (see Around the Area section below) about nearby legal fossil-collecting sites. ▲ Undesignated campsites; fee; water; primitive; open all year/full operation May-Sept; grills/fire rings; tables. Marina; groceries; fishing; boating. 25 miles N of Jordan on gravel road with steep, curvy sections. 406/232-4365.

▲ **Bone Trail** (Phillips County, MT)—Undesignated sites; free; **no** water; primitive; open all year; grills/fire rings; tables; 16' limit. Boat ramp; fishing. 7 miles W of Fort Peck on MT 24, 53 miles SW on Willow Creek Rd. 406/526-3411.

May 18, 1805

▲ **Fourchette Creek**—Undesignated sites; free; **no** water; primitive; open all year; grills/fire rings; tables; 16' limit. Boat ramp/dock; fishing. 60 miles S of Malta. 406/526-3411.

▲ **Devils Creek**—Undesignated sites; free; **no** water; primitive; open all year; grills/fire rings; tables; 16' limit. Boat ramp/dock; fishing. 45 miles NW of Jordan. 406/526-3411.

May 20, 1805

▲ **Crooked Creek**—Fort Musselshell Marina; fee; **no** water; open all year; tables, storm shelters. Boat rentals; tackle, bait available. 48 miles NE of Winnett on gravel road, signed; follow Crooked Creek Road. 406/429-2999.

May 21-June 3, 1805

[1] ★ Missouri Breaks National Back Country Byway—81-mile loop of gravel, unimproved roads begins in Winifred. Interpretation of Lewis and Clark, and Nez Perce National Historic Trail. Through Charles M. Russell National Wildlife Refuge (see below). Low-clearance vehicles not recommended. Roads impassable when wet. All year, weather permitting. 406/538-7461.

[2] ★ Wild and Scenic Upper Missouri Visitor Center (Fort Benton, MT)—Interpretive exhibits detail the historical impact of the Missouri River upon the area and the nation. Archaeological displays and a multi-media presentation on Lewis and Clark are part of this riverfront center. Daily 8 to 5 (May-Sept); free. 1718 Front. 406/622-5185.

[2] ★ Wild & Scenic Missouri River

Wildlife and dramatic scenery abound along the section of the river between here and Fort Benton: the longest section of the river preserved in its natural state. If you float any section of the Lewis and Clark Trail, this should be it. It's an easy paddle by early summer. It takes about 7 days to float downstream from Fort Benton to James Kipp Recreation Area, and the stretch from Fort Benton to Loma is best for a day trip. Weather and water hazards do exist and detailed information should be obtained from the River Manager, P.O. Box 1160, Lewistown, MT 59457, 406/538-7461 by anyone planning their own trip. Professional outfitters are available to handle the details. ▲ All public lands along the river are available for camping; however, the following campsites have some type of development. Mileages below are from Fort Benton; note that not all designated sites have take-out points.

Fort Benton (Mile 0)—Put-in.
Evans Bend (Mile 6.5)—Primitive restrooms.
Loma Bridge (Mile 21)—Boat launch; vehicle access; interpretive trail along river. Take-out point.

Coal Banks Landing (Mile 42)—Boat launch; water; primitive restrooms; ranger station; vehicle access. Take-out point.
Little Sandy (Mile 46.7)—Primitive restrooms.
Ordway Return July 29, 1806: White Cliffs Area (Mile 52)—No campsite.
Eagle Creek (Mile 55.7)—Primitive restrooms.
Hole-in-the-Wall (Mile 66.8)—Primitive restrooms.
Dark Butte (Mile 69)—Primitive restrooms.
Slaughter River (Mile 77)—Primitive restrooms; shelter.
Judith Landing (Mile 88)—Take-out point. ▲ 10 sites; free; water; primitive; open May-Oct; grills/fire rings; tables. Boat launch; fishing; ranger station; vehicle access. 26 miles NW of Winifred on MT 236. 406/454-3441.
Stafford Ferry (also called McClelland Ferry) (Mile 102)—Boat launch; primitive restrooms; vehicle access. Canoe take-out only; no boat ramp.
Cow Island Landing (Mile 125)—Primitive restrooms.
Woodhawk Bottom (Mile 131)—Primitive restrooms.
James Kipp Recreation Area (Mile 149)—Last take-out point in the Wild and Scenic Missouri River. ▲ 34 sites; water; primitive/&; open Apr-Nov; grills/fire rings; tables. Fishing; hiking trails, vehicle access. 64 miles NE of Lewistown on US 191. 406/538-7461. Take-out point.
● **Charles M. Russell National Wildlife Refuge**—Over a million acres along 125 miles of the Missouri River. Access roads are gravel and dirt. Elk, bighorn sheep and even black-footed ferrets are seen here. ▲ Primitive camping is possible throughout the refuge with established campgrounds at Crooked Creek and James Kipp. A 39-mile, gravel, scenic auto loop to Slippery Ann—local name for Siparyann—is 6 miles E of US 191. Enter refuge at James Kipp Recreation Area or 1 mile S of junction MT 66 & US 191. Information available at Refuge headquarters, Airport Rd., Lewistown or USF & W office, 4 miles S on US 191. 406/538-8706.

June 4, 1805
Ordway Return July 27, 1806
[3] ★ **Lewis and Clark Decision Point** (Fort Benton, MT)—Short trail to an overlook on the Missouri and Marias rivers. Interpretive exhibits. Always open; free. 11 miles northeast of Fort Benton on US 87, 0.5 mile on gravel road W of Loma Bridge.

June 10, 1805
● **Lewis and Clark Monument** (Fort Benton, MT)—Heroic bronze statue in nice park setting along the Missouri River. Picnic area. Always open; free. Front St. 406/622-5494.

AROUND THE AREA

TOWNS LISTED ALPHABETICALLY

Kings Hill National Scenic Byway—71-mile drive through the Little Belt Mountains. US 89 between US 12 and US 78. 406/547-3361.

Chinook, Montana
Chinook Chamber of Commerce, P.O. Box 744. 406/357-2100.
Bear Paw Battlefield (unit of Nez Perce National Historical Park)—After defeating the Army in Idaho, Chief Joseph and the Nez Perce began a 1,500-mile trek to Canada. Skirmishes with the troops along the way resulted in mounting casualties for the tribe. On October 5, 1877, 40 miles from the border, Chief Joseph could not stand to see his people suffer any longer and surrendered, saying, "from where the sun now stands, I will fight no more forever." Interpreted hiking trail and picnic area. Information at Blaine County Museum in Chinook. Always open; free. 16 miles S of US 2. 406/357-3130.
Blaine County Museum—Multimedia presentation on Bear Paw Battlefield (site of 1877 Nez Perce surrender), Indian and pioneer artifacts, reconstructed pioneer room settings. Mon-Sat 8 to 5, Sun 1 to 5 (June-Sept), Mon-Fri 1 to 5 (rest of year); free. 501 Indiana St. 406/357-2590.
⊞ **Chinook Motor Inn**—38 rooms, pets, ⊗ restaurant. Suites

are same price as doubles. 100 Indiana Ave. 406/357-2248, 800/603-2864. $ K12

Culbertson, Montana
Culbertson Chamber of Commerce, P.O. Box 639. 406/787-5821.
Culbertson Museum and Visitor Information Center—Historical settings detail life from 1890 through the 1920s in the shops, offices, and homes of Montana's early settlers. Also serves as state welcome center. Daily 8 to 8 (summer), 9 to 6 (May & Sept); donations. US 2 & US 16. 406/787-6320.
Medicine Lake National Wildlife Refuge—Waterfowl as well as deer and antelope can be seen across 31,000 acres. Auto tour, hiking trails and canoe trails. Several tipi rings are preserved in the Teepee Hills Natural Area. Daily dawn-dusk; free. 24 miles N on MT 16. 406/789-2305.
⊞ **The Kings Inn**—20 rooms. US 2, E of town. 406/787-6277. $

Fort Benton, Montana
Fort Benton Chamber of Commerce, P.O. Box 12, Fort Benton, MT 59442, 406/622-3864.
Fort Benton Heritage Complex—Reconstruction of the original fort is in progress here and a keelboat replica and statue commemorate the Expedition. Includes:
  Museum of the Northern Great Plains—Unusual collection of exhibits and information relating to agriculture and its historical impact. Daily 10 to 5 (May-Sept); admission fee. 406/622- 5316.
  Museum of the Upper Missouri—Located in the park, this museum focuses on the world of fur traders, steamboats and early Montana river runners. Daily 10 to 5 (May-Sept); admission fee. 406/622-5316.
Shep—A statue of the faithful dog who, even after his master's body was shipped away on the train, met every train for 5 years, waiting for him to return. He died after being hit by a train and is buried nearby.
⊞ **Grand Union Hotel**—27 rooms, pets, ⊗ restaurant, full breakfast, bike rentals. Historic

hotel on the Missouri River. Reduced rates weekdays and off-season. Downtown. 406/622-3840. $$ K12

Fort Peck, Montana
● **Fort Peck Museum/Dam**—History, geology and archaeological finds. Hundreds of fossils and dinosaur bones. Daily tours of the power-house. Daily 9 to 5 (June-Sept); free. On MT 24. 406/526-3411.
Fort Peck Summer Theater—Professional summer stock for audiences of all ages in a 1200-seat National Historic Register theater. Fri-Sun evenings. 406/228-9219.

Glasgow, Montana
Glasgow Area Chamber of Commerce, 740 US 2E. 406/228-2222, 800/228-2223.
Valley County Museum—Pioneer and Indian exhibits. Showcased are historic barroom and wildlife mounts. Lewis and Clark exhibits. Mon-Sat 10 to 7, Sun 1 to 5 (Memorial Day-Labor Day); free. 0.5 W on US 2. 406/228-8692.
⊞ **Cottonwood Inn**—92 rooms, pets, indoor pool, ⊗ restaurant, hot tub, coin laundry. US 2 E of town. 406/228-8213. $$ K12
⊗ **Sam's Supper Club**—Steaks, seafood & walleye. L & D daily. 307 First Ave. 406/228-4614. $$

Havre, Montana
Havre Area Chamber of Commerce, 518 First St. 406/265-4383.
Beaver Creek County Park—At 10,000 acres, this is the largest county park in the U.S. Extensive hiking trails and fishing on two lakes make this a popular spot along the Hi-Line. ▲ 254 sites; fee; water; modern; showers; open all year; grills/fire rings; tables. 10 miles S on 5th Ave. 406/395-4565.
Havre Beneath The Streets—Tour a hidden community created in the 1890s. Wah Sing Laundry, Tamale Jim's, bordello, opium den, bakery, stores. Tours daily; admission fee. 100 3rd Ave. 406/265-8888.
H. Earl Clack Memorial Museum—Emphasis on geological and archaeological history of the area. Guided tours of Fort Assiniboine at nearby **Wahkpa Chu'gn Bison Kill Archaeology Site.** Tours

of the archaeology site can also be arranged. Daily 8 to 6 (May-Sept); donations, admission fee for tours. 1 mile W on US 2. 406/265-4000.

▲ **Clack Museum Campground**—35 sites (26 w/hookups); fee; water; modern; showers; open May-Sept; grills/fire rings; tables; 3-day limit. Dump station; playground. Adjacent to museum. 1 mile W on US 2. 406/265-9641.

⊞ **Super 8**—64 rooms, pets. Off-season rates. 166 19th Ave W. 406/265-1411, 800/800-8000. $ K12

⊞ **Townhouse Inn**—105 rooms, pets, indoor pool, hot tub, coin laundry, exercise room. 629 W. 1st St. 406/265-6711. $$ K12

⊗ **Andy's Supper Club**—Steaks are the draw here. B L & D daily. 658 W. 1st St. 406/265-9963. $$$

⊗ **Uncle Joe's Steakhouse**—More steaks at local hangout. ♿ L & D Tue-Sun. 1400 1st St. 406/265-5111. $$$

Jordan, Montana

Garfield County Museum—Replica of a triceratops excavated 25 miles NE of Jordan is the main attraction. Fossils found in the area, homesteader memorabilia and other remnants of life in early Montana. Ask to see the one-room schoolhouse. Daily 1 to 5 (June-Labor Day); free. On MT 200 N of Jordan. 406/557-2517.

Lewistown, Montana

Lewistown Chamber of Commerce, 408 NE Main St, 406/538-5436, 800/216-5436.

Big Springs—Snowmelt from the Snowy Mountains feeds this spring, the third largest freshwater spring in the world. The water is so pure it feeds directly into the taps of Lewistown without treatment. Great picnic area along the wooded creek shore. Daily sunrise to sunset; free.

Big Springs Trout Hatchery—

More than 3 million fish are raised here annually. Interpretive signs and a self-guided tour give visitors an overview of the development process and its importance to the state. Daily 9 to 4; free. 4.5 miles S on MT 238, 2 miles E on MT 466. 406/538-5588.

Central Montana Historical Association Museum—Collection of homesteader and Indian artifacts defining life on the range in early Montana. Weekdays 9 to 5; weekends 10 to 4 (summer); donations. 408 NE Main. 406/538-5438.

Crystal Cascades Trail #445—5.2-mile trail to marvelous waterfall begins off FR 275 (elevation gain 1400'). Joins with Ulhorn Trail back to Crystal Lake Campground. 406/566-2292.

Crystal Lake Shoreline National Recreation Trail #404—1.7-mile interpretive loop trail begins at Crystal Lake Campground. Pick up a brochure and take the kids, there's lots to see and it's an easy hike. 406/566-2292.

Rocks and Fossils—This area abounds with mineral deposits and fossil beds located on public lands. Check out the Big Spring Area, particularly excellent for children since the ditches are almost totally fossils. Pick up a brochure with details and directions at the Chamber of Commerce.

▲ **Crystal Lake Campground**—28 sites; fee; water; primitive/♿; open May-Aug; grills/fire rings; tables; 22' limit. Fishing; boat ramp; Shoreline Trail #404; Crystal Cascades Trail # 445. 9 miles W on US 87, 16 miles S on CR, 8.5 miles S on FR 275. 406/566-2292.

⊞ **Historic Calvert Hotel**—45 rooms in 1917 high school dorm, some shared baths. 216 7th St S. 406/538-5411. $

⊞ **Yogo Inn**—124 rooms, indoor & outdoor pool, pets, ⊗ restaurant, hot tub. 211 E. Main. 406/538-8721. $$

⊗ **Bar Nine**—Watch your meal being prepared and then head for the dance floor. L & D daily. Fairgrounds Road. 406/538-3250. $$

⊗ **Pete's Drive Inn and Fireside Restaurant**—Standard fare in nostalgic drive-in. B L & D daily. 1308 W. Main. 406/538-9400. $

⊗ **The Whole Famdamily**—Homemade soups and enormous sandwiches. Smoke-free. L & D Mon-Fri, L only Sat. 206 W. Main. 406/538-5161. $

Malta, Montana

Malta Area Chamber of Commerce, 10½ S. 4th St. E. 406/654-1776, 800/704-1776.

Bowdoin National Wildlife Refuge—Hundreds of pelicans, white-faced ibises and night herons nest here. Over 200 bird species are protected here along with deer, elk and antelope. Self-guided auto and hiking tours. Open dawn to dusk; free. 8 miles E on US 2. 406/654-2863.

Phillips County Museum—Military exhibits, fossils, pioneers and mining history. Daily 10 to 6 (May-Sept); admission fee. 431 US 2E. 406/654-1037.

⊞ **Edgewater Inn**—32 rooms, pool, exercise room, hot tub, coin laundry. 101 US 2 N. 406/654-1302. $

⊞ **Maltana Motel**—19 rooms. 138 S. 1st Ave. W. 406/654-2610. $

Wolf Point, Montana

Wolf Point Chamber of Commerce, 201 4th Ave. S. 406/653-2012.

Wolf Point Area Historical Society—Pioneer and Indian clothing, arrowheads, rifle collection. Mon-Fri 10 to 5 (June-Aug); donations. 220 2nd Ave S. 406/653-1912.

⊞ **Sherman Motor Inn**—46 rooms, pets, ⊗ restaurant. 200 E. Main. 406/653-1100. $

CHAPTER 14

June 13 to July 14, 1805

AROUND THE GREAT FALLS

At today's city of Great Falls, Montana, the Missouri River of 1805 tumbled through a series of five waterfalls, with rapids between them. Ravines cut deeply into the high, steep riversides, leaving no banks to walk on. Today, five dams (including [2] Ryan Dam at the Great Falls itself) have changed the appearance of the Missouri in the area.

The Corps of Discovery needed to portage—or carry their boats overland—around this stretch of the river. The ravines prevented them from walking along the river, sending them south onto the plain to find a more level route.

Preparing for the portage, making it, and then preparing to go on, would take nearly a month of very hard work.

On June 13, Captain Meriwether Lewis reached [1] the falls many informants had said awaited them on the Missouri.

The next day, he sent Joseph Field back down the Missouri to Captain William Clark with the good news that they had correctly chosen the course of the Missouri River (see Chapter 13). Clark was to proceed upriver as far as the boats could travel, and then camp. He did so, creating Lower Portage Camp about two miles below the mouth of today's Belt Creek—which the men called Portage Creek—on June 16.

Meanwhile, after dispatching Field and assigning the other three men to dry bison meat, the eager Lewis went alone to see "where the rappids termineated above, and return to dinner"—the midday meal (in the evening they "supped"). He took his rifle and espontoon, a versatile metal-bladed spear that infantry officers carried. Besides being a weapon, it could serve as a hiking staff and as a prop to steady the heavy long-barreled rifles. The symbol for north on this book's maps is modeled after the top of an espontoon.

As soon as Lewis passed one waterfall, he heard still another beyond it, until he had viewed all five in amazement. He walked the rest of the day, finally reaching the mouth of today's Sun River (called Medicine River by the Mandans and also by the Corps), in the south central portion of today's Great Falls. Here the Missouri makes a large bend. It flows from the south past the mouth of the Sun, turning northeasterly in Great Falls.

The Hidatsas had told the Corps that a cottonwood tree held an eagle's nest on an island marking the falls. The eagle's nest was at the fifth falls, site of today's Black Eagle Dam. The Hidatsas also had said only a half day's portage would take the Corps around these falls, but they hadn't reckoned with portaging boats and goods.

Lewis wrote pages and pages in his journal about the "magnificence" and beauty of the waterfalls, concluding that he was sorry not to be a fine poet or painter in order to capture the scene.

A herd of a thousand bison grazed east of the Sun River. In case he couldn't make it back to camp that night, Lewis shot a bison and noted where he could shelter in "a few s[c]attering cottonwood trees" after he examined the Sun. [5] Before he reloaded his gun, a grizzly bear that had "perceived and crept on me" charged. (Reloading took a good 30 seconds, during which an average grizzly could run more than 800 feet on flat land.) There was nowhere to hide "from this monster" and no tree nearby. Lewis ran eighty yards, with the bear gaining on him, waist-deep right into the Missouri, then "faced about and presented the point of my espontoon…" The bear "sudonly wheeled about as if frightened, declined the combat on such unequal grounds, and retreated [toward the Sun River] with quite as great precipitation as he had…pursued me."

Lewis promptly reloaded his gun, vowing

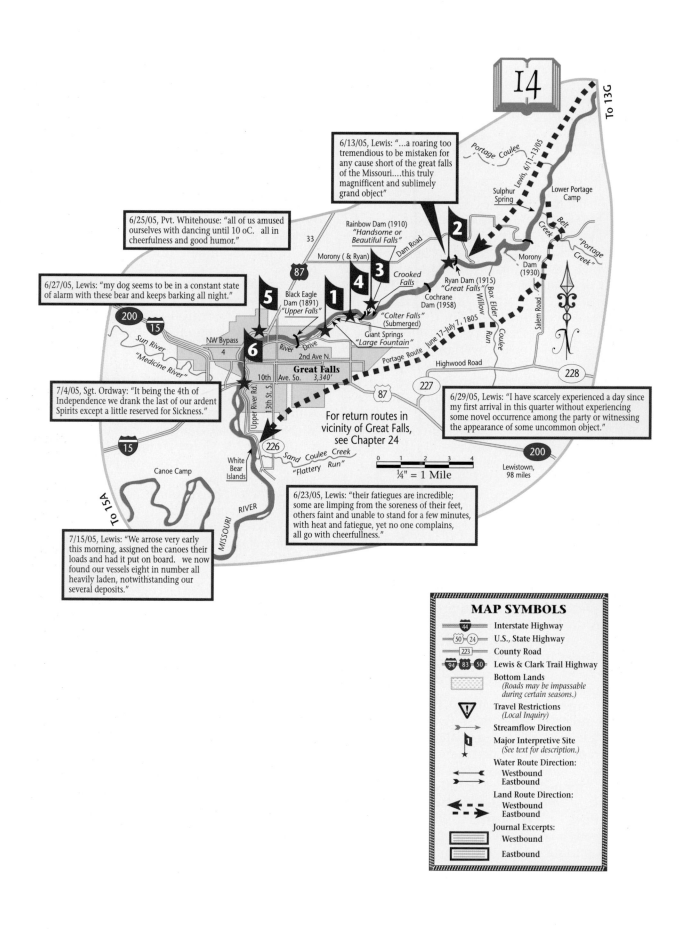

14

To 13G

Portage Coulee

Lewis, 6/11–13/05

6/13/05, Lewis: "...a roaring too tremendious to be mistaken for any cause short of the great falls of the Missouri....this truly magnificent and sublimely grand object"

Sulphur Spring

Lower Portage Camp

Belt Creek

"Portage Creek"

2

Morony Dam (1930)

6/25/05, Pvt. Whitehouse: "all of us amused ourselves with dancing until 10 oC. all in cheerfullness and good humor."

33

Rainbow Dam (1910) "Handsome or Beautiful Falls"

Dam Road

Crooked Falls

Morony (& Ryan)

87

Ryan Dam (1915) "Great Falls"

Box Elder

Willow

Coulee

Run

Salem Road

N

6/27/05, Lewis: "my dog seems to be in a constant state of alarm with these bear and keeps barking all night."

4 3

Cochrane Dam (1958)

5

Black Eagle Dam (1891) "Upper Falls"

1

"Colter Falls" (Submerged)

200 15

NW Bypass

4

Giant Springs "Large Fountain"

Portage Route June 17–July 7, 1805

Highwood Road

228

Sun River "Medicine River"

River Drive

2nd Ave N.

6

Great Falls Ave. So. 3,340'

10th

87

227

7/4/05, Sgt. Ordway: "It being the 4th of Independence we drank the last of our ardent Spirits except a little reserved for Sickness."

Upper River Rd.

13th St. S.

6/29/05, Lewis: "I have scarcely experienced a day since my first arrival in this quarter without experiencing some novel occurrence among the party or witnessing the appearance of some uncommon object."

15

226

For return routes in vicinity of Great Falls, see Chapter 24

200

To 15A

White Bear Islands

Sand Coulee Creek "Flattery Run"

0 1 2 3 4

¼" = 1 Mile

Lewistown, 98 miles

Canoe Camp

MISSOURI RIVER

7/15/05, Lewis: "We arrose very early this morning, assigned the canoes their loads and had it put on board. we now found our vessels eight in number all heavily laden, notwithstanding our several deposits."

6/23/05, Lewis: "their fatiegues are incredible; some are limping from the soreness of their feet, others faint and unable to stand for a few minutes, with heat and fatiegue, yet no one complains, all go with cheerfullness."

MAP SYMBOLS

44	Interstate Highway
50 24	U.S., State Highway
223	County Road
94 83 50	Lewis & Clark Trail Highway

Bottom Lands
(Roads may be impassable during certain seasons.)

Travel Restrictions
(Local Inquiry)

Streamflow Direction

Major Interpretive Site
(See text for description.)

Water Route Direction:
Westbound
Eastbound

Land Route Direction:
Westbound
Eastbound

Journal Excerpts:
Westbound
Eastbound

never to leave it empty again. He also decided the bear wouldn't stop him from seeing the Sun, and followed in the animal's path. He didn't see the bear again, but changed his mind about staying here overnight. It was well after dark by the time he got back to camp, where his three companions had already planned a search party for morning.

After Lewis's group rejoined the canoe party, the captains planned their portage. They hid the white pirogue north of the lower camp, and separately cached other items to retrieve on their return trip. Clark and five others surveyed a route on the south side of the Missouri, marking it with willow sticks. The prairie had been trampled by bison when it was wet, and now was covered with hard clay ridges of hoofprints. Low prickly pear cactus grew everywhere. Before beginning the portage, the men sewed more leather onto their moccasins; nevertheless, their feet were bruised and bloody every day.

From the camp northeast of Great Falls, the men dragged the canoes three fourths of a mile to Belt Creek, then one and three fourths miles up the creek, then walked overland for eighteen miles. They sliced wheels from logs, and built a carriage to hold the canoes. Made from soft cottonwood, the carriages broke frequently, and trees were scarce here. Most of the time the men pulling carriages walked bent into a hard west wind, but sometimes were able to put up the canoes' sails and let the wind help them.

After organizing the portage, Clark was kbased at the Lower Portage Camp, northeast of today's city of Great Falls, with most of the men and the Charbonneau family. Lewis formed Upper Portage Camp at the upstream end of the portage, on White Bear Islands in the Missouri. Now attached to the shore, one of those "islands" can be glimpsed during high water. Ferrying the canoes and their goods began on June 23 and took eight days. It was such exhausting work that the men fell asleep the moment they paused for rest, but they went at the work cheerfully. According to Clark, "to State the fatigues of this party would take up more of the journal than other notes..."

When rain made the ground too wet and slippery for the carriage on June 29, the men carried what they could on their backs. Clark wanted to replace notes he had lost, and his group from Lower Portage Camp went along to view the falls. When the rain began, all his group but York, hunting bison nearby, took shelter in a ravine. A flash flood washed down, and Clark, the Charbonneau family, and the others, barely survived. Watching from a different ravine, York thought them lost. The baby's mosquito netting and clothing washed away, as did Clark's surveying compass. The next day, men of the Corps located the compass, and saw the ravine now filled with rocks by the powerful flood.

Three men drew easier duty than hauling goods over the portage. Sergeant Patrick Gass and privates Joseph Field and John Shields were to put together a ninety-nine–pound, strap-iron boat frame that Lewis had designed, ordered built at the Harpers Ferry Arsenal in Virginia, and carried all this way. For its size and freight capacity, it would be light in weight. They had to hunt for hides to cover the frame—twenty-eight elk and four bison skins were needed—and gather wood to make interior parts.

All hands worked on the iron-frame boat on July 4, and in the evening held a party celebrating Independence Day. The last of the spirits were passed around, bacon, bison, beans, and dumplings comprised dinner, and dancing to Cruzatte's fiddle went on until a rain shower sent the Corps to bed.

Finished on July 9, the iron-frame boat was thirty-six feet long and expected to carry up to four tons of cargo. But when launched, the boat leaked and had to be abandoned. Unfortunately, Lewis had counted on having pine pitch to waterproof the seams, but there was none in this area. He wrote he was "mortified." The men had to find trees big enough to make two more dugout canoes to carry what the iron-frame boat would have.

Finally, on July 14, the two new canoes were finished and the Corps of Discovery could set off again upriver. They needed to cross the Rockies before winter. And they still had no idea how wide that mountain barrier would be.

TOURING TODAY

ᔇ AROUND THE GREAT FALLS ᔇ

[ ] Bracketed numbers key sites to maps	♿ Special-needs accessible	⚑ Bed & breakfast
★ L&C in-depth interpretation, unchanged landform	⊗ Restaurant	▲ Camping, RV park
● L&C interpreted site	⊞ Motel, hotel, cabin	

Bridges over the Missouri River in this area are in Great Falls, MT at 10th Avenue South, 9th Street; Central Avenue West; 15th Street.

ALONG THE EXPEDITION'S PATH

Driving tour of the portage from Willow Run to White Bear Islands is available; however, permission must be obtained in advance. Access can be arranged by contacting the Portage Route Chapter, P.O. Box 2424, Great Falls, MT 59403.

Audio driving tour is available from the Cascade County Historical Museum at Paris Gibson Square, 1400 1st Ave N. Detailed map and tape. Tour is 34 miles and takes about 90 minutes.

June 16 to July 9, 1805
(Lewis Return July 11-17, 1806)
(Ordway Return July 22-27, 1806)
[1] Lewis and Clark National Historic Trail Interpretive Center (Great Falls, MT)—Visits begin with an excellent half-hour film by Ken Burns and Dayton Duncan, which sets the stage for exhibits featuring the Corps' travels through Indian country, with emphasis on Indian cultures of 1800s. Life-size, 2-story portage diorama. Test your ability to pull a canoe upstream. Overlooks, ♿ interpretive trails, living history site, along south shore of Missouri River. Home to extensive archives and headquarters of the Lewis and Clark Trail Heritage Foundation. Daily 10 to 5, longer summer hours; admission fee. Adjacent to

Giant Spring State Park, 3 miles E of US 87 on River Drive. 406/727-8733.
Sacagawea Springs (Great Falls, MT)—See wildlife and native plants on the hike to the sulfur springs. Hike is a mile along the top of bluffs just above Morony Dam.
[2] ★ Ryan Dam Park (Great Falls, MT)—Extensive interpretation in a delightful park along the river. Hiking, fishing, picnic area. Daily dawn to dusk; free. 406/723-5454.
[3] ▲ Rainbow Dam and Overlook (Great Falls, MT)—Bike trails, interpretive exhibits, picnic area. Dawn to dusk; free. 406/454-5858.
[4] ★ Giant Springs State Park (Great Falls, MT)—Lewis was right—on June 18, 1805—when he thought Giant Springs the largest freshwater spring in the nation; it may be the largest in the world. A picnic and leisurely walk down River's Edge Trail (see below) are a delightful way to pass a summer day. Interpretive trail/♿ details the movements of Lewis and Clark. Interpretive displays and videos about the state's flora and fauna and the importance of the area to the Corps of Discovery. The **Lewis and Clark Encampment**, held the last weekend in June, affords visitors the opportunity to participate in a living interpretation of the expedition's portage around the great falls. Giant Springs provides ♿ mobility-impaired visitors with fishing and picnicking options as well as access to the visitor center and fish hatchery. Daily dawn to dusk; admission fee. 3 miles E of US 87 on River Drive. 406/454-3441.

River's Edge Trail (Great Falls, MT)—Ten-mile paved trail along the Missouri from Oddfellows Park at 9th Ave. S and River Drive past Black Eagle Falls, Giant Springs, and Rainbow Falls.
● **Black Eagle Falls** (Black Eagle, MT)—Overlook and interpretation. Always open; free. River Rd & 25th St N.
[5] ★ West Bank Park (Great Falls, MT)—Here is where the grizzly bear nearly caught Captain Lewis. Interpretation, wildlife viewing, picnic area. Daily dawn to dusk; free. 17 Ave NE & 3rd St NW.
[6] ★ Broadwater Portage Overlook (Great Falls, MT)—Heroic bronze sculpture, monument to the Corps. Information center and interpretive displays. Daily 8 to 8 (Memorial Day-Labor Day); free. 10th Avenue S & 2nd Street. 406/771-0885.

Ordway Return July 19, 1806
White Bear Islands (Great Falls, MT)—Viewpoint for the Lower Portage Camp and cache is on Upper River Road at 40th Ave S. Campsite was on south end of largest island and cache was on the knoll.

AROUND THE AREA

TOWNS LISTED ALPHABETICALLY

Belt, Montana
Sluice Boxes State Park—Dramatic limestone canyon with ghost towns, abundant wildlife and great fishing. Hiking is a worthwhile challenge; bring plenty of water, sunscreen and insect

repellent. No facilities. Daily dawn to dusk; free. 5 miles S on US 89, 2 miles W on Evans-Riceville Rd. 406/454-3441.

Bynum, Montana

Blackleaf Wildlife Management Area—Bears are frequent visitors here, as are elk and deer. Hike into dramatic Blackleaf Canyon from the end of the road to see a large mountain goat herd and several raptors' nests. Daily sunrise to sunset; free. 16 miles W of Bynum on Blackleaf Rd. 406/278-7754.

Great Falls, Montana

Great Falls Chamber of Commerce, 926 Central Ave. 406/761-4434.

Benton Lake National Wildlife Refuge—The 9-mile Prairie Marsh Drive is best for seeing enormous flocks of Canada geese and tundra swans. Interpretive signs are keyed to a brochure available at the Refuge office. Daily 9 to 4; free. 1 mile N on US 87, 12 miles N on Bootlegger Trail. 406/727-7400.

Cascade County Historical Museum—Permanent and rotating exhibits. Early Montana history and mining's impact on the area. Volunteers conduct tours to local historical sites. Mon-Fri 10 to 5, Sat/Sun noon to 5 (summer); donations. 1400 1st Ave. N (Paris Gibson Square) 406/452-3462.

Paris Gibson Square Museum of Arts—Rotating and permanent exhibits of contemporary art. Tue-Fri 10-5, Sat and Sun 12-5; donations. 1400 1st Ave. N (Paris Gibson Square) 406/727-8255.

Malmstrom Air Force Base Museum and Air Park—Military buffs will enjoy this display recounting the base's history. Outside is the air park with examples of the hardware used on the base since the 1950s. Base tours given on Fridays. Mon-Sat noon to 3 (Memorial Day-Labor Day), Mon/Wed/Fri noon to 3 (rest of year); free. East end of 2nd Ave. S, 406/731-2705; 406/731-2427 (tours).

C.M. Russell Museum—Museum complex includes Russell's log cabin studio and home. The studio houses his collection of cowboy memorabilia and the home itself is furnished as it was during his life. Along with his paintings and sculptures, illustrated letters displayed in the museum offer a unique glimpse into the character of this artist. Kids will enjoy the feel of life in the old west. Open 9 to 6, Sunday 1 to 5 in the summer; winter hours are 10 to 5, 1 to 5 Sunday, closed on Monday; fee. 400 13th St. N, 406/727-8787.

▲ **KOA Great Falls**—150 sites; fee; water; modern; open all year; grills/fire rings; tables. Dump station; playground; hot tub; water slides; groceries; hiking; coin laundry. 4.5 miles SE on US 87. 1500 51st St. 406/727-3191.

▲ **Thain Creek**—20 sites; fee; water; primitive; open June-Sept; grills/fire rings; tables; 22' limit. Fishing; 5 interconnecting trails for day hikes. 6 miles E on US 89, 13 miles E on MT 228, 16 miles E on CR 121, 2 miles E on FR 8841. 406/566-2292.

▦ **Comfort Inn**—64 rooms, pets, indoor pool, continental breakfast, hot tub. Off-season rates. 1120 9th St. S. 406/454-2727. $$ K18

▦ **Fairfield Inn**—63 rooms, indoor pool, continental breakfast, hot tub. Off-season rates. 1000 9th Ave. S. 406/454-3000. $$ K16

▦ **Heritage Inn**—239 rooms, pets, indoor pool, tennis courts, jogging, ⊗ restaurant, hot tub, coin laundry. 1700 Fox Farm Rd. 406/791-1900, 800/548-0361. $$$ K12

▦ **Townhouse Inn**—109 rooms, pets, pool, ⊗ restaurant, hot tub, coin laundry. 1411 10th Ave. S. 406/761-4600. $$ K12

⊗ **Borries**—Hearty servings of pasta, steak and seafood. D daily. 1800 Smelter Ave. 406/761-0300. $$$

⊗ **Eddies**—Campfire steaks & burgers. B L & D daily. 38th & 2nd Ave N. 406/456-1616. $$

⊗ **Jaker's**—Cozy steak and seafood place; kids' menu. L & D weekdays, D only S/S. 10 Ave. S & 15th St. 406/727-1033. $$

Neihart, Montana

Memorial Falls Trail #738—Half-mile hike to 2 waterfalls. Get out of the car and stretch your legs. 1.5 miles SE on US 89. 406/547-3361.

▲ **Aspen**—6 sites; fee; water; primitive; open May-Aug; grills/fire rings; tables; 22' limit. Fishing; hiking. 6 miles N on US 89. 406/547-3361.

▲ **Kings Hill**—23 sites; fee; water; primitive; open May-Oct; grills/fire rings; tables; 22' limit. Hiking trails. 9 miles S on US 89. 406/547-3361.

▲ **Many Pines**—23 sites; fee; water; primitive; open May-Oct; grills/fire rings; tables; 22' limit. Fishing; hiking. 4 miles S on US 89. 406/547-3361.

▦ **Kings Hill Forest Service Cabin**—6 beds; available all year. 5 miles S on US 89, year-round access. 406/547-3361. $

Ulm, Montana

Ulm Pishkun State Park—Before they had the horse, Indians hazed bison to nearby grazing areas, then stampeded them over this cliff. Animals that survived the 30' fall were killed with bows and arrows or stone clubs. Interpretive trail atop the cliff. Visitor center below the jump offers a hands-on interpretation of daily life and the buffalo's significance as the Indians' main source of food, clothing, and shelter. I-15 exit 270 (Ulm), 6 miles NW on Ulm-Vaughn Rd. Parts of the gravel road to the pishkun are steep and large trailers may be tough to maneuver. Pishkun area open daily dawn to dusk (entrance road closed mid-Oct to mid-Apr), visitor center open daily 10 to 6 (Memorial Day-Sept), Wed-Sat 10 to 4, Sun noon to 4 (rest of year); admission fee. 406/866-2217.

CHAPTER 15

July 15 to 29, 1805

THREE FORKS OF THE MISSOURI

With eight canoes heavily loaded, the Corps of Discovery were happy to head up the Missouri River by water again, now traveling south across Montana. Even so, as many men as could be spared from manning the canoes walked ashore to lighten the boats' loads and to hunt. Near today's town of Ulm, they passed the mouth of and named Smith River after Secretary of the Navy Robert Smith. Where they didn't learn Indian names, they named creeks and rivers for relatives, men in Jefferson's cabinet, and members of the Corps. Most of these names have been changed, but not those of the Marias, Judith (for the future Mrs. Clark, called both Judith and Julia Hancock), Smith, Dearborn, Gallatin, Madison, and Jefferson, and a few other rivers.

The Corps trudged over blooming prickly pear cactus, which Captain Meriwether Lewis called "one of the beauties as well as the greatest pests of the plain." To the west rose a large butte they named Fort Mountain. Today called Square Butte, it is visible from Interstate 15. South of there, on July 18, they named a river for Secretary of War Henry Dearborn.

As always, the captains made astronomical observations necessary for accurate maps, and noted all plants and animals new to them. They recorded descriptions of each creature, how many were seen, and their habitats. Along this stretch of the Missouri, they noted the abundance of otters and beavers.

They also were eagerly watching for Sacagawea's people, the Shoshones, who might be hunting along here. But the Corps had to fire guns to hunt for food, and were afraid the Shoshones would think them an enemy war party—and hide. The Corps needed to trade for Shoshone horses to carry supplies over the short portage they expected across a single mountain range between the headwaters of the Missouri and those of the Columbia.

So, on July 18, Captain William Clark took his servant York and privates Joseph Field and John Potts ahead of the main party, to search for the Shoshones. They followed a well worn Indian trail on the west side of the Missouri. Camping on "Pryor's Creek" (named for Private Nathaniel Pryor, it later became Spokane Creek) on the 19th, Clark wrote that he pulled 17 cactus spines from his feet.

That day Lewis and party entered "dark and gloomy" cliffs the Missouri had "forced" its way through. For nearly six miles, they rowed in swift current where the river was narrowed by what Lewis called **[2]** "The Gates of the Rocky Mountains." They saw bighorn sheep walking comfortably along narrow shelves, high up perpendicular cliffs. It was hard to find a flat spot on shore to camp that night.

Lewis and the main party came out of this canyon the next day, and traveled into the broad Prickly Pear Valley that is north of today's Helena (Montana's capital—in the nation's only Lewis and Clark County). He took special notes on the many birds he saw: geese, cranes, curlews, sharp-tailed grouse, and more. Ahead, Clark needed to hunt for food. Just to make sure his men didn't scare off the Shoshones, he walked three miles farther up the Missouri looking for them, then backtracked *four* miles before allowing guns to be fired.

Lewis collected wild onions on the 22nd and the main party ate them for breakfast, enjoying the treat of a fresh vegetable. Even better, Sacagawea recognized the country around Beaver Creek north of today's Townsend, and said the Three Forks were not far ahead. Lewis feared more unforeseen delays like that of the Great Falls, but Sacagawea reassured him. That afternoon, Lewis and the canoe flotilla caught up with Clark's advance party, which had stayed in camp to hunt and rest their stone-bruised, cactus-pierced feet. Lewis offered to spell his co-captain, but Clark set off again next day leading a different group. Lewis ordered flags raised on the canoes, hoping the Shoshones would understand they were not a war party.

Both the main party and the smaller advance one suffered tremendously from mosquitoes, gnats, and prickly pear cactus.

Before stopping for breakfast on July 25, Clark's

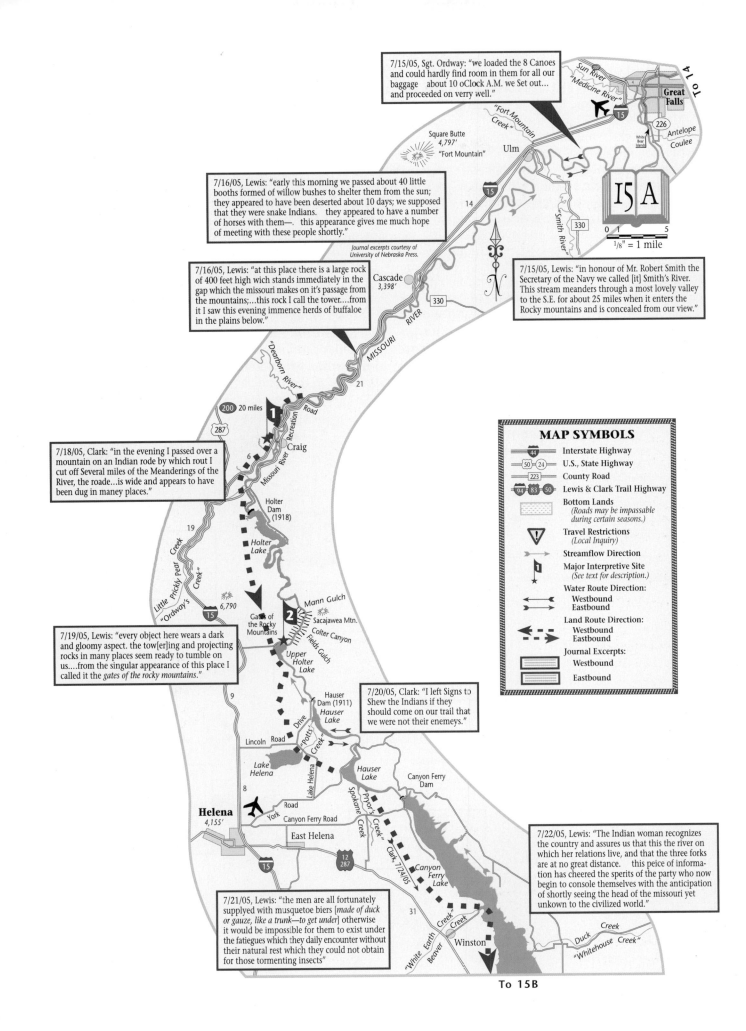

7/15/05, Sgt. Ordway: "we loaded the 8 Canoes and could hardly find room in them for all our baggage   about 10 oClock A.M. we Set out... and proceeded on verry well."

7/16/05, Lewis: "early this morning we passed about 40 little booths formed of willow bushes to shelter them from the sun; they appeared to have been deserted about 10 days; we supposed that they were snake Indians.   they appeared to have a number of horses with them—.   this appearance gives me much hope of meeting with these people shortly."

Journal excerpts courtesy of University of Nebraska Press.

7/16/05, Lewis: "at this place there is a large rock of 400 feet high wich stands immediately in the gap which the missouri makes on it's passage from the mountains;...this rock I call the tower....from it I saw this evening immence herds of buffaloe in the plains below."

7/15/05, Lewis: "in honour of Mr. Robert Smith the Secretary of the Navy we called [it] Smith's River. This stream meanders through a most lovely valley to the S.E. for about 25 miles when it enters the Rocky mountains and is concealed from our view."

7/18/05, Clark: "in the evening I passed over a mountain on an Indian rode by which rout I cut off Several miles of the Meanderings of the River, the roade...is wide and appears to have been dug in maney places."

7/19/05, Lewis: "every object here wears a dark and gloomy aspect. the tow[er]ing and projecting rocks in many places seem ready to tumble on us....from the singular appearance of this place I called it the *gates of the rocky mountains*."

7/20/05, Clark: "I left Signs to Shew the Indians if they should come on our trail that we were not their enemeys."

7/22/05, Lewis: "The Indian woman recognizes the country and assures us that this the river on which her relations live, and that the three forks are at no great distance.   this peice of information has cheered the sperits of the party who now begin to console themselves with the anticipation of shortly seeing the head of the missouri yet unknown to the civilized world."

7/21/05, Lewis: "the men are all fortunately supplied with musquetoe biers [*made of duck or gauze, like a trunk—to get under*] otherwise it would be impossible for them to exist under the fatiegues which they daily encounter without their natural rest which they could not obtain for those tormenting insects"

MAP SYMBOLS

Interstate Highway
U.S., State Highway
County Road
Lewis & Clark Trail Highway
Bottom Lands *(Roads may be impassable during certain seasons.)*
Travel Restrictions *(Local Inquiry)*
Streamflow Direction
Major Interpretive Site *(See text for description.)*
Water Route Direction: Westbound / Eastbound
Land Route Direction: Westbound / Eastbound
Journal Excerpts: Westbound / Eastbound

1/8" = 1 mile

Great Falls

Ulm

Cascade 3,398'

Square Butte 4,797' "Fort Mountain"

Craig

Holter Dam (1918)

Holter Lake

Gates of the Rocky Mountains

Upper Holter Lake

Mann Gulch

Sacajawea Mtn.

Colter Canyon

Fields Gulch

Hauser Dam (1911) Hauser Lake

Lake Helena

Helena 4,155'

East Helena

Canyon Ferry Dam

Hauser Lake

Canyon Ferry Lake

Winston

To 15B

party reached the **[3]** Three Forks of the Missouri and faced the same big decision they had at the Marias River: which was the "main" fork to follow to the Rockies and the hoped-for easy passage to the Columbia River? From the writings of earlier coastal explorers, they knew that the Columbia would take them to the Pacific Ocean, but not where to connect with its tributaries.

The Three Forks were nearly of equal size. Clark quickly decided to investigate what he called the north fork—which actually flowed from the west—as recommended by the Mandans. Leaving a note for Lewis, he pushed on for another fifteen miles before camping. The next day he and privates Reubin Field and Robert Frazer made a twenty-five–mile round trip, including a 2,175-foot climb up a mountain, to scout the way ahead and look for Shoshones.

En route up the mountain Clark and the two

privates passed above, but did not see, the entrance to the spectacular Lewis and Clark Caverns, which weren't found until 1892. President Theodore Roosevelt named them Lewis and Clark National Monument in 1908.

Back down from the mountain, thirsty in the hot sun, they found a cold spring and drank freely, following the medical recommendation of the day: wetting face, hands, and feet before taking an icy drink on a warm day.

Clark became ill from what Lewis later thought were "the effects of the water," and suffered several days with a high fever, chills, weakness, and "a general soarness." Some scholars think he may have contracted what we today call Colorado tick fever.

Clark's party went back for Charbonneau and Joseph Field, who were waiting below, and crossed overland to the "middle" fork before camping.

MAP SYMBOLS

- Interstate Highway
- U.S., State Highway
- County Road
- Lewis & Clark Trail Highway
- Bottom Lands (Roads may be impassable during certain seasons.)
- Travel Restrictions (Inquire Locally)
- Streamflow Direction
- Major Interpretive Site (See text for description.)
- Water Route Direction: Westbound / Eastbound
- Land Route Direction: Westbound / Eastbound
- Journal Excerpts: Westbound / Eastbound

To 15A

To 16A

$^1/_8$" = 1 mile

7/24/05, Lewis: "our trio of pests still invade and obstruct us on all occasions, these are the Musquetoes eye knats and prickley pears, equal to any three curses that ever poor Egypt laiboured under, except the *Mahometant yoke*."

7/26/05, Lewis: "these barbed seed penetrate our mockersons and leather legings and give use great pain untill they are removed. my poor dog suffers with them excessively, he is constantly [biting] and scratching himself as if in a rack of pain."

7/27/05, Lewis: "we are now several hundred miles within the bosom of this wild and mountanous country, where game may rationally be expected shortly to become scarce and subsistence precarious without any information with rispect to the country not knowing how far these mountains continue, or where to direct our course to pass them to advantage or intersept a navigable branch of the Columbia."

Journal excerpts courtesy of University of Nebraska Press.

7/26/05, Clark: "We Contind. thro a Deep Vallie without a Tree to Shade us Scorching with heat,...I was fatigued my feet with Several blisters & Stuck with prickley pears."

7/28/05, Lewis: "Our present camp is precisely on the spot that the Snake Indians were encamped at the time the Minnetares of the Knife R. first came in sight of them five years since ....*Sah-cah-gar-we-ah* o[u]r Indian woman was one of the female prisoners taken at that time."

About nine the next morning, July 27, Lewis's party reached the Three Forks. The men camped and started curing deerskins for clothing. Clark's group arrived at midafternoon.

In his journal for the 27th, Lewis worried about finding the Shoshones and getting information and horses. The Corps didn't know "how far these mountains continue, or wher to direct our course" to reach the Columbia. Game was abundant here, but in the "wild and mountanous country" ahead, meat would become scarce. Lewis decided that if the Shoshones could survive in such country, so could the Corps.

The captains soon would name the Three Forks of the Missouri: from the southeast came the Gallatin River, for Secretary of the Treasury Albert Gallatin. The "middle" fork was the Madison for Secretary of State, and future president, James Madison. The third fork, which flowed from the southwest, they decided correctly was the main branch. So they named it for Thomas Jefferson.

At the Three Forks, the Corps of Discovery was camped exactly where Sacagawea's people had been five years earlier when the enemy Hidatsas arrived. She told how the Shoshones recognized enemies and ran (about three miles) up the Jefferson River before being attacked, with several men, women, and boys killed, and four women and four boys captured. Lewis marveled at how she seemed to show neither sadness at the memory nor happiness at being in home country.

TOURING TODAY

⇜ THREE FORKS OF THE MISSOURI ⇝

[ ] Bracketed numbers key sites to maps	♿ Special-needs accessible ⊨ Bed & breakfast
★ L&C in-depth interpretation, unchanged landform	⊗ Restaurant ▲ Camping, RV park
● L&C interpreted site	⊞ Motel, hotel, cabin

Bridges over the Missouri River in this area are in Ulm, MT (County 330); Cascade, MT (County 330); Craig, MT area (I-15 and Recreation Rd.); Wolf Creek, MT (Holter Dam); Helena, MT area (County 280 and Canyon Ferry Dam); Townsend, MT (US 12/287); Three Forks, MT (I-90 and County 286).

ALONG THE EXPEDITION'S PATH

July 16,1805
[1] Recreation Road—Exit I-15 at Dearborn and take this road for a scenic drive along the Missouri River.
▲ **Craig** (Craig, MT)—8 sites plus undesignated area; fee; water; primitive; open all year, grills/fire rings; tables. Fishing; boat ramp. I-15 exit at Craig. 406/454-3441.

July 17, 1805
▲ **Log Gulch** (Wolf Creek, MT)—90 sites; fee; water; primitive; showers; open May-Sept; grills/fire rings; tables; 14-day limit; 50' trailer limit. Fishing; boating. On Recreation Road, east side of river. 406/235-4314.

July 19, 1805
(Ordway return July 16, 1806)
[2] ★ **Gates of the Mountains Boat Tour** (Helena, MT)—A narrow gorge on the Missouri River with 1200' sheer cliffs that appear to close behind you. You'll see about the same sights that awed Lewis and Clark. Mountain goats and osprey sightings are common. Pack a lunch, take an early boat and spend some time at the ● **Meriwether Picnic Area** landing. Tours daily May-Sept; admission fee. 17 miles N on I-15. 406/458-5241.
▲ **Coulter** (Holter Lake)—Accessible only by boat or foot. 7 sites; free; water; primitive; open June-Sept; grills/fire rings; tables. Fishing; boating/docks; hiking; access to Gates of the Mountains Wilderness. 406/449-5490.

Hauser Lake State Park/Black Sandy—Fish for kokanee salmon and rainbow trout or enjoy boating access to the Missouri River Canyon between Hauser and Canyon Ferry dams. ▲ 33 sites (4 tent-only); fee; water; modern; showers; open all year/full operation May-Sept; grills/fire rings; tables. Interpretive signs and accessible fishing and swimming areas. Hiking trails. I-15 exit 200, 4 miles E on Lincoln Rd., left on Hauser Dam Road, park is 3 miles down road. 406/444-4720.
▲ **York Bridge** (Helena, MT)—14 sites; fee; **no** water; primitive; open all year; grills/fire rings; tables. Fishing; boat ramp. 5 miles E of Helena on York Rd. 406/444-4720.

July 22, 1805
▲ **White Earth** (Canyon Ferry Reservoir)—12 sites; fee; water; primitive; open all year; grills/fire rings; tables. Fishing; boating; boat ramp. 21 miles S of Helena on US 12, 5.5 miles E on gravel road. 406/475-3310.

July 23, 1805

⚊ **Indian Road** (Canyon Ferry Reservoir)—12 sites; fee; water; primitive; open all year; grills/fire rings; tables. Fishing; boating. 31 miles S of Helena on US 12, E to park. 406/475-3310.

● *Canyon Ferry Reservoir*

⚊ **Chinaman's**—50 sites; fee; water; primitive; open all year; grills/fire rings; tables. Fishing; boating; boat ramp; dock. 11 miles S on US 12; 11.2 miles E on Sec 284. 406/475-3310.

⚊ **Court Sheriff**—40 sites; fee; water; primitive; open all year; grills/fire rings; tables. Fishing; boating; swimming. 11 miles S of Helena on US 12, 11 miles E on Sec 284. 406/475-3310.

⚊ **Hellgate**—47 sites; fee; water; modern; open all year; grills/fire rings; tables. Fishing; boat ramp/dock; swimming. 11 miles S of Helena on US 12; 17 miles E on Sec 284, 0.75 mile on access road. 406/475-3310.

⚊ **Jo Bonner**—15 sites; fee; water; primitive; open all year; grills/fire rings; tables. Fishing; boating; playground; boat ramp; dock. 11 miles S of Helena on US 12, 13 miles E on Sec 284. 406/475-3310.

⚊ **Riverside**—18 sites; fee; water; primitive; open all year; grills/fire rings; tables. Fishing; fishing platform/♿; boating; boat ramp; dock; eagle viewing. 11 miles S of Helena on US 12, 10 miles E on Sec 284, 1 mile N on CR. 406/475-3310.

⚊ **Silos**—15 sites; fee; water; primitive; open all year; grills/fire rings; tables. Fishing; boat ramp. 26 miles S of Helena on US 12, 1.1 miles east on gravel road. 406/475-3310.

July 24, 1805

⚊ **Toston Dam** (Toston, MT)—7 sites; free; **no** water; primitive; open all year; grills/fire rings; tables. Fishing; boating. 2 miles S on US 287, 5 miles SE on gravel road. 406/494-5059.

July 25-29, 1805
(Clark return July 13, 1806)

[3] ★ **Missouri Headwaters State Park** (Three Forks, MT)—It wasn't exactly what they expected, but this is where the Corps achieved their goal of finding the Missouri's source. A variety of interpretive exhibits relate the impact of Lewis and Clark, gold mining, and native plants. Well developed picnic area with paved trails/♿. The park lines both sides of Secondary 286 and runs along the east shore of the Madison and Missouri rivers. Across the road from the campground is a paved interpretive area/♿ and the weathered remains of the second Gallatin City. Several trails lead to the rivers, vista points and a Montana Centennial Acre. Additional interpretation and enhanced exhibits are in progress. ⚊ 21 sites; fee; water; primitive; open all year/full operation May-Sept; grills/fire rings; tables. Fishing; biking; boating. 3 miles E on US 10; 3 miles N on Secondary 286. 406/994-4042.

AROUND THE AREA

TOWNS LISTED ALPHABETICALLY

Boulder, Montana

Radon Mines—Thousands visit these controversial mines annually to "take the cure" for maladies from arthritis to allergies. The level of radon gas is considered safe for miners. Details available from Chamber of Commerce, P.O. Box 67, Boulder, MT 59632.

Helena, Montana

Helena Area Chamber of Commerce, corner of Sixth and Cruse avenues, 406/442-4120.

Archie Bray Foundation—Ceramic artists from around the world teach, study and work here. Walking tour of outdoor gallery. Gallery/gift shop. Daily, 9 to 5; free. 2915 Country Club Dr. 406/443-3502.

Continental Divide Trail #348 (Helena, MT)—Easy 2.5-mile trail up to the Continental Divide with gradual elevation changes. Trailhead is across Ten Mile Creek from the Ten Mile Picnic Area. 406/449-5490.

Gold Collection—To see what drew so many to Montana in the 1860s, visit Wells Fargo Bank, 350 N. Last Chance Gulch or the Federal Reserve, 100 Neill. Both have displays of gold in various forms, including large nuggets found in the area.

Grandstreet Theater—Stone building with a Tiffany window is home to a year-round community theater and children's theater school. 325 N. Park. 406/447-1574.

Hanging Valley National Recreation Trail #247-248—Challenging 6-mile trail with spectacular views (2200' elevation change). Begins at Vigilante Campground by the water pump. 406/449-5490.

Holter Museum of Art—Changing exhibits of regional and national artists as well as workshops and literary readings. Gift shop contains work by local artists and related items. Tue-Sat noon to 5, Sun 1 to 4; admission fee. 12 E. Lawrence 406/442-6400.

Kleffner Ranch—Tour the three-story barn and octagonal stone house built in 1888 on this working cattle ranch east of town. Call for tour times; admission fee. 3 miles E of I-15 on US 12, 1 mile S on Hwy 518. 406/227-6645.

MacDonald Pass—Take US 12 west out of town for a dramatic look at the Continental Divide. The spectacular view is much the same as that seen by Natives Americans and early explorers.

Montana Capitol—Built in 1899, the original dome (encased in Butte copper) and a statue representing Liberty still top the rotunda. Follow signs to the third floor to see the immense mural by Charles M. Russell, ● "Lewis and Clark Meeting Indians at Ross' Hole," portraying the Salish Indians' greeting of September 1805 (See Chapter 17). Daily 8 to 5; free tours. 1301 Sixth Ave.

● **Montana Historical Society Museum**—Permanent and temporary exhibits document the history of Montana and its people. A gallery dedicated to work by Charles M. Russell includes paintings and sculptures as well as illustrated letters to friends. The F. Jay Haynes exhibit tells the story of Yellowstone National Park's official photographer from 1887 to 1916. Group tours are available. Daily 8 to 5, closed on Sun (Sept-May); donations. 225 N. Roberts 406/444-2694.

Mount Helena City Park—700 acres of this 5,486' mountain on the southwest edge of town are a city park. Several marked trails take hikers through a variety of terrain. Portions of all trails are steep, but there are plenty of beautiful spots to stop and rest. Park Ave S of Reeder's Alley, follow Reeder's Village Dr to trailhead parking lot.

Original Governor's Mansion— Home to nine Montana governors and their families, 1913-1959. The 20 rooms and 7 fireplaces reflect the early 1900s. Tue-Sun 12 to 5 (May-Sept), guided tours on the hour; free. 304 N. Ewing, 406/442-3115.

Reeder's Alley—Miners' brick lodgings built during the gold rush of the 1870s line this winding street which houses shops and a ⊗ restaurant. A pioneer cabin is open for tours. On the south end of Park Ave.

St. Helena Cathedral—Fashioned after the Cologne Cathedral, its 230-foot twin spires are visible from afar. Open to the public daily 10 to 4; free. Group tours are available. 509 N. Warren 406/442-5825.

Spring Meadow Lake—Clear, cool water and sandy beaches attract hundreds of visitors even on weekdays with a grassy area for picnics, sunbathing and a game of volleyball. Interpretive nature trail. Daily dawn to dusk; admission fee. US 12 to west side of Helena, N on Joslyn and curve to left on Country Club for 0.5 mile. 406/444-4720.

Tour Train—Catch the train for a narrated historical tour. Trains depart hourly from the 6th Ave. side of the Historical Society Museum from May through September; admission fee. 406/442-1023.

Trout Creek Canyon Trail—Easy 3-mile trail through a scenic canyon starts near the entrance to Vigilante Campground. 406/449-5490.

▲ **Cromwell Dixon**—14 sites; fee; water; primitive; open June-Sept; grills/fire rings; tables; 25' trailer limit. Trail #348 to Moose Creek Campground. 15 miles W on US 12. 406/449-5490.

▲ **Helena Campground**—118 sites (76 w/hookups); fee; water; modern; showers; open all year; grills/fire rings; tables; ⊞ cabins. Pool; hot tub; playground; groceries; coin laundry; dump station. 5820 N. Montana. 406/458-4714.

▲ **Moose Creek**—10 sites; fee; water; primitive; open June-Sept;

grills/fire rings; tables; 20' trailer limit. Fishing; trail #348 to Cromwell Dixon Campground. 10 miles W of Helena on US 12, 5 miles S on Rimini Rd. 406/449-5490.

▲ **Park Lake**—21 sites; fee; water; primitive; open June-Aug; grills/fire rings; tables; 25' trailer limit. Fishing; swimming; non-motorized boating; hiking. Clancy exit off I-15 (S of Helena), 11 miles W on Lump Gulch Rd. 406/449-5490.

▲ **Vigilante Campground**—22 sites; no fee; water; primitive; open May-Aug; grills/fire rings; tables; 20' trailer limit. Fishing; hiking on Hanging Valley National Recreation Trail; Trout Creek Canyon Trail. 20 miles NE on MT 280; 12 miles NE on county road. 406/449-5490.

⊞ **Cavanaugh's Colonial Hotel**— 149 rooms, indoor pool, hot tub, ⊗ restaurant, coin laundry. 2301 Colonial Dr. 406/443-2100. $$$ K18

⊞ **Comfort Inn**—56 rooms, indoor pool, pets, continental breakfast, hot tub. Off-season rates. 750 Fee St. 406/443-1000, 800/228-5150. $$ K18

⊞ **Holiday Inn Express**—75 rooms, continental breakfast, exercise room, coin laundry. Smoke-free/ᶜ. Off-season rates. I-15 exit 92B. 406/449-4000. $$ K18

⊞ **Jorgenson's Holiday Motel**—117 rooms, indoor pool, ⊗ restaurant, exercise room, coin laundry. 1714 11th Ave. 406/442-1770. $$ K10

⊞ **Shilo Inn**—47 rooms, indoor pool, pets, continental breakfast, microwaves, refrigerators, hot tub, coin laundry. Off-season rates. 2020 Prospect Ave. 406/442-0320, 800/222-2244. $$ K12

⊨ **Mountain Meadow Inn**—16 rooms in rural mansion, hot tub, full breakfast, restaurant. Smoke-free. Children welcome. 406/443-7301, 888/776-6466. $$$

⊨ **The Sanders**—7 rooms in restored 1875 mansion, full breakfast. Smoke-free. 6th & Ewing. 406/422-3309.

⊗ **Parrot Confectionery**—Ice cream specialties and handmade chocolates. Mon-Sat 9 to 6. 42 N. Last Chance Gulch. 406/442-1470. $

⊗ **Stonehouse**—Intriguing menu in historic mining area, kids' menu, smoke-free. L & D Mon-Sat, D only Sun, some buffets. 120 Reeders Alley. 406/449-2552. $$

⊗ **Windbag Saloon and Grille**— Fresh-made hamburgers, whole-potato fries, seafood and steak, in a former bordello. L & D Mon-Sat. 19 S. Last Chance Gulch. 406/443-9669. $$

Montana City, Montana

⊞ **Elkhorn Mountain Inn**—22 rooms, pets, continental breakfast. ᶜ. Off-season rates. I-15 exit 187. 406/442-6625. $$ K12

Three Forks, Montana

Three Forks Chamber of Commerce, P.O. Box 1103. 406/285-4556.

● **Headwaters Heritage Museum**—Explore the recreated railroad dispatch office as you learn about the impact of railroads on Montana's early settlements. Open daily 1 to 5 (June-Aug); free. On Main Street, 406/285-3495.

▲ **Three Forks KOA**—70 sites (50 w/hookups); fee; water; modern; showers; open May-Sept; grills/fire rings; tables; ⊞ cabins. Pool; playground; groceries; coin laundry; dump station. I-90 exit 274, 1 mile S on US 287. 406/285-3611.

⊞ **Sacajawea Inn**—33 rooms in historic hotel, full breakfast; pets, hot tub, playground. Smoke-free. $$$ K12. ⊗ Dining room offers beef and pasta specialties. Sun brunch, kids' menu. $$ 5 N. Main St. 406/285-6515, 800/821-7326.

⊨ **Madison River Inn**—5 rooms in stone mansion in mountain valley, full breakfast, fishing, hiking trails, horseback riding. Smoke-free. 406/285-3914. $$$+ K12

Townsend, Montana

Broadwater County Museum— Among the pioneer and Indian artifacts is a huge assortment of barbed wire collected from Montana ranches over the years. How many different types did you think there were? Daily noon to 5 (May-Sept); donations. 133 N. Walnut 406/266-5252.

Wolf Creek, Montana

⊨ **Bungalow B & B**—4 rooms in historic log lodge in the mountains. Full breakfast. Open Apr-Dec. 4 miles N on US 287. 406/235-4276, 888/286-4250. $$

CHAPTER 16

July 30 to August 19, 1805

TO CAMP FORTUNATE

On July 30, 1805, the Corps of Discovery moved up the Jefferson River from their great landmark, the Three Forks of the Missouri in today's Montana. Next goal: find the Shoshones, get horses, and learn where to cross the Rocky Mountains.

Captain Meriwether Lewis walked ahead by himself that day. Near dark, he shot a duck for supper, and "looked...for a suitable place to amuse myself in combating the musquetoes for the ballance of the evening." He built a driftwood fire and slept beside it. The main party caught up next morning just as Lewis had begun to consider proceeding upstream, thinking they had passed by.

Now in Shoshone country, the Corps *had* to find Sacagawea's people before winter set in. The captains decided that Lewis and a small group would go ahead up the Jefferson to "spy," or scout, for them. Captain William Clark, suffering from a "tumor" in one foot, and the rest would continue in the canoes up the rocky, rapid, and increasingly shallow river.

Lewis wrote "we have a lame crew just now..." including "one [John Shields] with his arm accidently dislocated but fortunately well replaced..." From the injured came his advance party: Sergeant Patrick Gass and interpreters Toussaint Charbonneau and George Drouillard. They set out on August 1, and wasted time "thrown several miles out of our rout" by traveling up one of the river's many side channels instead of along its main stream. They camped west of today's Cardwell. Clark and party camped only a few miles east of Cardwell, supping on an elk Lewis's group had killed and left for them. Game was very scarce, and they had had no fresh meat for two days.

In a couple of days Lewis's men reached the mouth of today's Big Hole River, the Wisdom River to them. He noted the wildlife seen, and the various types of berries his group enjoyed. His party was now two days ahead of Clark's.

On August 4, upriver from today's Twin Bridges, Lewis reached a definite fork in the Jefferson River. He concluded—correctly—which was the main stream: today's Beaverhead River. At the fork, Lewis put up a pole with a note for Clark, telling him to proceed up the Beaverhead.

Unfortunately, the pole was green, and a beaver must have chewed it through and carried pole and note away before Clark and the main party arrived.

When they reached the Big Hole River on August 5, Clark thought *this* was the main stream of the Jefferson and traveled ten miles up it before meeting Drouillard, whom Lewis had sent out to hunt. Lewis heard the main group "whooping" and joined them. Just before he arrived, a canoe had tipped over and its baggage got wet, including the medicine box, parched meal and corn, and presents for Indians. Private Joseph Whitehouse was thrown under the canoe, and Lewis thought he would have been crushed if the water were two inches shallower. The reunited Corps camped at the mouth of the Big Hole until noon on August 7 to dry out their goods.

Before meeting Lewis, Clark had sent Private George Shannon hunting ahead up the Big Hole. Shannon had not come back, and Lewis wrote "I am fearful he is lost again." (see Chapter 8). Shannon finally found the Corps three days later. Unlike the time he was lost and starving in South Dakota, "he had lived very plentifully this trip but looked a good deel worried with his march."

The Beaverhead had many meanders and side channels obstructed by beaver dams that made slow going with the canoes. On August 8, Lewis noted that geese "begin to fly," an alarming sign of autumn, which would come early at this elevation. But Sacagawea had good news. In the distance, she recognized a large rock (on today's Madison County–Beaverhead

County line), the one her Shoshone people called The Beaver's Head because of its shape, today known as Beaverhead Rock. She said it was near "the summer retreat of her nation on a river beyond the mountains which runs to the west." The captains thought that river might be the Columbia, just what they sought.

Lewis "determined" to take a small party to "pass the mountains to the Columbia" and find the Shoshones, even if it took a month, "for without horses we shall be obliged to leave a great part of our stores, of which…we have a stock already sufficiently small for the length of the voyage before us."

The next day, after the Corps stopped for an 8:00 a.m. breakfast, Lewis left with Drouillard and privates John Shields and Hugh McNeal. During the day, Lewis climbed the prominence now called Lewis's Lookout to view the land ahead. They camped that night near today's Dillon. On the 10th, they found an Indian trail and followed it to what they named Rattlesnake Cliffs because of the inhabitants.

They soon arrived at splits in both the

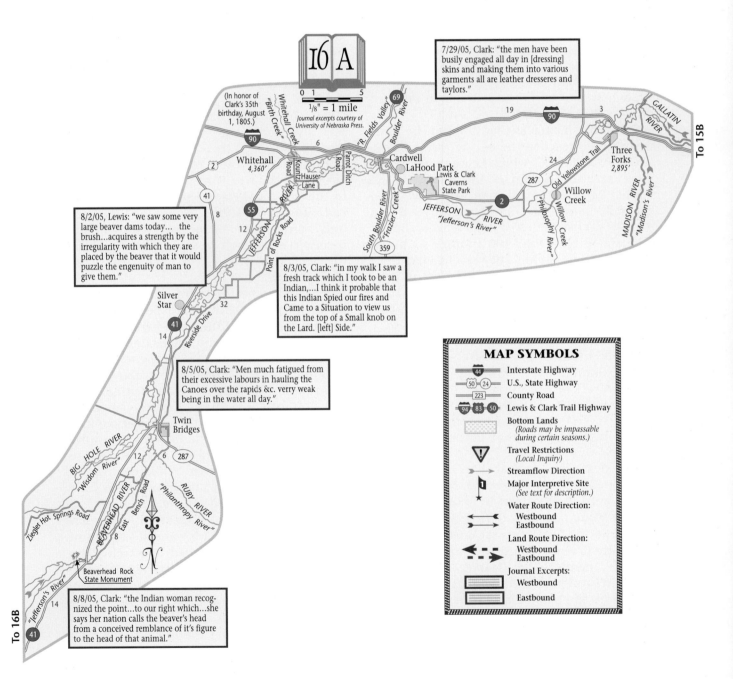

16 A

$\frac{1}{8}$" = 1 mile

(In honor of Clark's 35th birthday, August 1, 1805.)

Journal excerpts courtesy of University of Nebraska Press.

7/29/05, Clark: "the men have been busily engaged all day in [dressing] skins and making them into various garments all are leather dresseres and taylors."

8/2/05, Lewis: "we saw some very large beaver dams today… the brush…acquires a strength by the irregularity with which they are placed by the beaver that it would puzzle the engenuity of man to give them."

8/3/05, Clark: "in my walk I saw a fresh track which I took to be an Indian,…I think it probable that this Indian Spied our fires and Came to a Situation to view us from the top of a Small knob on the Lard. [left] Side."

8/5/05, Clark: "Men much fatigued from their excessive labours in hauling the Canoes over the rapids &c. verry weak being in the water all day."

8/8/05, Clark: "the Indian woman recognized the point…to our right which…she says her nation calls the beaver's head from a conceived remblance of it's figure to the head of that animal."

MAP SYMBOLS

Interstate Highway
U.S., State Highway
County Road
Lewis & Clark Trail Highway

Bottom Lands
(Roads may be impassable during certain seasons.)

Travel Restrictions
(Local Inquiry)

Streamflow Direction

Major Interpretive Site
(See text for description.)

Water Route Direction:
Westbound
Eastbound

Land Route Direction:
Westbound
Eastbound

Journal Excerpts:
Westbound
Eastbound

Beaverhead River and the Indian trail. From the west came today's Horse Prairie Creek, from the east Red Rock River (the junction is now under [2] Clark Canyon Reservoir). Neither creek was navigable with their canoes. After exploring, Lewis decided to follow Horse Prairie Creek to the west. He left a note at the forks telling Clark to camp there—this time careful to choose a *dry* willow pole.

On August 11, about six miles west of today's Clark Canyon Reservoir, Lewis finally saw an Indian. Through his telescope, he could see that the man's clothing was different from any seen so far, and believed this was a Shoshone. And he was riding "an eligant horse." From about 100 paces away, Lewis made the Plains sign for friendship, and yelled what he thought was the Shoshone word for white man, but to no effect. The man galloped off into the brush.

Following his tracks that day and the next, Lewis's men reached the end of Horse Prairie Creek on August 12, which Lewis thought "the most distant fountain of the waters of the mighty Missouri in surch of which we have spent so many toilsome days and wristless nights." (Actually, the Missouri's "most distant fountain" is more than 100 air-miles southeast of where Lewis stood.) They reached the Continental Divide at today's [1] Lemhi Pass, where Lewis saw "immence ranges of high mountains still to the West of us with their tops partially covered with snow."

Less than a mile downhill from the Divide, Lewis and his men "first tasted the water of the great Columbia river," drinking from today's Agency Creek or Horseshoe Bend Creek. When they crossed the Divide into today's Idaho, they also left the Louisiana Purchase and moved into territory that European nations claimed.

The next day, August 13, they met the Shoshones. First, two women and a man, who fled to warn their village. In another mile, an elderly woman and two girls. One girl ran away, and the other two sat down to be captured—they were sure this was a raiding party of their enemies, the Blackfeet. Lewis gave them gifts and persuaded them to call back the girl before she could alarm others. The three agreed to take Lewis's party to their village.

After a couple of miles, here came sixty warriors galloping on fast horses, ready for battle.

Lewis put down his gun and walked toward them carrying a flag, while the women "exultingly" displayed their presents. The warriors and their chief, Cameahwait, hugged in welcome the first whites they had ever met. At their village on the Lemhi River, they fed Lewis and his men the only food they had: cakes of dried serviceberries and chokecherries. Lewis noticed how thin the Shoshones were, but gladly accepted his first food in twenty-four hours.

Shields and Drouillard went hunting—unsuccessfully—with the village's young men the next day. Through Drouillard's sign language, Lewis quizzed Cameahwait about the way west. The chief said his people never went down the river from here, because the mountains were impassable for men or horses, but the Nez Perce had told him that the river "finally lost itself in a great lake of water which was illy taisted, and where the white men lived."

How should they proceed? How, asked Lewis, did the Nez Perce cross the mountains to the Missouri? Cameahwait said via a very bad route north of here, which had no game, only berries, and timber so thick you could barely pass through it. Lewis thought that if the Nez Perce could make it, so could the Corps of Discovery.

He asked Cameahwait to take thirty horses to trade, and go back with him to meet Clark—"my brother chief"—and the main party. The chief spoke to his village, who agreed, but by morning all but Cameahwait feared the whites were working with the Blackfeet to ambush them. Lewis promptly lied that white men didn't do that sort of thing. After Lewis accused the Shoshones of cowardice, Cameahwait mounted up for the trip, saying he hoped some others would join him. At first a few men, and eventually many men, women and children, followed over the Divide. They camped near Trail Creek west of today's Grant, Montana, that night.

On the morning of August 16, Lewis sent Drouillard and Shields ahead to hunt. Shoshone warriors followed to watch them. After Lewis and the village started the day's trek, a Shoshone rider galloped back, making Lewis fear enemies had been seen and no one would believe he had nothing to do with it. But no—the news was that a white man had killed a deer!

The people whipped their horses a mile to the site, and devoured the animal raw. Lewis looked on "with pity and compassion" at their hunger. Two more deer were consumed, "even to the soft parts of the hoofs."

Cameahwait thought the whites and his men should exchange clothing as protection from an ambush, which was done. When they reached the forks of the Beaverhead, Clark wasn't there as Lewis had promised, and the Shoshones

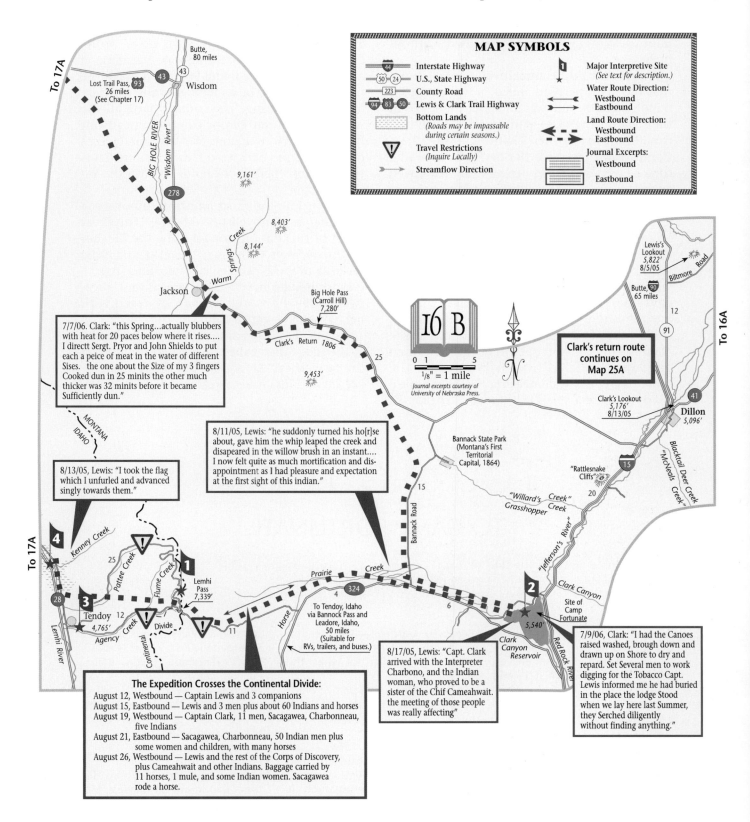

MAP SYMBOLS

- Interstate Highway
- U.S., State Highway
- County Road
- Lewis & Clark Trail Highway
- Bottom Lands *(Roads may be impassable during certain seasons.)*
- Travel Restrictions *(Inquire Locally)*
- Streamflow Direction

- Major Interpretive Site *(See text for description.)*
- Water Route Direction:
  Westbound
  Eastbound
- Land Route Direction:
  Westbound
  Eastbound
- Journal Excerpts:
  Westbound
  Eastbound

1/8" = 1 mile
0 1   5
Journal excerpts courtesy of University of Nebraska Press.

Clark's return route continues on Map 25A

7/7/06. Clark: "this Spring...actually blubbers with heat for 20 paces below where it rises.... I directt Sergt. Pryor and John Shields to put each a peice of meat in the water of different Sises. the one about the Size of my 3 fingers Cooked dun in 25 minits the other much thicker was 32 minits before it became Sufficiently dun."

8/11/05, Lewis: "he suddenly turned his ho[r]se about, gave him the whip leaped the creek and disapeared in the willow brush in an instant.... I now felt quite as much mortification and disappointment as I had pleasure and expectation at the first sight of this indian."

8/13/05, Lewis: "I took the flag which I unfurled and advanced singly towards them."

8/17/05, Lewis: "Capt. Clark arrived with the Interpreter Charbono, and the Indian woman, who proved to be a sister of the Chif Cameahwait. the meeting of those people was really affecting"

7/9/06, Clark: "I had the Canoes raised washed, brough down and drawn up on Shore to dry and repard. Set Several men to work digging for the Tobacco Capt. Lewis informed me he had buried in the place the lodge Stood when we lay here last Summer, they Serched diligently without finding anything."

The Expedition Crosses the Continental Divide:

August 12, Westbound — Captain Lewis and 3 companions

August 15, Eastbound — Lewis and 3 men plus about 60 Indians and horses

August 19, Westbound — Captain Clark, 11 men, Sacagawea, Charbonneau, five Indians

August 21, Eastbound — Sacagawea, Charbonneau, 50 Indian men plus some women and children, with many horses

August 26, Westbound — Lewis and the rest of the Corps of Discovery, plus Cameahwait and other Indians. Baggage carried by 11 horses, 1 mule, and some Indian women. Sacagawea rode a horse.

became suspicious again. Lewis and his men handed their guns to Cameahwait and his warriors. Then Lewis sent Drouillard for the note he himself had left for Clark, and "read" it to Cameahwait, lying that it was *from* Clark and said to wait here. Lewis was fearful that the Shoshones would disappear into the mountains, leaving the Corps stranded without horses.

Lewis had told Cameahwait several times that the main party included "a woman of his nation" who would explain about the Corps in their own language, if only the Shoshones would wait to hear her. That night, August 16, Cameahwait lay close beside Lewis to watch him. Lewis "slept but little as might be well expected, my mind dwelling on the state of the expedition..."

In the morning, Lewis sent Drouillard and a Shoshone guard downriver with a note for Clark. Since they had split up on August 9, a week before, Clark and the main party had progressed only four or five land miles most days—but several times that in river miles—having to tow the canoes up the Beaverhead. Clark wrote that the water was as cold as the "best springs in our country" and the men must have suffered from hypothermia. The same day Lewis was meeting the Shoshones, Clark climbed a steep hill to "spy" ahead; it's known today as Clark's Lookout. On the 14th, they didn't set out until the late hour of 7:00 a.m. because the men were so stiff and sore. The canoes finally reached the forks of the Beaverhead at noon on August 17.

Charbonneau and Sacagawea were walking ahead of Clark that morning, when several Shoshones rode up. Sacagawea, Clark wrote, "made signs to me that they were her nation" and "danced for the joyful Sight..." One of the Indians proved to be a member of the Corps in Shoshone clothing. The Indians sang all the way back to their camp, where Cameahwait hugged Clark in welcome, and tied small pieces of seashells in Clark's red hair, precious items traded from "the nations resideing near the *Sea Coast.*"

Then came the most amazing discovery, a coincidence no novelist could dare: "The Great Chief of this nation proved to be the brother of the *Woman* with us..." (Clark) and "the meeting of those people was really affecting..." (Lewis). Besides her brother Cameahwait, Sacagawea met the young woman captured with her, who had escaped from the Hidatsas.

Part of the Corps and the Shoshones rested at the place they called "Camp Fortunate" on the Beaverhead River. The site today is under [2] Clark Canyon Reservoir.

TOURING TODAY

∽ TO CAMP FORTUNATE ∾

[ ] Bracketed numbers key sites to maps	♿ Special-needs accessible	⚑ Bed & breakfast
★ L&C in-depth interpretation, unchanged landform	⊗ Restaurant	⚠ Camping, RV park
• L&C interpreted site	⊞ Motel, hotel, cabin	

Bridge over the Jefferson River in this area is in Twin Bridges, MT (MT 41). **Bridge** over the Beaverhead River in Dillon, MT (I-15 and MT 41).

ALONG THE EXPEDITION'S PATH

August 1, 1805
MT 2 from Lewis and Clark Cav-

erns to Cardwell—This section hugs the Jefferson River shore; landscape similar to what the Corps saw.
LaHood Park—Interpretive signs about nearby campsite. On MT 2.

August 10, 1805
(Clark return July 11, 1806)
Beaverhead Rock State Park (Dillon, MT)—Sacagawea's landmark is still visible. Interpretation is

planned. Always open; free. 13 miles N on MT 41. 406/834-3413.
Lewis's Lookout (Dillon, MT)—Pullout area for viewing the cliff which is on private land. Lots of rattlesnakes in the area so it's best to stay in the car. 24 miles NW on MT 91, E on Beltmore Rd.

August 12, 1805
[1] ★ **Lemhi Pass National Historic Landmark/Sacajawea Me-**

morial Campground—Day-use only; free; water must be treated; primitive; open June-Sept; grills/fire rings; tables. Hiking; view and interpretation of travel along Horse Prairie and Trail creeks. 10 miles W of Grant on MT 324, 2 miles N on FR 3909 to fork, take left fork for 10 miles. No vehicles over 26 feet permitted; one-lane road with steep, difficult terrain, impassable if wet. Alternative route for wet roads or those towing trailers is to continue on MT 324 to Bannock Pass. From there it is 13 miles to ID 28 and another 26 miles NW to Tendoy. 406/683-3900 or 208/768-2500 for current information and road conditions.

• **Route to First Idaho Camp**—0.75-mile, steep hiking trail down west side of pass to Agency Creek, steep narrow access road requiring 4WD, hiking, along the Byway (see below). Signs at Lemhi Pass leading to trail. Campsite itself is on private property and not accessible. 208/756-5400.

August 13-20, 1805
[3] ★ **Lewis and Clark Back Country Byway Kiosk**—Information on 39-mile loop route through the treacherous terrain encountered by the Corps. Winding, sometimes steep gravel road. Interpretation, hiking trails, picnic areas, overlooks along the route that takes 3 to 4 hours to drive. ▲ Primitive camping. Wildlife viewing; road is gravel and access is limited during rain; inaccessible during winter. Access to Byway near Tendoy Store; see August 13 below.

August 13, 1805—Clark
Clark's Lookout State Park (Dillon, MT)—Undeveloped area that can be easily climbed for the same view Clark had. Interpretive signs are planned. 1 mile N on old Hwy. 91. Always open; free. 406/944-4042.

August 13, 1805—Lewis
[4] • **Sacajawea Monument/ Kenney Creek**—Interpretation about Sacagawea's birthplace. 0.5 mile E of Tendoy/ID 28. 208/756-4562.

• **Tendoy Store**—About where Lewis met the Shoshones. Access to Lewis and Clark Back Country Byway. Primitive camping, wildlife viewing, hiking, fishing. 20 miles S of Salmon on ID 28. 208/756-5400.

August 13-15, 1805
• **Shoshone Camp**—Interpretation about this camp and hiking trails. ID 28, mile markers 122-123. 208/756-3313.

August 17-19, 1805
(Clark return July 8, 1806)
[2] *Clark Canyon Reservoir*
West Shore
▲ **Hap Hawkins**—Primitive camping; free; water; primitive/ &; open all year; grills/fire rings. Hiking; fishing; birding; picnic area. 20 miles S of Dillon off I-15. 406/683-6472.

▲ **Lonetree**—Primitive camping; free; water; primitive/&; open all year; grills/fire rings. Hiking; fishing; boat ramp; birding; picnic area. 20 miles S of Dillon off I-15. 406/683-6472.

East Shore
▲ **West Cameahwait**—Primitive camping; free; water; primitive/&; open all year; grills/fire rings. Hiking; fishing; birding; picnic area. 20 miles S of Dillon off I-15. 406/683-6472.

▲ **Cameahwait**—Primitive camping; free; water; primitive/&; open all year; grills/fire rings. Hiking; fishing; birding; picnic area. 20 miles S of Dillon off I-15. 406/683-6472.

▲ **Horse Prairie**—Primitive camping; free; water; primitive/&; open all year; grills/fire rings. Hiking; fishing; boat ramp; birding; picnic area. 20 miles S of Dillon off I-15. 406/683-6472.

▲ **Lewis & Clark**—Primitive camping; free; water; primitive/ &; open all year; grills/fire rings. Hiking; fishing; birding; picnic area. 20 miles S of Dillon off I-15. 406/683-6472.

▲ **Fishing Access**—Primitive camping; free; water; primitive/&; open all year; grills/fire rings. Hiking; fishing; boat ramp; birding; picnic area. 20 miles S of Dillon off I-15. 406/683-6472.

• **Beaverhead** (Dillon, MT)—Memorial to Sacagawea, expedition interpretation. ▲ Primitive camping; free; water; primitive/&; open all year; grills/fire rings. Hiking; fishing; boat ramp; birding; picnic area. 20 miles S of Dillon off I-15. 406/683-6472.

• **Camp Fortunate Overlook** (Dillon, MT)—Picnic area with view of Shoshone meeting site. Always open; free. 17 miles S on I-15, on Clark Canyon Reservoir. 406/683-6472.

AROUND THE AREA

TOWNS LISTED ALPHABETICALLY

Alder, Montana
▲ **Alder-Virginia City KOA**—50 sites (32 w/hookups); fee; water; modern; showers; open all year; grills/fire rings; tables. Fishing; playground; coin laundry; groceries. 0.25 mile E on MT 287. 406/842-5677, 800/562-1898.

▲ **Ruby Reservoir**—10 sites; free; water; primitive; open all year; grills/fire rings; tables; 36' trailer limit; 14-day limit. Boating; fishing; dig for rubies. 9 miles S to E side of reservoir. 406/494-5059.

Butte, Montana
Butte-Silver Bow Convention and Visitor Bureau—See display of over 700 hand-tied flies from the George Grant collection. Daily 8 to 8 (Memorial Day-Labor Day), Mon-Fri 8 to 5 (rest of year). 1000 George St. 406/494-3177, 800/735-6814.

Arts Chateau—Formerly home to a copper baron's son, this massive structure offers rotating exhibits by area and regional artists. The architecture alone is worth the visit. Tue-Sat 10 to 5, Sun 12 to 5 (summer); Tue-Sat 11 to 4 (rest of year) admission fee. 321 W. Broadway. 406/723-7600.

Bear Gulch Trail #123—Easy 4-mile trail along the gulch to Bear Meadows. I-15 exit 151, 2 miles S on FR 8481. 406/494-2147.

Butte Trolley—Journey through Butte's past on a replica of the original electric trolley system. Tours daily June 1 through Labor Day; admission fee. 2950 Harrison Ave. 406/723-3177, 800/735-6814.

Copper King Mansion—William Clark, one of Montana's early copper barons, spared no expense in building this 34-room mansion. You can even spend the night in one of the four bedrooms used as a ⚑ bed and breakfast. Daily 9 to 4 (May-Sept); admission fee. 219 W. Granite St. 406/782-7580.

Mineral Museum—1,300 specimens including a 27.5-ounce gold nugget found south of Butte. Be sure to ask the curator about local digging spots. Daily 9 to 6 (Memorial Day to Labor Day), Mon-Fri, 8 to 5 Sun 1 to 5 (rest of year); free. On the Montana Tech campus, at the top of the hill near the Marcus Daly statue, 406/496-4414.

Sheepshead Trail System—5-mile system of trails/♿ begins at Sheepshead Mountain Recreation Area. Waterfowl, birds and small mammals are common here along with deer and sometimes moose or elk. Fishing area/♿. ♿ campsites available nearby at ▲ Lowland and Freedom Point campgrounds. I-15 exit 138, 6 miles W on FR 442. 406/494-2147.

U.S. High Altitude Sports Center—Athletes from around the world train here using biking, roller and ice skating, running and weight training programs. The world class speed skating oval is the site of national and international competition. For information or a schedule of events call 406/723-7060.

World Museum of Mining and Hell Roarin' Gulch—Outdoor museum of more than 20 buildings provides an opportunity for visitors to wander the brick streets of a mining camp and tour the mine's hoist house. The Neversweat and Washoe RR takes you on a guided tour past mines and headframes. Daily 9 to 9 (June-Labor Day), 9 to 5 (spring and fall); admission fee. West end of Park and Granite Streets, signs near the Marcus Daly statue, 406/723-7211.

▲ **Freedom Point**—5 tent sites/all ♿; free; water; primitive; June-Aug; grills/fire rings; tables; group camping/♿ and picnic area/♿. Fishing. I-15 exit 138, 9 miles W on FR 442. 406/494-2147.

▲ **KOA-Butte**—111 sites (85 w/hookups); fee; water; modern; showers; open Apr-Oct; grills/fire rings; tables. Pool; fishing; playground; coin laundry; groceries; dump station. I-90 exit 126, follow signs. 406/782-8080, 800/562-8089.

▲ **Ladysmith**—6 sites; free; **no** water; primitive; open Memorial Day-Nov; grills/fire rings; tables; 16' trailer limit. Fishing. I-15 exit 151, 4 miles W on FR 82. 406/494-2147.

▲ **Lowland**—11 sites/all ♿; free; water; primitive; open Memorial Day-Labor Day; grills/fire rings; tables; 22' trailer limit. I-15 exit 138, 8 miles W on FR 442, 1.5 miles S on FR 9485. 406/494-2147.

▲ **Mormon Gulch**—16 sites; free; **no** water; open Memorial Day-Labor Day; grills/fire rings; tables; 16' trailer limit. Fishing. I-15 exit 151, 2 miles W on FR 82. 406/494-2147.

▲ **Whitehouse**—5 sites; free; water; vault toilets; open Memorial Day-Nov; grills/fire rings; tables; 22' trailer limit. Fishing; hiking. I-15 exit 151, 8 miles W on FR 82. 406/494-2147.

⊞ **Comfort Inn**—150 rooms, pets, continental breakfast, hot tub, coin laundry. Off season rates. I-90/I-15 exit 127. 406/494-8850. $$ K18

⊞ **Copper King**—150 rooms, pool, pets, continental breakfast, ⊗ restaurant, coin laundry, tennis courts, hot tub. Off season rates. I-15 & I-90 exit 127A. 406/494-6666. $$$ K18

⊞ **Holiday Inn Express**—82 rooms, continental breakfast, coin laundry. Off season rates. I-90 exit 127. 406/494-6999. $$

⊞ **War Bonnet Inn**—134 rooms, indoor pool, pets, hot tub, ⊗ restaurant. Off-season rates. I-15 & I-90 exit 127B. 406/494-7800. $$$ K18

⊗ **Lydia's**—Full Italian dinners, kids' menu. D daily. 4915 Harrison 406/494-2000. $$

⊗ **Metals Banque**—Standard fare in restored 1906 bank, kids' menu. L & D daily. 8 W. Park St. 406/723-6160. $$

⊗ **Uptown Cafe**—Continental fare in modern setting, L buffet. L & D daily. Smoke-free. 47 E. Broadway. 406/703-4735. $$

Lewis and Clark Caverns State Park—The Corps just missed this labyrinth of caverns along the Jefferson River west of Three Forks. Visitor center and caverns are at the top of a steep, winding 3-mile paved road with breathtaking views of the Tobacco Root Mountains and Jefferson River Valley. Tours last 2 hours; cover 2 miles and hundreds of stairs. Get your tickets early in the day. ♿ Special tours of the Paradise Room are available to people with mobility impairments; advance reservations are requested during July and August. Tours daily May-Oct.

▲ 45 sites; fee; water; modern; showers; open all year/full operation May-Sept; grills/fire rings; tables; ⊞ three 1-room cabins/♿. Interpretive and campfire programs. Admission fee. I-90 exit 256, 7 miles E on Hwy 2 or I-90 exit 274, 20 miles W on Hwy 2. 406/287-3541 or 406/994-4042.

Beaverhead County Museum—Large collection dedicated to local and Montana history. Alaskan brown bear mount. Outdoor interpretive center on pioneer life. Daily 8 to 6 (June-Aug), weekdays 1 to 5 (rest of year); donations. 15 S. Montana. 406/683-5027.

Cattail Marsh Nature Trail—Waterfowl and shorebirds at north edge of Clark Canyon Reservoir. ♿ trail below the dam. I-15 exit 44, follow signs. 406/683-6472.

Dillon Visitor Center—Restored Union Pacific Depot contains travel information, a Lewis and Clark diorama and an interpretive display about the Mammoth Digs. Adjacent to the center is a summer theater running July through Labor Day. Open daily, 125 S. Montana, Dillon; 406/683-5511.

Seidensticker Wildlife Collection—Within the Western Montana College Gallery and Museum is this collection of North American, African and Asian animals. Mon-Thurs 10 to 3, Tue/Thurs 7 to 9; free. 710 S. Atlantic, Dillon; 406/683-7126.

▲ **Dillon KOA**—98 sites (68 w/hookups); fee; water; modern; showers; open all year; grills/fire rings; tables. Pool; ⊞ cabins; playground; coin laundry; groceries; fishing. I-15 exit 63, 735 W. Park. 406/683-2749, 800/562-2751.

▲ **Dinner Station**—7 tent sites; free; water; primitive; open May-Sept; grills/fire rings; tables; group picnic area. Fishing; hiking. 12 miles N on I-15, 12 miles NW on Birch Creek Rd. 406/683-3900.

▲ **Miner Lake**—18 sites; free; water; primitive; open Jul-Aug; grills/fire rings; tables; 32' trailer length. Fishing; hiking; boat ramp. 10 miles W of Jackson on FR 182. 406/689-3243.

▲ **Twin Lakes**—17 sites; free; water; primitive; open Jul-Aug; grills/fire rings; tables; 32' trailer limit. Fishing; hiking; boat ramp. 8 miles W on CR 1290, 5 miles S of FR 945, 6 miles SW on FR 183. 406/689-3243.

⊞ **Comfort Inn**—46 rooms, pool, pets, continental breakfast, playground, coin laundry. Off-season rates. 450 N. Interchange. 406/683-6831, 800/442-4667. $$ K12

⊞ **Paradise Inn**—65 rooms, pets, indoor pool, hot tub, ⊗ restaurant. Off-season rates. I-15 exit 63, S on MT 41. 406/683-4214. $$

⊗ **Pappa T's**—Variety of burgers amid old-time Montana photos, kids' menu. L & D daily. 10 N. Montana. 406/683-6432. $

Lemhi, Idaho

▲ **McFarland**—10 sites; free; **no** water; primitive; open May-Nov; grills/fire rings; tables; 14-day limit. Fishing. 5 miles S on ID 28. 208/456-5400.

Sheridan, Montana

▲ **Branham Lake**—6 sites; free; water; primitive; open Jul-Sept; grills/fire rings; tables; no trailers. Fishing; hiking. 6 miles E on Mill Creek Rd, 5 miles E on FR 1112, 3 miles N on FR 1110. 406/842-5432.

▲ **Mill Creek**—9 sites; free; water; primitive; open Memorial Day-Sept; grills/fire rings; tables; 22' trailer limit. Fishing. 6 miles E on Mill Creek Rd. 406/842-5432.

Virginia City, Montana

This 1860s mining town along both sides of MT 287 served as one of Montana's territorial capitals. Dozens of buildings here and in neighboring Nevada City have been restored or rebuilt with many still operating as businesses serving the town's remaining residents. Visitor centers at the depot and the schoolhouse provide information, souvenirs, and tours. 406/843-5247.

Alder Gulch Steam Railroad—Narrow gauge train powered by Locomotive No. 12 (a meticulously restored antique steam engine) makes the mile trip between Virginia City and Nevada City on selected weekends. 406/843-5247.

Brewery Follies—At the Gilbert Brewery the fare is vaudeville. Families are welcome for all performances but things do get a bit ribald. Get your tickets early, they sell out quickly. Daily except Tue. (June through Sept). Hamilton and Cover Sts. 406/843-5218.

Madison County Museum—Get a factual taste of the early mining days before heading out to explore the area. Daily 10 to 5 (Memorial Day through Sept); admission fee. 219 W. Wallace. 406/843-5500.

Nevada City Music Hall—This assortment of early mechanical music machines is a delight. Not a computer chip in sight, but you'll still be intrigued by the unique qualities of these contraptions. Daily 9 to 7 (mid-May to mid-Sept); free. 406/843-5300.

Nevada City Museum—Several original buildings from Montana's early days have been assembled into an outdoor museum behind the Music Hall. Daily 9 to 7 (mid-May to mid-Sept); admission fee.

Thompson-Hickman Memorial Museum—Vigilantes and their antics are the focus of this collection. Daily 10 to 5 (May-Sept); donations. 300 E. Wallace. 406/843-5238.

Virginia City Players—A talented troupe performs melodramas and comedies nightly at the Opera House from June through Labor Day; admission fee. 340 W. Wallace. 406/843-5314, 800/648-7588.

▲ **Virginia City Campground**—49 sites (19 w/hookups); fee; water; modern; showers; open May-Oct; grills/fire rings; tables; firewood. Recreation; dump station. 0.5 mile E on MT 287. 406/843-5493.

⊞ **Fairweather Inn**—15 rooms in historic hotel. Shared baths. Hwy 287. 406/843-5377, 800/648-7588.

⊞ **Nevada City Hotel**—14 rooms/17 cottages in log buildings, pets. MT 287. 406/843-5377, 800/648-7588. $$ K12

⊨ **Bennett House Country Inn**—5 antique-filled rooms in 1879 Victorian. 115 E. Idaho. 406/843-5220, 877/843-5220. $$

Whitehall, Montana

▲ **Toll Mountain**—5 sites; free; **no** water; primitive; open May-Sept; grills/fire rings; tables; 22' trailer limit. Fishing; hiking. 15 miles W on MT 2, 3 miles N on FR 240. 406/287-3223.

▲ **Pigeon Creek**—6 tent sites; free; water; primitive; open Memorial Day-Sept; grills/fire rings; tables. Fishing. 15 miles W on MT 2, 5 miles S on FR 668. 406/287-3223.

⊞ **Hells Canyon Forest Service Cabin**—Located 30 miles SW of Whitehall; available all year; 4 beds. Access road not plowed, accessibility varies with snow conditions. 406/287-3223.

⊞ **Super 8**—33 rooms, pets, continental breakfast, hot tub. 515 N. Whitehall St. 406/287-5588, 800/800-8000. $$ K18

CHAPTER 17

August 20 to September 10, 1805

ROCKY MOUNTAINS CHALLENGE

With autumn approaching the mountains, the Corps of Discovery was on the east side—the wrong side for them—of the Continental Divide. They needed to go west over the Divide to find streams flowing toward the Pacific Ocean. The Shoshones could supply horses, but their information about routes to the west was all about where *not* to go. Time to split up again, the captains decided.

Captain William Clark and eleven men with axes for making canoes would go back over Lemhi Pass into today's Idaho, taking along Sacagawea and Charbonneau. Those two would bring Shoshones with horses back to Camp Fortunate, and Captain Meriwether Lewis and the rest could pack their goods over the Divide to the Shoshone camp. Clark and his men would meet them there after checking to see whether the Salmon River seemed navigable despite what the Shoshones had said. They took tools in hopes of building canoes if the river looked promising.

Clark's party, including three or four Shoshones who stayed when the others had returned to the Lemhi Valley, had left Camp Fortunate on August 18. In two days, they reached the Shoshone village, which had been moved to about three miles north of modern Tendoy. Clark asked that the entire village take their horses over the mountains and help Lewis and the others cross. He also asked for a guide for his own group. Of all the Shoshones, none knew more about the land west of here than one old man. Although his name meant Swooping Eagle, the captains nicknamed their guide Toby, an abbreviation of one of his names meaning "furnished... white-man brains." He set off with Clark's men that same afternoon, August 20. He and his son would stay with the Corps for nearly eight weeks.

Over the next four days, Clark's group went down today's Lemhi River, reaching the Salmon River near Tower Creek on the 21st. He named the Salmon "Lewis's River."

On August 22, they named today's North Fork of the Salmon River "Fish Creek." Here they appeared out of the thick woods, terrifying a few Indian families who were drying fish and berries for winter. Several women and children ran away fearing for their lives, but Toby calmed those who stayed, and an exchange of trade goods was made.

These four days took Clark far enough down the Salmon River to see how dangerous its rapids were. Toby told him the river only got worse farther west; even today, its nickname is "The River of No Return." Clark wrote that "every man appeared disheartened from the prospects of the river, and nothing to eat." There was no game, and the trees weren't big enough to make dugout canoes.

Clark sent Private John Colter as messenger to Lewis on August 24, with the bad news about the Salmon River. He and his men headed back the way they had come. In two days they camped southeast of today's town of Salmon, and waited there to hear from Lewis.

After Clark's party left them on August 18—Lewis's thirty-first birthday—Lewis created a new cache at Camp Fortunate, emptying some wooden storage boxes. The men used rawhide plus the wood to make twenty packsaddles, while the visiting Shoshone women made and mended moccasins. One of the items cached here was part of the tobacco supply, to reserve it for the return trip. On the 22nd, Camp Fortunate welcomed Sacagawea, Charbonneau, Cameahwait, and fifty Shoshone men, plus some women and children. They had answered Clark's request to help the Corps cross to their village in Idaho.

Lewis wrote that day of how hungry the Shoshones were, and how much they enjoyed the game and fish the whites killed. Neverthe-

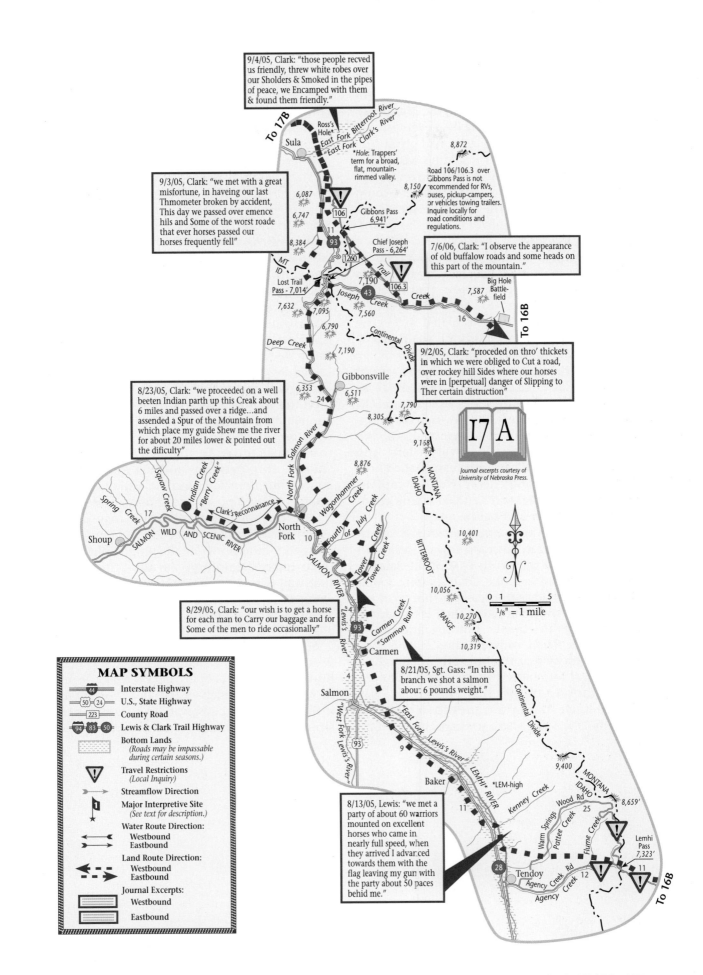

less, the Indians insisted on sharing what little food they had. Cameahwait tasted squash for the first time (dried, it was from the Mandans), and said it was the best thing he'd ever tasted—except for some sugar his sister had given him from the Corps' supply. He said he wished his people could live safely in a land of plenty, and Lewis assured him that soon whites would make peace among all the native peoples. Then the Shoshones could move out of the mountains and raise squash.

The Shoshones and Lewis's group left Camp Fortunate on August 24, and in two days reached what Lewis already had labeled (wrongly; see Chapter 16) the "extreem source of the Missouri." They traveled over the Divide, arriving at the Shoshone camp just as Colter showed up with Clark's letter.

After Clark reached the camp in the area of today's Tendoy, the captains traded for as many horses as the Shoshones would spare. On August 30, with twenty-nine horses that were poorly fed and unused to packsaddles, the reunited Corps of Discovery left the Shoshones, who were heading east to the Three Forks of the Missouri River. Neither captain recorded how Sacagawea handled saying goodbye to her brother and her people.

Toby led the Corps north down the Lemhi River to the Salmon River, up Tower Creek, and cross-country to the North Fork of the Salmon near today's Gibbonsville, Idaho, along a well used Indian road. After leaving that road on September 2, they had to cut their own narrow path through the brushy bottom land of the North Fork. Then they climbed hillsides so steep and rocky that the horses kept falling.

We don't know their precise path the next day, in the area of Lost Trail Pass—which was named much later by a white settler who had read the Lewis and Clark journals as edited by Reuben Gold Thwaites (published 1905). The mountains, bad weather, and hunger led to confusion, and so the journals are confused. This area of the Corps of Discovery's path is among those still attracting much discussion and speculation.

They again crossed the Salmon-Bitterroot divide, today's Idaho-Montana border, and went down the north side to Ross's Hole, near Sula, Montana. Here they were the first whites to meet those allies of the Shoshones, the Salish people who "recved us friendly." The Corps stayed for two days, visiting, taking down Salish vocabulary, purchasing eleven horses and exchanging seven others. Lewis and Clark, like many other whites, mistakenly called the Salish "Flathead" Indians; today the Confederated Salish and Kootenai Tribes share the Flathead Indian Reservation in northwest Montana.

On September 6, the Salish headed off to meet the Shoshones at the Three Forks for their annual bison hunt, and the Corps went northward on the Pacific side of the Bitterroots. It wasn't a good day for the menu. Clark wrote: "rained this evening nothing to eate but berries, our flour out, and but little Corn, the hunters killed 2 pheasents [grouse] only—"

The traveling was relatively easy on an established Indian "road" to where they camped a mile north of Sleeping Child Creek (near today's Hamilton) on the 7th. Still on that trail they moved north the next day and camped near present Stevensville. There they suffered "a hard rain all the evening[;] we are all Cold and wet."

September 9 brought them to [1] Lolo Creek—which they called Travelers' Rest Creek—near today's town of Lolo. The skies had cleared, so for a day the men rested and the captains made astronomical observations to establish the latitude and longitude of the location.

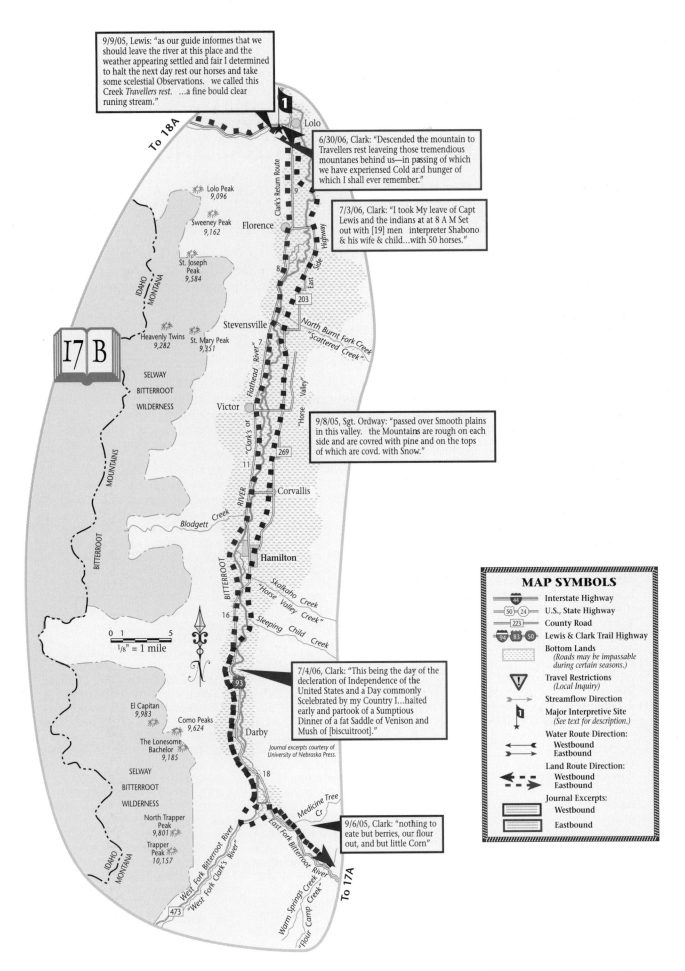

9/9/05, Lewis: "as our guide informes that we should leave the river at this place and the weather appearing settled and fair I determined to halt the next day rest our horses and take some scelestial Observations. we called this Creek *Travellers rest.* ...a fine bould clear runing stream."

6/30/06, Clark: "Descended the mountain to Travellers rest leaveing those tremendious mountanes behind us—in passing of which we have experiensed Cold and hunger of which I shall ever remember."

7/3/06, Clark: "I took My leave of Capt Lewis and the indians at 8 A M Set out with [19] men interpreter Shabono & his wife & child...with 50 horses."

9/8/05, Sgt. Ordway: "passed over Smooth plains in this valley. the Mountains are rough on each side and are covred with pine and on the tops of which are covd. with Snow."

7/4/06, Clark: "This being the day of the decleration of Independence of the United States and a Day commonly Scelebrated by my Country I...halted early and partook of a Sumptious Dinner of a fat Saddle of Venison and Mush of [biscuitroot]."

Journal excerpts courtesy of University of Nebraska Press.

9/6/05, Clark: "nothing to eate but berries, our flour out, and but little Corn"

To 18A

Lolo

Lolo Peak
9,096

Sweeney Peak
9,162

St. Joseph Peak
9,584

Florence

IDAHO
MONTANA

Clark's Return Route

East Side Highway

Heavenly Twins
9,282

St. Mary Peak
9,351

Stevensville

North Burnt Fork Creek "Scattered Creek"

SELWAY

BITTERROOT

WILDERNESS

"Clark's or Flathead River"

"Horse Valley"

Victor

269

BITTERROOT

MOUNTAINS

Corvallis

Blodgett Creek

RIVER

BITTERROOT

Hamilton

Skalkaho Creek

"Horse Valley Creek"

Sleeping Child Creek

0 1 ... 5
1/8" = 1 mile

N

El Capitan
9,983

Como Peaks
9,624

93

Darby

The Lonesome Bachelor
9,185

SELWAY

BITTERROOT

WILDERNESS

18

Medicine Tree Cr

North Trapper Peak
9,801

Trapper Peak
10,157

West Fork Bitterroot River

"West Fork Clark's River"

East Fork Bitterroot River

IDAHO
MONTANA

473

"West Springs Creek"

Warm Springs Creek

"Hour Camp Creek"

To 17A

I7 B

MAP SYMBOLS

44	Interstate Highway
50 24	U.S., State Highway
223	County Road
94 83 50	Lewis & Clark Trail Highway
	Bottom Lands *(Roads may be impassable during certain seasons.)*
⚠	**Travel Restrictions** *(Local Inquiry)*
→	**Streamflow Direction**
⚑	**Major Interpretive Site** *(See text for description.)*
	Water Route Direction: Westbound Eastbound
	Land Route Direction: Westbound Eastbound
	Journal Excerpts: Westbound Eastbound

TOURING TODAY

⤳ ROCKY MOUNTAINS CHALLENGE ⤳

[ ] Bracketed numbers key sites to maps	♿ Special-needs accessible ⚑ Bed & breakfast
★ L&C in-depth interpretation, unchanged landform	⊗ Restaurant ⚑ Camping, RV park
● L&C interpreted site	⊞ Motel, hotel, cabin

ALONG THE EXPEDITION'S PATH

August 20, 1805
★ **Lewis and Clark Monument** (Tendoy, ID)—Interpretation about Sacagawea. Always open; free. ID 28, S of mile marker 120. 208/756-3313.

● **Withington Creek Campsite** (Salmon, ID)—Interpretation turnout near actual site. Always open; free. 10 miles S on ID 28 (mile markers 125-126). 208/756-2523.

August 21, 1805
Tower Rock (Salmon, ID)—Interpretation on campsite. 6 sites; fee; no water; primitive; open all year; grills/fire rings; tables. Fishing, boating. 11 miles N on US 93. 208/756-5401.

Shoshoni Trail Segment/Wagonhammer Springs (North Fork, ID)—Hike takes you 2 miles to Thompson Gulch to 6 mile trail back to US 93 at Trail Gulch with inspiring views. Hike is difficult with steep elevation gains. Bring plenty of water and start early in the day. Park at gate on Wagonhammer Road, S of town on US 93 (mile markers 324-325).

August 22, 1805
(Return June 16, 1806)
Fish Creek (North Fork, ID)—Interpretive site. ⚑ 11 sites; fee; water; primitive; open all year/full operation May-Sept; grills/fire rings; tables; 14-day limit. Floating, boating, hiking trails, wildlife viewing, fishing. US 93 in town. 208/983-1963.

August 23, 1805
● **Ridge Route Site/Nez Perce Trail** (Gibbonsville, ID)—Not part of actual trail, but good place to see the trail along the ridges toward Lost Trail Pass. 15 miles S of North Fork on US 93. 208/865-2383.

Salmon Scenic Byway—US 93 for 25 miles along the Salmon River from Lost Trail Pass to North Fork. Historic markers for the trail.

September 2, 1805
● **Deep Creek** (North Fork, ID)—Interpretation, hiking, wildlife viewing. Always open; free. 2 miles N on US 93 (mile markers 321-322). 208/865-2383.

September 3, 1805
★ **Lost Trail Pass**—Interpretive sign, information center. US 93 at ID/MT border. 208/865-2383.

September 6, 1805
● **Spring Gulch** (Sula, MT)—Fishing; hiking trails. ⚑ 10 sites; fee; water; primitive; showers; open June-Sept; grills/fire rings; tables. 4 miles N on US 93. 406/821-3201.

● **Fort Owen State Park** (Stevensville, MT)—Converting a mission to a trading post in 1852, John Owen replaced adobe buildings with the log ones standing today. It was an important place until the Mullan Road was established 30 miles to the north. A homesteader's cabin and several original fort buildings remain. Museum contains interpretive displays, artifacts from archaeological studies at the site and dioramas of the fort, mill and Major Owen's office/library. Daily dawn to dusk; free. 0.5 mile E of Sec 269 and US 93 junction. 406/542-5500.

September 9-10, 1805
(Return June 30–July 3, 1806)
[1] ★ **Travelers' Rest**—Site of Travelers' Rest camp is not currently open to the public. Interpretive sign. In Lolo on US 12. 406/329-3962.

AROUND THE AREA

TOWNS LISTED ALPHABETICALLY

Darby, Montana
Painted Rocks State Park—An isolated but delightful park. It's not crowded, but the water level by late July is too low for motorboats. ⚑ 32 sites; fee; no water; primitive; open all year/full operation May-Sept; grills/fire rings; tables. Picnic area; boat ramp; hiking. 21 miles S on US 93, 23 miles SW on Sec 473. 406/542-5500.

Pioneer Memorial Museum—Explore the history of Darby's settlement during the 1800s. Tue-Sat 1 to 5 (Memorial Day-Labor Day); free. US 93 at Council Park. 406/821-4503.

⚑ **Alta**—15 sites; fee; water; primitive; open Jul-Aug; grills/fire rings; tables; 50' trailer limit. Fishing; hiking; site of nation's first ranger station. 4 miles S on US 93, 21.5 miles SW on CR 473, 6 miles S on CR 96. 406/821-3269.

⚑ **Billings Memorial**—11 sites; free; no water; primitive; open June-Sept; grills/fire rings; tables; 30' trailer limit. Fishing. 4 miles S on US 93, 13 miles SW on CR 473, 1 mile NW on FR 5631. 406/821-3269.

⚑ **Lake Como**—11 sites; fee; water; primitive; open June-Sept; grills/fire rings; tables; 22' trailer limit. Fishing; hiking; boat ramp. 5 miles N on US 93, 3 miles W on Lake Como Rd. 406/821-3913.

⚑ **Rombo Creek**—14 sites; fee; water; primitive; open Jul-Labor

Day; grills/fire rings; tables; 40' trailer limit. Fishing; hiking. 4 miles S on US 93, 18 miles SW on CR 473. 406/821-3269.

⚑ Slate Creek—13 sites; fee; water; primitive; open Jul-Labor Day; grills/fire rings; tables; 30' trailer limit. Fishing; hiking; swimming; boat ramp. 4 miles S on US 93, 22 miles W on CR 473, 2 miles S on CR 96. 406/821-3269.

Gibbonsville, Idaho

⚑ Twin Creeks—44 sites; fee; water; primitive; open May-Sept; grills/fire rings; tables; firewood; 22' trailer limit. Fishing; hiking; rafting; scenic drive 5 miles NW on US 93, 0.5 mile NW on FR 604. 208/865-2383.

Hamilton, Montana

Daly Mansion—1890 copper baron mansion with 24 bedrooms, 15 bathrooms and 24,213 square feet of space. Tue-Sun, 11 to 4 (May-Sept); fee. 2 miles N on MT 269. 406/363-6004.

• Ravalli County Museum—Homesteader and Flathead Indian memorabilia. Interpretive exhibits on the history of Rocky Mountain spotted fever research, along with an assortment of wood ticks. Mon-Fri 10 to 4 (May-Sept); donations. In the old courthouse, 205 Bedford. 406/363-3338.

Bitterroot Family Campground—52 sites (40 w/hookups); fee; water; modern; showers; open all year; grills/fire rings; tables. Fishing; playground; coin laundry; groceries; dump station. 9 miles S on US 93. 406/363-2430, 800/453-2430.

⚑ Blodgett Canyon—6 sites; free; no water; primitive; open May-Sept; grills/fire rings; tables; 30' trailer limit. Fishing and swimming. 5 miles NW of Hamilton on Blodgett Camp Rd, adjacent to Selway-Bitterroot Wilderness. 406/363-3131.

⚑ Lick Creek Campground—65 sites (44 w/hookups); fee; water; modern; showers; open Apr-Sept; grills/fire rings; tables; firewood. Fishing; hiking; coin laundry; dump station. 11.75 miles S on US 93. 406/821-3840.

⊞ Best Western Hamilton Inn—36 rooms, continental breakfast,

hot tub. Off-season rates. In town on US 93. 406/363-2142. $$

⊞ Comfort Inn—65 rooms, pets, continental breakfast, coin laundry. Off-season rates. In town on US 93. 406/363-6600. $$ K18

Missoula, Montana

Missoula Chamber of Commerce—Stop at the office at Van Buren and Front streets for brochures and walking/driving tour information. 406/543-6623, 800/526-3465.

Art Museum of Missoula—Rotating exhibits of regional and national artists with an emphasis on works of Western art. Tue-Sat 12 to 5; donations. 335 N. Pattee, 406/728-0447.

Sam Braxton National Recreation Trail—3.5-mile loop trail through old homesteading area in the Pattee Canyon Recreation Area southeast of Missoula off Pattee Canyon Rd. 406/329-3814.

A Carousel for Missoula—First fully hand-carved carousel built in U.S. since Great Depression. One of the fastest, with largest band organ in continuous use in U.S. Building and carousel ♿. Fee per ride. 11 to 7 (June-Aug), 11 to 5:30 (rest of year). From I-90, take Orange St exit, then S onto Orange, left on Broadway, and right on Ryman, which leads into parking lot. 406/549-8382.

Council Grove State Park—Site where Washington territorial governor Isaac Stevens convened the Salish Council with the Pend d'Oreille, Kootenai and Salish Indians to obtain the land along the Clark Fork, Bitterroot and Flathead rivers for settlement by whites. Interpretive signs describe the impact and significance of this agreement. Picnic area; fishing; hiking trail. Open dawn to dusk; free. I-90 exit 101, 2 miles S on Reserve St., 10 miles W on Mullan Rd. 406/542-5500.

• Fort Missoula—Renovated fort built in 1877 during the flight of the Nez Perce. 12 buildings contain indoor exhibits. Outdoor interpretive displays tell the area's history. Tue-Sat 10 to 5, Sun 12 to 5 (Memorial Day to Labor Day), Tue-Sun, 12 to 5 (rest of the year); donations. On Fort Missoula Rd. 406/728-3476.

Garnet—Experience this 1870s ghost town up close by renting one of the two ⊞ BLM cabins between 12/1 and 4/30. During the summer a visitor center provides maps and interpretive information. I-90 exit 153, 12 miles W on frontage road, 11 miles N on County Rd. 406/ 494-5059.

Kelly Island—Undeveloped island in the Clark Fork River. Red-tailed hawks, great horned owls and white-tail deer. Access by boat or wading across the river when the water is low enough. Spurgin Rd to Kelly Island FAS. 406/542-5500.

Lion Creek Trail #28—4.5-mile moderately easy trail to mountain lakes, begins in Lion Creek Canyon. Steep sections alternate with level ones. I-15 exit 93, 6 miles W on FR 188, 12 miles N on FR 7401. 406/832-3178.

Maclay Flat Nature Trail—1.75-mile paved trail (take the cut-off to shorten it to 1.25 miles) along the Bitterroot River with interpretive signs. 2 miles S on US 93, 1.5 miles W on Blue Mountain Rd. 406/329-3814.

Memorial Rose Garden—Beautiful area with 2,500 rose bushes dedicated as a memorial to Montana enlistees of World Wars I & II, Korea, Vietnam, conflicts of 1980s, Persian Gulf. A bronze statue is the official Montana state Vietnam Veterans Memorial; follow signs for it from I-90. On Brooks St (US 93 S).

Nine Mile Remount Station—Built, and still used, as a Forest Service center to supply mules for back country tasks. Take a self-guided tour and then hike into the mountains for lunch at the **Grand Menard Picnic Area**. Maps available for 5 mountain bike trails around **Kreis Pond**. Weekdays 8 to 4:30 (guided tours on the hour); free. I-90 exit 82, north 6 miles. 406/626-5201.

Rocky Mountain Elk Foundation—Incredible display of trophy game mounts, wildlife videos and art gallery. What you see here may enhance your appreciation or simply broaden your perspective. Weekdays 8 to 5, weekends 11 to 4:30; donations. 2291 W. Broadway, 406/721-0010.

Smokejumper Visitor Center and

Aerial Fire Depot—A smokejumper is a highly trained person who fights large forest fires. A tour, often led by a smokejumper, through this base facility gives you a solid appreciation for their difficult and dangerous work. Daily 8:30 to 5 (May-Sept); free. US 93 and I-90, 406/329-4934.

St. Francis Xavier Church—Built in 1889 with a 144-foot steeple, intricate stained glass windows and magnificent interior paintings by Brother Joseph Carignano. Mon-Sat 7 to 5; free. 420 W. Pine, 406/542-0321.

Kim Williams Nature Trail—2.5-mile level trail along the Clark Fork River with great wildlife viewing. Trailhead is east of the footbridge behind the Chamber of Commerce Building.

▲ **Jellystone Park**—110 sites (all w/hookups); fee; water; modern; showers; open May-Oct; grills/fire rings; tables; firewood. Pool; mini golf; playground; hiking trails; groceries; coin laundry; dump station. I-90 exit 96, 0.5 mile N on US 93. 406/543-9400, 800/318-9644.

▲ **Missoula/El Mar KOA**—210 sites (174 w/hookups); fee; water; modern; showers; open all year/full operation June-Sept; grills/fire rings; tables; firewood. Pool; playground; groceries; coin laundry; dump station. I-90 exit 101, 1.5 miles S on Reserve St, 0.25 mile NW on Tina Ave. 406/549-0881.

⊞ **Best Western Executive Inn**—51 rooms, pool, pets, ⊗ restaurant. Off-season rates. 201 E. Main. 406/543-7221, 800/528-1234. $$ K12

⊞ **Best Western Grant Creek Inn**—126 rooms in mountain setting, pool, continental breakfast, exercise room, coin laundry. I-90 exit 101, 5280 Grant Creek Rd. 406/543-0700. $$$ K18

⊞ **Doubletree Hotel**—172 large rooms, pets, pool, ⊗ restaurants, hot tub. ♿. Off-season rates. 100 Madison Ave. 406/728-3100. $$$

⊞ **Holiday Inn Express**—95 rooms, continental breakfast, exercise room, coin laundry. ♿. Along Clark Fork river. I-90 exit 105. 406/549-7600. $$

⊞ **Holiday Inn Parkside**—200 rooms, pool, exercise room, hot tub, restaurant. Adjoins Riverfront Park. 200 S. Pattee. 406/721-8550. $$$ K18

⊞ **Rodeway Inn Southgate**—81 rooms, pool, continental breakfast, river raft trips, exercise room, hot tub, coin laundry. Family suites and off-season rates. I-90 exit 101, 5 miles S to Brooks. 406/251-2250.

⊭ **Goldsmith's Bed and Breakfast Inn**—3 rooms and 4 suites in turn-of-the-century mansion along the Clark Fork River, full breakfast. 406/721-6732. $$$

⊗ **Goldsmith's**—Hearty food, homemade bagels & ice cream, kids' menu, smoke-free. B L & D daily, 809 E. Front at the footbridge. 406/721-6732. $

⊗ **McKay's on the River**—Seafood and steak in historic river setting, kids' menu. B L & D daily, Sun brunch. 1111 E. Broadway. 406/728-0098. $$

⊗ **The Mustard Seed**—Fresh, light oriental-style menu, kids' menu. L & D daily. 419 W. Front. 406/728-7825. $$

⊗ **The Shack**—Freshly-prepared unusual items, kids' menu, smoke-free. B L & D daily. 222 W. Main. 406/549-9903. $$

⊗ **Zimorino's Red Pies over Montana**—Pizza and fresh pasta. D only. 424 N. Higgins. 406/549-7434. $$

Salmon, Idaho

Lemhi County Historical Museum—Indian and pioneer artifacts. Asian antiques collection. Mon-Sat 10 to 5 (Jul/Aug), 1 to 5 (Apr-June, Sept/Oct); donations. 210 Main. 208/756-3342.

White Water Rafting—Information on outfitters and trips available from Chamber of Commerce, 200 Main St, Suite #1. 208/756-2100.

▲ **Heald's Haven**—24 sites (all w/hookups); fee; water; modern; showers; open all year/full operation May-Nov; grills/fire rings; tables; firewood. Boating; fishing; hiking trails. 12 miles S of ID 28 on US 93. 208/756-3929.

▲ **Salmon Meadows Campground**—76 sites (50 w/hookups); fee; water; modern; showers; open Apr-Oct; grills/fire rings; tables. Playground; hiking trails; coin laundry; dump station. 0.5 mile W of ID 28 on US 93. 208/756-2640.

▲ **Williams Lake**—11 sites; free; no water; primitive; open May-Oct; grills/fire rings; tables; 28' trailer limit. Boating; fishing; hike Thunder Mountain Historic Trail. 4 miles S on US 93, 7 miles on FR 028. 208/756-5400.

⊞ **Stagecoach Inn**—100 rooms, pool, continental breakfast, coin laundry. 10.5 mile N on US 93. 208/756-2919. $$ K12

⊞ **Suncrest Motel**—20 rooms, pets, continental breakfast, refrigerators. US 93 & ID 28. 208/756-2294. $

⊗ **Shady Nook**—steak & seafood in the company of big game mounts; kids' menu. D only. 0.75 mile N on US 93. 208/756-4182.

Stevensville, Montana

St. Mary's Mission—The original mission was built in 1841 and later evolved into Fort Owen. A second mission was built by Father Anthony Ravalli in 1866, and it is that chapel, along with the mission pharmacy, that survives. Other buildings include the priests' living quarters, and home of Charlo, the last pre-reservation chief of the Flathead Indians. Open daily 10 to 4 (Apr-Oct); admission fee. Fourth and Charlo Streets, 406/777-5734.

▲ **Charles Waters**—20 sites; fee; water; primitive; open Memorial Day-Labor Day; grills/fire rings; tables; 45' trailer limit. Fishing; trails. 2 miles NW on CR 269; 4 miles N on US 93, 2 miles W on CR 22, 1 miles NW on FR 1316. 406/777-5461.

Sula, Montana

▲ **Crazy Creek**—16 sites; free; water; primitive; open June-Sept; grills/fire rings; tables; 26' trailer limit. Fishing; hiking; horse camp. 5 miles NW on US 93, 1 mile SW on CR 100, 3 miles SW on FR 370. 406/777-5461.

▲ **Indian Trees**—17 sites; fee; water; primitive; open Memorial Day-Labor Day; grills/fire rings; tables; 30' trailer limit. Fishing; hiking; nearby hot springs. 6 miles S on US 93, 1 mile SW on FR 729. 406/777-5461.

▲ **Moosehead Campground**—18

sites (all w/hookups); fee; water; modern; showers; open Apr-Nov; grills/fire rings; tables; firewood. Fishing. 15 miles N of MT 43 on US 93. 406/821-3327.

▲ **Spring Gulch**—10 sites; fee; water; primitive; open June-Sept; grills/fire rings; tables; 22' trailer limit. Fishing; hiking; swimming. 3 miles NW on US 93. 406/777-5461.

▲ **Warm Springs**—14 sites; fee; water; primitive; open Memorial Day-Labor Day; grills/fire rings; tables; 26' trailer limit. Fishing; hiking; swimming. 3 miles NW on US 93, 1 mile SW on CR 100. 406/777-5461.

⊞ **East Fork Guard Station Cabin**—available all year; sleeps 8. Last 0.75 mile access by skis or snowmobile in the winter. 15 miles NE. 406/821-3201.

⊞ **McCart Lookout Forest Service Cabin**—available Apr-Oct, sleeps 4. Easy 1.5-mile hike to lookout. 22 miles E. 406/821-3201.

CHAPTER 18

September 11 to October 7, 1805

TRIAL AND TRYUMPH

Leaving Travelers' Rest on September 11, 1805, the Corps of Discovery began the very worst part of the entire journey, over mountains nearly as uninhabited today as they were then.

Following the Nez Perce trail (now also called Lolo Trail), they moved up today's Lolo Creek in the Bitterroot Range of the Rocky Mountains. On the next day, Captain William Clark wrote that the trail was "verry bad passing over hills & thro' Steep hollows, over

falling timber...most intolerable...on the Sides of the Steep Stoney mountains."

Having set out at 7 a.m. on the 12th, Clark made camp at 8 p.m.; some men didn't reach camp for another two hours.

While Captain Meriwether Lewis and four men hunted for their lost horses on the 13th, Clark proceeded to today's Lolo Hot Springs (Montana), where the water was "hot & not bad tasted." More ominously: "mountains in view...[were] Covered with Snow." The Corps

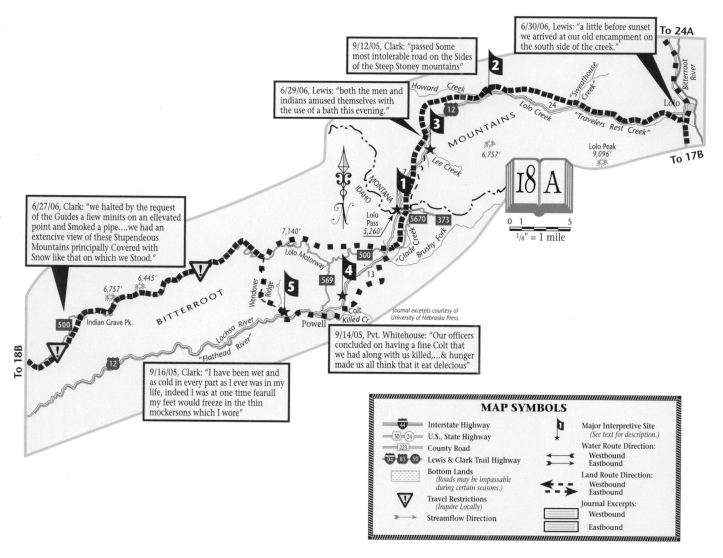

6/30/06, Lewis: "a little before sunset we arrived at our old encampment on the south side of the creek." — To 24A

9/12/05, Clark: "passed Some most intolerable road on the Sides of the Steep Stoney mountains"

6/29/06, Lewis: "both the men and indians amused themselves with the use of a bath this evening."

6/27/06, Clark: "we halted by the request of the Guides a fiew minits on an ellevated point and Smoked a pipe....we had an extencive view of these Stupendeous Mountains principally Covered with Snow like that on which we Stood."

9/16/05, Clark: "I have been wet and as cold in every part as I ever was in my life, indeed I was at one time fearull my feet would freeze in the thin mockersons which I wore"

9/14/05, Pvt. Whitehouse: "Our officers concluded on having a fine Colt that we had along with us killed,...& hunger made us all think that it eat delecious"

Journal excerpts courtesy of University of Nebraska Press.

BITTERROOT MOUNTAINS — Howard Creek, Lolo Creek, Sweathouse Creek, Travelers Rest Creek, Lolo Peak 9,096', 6,757', Lee Creek, Lolo Pass 5,260', Glade Creek, Brushy Fork, 7,140', Lolo Motorway, Wendover Ridge, 6,445', 6,757', Indian Grave Pk., Lochsa River, "Flathead River", Powell, Colt Killed Cr., MONTANA / IDAHO

0 1 5 1/8" = 1 mile

To 17B — To 18B

MAP SYMBOLS

44	Interstate Highway
50 24	U.S., State Highway
223	County Road
94 83 50	Lewis & Clark Trail Highway
(shaded)	Bottom Lands (Roads may be impassable during certain seasons.)
!	Travel Restrictions (Inquire Locally)
→	Streamflow Direction

Major Interpretive Site (See text for description.)

Water Route Direction:
Westbound
Eastbound

Land Route Direction:
Westbound
Eastbound

Journal Excerpts:
Westbound
Eastbound

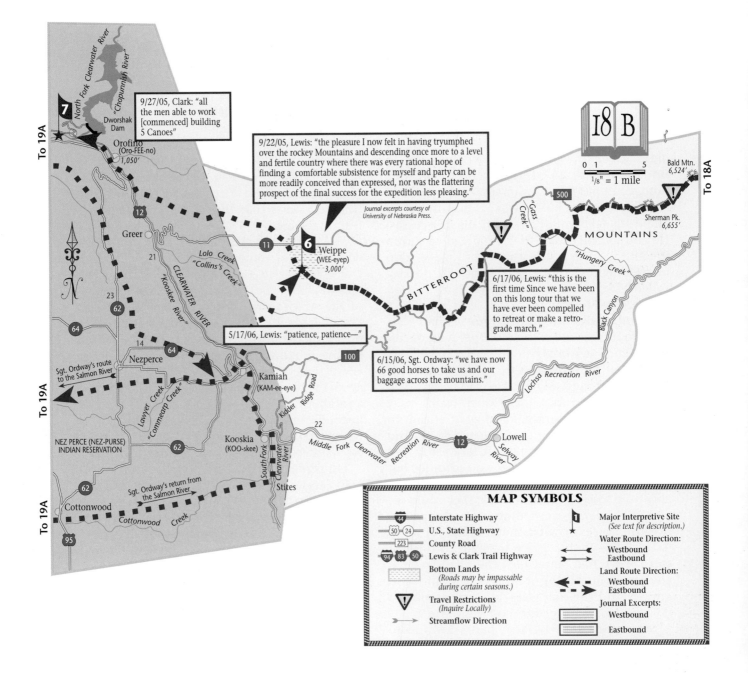

9/27/05, Clark: "all the men able to work [commenced] building 5 Canoes"

9/22/05, Lewis: "the pleasure I now felt in having tryumphed over the rockey Mountains and descending once more to a level and fertile country where there was every rational hope of finding a comfortable subsistence for myself and party can be more readily conceived than expressed, nor was the flattering prospect of the final success for the expedition less pleasing."

Journal excerpts courtesy of University of Nebraska Press.

5/17/06, Lewis: "patience, patience—"

6/17/06, Lewis: "this is the first time Since we have been on this long tour that we have ever been compelled to retreat or make a retrograde march."

6/15/06, Sgt. Ordway: "we have now 66 good horses to take us and our baggage across the mountains."

Sgt. Ordway's route to the Salmon River

Sgt. Ordway's return from the Salmon River

NEZ PERCE (NEZ-PURSE) INDIAN RESERVATION

MAP SYMBOLS

44	Interstate Highway
50 24	U.S., State Highway
223	County Road
94 83 50	Lewis & Clark Trail Highway
	Bottom Lands *(Roads may be impassable during certain seasons.)*
!	Travel Restrictions *(Inquire Locally)*
→	Streamflow Direction

1 Major Interpretive Site *(See text for description.)*

Water Route Direction:
←→ Westbound
→ Eastbound

Land Route Direction:
Westbound
Eastbound

Journal Excerpts:
Westbound
Eastbound

¹/₈" = 1 mile

then crossed back into today's Idaho via **[1]** Lolo Pass and camped at Packer Meadows.

The next day, "in the Valies it rained and hailed, on the top of the mountains Some Snow fell" and their Shoshone guide, Toby, accidentally led them down to the vicinity of the present Powell Ranger Station. Camping on the Lochsa River that night, "we were compelled to kill a Colt...to eat for the want of meat." Having passed the mouth of a creek two miles before, the captains named it Colt Killed Creek; this is today's White Sand Creek. Before settlement on the plains drove deer and elk herds into the mountains, the Rockies in any weather were not a place to live off the land on a meat diet.

The Corps spent all the next day climbing the steep mountainside back up to the trail that followed the ridge. For drinking water and to boil the rest of the horsemeat that night, they melted snow. Clark wrote, "From this mountain I could observe high ruged mountains in every direction as far as I could See."

They had expected a single range, and one that was like the Alleghenies back home—which were geologically much older, eroded smoother, and rose only to 3,000 feet or so. Not only did they find range after range, but the Bitterroots were much younger, jagged and craggy. Passes were few and far apart. Although the Bitterroots' highest peak along their route, at 9,000 feet, was 3,000 to 5,000 feet lower than some Colorado Rockies peaks, the Corps would find no easy crossing like the great South Pass in future Wyoming.

September 16 brought an all-day snow-storm, putting 4" of new snow atop 6"–8" of old, and making the trail harder than ever to find. Snow dropped from branches they bumped in passing. Clark was "wet and as cold in every part as I ever was in my life," and afraid his feet would freeze in his moccasins. He and another man hurried ahead to start a fire and use the rest of the colt to make soup for that night's camp, near the rock cairn today called Indian Post Office. It was hard to find level ground for camp.

By morning, the precious horses had scattered to forage, and it took till 1:00 p.m. to collect them. The Corps could see that the valleys below had no snow, but their trail kept them up on top of rugged knobs covered with it. The captains decided to split the party again.

Clark took six hunters and went ahead on September 18, hoping to find game to kill and hang up for the main party. Clark estimated his men traveled thirty-two rugged miles but found no game. In the distance, though, probably from today's Sherman Peak, they could see a prairie. They proceeded on, then stopped to rest the horses at what they named "Hungry Creek," "as at that place we had nothing to eate." They had better luck the next day, discovering and killing a stray horse and two grouse. And the trail was—for the last time—descending, and the air becoming warmer.

September 20 saw Clark's party down from the mountains to "leavel pine country...a butifull Countrey," today's **[6]** Weippe Prairie, where they found a camp of Nez Perce Indians collecting camas roots. The starchy bulb of this lily was a staple of the Indians' diet, of which "they make bread & Supe," Clark noted.

The Nez Perce welcomed them with a feast of dried berries, a little bison meat, some fish, and camas roots cooked various ways. Clark became ill, he thought "from eateing the fish & roots too freely." The next day, he sent out all the hunters while he quizzed the Nez Perce about the country. They drew a chart of the rivers ahead, and of the Indian nations there. The hunters returned empty-handed, but Clark sent Private Reubin Field, with a Nez Perce, back to Lewis and the main party with a horse-load of roots and three large salmon. Clark and

the other five pushed on to the Clearwater River and reached the camp of Chief Twisted Hair late at night. Clark presented a medal and conversed with the chief by sign language until 1:00 a.m.

With Twisted Hair and his son, Clark set out on September 22 to return to the main party, leaving his hunters to their work around the Nez Perce camp. He reached Lewis at dark, despite a horse that "threw me 3 times which hurt me Some."

The main party, with Lewis, had had five bad days while Clark and his men were gone ahead. On September 18, they had eaten the last of the second colt in the morning, with small portions of the now-rancid "portable soup" bought in Philadelphia for dinner and supper. From Sherman Peak the next day, they too saw the prairie far ahead. But the men were weak from hunger and dysentery. September 20 brought the discovery of the horse Clark had killed and left, but now a packhorse was missing, which, Lewis noted, carried some Indian trade items as well as all his own winter clothing. Even so, he took time to make careful notes of birds new to science.

On September 21, Lewis's party camped on Lolo Creek, and ate a few grouse, a coyote, and some crayfish from the creek. He and the men were still very weak from hunger and cold, but they hoped to reach open country the next day. Even better, that day brought Reubin Field with the horseload of food.

After eating, they went down out of the mountains to the first Nez Perce camp. Lewis wrote that it was easier to imagine than to describe "the pleasure I now felt in having tryumphed over the rocky Mountains..."

Now everyone was sick from overeating after their mountain fast, or simply from the abrupt change of diet. They presented medals among the Nez Perce, and traded whatever they could for as much food as their tired horses could carry.

It was time to make canoes for the final trek to the Pacific, so they moved down the Clearwater River until they found good timber, and set up **[7]** "Canoe Camp" on September 26, five miles west of today's Orofino.

Here they stayed for a week and a half, recovering from the terrible trek over the Rocky Mountains, and carving and burning out five canoes from huge ponderosa pine logs. Clark noted "Capt Lewis very Sick nearly all the men Sick" from the new diet of fish and camas roots. Also affecting them was the change from the mountains' cold to Clearwater Canyon's heat. Sergeant John Ordway wrote on the 26th that they were ill from "a Sudden change of diet and water as well as the change of climate also." By the 30th, all but two men were working on the canoes, and two days later a horse was killed for soup to nourish the sick.

Meriwether Lewis must have been one of the hardest-hit, because it was not until October 4 that Clark noted Lewis was "able to walk about a little," although the next day, "Capt Lewis not So well to day as yesterday."

Meanwhile, Private John Colter went out on September 24 and returned three days later with one of the two lost horses, but apparently not the one carrying Lewis's winter clothing. Happily, Colter also brought back a deer that was shared between Nez Perce visitors and the sick men.

The Nez Perce agreed to take care of the Corps' horses until they returned the next year, so all 38 horses were branded with an iron that read "U.S. Capt. M. Lewis." This brand is now at the Oregon Historical Society in Portland.

A cache was dug and filled with ammunition and the mountain packsaddles, to be retrieved next spring. On October 7, they set out down the Clearwater River, even though not everyone was well yet. Clark, in the lead canoe, was ill again, too.

TOURING TODAY

ॐ TRIAL AND TRYUMPH ॐ

[ ] Bracketed numbers key sites to maps	♿ Special-needs accessible	⊨ Bed & breakfast
★ L&C in-depth interpretation, unchanged landform	⊗ Restaurant	▲ Camping, RV park
● L&C interpreted site	⊞ Motel, hotel, cabin	

ALONG THE EXPEDITION'S PATH

Lolo Motorway follows Forest Service Road 500 and takes you as close as you can get with a vehicle to the actual trail. Access is off US 12 west of Lolo; Forest Service Road 569 north of Powell Ranger Station; Forest Service Road 100 east from Kamiah. This is a rough, single-lane road and not for the faint-hearted. Before starting out you'll need a detailed map, a high clearance vehicle (preferably 4-wheel drive), a full tank and water. The road is open only mid-July to September, and this is subject to weather conditions. Check with the Forest Service for closure information. A permit system is being implemented to lessen the impact on this fragile resource during the Bicentennial. Procedures are being finalized and a lottery system will begin when the number of visitors warrants the precautions. On-line applications and informa-

tion are available at www.fs.fed.us /rl/clearwater/LewisClark.LewisClark .htm or 208/476-4541.

September 11, 1805
● **Lewis and Clark Campground** (Lolo, MT)—Interpretive display; picnic area; fishing; hiking. ▲ 18 sites; fee; water; primitive; open Memorial Day-Sept; grills/fire rings; tables; 22' trailer limit. 15 miles W on US 12. 406/329-3750.

September 12, 1805
[2] ★ **Howard Creek** (Lolo, MT)—Interpretive exhibit and trails along the actual route. 18.5 miles W on US 12. 406/329-3962.

September 13, 1805
(Return June 29, 1806)
● **Lolo Hot Springs Resort** (Lolo, MT)—The same springs that soothed the Corps. ▲ Ten 18'-diameter tipis sleep 6-8 people (flat rate); pets; 116 sites (86 w/hookups); fee; water; modern; showers; open May-Sept; grills/fire rings; tables. Indoor/outdoor hot spring

pools; fishing; hiking; ⊗ restaurant; playground. 26 miles W on US 12. 406/273-2290, 800/273-2290.
[3] ★ **Lee Creek** (Lolo, MT)—Interpretive displays, 2.5-mile hike along what may have been part of the actual route. ▲ 22 sites; fee; no water; primitive; open May-Sept; grills/fire rings; tables; 22' trailer limit. Fishing. 26 miles W on US 12. 406/329-3750.
[1] ★ **Lolo Pass Visitor Center**—Interpretive exhibits. Summer only; free. 28 miles W of Lolo on US 12. 406/329-3962.
● **Packer Meadows**—Interpretive sign 1 mile E of Visitor Center on FR 373.
[4] ★ **De Voto Memorial Grove of Cedars**—Alongside Crooked Creek is this memorial to historian Bernard De Voto who spent time here in 1953 while working on a one-volume version of the Lewis and Clark journals; his ashes were scattered here in 1955. Always open; free. 5 miles W of Powell Ranger Station on US 12.

September 14, 1805
(Return June 28, 1806)
- **Powell**—Interpretive exhibit. ▲ 39 sites; fee; water; modern/primitive; open May-Oct; grills/fire rings; tables; 14-day limit; firewood. Fishing; hiking. 12 miles W of Lolo Pass on US 12. 208/942-3113.
- **Colt Killed Camp/Powell Ranger Station**—Interpretive exhibits. Daily dawn to dusk; free. 18 miles W of Lolo Hot Springs on US 12. 208/942-3113.

September 15, 1805
[5] ★ **Whitehouse Pond**—Trail interpretation. ▲ 14 sites; fee; water; primitive; open May-Sept; grills/fire rings; tables; 14-day limit; firewood. Fishing; hiking; off-road vehicle trails. 16 miles W of Lolo Pass on US 12. 208/942-3113.
- **Wendover Campground**—Fishing; hiking. ▲ 28 sites; fee; water; primitive; open June-Sept; grills/fire rings; tables; 10-day limit; firewood; 32'. 16 miles W of Lolo Pass on US 12. 208/942-3113.

September 17, 1805
- **Sinque Hole Camp**—Hiking trail. Access is by 4-wheel drive only, often impassable until mid- or late summer, then a half-mile hike. 80 miles from Kooskia on FR 500. 208/476-454 on the Lolo Motorway.

September 20, 1805
(Return June 21-24 & 10-15, 1806)
[6] ★ **Weippe Prairie/Nez Perce National Historic Park** (Weippe, ID)—Interpretation of the Corps' visits. Daily dawn-dusk; free. 18 miles E of US 12 on ID 11. 208/843-2261.

September 26 to October 5, 1805
(Return May 9, 1806)
[7] ★ **Canoe Camp/Nez Perce National Historic Park** (Orofino, ID)—Interpretation of the camp here includes replica of a dugout canoe. Hiking trails, fishing access. Open dawn-dusk; free. 5 miles W on US 12. 208/843-2261.

AROUND THE AREA

TOWNS LISTED ALPHABETICALLY

Kamiah, Idaho
East Kamiah—Volcanic rock formation known as the Heart of the Monster to the Nez Perce, who consider it their point of origin. Daily dawn-dusk; free. 2 miles E on US 12.

▲ **Lewis and Clark Resort**—231 sites (all w/hookups); fee; water; modern; showers; open all year; grills/fire rings; tables. Pool; fishing; coin laundry; groceries. 1.5 miles E on US 12. 208/935-2556.

⊞ **Clearwater 12 Motel**—29 large rooms, pets. US 12 & Cedar St. 208/935-2671. $

⊞ **Lewis-Clark Motel**—21 rooms in log building, pets, full breakfast, hot tub, ⊗ restaurant, coin laundry. & E on US 12. 208/935-2556. $ K3

Kooskia, Idaho
▲ **Apgar**—7 sites; fee; water; primitive; open May-Oct; grills/fire rings; tables; 14-day limit; firewood. Fishing and river rafting. 30 miles E on US 12. 208/926-4275.

▲ **Ohara Bar**—34 sites; fee; water; primitive; open June-Sept; grills/fire rings; tables; 14-day limit; firewood; 32' trailer limit. Swimming; boating; fishing. 23.5 miles E on US 12, 7 miles SE on Co 223, 0.25 mile S on FR 651. 208/926-4258.

▲ **Wilderness Gateway**—89 sites; fee; water; modern/primitive; open June-Sept; grills/fire rings; tables; 14-day limit; firewood. Lochsa Historic Ranger Station (exhibits and tours); playground; river trail; amphitheater. 48 miles E on US 12. 208/926-4275.

⊨ **Looking Glass Inn**—7 rooms in rustic guest house. No TV or phone in rooms. Full breakfast. W of Lolo on US 12. 208/926-0855, 888/926-0855. $$

Lolo Pass
▲ **Jerry Johnson**—15 sites; fee; water; primitive; open June-Aug; grills/fire rings; tables; 14-day limit; firewood; 22'. Fishing; hiking; off-road vehicle trails. 24 miles W on US 12. 208/942-3113.

Lolo, Montana
Fort Fizzle Historic Site—Interpretive signs and picnic area near Lolo Creek. Trail/& to fishing access. Daily dawn to dusk; free. 5 miles W on US 12. 406/329-3750.

⊞ **Lolo Hot Springs**—34 rooms, indoor/outdoor hot spring pools, pets, trail rides, hiking, mountain biking. Deluxe rooms are larger, executive rooms have best views. 25 miles W on US 12. 406/273-2290, 800/273-2290. $$

⊞ **West Fork Butte Forest Service Cabin**—Available Oct. through May, 4 beds. Winter access by snowmobile last 7.5 miles, elevation rise of 2,300'. 25 miles W. 406/329-3814.

⊗ **Guy's Lolo Creek Steakhouse**—Western fare in hand-hewn log building. & D only Tue-Sun. Just W of US 93 on US 12. 406/273-2622. $$$

⊗ **Lolo Hot Springs Eatery and Saloon**—Barbecued pork and half-pound Lolo Burger; soak in the hot springs; kids' menu, country music. & B L & D daily. 25 miles W on US 12. 406/273-2290. $$

Orofino, Idaho
▲ **Dent Acres**—50 sites (all w/hookups); fee; water; modern; showers; open May-Sept; grills/fire rings; tables; 35' trailer limit. Swimming; boat dock/ramp; nature trail; fishing; hiking; dump station. 20 miles N on Elk River Rd. 208/476-3294.

▲ **Dworshak State Park**—106 sites (50 w/hookups); fee; water; modern/primitive; showers; open June-Oct; grills/fire rings; tables. Swimming; boat ramp; fishing; playground; hiking. 26 miles NW on Co P1. 208/476-5994.

⊞ **Konkolville Motel**—40 rooms, pets, pool, hot tub, coin laundry. 3 miles E of US 12 on ID 7. 208/476-5584. $ K10

⊞ **White Pine Motel**—18 rooms, pets. US 12 E of ID 7. 208/476-7093. $ K12

CHAPTER 19

October 7 to 16, 1805

TO THE COLUMBIA RIVER

On the Great Plains during the summer of 1804, it had been hard to meet certain Indian nations who were out hunting bison for their winter food supply. Now, on rivers feeding the Pacific, the autumn salmon run was on, and Indian nations were camped right beside the Clearwater River, catching and drying abundant fish.

After the Corps of Discovery passed fifteen rapids on October 8 alone, one canoe split and sank, spilling goods and men—including non-swimmers. The men hung onto pieces of the canoe until the precious Indian presents were collected, and everyone was rescued. The Corps went into camp near today's **[1]** Spalding, Idaho, for two days to patch the canoe and dry out cargo. They were near the mouth of the Potlatch River, which they named Colter Creek for Private John Colter.

Nez Perce chiefs Twisted Hair and Tetoharsky, who had promised to accompany the Corps downriver, joined them, and Shoshone guide Toby and his son left for home without payment because Toby said enemies would steal it before he got home, anyway.

On October 10, the party set out again down the Clearwater River. They made only twelve river miles that day, having to stop for an hour to free and repair one canoe that became stuck on a rock.

From some Nez Perce people camped at the site, the Corps purchased dogs and dried fish for food. Captain William Clark wrote that all the others "relish the flesh of the dogs..." but he stayed on a diet of fish.

The day's long journey downstream took them to the Snake River, which Clark considered an extension of his "Lewis's River," the Salmon. They camped that night across from today's Lewiston, Idaho, and Clarkston, Washington at the confluence of the Clearwater and the Snake River. Making thirty miles each of the next two days brought them to a bad rapid near Riparia

on October 12, where they camped overnight to decide how to proceed.

In the morning, Captain Meriwether Lewis took two canoes and made it through the rapid, and the others followed safely. Clark wrote that they would have portaged more often, for safety's sake, "if the Season was not So far advanced and time precious with us."

Sacagawea, useful as an interpreter only in Shoshone country, now assisted the Corps by her very presence. Clark noted that, to the native peoples in this country (including the Nez Perce already met), a woman among strangers meant the party came in peace.

Passing the mouth of today's Palouse River, the Corps called it Drewyer's River from the phonetic way they spelled the name of interpreter George Drouillard.

After camping near Ayer in Franklin County on the 13th, they passed Monumental Rock, labelling it Ship Rock because it looked to them like a ship's hull. Dinner on October 14—their midday meal—was blue-winged teal; Clark wrote "for the first time for three weeks past I had a good dinner..."

Shortly, downstream from today's Burr Canyon, the last canoe in line got stuck on a rock. Its passengers jumped out onto the stone, and one of the Nez Perce chiefs swam to shore, but the canoe sank, and out floated food, bedding, skins, and a tent. Some of the goods were caught by men in the canoes ahead, but all the roots were lost. Another canoe rescued the crew. The Corps camped to dry out what had been saved. But the night at this site now under Lake Sacajawea was frosty, and cargo didn't dry enough to reload until midafternoon of the next day. While they were waiting, Lewis walked out onto the plains and reported he could see mountains ahead, which were probably the Blue Mountains of Washington and Oregon.

Although the 15th took them through seven rapids successfully, day's end brought them to

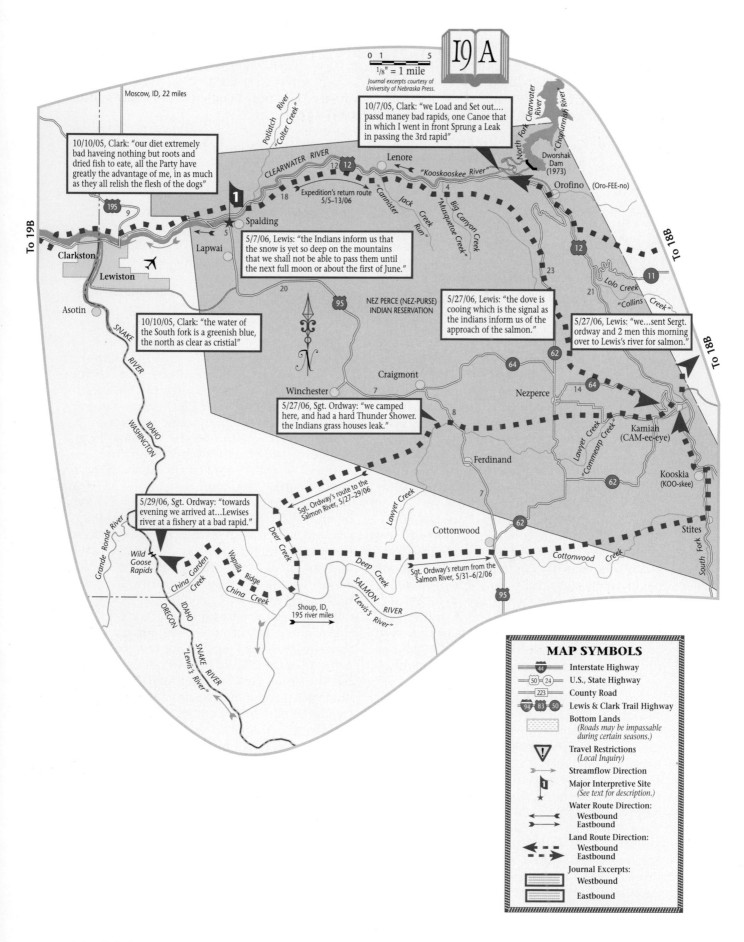

0 1   5
1/8" = 1 mile

Journal excerpts courtesy of
University of Nebraska Press.

19 A

Moscow, ID, 22 miles

10/7/05, Clark: "we Load and Set out…. passd maney bad rapids, one Canoe that in which I went in front Sprung a Leak in passing the 3rd rapid"

10/10/05, Clark: "our diet extremely bad haveing nothing but roots and dried fish to eate, all the Party have greatly the advantage of me, in as much as they all relish the flesh of the dogs"

Potlatch River
"Colter Creek"

North Fork Clearwater River

"Chopunnish River"

Dworshak Dam (1973)

Lenore

CLEARWATER RIVER

"Kooskooskee River"

Orofino (Oro-FEE-no)

12 12

18 Expedition's return route 5/5–13/06

"Cannister Run"

Jack Creek

"Musquetoe Creek"

Big Canyon Creek

195 9

1

To 19B

Spalding

5

Lapwai

To 18B

12

23

11

Lolo Creek

21 "Collins Creek"

Clarkston

Lewiston

5/7/06, Lewis: "the Indians inform us that the snow is yet so deep on the mountains that we shall not be able to pass them until the next full moon or about the first of June."

Asotin

20

NEZ PERCE (NEZ-PURSE) INDIAN RESERVATION

95

5/27/06, Lewis: "the dove is cooing which is the signal as the indians inform us of the approach of the salmon."

5/27/06, Lewis: "we…sent Sergt. ordway and 2 men this morning over to Lewis's river for salmon."

62

64

To 18B

10/10/05, Clark: "the water of the South fork is a greenish blue, the north as clear as cristial"

N

Craigmont

Nezperce

14 64

Kamiah (CAM-ee-eye)

Winchester

7

5/27/06, Sgt. Ordway: "we camped here, and had a hard Thunder Shower. the Indians grass houses leak."

8

Ferdinand

Lawyer Creek

"Commearp Creek"

62

Kooskia (KOO-skee)

SNAKE RIVER

WASHINGTON IDAHO

5/29/06, Sgt. Ordway: "towards evening we arrived at…Lewises river at a bad rapid."

Sgt. Ordway's route to the Salmon River, 5/27–29/06

Lawyer Creek

7

Cottonwood

62

Cottonwood Creek

Stites

Grande Ronde River

Wild Goose Rapids

China Garden Creek

Wapilla Ridge

Deer Creek

Deep Creek

SALMON RIVER

"Lewis's River"

Sgt. Ordway's return from the Salmon River, 5/31–6/2/06

95

South Fork

China Creek

OREGON IDAHO

Shoup, ID, 195 river miles

SNAKE RIVER

"Lewis's River"

MAP SYMBOLS

44	Interstate Highway
50 24	U.S., State Highway
223	County Road
94 83 50	Lewis & Clark Trail Highway
	Bottom Lands *(Roads may be impassable during certain seasons.)*
▽	**Travel Restrictions** *(Local Inquiry)*
	Streamflow Direction
1	**Major Interpretive Site** *(See text for description.)*
	Water Route Direction: Westbound Eastbound
	Land Route Direction: Westbound Eastbound
	Journal Excerpts: Westbound Eastbound

Fishhook Rapids, now submerged under Lake Sacajawea, above Ice Harbor Dam. Chiefs Twisted Hair and Tetoharsky, traveling ahead, had waited here to warn the Corps how bad these rapids were. After camping overnight, they ran the rapids successfully. Sergeant Nathaniel Pryor's canoe got stuck on a rock, but unloading was enough to free it. Later in the day, though, a worse rapid near today's Strawberry Island required a short portage. McNary Dam near Pendleton since has tamed the river here.

But that day, October 16, brought them at last to the "great Columbia river."

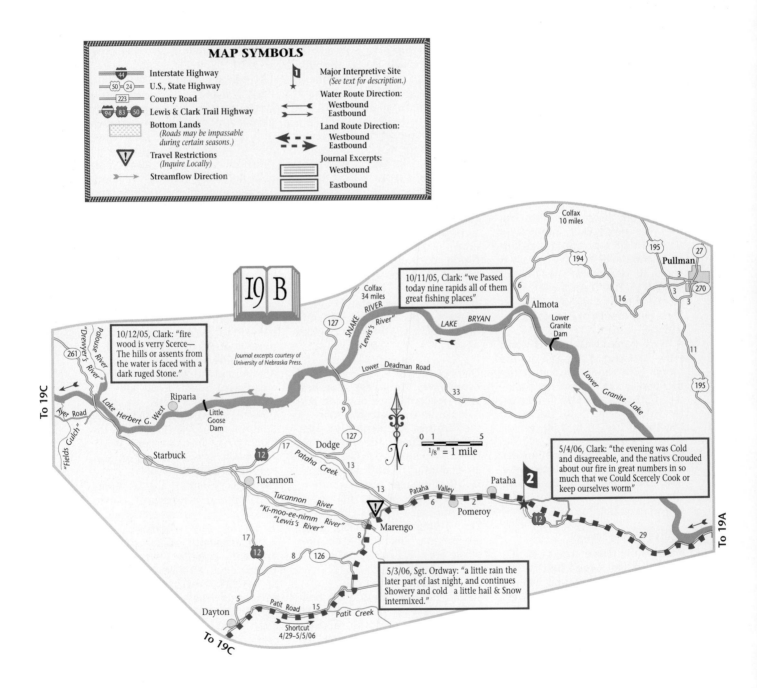

MAP SYMBOLS

Interstate Highway
U.S., State Highway
County Road
Lewis & Clark Trail Highway
Bottom Lands
(Roads may be impassable during certain seasons.)
Travel Restrictions
(Inquire Locally)
Streamflow Direction

Major Interpretive Site
(See text for description.)
Water Route Direction:
Westbound
Eastbound
Land Route Direction:
Westbound
Eastbound
Journal Excerpts:
Westbound
Eastbound

10/11/05, Clark: "we Passed today nine rapids all of them great fishing places"

10/12/05, Clark: "fire wood is verry Scerce—The hills or assents from the water is faced with a dark ruged Stone."

Journal excerpts courtesy of University of Nebraska Press.

5/4/06, Clark: "the evening was Cold and disagreeable, and the nativs Crouded about our fire in great numbers in so much that we Could Scercely Cook or keep ourselves worm"

5/3/06, Sgt. Ordway: "a little rain the later part of last night, and continues Showery and cold a little hail & Snow intermixed."

$1/8" = 1$ mile

TOURING TODAY

❧ TO THE COLUMBIA RIVER ❧

[ ] Bracketed numbers key sites to maps	♿ Special-needs accessible	⊫ Bed & breakfast
★ L&C in-depth interpretation, unchanged landform	⊗ Restaurant	⚊ Camping, RV park
● L&C interpreted site	⊞ Motel, hotel, cabin	

Bridges over the Clearwater River in this area are near Spalding, ID (US 95); Lewiston, ID (US 12); over the Snake River at Clarkston, WA (WA 129).

ALONG THE EXPEDITION'S PATH

October 10, 1805

[1] ★ **Nez Perce National Historic Park/Headquarters & Visitor Center** (Spalding, ID)—Exhibits about the cultural history of the Nez Perce and information about the 38 separate sites included in the multi-state park. Daily 8 to 5:30 (Memorial Day-Labor Day), 8 to 4:30 (rest of year); free. US 95 on north bank of Clearwater River near mouth of Potlatch River. 208/843-2261.

● **Nez Perce National Historic Park/Spalding Site**—Self-guided tour of 1838 Lapwai Mission, cemetery and Indian Agency headquarters. 0.25 mile E of park headquarters. Daily 8 to 5:30 (Memorial Day-Labor Day), 8 to 4:30 (rest of year); free. 208/843-2261.

● **Sacajawea Fountain/Pioneer Park** (Lewiston, ID)—Interpretation, picnic area, playground at city park. Always open; free. 5th St & 2nd Ave. 208/746-6857.

(Return May 5, 1806)
● **Lewiston Levee** (Lewiston, ID) and **Clarkston Green Belt** (Clarkston, WA)—Hiking and biking area along the Snake/Clearwater rivers confluence. 208/758-9676.

October 11, 1805

★ **Chief Timothy State Park** (Clarkston, WA)—**Alpowai Interpretive Center** contains audiovisual presentations and exhibits on Indian history and culture, and on the Lewis and Clark Expedition. Open Wed-Sun 1 to 5 (Memorial Day-Labor Day). ⚊ 66 sites (33 w/hookups); fee; water; modern; showers; open all year/full operation May-Sept; grills/fire rings; tables; firewood; 10-day limit. Fishing; boat ramp/dock; playground; beach; hiking; dump station; concessions. 8 miles W of Clarkston on US 12. Park is on Silcott Island across causeway. 509/758-9580.

(Return Shortcut May 3, 1806)
Central Ferry State Park (Pomeroy, WA)—Swimming; boating; hiking; birdwatching; large picnic area with shelters; beach; Snake River Canyon. ⚊ 60 sites (all w/hookups); fee; water; modern; showers; open all year; grills/fire rings; tables; 10-day limit. 22 miles W on WA 127. 509/549-3551.

October 13, 1805

Lyons Ferry State Park (Starbuck, WA)—At confluence of Snake and Palouse rivers. Interpretation of the **Marmes Archaeological Site**, which contained the cultural remains of people who lived in the area about 10,000 years ago. ⚊ 50 sites; fee; water; modern; showers; open all year/full operation Apr-Sept; grills/fire rings; tables; 10-day limit. Fishing; boating/marina; hiking; beach and picnic area. 7.5 miles NW on WA 261. 509/646-3252.

Lyons Marina (Starbuck, WA)—Swimming; boat ramp/dock; boat rentals; fishing. ⚊ 38 sites (18 w/hookups); fee; water; modern; showers; open all year; grills/fire rings; tables; groceries. 14 miles NW of US 12 on WA 261. 509/399-2001.

(Return Shortcut May 2, 1806)
[2] ● **3 Forks Indian Trail Turnout** (Dayton, WA)—Interpretation of nearby trails. 15 miles E on US 12. 509/758-9580.

[3] ★ **Lewis and Clark Trail State Park** (Dayton, WA)—Interpretive kiosks and 1-mile interpretive trail. Birdwatching trail; interpretive programs Sat evenings. ⚊ 25 sites; fee; water; modern; open all year/full operation May-Sept; grills/fire rings; tables; firewood; 10-day limit. Hiking trails; dump station. 5 miles W on US 12. 509/337-6457.

October 15, 1805

Ice Harbor Dam (Pasco, WA)—Self-guided tours of dam, powerhouse, fish ladders and locks. Slide show and videotape presentation on salmon. Visitor center open daily 9 to 5 (Apr-Oct); free. 12 miles E of Pasco. 509/547-7781.

Charbonneau (Burbank, WA)—Boating; fishing; swimming; picnic area; playground. ⚊ 54 sites (all w/hookups); fee; water; modern; showers; open all year/full operation Apr-Oct; grills/fire rings; tables; 14-day limit. 8 miles E of US 12 on WA 124, 2 miles N on Sun Harbor Dr. 509/547-7781.

Fishhook (Burbank, WA)—Boating; fishing; swimming; picnic area; hiking; beach; playground. ⚊ 61 sites (41 w/hookups); fee; water; modern; showers; open Apr-Sept; grills/fire rings; tables; 14-day limit. 15 miles E of US 12 on WA 124, 4 miles N on Fishhook Park Rd. 509/547-7781.

Hood (Burbank, WA)—Hiking; boat ramp; playground; picnic area; beach. ⚊ 69 sites (all w/hookups); fee; water; modern; showers; open Apr-Oct; grills/fire rings; tables; 14-day limit. In Burbank at US 12 & WA 124. 509/547-7781.

Around the Area

TOWNS LISTED ALPHABETICALLY

Ahsahka, Idaho
Dworshak Fisheries Complex—Steelhead trout and chinook salmon are produced here in record numbers. Tours and exhibits. Daily 7:30 to 4:30; free. On ID 7. 208/476-4591.

▲ **Freeman Creek**—101 sites; fee; water; modern; showers; open May-Sept; grills/fire rings; tables; 14-day limit, 35' limit. Boat ramp; lake fishing; dump station. 24 miles W of Orofino on ID 7 (many steep and narrow sections). 208/476-3294.

Anatone, Washington
Fields Spring State Park—Take 1-mile hike up 4,500' **Puffer Butte** for panoramic view. Don't miss the steep, but spectacular, 10-mile drive through the canyon on WA 129 south of the park. ▲ 20 sites; fee; water; modern; showers; open all year/full operation May-Sept; grills/fire rings; tables; 10-day limit; firewood. Nature trail;

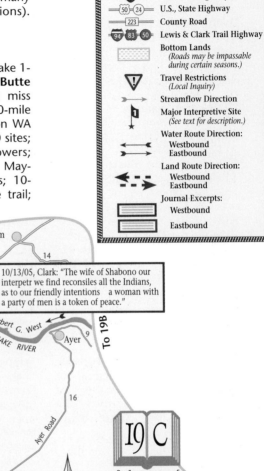

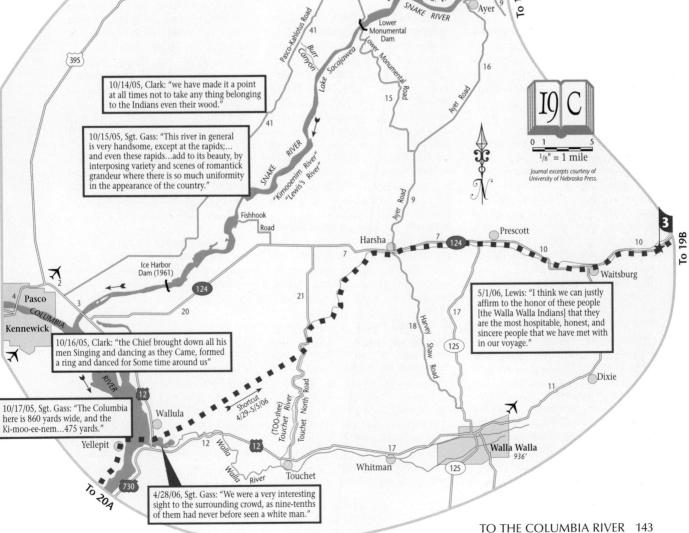

10/13/05, Clark: "The wife of Shabono our interpetr we find reconsiles all the Indians, as to our friendly intentions   a woman with a party of men is a token of peace."

10/14/05, Clark: "we have made it a point at all times not to take any thing belonging to the Indians even their wood."

10/15/05, Sgt. Gass: "This river in general is very handsome, except at the rapids;… and even these rapids…add to its beauty, by interposing variety and scenes of romantick grandeur where there is so much uniformity in the appearance of the country."

10/16/05, Clark: "the Chief brought down all his men Singing and dancing as they Came, formed a ring and danced for Some time around us"

10/17/05, Sgt. Gass: "The Columbia here is 860 yards wide, and the Ki-moo-ee-nem…475 yards."

5/1/06, Lewis: "I think we can justly affirm to the honor of these people [the Walla Walla Indians] that they are the most hospitable, honest, and sincere people that we have met with in our voyage."

4/28/06, Sgt. Gass: "We were a very interesting sight to the surrounding crowd, as nine-tenths of them had never before seen a white man."

playground; hiking. 26 miles S of Clarkston on WA 129. 509/256-3332.

Asotin, Washington
Asotin County Historical Museum—1882 log cabin and barn with carriages, pioneer memorabilia. Tue-Sat 1 to 5; donations. 3rd & Filmore. 509/243-4659.

Clarkston, Washington
Clarkston Chamber of Commerce, 502 Bridge St. 509/758-7712, 800/933-2128.
⊞ **Best Western Rivertree Inn**—61 rooms, pool, hot tub, exercise room. 6 blocks W of WA 129 on US 12. 509/758-9551. $$ K18
⊞ **Motel 6**—87 rooms, pool, pets, coin laundry. Off season rates. 222 Bridge St. 509/758-1631. $ K18
⊞ **Quality Inn**—75 rooms, pool, ⊗ restaurant, coin laundry. On Snake River. N on 5th St off US 12. 509/758-9500. $$ K18

Cottonwood, Idaho
Nez Perce National Historic Park—Interpretive markers about 1877 battles between the Nez Perce and U.S. cavalry. Daily dawn-dusk; free. SE of town. 208/843-2261.

Dayton, Washington
Dayton Chamber of Commerce, 166 E. Main. 509/382-4825.
▲ **Last Resort RV Campground**—41 sites (36 w/hookups); fee; water; modern; showers; open all year; grills/fire rings; tables. Along Tucannon River. Coin laundry; groceries; dump station. 14 miles N on US 12, 19 miles SE on Tucannon Rd. 509/843-1556.
⊞ **The Weinhard Hotel**—15 rooms, full breakfast, smoke-free, TV. 509/382-4032. $$$
⊗ **Patit Creek**—Intriguing continental menu. Smoke-free. L & D Tue-Sat. US 12. 509/382-2625. $$$

Grangeville, Idaho
Nez Perce National Historic Park/White Bird Battlefield—Interpretation of first confrontation in the Nez Perce War of 1877. Daily dawn-dusk; free. 16 miles S on US 95. 208/843-2261.

Kahlotus, Washington
Lower Monumental Lock and Dam—Viewing room for fish ladder in visitor center. Powerhouse and lock overlook. Daily dawn to dusk (Apr-Oct); free. 6 miles S on Devils Canyon Rd. 509/282-3219.

Lapwai, Idaho
Northern Idaho Indian Agency—Bureau of Indian Affairs headquarters of the Nez Perce, Coeur d'Alene and Kootenai Indians. Near the site of Fort Lapwai, abandoned in 1884. Some buildings are still in use. Weekdays 8 to 4:30. 208/843-2300.

Lewiston, Idaho
Lewiston Chamber of Commerce, 2207 E. Main St. 208/743-3531, 800/473-3543.
Hells Canyon Boat Trips—Deepest river gorge in the country. Information on day trips and longer floats available at the Chamber of Commerce, 208/743-3531, 800/473-3543.
Hells Gate State Park—Highly developed, popular park on the Snake River. Snake River Canyon float trips. ▲ 96 sites (64 w/hookups); fee; water; modern; showers; open Mar-Nov; grills/fire rings; tables; 15-day limit. Fishing; marina; swimming; playground; bike trail; visitor center; dump station. 3.5 miles S of Snake River Bridge on US 12. 208/879-5204.
● **Nez Perce County Museum**—Indian and pioneer history. Tue-Sat 10 to 4; donations. 3rd & C Streets. 208/743-2535.
● **North Central District Health Department**—Tile mosaics of Canoe Camp and Lewis and Clark with the Nez Perce decorate the outside of this building. Always open; free. 10th St. 208/799-3100.
⊞ **Howard Johnson Express**—66 rooms, pets, pool, continental breakfast, free laundry, hot tub. Ask about special discounts. 1716 Main. 208/743-9526. $$ K12
⊞ **Red Lion Hotel**—136 rooms, pets, pool, ⊗ restaurant, hot tub, coin laundry. Off-season rates. US 12 & 21st St. 208/799-1000. $$$ K18
⊞ **Riverview Inn**—75 rooms, pets, pool, continental breakfast.

Off-season rates. US 12 & 21st St. 208/746-3311.
⊞ **Sacajawea Motor Inn**—90 rooms, pets, pool, ⊗ restaurant, exercise room, hot tub, coin laundry. Near Dike Bypass and Walk. 1824 Main. 208/746-1393, 800/333-1393. $$
⊗ **Bojack's**—Hearty down-home meals. D only Mon-Sat. 311 Main St. 208/746-9532. $$

Moscow, Idaho
Moscow Chamber of Commerce, 411 S. Main. 208/882-1800, 800/380-1801.
Appaloosa Museum—Nez Perce memorabilia and history of the Appaloosa horse. Mon-Fri 10 to 5; donations. On WA 8. 208/882-5578 x 279.
McConnell Mansion/Latah County Historical Society—Victorian furnishings and exhibits. Tue-Sat 1 to 4; donations. 110 S. Adams. 208/882-1004.
▲ **Little Boulder**—17 sites; fee; water; primitive; open June-Aug; grills/fire rings; tables; 14-day limit; 40' trailer limit. Fishing. 26 miles E on ID 8. 208/875-1311.
⊞ **Mark IV**—86 rooms, pets, indoor pool, hot tub, ⊗ restaurant. ⅖. 414 N. Main. 208/882-7557, 800/833-4240. $$ K10
⊞ **Motel 6**—110 rooms, pool, pets, coin laundry. Off season rates. 101 Baker. 208/882-5511. $ K17
⊞ **University Inn**—173 rooms, pool, pets, continental breakfast, weight room. Ask about discounts. 1516 Pullman Rd. 208/882-0550, 800/325-8765. $$$ K17

Pomeroy, Washington
▲ **Tucannon**—15 sites; free; water; primitive; open May-Nov; grills/fire rings; tables; 14-day limit; 16' maximum length. 17 miles SW on Co 101, 8 miles SW on FR47, S on FR 160. 509/843-1891.

Pullman, Washington
Pullman Chamber of Commerce, 415 Grand Ave. 509/334-3565, 800/365-6948.
▲ **City of Pullman RV Park**—24 sites (all w/hookups); fee; water; primitive; open Apr-Nov; grills/fire rings; tables. 1 mile E of WA 27 on WA 270. 509/334-4555.

⊞ **American Travel Inn**—35 rooms, pool, pets. Family rooms. 515 S. Grand. 509/334-3500. $$ K12

⊞ **Holiday Inn Express**—85 rooms, pets, indoor pool, continental breakfast, hot tub, coin laundry, bike rental. &. 1190 Bishop Blvd. 509/334-4437. $$$ K18

⊞ **Quality Inn Paradise Creek**—66 rooms, pets, pool, continental breakfast, hot tub, coin laundry. 1050 SE Bishop Blvd. 509/332-0500. $$$ K18

⊗ **Swilly's Cafe & Gathering Place**—Upscale deli & more. L & D Mon-Sat, smoke-free. 200 Kamiaken. 509/334-3395. $$

Washtucna, Washington

Palouse Falls State Park—Adjacent to Lyons Ferry State Park, trail/& to overlook and observation shelter above 190' Palouse Falls. ▲ 9 sites; fee; water; primitive; open all year; grills/fire rings; tables; 10-day limit. 17 miles SE on WA 261. 509/646-3252.

Walla Walla, Washington

Walla Walla Chamber of Commerce, 29 E. Sumach. 509/525-0850.

Fort Walla Walla Museum—Sixteen buildings recreate pioneer life in the area. Diorama of Lewis & Clark meeting with the Walla Walla Tribe. Tue-Sun 10 to 5 (Apr-Oct); admission fee. 755 Myra Rd. 509/525-7703.

Whitman Mission National Historic Site—Dr. Marcus Whitman and his wife, Narcissa, established a Protestant mission here in 1836. It served Indians in the area and travelers along the Oregon Trail until 1847 when the Whitmans and 11 others were killed by Cayuse Indians. Excavations reveal the sites of original buildings and the visitor center contains a museum and a slide show. Audio stations along a 1-mile trail/& retell the story. Daily 8 to 6 (June-Aug), 8 to 4:30 (rest of year); admission fee. 7 miles W on US 12. 509/522-6360.

⊞ **Comfort Inn**—61 rooms, indoor pool, pets, continental breakfast, hot tub, exercise room, coin laundry. US 12 at 2nd St exit. 509/525-2522. $$$ K18

⊞ **Walla Walla Suites Inn**—78 rooms, pets, continental breakfast, indoor pool, refrigerators, microwaves, exercise room, coin laundry. &. US 12, 2nd Ave exit. 509/525-4700. $$$ K15

⊨ **Green Gables Inn**—6 rooms, full breakfast, smoke-free, bicycles, refrigerators. Weekday discounts. 509/525-5501. $$$

⊗ **The Homestead**—Casual but elegant dining, kids' menu, smoke-free. L & D Mon-Fri, D only Sat, B L D on Sun. 1528 Isaacs. 509/522-0345.

⊗ **Jacobi's Cafe & Dining Car**—Historic railroad depot and car, kids' menu, smoke-free. L & D daily. S of US 12, 2nd Ave exit. 509/525-2677. $$

⊗ **Merchants Ltd**—Upscale deli, dress code, smoke-free. &. B & L Mon-Sat, B only Sun. 21 E. Main. 509/525-0900. $

Winchester, Idaho

Winchester Lake State Park—0.5 mile W on Joseph Avenue.

▲ **Lapwai Campground**—28 wooded primitive sites; fee; water; primitive; open all year/full operation May-Aug; grills/fire rings; tables; 15-day limit. Fishing; hiking; nature trails; boating; interpretive programs. 208/924-7563.

▲ **Nez Perce Campground**—32 primitive sites; fee; water; primitive; open all year/full operation May-Aug; grills/fire rings; tables; 15-day limit. Fishing; hiking; nature trails; boating; interpretive programs. 208/924-7563.

CHAPTER 20

October 16 to 29, 1805

DOWN THE COLUMBIA

The Corps of Discovery paused on October 17 and 18 at the site of today's **[1]** Sacajawea State Park, where the Snake River joins the Columbia River. Nez Perce chiefs Twisted Hair and Tetoharsky, traveling ahead, had notified Yakama and Wanapam people, who gathered to welcome the travelers with singing and drumming, and gifts of fish and dried horse meat.

On the 17th, Captain William Clark and two men explored upstream on the Columbia far enough to see the mouth of the Yakima River near today's Richland before returning to camp. This was dry country covered with prickly pear cactus "much worst than I have before Seen." Clark concluded that this area received little rain when he noted flat roofs on the Indians' marsh-grass longhouses.

Later that day, the Corps of Discovery held council with the Yakamas and Wanapams, and the captains bestowed medals, shirts, and handkerchiefs upon the chiefs. Even though

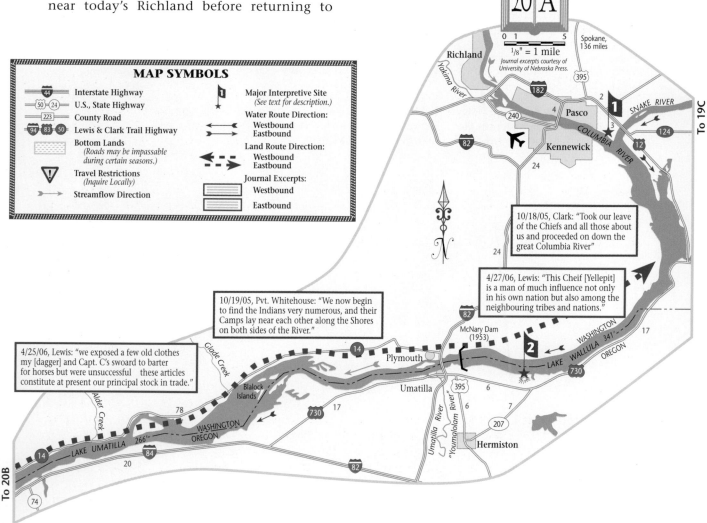

MAP SYMBOLS

Interstate Highway
U.S., State Highway
County Road
Lewis & Clark Trail Highway
Bottom Lands
(Roads may be impassable during certain seasons.)
Travel Restrictions
(Inquire Locally)
Streamflow Direction

Major Interpretive Site
(See text for description.)
Water Route Direction:
Westbound
Eastbound
Land Route Direction:
Westbound
Eastbound
Journal Excerpts:
Westbound
Eastbound

20 A
0 1 5
1/8" = 1 mile
Journal excerpts courtesy of University of Nebraska Press.

Spokane, 136 miles

Richland

Yakima River

Pasco

Kennewick

SNAKE RIVER

COLUMBIA RIVER

To 19C

10/18/05, Clark: "Took our leave of the Chiefs and all those about us and proceeded on down the great Columbia River"

4/27/06, Lewis: "This Cheif [Yellepit] is a man of much influence not only in his own nation but also among the neighbouring tribes and nations."

10/19/05, Pvt. Whitehouse: "We now begin to find the Indians very numerous, and their Camps lay near each other along the Shores on both sides of the River."

McNary Dam (1953)

Plymouth

LAKE WALLULA 341'

WASHINGTON
OREGON

4/25/06, Lewis: "we exposed a few old clothes my [dagger] and Capt. C's swoard to barter for horses but were unsuccessful   these articles constitute at present our principal stock in trade."

Glade Creek

Blalock Islands

Umatilla

Umatilla River

"Youmalolam River"

Hermiston

Alder Creek

WASHINGTON
OREGON

LAKE UMATILLA 266'

To 20B

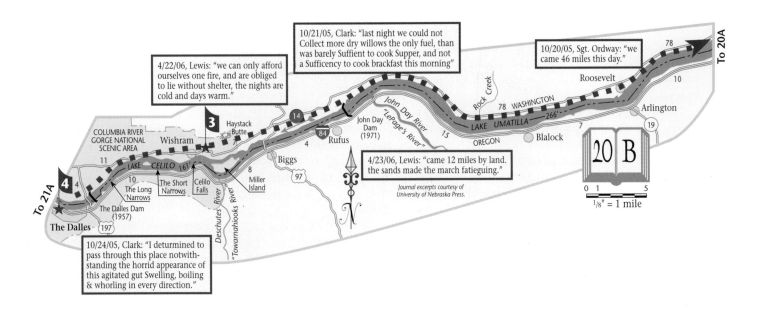

10/21/05, Clark: "last night we could not Collect more dry willows the only fuel, than was barely Suffient to cook Supper, and not a Sufficency to cook brackfast this morning"

4/22/06, Lewis: "we can only afford ourselves one fire, and are obliged to lie without shelter, the nights are cold and days warm."

10/20/05, Sgt. Ordway: "we came 46 miles this day."

4/23/06, Lewis: "came 12 miles by land. the sands made the march fatieguing."

Journal excerpts courtesy of University of Nebraska Press.

10/24/05, Clark: "I deturmined to pass through this place notwith-standing the horrid appearance of this agitated gut Swelling, boiling & whorling in every direction."

now in land the United States had no claim to—as they had been since they crossed the Continental Divide—Clark and Captain Meriwether Lewis made the speech about "our friendly intentions towards them and all other of our red children." The captains wrote thorough descriptions of the newly met Indians, their vocabulary, how they dressed and how they lived, their respect for elders, and the way men and women shared work. Clark found these people "of a mild disposition and friendly…" They had few horses, and canoes were their main transport. They also were the first Indians met who shaped their children's foreheads by bands and boards attached to their cradleboards. It was a mark of beauty reserved for the upper class among various nations of the Columbia and Pacific Northwest.

Also apparently new to the captains here was the sage grouse, which Clark wrote "I have only Seen on this river" even though this fowl is found in Montana and Idaho. Not understanding that salmon died after their spawning run, Clark wondered why so many dead fish lay along the river. Considering them unsafe to eat, the captains refused to buy any fresh salmon.

Early on the 18th, for forty dogs to eat, the Corps traded items such as knitting needles, brass wire, and thimbles—items of great value to people who couldn't manufacture them.

At 4 p.m., they set off, passing the mouth of the Walla Walla River. Soon after, the Columbia River turned west. From here to the Pacific Coast, the Columbia is the border between today's Washington and Oregon, and as far downstream as McNary Dam, the river forms Lake Wallula.

The Corps of Discovery knew that they were approaching territory explored by the party of George Vancouver of Great Britain thirteen years before. (In slightly more than two weeks, at Beacon Rock, they'd reach the farthest point his men traveled up the Columbia.) Lewis carried copies of Vancouver's published maps, and the captains now began watching for landmarks confirming that the Pacific Ocean was near. When they saw a conical, snow-covered mountain to the southwest on the 18th, Clark didn't name it; now scholars think that it was Mount Hood, named by a member of Vancouver's party. The next day, spying "a high mountain covered with snow" to the west, Clark thought it was Mount St. Helens, named by Vancouver's lieutenant—today's geographers think it was Mount Adams.

The river banks were well populated, and almost daily the Corps visited native villages. Overnight on the 18th, they stayed with Chief Yelleppit's village of Wallula, or Walla Walla Indians. Private Pierre Cruzatte "pleasd and astonished" the Indians with his violin. The captains promised to stay longer on their return next spring.

After passing and naming [2] Hat Rock, they came to a two-mile-long rapid at the end of which McNary Dam is today. Clark went ashore on the south side to study the rapid, walking with Nez Perce chiefs Twisted Hair and Tetoharsky, and Sacagawea, her husband and baby. Clark waited below the rapid for two hours while the main party came through it, dragging canoes over rocks.

Clark saw Indians across the river discover Lewis and the Corps, then return "to their Lodges as fast as they could run..." He took a canoe that already had passed the rapids, with interpreter George Drouillard and privates Joseph and Reubin Field, and headed downriver.

They reached a village of Umatilla people near today's Plymouth, Washington. The lodges were of woven mats, and their mat doors were closed. Clark entered one and found thirty-two men, women, and children hiding in terror. He made signs of peace, and offered gifts of whatever he found in his pockets. Clark sent the three others to do the same.

Clark waited boldly on a rock out in the open, inviting Umatilla men to smoke with him. But the Umatillas waited until Lewis and the others came up—with Sacagawea, whose very presence indicated to people of this area that the Corps came in peace. Then the Umatillas relaxed, and all ate and traded together before the Corps moved on.

That night, camping possibly on Blalock Island—now partially under the waters of Lake Umatilla—the Corps hosted another village, which was delighted when Cruzatte and Private George Gibson played the violin. One Umatilla man was wearing a sailor's jacket, a heartening sign that these people were part of a trading network that extended to the coast.

On October 20, they made their way through a bad rapid near today's Crow Butte State Park, Washington, where a chain of huge black rocks extending from the north side nearly choked the river.

Now, on the Washington side, stood "high rugid hills..." and on the Oregon side "a low plain and not a tree to be Seen in any Direction" except small willows on the banks. The Corps had ducks for supper on the 20th, but barely enough fuel to cook them. Wood would be in short supply for the next hundred miles or more, and there's not much more of it on these brush- and grass-covered hills today. The next day, the Corps met Indians who sold them wood and, notably, wore some articles of European clothing. The wood-sellers warned the Corps of a great falls ahead on the Columbia. Near that falls, they said, stood that large conical mountain visible in the distance—Mount Hood.

After passing another bad rapids near the mouth of the John Day River, the Corps had a pleasant surprise at camp the next night near today's John Day Dam. Private John Collins "presented us with Some verry good beer" made of bread the Nez Perce gave them a month ago, which had gotten wet and fermented.

October 22 took the Corps past lodges near today's Maryhill State Park, Washington, where Indians dried fish, then through a bad rapid, and past still more lodges. They explored a couple miles up today's Deschutes River into Oregon, and Clark named it with the Chinook word for enemies, because the local people's enemies lived upstream to the south. Another four miles brought them near the great falls—later [3] Celilo Falls, and now under the waters of Lake Celilo—between Wishram, Washington, and Celilo, Oregon.

The captains decided to portage 1,200 feet on the Washington side, crossing rock and loose sand. Indians living below the falls brought horses to carry heavy items. After camping overnight, the Corps took most of the day to make the portage, while many Indians watched. Empty canoes were carried around the falls on the Oregon side, then lowered into the rough water to float wildly downriver. On the evening of October 23, the Nez Perce guides overheard local Indians saying that people downriver planned to attack the expedition. After the locals ended their evening visit earlier than usual, Lewis and Clark ordered the men to inspect their guns.

Below Celilo Falls, they met the Wishram-Wasco people, whose canoes were "neeter made than any I have ever Seen and Calculated to ride the waves, and carry emence burthens." With figureheads carved on the bows, these canoes were light dugouts reinforced with crosspieces. Lewis promptly traded their small canoe—plus a hatchet and trinkets—for one.

The captains referred to the Wishram-Wasco as the Echelutes and the Che-luc-it-te-quars, thinking them different tribes. In fact, the first name came from the Chinook for "I am a Wishram Indian," and the second from that meaning "He is pointing at him." Perhaps, in the second case, instead of getting an answer to "Who are these people?" they got a translation of what they were doing while they asked!

The Nez Perce chiefs now said they were at war with people of this area, and proposed returning home. The captains persuaded the Nez Perce to stay two more nights until they could arrange a peace negotiation.

October 24 brought the Corps to the Columbia's Short Narrows—one quarter mile long and 45 yards wide—followed by the Long Narrows, five miles long and 200 yards wide. Since then, The Dalles Dam has raised the Columbia above this dangerous stretch. Clark wrote: "the water was agitated in a most Shocking manner..."

They camped at a Wishram-Wasco village near today's Horsethief Lake State Park, Dallesport, Washington, while planning how to proceed through the narrows. That night, Clark was satisfied that a lasting peace had been made in council between the Nez Perce and the Wishrams. Crluzatte brought out his violin, and the Wishrams stayed the night.

The next morning, men on shore stood ready to throw lifeline ropes to the canoeists. Men who couldn't swim walked halfway around the Long Narrows carrying guns and important papers. With Indians watching from the rocks, the first canoe, and then the second, came through the worst stretch of water to this halfway point. The third filled with water but got to shore, and the last one had no trouble. After reloading the canoes, the Corps proceeded down the Columbia. At the mouth of Mill Creek, they camped on a rock at today's city of The Dalles, Oregon.

They called this camp **[4]** "Fort Rock," posted a night guard in case the attack rumors were true, and stayed until October 28 to dry out cargo and patch canoes. Hunting was good for deer and geese, and Indian visitors seemed friendly. York danced to violin music as part of the entertainment.

The Corps traveled only four miles the next day because of high winds, and realized that canoe design was the problem. The native canoes rode high and kept going; waves easily swamped their own heavy dugouts. Camping near another Wishram village, the Corps saw more signs of coastal trade: brass tea kettles and a British musket. They were forced to sleep on a wet sandy beach that night, near present-day Crate's Point, Oregon.

TOURING TODAY

☞ DOWN THE COLUMBIA ☜

[ ] Bracketed numbers key sites to maps	♿ Special-needs accessible ⊨ Bed & breakfast
★ L&C in-depth interpretation, unchanged landform	⊗ Restaurant ▲ Camping, RV park
• L&C interpreted site	⊞ Motel, hotel, cabin

Bridges across the Columbia River in this area are at Maryhill, WA (US 97), and The Dalles, OR (US 197).

ALONG THE EXPEDITION'S PATH

October 16-18, 1805
[1] ★ **Sacajawea State Park** (Pasco, WA)—At confluence of the Columbia and Clearwater rivers. Interpretive center with exhibits related to the expedition, Saca-gawea, and stone and bone tools and toolmaking. Playground; picnic area; fishing; boating. Daily (limited access in winter); free. 2 miles E of Pasco on US 12. 509/545-2361.

Two Sisters (Wallula, WA)—A natural monument overlooking the Columbia Gorge. Two basalt pillars formed by floods over 15,000 years ago. Cayuse legend is that Coyote, an animal spirit, turned two beautiful sisters to stone in a rage of jealousy. 2 miles SW on WA 73.

October 19, 1805
(Return April 27, 1806)
[2] ★ **Hat Rock State Park** (Hermiston, OR)—This formation, mentioned by Clark, is now a day-use park with interpretive markers, hiking trails, swimming, boating, fishing and picnic area. Daily 6am to 10pm; fee. 9 miles E of Umatilla on US 730. 541/567-5032.

October 20, 1805
Crow Butte State Park (Paterson, WA)—Focus here is on the water. ▲ 50 sites (all w/hookups); fee;

water; modern; showers; open Mar-Oct; grills/fire rings; tables; 60' trailer limit. Beach; ramp/dock; fishing; nature trails. 14 miles W on WA 14. 509/875-2643.

Arlington State Wayside (Arlington, OR)—Picnic area and restrooms. 2 miles E on I-84.

October 21, 1805
Lepage Park (Rufus, OR)—Extensive day-use facilities for swimming, boating and fishing. ▲ 20 sites; fee; water; modern; showers; open all year; grills/fire rings; tables. Fishing; boating. I-84 exit 114, mouth of John Day river. 541/296-1181.

October 22, 1805
[3] ★ **Celilo Falls Overlook** (Wishram, WA)—View where the once-mighty falls raged, causing the Corps and their local helpers an entire day's portage. Above Wishram on US14.

October 22-24, 1805
(Return April 22, 1806)
● **Maryhill State Park** (Goldendale, WA)—▲ 50 sites (all w/hookups); fee; water; modern; showers; open May-Aug; grills/fire rings; tables. Interpretive exhibits; swimming; boat ramp; fishing; picnic area. 12 miles S on US 97. 509/773-5007.

Deschutes River State Park (The Dalles, OR)—Extensive hiking and biking trail system, Oregon Trail interpretive center. ▲ 33 primitive sites; fee; water; modern; showers; open all year; grills/fire rings; tables. Fishing; boating. 17 miles W on I-84. 541/739-2322.

October 24, 1805
Horsethief Lake State Park (Goldendale, WA)—Former Indian village site contains some of the oldest pictographs in the northwest. Interpretation of Indian cultures. Interpretive walks; fee. ▲ 12 sites; fee; water; modern; open all year; grills/fire rings; tables. Fishing; boat rental; lake and river ramps; underwater park for divers. 28 miles W on WA 14. 509/767-1159.

October 25-28, 1805
(Return April 15-18, 1806)
[4] ★ **Fort Rock Campsite** (The

Dalles, OR)—Locally known as "Rock Fort." Interpretation. I-84 exit 83 at The Dalles, then Webber St. N to First St., then E to Overlook. 541/296-9533.
● **The Dalles Dam** (The Dalles, OR)—Guided tours, including one by train, of the powerhouse, fish ladder, lock and dam. Interpretive center with exhibits on water-generated power. Picnic areas, beach, fishing and boating access. Daily 9 to 5 (June-Labor Day), hours vary rest of year; free. E side of town. 541/296-9778.

AROUND THE AREA

TOWNS LISTED ALPHABETICALLY

Goldendale, Washington
Goldendale Chamber of Commerce, 105 W. Main. 509/773-3400.
Goldendale Observatory State Park—Home to a 24.5-inch reflecting telescope, which is one of the largest available in the U.S. for use by the public. An 8-inch Celestron telescope is in a second dome; portable telescopes and camera attachments are available. Lectures and interpretive exhibits. Wed-Sun 2 to 5, 8 to midnight (Apr-Sept), Sat 1 to 5, 7 to 9, Sun 1 to 5 (rest of year); donations. 1.5 miles N of Main on Columbus Ave. 509/773-3141.
Klickitat County Historical Museum—Pioneer exhibits, branding iron and coffee mill collections in the 20-room Presby mansion. Daily 9 to 5 (Apr-Oct); admission fee. 127 W. Broadway. 509/773-4303.
▲ **Brooks Memorial State Park**—55 sites (22 w/hookups); fee; water; modern; showers; open all year; grills/fire rings; tables. Nine miles of hiking trails; fishing. 12 miles N on WA 97. 509/773-4611.
▲ **Sunset RV Park**—32 sites (19 w/hookups); fee; water; modern; showers; open Apr-Nov; grills/fire rings; tables. Pool, dump station. 821 Simcoe Dr. 509/773-3111.
⊞ **Farvue Motel**—49 rooms, pool, ⊗ restaurant. 808 E. Simcoe Dr. 509/773-5881. $$ K5
⊞ **Highland Creeks Resort**—23

rooms in chalets, smoke-free, hiking and fishing. 509/773-4026. $$$+ K12

Hermiston, Oregon
▲ **Hat Rock Campground**—65 sites (all w/hookups); fee; water; modern; showers; open all year; grills/fire rings; tables; firewood. Pool; coin laundry; dump station. 7 miles NE of US 395 on OR 207, 1 mile E on US 730, 0.75 mile on Hat Rock Rd. (adjacent to state park). 541/567-4188.
⌐ **Hermiston Inn**—33 rooms, indoor pool, continental breakfast. 2255 US 395S. 541/564-0202. $$ K12
⊞ **Oxford Suites**—91 rooms, indoor pool, continental breakfast, hot tub, exercise room, refrigerators, microwaves. US 395S. 541/564-8000. $$ K10

Kennewick, Washington
Tri-Cities Visitor & Convention Bureau serves Kennewick, Pasco, and Richland. 6951 E. Grandridge Blvd. 509/735-8486, 800/254-5824.
East Benton County Historical Museum—Exhibits depict hardships and successes of area's pioneer families. Tue-Sat noon to 4; admission fee. 205 Keewaydin Drive. 509/582-7704.
▲ **Columbia Park**—81 sites (30 w/hookups); fee; water; modern; showers; open Apr-Sept; grills/fire rings; tables. Columbia River shoreline park. Beach; fishing; boating. 5515 Columbia Dr SE, off WA 240. 509/783-3711.
⊞ **Clearwater Inn**—59 suites, pets, continental breakfast, coin laundry, refrigerators, microwaves. &. 5616 W. Clearwater. 509/735-2242. $$ K16
⊞ **Comfort Inn**—56 rooms, indoor pool, pets, continental breakfast, hot tub, coin laundry. 0.5 mile S of WA 240 on Columbia Center Blvd. 509/783-8396. $$ K18
⊞ **Kennewick Silver Cloud Inn**—125 rooms, pool, pets, continental breakfast, hot tub, exercise room, coin laundry. Off-season rates. 0.5 mile S of WA 240 on Columbia Center Blvd. 509/735-6100. $$ K18
⊞ **Ramada Inn Clover Island**—149 rooms, pets, ⊗ restaurant, coin laundry. Off-season rates. 435

Clover Island. 509/586-0541. $$$ K18

⊞ **Shaniko Suites**—47 suites, pool, pets, continental breakfast, kitchen, coin laundry. 0.5 mile W of US 395 on Clearwater Ave. 509/735-6385. $$ K12

⊞ **Tapadera Inn**—61 rooms, pool, pets, continental breakfast, coin laundry. US 395 & Clearwater. 509/783-6191. $$ K12

⊗ **Cedars Pier One**—Steak and seafood overlooking the Columbia River, smoke-free. D daily. 7 Clover Island. 509/582-2143. $$$

Maryhill, Washington

Maryhill Museum of Art—Chateau home of entrepreneur Sam Hill, dedicated by Queen Marie of Romania in 1929 and opened as a museum in 1940. European and American paintings, Rodin sculptures and watercolors. Personal items and royal furnishings donated by Queen Marie. Native American tools, baskets. Weapons collection and special exhibitions. Picnic area. Daily 9 to 5 (Mar-Nov); admission fee. 3 miles W of US 97 on WA 14. 509/773-3733.

Stonehenge—Concrete replica of the 4,000-year-old English monument built as a memorial to local men killed in WWI. Daily 7am to 10pm; free. 1 mile E of US 97 & WA 14, 0.75 mile S on cliff overlooking Columbia River.

Pasco, Washington

Tri-Cities Visitor & Convention Bureau serves Pasco, Kennewick, and Richland, 6951 Grandridge Blvd., Kennewick. 509/735-8486, 800/254-5824.

Franklin County Historical Museum—In a former Carnegie library listed on National Register of Historic Places. Indian, pioneer, aviation, railroad exhibits of the area, plus archives of Hollywood cinematographer James Wong Howe. Tue-Fri 1 to 5; Sat 10 to 5; donations. 305 N. 4th Ave. 509/547-3714.

McNary National Wildlife Refuge—Mile-long hiking trail through area with hawks, eagles and falcons. Fishing Feb-Sept. Daily dawn to dusk, headquarters weekdays 7 to 4:30; free. 0.25

mile N of US 12 near Burbank. 509/547-4942.

⊞ **Doubletree at Pasco**—79 rooms, balcony/lanai, pools, ⊗ restaurant, hot tub, exercise room. ♿. Off-season and weekend rates. I-182 exit 12B. 509/547-0701. $$$ K18

⊞ **Vineyard Inn**—165 rooms, indoor pool, pets, continental breakfast, hot tub, ⊗ restaurant. US 395 Lewis St. exit. 509/547-0791. $$ K12

Pendleton, Oregon

Pendleton Chamber of Commerce, 501 S. Main St. 541/276-7411, 800/547-8911.

Pendleton Woolen Mill—The story of making wool blankets and clothing from dyeing to spinning and weaving. Plant tours weekdays 9, 11, 1:30 and 3; free. I-84 exit 207 (1307 SE Court Place). 541/276-6911, 800/568-3156.

Tamastslikt Cultural Institute—Past, present and future impact of white settlers on tribal life and the environment. Gift shop. Daily 10 to 5; admission fee. I-84 exit 216, 1 mile N. 541/966-9748.

Umatilla County Historical Society Museum—Former railway station now harbors Oregon Trail and Indian collections. Tue-Sat 10 to 4; admission fee. 108 SW Frazier. 541/276-0012

⊞ **Best Western Pendleton Inn**—69 rooms, continental breakfast, pool, hot tub, exercise room, coin laundry. 2-bedroom units are reasonable. I-84 exit 210. 541/276-2135. $$ K12

⊞ **Red Lion Inn/Indian Hills**—170 rooms, pool, hot tub, restaurant, coin laundry. Coffeemakers and ironing boards in all rooms. I-84 exit 210. 541/276-6111. $$$ K17

⊞ **Super 8**—50 rooms, continental breakfast, pets, indoor pool, hot tub. I-84 exit 210. 541/276-8881. $$ K12

Plymouth, Washington

⚠ **Plymouth Park**—32 sites (16 w/hookups); fee; water; modern; showers; open Apr-Sept; grills/fire rings; tables; 31' trailer limit. Swimming; fishing; boating. 1 mile E of I-82 & Umatilla Bridge, 0.5 mile S off WA 14. 541/298-7542.

Richland, Washington

Tri-Cities Visitor & Convention Bureau serves Richland, Kennewick, and Pasco. 6951 Grandridge Blvd., Kennewick. 509/735-8486, 800/254-5824.

Columbia River Exhibition of History, Science and Technology—Interactive exhibits about history/science of nuclear technology. Scale models and historical exhibits. Mon-Sat 10 to 5, Sun noon to 5; admission fee. 95 Lee Blvd. 509/943-9000.

Plant 2 Visitors Center—Video tour of how a commercial nuclear power plant works. Exhibits compare nuclear power to traditional modes. Thur/Fri 11 to 4, Sat/Sun noon to 5; free. 12 miles N in Hanford Site of the Department of Energy. 509/372-5860.

Three Rivers Children's Museum—Hands-on educational exhibits for children. Rotating activities emphasize different themes. Tue-Sat 10 to 5, Sun noon to 5; admission fee. 650 George Washington Way. 509/946-5437.

⊞ **Hampton Inn**—130 rooms on the Columbia River, indoor pool, continental breakfast, hot tub, exercise room, coin laundry, microwaves, refrigerators. I-182 exit 5B. 509/943-4400. $$$

⊞ **Nendel's Inn**—98 rooms, pool, pets, continental breakfast. Efficiencies are same price as a double room. I-182 exit 5B. 509/943-4611. $$ K12

⊞ **Red Lion Hotel**—150 rooms, pets, pool, fishing, biking, jogging, ⊗ restaurant. ♿. Off-season and package rates. I-182 exit 5B. 509/946-7611. $$$ K18

⊞ **Shilo Inn Rivershore**—150 rooms, pets, pool, ⊗ restaurant, hot tub, coin laundry, marina. ♿. Off-season rates. Off US 12 along Columbia River. 509/946-4661, 800/222-2244. $$$ K12

⊞ **Vagabond Inn**—40 rooms, pool, pets, continental breakfast. Off-season rates. I-182 exit 5B. 509/946-6117. $$$ K18

⊗ **The Boulevard**—Rustic, colonial river setting, kids' menu. L & D Mon-Fri, D only Sat/Sun. 240 Columbia Center exit. 509/735-6575. $$

⊗ **Emerald of Siam**—Thai lunch buffet and dinners, dress code, kids' menu. ♿. Smoke-free. L & D weekdays, D only Sat. 1314 Jadwin. 509/946-9328. $$

⊗ **R.F. McDougalls**—Burgers & pasta, kids' menu. L & D daily. 1705 Columbia Dr. SE. 509/735-6418. $

The Dalles, Oregon

The Dalles Chamber of Commerce, 404 W. 2nd St. 541/296-2231, 800/255-3385. Self-guided walking tour maps available.

Columbia Gorge Discovery Center/Wasco County Historical Museum—Geology, natural history, Native American culture, local history of the Gorge. Lewis and Clark exhibits and Oregon Trail interpretation. Trails, overlooks and picnic area. Daily 10 to 6; admission fee. 5000 Discovery Drive. 541/296-8600.

• **Fort Dalles Museum**—Military, pioneer and medical history exhibits in the last building that remains from the fort. Daily 10 to 5 (Apr-Oct), Thur-Mon 10 to 4 (rest of year); admission fee. 500 W. 15th St. 541/296-4547.

Old St. Peter's Landmark—1897 Gothic church with 170-foot steeple. Dozens of stained glass windows, unusual marble carvings and tin ceilings. Tue-Fri 11 to 3, Sat/Sun 1 to 3; donations. 3rd & Lincoln. 541/296-5686.

Wonder Works Children's Museum—Creative building materials and play experiences. Special infant and toddler area. Mon-Sat 10 to 6, Sun 12 to 4; admission fee. 419 E. 2nd St. 541/296-2444.

⊞ **Lone Pine Motel**—56 rooms, indoor pool, pets, breakfast, hot tub, coin laundry, microwaves, refrigerators. Off-season rates. 2.5 miles E of I-84 & US 197 exit 87. 541/298-2800. $$ K12

⊞ **Quality Inn**—85 rooms, pool, pets, hot tub, ⊗ restaurant, coin laundry. Off-season rates. 1.5 miles W of I-84 exit 83/84. 541/298-5161. $$ K18

⊞ **Shilo Inn**—112 rooms, pets, continental breakfast, pool, microwaves, ⊗ restaurant, hot tub, coin laundry. ♿. Off-season rates. I-84 exit 87. 541/298-5502, 800/222-2244. $$$ K13

Toppenish, Washington

Toppenish Chamber of Commerce, 5A S. Toppenish, 509/865-3262, 800/569-3982.

American Hop Museum—Everything you ever wanted to know about the history of hops. Daily 11 to 4 (May-Sept); donations. 22 S. B Street. 509/865-4677.

Fort Simcoe State Park—Tour on your own or with a guide through this restoration/reconstruction of an 1856 army fort. This day-use area is located on the Yakama Indian Reservation and provides an interpretive center with insight into the Army's relationship with the Indians. Spend the day and have a picnic on the grounds. Grounds only Wed-Sun 10 to 5 (Apr-Oct), weekends only (rest of year), interpretive center (Apr-Oct only); admission fee. 30 miles W on Fort Rd. 509/874-2372.

Toppenish Museum—Extensive collection of Native American handcrafts and artwork. Tue-Thur 1:30 to 4, Fri/Sat 2 to 4; admission fee. 1 S. Elm. 509/865-4510.

Toppenish National Wildlife Refuge—Hundreds of bird species, interpretive center and nature trail. Daily dawn to dusk; free. 5 miles S on US 97, 0.5 mile W on Pump House Rd. 541/922-3232.

Yakama Nation Cultural Center—Tribal history from its beginning, research library, gift shop. 76-foot high winter lodge replica is used as a meeting hall. Daily 8 to 6; admission fee. 0.5 mile N on US 97. 509/865-2800.

⊞ **Oxbow Motor Inn**—44 rooms, some with kitchens. 511 S. Elm. 509/865-5800. $$

⊞ **Toppenish Inn Motel**—41 rooms, continental breakfast, pets, indoor pool, hot tub, exercise room, coin laundry, refrigerators, microwaves. Off season rates. 515 S. Elm. 509/865-7444. $$ K12

Wallula, Washington

▲ **Madame Dorion**—30 sites; free; water; primitive; open all year; grills/fire rings; tables; 14-day limit. Boating; swimming; fishing. 1 mile S on US 12. 541/922-3211.

Warm Springs, Oregon

The Museum at Warm Springs—Broad assortment of ceremonial items and artifacts from the daily lives of the Wasco, Pauite and Warm Springs tribes. Crafts and demonstrations. Daily 10 to 5; admission fee. 2189 OR 26. 541/553-3331.

CHAPTER 21

October 29 to November 7, 1805

OCIAN IN VIEW

As the Corps of Discovery neared the Pacific Ocean via the Columbia River, they had to portage many rapids since inundated by dams. Captain William Clark noted several times that a certain place might be good for winter quarters—already keeping his eyes open for shelter.

Passing the mouth of Hood River on October 29, they named it Labiche River for Private Francois Labiche—another of their names that didn't stick. Now they moved through the **[1]** Columbia River Gorge, its waters so different today from what the explorers faced.

They passed, and visited with, villages of different Indian nations, camped here for the fall salmon runs. In the evenings, Private Pierre Cruzatte entertained Indian visitors with his violin. Undoubtedly, others of the Corps danced and sang, too.

To get around the Cascades of the Columbia on November 1, the men carried baggage on their backs and walked "940 yards of bad Slippery and rocky way," Clark wrote. Then they laid poles on rocks and slid the four large canoes over these rollers. The small canoe could go by water, but all the boats were banged up and had to be patched.

Seeing more and more trading-ship goods at each village, Clark tried to find out if the people traded directly with whites, or got the items from other tribes. No one in the Corps spoke the local languages, and Clark couldn't get an answer. People of the region didn't use signing to overcome language differences the way the

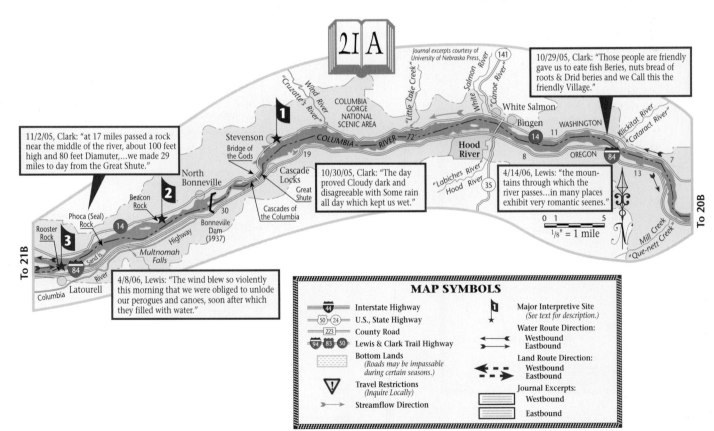

21 A

Journal excerpts courtesy of University of Nebraska Press.

10/29/05, Clark: "Those people are friendly gave us to eate fish Beries, nuts bread of roots & Drid beries and we Call this the friendly Village."

11/2/05, Clark: "at 17 miles passed a rock near the middle of the river, about 100 feet high and 80 feet Diamuter,...we made 29 miles to day from the Great Shute."

10/30/05, Clark: "The day proved Cloudy dark and disagreeable with Some rain all day which kept us wet."

4/14/06, Lewis: "the mountains through which the river passes...in many places exhibit very romantic seenes."

4/8/06, Lewis: "The wind blew so violently this morning that we were obliged to unlode our perogues and canoes, soon after which they filled with water."

MAP SYMBOLS

44	Interstate Highway
50 24	U.S., State Highway
223	County Road
94 83 50	Lewis & Clark Trail Highway
	Bottom Lands *(Roads may be impassable during certain seasons.)*
▽	Travel Restrictions *(Inquire Locally)*
→	Streamflow Direction

Major Interpretive Site *(See text for description.)*

Water Route Direction:
Westbound
Eastbound

Land Route Direction:
Westbound
Eastbound

Journal Excerpts:
Westbound

Eastbound

Plains tribes did; they had developed Chinook Jargon, a practical, spoken trade language drawn from many different tongues including Chinook, English, French, and Nootka.

The day after the Cascades portage, the Corps carried their baggage around another rapid. The lightened canoes ran through without much damage, although one hit a rock and "Split a little…" In the area of today's Cascade Locks on the Columbia, the Cascades of the Columbia is now under the waters of Bonneville Dam. The Corps passed and named **[2]** Beacon Rock before camping for the night near today's **[3]** Rooster Rock State Park. They named Phoca Rock, using the Greek word for seal because of all the harbor seals around.

Here, at last, they could see the Columbia River rising and falling with the tide of the Pacific Ocean.

When they passed modern-day Reed Island on November 3, it was the first time in seven months the Corps had been where Europeans previously had visited. This island was as far upriver as any member of Captain George Vancouver's party of Great Britain had come in the fall of 1792.

That night they camped on what they called "Dimond Island." Since then, the Columbia has carved it into two smaller islands—Government and McGuire—near today's Portland, Oregon. Ducks and swans were on the supper menu.

The next night, they were introduced by Chinookan-speaking Watlala people to the wapato

To 21C

11/5/05, Clark: "This is certainly a fertill and a handsom valley, at this time Crouded with Indians."

3/28/06, Sgt. Gass: "The Columbia river is now very high, which makes it more difficult to ascend."

Journal excerpts courtesy of University of Nebraska Press.

3/30/06, Sgt Gass: "The natives of this country ought to have the credit of making the finest canoes, perhaps in the world, both as to service and beauty; and are no less expert in working them when made."

11/4/05, Sgt. Ordway: "came to a large new village… consisting of about 35 Cabbens and have 50 fine canoes."

4/2/06, Clark: "The Current of the Multnomar is as jentle as that of the Columbia glides Smoothly with an eavin surface, and appears to be Sufficiently deep for the largest Ship."

MAP SYMBOLS

Interstate Highway
U.S., State Highway
County Road
Lewis & Clark Trail Highway
Bottom Lands
(Roads may be impassable during certain seasons.)
Travel Restrictions
(Local Inquiry)
Streamflow Direction
Major Interpretive Site
(See text for description.)
Water Route Direction:
Westbound
Eastbound
Land Route Direction:
Westbound
Eastbound
Journal Excerpts:
Westbound
Eastbound

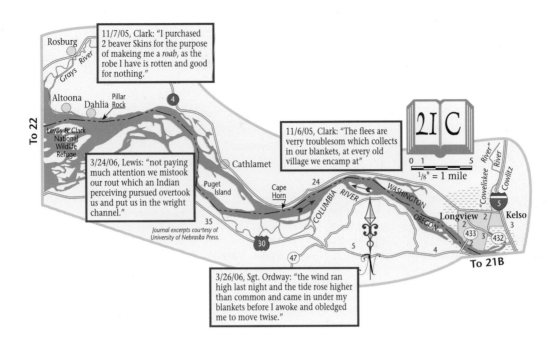

11/7/05, Clark: "I purchased 2 beaver Skins for the purpose of makeing me a *roab*, as the robe I have is rotten and good for nothing."

11/6/05, Clark: "The flees are verry troublesom which collects in our blankets, at every old village we encamp at"

3/24/06, Lewis: "not paying much attention we mistook our rout which an Indian perceiving pursued overtook us and put us in the wright channel."

3/26/06, Sgt. Ordway: "the wind ran high last night and the tide rose higher than common and came in under my blankets before I awoke and obledged me to move twise."

Journal excerpts courtesy of University of Nebraska Press.

21C

0   1   5
$^1/_8$" = 1 mile

MAP SYMBOLS

44 Interstate Highway	Major Interpretive Site *(See text for description.)*
50 24 U.S., State Highway	Water Route Direction: Westbound Eastbound
223 County Road	
94 83 50 Lewis & Clark Trail Highway	Land Route Direction: Westbound Eastbound
Bottom Lands *(Roads may be impassable during certain seasons.)*	Journal Excerpts: Westbound
Travel Restrictions *(Inquire Locally)*	Eastbound
Streamflow Direction	

root, the North American or broadleaf arrowhead. Clark wrote "it has an agreeable taste and answers verry well in place of bread." Very important in the regional diet, it also would feed the Corps in the coming winter. Wapato grew underwater, and was harvested by women who waded while pulling a small canoe. They used their feet to loosen the roots, which floated to the surface and were thrown into the boat.

Because a combination tomahawk-pipe and a capote (hooded coat) disappeared during supper, Clark decided he didn't like the people of this village. One of the Corps' interpreters found the coat hidden nearby, but it would be months before the tomahawk came back into the Corps' hands. It had belonged to Sergeant Charles Floyd, and Clark hoped to return it to his parents.

Going downstream, they easily traveled thirty miles in a day, but constant rain made Clark write that "we are all wet Cold and disagreeable, rain Continues & encreases." After stopping near today's Rainier, Oregon, the Corps arrived at the upper end of the Columbia estuary on November 7. They set up camp on the Washington side, opposite Pillar Rock, watching the tidal play of the Columbia and hearing waves break on the shores of Gray's Bay off to the west. Clark wrote:

Great joy in camp we are in View *of the* Ocian, *this great Pacific Octean which we been So long anxious to See. and the roreing or noise made by the waves brakeing on the rockey Shores (as I Suppose) may be heard distictly*[.]

TOURING TODAY

↷ OCIAN IN VIEW ↶

[ ] Bracketed numbers key sites to maps	♿	Special-needs accessible	⚑ Bed & breakfast
★ L&C in-depth interpretation, unchanged landform	⊗	Restaurant	▲ Camping, RV park
● L&C interpreted site	⊞	Motel, hotel, cabin	

Bridges across the Columbia River in this area are at Hood River, OR (US 26); Cascade Locks, OR/ Stevenson, WA; Portland, OR/ Vancouver, WA (I-205, I-5); Lewis and Clark Bridge at Longview, WA.

ALONG THE EXPEDITION'S PATH

October 29 to November 1, 1805
[1] Columbia River Gorge
Mayer State Park (The Dalles, OR)—Hike to Rowena Crest and view the gorge or explore the **Tom McCall Nature Preserve.** Picnic area, beach access, fishing, boat ramp. Daily dawn to dusk; admission fee. 10 miles W on I-84. 800/551-6949.

Memaloose State Park—Hiking; fishing. ▲ 110 sites (43 w/hookups); fee; water; modern; showers; open Apr-Oct; grills/fire rings; tables; 10-day limit; dump station. Access from rest area between Hood River and The Dalles on westbound I-84. 541/478-3008.

Vinzenz Lausmann State Park (Hood River, OR)—Day use area adjoining Wygant with hiking trails along the Gorge. I-84 exit 58 (eastbound only), 5 miles W. 800/551-6949.

Wygant State Park (Hood River, OR)—Day-use park with 6-mile trail through the gorge. 7 miles W, I-84 Fouts-Lausmann exit (eastbound only). 800/551-6949.

Viento State Park (Hood River, OR)—Hike in the Old Wagon Road historic area. Even on busy summer weekends, you can often find a site here. ▲ 75 sites (58 w/hookups); fee; water; modern; showers; open Apr-Oct; grills/fire rings; tables; hiking trails/♿; river access. I-84 exit 84. 541/374-8811.

Starvation Creek State Park (Hood River, OR)—Easy hike to waterfall, picnic area. 10 miles W on I-84 (eastbound access only). 800/551-6949.

● **Bonneville Dam**—Access between the Washington and Oregon sides is across the **Bridge of the Gods,** 3 miles E of the Dam. **Washington Shore Visitor Center**—Fish Viewing Building has underwater windows and exhibits on history of the fishing industry. Exhibits on the expedition. Self-guided tours. Picnic areas and hiking trails. Summer interpretive programs. Center open daily 9 to 5; free. N end of dam off WA 14. 509/427-4281. **Fort Cascades National Historic Site**—1.5-mile interpretive trail through remains of the old Portage railroad, a Chinook Indian village and the military fort. Summer interpretive programs.

Bradford Island (Cascade Locks, OR)—Referred to as "Brandt Island" in the journals. Broad range of interpretive displays about the dam's history and operation and the expedition. Powerhouse viewing area. Center's glass walls overlook the Gorge. Summer interpretive programs. Daily 9 to 5; free. Route 84, exit 40. 541/374-8820.

Historic Columbia Road Trail—Hiking, biking, ♿ wheelchair trail is being constructed along the old Columbia Road Highway. 800/ 275-6368 for updated information. Sections currently completed are: *Bridge of the Gods* (I-84 exit 44 access road) 2.4 miles W to

Eagle Creek trailhead at the Cascade Fish Hatchery. *Cascade Fish Hatchery,* 1.4 miles W to Bonneville Dam. *Bonneville Dam,* 1.4 miles W to Moffett Creek Bridge. *Hatfield Trailhead East* (W of Mosier on the Historic Hwy) 4.6 miles to Hatfield Trailhead West (E of Hood River). This section runs through the twin tunnels segment.

November 2, 1805
(Return April 6, 1806)
[2] ★ **Beacon Rock State Park** (North Bonneville, WA)—14 miles of trails through hilly and steep park, an important historic/geologic site. One-mile trail to top of this 848' rock (documented by Clark) has 15% grade. 8.5-mile loop trail to Hamilton Mountain. ▲ 35 primitive sites; fee; water; modern; showers; open Apr-Oct; grills/fire rings; tables; firewood; 10-day limit. Playground; boat ramp; fishing; rock climbing; horseback riding; mountain bike trails; dump station. 3 miles W on WA 14. 509/427-8265.

Ainsworth State Park (Cascade Locks, OR)—Connected by trail to ● **John Yeon State Park** (2 miles). ▲ 45 sites (all w/hookups); fee; water; modern; showers; open Apr-Oct; grills/fire rings; tables; 10-day limit. 9 miles W on US 30. 800/551-6949.

● **Portland Women's Forum State Park** (Troutdale, OR)—Scenic overlook with interpretation. Daily 6am to 10pm; free. 10 miles E on US 30. 800/551-6949.

● **Crown Point State Park** (Troutdale, OR)—Vista House was built here in 1918 as a memorial to the pioneers who traveled the Columbia River. Offers expansive views

of the gorge. Interpretive programs, museum, and gift shop. Daily 9 to 6 (Apr-Oct); free. 11 miles E on US 30. 800/551-6949.
Bridal Veil Falls (Troutdale, OR)—Picnic area and 1 mile trail to falls. Trail to gorge overlook. 16 miles E on US 30. 800/551-6949.
George W. Joseph State Park/Guy W. Talbot State Park (Portland, OR)—Adjacent day use parks with picnic areas and trail to **Latourell Falls**—the 2nd highest in the gorge. Daily dawn to dusk; fee. 27 miles E on US 30. 800/551-6949.
[3] ★ Rooster Rock State Park (Portland, OR)—Picnic area, sand beach when the river is down (including clothing-optional beach at far end of park), boating and hiking trails. Interpretation. Daily 7am to 10pm; admission fee. 22 miles E on I-84 (exit 28). 800/551-6949.
Dabney State Park (Portland, OR)—Picnic area, boating and fishing access, swimming, folf course. 1.5-mile trail along the river. 19 miles E on US 30. 800/551-6949.

November 3, 1805
(Return March 31–April 6, 1806)
● **Lewis and Clark State Park** (Portland, OR)—Located on the Sandy River, named Quicksand River by Lewis and Clark. Day use park with picnic area, swimming, boating, fishing, and hiking trails. Self-guided trail provides interpretation and identification of nearly 200 plants identified by Lewis and Clark. Open 6am to 9pm; free. 16 miles E, off US 30. 800/551-6449.
● **Kelley Point Park** (Portland, OR)—Biking, hiking, fishing at the confluence of the Willamette River. Canoe trail. Daily 8 to 8; free. End of N Marine Dr. 503/823-3643.
Sauvie Island Wildlife Area and Howell Territorial Park (Portland, OR)—Interpretive tours of pioneer house and adjacent agricultural museum (summer only). Fishing, swimming, hiking, clothing-optional beach. Daily 4am to 10pm, free. 1 mile N on US 30, E on Sauvie Island Bridge. 503/621-3488.

November 5, 1805
● **Deer Island** (Deer Island, OR)—Use pullout area on US 30 in town

to see island called E-Lal-Lar ("deer" in Upper Chinookan) by the Cathlapotle Indians. Always open; free. US 30.

Ridgefield National Wildlife Refuge (Vancouver, WA)—Two-mile Oaks to Wetlands Wildlife Trail. Hiking trails, canoeing. More than 200 bird species have been identified. Daily dawn to dusk; free. 3 miles W of I-5 exit 14. 360/887-4106.

November 7, 1805
Pillar Rock—Visible from WA 401, east of Dahlia. It now bears a navigation light on its top.

AROUND THE AREA

TOWNS LISTED ALPHABETICALLY

● **Mount Hood/Columbia River Gorge Loop** (Oregon side)—This drive takes at least 4 hours and passes 70 waterfalls. Begin at The Grotto on Sandy Blvd. in Portland. Follow US 26 east around the base of Mt. Hood to WA 35 and continue north to Hood River. West on I-84 past Bonneville Dam. Get off I-84 when 6 miles W of the Dam (exit 35) onto the Historic Columbia River Highway to Troutdale. This section passes dozens of waterfalls and Vista House at Crown Point State Park. I-84 returns you to Portland.
Columbia River Gorge Scenic Highway (Washington side)—WA 14 follows the river through this National Scenic Area from Vancouver, WA to Maryhill, WA.

Aurora, Oregon
▲ **Isberg RV Park**—84 sites (all w/hookups); fee; water; modern; showers; open all year; grills/fire ring; tables. Pool; groceries; jogging trail; basketball. 2.5 miles W of I-5 exit 278. 503/678-2646.

Carson, Washington
Wind River Arboretum & Canopy Crane—Hike interpretive trails through this experimental forest established in 1912 to test adaptability of non–North American trees. Tours of Canopy Crane. Tue-Sat 7

to 3:30 (May-Oct); free. 8 miles NW on Wind River Hwy, 1 mile W on Hemlock Rd. 509/427-3200.

Cascade Locks, Oregon
Cascade Locks Historical Museum—Located in an old lockkeeper's home. Indian and pioneer memorabilia. Mon-Wed noon to 5, Thur-Sun 10 to 5 (June-Sept), weekends only 10 to 5 (May); admission fee. Marine Park, 355 Wanapa St. 541/374-8535.
Columbia Gorge Sternwheeler—Two-hour narrated cruises along the Columbia River complete with colorful legends and relaxing scenery. Tours begin in Marine Park. Daily May-Oct; admission fee. 541/374-8427.
Eagle Creek Trail—14-mile trail to Wahtum Lake and Pacific Crest Trail that passes 7 waterfalls including Punchbowl and Tunnel. ▲ Primitive campground at halfway point. Begins at Eagle Creek Campground (I-84 exit 41; see listing below).
Eagle Creek Trail 440—2-mile day hike to Punchbowl Falls. Begins at Eagle Creek Campground (see below). I-84 exit 41.
▲ **Cascade Locks KOA**—100 sites (75 w/hookups); fee; water; modern; showers; open Mar-Oct; grills/fire rings; tables; ⊞ 1 & 2 room cabins. Pool; hot tub; groceries; playground; coin laundry; dump station. I-84 exit 44, 1.5 miles E on US 30. 541/374-8668.
▲ **Cascade Locks Marine Park**—38 sites; fee; water; modern; open all year; grills/fire rings; tables. Boat ramp/dock; fishing; hiking; playground. I-84 exit 44. 541/374-8619.
▲ **Eagle Creek**—19 sites; fee; water; modern; open May-Oct; grills/fire rings; tables; firewood; 7-day limit, 22' limit. Hiking and biking trails; swimming; interpretive trail; suspension bridge over creek. I-84 exit 41 (eastbound), exit 44 westbound, follow signs. 541/386-2333.
▲ **Wyeth**—17 sites; fee; water; modern; open May-Sept; grills/fire rings; tables; firewood; group sites; 14-day limit, 32' limit. Hiking; swimming; fishing. I-84 exit 51, 0.5 mile on County road. 541/386-2333.

⊞ **Columbia River Inn**—63 rooms; indoor pool; pets; continental breakfast; coin laundry; exercise room; hot tub. Reduced rates weekdays and off-season. I-84 exit 44. 541/374-8777. $$$ K12

Clackamas, Oregon
⊞ **Days Inn**—110 rooms, pool, continental breakfast, exercise room, hot tub. Smoke-free. I-205 exit 14. 503/654-1699. $4 K12

Corbett, Oregon
⋏ **Crown Point RV Park**—26 sites (20 w/hookups); fee; water; modern; showers; open all year; grills/fire rings; tables. Coin laundry; dump station. 7.25 miles E of I-84 on US 30. 503/695-5207.

Estacada, Oregon
⋏ **Milo McIver State Park**—44 sites (all w/hookups); fee; water; modern; showers; open Mar-Oct; grills/fire rings; tables. Boat ramp; folf course; nature trails; fishing; dump station. 5 miles W on OR 211. 503/630-7150.

Government Camp, Oregon
⋏ **Alpine**—16 sites; free; water; primitive; open Jul-Sept; grills/fire rings; tables; no trailers. Hike Pacific Crest Trail or into Mount Hood wilderness. On south slope of Mount Hood. 1 mile E on US 26, 4.5 miles on road to Mt. Hood ski area. 503/622-3191.

⋏ **Barlow Creek**—5 sites; free; **no** water; primitive; open May-Sept; grills/fire rings; tables; no trailers. Hiking; fishing. 2 miles E on US 26, 4.5 miles N on OR 35, 4 miles SE on FR 3530. 503/328-6211.

⋏ **Barlow Crossing**—5 sites; free; **no** water; primitive; open May-Sept; grills/fire rings; tables; no trailers. Fishing. 2 miles E on US 26, 6 miles N on OR 35, 9 miles S on FR 48. 503/328-6211.

⋏ **Clear Lake**—26 sites; fee; water; primitive; open May-Sept; grills/fire rings; tables; firewood. Boat ramp; windsurfing; hiking. 10 miles S on OR 26. 503/666-0700.

⋏ **Devil's Half Acre**—5 sites; free; **no** water; primitive; open May-Sept; grills/fire rings; tables; no trailers. Hike Pacific Crest Trail or the Old Barlow Road wagon trail;

fishing. 2 miles E on US 26, 4.5 miles N on OR 35, 1 mile SE on FR 3530. 503/328-6211.

⋏ **Frog Lake**—22 sites; fee; water; primitive; open May-Sept; grills/fire rings; tables; firewood; 14-day limit. Fishing; canoeing; hiking; trail to Pacific Crest Scenic Trail. 7 miles S on US 26. 503/666-0700.

⋏ **Grindstone**—5 sites; free; **no** water; primitive; open May-Oct; grills/fire rings; tables; 22' maximum length. Hiking. 2 miles E on US 26, 4.5 miles N on OR 35, 2 miles SE on FR 3530. 503/328-6211.

⋏ **Still Creek**—27 sites; fee; water; primitive; open June-Aug; grills/fire rings; tables; 14-day limit; 16' maximum length; firewood. Fishing; canoeing; swimming; groceries. 1.5 miles E on US 26, 0.5 mile S on FR 2650. 503/666-0704.

⋏ **Trillium Lake**—39 sites; fee; water; primitive; open June-Aug; grills/fire rings; tables; 14-day limit; 22' maximum length; firewood. Boat ramp; swimming; hiking; fishing; bike trails. 2.5 miles SW on US 26, 1.25 miles S on FR 2656 (this road is quite steep). 503/666-0704.

⋏ **White River Station**—5 sites; fee; **no** water; primitive; open May-Sept; grills/fire rings; tables; no trailers. Fishing; hiking. 2 miles E on US 26, 4.5 miles N on OR 35, 7 miles NE on FR 30. 503/328-6211.

⊞ **Mt. Hood Inn**—56 rooms, continental breakfast, hot tub. ♿. 87450 E. Government Camp Loop. 503/272-3205, 800/443-7777. $$$ K12

⊞ **The Resort at the Mountain**—160 rooms, terraces, pool, biking, fishing, golf course, tennis courts, ⊗ restaurants. ♿. Off-season rates. 68010 E. Fairway in Welches. 503/622-3101, 800/669-7666. $$$+ K18

⊞ **Timberline Lodge**—60 rooms in historic mountain lodge on Mt. Hood, pool, ⊗ restaurant, hot tub. ♿. Timberline Ski Area. 503/272-3311, 800/547-1406. $$$+ K11

Gresham, Oregon
⋏ **Oxbow Park**—45 sites; fee; water; primitive; open all year;

grills/fire rings; tables; 5-day limit; 35' maximum length. Beach; canoeing; nature trails; interpretive program; fishing; hiking trails. I-84 exit 17, 4 miles S on SE 257th St, 8 miles E on Division St. 503/663-4708.

⊞ **Quality Inn**—73 rooms, pool, continental breakfast, coin laundry. Smoke-free. 1545 NE Burnside. 503/666-9545. $$ K18

Hood River, Oregon
Hood River County Chamber of Commerce, Port Marina Park. 541/386-2000, 800/366-3530.

Hood River County Historical Museum—Pioneer artifacts and area history exhibits. Mon-Sat 10 to 4, Sun noon to 4; donations. I-84 exit 64, in Port Marina Park. 541/386-6772.

Luhr Jensen & Sons, Inc.—Tour this facility that manufactures fishing lures and related gear. Mon-Thu 7:30 to 4:30, Fri 7:30 to 4, guided tours at 11 and 1:30; free. 400 Portway. 541/386-3811, 800/535-1711.

Mount Hood Scenic Railroad—Diesel locomotive pulls 1910-era railcars through the valley between Mt. Hood and Columbia River. Two- or four-hour trip; admission fee. Reservations recommended. 110 Railroad. 541/386-3556; 800/872-4661.

⋏ **Tucker Park**—70 sites (10 w/hookups); fee; water; modern; showers; open Apr-Oct; grills/fire rings; tables; 7-day limit. Playground; nature trails; fishing. 4 miles S on OR 281. 541/386-4477.

⊞ **Columbia Gorge Hotel**—44 rooms overlooking waterfall, pets, full breakfast, bathrobes, ⊗ restaurant, walking paths. ♿. Weekday discounts. I-84 exit 62. 541/386-5566, 800/345-1921. $$$+ K5

⊞ **Hood River Inn**—149 rooms, pool, windsurfing, ⊗ restaurant, coin laundry. ♿. Off-season rates. 1108 E. Marina Way. 541/386-2200, 800/828-7873. $$$ K18

⊞ **Vagabond Lodge**—40 rooms, pets, playground. 5 two-bedroom units. Off-season rates. I-84 exit 62, 2.5 miles W on US 30. 541/386-2992. $$

⊗ **Columbia River Court**—Nouvelle cuisine with jazz in the background, dress code, smoke-free. &. BLD daily. I-82 exit 62 (in Columbia Gorge Hotel). 541/386-5566. $$$

⊗ **Full Sail Brew Pub**—English-style pub overlooking the Columbia River Gorge features 14 beer varieties. Daily noon to 8 (May-Oct), Thur-Sun noon to 8 (Nov-Apr); free. 506 Columbia Street. 541/386-2247.

⊗ **Sixth Street Bistro & Loft**—Regional specialties, kids' menu, smoke-free. &. L & D daily. 509 Cascade St. 541/386-5737. $$

Kalama, Washington

▲ **Camp Kalama RV Park**—84 sites (all w/hookups); fee; water; modern; showers; open all year; grills/fire rings; tables; firewood. Swimming; boating; fishing; playground. Dump station. I-5 exit 32. 360/673-2456, 800/750-2456.

▲ **Louis Rasmussen RV Park on the River**—28 sites (22 w/hookups); fee; water; modern; showers; open all year; grills/fire rings; tables. Swimming; boat ramp/dock; fishing; playground. I-5 exit 30. 360/673-2626.

Kelso, Washington

Cowlitz County Historical Museum—Pioneer room recreations, exhibits on settlement and the evolution of transportation. Tue-Sat 9 to 5, Sun 1 to 5; donations. 405 Allen St. 360/577-3119.

Kelso Volcano Tourist Information Center—Drama of the 1980 Mount St. Helens eruption retold through exhibits, memorial to those who died and an audio narrative. Daily 8 to 6; donations. I-5 exit 39. 360/577-8058.

⊞ **Comfort Inn**—57 rooms, indoor pool, continental breakfast, hot tub. I-5 exit 39. 360/425-4600. $$ K18

⊞ **Motel 6**—63 rooms, pool, pets. I-5 exit 39. 360/425-3229. $ K17

Longview, Washington

Longview Chamber of Commerce, 1563 Olympia Way. 360/423-8400.

Monticello Convention Site—Park commemorating 1852 meeting to petition for a territory north of the Columbia River. 18th, Olympia & Columbia Avenues.

Nutty Narrows Bridge—60-foot skybridge built for squirrels to safely cross Olympia Way. Near the Civic Center.

Port of Longview—Tour the port and see how they move all that cargo. Mon-Fri 10:30 and 1:30; free, reservations required. 2 miles S on WA 433. 360/425-3305.

⊞ **Holiday Inn Express**—50 rooms, indoor pool, pets, continental breakfast, hot tub. I-5 exit 36, 3 miles W on WA 432. 360/414-1000. $$ K18

⊞ **Townhouse Motel**—28 rooms, pool, pets. Downtown, 744 Washington Way. 360/423-7200. $

Mosier, Oregon

Wahkeena-Multnomah Loop—Multi-trail hiking complex leading to several waterfalls and Larch Mountain. Begin at the parking lot on US 30, off I-84 exit 28.

Multnomah Falls, Oregon

★ **Multnomah Falls**—Trail leads to this 620' falls. Visitor Center and interpretation. ⊞ Historic lodge and ⊗ restaurant at base. Always open; free. 3 miles N on US 30.

Oregon City, Oregon

End of the Oregon Trail Interpretive Center—Interpretive exhibits and multimedia experiences bring the Oregon Trail to life. Mon-Sat 9 to 5, Sun 10 to 5 (Memorial Day-Labor Day), Mon-Sat 10 to 5, Sun 11:30 to 5 (rest of year); admission fee. 1726 Washington St. 503/657-9336.

Parkdale, Oregon

▲ **Rainy Lake**—4 sites; free; **no** water; primitive; open June-Sept; grills/fire rings; tables; 16' maximum length. Canoeing, swimming, fishing on secluded lake. 6 miles N on Co 281, 10 miles W on FR 205. 503/352-6002.

▲ **Robinhood**—24 sites; fee; water; primitive; open Apr-Oct; grills/fire rings; tables; 14-day limit; firewood; 16' maximum length. Fishing; hiking trails; swimming. At the base of Mount Hood. 15 miles S on OR 35. 503/666-0701.

▲ **Routson**—14 sites; fee; water; modern; showers; open Apr-Oct; grills/fire rings; tables. Boating;

beach; hiking. 20 miles S on OR 35. 503/386-6323.

▲ **Sherwood**—18 sites; fee; water; primitive; open May-Oct; grills/fire rings; tables; 14-day limit; firewood; 16' maximum length. Fishing; hiking; trail to Tamanawas Falls; East Fork River trail; picnic area. 11 miles S on OR 35. 503/666-0701.

▲ **Tollbridge**—65 sites (20 w/hookups); fee; water; modern; showers; open Apr-Oct; grills/fire rings; tables; 7-day limit. Fishing; hiking; picnic area; play area. 17 miles S on OR 35. 503/352-6300.

Portland, Oregon

Portland Visitors Association, 26 SW Salmon St. 503/222-2223, 800/345-3214.

American Advertising Museum—Evolution of influencing the consumer. Weekdays by appt., Sat noon to 5; admission fee. 524 NE Grand Ave. 503/230-1090.

The Children's Museum—Creativity and imagination are key here as children make-believe and problem-solve. Daily 9 to 5; admission fee. 3037 SW Second Ave. 503/823-2227.

Church of Elvis—The "King of Rock 'n' Roll" lives on at this flashy house of worship. Open 24 hours; free. 720 SW Ankeny. 503/226-3671.

The Grotto—A Catholic spiritual retreat of trails lined with statuary and shrines. Large chapel; outdoor services also held. Daily 9 to 8 (May-Sept), daily 9 to 5 (Oct-Apr); free. Sandy Blvd & NE 85th Ave. 503/254-7948.

Japanese Gardens—Five traditional gardens, a tea house and a pavilion with views of the city. Guided tours available. Daily 10 to 7 (May-Aug), 10 to 4 (rest of year); admission fee. 611 SW Kingston. 503/223-1321.

[4] ★ **Oregon History Center**—The state and Portland's past, present and future. Tue-Sat 10 to 5, Sun noon to 5; admission fee. 1200 SW Park Ave. 503/222-1741.

Oregon Maritime Center and Museum—Board the sternwheeler *Portland* and step back to the past. Museum of ship models, navigational instruments and photos. Fri-Sun 11 to 4; admission fee. 113

SW Front Ave. 503/224-7724.
Oregon Museum of Science and Industry—You'll need an entire day to experience the variety of interactive exhibits here. **Murdock Sky Theatre** laser light shows, a submarine and OMNIMAX theatre. Daily 9:30 to 7 (summer), Tue-Sun 9:30 to 7 (rest of year); admission fee. 1945 SE Water Ave. 503/797-4000.

Portland Art Museum—Over 3,000 years of art from around the world. Special collections of Indian, regional and contemporary works. Tue-Sun 10 to 5; admission fee. 1219 SW Park Ave. 503/226-2811.

Portland Audubon Interpretive Center—Rehabilitation center allows close-up viewing of wildlife, walking trails and interpretation areas. Mon-Sat 10 to 6, Sun 10 to 5; free. 5151 NW Cornell Rd. 503/292-6855.

Tom McCall Waterfront Park—Outdoor concerts and other activities make this a popular place. A 2-mile greenway between River-Place Marina and the Japanese American Historical Plaza. Daily 5am to midnight; free admission.

Portland Trailblazers—Professional basketball (NBA). Nov to May. Rose Garden Arena, 1 N. Center Ct. 503/797-9619.

Tryon Creek State Park—Eight miles of hiking trails through forests. Nature center and 3-mile barrier-free trail. Daily dawn-dusk; free. Off I-5 on Terwilliger Blvd. 503/636-9886.

Vintage Trolley—Free rides between Lloyd Center and downtown. Weekdays 10 to 3, weekends 10 to 6 (June-Dec), weekends only (Dec-Mar). 503/323-7363.

Washington Park
145-acre oasis of gardens and recreation. Statues here were unveiled during 1905 Lewis and Clark Exposition. Outdoor concerts. Main entrance on Park Place, S of Burnside Rd. 503/823-2223.

International Rose Test Garden—Thousands of roses create an explosion of color to explore. Daily 7am to 9pm; free. 400 SW Kingston Ave. 503/823-3636.

Metro Washington Park Zoo—Over 800 animals in natural jungle, desert, rain forest and tun-

dra environments. Daily 9:30 to dusk; admission fee. 4001 SW Canyon Rd. 503/226-1561.

World Forestry Center—Experience a Central African rain forest, old-growth Pacific Northwest forests or petrified woods from millions of years ago. Daily 9 to 5 (Memorial Day-Labor Day), 10 to 5 (rest of year); admission fee. 4033 SW Canyon Rd. 503/228-1367.

⊞ **Best Western Fortnighter Motel**—52 1- & 2-bedroom suites, pool, continental breakfast, coin laundry. I-84 exit 5 (82nd Ave), 2.5 miles N. 503/255-9771. $$ K12

⊞ **Comfort Inn Lloyd Center**—79 rooms, pool, pets, continental breakfast. Off-season rates. 431 NE Multnomah. 503/233-7933. $$$ K18

⊞ **Comfort Suites**—81 suites, indoor pool, continental breakfast, exercise room, hot tub, coin laundry. I-205 exit 24. 503/261-9000. $$ K17

⊞ **Four Points Portland Downtown**—139 rooms, pets, fitness center. Great location. 50 SW Morrison. 503/221-0711, 800/899-0247. $$$ K17

⊞ **Governor Hotel**—100 rooms, pool, bathrobes, ⊗ restaurants, health club, hot tub. Lewis and Clark mural in lobby. 611 SW 10th at Alder. 503/224-3400, 800/544-3456. $$$+ K18

⊞ **Hotel Vintage Plaza**—107 rooms, continental breakfast, bathrobes, exercise room, ⊗ restaurant. Specialty rooms and suites. 422 SW Broadway. 503/228-1212, 800/243-0555. $$$+ K16

⊯ **Heron House**—6 large rooms, continental breakfast, pool, bathrobes, TV. No children under 10. 503/274-1846. $$$+

⊯ **The Lion and the Rose**—6 rooms, full breakfast, afternoon tea, cold drinks, garden. Smoke-free. 503/287-9245, 800/955-1647. $$$ K6

⊗ **Atwater's**—Regional and nouvelle specialties, kids' menu, smoke-free, dress code. L & D weekdays, D only Sat/Sun, Brunch on Sun. 111 SW 5th Ave. 503/275-3600. $$$

⊗ **Doris Cafe**—Barbecue and jazz,

kids' menu, . L & D daily, B on weekends. 325 NE Russell. 503/287-9249. $$

⊗ **Esparza's Tex Mex Cafe**—The real thing from scratch. Smoke-free. L & D daily. 2725 SE Ankeny. 503/234-7909. $

⊗ **The Heathman Restaurant**—Regional cuisine, smoke-free. BLD daily. 1001 SW Broadway at Salmon. 503/790-7752. $$$

Rhododendron, Oregon
▲ **Camp Creek**—24 sites; fee; water; primitive; open June-Aug; grills/fire rings; tables; 14-day limit; firewood; 16' limit. Fishing; hiking; nature trails. 2.5 miles E on US 26. 503/666-0704.

▲ **Toll Gate**—15 sites; fee; water; primitive; open May-Sept; grills/fire rings; tables; 14-day limit; firewood; 22' maximum length. Fishing; picnic area; hiking; trails into Mount Hood Wilderness Area. 0.5 mile E on US 26. 503/666-0704.

Silver Lake, Washington
Seaquest State Park—Eight miles of hiking trails provide views of Mount St. Helens. Interpretive center and 116-acre wetland area. Fishing for trout and salmon; ▲ 92 sites (16 w/hookups); fee; water; modern; showers; open all year; grills/fire rings; tables. Fishing; playground; hiking trails. 5.5 miles E of Castle Rock on WA 504. 360/274-8633.

St. Paul, Oregon
Champoeg State Park—Site where French settlers met on May 2, 1843, to establish a provisional government for the Oregon Territory. Museum with interpretive exhibits. 10 miles of hiking trails. ▲ 48 sites (all w/hookups); fee; water; modern; showers; open all year; grills/fire rings; tables; 10-day limit. Boat dock; playground; nature trails; fishing; dump station. 8 miles W of I-5 exit 278. 503/633-8170.

Stevenson, Washington
★ **Columbia Gorge Interpretive Center**—History of the gorge, 37' replica of 1900s fishwheel, multimedia geology theatre, Lewis and Clark and Oregon Trail interpreta-

tion and exhibits. Daily 10 to 5; admission fee. 990 Rock Creek Drive. 509/427-8211.

⊞ **Skamania Lodge**—195 rooms in resort and conference center overlooking Columbia River Gorge, pool, restaurant, hot tub, fitness center, walking trails. Off season rates. 1 mile W of town, 1131 Skamania Lodge Way. 509/427-7700, 800/221-7117. $$$+ K12

Vancouver, Washington

Clark County Historical Museum—Pioneer and Chinook Indian life. Tue-Sun 1 to 5; donations. 1511 Main St. 360/695-4981.

● **Fort Vancouver National Historic Site**—Preservation of the Hudson's Bay Company's headquarters takes visitors back to the days of trappers and traders. 3-story bastion with 8 cannons welcomed ships. Daily tours, interpretive exhibits and programs. Daily 9 to 5 (Memorial Day-Labor Day), daily 9 to 4 (rest of year); admission fee. 612 E. Reserve St. 360/696-7655, 800/832-3599.

Mount St. Helens National Volcanic Monument—Walk-in model of volcano; exhibits including films. Short trail leads to overlook of Mount St. Helens, 34 miles in the distance. Daily 9-5 (Apr-Sept), closed Wed-Thur (Nov-Dec), closed Mon-Thur (Jan-Apr); admission fee. Take I-5 exit 49, then 5 miles E on S504. 360/274-2100.

Officer's Row National Historic District—Neighborhood of 21 late 1800s homes built as part of Fort Vancouver army base. Walking tours include an orientation video. Mon-Fri 9 to 5; donations. E. Evergreen Blvd. 360/693-3103.

Pearson Air Museum—History of aviation at the country's oldest operating airfield. Wed-Sun noon to 5; admission fee. 1115 E. 5th. 360/694-7026.

Λ **Battleground Lake State Park**—35 sites; fee; water; modern; showers; open all year/full operation May-Oct; grills/fire rings; tables; 10-day limit. Fishing; boating; sandy beach; nature trails; horse trails and camp; picnic area. 8 miles N on I-5, 8 miles E on WA 502, 3 miles on county road. 360/687-4621.

⊞ **Best Western Ferryman's Inn**—133 rooms, pool, pets, continental breakfast, coin laundry. 10 rooms with kitchens. Off-season rates. I-5 exit 4. 360/574-2151. $$ K12

⊞ **Comfort Suites**—68 suites, indoor pool, continental breakfast, hot tub, exercise room. I-205 exit 30. 360/253-3100. $$$ K18

⊞ **Quality Inn**—72 suites, pool, pets, continental breakfast, hot tub, coin laundry. All rooms have kitchens. I-5 exit 4. 360/696-0516. $$$ K18

⊞ **Red Lion at the Quay**—160 rooms along the Columbia River, pets, pool, restaurant. Off-season rates. 100 S. Columbia (on the dock). 360/694-8341. $$$ K18

⊞ **Rodeway Inn Cascade Park**—117 rooms, indoor pools, pets, continental breakfast, hot tub. I-205 exit 28. 360/256-7044. $$ K16

Washougal, Washington

Λ **Dougan Creek**—7 sites; free; water; primitive; open all year; grills/fire rings; tables; 14-day limit. Hiking; fishing. 9.5 miles E on WA 14, 5 miles N on WA 140, 7 miles E on Washougal River Rd. 360/753-2400.

Welches, Oregon

Λ **Green Canyon**—15 sites; free; water; primitive; open May-Sept; grills/fire rings; tables; 14-day limit; 22' maximum length. Swimming; hiking trails; fishing. 4.5 miles S on FR 2618. 503/666-0704.

Λ **McNeil**—34 sites; free; **no** water; primitive; open June-Aug; grills/fire rings; tables; 14-day limit; 22' maximum length. Nature trails; bike trails; fishing. 1 mile E on US 26, 5 miles NE on Co 18, E on FR 1825. 503/666-0704.

Λ **Mt. Hood Village**—420 sites (360 w/hookups); fee; water; modern; showers; open all year; grills/fire rings; tables. Indoor pool; concessions; groceries; hot tub; playground; coin laundry; fishing; recreation programs; nature programs. 3 miles W on US 26. 503/622-4011.

Wilsonville, Oregon

⊞ **Comfort Inn**—63 rooms, indoor pool, continental breakfast, exercise room, coin laundry. Off-season rates. I-5 exit 283. 503/682-9000. $$ K18

⊞ **Phoenix Inn**—56 rooms, indoor pool, continental breakfast, exercise room, waterslide, coin laundry. Weekend rates. I-5 exit 283. 503/580-9700. $$$ K17

Woodland, Washington

Hulda Klager Lilac Gardens—Be here for the spectacular display of blooms from mid-April to mid-May and tour the 1889 Victorian farmhouse. Gardens dawn to dusk, house daily 10 to 4 during blooming season; admission fee. 1.5 miles W of I-5 exit 21. 360/225-8996.

Λ **Paradise Point State Park**—70 sites; fee; water; modern; showers; open all year/weekends only in winter; grills/fire rings; tables; 10-day limit. Boat ramp; fishing; hiking; dump station. I-5 exit 16, frontage road on E side. 360/263-2350.

Λ **Woodland**—10 sites; free; water; primitive; open all year; grills/fire rings; tables; 14-day limit. Hiking; playground. I-5 exit 21, E on WA 503, right on E CC St, go to S of bridge, right 2.5 miles on Co 38. 360/753-2400.

⊞ **Woodlander Inn**—61 rooms, indoor pool, pets, hot tub. I-5 exit 21. 360/225-6548. $$ K16

CHAPTER 22

November 8, 1805 to March 22, 1806

WINTER AT FORT CLATSOP

So close and yet so far, the Corps of Discovery faced ten days of travel before they reached the Pacific coast.

Beginning November 8, 1805, they had great trouble finding flat camping sites on the Columbia estuary's steep rocky shores. At Grays Point, several men and Sacagawea were ill, possibly from drinking the Columbia's water that mixed with saltwater. Captain William Clark wrote, "we are all wet and disagreeable, as we have been Continually for Severl. days past...& cannot find out if any Settlement is near the mouth of this river." The tide flooded camp, and wind and rain made "our party all wet and cold...[but] they are chearfull and anxious to See further into the Ocean[.]" At least, they could drink the plentiful rainwater.

The captains thought briefly that Grays Point was the "Cape Disappointment" named by British captain John Meares seventeen years earlier, when he concluded that no great river came into the Pacific here. Robert Gray finally located, and named, the Columbia River in 1792, calling the point "Cape Hancock," but the more colorful name is not forgotten.

A few days later, with their leather clothes rotting from the moisture, Clark wrote, "It would be distressing to a feeling person to See our Situation at this time all wet and cold with our bedding &c. also wet..."

The Corps took shelter from November 10 to 15 on the eastern side of Point Ellice in today's Washington, east of the current Astoria-Megler Bridge. Clark called the site a dismal niche. The captains sent privates John Colter, Alexander Willard, and George Shannon downriver in the Indian canoe bought back at Celilo Falls to look for "the Bay...and good harbers..."

Colter returned by land on the 14th, reporting "a butifull Sand beech..." but neither vessels nor permanent trading posts. The captains decided, correctly, that traders stopped in their ships during the summers and then moved on. Captain Meriwether Lewis and a small party paddled downstream with the outgoing tide in one of the large canoes to explore today's Baker Bay.

Ahead of Lewis, Chinook Indians stole the sleeping Willard's and Shannon's rifles right from under their heads. The privates threatened that a large party was on its way to join them. Just then, Lewis and his men arrived—and the guns were returned.

Ready to go but pinned down by wind and high waves until 3:00 p.m. on November 15, Clark and the main party finally left Point Ellice. Then waves stopped them after only three miles, and they camped on the east side of Baker Bay, near Chinook Point. Clark wrote: "This I could plainly See would be the extent of our journey by water..." He thought they were still fourteen miles from Cape Disappointment, on the coast.

From Chinook Point, they scouted for a good place to winter. Their ideal location would offer: a harbor where a trading vessel could stop if one appeared, so the Corps could buy trade goods for the trip back and send their writings to the "U' States"; somewhere to make salt for their diet, to preserve food and to trade during the return down the Missouri River; friendly neighbors; and enough food.

Clark took York and ten others on foot to see the Pacific, November 18-20, and explore north up today's Washington coast. The men, he wrote, "appear much Satisfied with their trip beholding with estonishment...this emence ocian." Their camp was within today's **[2]** Fort Canby State Park.

The party also planned to explore the south, now Oregon, side of the estuary, but waves prevent crossing. The captains decided to poll expedition members (excluding those out hunting) for opinions about the winter's camp.

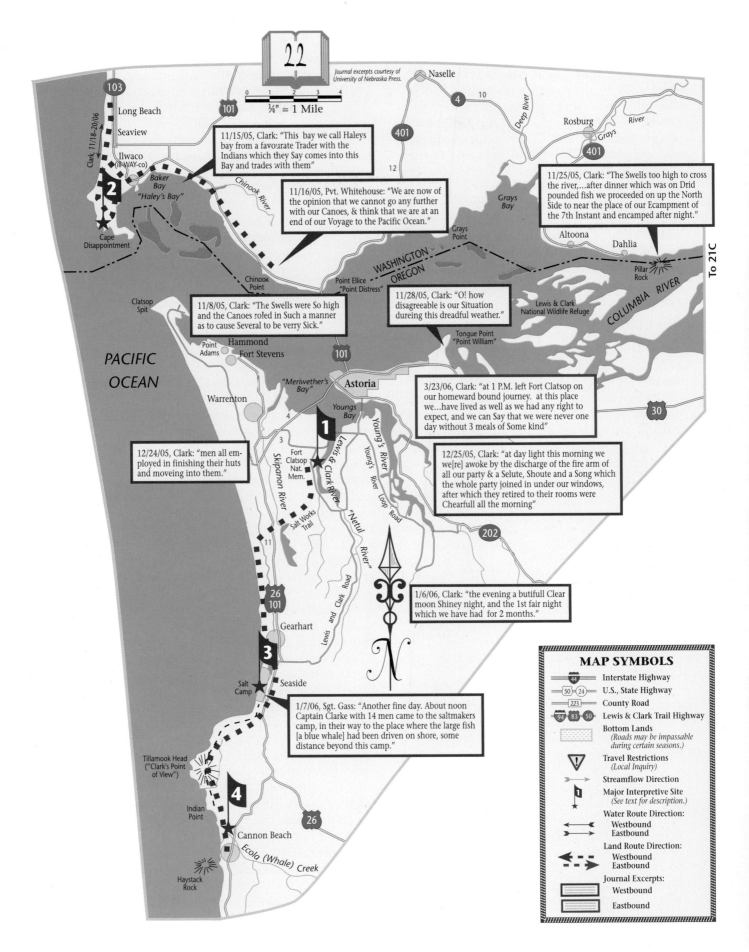

22

Journal excerpts courtesy of University of Nebraska Press.

¼" = 1 Mile

0 1 2 3 4

Naselle

Long Beach

Seaview

Ilwaco (ill-WAY-co)

Clark, 11/18–20/06

Baker Bay "Haley's Bay"

Cape Disappointment

Chinook River

Chinook Point

Clatsop Spit

Point Adams

Hammond

Fort Stevens

Warrenton

PACIFIC OCEAN

"Meriwether's Bay"

Astoria

Youngs Bay

Young's River

Young's River Loop Road

Skipanon River

Fort Clatsop Nat. Mem.

Lewis & Clark River

Salt Works Trail

"Netul River"

Salt Camp

Gearhart

Seaside

Lewis and Clark Road

Tillamook Head ("Clark's Point of View")

Indian Point

Cannon Beach

Ecola (Whale) Creek

Haystack Rock

WASHINGTON
OREGON

Rosburg

Deep River

Grays River

Grays Bay

Grays Point

Altoona

Dahlia

Pillar Rock

Lewis & Clark National Wildlife Refuge

Tongue Point "Point William"

Point Ellice "Point Distress"

COLUMBIA RIVER

To 21C

11/15/05, Clark: "This bay we call Haleys bay from a favourate Trader with the Indians which they Say comes into this Bay and trades with them"

11/16/05, Pvt. Whitehouse: "We are now of the opinion that we cannot go any further with our Canoes, & think that we are at an end of our Voyage to the Pacific Ocean."

11/25/05, Clark: "The Swells too high to cross the river,...after dinner which was on Drid pounded fish we proceeded on up the North Side to near the place of our Ecampment of the 7th Instant and encamped after night."

11/8/05, Clark: "The Swells were So high and the Canoes roled in Such a manner as to cause Several to be verry Sick."

11/28/05, Clark: "O! how disagreeable is our Situation dureing this dreadful weather."

3/23/06, Clark: "at 1 P.M. left Fort Clatsop on our homeward bound journey. at this place we...have lived as well as we had any right to expect, and we can Say that we were never one day without 3 meals of Some kind"

12/24/05, Clark: "men all employed in finishing their huts and moveing into them."

12/25/05, Clark: "at day light this morning we we[re] awoke by the discharge of the fire arm of all our party & a Selute, Shoute and a Song which the whole party joined in under our windows, after which they retired to their rooms were Chearfull all the morning"

1/6/06, Clark: "the evening a butifull Clear moon Shiney night, and the 1st fair night which we have had for 2 months."

1/7/06, Sgt. Gass: "Another fine day. About noon Captain Clarke with 14 men came to the saltmakers camp, in their way to the place where the large fish [a blue whale] had been driven on shore, some distance beyond this camp."

MAP SYMBOLS

44	Interstate Highway
50 24	U.S., State Highway
223	County Road
94 83 50	Lewis & Clark Trail Highway
	Bottom Lands (Roads may be impassable during certain seasons.)
	Travel Restrictions (Local Inquiry)
	Streamflow Direction
1	Major Interpretive Site (See text for description.)
	Water Route Direction: Westbound Eastbound
	Land Route Direction: Westbound Eastbound
	Journal Excerpts: Westbound Eastbound

On November 24, six men voted to return to The Dalles, nine chose Sandy River (on the Oregon side), and fourteen (including York and the captains) wanted to explore further. Sacagawea voted for any place with plenty of wapato roots to eat, and Charbonneau expressed no opinion. Clark thought that two or three weeks wasn't too long to explore on the Oregon side of the Columbia.

To cross the estuary, the Corps went back upriver to near Pillar Rock and today's Lewis and Clark National Wildlife Refuge, and on November 27 canoed west to Tongue Point, Oregon, which they named Point William. Base camp was here until December 7. The rain was constant, but Chinook Indians on the north side had said winters brought little snow.

Rain continued and their clothing and tents were "So full of holes & rotten" that the men at Tongue Point hunted and tanned hides constantly.

On November 29, Lewis and five men traveled the shore of Youngs Bay within today's Astoria and set up a base camp for further exploring. Only six years after the expedition, John Jacob Astor's Pacific Fur Company would build a trading post here.

Two days later, joking about weather conditions on the ocean whose name means "peaceful," Clark wrote: "now 24 Days Since we arrived in Sight of the Great Western Ocian, I cant Say Pasific as Since I have Seen it, it has been the reverse."

But he was proud of the expedition's success so far. He carved on an evergreen tree:

William Clark December 3rd 1805. By Land from the U. States in 1804 & 1805.

By land—how much effort those two words signified.

About Lewis's party, Clark wrote "a 1000 conjectures has crouded into my mind," but they returned on December 5, having left two men where they "found a good Situation and Elk Suffi[c]ient to winter on..."

On December 7, the whole Corps moved to where they would build **[1]** Fort Clatsop and stay until March 23, 1806. It was about two miles up the Netul—now Lewis and Clark—River from Youngs Bay. The next day, Clark took five men to seek a place to make salt, and blaze a trail to it. But it wouldn't be until nearly New Year's Day that they began **[3]** Salt Works on the Necanicum River within the

present city of Seaside, Oregon, fifteen miles by trail and rivers from their main fort. Privates Willard, Joseph Field, William Bratton, George Gibson, and Peter Weiser built the camp, and the first three stayed to produce salt.

In the rain on the 8th, men began clearing land for Fort Clatsop. Felling trees, splitting logs for boards, raising buildings, and chinking log walls took until Christmas Eve, when most of the men moved into their "huts," as Sergeant John Ordway called them. They had built the smokehouse first, to preserve elk meat that spoiled quickly in the damp—some of it even while being smoked because the firewood was damp.

That Christmas Eve, Clark recorded that Private Joseph Field completed for each captain "a wide Slab hued [hewed] to write on." Two days later, Field finished "a Table & 2 Seats for us." The captains would use these well, with Clark primarily drawing maps of the journey since Fort Mandan, and Lewis mostly writing what the expedition had learned this past year about native cultures, animals, and plants new to science.

Christmas 1805 was a poor one. The men awakened their captains with "a Selute, Shoute and a Song" and small personal presents were exchanged before they ate spoiled elk, spoiled fish, and "Some roots, a bad Christmass diner... we would have Spent this day the nativity of Christ in feasting, had we any thing either to raise our Sperits or even gratify our appetites..."

All this winter, the dreary refrain that the hunters found no, or only one elk, runs through this journals.

Two days after Christmas, the men completed Fort Clatsop's chimneys and bunks, and its fence and gates. On December 30, the fort was finished, with a sentinel at the gate. Indian visitors—who came daily—now had to leave at sunset, when the gate closed.

The Indians of this area, like those of the lower Missouri, had traded with whites before. And, like the Sioux, they wanted good returns for their wares. All winter, the journals would complain about the "prices" asked for wapato roots and dried fish—which locals had and the Corps needed. It also turned out that the Clatsops wouldn't take red beads in trade, only blue—which were getting scarce. Luckily, the Wahkiakum would accept the red beads.

January 1, 1806, was greeted at an early hour by a volley of small arms fire. The Corps' food was better than at Christmas, but their biggest happiness came from looking forward to next New Year's Day, Lewis wrote, "when in the bosom of our friends we hope to participate in the mirth and hilarity of the day, and when with the zest given by the recollection of the present, we shall completely... enjoy the repast which the hand of civilization has prepared..."

On December 29, they had heard about a whale beached to the south, where the Tillamook people lived. A week later, Willard and Weiser returned from Salt Works, bringing blubber the Tillamooks had given them. Lewis wrote that blubber was like pork fat, but spongier and coarser. When cooked, "it resembled the beaver or the dog in flavour."

Hoping to trade for blubber, Clark set out on January 7, with 11 men. Joining the party was Sacagawea (and her baby), who had to argue with Lewis "that she had traveled a long way with us to see the great waters, and now that monstrous fish was also to be seen." Following an Indian guide, they climbed over steep Tillamook Head en route to the whale. Clark's party found the Tillamooks at the mouth of [4] Ecola Creek at today's Cannon Beach. By then, the whale was just a skeleton, and the Indians were boiling blubber for its oil. The Tillamooks didn't want to give up any blubber or oil, but finally agreed to trade. Clark got 300 pounds of blubber, which supplemented the Fort Clatsop diet for three weeks.

With a twinkle, Clark wrote that he thanked "providence for...having Sent this monster to be *Swallowed by us* in Sted of *Swallowing of us* as jonah's [whale] did."

When the Corps used the last of their candles on January 13, Lewis noted that they had carried molds and wick all this way, and now used elk fat to make "this necessary article."

The rest of the winter was constant work: hunting for food, preserving meat, and making moccasins and leather clothing. By March 12, they had made about 350 pairs of moccasins, plus elk hide shirts, pants, hooded coats, and luggage bags.

By February 3, Salt Works had produced eight gallons—a bushel—of salt, but the captains thought they needed three times that much until they reached caches on the Missouri. The men at Salt Works weren't doing well. On the 10th, Willard arrived at Fort Clatsop after hunting his way to Salt Works, and Lewis wrote he "had cut his knee very badly with his tommahawk" when butchering an elk there. Willard said that Bratton was very unwell and Gibson so sick he "could not set up or walk alone" and wanted to be called back to Clatsop. The captains sent Colter and Weiser the next day to replace Gibson and Bratton; and Sergeant Nathaniel Pryor with four men in a canoe to bring both Gibson and Bratton in. When the salt produced totalled about twenty gallons, on February 21, Salt Works would be abandoned.

Gibson, it turned out, was suffering from a severe cold after hunting in marshes near Salt Works. Bratton had back pain and an obstinate cough, and continued to weaken. The bad diet of lean elk didn't help, although hunters brought Bratton cranberries when they found them. Bratton was worse after a month, and then Lewis began applying liniment and wrapping his chest in flannel. It helped, but Bratton remained ill. Lewis decided he would improve when they set out for the U' States, the departure planned for April 1.

In late February, the small candlefish, or eulachon (Lewis called them "anchovies"), began running up the shallower rivers, where they were scooped up in nets. Indians traded these and wapato at reasonable prices, but the Corps' supply of trade goods was very low. In mid-March, Lewis wrote that "two handkercheifs would now contain all the small articles of merchandize which we possess." Elk were moving away from the coast, so the men had to fish as well as hunt. Early in March, Lewis wrote that for a while they lived "sumptuously" on wapato, candlefish, and fresh sturgeon. This winter's pattern seems to have been feast and famine. And yet, when Clark would sum up the winter in his journal entry of March 20, he'd write: "Altho' we have not fared Sumptuously this winter & Spring at Fort Clatsop, we have lived quit[e] as comfortably as we had any reason to expect."

Every day was cloudy, foggy, or rainy. Lewis was "mortified" by February 25 that he hadn't been able to make more astronomical observations at Fort Clatsop. Bad weather and lack of game as March came on made them decide to start out early for the Rockies. The Nez Perce Indians had said June 1 was as early as they should try the crossing, because of snow, and the captains figured it would take two months to reach the mountains. Now they decided that any place was better than Fort Clatsop.

On March 20, the men tested gunsights, and John Shields made adjustments. Two days later, all hunters except Colter failed to locate game, but the men bought a dog and some dried candlefish from Indians. They presented Fort Clatsop and its furniture to Chief Coboway on the 22nd, because he had been "much more kind and hospitable to us" than any other neighbor. The chief and his family lived there for a while, and ninety-three years later his grandson Silas B. Smith led historians to the site he recalled. Archaeological studies are again under way.

TOURING TODAY

❧ FORT CLATSOP AREA ❧

[ ] **Bracketed numbers key sites to maps**
★ **L&C in-depth interpretation, unchanged landform**
● **L&C interpreted site**

    ⛌ Special-needs accessible   ⊨ Bed & breakfast
    ⊗ Restaurant   ▲ Camping, RV park
    ⊞ Motel, hotel, cabin

Bridge across the Columbia River in this area is on US 101.

Ferry—Wahkiakum County Ferry runs between Cathlamet and Westport, OR on the hour, 5am to 10pm; admission fee. 360/795-3301.

ALONG THE EXPEDITION'S PATH

November 10, 1805
● **Lewis and Clark National Wildlife Refuge** (Knappa, OR)—Columbia River islands accessible by boat only. Self-guiding canoe trail. 360/795-3915.

November 15-25, 1805
● **Lewis and Clark Campsite State Park** (Ilwaco, WA)—Picnic area and interpretation of campsite. Always open; free. 5 miles E of Ilwaco on US 101. 360/642-3078.
Fort Columbia State Park (Chinook, WA)—Military post from the Spanish-American War. 12 buildings remain for exploration including bunkers, the hospital and theater, lookouts. Interpretive center atop Cape Disappointment brings additional perspective. Self-guiding trail and hiking trail to Scar-

boro Hill. Picnic area. ⊞ Hostel lodging available. 360/777-8755. Park open daily 8 to dusk, center open Wed-Sun 10 to 5 (Apr-Sept); donations. 1.75 miles E on US 101. 360/777-8221.
[2] ★ **Fort Canby State Park** (Ilwaco, WA)—Lewis and Clark Interpretive Center details the expedition with exhibits on medical treatments, food, entertainment, discipline and tribal impacts on the Corps. Multimedia presentations and actual artifacts. Daily 10 to 5; donations. Tours of North Head Lighthouse daily 10 to 6 (June-Aug); admission fee. Swimming beach, 4 nature trails, boat ramp, virgin Sitka spruce–western hemlock forest. ▲ 250 sites (60 w/hookups); fee; water; modern; showers; open all year; grills/fire rings; tables; 10-day limit. Dump station. 2.5 miles SW off US 101. 360/642-3078.

December 7, 1805
[1] ★ **Fort Clatsop National Memorial** (Astoria, OR)—Construction reminiscent of the fort, living history programs 9:30 to 5:30 during the summer. Visitor center with exhibits and multimedia programs. Picnic area, hiking trails, canoe landing. Daily 8 to 6 (June-Labor Day), 8 to 5 (rest of

year); admission fee. 5 miles SW near US 101. 503/861-2471.
● **Fort Stevens State Park** (Warrenton, OR)—Erected to protect Columbia River entrance from the Civil War until WWII. Historical Area and Military Museum has a war games building, summer tours of underground gun batteries and guardhouse. Living history programs. Wreck of 1906 schooner *Peter Iredale* is now accessible by a paved road. Summer tours are given aboard a military truck. Daily 10 to 6 (May-Sept), 10 to 4 (rest of year); donations, admission fee for tours. Swimming, fishing and boating on the ocean and at Coffenbury Lake. Miles of biking and hiking trails. Very popular park. ▲ Yurts can be rented. 600 sites (350 w/hookups); fee; water; modern; showers; open all year; grills/fire rings; tables; 10-day limit; firewood. 2.5 miles N of Main St. on Warrenton Drive. 503/861-1671, 503/861-2000.

January 10, 1806
[3] ★ **Salt Works** (Seaside, OR)—Near the south end of the Promenade is a memorial, not a replica, of Salt Works. Monument at the foot of Broadway commemorates the journey. Always open; free. A challenging trail leads from Sea-

side over Tillamook Head to Indian Beach.

[4] ★ **Ecola State Park** (Cannon Beach, OR)—Day-use park with sea lion and bird rookeries offshore. Herd of elk, 7.5 mile scenic cliff hiking trail over **Tillamook Head**, picnic area. Interpretive marker. Daily dawn to dusk; admission fee. 2 miles N off US 101. 503/436-2844.

Oswald West State Park (Cannon Beach, OR)—Accessible only by foot. Explore the rain forest of giant spruce and cedar trees. 13-mile segment of Oregon Coast Trail. ▲ 36 primitive sites; fee; water; modern; open Mar-Oct; grills/fire rings; tables; firewood. Fishing; hiking trails. 7 miles S on US 101. 503/436-2844.

AROUND THE AREA

TOWNS LISTED ALPHABETICALLY

Astoria, Oregon

Astoria-Warrenton Chamber of Commerce, 111 W. Marine Dr. 503/325-6311, 800/875-6807.

Astoria Children's Museum—Permanent and rotating exploration centers encourage children to use their imagination. Mon/Thur/Fri 11 to 3, Sat 11 to 4, Sun 1 to 4; admission fee. 11th & Exchange streets. 503/325-8669.

● **Astoria Column**—Spiral mural around outer wall portrays the history of the Oregon Country. 164 steps to observation platform. Daily 8 to dusk; free. Coxcomb Hill. 503/325-6311.

Columbia River Maritime Museum—History of the river and Pacific coast. Tours of a seagoing lightship. Daily 9:30 to 5; admission fee. 1792 Marine Dr. 503/325-2323.

● **Fort Astoria**—A portion of the 1811 fort has been rebuilt. It was the first permanent U.S. settlement west of the Mississippi. Always open; free. Exchange & 15th streets. 503/325-2203.

Heritage Museum—Regional history and photographs. Daily 10 to 5 (May-Sept), 11 to 4 (rest of year); admission fee. 1618 Exchange St. 503/325-2203.

The Uppertown Firefighters Museum—Vintage fire engines and equipment in an 1896 firehouse. Fri-Sun 10 to 5 (May-Sept), 11 to 4 (rest of year); admission fee. 30th & Marine Dr. 503/325-2203.

▲ **Astoria-Warrenton-Seaside KOA**—259 sites (232 w/hookups); fee; water; modern; showers; open all year; grills/fire rings; tables; firewood. Indoor pool; hot tub; bike rentals; playground; hiking trails; ⊞ cabins; coin laundry; dump station; groceries. 3 miles S on US 101, 4.5 miles W on Alt US 101. 503/861-2606.

▲ **Kampers West Kamp Ground**—232 sites (222 w/hookups); fee; water; modern; showers; open all year; grills/fire rings; tables; firewood. Fishing; playground; dump station; coin laundry; groceries. 1.5 miles NW of US 101 on Harbor St, 1.75 miles N on Warrenton Dr. 503/861-1814.

⊞ **Rosebriar Hotel**—11 rooms, full breakfast, TV. ₺. Kids not encouraged. Off-season rates. 636 14th St. 503/325-7427, 800/487-0224. $$$

⊞ **Shilo Inn**—62 rooms, pets, pool, hot tub, ⊗ restaurant, coin laundry. ₺. Off-season rates. 1609 E. Harbor Dr. 503/861-2181, 800/222-2244. $$$ K12

⊗ **Columbian Cafe**—Fresh home cooking, vegetarian style. B & D daily (B only Sun). 1114 Marine Dr. 503/325-2233. $$

⊗ **Pier 11 Feed Store**—American food on the river, kids' menu. B L & D daily. 10th St. on the pier. 503/325-0279. $$

Cathlamet, Washington

Wahkiakum County Historical Museum—County, Indian and logging history. Tue-Sun 11 to 4 (June-Sept), Thur-Sun 1 to 4 (rest of year); admission fee. 65 River St. 360/795-3954.

Chinook, Washington

▲ **River's End Campground & RV Park**—97 sites (77 w/hookups); fee; water; modern; showers; open all year/full operation Apr-Oct; grills/fire rings; tables; firewood. Fishing. Coin laundry; groceries; dump station. 0.75 mile N on US 101. 360/777-8317.

⊗ **Sanctuary Restaurant**—Ameri-

can food in restored historic church, kids' menu. D daily. US 101 & Hazel St. 360/777-8380. $$

Clatskanie, Oregon

Historical Flippin Castle—Tours of 19th century Victorian mansion. Daily 10 to 2 (Mar-Dec); admission fee. 620 Tichenor St. 503/728-2026.

Grays River, Washington

Covered Bridge—This 158-foot bridge is the only one of its kind in Washington. 1.75 miles S on WA 4.

Hammond, Oregon

⊩ **Officer's Inn Bed & Breakfast**—8 rooms in former officers' quarters adjacent to Fort Stevens. Full breakfast. 540 Russell Pl. 503/861-2524, 800/377-2524. $$

Ilwaco, Washington

Ilwaco Heritage Museum—Shipwrecks, fishing and forestry exhibits. Daily 10 to 5; admission fee. 115 SE Lake St. 360/642-3446.

▲ **KOA-Ilwaco**—164 sites (114 w/hookups); fee; water; modern; showers; open May-Oct; grills/fire rings; tables. Fishing; playground; dump station; coin laundry; groceries. US 101 & Alt US 101. 360/642-3292, 800/562-3258.

⊞ **Heidi's Inn**—25 rooms, pets, ⊗ restaurant. 126 Spruce St. 360/642-2387. $$

⊩ **Chick-A-Dee Inn**—12 rooms in a renovated historic church, full breakfast. Smoke-free. 120 Williams St. NE. 360/642-8686.

Jewell, Oregon

Jewell Meadows Wildlife Area—Protected environment for Roosevelt elk with 3 viewing areas. Always open; free. 1.5 miles W on OR 202. 503/755-2264.

Long Beach, Washington

Long Beach Peninsula Visitors Bureau—Hwys 101 & 103. 360/642-2400, 800/451-2542.

Boardwalk—10-block boardwalk along the beach with observation platforms, telescopes and interpretive exhibits. Bolstad Street off WA 103.

Pacific Coast Cranberry Research Foundation Museum—Guided tours of museum and bog. Exhibits include antique and modern machinery. Fri-Sun 10 to 3; free. 1 mile N on WA 103, 0.75 mile E on Pioneer Rd. 360/642-4938.

World Kite Museum & Hall of Fame—Kites, designs, and the people who fly them. Daily 11 to 5 (June-Aug), Sat/Sun 11 to 5 (rest of year); admission fee. 3rd St N & Boulevard. 360/642-4020.

⛺ Andersen's on the Ocean—75 sites (60 w/hookups); fee; water; modern; showers; open all year; grills/fire rings; tables. Fishing; playground; coin laundry. 3 miles N on US 101 on WA 103. 360/642-2231, 800/645-6795.

⛺ Pacific RV Park—50 sites (all w/hookups); fee; water; modern; showers; open all year; grills/fire rings; tables. Fishing; playground; hiking trails; coin laundry. 3.5 miles N on WA 103. 360/642-3253.

⛺ Pegg's Oceanside RV Park—30 sites (all w/hookups); fee; water; modern; showers; open Apr-Sept; grills/fire rings; tables. Fishing; hiking trails; coin laundry. 5.5 miles N on WA 103. 360/642-2451.

⛺ Pioneer RV Park—34 sites (all w/hookups); fee; water; modern; showers; open all year; grills/fire rings; tables; 35' maximum length. Fishing; hiking trails. 2.5 miles N on WA 103. 360/642-3990.

⊞ The Breakers—106 rooms, pool, hot tub. 1 mile N on WA 103. 800/288-8890. $$$

⊞ Chautauqua Lodge—180 rooms, indoor pool, hot tub. 304 14th St NW. 800/869-8401. $$$

⊞ Our Place at the Beach—25 rooms, pets, hot tub, exercise room, refrigerators. Off-season rates. 1309 S Blvd. 360/642-3793. $$ K9

⊞ Super 8—50 rooms, coin laundry. Off-season rates. 500 Ocean Beach Blvd. 360/642-8988. $$$ K18

⌂ Scandinavian Gardens Inn—5 rooms, full breakfast, hot tub, smoke-free. 360/642-8877. $$$

⌂ Shelburne Country Inn—15 rooms in 1896 Inn, full breakfast,

⊗ restaurant, smoke-free. Off-season rates. ♿. 360/642-2442. $$$

⊗ Cottage Bakery & Delicatessen—Hundreds of different pastries. B & L daily. Downtown. 360/642-4441.

Naselle, Washington

Naselle Hatchery—Exhibits and tours of this facility for coho and chinook salmon and steelhead trout. Daily 8 to 4:30; free. 1.5 miles E of WA 4 on North Valley Rd. 360/665-4547.

Ocean Park, Washington

Loomis Lake State Park—Picnic area, hiking trail to beach. Collecting driftwood and beachcombing allowed. Freshwater lake for fishing is a bit north. 4 miles S on WA 103. 360/642-3078.

Pacific Pines State Park—Picnic area, hiking trail to beach. Collecting driftwood and beachcombing allowed. 1 mile N on WA 103. 360/642-3078.

⛺ Ocean Park Resort—83 sites (76 w/hookups); fee; water; modern; showers; open all year; grills/fire rings; tables; firewood. Pool; hot tub; playground; ⊞ cabins; coin laundry. 2 blocks E of WA 103 on 259th Place. 360/665-4585, 800/835-4634.

⌂ Caswell's on the Bay—5 rooms, full breakfast. 360/665-6535. $$$

Oysterville, Washington

Leadbetter Point State Park—Day-use park on Long Beach Peninsula. Trails for hiking and wildlife study through dunes and forested areas. Beachcombing and clamming along the ocean; waterfowl, birding, hiking trails through dunes & forested areas. 4 miles N on WA 103. 360/642-3078.

Seaside, Oregon

Seaside Visitors Bureau, 415 1st. 503/738-3097, 888/306-2326.

Seaside Aquarium—Focus on coastal marine life. Feed the seals or explore the touch tanks. Daily 9 to 5 (Mar-Oct), Wed-Sun 9 to 5 (rest of year); admission fee. 2nd Ave at the Promenade. 503/738-6211.

Seaside Museum and Historical Society—Local history, Clatsop Indians, logging, restored beachside cottage. Daily 10:30 to 4:30; admission fee. 570 Necanicum Dr. 503/738-7065.

⊞ Ocean View Resort—84 rooms, pets, indoor pool, hot tub, efficiencies, ⊗ restaurant, coin laundry. Off-season rates. 414 N. Promenade. 503/738-3334. $$$

⊞ Seashore Resort Motel—51 large rooms, indoor pool, hot tub. Off-season rates. 60 N. Promenade. 503/738-6368. $$$ K12

⌂ Beachwood Bed & Breakfast—4 rooms, full breakfast, bicycles, smoke-free, TV. Off-season rates. 503/738-9585. $$$

⊗ Dooger's Seafood & Grill—You'll feel at home here, kids' menu. L & D daily. 505 Broadway. 503/738-3773. $$

Seaview, Washington

Willapa National Wildlife Refuge—All of Long Island and parts of Leadbetter Point. Waterfowl, reptiles and amphibians. Access by boat, 7 primitive campgrounds, miles of hiking trails. Headquarters 8 miles NE of Seaview on US 101. 360/484-3482.

⛺ Sou'wester Lodge—65 sites (60 w/hookups); fee; water; modern; showers; open all year; grills/fire rings; tables. ⊞ Lodge and cabins, beach, coin laundry, fishing. US 101 & WA 103. 360/642-2542.

Skamokawa, Washington

River Life Interpretive Center at Redmen Hall—Interpretation of the building's history and life along the Columbia. See the view from the bell tower. Tue-Sat 11 to 5, Sun 1 to 5 (June-Sept), Wed-Sat noon to 4, Sun 1 to 4 (rest of year); admission fee. 1384 W WA 4. 360/795-3007.

⛺ Skamokawa Vista Park—25 sites (all w/hookups); fee; water; modern; showers; open all year; grills/fire rings; tables. Boating, scenic view. 13 School Rd. 360/795-8605.

CHAPTER 23

March 23 to July 2, 1806
RETURN TO TRAVELERS' REST

Captain William Clark's journal, Sunday, March 23, 1806:...*left Fort Clatsop on our homeward bound journey. at this place we had wintered ...and have lived as well as we had any right to expect...not withstanding the repeated fall of rain which has fallen almost Constantly...indeed w[e] have had only [   ] days fair weather.*

Clark never filled in the blank, but it would have been a single-digit number. In 106 days at Fort Clatsop, only 12 were without rain, and only six of those had clear skies.

They retraced their route to Tongue Point, Oregon, and then, traveling fifteen to eighteen miles a day, headed back up the Columbia. They hunted and also traded for food at Indian villages.

As Captain Meriwether Lewis expected, invalid Private William Bratton became stronger.

On March 30, Lewis wrote, "we had a view of mount St. helines...the most noble looking object of it's kind in nature...a regular cone." That volcano and Mount Hood were "perfectly covered with snow."

They had hoped to harvest salmon from the spring run, but Indians said that was a month away. To wait, Lewis wrote on April 1, "would detain us so large a portion of the season that it is probable we should not reach the United States before the ice would close the Missouri..." Also, they needed to find the Nez Perce, who held the Corps' horses, before those people moved away from winter camp.

When they reached "Indian Island" at today's Portland, some Watlala men visited and described a large river flowing into the Columbia from the south. Because the Corps was on the other side of the island when headed to the Pacific, they hadn't seen it. Now, on April 2, Clark took seven men to explore up the Willamette River, which they called the Multnomah. Having gone 10 miles upstream and

camped in what is today northwest Portland, Clark proclaimed the Willamette deep enough "for a Man of War or Ship of any burthen."

Spring snowmelt was raising the Columbia, and when they could see Beacon Rock ahead on April 6, Lewis observed that the waterline was 12 feet higher than it had been the previous autumn. By now, they had stored up enough meat for sustanance till they reached the Nez Perce villages on the Clearwater, they figured. Camping for three nights in the area of today's Shepperd's Dell State Park, they dried more meat, tuned their weapons, and made their canoes shipshape.

April 9 brought them back to the Watlala village visited last November 4, where they had been introduced to wapato, and where Charles Floyd's tomahawk was stolen (see Chapter 23). Now, "John Colter...observed the tomehawk in one of the lodges...; the natives attempted to wrest the tomahawk from him but he retained it."

Their portage around the Cascades of the Columbia on April 11 was difficult—in the rain, with Bratton and three others "lamed by various accedents," and Indians throwing stones down on them. After dragging four boats up the cascades, they decided to wait until the next day for the last one. Indians surrounded the camp, and Lewis wrote "these are the greates theives and scoundrels we have met with" after they stole his Newfoundland dog, Seaman, and other items. Members of the Corps pursued the thieves and retrieved Lewis's pet. A friendly chief blamed two very bad men, and "appeared mortified at the conduct of his people." Lewis wrote that perhaps the chief's visit had calmed things down, but "our men seem well disposed to kill a few of them."

The next day wasn't much better. The men carried their rifles while they portaged baggage, but had no trouble. However, when they were hauling the last boat over the rocks, it turned sideways and broke up in the current. That cost another day dividing the baggage among the remaining boats.

While half the party went ahead, Lewis and half stayed to trade hides for two small canoes, and for dogs to eat. Lewis, who added to the hunters' burden by taking his very large dog on the expedition, wrote "with most of the party [dog] has become a favorite food...I prefer it to lean venison or Elk...very far superior to the horse in any state." One wonders if Seaman's big dark eyes ever caught his master's while the latter munched happily on a dinner of dog haunch.

They stayed at Fort Rock (of last October) from April 15 to 18—hunting, building pack-saddles, and trading for horses. Indian people were gathering along the Columbia for the spring salmon run, but it hadn't begun yet, "a serious inconvenience to us." Clark obtained only five horses after a full day of bargaining. The two dugouts were cut up for fuel.

Near today's Horsethief Lake State Park, they camped April 19 to 21, and got more horses. But the Indian man who owned one of those had lost it gambling, and its new owner took it away. The ailing Bratton was to ride one horse, while nine carried packs.

From that camp, Clark and four men visited an Indian village near today's Wishram, Washington. There, on April 20, the first salmon arrived. To ensure that more salmon would come soon, the village performed their first-salmon ceremony, sacred to all in this region, which included giving each child a taste of the fish.

Keeping the horses was a constant struggle, between thieves along the way and horses wandering back to their former homes. The Corps spent time many mornings hunting for lost horses.

After passing today's McNary Dam, they stopped for a scanty noon dinner. Walla Walla chief Yelleppit arrived, reminding them that last fall they had promised a longer visit on their return. At his village opposite the mouth of the Walla Walla River on April 27, he urged the people to share fuel (only dried shrubs were available here) and food with the Corps, then set the example himself. The shared food was welcome.

The next day, Chief Yelleppit offered a "very eligant white horse" for a kettle—but now the Corps had none to spare. Clark counter-offered his sword, which was accepted. With neighboring Yakamas visiting, the Corps and the Walla Wallas danced and sang until midnight.

Borrowing canoes from Yelleppit's village on the 29th, the expedition transported their goods across the Columbia, but agreed to Chief Yellepit's invitation to spend just one more night at his village. They now had twenty-three horses for the trek to the Rockies. Upon leaving the Walla Wallas on April 30, Lewis called them the "most hospitable, honest, and sincere people that we have met with in our voyage."

The best gift of all from the Walla Wallas and their chief was information about a short-cut back to the Clearwater River. Generally paralleling the Snake River, but south of it, the route—Lewis thought—would save at least eighty miles. It passed by the future site of Dayton, Washington.

The Corps traveled uneventfully across the southeastern tip of today's Washington back into Idaho and to the Clearwater River. When they began meeting Nez Perce Indians, they traded medical care for more horses. They heard the unwelcome news that snow was still deep in the Rockies—just as the Nez Perce had predicted last fall.

On May 8 they met Twisted Hair, the Nez Perce chief who had guided them down the Columbia to Celilo Falls and cared for their horses over winter. With him was another chief, Broken Arm, who had been on a hunting party last fall and hadn't met the Corps. Twisted Hair was surprisingly cool toward the captains.

At camp near Orofino, Idaho, Twisted Hair told the captains Broken Arm was angry because he was left out of the horse-care arrangement. But Broken Arm told them he had to take over the horses because Twisted Hair was letting his young men overuse them.

The next day, the Corps collected most of their horses, and the chiefs seemed to be friends again. Traveling to Broken Arm's village, where their words were as usual translated through several languages, the captains told his people about their expedition and the new government they were subject to. Gradually collecting their horses, and giving medical treatments all the while, the expedition stayed there until May 13.

They moved on, camping overnight near the site of the train depot in today's Kamiah, Idaho, then crossing to the east bank of the Clearwater River, northwest of today's U.S. Highway 12 bridge. Here they stayed until June 10, waiting for the snow to melt. Other than at the two winter forts, this was their longest stay in one place. They didn't name the camp, but historians have called it Long Camp, and also Camp Chopunnish, which was the name Lewis and Clark used for the people known now as Nez Perce.

At this camp, they hunted, ran foot and horse races to strengthen themselves for the coming climb, and waited. On May 17, Lewis fumed in his journal about "that icy barrier which seperates me from my friends and Country, from all which makes life esteemable.— patience, patience—"

Pomp—Jean Baptiste Charbonneau—now 14 months old, was cutting teeth, and developed a throat infection and fever that lasted three weeks. Bratton still found it hard to sit up, much less to walk, until John Shields had the idea of building him a sauna. After sweating inside for twenty minutes, he plunged into a cold creek, then repeated the treatment. Bratton also drank "copious draughts" of a strong horse-nettle tea. The next day, May 25, he claimed to feel much better. Nine days later, he was walking with ease, and on June 5 went with Colter to trade at Broken Arm's village. Trade goods were now reduced to brass buttons cut from dress uniforms.

On May 31, Lewis noted that they had sixty-five horses—a saddle mount plus a packhorse for each person, with some animals to spare for replacements, or meat.

On June 10, the Corps of Discovery set out for the Bitterroot Mountains, despite the Nez Perces' warning to wait another month. The men were "elated with the idea of moving on towards their friends and country" in "this delightfull season for traveling."

To gather food and strength for their assault on the formidable mountains ahead, they camped for four days at Weippe Prairie, where they had first met the Nez Perce last September. On the 15th they proceeded on, But it had been a big mistake to disregard the Nez Perce. They found twelve to fifteen feet of snow in the mountains and had to turn back after stowing some of the baggage.

By June 21 they were again at "the flats" of Weippe Prairie, convinced of the need for a guide. Lewis noted: "This is the first time since we have been on this long tour that we have ever been compelled to retreat or make a retrograde march."

Then five Nez Perce young men arrived and joined the travelers. Three said they were going to the Great Falls, chosen by their people at the captains' invitation, to try to make peace with the Blackfeet. The other two were going to visit their allies, the Salish. They would be excellent guides over the rugged Indian trail.

Back at their stowed baggage on June 26, the men took two hours to repack it, then followed the trail along the ridge dividing the North Fork of the Clearwater and the Lochsa River. Lewis wrote on the 27th, "We were entirely surrounded by those mountains...it would have seemed impossible ever to have escaped; in short, without the assistance of our guides I doubt much whether we...could find our way." The sight would "damp the sperits of any except such hardy travellers as we have become."

By the time they "bid adieu to the snow" on June 29, their only food was roots without salt or oil for cooking. At Lolo Hot Springs in today's Montana that night, the men enjoyed "the baths."

Travelers' Rest, reached the next day, again lived up to its name. They rested for a couple of days and planned the journey's next phase. Now Clark wrote that they had put "those tremendious mountanes behind us—in passing of which we have experiensed Cold and hunger of which I shall ever remember."

Touring information for this area is given in Chapters 16 through 22.

CHAPTER 24

July 3 to August 12, 1806

LEWIS'S RETURN VIA THE MARIAS

During the winter at Fort Clatsop, the captains had worked out a plan that enabled them to explore more land (in today's Montana) on the return trip. They would split into two main groups, Captain Meriwether Lewis's to seek the mysterious Marias River's headwaters and Captain William Clark's to map the Yellowstone River.

Captain Meriwether Lewis, with nine men, would return to the Great Falls of the Missouri River via the shortcut the Mandans and the Salish had described: up the Blackfoot River, over the Continental Divide, and down the "Medicine," or Sun, River to its mouth on the Missouri. Most of Lewis's men would wait there for a part of Clark's group, who meanwhile would retrieve cached canoes and paddle down the Missouri. Once joined with Lewis's men,

they'd portage the Great Falls, while Lewis and a few volunteers explored up the Marias.

When the captains outlined this plan, many volunteers to go with Lewis, who selected Sergeant Patrick Gass, privates William Werner, Robert Frazer, Joseph and Reubin Field, and interpreter George Drouillard. Going along to camp on the Missouri at the Great Falls and await the Missouri River party were privates John B. Thompson, Silas Goodrich, and Hugh McNeal.

Clark's larger group would return to Camp Fortunate, then take canoes and horses down the Beaverhead River to the Three Forks of the Missouri. From there, Sergeant John Ordway would lead nine men down the Missouri to meet Lewis's men at the Great Falls. Meanwhile, Clark would take the remaining ten people, including his servant York and the

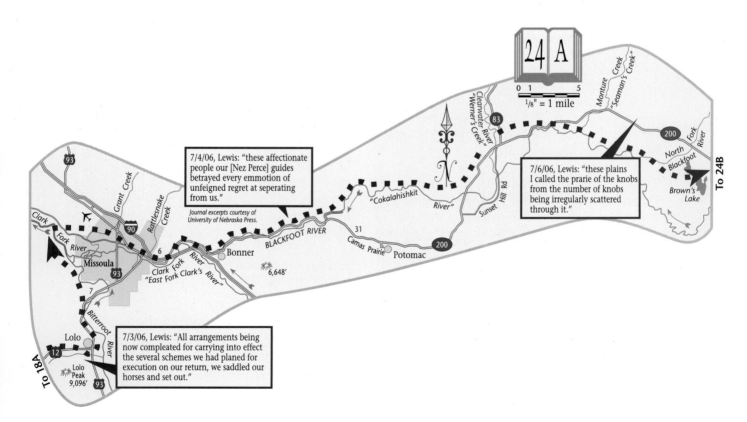

7/4/06, Lewis: "these affectionate people our [Nez Perce] guides betrayed every emmotion of unfeigned regret at seperating from us."

Journal excerpts courtesy of University of Nebraska Press.

7/6/06, Lewis: "these plains I called the prarie of the knobs from the number of knobs being irregularly scattered through it."

7/3/06, Lewis: "All arrangements being now compleated for carrying into effect the several schemes we had planed for execution on our return, we saddled our horses and set out."

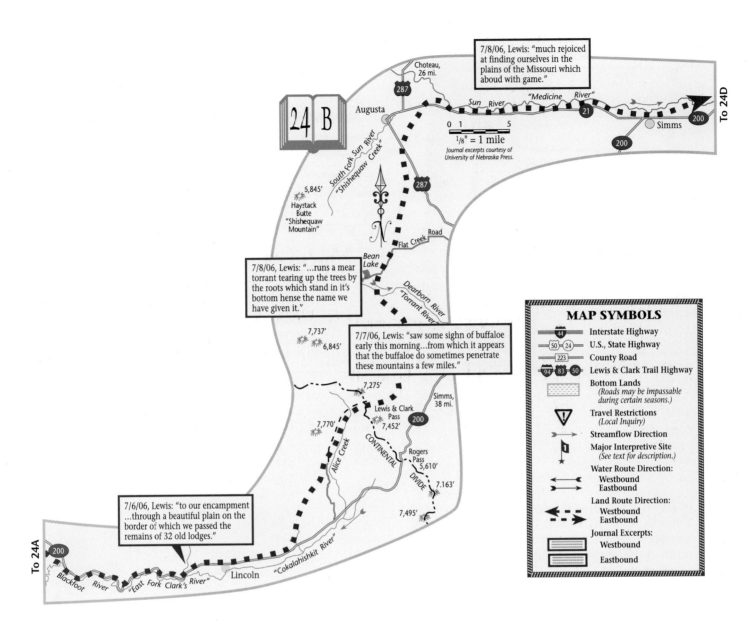

7/8/06, Lewis: "much rejoiced at finding ourselves in the plains of the Missouri which aboud with game."

Choteau, 26 mi.

287

Augusta

Sun River "Medicine River"

21

Simms

200

200

To 24D

24 B

0 1 5
1/8" = 1 mile
Journal excerpts courtesy of University of Nebraska Press.

South Fork Sun River "Shishequaw Creek"

5,845'
Haystack Butte "Shishequaw Mountain"

287

Flat Creek Road

Bean Lake

7/8/06, Lewis: "...runs a mear torrant tearing up the trees by the roots which stand in it's bottom hense the name we have given it."

Dearborn River "Torrant River"

7,737'
6,845'

7/7/06, Lewis: "saw some sighn of buffaloe early this morning...from which it appears that the buffaloe do sometimes penetrate these mountains a few miles."

7,275'

Lewis & Clark Pass
7,452'

Simms, 38 mi.

200

7,770'

Alice Creek

CONTINENTAL DIVIDE

Rogers Pass 5,610'

7.163'

7,495'

7/6/06, Lewis: "to our encampment ...through a beautiful plain on the border of which we passed the remains of 32 old lodges."

To 24A

200

Blackfoot River "East Fork Clark's River"

Lincoln

"Cokalahishkit River"

MAP SYMBOLS

44 — Interstate Highway
50 24 — U.S., State Highway
223 — County Road
94 83 50 — Lewis & Clark Trail Highway

Bottom Lands
(Roads may be impassable during certain seasons.)

Travel Restrictions
(Local Inquiry)

Streamflow Direction

Major Interpretive Site
(See text for description.)

Water Route Direction:
Westbound
Eastbound

Land Route Direction:
Westbound
Eastbound

Journal Excerpts:
Westbound
Eastbound

Charbonneau family, overland to the Yellowstone River, then explore downstream to its mouth on the Missouri.

The whole Corps was to reunite at the mouth of the Yellowstone.

The captains had two serious reasons for spreading out and seeing more country on the way back. One was to establish a geographical reference point for the northern boundary of the Louisiana Territory. According to the treaty, that was 49° 37', or roughly 45 miles north of the U.S.-Canada boundary west of the Great Lakes. But no one had yet surveyed that line on the ground. Secondly, Lewis hoped to find a workable trade route up a northern tributary of the Missouri so the United States could compete with the British in the Canadian fur trade.

With 17 horses, and the Nez Perce guides, Lewis's party left Travelers' Rest on July 3.

Lewis wrote, "I took leave of my worthy friend and companion Capt. Clark and the party that accompanyed him. I could not avoid feeling much concern on this occasion although I hoped this seperation was only momentary."

It would last nearly six weeks and almost cost Lewis and some of his volunteers their lives.

The five Nez Perce who had guided the Corps back over the Bitterroot Mountains left the Corps on July 4. But first they pointed the way—across the site of today's Missoula, Montana, and up the Clark Fork and Blackfoot rivers. From the Blackfoot River, they promised a well beaten path overland to the Sun River, whose mouth the Corps had passed last year west of the Great Falls.

Lewis didn't mention the nation's birthday in his journal entries for this July 4. Three days later, his party crossed the Continental Divide

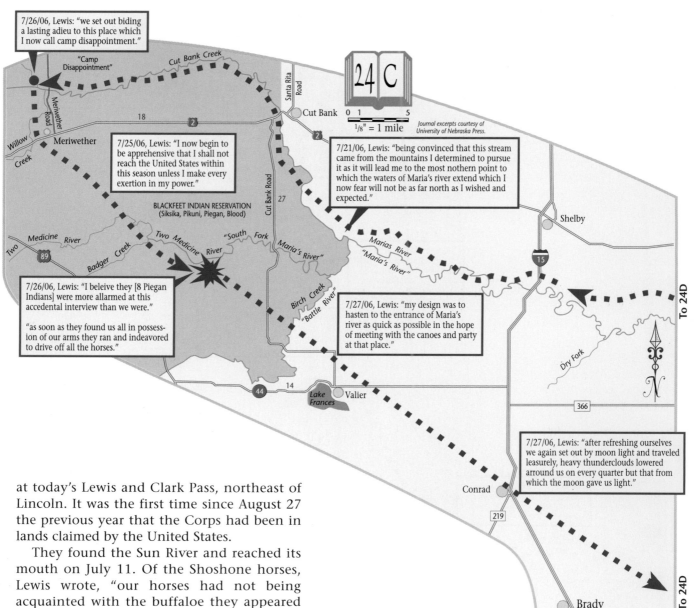

7/26/06, Lewis: "we set out biding a lasting adieu to this place which I now call camp disappointment."

"Camp Disappointment"

Cut Bank Creek

Santa Rita Road

24 C

0   1   5

1/8" = 1 mile

Journal excerpts courtesy of University of Nebraska Press.

Cut Bank

18

Meriwether Road

Willow Creek

Meriwether

7/25/06, Lewis: "I now begin to be apprehensive that I shall not reach the United States within this season unless I make every exertion in my power."

Cut Bank Road

27

7/21/06, Lewis: "being convinced that this stream came from the mountains I determined to pursue it as it will lead me to the most nothern point to which the waters of Maria's river extend which I now fear will not be as far north as I wished and expected."

Shelby

BLACKFEET INDIAN RESERVATION
(Siksika, Pikuni, Piegan, Blood)

Medicine River

Two

Badger Creek

Two Medicine River

"South Fork Maria's River"

Marias River
"Maria's River"

15

7/26/06, Lewis: "I beleive they [8 Piegan Indians] were more allarmed at this accedental interview than we were."

"as soon as they found us all in possession of our arms they ran and indeavored to drive off all the horses."

Birch Creek
"Battle River"

7/27/06, Lewis: "my design was to hasten to the entrance of Maria's river as quick as possible in the hope of meeting with the canoes and party at that place."

To 24D

Dry Fork

N

44   14

Lake Frances   Valier

366

7/27/06, Lewis: "after refreshing ourselves we again set out by moon light and traveled leasurely, heavy thunderclouds lowered arround us on every quarter but that from which the moon gave us light."

Conrad

219

To 24D

Brady

Dutton

15

at today's Lewis and Clark Pass, northeast of Lincoln. It was the first time since August 27 the previous year that the Corps had been in lands claimed by the United States.

They found the Sun River and reached its mouth on July 11. Of the Shoshone horses, Lewis wrote, "our horses had not being acquainted with the buffaloe they appeared much allarmed at their appearance and bellowing." West of today's city of Great Falls on the 11th, Lewis saw "10 thousand buffaloe within a circle of 2 miles."

Opening the cache at the White Bear Islands on July 13 was disappointing. High ground water had flooded it, ruining bearskins and "all my specimens of plants." At least the carriage wheels, dug up the next day, were in good shape. And the men were happy to be eating bison again, a great improvement to the mush of roots and fish.

Seven of the seventeen horses were missing. Drouillard went after them on July 12 and didn't return until the 15th. By then Lewis had been ready to abandon the Marias route and search for the interpreter's dead body. "I felt so perfectly satisfyed that he had returned in safety that I thought but little of the horses."

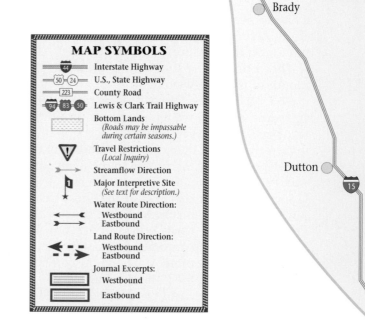

MAP SYMBOLS

44	Interstate Highway
50 24	U.S., State Highway
223	County Road
94 83 50	Lewis & Clark Trail Highway
	Bottom Lands *(Roads may be impassable during certain seasons.)*
∇!	**Travel Restrictions** *(Local Inquiry)*
	Streamflow Direction
	Major Interpretive Site *(See text for description.)*
	Water Route Direction: Westbound / Eastbound
	Land Route Direction: Westbound / Eastbound
	Journal Excerpts: Westbound / Eastbound

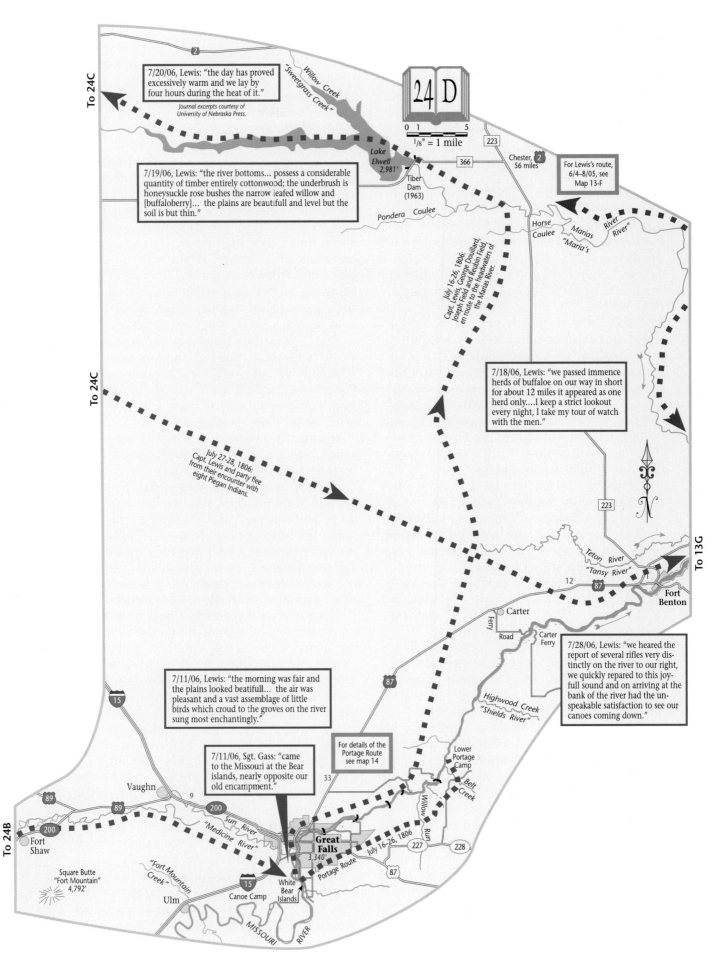

To 24C

7/20/06, Lewis: "the day has proved excessively warm and we lay by four hours during the heat of it."

Journal excerpts courtesy of University of Nebraska Press.

Willow Creek

"Sweetgrass Creek"

2

223

0   1   5
⅛" = 1 mile

Chester, 56 miles

2

For Lewis's route, 6/4–8/05, see Map 13-F

7/19/06, Lewis: "the river bottoms… possess a considerable quantity of timber entirely cottonwood; the underbrush is honeysuckle rose bushes the narrow leafed willow and [buffaloberry]… the plains are beautifull and level but the soil is but thin."

Lake Elwell 2,981'

Tiber Dam (1963)

366

Pondera Coulee

Horse Coulee

Marias River

"Maria's River"

Capt. Lewis, George Drouillard, Joseph Field and Reubin Field, en route to the headwaters of the Marias River.
July 16-26, 1806:

To 24C

July 27-28, 1806: Capt. Lewis and party flee from their encounter with eight Piegan Indians.

7/18/06, Lewis: "we passed immence herds of buffaloe on our way in short for about 12 miles it appeared as one herd only….I keep a strict lookout every night, I take my tour of watch with the men."

223

N

12

Teton River "Tansy River"

87

To 13G

Fort Benton

Carter

Ferry Road

Carter Ferry

7/28/06, Lewis: "we heard the report of several rifles very distinctly on the river to our right, we quickly repared to this joyfull sound and on arriving at the bank of the river had the unspeakable satisfaction to see our canoes coming down."

7/11/06, Lewis: "the morning was fair and the plains looked beatifull… the air was pleasant and a vast assemblage of little birds which croud to the groves on the river sung most enchantingly."

15

87

Highwood Creek "Shields River"

For details of the Portage Route see map 14

7/11/06, Sgt. Gass: "came to the Missouri at the Bear islands, nearly opposite our old encampment."

Vaughn

89

89

200

9

Sun River "Medicine River"

Lower Portage Camp

Belt Creek

33

Willow Run

227

228

To 24B

200

Fort Shaw

Square Butte "Fort Mountain" 4,792'

"Fort Mountain Creek"

Ulm

Great Falls 3,340'

July 16-26, 1806

Portage Route

87

15

White Bear Islands

Canoe Camp

MISSOURI RIVER

Lewis decided now to take only the Field brothers and Drouillard up the Marias, with six horses. They set out July 16 and camped on the north side of the Missouri at the Great Falls. Lewis drew sketches of the falls, which unfortunately have been lost.

On the 19th, the men began moving up the Marias River, fearful of "the blackfoot indians...vicious lawless and reather...abandoned," as the Shoshones (enemies of the Blackfeet) had told Lewis. "I keep a strict lookout every night, I take my tour of watch with the men."

When they came to the "north branch" of the Marias (today's Cut Bank Creek) on July 21, they followed it for a day. Lewis feared it wouldn't go as far north as hoped—50° latitude—and soon concluded he was right. On the 22nd they "encamped resolving to rest ourselves and horses a couple of days...and take the necessary observations." Cloudy weather prevented Lewis from determining the camp's latitude, so on the 26th they packed up and headed downstream toward the Missouri River, "biding a lasting adieu to this place which I now call camp disappointment."

His party crossed overland to the other branch of the Marias River, today's Two Medicine River flowing from Glacier National Park. Sending Drouillard downstream hunting, Lewis and the Field brothers followed overland. Cresting a hill, Lewis saw thirty horses a mile away—half of them saddled—their riders evidently watching Drouillard. "I halted and used my spye glass...discovered several indians...this was a very unpleasant sight."

They were in the territory of the Blackfeet, on land that was to become the Blackfeet Indian Reservation. And Drouillard, unaware, was alone.

Lewis decided a friendly approach was best, and advanced slowly toward the Indians, who probably were Piegan Blackfeet. From a quarter mile, one Piegan rode full speed at Lewis, who coolly dismounted his horse and beckoned for the man to approach. At "a hundred paces," the Piegan halted, looked over Lewis and his two companions, and galloped back to his own. At this range, Lewis saw only eight Piegans among the 15 saddled horses, but thought more warriors might be hiding.

The two groups drew closer, and finally the Piegan came forward and shook hands with Lewis and the Field brothers. They sat down and the Piegan asked in sign language to smoke. Lewis said Drouillard had his pipe, so a Piegan and Reubin Field went to fetch the hunter. Lewis presented the three men who claimed to be chiefs with a medal, a flag, and a handkerchief.

The Piegans agreed when Lewis suggested they camp together. During the evening, Lewis said he had been looking for these people to ask them to make peace with their neighbors and to trade with the Americans and stop going north to British posts. He said that he had made peace among all the tribes met, and asked these men to go back to their people and bring their chiefs and warriors to a council at the mouth of the Marias, where more of his men waited.

The Piegans didn't reply. What they understood Lewis to say was that the Americans had consolidated the Blackfeet's enemies—the Shoshones, the Nez Perce, and the Salish—and now would be supplying them with guns and other goods. This was bad news.

During the night, Lewis warily took first watch and Ruebin Field the next, but the night passed uneventfully.

At dawn, though, the Piegan given a medal grabbed Joseph Field's rifle that he "had carelessly laid...down," and grabbed a rifle from under the head of the still-sleeping Reubin. At the same moment, two others took Drouillard's and Lewis's guns. Joseph and Reubin ran after the medal-wearing Piegan and retrieved their rifles; Reubin stabbed the man to death.

Lewis was awakened by Drouillard's swearing at the Piegan who took his rifle. Finding his own stolen, Lewis drew his pistol and chased the man carrying it away. The man dropped Lewis's rifle, and Lewis refused to allow the Field brothers and Drouillard to shoot him.

Now the Piegans tried to drive off the horses, another way of defeating enemies in this inhospitable terrain. Lewis hollered for help and pursued two Piegans taking the remaining horses. He shot one "through the belly." The man raised himself up and fired at Lewis, who felt "the wind of his bullet very distinctly" pass his head. Whether that warrior survived is unknown.

Lewis didn't have his shot pouch, so couldn't reload. He returned to the campsite. The Field brothers returned with four of their own horses. Lewis burned Piegan shields and bows and arrows, and took four Piegan horses, plus some bison meat from the Indians' baggage.

"I also retook the flagg but left the medal about the neck of the dead man that they might be informed who we were."

Galloping away, they feared that more Piegans soon would follow. Lewis estimated they traveled sixty-three miles before resting for an hour and a half at 3:00 p.m. They went seventeen more miles, rested for two hours, and killed a bison to eat. They rode about twenty more miles by moonlight, finally stopping at 2:00 a.m., "very much fatiegued as may be readily conceived." They slept on the plains somewhere west of today's Fort Benton.

When Lewis awakened them at dawn, all the men—himself included—were so sore they could scarcely stand, but resumed their march to the Missouri. They hoped to intercept the river party before it encamped at the mouth of the Marias, since Lewis had told the Piegans about them.

Amazingly, Lewis's group reached the Missouri just as Sergeant John Ordway's canoe party arrived from the Lower Portage Camp, hastily unloaded and released the horses, and leaped into the canoes.

They descended the Missouri at a good pace, and without more trouble. On August 7 at 4 p.m. they reached the mouth of the Yellowstone, only to find a remnant of a note from Clark that game was scarce and mosquitoes troublesome, so he had gone downriver. Privates John Colter and John Collins were hunting behind Clark's party; in case they were also behind him, Lewis left them a note and went on.

Passing into today's North Dakota, they still hadn't met Clark. Lewis decided to slow the pace, "proceed as tho' he was not before me and leave the rest to the chapter of accedents." They camped southwest of Williston, on August 8, to dress skins and make clothing since the men's was wearing out "and most of them are therefore extreemly bare."

No Captain Clark, no pitch to caulk the canoes, "nor was there a buffaloe to be seen...as far as the eye could reach." They proceeded downriver.

In the vicinity of Lewis and Clark State Park, just after noon on August 11, Lewis saw a herd of elk on a sandbar where willows grew. (Today the site is covered by Lake Sakakawea.) He and Private Pierre Cruzatte each shot an elk and reloaded their guns before separating to hunt through the willows.

As Lewis aimed again, a bullet passed through his left thigh and grazed his right thigh. He instantly thought Cruzatte, who "cannot see very well," had mistaken him in his brown leather garb for an elk. Cruzatte, who had lost an eye before the expedition, would have had trouble with depth perception. But when Lewis shouted to Cruzatte, there was no answer, and he feared an Indian attack. Lewis called the men to arms and ordered them to save Cruzatte, saying he himself was "wounded but I hoped not mortally."

Lewis "returned about a hundred paces" to the boat, by then in such pain he could barely board it. He armed himself with pistol, rifle and air-gun, planning "to sell my life as deerly as possible. in this state of anxiety and suspense remained about twenty minutes when the party returned with Cruzatte and reported that there were no indians."

Lewis thought Cruzatte knew he had shot him and was pretending innocence, but both Ordway and Gass believed Cruzatte's protests.

With Gass's help Lewis took off his clothing, and then dressed his own wounds, he wrote, sending the men to butcher the elk. Lewis spent a feverish night on board the pirogue because it was too painful to move ashore. Writing in his journal the next day, he worried mainly about whether the Corps still had time to send trader Hugh Heney to the Sioux chiefs (see Chapter 25).

On August 12, Lewis's party met two trappers from Illinois, heading upriver. Lewis shared his knowledge of major landmarks and beaver sites. Now Colter and Collins arrived, saying they thought they were ahead of Lewis's group and had waited several days for them before deciding to push on.

Lewis noted that now his wounds made him stiff and sore "but gave me no considerable pain." At 1:00 p.m., his party overtook Clark's.

Lewis stated that, "as wrighting in my present situation is extreemly painfull to me I shall desist untill I recover and leave to my frind Cpt. C. the continuation of our journal." But first, "however I must notice a singular Cherry, which is found on the Missouri." Lewis's thorough, and lengthy, botanical description of it is the last journal entry we have from him.

TOURING TODAY

᠀ LEWIS'S RETURN VIA THE MARIAS ᠀

[ ] Bracketed numbers key sites to maps
★ L&C in-depth interpretation, unchanged landform
● L&C interpreted site

  ♿ Special-needs accessible ⚐ Bed & breakfast
  ⊗ Restaurant   Ⓐ Camping, RV park
  ⊞ Motel, hotel, cabin

ALONG THE EXPEDITION'S PATH

July 18, 1806
Lake Elwell (Chester, MT)—Ⓐ Undesignated primitive campsites above and below the dam; free; **no** water; open all year; 14-day limit. Boat ramp; fishing. 12 miles S on MT 223, 7 miles W on county road.

July 20, 1806
Williamson Memorial Park (Shelby, MT)—Swimming; playground; fishing; dump station. Ⓐ 25 sites; fee; water; modern; open June-Sept; grills/fire rings; tables; 14-day limit. I-15 exit 358, 7 miles S on frontage rd. 406/434-5222.

July 22, 1806
● **Camp Disappointment** (Browning, MT)—The northernmost point reached by Captain Lewis is on private land. To the southeast (about 8 miles) is the Two Medicine Fight Site. Interpretive signs. 13 miles E on US 2 (mile marker 233).

AROUND THE AREA

TOWNS LISTED ALPHABETICALLY

Augusta, Montana
Ⓐ **Benchmark**—25 sites; fee; water; primitive; open June-Nov; grills/fire rings; tables; 14-day limit. Nature trails; fishing. 14 miles SW on Co 235, 15.5 miles SW on FR 235. 406/466-5341.
Ⓐ **Home Gulch**—15 sites; fee; water; primitive; open May-Nov; grills/fire rings; tables; 14-day limit. Swimming; boat ramp; nature trails; fishing. 20 miles NW on Co 1081, 2 miles W on FR 1082. 406/466-5341.
Ⓐ **Mortimer Gulch**—28 sites; fee; **no** water; primitive; open May-Nov; grills/fire rings; tables; 14-day limit. Trailhead into Bob Marshall Wilderness Area. Swimming; boating; fishing; groceries. 20 miles NW on Co 1081, 4 miles W on FR 1082, 3 miles N on FR 8984. 406/466-5341.
Ⓐ **Wagons West**—75 sites (50 w/hookups); fee; water; modern; showers; open Mar-Oct; grills/fire rings; tables. ⊞ Motel; ⊗ restaurant. US 287 in town. 406/562-3295.

Babb, Montana
Ⓐ **Chewing Blackbones Campground**—100 sites (60 w/hookups); fee; water; modern; showers; open May-Sept; grills/fire rings; tables. Boat ramp; playground; coin laundry; fishing; dump station. 6 miles N of St. Mary entrance on US 89. 406/732-5577.

Browning, Montana
Blackfeet Historic Site & Tipi Village Tours—Explore the Blackfeet Indian Reservation with a Blackfeet guide. Advance booking required. 800/215-2395.
Museum of the Plains Indian—Artwork, dioramas and exhibits on history and culture of the Blackfeet. 5-screen multimedia presentation. Daily 9 to 5 (June-Sept), Mon-Fri 10 to 4:30 (rest of year); admission fee. US 2 & US 89. 406/338-2230.
⊗ **Old Nine Mile Inn**—Native American menu. Smoke-free. B L & D daily. 10 miles W on US 89. 406/338-7911. $$

Chester, Montana
Liberty County Museum—History of homesteading on the Hi-Line. Daily 2 to 5, 7 to 9 (Memorial Day-Labor Day); donations. 210 2nd St E. 406/759-5256.

Choteau, Montana
Egg Mountain—Free tours of the site where nests of baby dinosaurs were discovered. A Dinosaur School for amateur paleontologists is held each summer. Daily (Jul-Aug); free. US 287 S to Triangle Meat Packing Plant (follow signs), go right at the fork. 406/994-5257.
Freezeout Lake Wildlife Management Area—During migrations, this 11,350-acre wetland is home to the state's largest concentration of waterfowl. Ⓐ Primitive camping. Daily sunrise to sunset; free. 10 miles S on US 89. 406/467-2646.
Teton Trail Village and Old Trail Museum—History of pioneers, gold rush days and dinosaur discoveries at Egg Mountain. Daily 9 to 6 (Memorial Day-Labor Day), Tue-Sat 10 to 3 (rest of year); admission fee. US 89 & US 287. 406/466-5332.
Ⓐ **Cave Mountain**—14 sites; fee; water; primitive; open Memorial Day-Nov; grills/fire rings; tables. Hiking trails; fishing; trailhead to Bob Marshall Wilderness. 5 miles NW on US 89, 22 miles W on Teton Canyon Rd. 406/466-5341.
Ⓐ **Choteau City Park**—25 sites; free; water; modern; open May-Sept; grills/fire rings; tables. Swimming; tennis; groceries; boating; fishing; golf course. Main St. 406/466-2510.
Ⓐ **KOA-Choteau**—85 sites (55 w/hookups); fee; water; modern; showers; open May-Sept; grills/fire rings; tables; firewood. Playground; mini golf; groceries; ⊞ cabins. 2 mile E of US 89 on MT 221. 406/466-2615, 800/562-4156.
⊞ **Best Western Stage Stop Inn**—43 rooms, pool, hot tub, coin laun-

dry. 1005 Main. 406/466-5900. $

⌐ Country Lane Bed & Breakfast—4 rooms in game reserve, full breakfast, indoor pool, TV. Open May-Sept, smoke-free. 406/466-2816. $$ K6

Conrad, Montana

⊞ Super 8 Townhouse Inns—49 rooms, pets, coin laundry. I-15 exit 339. 406/278-7676. $$ K12

Cut Bank, Montana

Glacier County Historical Museum—Exhibits on area Blackfeet and white settlers history, including homestead-era railroads, oil production, farming, town life, school. Tue-Sat 1 to 5; weekends by appointment. Donation suggested. E on US 2, follow signs. 406/873-4904.

▲ Riverview Campground—▲ 36 sites (27 w/hookups); fee; water; modern; showers; open May-Sept; grills/fire rings; tables. Hot tub; fishing; groceries; coin laundry. End of 4th Ave. SW. 406/873-4151.

⊞ Glacier Gateway Inn—18 rooms, pets, continental breakfast. US 2. 406/873-5544. $$ K7

⊞ Northern Motor Inn—61 rooms, pool, hot tub. 609 W. Main. 406/873-5662. $$

East Glacier Park, Montana

▲ Summit Campground—17 sites; fee; water; primitive; open June-Labor Day; grills/fire rings; tables; 14-day limit. Nature trails; fishing. 13 miles SW on US 2. 406/466-5431.

⊞ Dancing Bears Inn—14 rooms, cabins and house, pets. Off-season rates. 147 Montana. 406/226-4402. $$

⊞ Jacobson's Scenic View Cottages—12 rooms, pets. Reasonable 2-bedroom unit, kitchen. Open May-Sept, off-season rates. 0.75 mile N on MT 49. 406/226-4422. $$ K6

⊞ Mountain Pine Motel—27 rooms, multi-room units and homes. Off-season rates. 0.5 mile N on MT 49. 406/226-4403. $$

⊗ Glacier Village Restaurant—Generous home-cooked portions in cafeteria setting, kids' menu. B L & D daily. Closed Oct-Apr. US 2 and MT 49. 406/226-4464. $

⊗ The Restaurant Thimble-berry—Hearty American and Native American food in a log building; kids' menu. B L & D daily. Closed Labor Day-Mother's Day. US 2 and MT 49. 406/226-5523. $

Glacier National Park

A million acres of sculpted peaks and lakes created during the ice age. Hundreds of wildflower and bird species along with most large mammals native to North America. Going-to-the-Sun Road is one of the most scenic drives in the world. With 52 miles of magnificent views, it is open from about mid-June to October (weather permitting). Along the road, Avalanche Creek is a gorge with several waterfalls, a 2-mile hiking trail and a boardwalk nature trail. 700 miles of hiking and equestrian trails create enormous variety for day trips and longer. Bus and boat tours, trail rides and rafting trips available. Open year-round; however, many roads are closed in the winter. Park is bounded by US 89, US 12 and the Canadian border with main entrances at West Glacier and St. Mary.

▲ Apgar—196 sites (39 w/hookups); fee; water; modern; open May-Oct; grills/fire rings; tables; 35' trailer limit; 7-day limit. Dump station; groceries; boating. 1 mile NW of West Glacier on Going-to-the-Sun Rd. 406/888-7800.

▲ Avalanche—87 sites; fee; water; modern; open June-Aug; grills/fire rings; tables; 26' trailer limit; 7-day limit. Dump station. 14 miles NE of West Glacier on Going-to-the-Sun Rd. 406/888-7800.

▲ Bowman Lake—48 sites; fee; water; primitive; open May-Sept; grills/fire rings; tables; 22' trailer limit; 7-day limit. Dump station, boat ramp. 32 miles NW of West Glacier on North Fork Rd., 6 miles on dirt road. 406/888-7800.

▲ Fish Creek—180 sites; fee; water; modern; open June-Aug; grills/fire rings; tables; 26' trailer limit; 7-day limit. Swimming; boating; dump station. 4 miles NW of West Glacier on Camas Creek Rd. 406/888-7800.

▲ Kintla Lake—13 sites; fee; water; primitive; open May-Sept; grills/fire rings; tables; 18' trailer limit; 7-day limit. Boat ramp. 47 miles N of West Glacier on North Fork Rd. 406/888-7800.

▲ Many Glacier—112 sites; fee; water; modern; showers; open June-Sept; grills/fire rings; tables; 35' trailer limit; 7-day limit. Swimming; horseback riding; boating; dump station; groceries. 13 miles W of Babb on Many Glacier Rd. 406/888-7800.

▲ Rising Sun—83 sites; fee; water; modern; showers; open June-Sept; grills/fire rings; tables; 7-day limit. Swimming; groceries; dump station. 6 miles SW of St. Mary on Going-to-the-Sun Rd. 406/888-7800.

▲ St. Mary—156 sites; fee; water; modern; showers; open June-Sept; grills/fire rings; tables; 7-day limit. Dump station. US 2, east entrance. 406/888-7800.

▲ Sprague Creek—25 sites; fee; water; modern; open June-Sept; grills/fire rings; tables; no towed units; 7-day limit. Swimming. 10 miles NW of West Glacier on Going-to-the-Sun Rd. 406/888-7800.

▲ Two Medicine—99 sites; fee; water; modern; open June-Labor Day; grills/fire rings; tables; 26' trailer limit; 7-day limit. Swimming; boating; groceries; dump station. 11.5 miles N of East Glacier Park on MT 49 & Two Medicine Rd. 406/888-7800.

⊞ Apgar Village Lodge—48 rooms, cabins and cottages overlooking Lake McDonald, beach, bike rentals, nature trails. Closed Oct-May. 2 miles NW of US 2 on Going-to-the Sun Rd. 406/888-5484. $$$ K12

⊞ Izaak Walton Inn—33 rooms, caboose efficiencies in historic inn built in 1939 to house workers on the Great Northern Railroad, ⊗ restaurant, coin laundry, bike rentals. Amtrak stop. US 2. 406/888-5700. In Essex. $$$ K2

⊞ Glacier Park Lodge—161 rooms, pool, bike rentals, horse rentals, social director, interpretive programs. Wide range of accommodations. Amtrak station. Closed Sept-May. US 2 and MT 49. 602/207-6000. $$$+ K12

⊞ Lake McDonald Lodge—100 rooms, beach, ⊗ restaurant,

boat cruises, horse rentals, bike rentals, interpretive programs. Wide range of accommodations. Closed Sept-May. Going-to-the Sun Rd. 602/207-6000. $$$ K12

▥ **Many Glacier Hotel**—208 rooms, beach, ⊗ restaurant, bus tours, boat cruises, interpretive programs. Wide range of accommodations. Closed Sept-May. Swiftcurrent Lake. 602/207-6000. $$$+ K12

Lincoln, Montana

▲ **Aspen Grove**—20 sites; fee; water; primitive; open Memorial Day-Oct; grills/fire rings; tables; 50' trailer limit; 14-day limit. Fishing. 7 miles E on MT 200, SE on FR 1040. 406/362-4265.

▲ **Copper Creek**—20 sites; fee; water; primitive; open Memorial Day-Oct; grills/fire rings; tables; 50' trailer limit; 14-day limit. Fishing; trailhead to Scapegoat Wilderness. 6.5 miles E on MT 200, 8.5 miles NW on FR 330. 406/362-4265.

St. Mary, Montana

▲ **Johnson's**—115 sites (65 w/hookups); fee; water; modern; showers; open Apr-Oct; grills/fire rings; tables. Coin laundry; groceries; mini golf; ⊗ restaurant. N on the hill. 406/732-5565.

▲ **St. Mary-Glacier Park KOA**—219 sites (117 w/hookups); fee; water; modern; showers; open May-Sept; grills/fire rings; tables. Playground; coin laundry; horseback riding; dump station. 1 mile W of US 89 at north edge of town. 406/732-4122.

Seeley Lake, Montana

Seeley Lake Chamber of Commerce, P.O. Box 516. 406/677-2880.

Clearwater Canoe Trail—4-mile float on Clearwater River. Common loons and great blue heron. 4 miles N on MT 83. Sign on W side for put-in point. 1.5 mile hike back from take-out point. 406/677-2233.

Placid Lake State Park—Forested, peaceful site on the lake. Fishing is excellent; boat ramp and docks. Separate day use swimming and picnic area. Interpretive panels about the area's logging history. ▲ 40 sites; fee; water; modern/primitive; open May-Nov/full oper-

ation May-Sept; grills/fire rings; tables. 3 miles S on MT 83, 3 miles W on North Placid Lake Rd, left at fork onto South Placid Lake Rd. 406/542-5500.

Salmon Lake State Park—Heavily forested, quiet park. Day use picnic and swimming areas, fishing access, boat docks/ramp. Several trails follow the river's edge and lead from the campground to the day use areas. ▲ 25 sites; fee; water; modern/primitive; open May-Nov/full operation May-Sept; grills/fire rings; tables; 25' trailer limit. 5 miles S on MT 83. 406/542-5500.

▲ **Big Larch**—50 sites/♿; fee; water; primitive; open all year; grills/fire rings; tables; 32' trailer limit. Fishing; hiking; swimming; boat ramp. 1 mile N on MT 83. 406/677-2233.

▲ **Holland Lake**—41 sites; fee; water; primitive; Memorial Day to Labor Day; grills/fire rings; tables; 22' trailer limit. Fishing; hiking; swimming; boat ramp. 9 miles SE of Condon on MT 83, 3 miles E on Holland Lake Rd. 406/837-5081.

▲ **Lake Alva**—41 sites; 2 small group sites; fee; water; primitive; grills/fire rings; tables; 22' trailer limit. Fishing; swimming; trail/♿ to beach. 12 miles N on MT 83. 406/677-2233.

▲ **River Point**—26 sites; fee; water; primitive; open Jul-Labor Day; grills/fire rings; tables; 22' trailer limit. Fishing; swimming; canoeing. 3 miles NW on MT 83. 406/677-2233.

▲ **Seeley Lake**—29 sites; fee; water; modern; open Memorial Day-Labor Day; grills/fire rings; tables; 32' trailer limit. Fishing; swimming; boat ramp. 4 miles NW on MT 83. 406/677-2233.

▲ **Wapiti Resort**—10 sites (all w/hookups); fee; water; modern; open all year; grills/fire rings; tables. Swimming; boating; fishing; ⊗ restaurant; coin laundry; groceries. 1 mile N on MT 83. 406/677-2775.

▥ **Wilderness Gateway Inn**—19 rooms, pets, hot tub. 0.5 mile S on MT 83. 406/677-2095. $$ K6

⚑ **The Emily A**—5 rooms in log home on Clearwater River, pets, full breakfast, fishing, smoke-free. 406/677-3474. $$$+ K2

Shelby, Montana

Shelby Chamber of Commerce, 100 2nd Ave. S. 406/434-7184.

Marias Museum of History and Art—Exhibits on the oil industry, homesteading, the 1923 Dempsey-Gibbons prize fight here, dinosaurs and fossils. Mon-Fri 10 to 5 and 7 to 9 (Memorial Day-Labor Day), Tue 1 to 5 (rest of year); free. 206 12th Ave. 406/434-2551.

▲ **Lake Shel-oole Park**—37 sites (27 w/hookups); fee; water; modern; open May-Sept; grills/fire rings; tables; 7-day limit. Fishing; dump station. I-15 exit 364. 406/434-5564.

▥ **Comfort Inn**—72 rooms, pool, pets, continental breakfast, hot tub. Off-season rates. I-15 exit 363. 406/434-2212. $$ K18

▥ **Crossroads Inn**—52 rooms, indoor pool, pets, continental breakfast, hot tub, coin laundry. US 2. 406/434-5134. $$ K15

West Glacier, Montana

▲ **Devil Creek**—14 sites; fee; water; primitive; open June-Sept; grills/fire rings; tables; 30' trailer limit; 14-day limit. Nature trails; fishing. 45 miles SE on US 2. 406/387-5243.

▲ **Glacier Campground**—175 sites (156 w/hookups); fee; water; modern; showers; open May-Oct; grills/fire rings; tables. Playground; ▥ cabins; groceries; coin laundry; dump station. 1 mile W on US 2. 406/387-5689.

▲ **West Glacier KOA**—153 sites (all w/hookups); fee; water; modern; showers; open May-Sept; grills/fire rings; tables. ▥ Cabins; ⊗ restaurant; playground; groceries; coin laundry; dump station. 2.5 miles W on US 2, follow signs. 406/387-5341.

▥ **Great Northern Whitewater Resort**—5 rooms, outdoor recreation, Amtrak service, microwaves, refrigerators. Off-season rates. 406/387-5340. $$$+

▥ **Village Inn Motel**—36 rooms with views, outdoor recreation, efficiencies and family units. Open May-Sept. 2 miles on US 2 in Apgar Village. 602/207-6000. $$$ K12

⚑ **Mountain Timbers Wilderness Lodge**—7 rooms in log home, full breakfast, hot tub, hiking. 406/387-5830. $$$

CHAPTER 25

July 3 to 15, 1806

CLARK'S OVERLAND RETURN

At Travelers' Rest on July 1, the co-captains had explained the plan they had discussed for months (see Chapter 24): for part of the return, the Corps would split into two groups and thus explore more land and more river miles. Captain Meriwether Lewis would take a small group to explore the Marias River country.

Most expedition members would go overland and down the Yellowstone River with

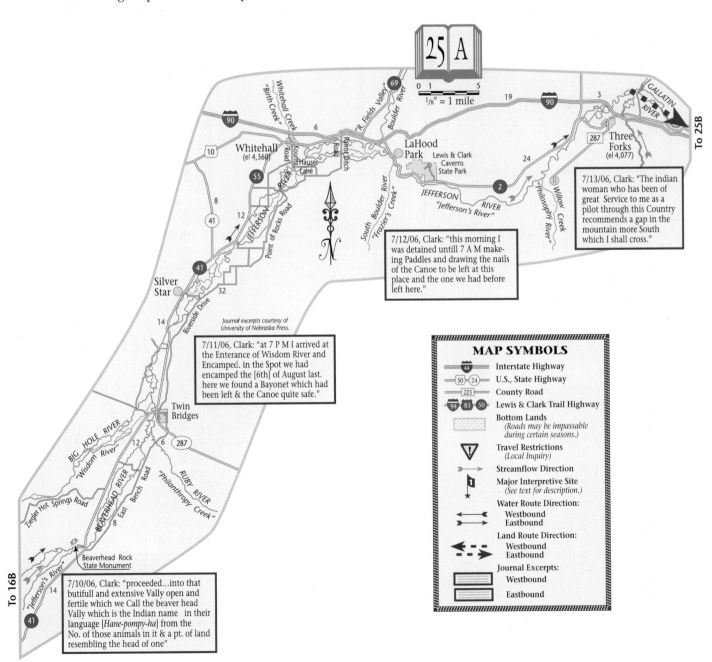

7/13/06, Clark: "The indian woman who has been of great Service to me as a pilot through this Country recommends a gap in the mountain more South which I shall cross."

7/12/06, Clark: "this morning I was detained untill 7 A M making Paddles and drawing the nails of the Canoe to be left at this place and the one we had before left here."

7/11/06, Clark: "at 7 P M I arrived at the Enterance of Wisdom River and Encamped. in the Spot we had encamped the [6th] of August last. here we found a Bayonet which had been left & the Canoe quite safe."

7/10/06, Clark: "proceeded...into that butifull and extensive Vally open and fertile which we Call the beaver head Vally which is the Indian name in their language [Hane-pompy-ha] from the No. of those animals in it & a pt. of land resembling the head of one"

Journal excerpts courtesy of University of Nebraska Press.

MAP SYMBOLS

44	Interstate Highway
50 24	U.S., State Highway
223	County Road
94 83 50	Lewis & Clark Trail Highway
	Bottom Lands *(Roads may be impassable during certain seasons.)*
	Travel Restrictions *(Local Inquiry)*
	Streamflow Direction
	Major Interpretive Site *(See text for description.)*
	Water Route Direction: Westbound Eastbound
	Land Route Direction: Westbound Eastbound
	Journal Excerpts: Westbound
	Eastbound

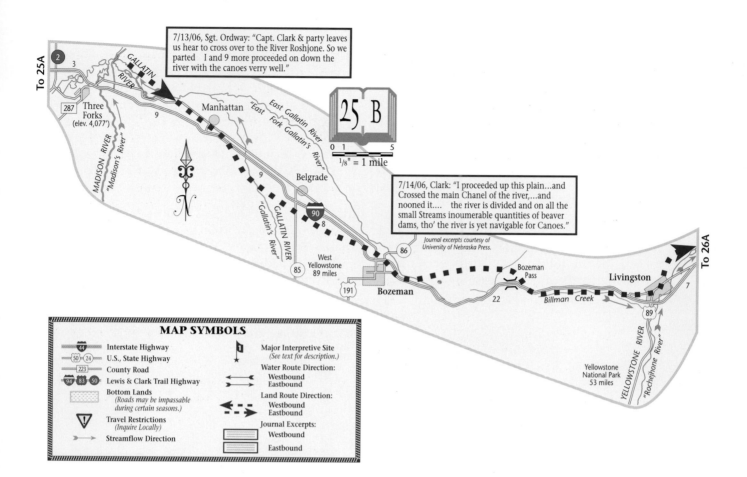

Journal excerpts courtesy of University of Nebraska Press.

Captain William Clark. But Sergeant Nathaniel Pryor and some others would break off from Clark's party to ride to the Mandan villages, then turn north to British posts on the Assiniboine River. Pryor's men would drive fifty horses to exchange for supplies with British trader Hugh Heney, met at Fort Mandan the winter before last. They also would deliver a letter asking Heney to persuade some Sioux chiefs to return with the expedition to Washington, D.C., and witness firsthand the power of the United States.

Clark's return from Travelers' Rest to Camp Fortunate is shown on maps 17B, 17A, and 16B, in that sequence.

Clark's party took off at 8:00 a.m. on July 3, heading south up the Bitterroot River and camping north of today's Hamilton, Montana. Unlike Lewis, Clark recorded honoring his country's thirtieth birthday:

This being the day of the decleration of Independence of the United States and a Day commonly Scelebrated by my Country I had every disposition to Selebrate this day and therefore halted early and partook of a Sumptious Dinner… at midday before traveling on.

They passed through Ross's Hole, where they had met the Salish people last September, and then crossed into the Big Hole on July 6, "an extensive open Leavel plain in which the Indian trail Scattered in Such a manner that we Could not pursue it." Sacagawea knew this territory from camas-gathering trips here in her childhood and, for the single time on the trip, actually guided the way—directing Clark until July 15 to today's Bozeman Pass.

The next morning the "horses were very much Scattered" and nine were missing. Clark left a small party behind under Sergeant John Ordway to hunt for them, and went on to where they had sunk their canoes last August, to raise and dry the boats. That night he ordered more care to be taken with the horses.

The animals were scattered again on the morning of July 8, but easily rounded up by 8:00 a.m. Clark's group reached the canoes at Camp Fortunate at the forks of the Beaverhead River. Clark thought the trail they followed here would make an excellent wagon road if a few trees were removed. Most of the party made a dash for the cache, to get the tobacco buried there. Clark gave each chewer two feet of it, took some for himself, and sent the rest with the canoes to Lewis.

They stayed two days at Camp Fortunate, fixing canoes. Ordway's party finally caught up, bringing the lost horses.

The night of July 9-10 was chilly, and they woke to "frost and the grass Stiff Frozend." All set off together down the Jefferson, with Ordway in charge of the canoe party and Clark of the horse party. They passed Beaverhead Rock on the 11th, and camped where they had last August 6: on the Jefferson River opposite the mouth of the Big Hole River.

The next morning, Clark wrote they were "detained untill 7 A M" making canoe paddles and salvaging precious nails from one canoe to be left behind and another stashed there last year. Despite a minor accident when Clark's canoe was driven into some trees, the day's travel was uneventful.

The 13th brought the canoeists and the horsemen together at the Three Forks of the Missouri. Following a shared midday meal, Ordway and his nine men set out down the Missouri.

After seven days canoeing downstream, Ordway's party would meet Sergeant Patrick Gass and his portion of Lewis's men, at the White Bear Islands camp upriver from the Great Falls. They completed the portage on July 26, and set off down the Missouri. Two days later, they were a welcome sight to Lewis, who had just ridden 120 miles on horseback in a little more than twenty-four hours (see Chapter 24).

Traveling across southwestern Montana, after Ordway's men had sailed off, Clark found Sacagawea "of great Service to me as a pilot through this Country." She led the men over the Bridger Range at today's Bozeman Pass on July 15. It lay on a trail she remembered from her Shoshone childhood. At 2 p.m. that same day, Clark's party came to the Yellowstone River, which Clark knew by its French name, Roche Jaune. On the Yellowstone, they soon passed and named Shields River for Private John Shields, their blacksmith and gunsmith. It's one of the few names of an expedition member that stuck.

TOURING TODAY

↭ CLARK'S OVERLAND RETURN ↭

[ ] Bracketed numbers key sites to maps	⟁ Special-needs accessible ⊨ Bed & breakfast
★ L&C in-depth interpretation, unchanged landform	⊗ Restaurant ⚠ Camping, RV park
● L&C interpreted site	⊞ Motel, hotel, cabin

Bridge across the Yellowstone River in this area is in Livingston, MT (US 89).

ALONG THE EXPEDITION'S PATH

July 6, 1806 (see Map 17A)
★ **Big Hole Battlefield National Monument/Nez Perce National Historic Park** (Wisdom, MT)—Site of major 1877 battle between the U.S. 7th Infantry and the Nez Perce. While leading his tribe in their flight from Idaho toward the Canadian border to escape conflict, Chief Joseph and the 800 sleeping Indians were attacked with many casualties among the women and children. Self-guided

trails/⟁ and interpretive center document the tragedy. Daily 8 to 8 (Memorial Day-Labor Day), 8 to 5 (rest of year); admission fee in summer only. 10 miles W on MT 43; 406/689-3155.

July 7, 1806
Bannack State Park (Dillon, MT)—Gold discovered here in 1862 sired a town that grew to 5,000 in less than 10 months and served as Montana Territory's first capital. Take the self-guided walking tour or a free mill tour. Hiking trails and fishing in Grasshopper Creek. ⚠ 30 sites; fee; water; modern/primitive; open all year/full operation May-Sept; grills/fire rings; tables. I-15 exit 59, 21 miles W on MT 278, 4 miles S on CR. 406/834-3413.

July 13, 1806
Three Forks of the Missouri (see Chapter 15)

July 14, 1806
● **Lindley Park** (Bozeman, MT)—City park with picnic areas. Daily dawn to dusk; free. In town, east off Main St. 406/585-1311.

July 15, 1806
● **Shields River Valley** (Wilsall, MT)—River named by Clark for Pvt. John Shields. Interpretive sign. Just N on US 89. 406/444-6258.
● **Judson Park/Depot Center Museum** (Livingston, MT)—Permanent exhibit "Rails Across the Rockies: A Century of People and Places." Picnic area. Mon-Sat 9 to 5, Sun 1 to 5 (May-Sept); admission fee. 200 W. Park. 406/222-2300.

Big Sky, Montana

▲ **Greek Creek**—14 sites; fee; water; primitive; open June-Sept; grills/fire rings; tables. Fishing. 9.5 miles N on US 191. 406/587-6920.

▲ **Moose Flat**—14 sites; fee; water; primitive; open June-Sept; grills/fire rings; tables; 16' trailer limit. Fishing. 7 miles N on US 191. 406/587-6920.

▲ **Red Cliff**—68 sites; fee; water; primitive; open June-Sept; grills/ fire rings; tables; 40' trailer limit. Fishing. 6.5 miles S on US 191. 406/587-6920.

▲ **Swan Creek**—11 sites; fee; water; primitive; open June-Sept; grills/fire rings; tables. Fishing. 8.5 miles N on US 191, 1 mile E on FR 481. 406/587-6920.

⊞ **Buck's T-4 Lodge**—75 spacious rooms, pets, outdoor recreation, hot tub, ⊗ restaurant. ♿. Off-season rates. 1 mile S on US 191. 406/995-4111. $$$ K10

⊞ **Huntley Lodge**—200 rooms, indoor/outdoor pools, full breakfast, outdoor recreation, coin laundry, full-scale resort. Off-season rates, closed Oct-Thanksgiving and Apr-May. Big Sky turnoff on US 191. 406/995-4211, 800/548-4486. $$$+ K10

⊞ **320 Guest Ranch**—59 rooms and multi-room units, pets, outdoor recreation, hot tub, playground, ⊗ restaurant, coin laundry. Off-season rates. 12 miles S on US 191. 406/995-4283. $$$+

Bozeman, Montana

Bozeman Chamber of Commerce, 2000 Commerce Dr. 406/586-5421 or 800/228-4224.

American Computer Museum—History of computers from early calculating machines to CD-ROM. Daily 10 to 4 (Memorial Day-Labor Day), Tue/Wed/Fri/Sat 12 to 4 (rest of year); admission fee. 234 E. Babcock. 406/587-7545.

Gallatin Pioneers' Museum—Located in the old county jail. Indian and homesteader artifacts. Collection of agates is worth seeing. Weekdays 2 to 5 (Memorial Day-Labor Day), Tue/Thur 2 to 4 (rest of year); free. 317 W. Main. 406/522-8122.

Grotto Falls Trail—1 mile trail/♿ to the falls. 18 miles S on Hyalite Canyon Rd., at Chisholm Campground 1 mile on East Fork Rd. 406/587-6920.

Kirk Hill—Several short interpreted hikes in area managed by the Museum of the Rockies. Lots of birds and wildflowers. 5 miles S on S. 19th Ave., at the sharp curve. 406/994-5257.

Museum of the Rockies—Home to paleontologist Dr. Jack Horner with several hands-on exhibits for exploring paleontology and dinosaurs. Traveling and permanent exhibits on Indians and pioneer history. A planetarium provides laser light shows and sky shows. Pioneer homestead outside the front door provides contrast. Daily 9 to 8:30 (Memorial Day-Labor Day), Mon-Sat 9 to 4:30, Sun 1 to 4:30 (rest of year); admission fee. On the Montana State campus at the corner of S. 7th Ave. and Kagy Blvd. 406/994-2251.

Palisades Falls Trail—0.5-mile paved nature trail to falls on Palisade Mountain. Environmental education area/♿. 18 miles S on Hyalite Canyon Rd., at Chisholm Campground go 2 miles on Main Hyalite Creek Rd. 406/587-6920.

West Shore Trail—0.5-mile trail/♿ from the **Blackmore Recreation Site** to a point overlooking the reservoir. Continue on to the **Crescent Lake Trail** and make 2.9-mile loop along west shore of reservoir. 16 miles S on Hyalite Canyon Rd. 406/587-6920.

▲ **Bear Canyon Campground**—104 sites (81 w/hookups); fee; water; modern; showers; open May-Oct; grills/fire rings; tables. Pool; playground; groceries; coin laundry. I-90 exit 313, 4 miles E on Bear Canyon Rd. 406/587-1575.

▲ **Bozeman Hot Springs KOA**—145 sites (100 w/hookups); fee; water; modern; showers; open all year; grills/fire rings; tables. ⊞ Cabins; tipis; hot springs; playground; hayrides; groceries; laundry. 7 miles W on US 191. 406/587-3030.

▲ **Chisholm**—9 sites; fee; water; primitive; open June-Sept; grills/fire rings; tables; 55' trailer limit. Fishing; hiking. 18 miles S on 19th Ave and Hyalite Canyon Rd/FR 62. 406/587-6920.

▲ **Hood Creek**—18 sites; fee; water; primitive; open June-Sept; grills/fire rings; tables; 16' trailer limit. Fishing; boat ramp; hiking. 17 miles S on 19th Ave and Hyalite Canyon Rd/FR 62. 406/587-6920.

▲ **Langohr**—11 sites; fee; water; primitive; open June-Sept; grills/fire rings; tables; 32' trailer limit. Fishing/♿; hiking. 11 miles S on 19th and Hyalite Canyon Rd. 406/587-6920.

▲ **Spanish Creek**—6 tent sites; free; water; primitive; open June-Sept; grills/fire rings; tables; no trailers. Fishing. 21 miles S on US 191, 3.5 miles W on Spanish Creek Rd. 406/587-6920.

▲ **Spire Rock**—16 sites; free; **no** water; primitive; June-Sept; grills/fire rings; tables; 16' trailer limit. Fishing. 26 miles S on US 191, 3 miles E on FR 1321. 406/587-6920.

⊞ **Battle Ridge Forest Service Cabin**—available all year; 4 beds. Road access to cabin, plowed within 0.25 mile in winter. 20 miles NE. 406/587-6920.

⊞ **Comfort Inn**—87 rooms, pool, continental breakfast, hot tub, exercise room, coin laundry. Off-season rates. 1370 N. 7th Ave. 406/587-2322, 800/587-3833. $$$ K16

⊞ **Fairfield Inn**—57 rooms, pool, pets, continental breakfast, hot tub. Off-season rates. I-90 exit 306. 406/587-2222, 800/228-2800. $$$ K18

⊞ **Mystic Lake Forest Service Cabin**—open Dec-Sept; 4 beds. 2 access routes: 5.3 miles is difficult, easier route is 10 miles. Area closed to motorized vehicles. 8 miles SE 406/587-6920.

⊞ **Window Rock Forest Service Cabin**—available year round; 4 beds. Road access in summer, winter access varies with road condition. Both cabin and outhouse facilities are ♿ accessible. 15 miles S near Hyalite Reservoir. 406/587-6920.

⊞ **Windy Pass Forest Service Cabin**—available June 1-Oct 15; 4 beds. Trail access is 2.5 miles with 1,300' elevation gain. Firewood not provided. 28 miles S. 406/587-6920.

⊨ **Lindley House**—7 rooms, full breakfast, afternoon tea, hot tub. Off-season rates. 406/587-8403, 800/787-8404. $$$

⊗ **John Bozeman's Bistro**—Fresh,

eclectic menu, kids' menu, smoke-free. L & D Mon-Sat. Sun Brunch only. 42 E. Main. 406/587-4100. $$

⊗ **MacKenzie River Pizza**—Gourmet pizza. L & D Mon-Sat. D only Sun. 406/587-0055. $$

⊗ **Spanish Peaks Brewery**—Pizza and Italian specialties. Smoke-free. L & D daily. 120 N. 19th Ave. 406/585-2296. $$

Divide, Montana

Humbug Spires Wilderness Study Area—2-mile trail to popular rock climbing area. ▲ Several undesignated sites; free; **no** water; primitive; open all year; 24' maximum length. N of I-15, exit 99. 406/494-5059.

▲ **Beaverdam**—15 sites; free; water; primitive; open Memorial Day-Sept; grills/fire rings; tables; 22' trailer limit. Fishing, hiking. I-15 exit 111, 8 miles W on Divide Creek Rd. 406/494-2147.

Ennis, Montana

Ennis Chamber of Commerce, P.O. Box 291. 406/682-4388.

Ennis National Fish Hatchery—Tour the facility and learn about rainbow trout that are bred here for release across the West. 12 miles SW on Varney Rd. 406/682-4847.

Lions Club Park—A stocked kids' fishing pond makes this a great place for families to spend an afternoon.

Wildlife Museum of the West—Owned by a local taxidermist, this museum is filled with mounts from Montana and other western states. Hours vary. On Main Street. 406/682-7141.

▲ **Ennis Fishing Access Site**—22 sites; fee; water; primitive; open all year/full operation May-Sept; grills/fire rings; tables. Boating; ramp; fishing. 0.25 mile SE on US 287. 406/994-4042.

▲ **West Madison**—28 sites; fee; water; primitive; open all year; grills/fire rings; tables. Fishing. 18 miles S on US 287, 3 miles S on county rd. 406/683-2337.

⊞ **El Western Resort**—28 rooms/log cabins, pets, kitchens available, fishing. Off-season rates. US 287. 406/682-4217. $$$ K10

⊞ **Rainbow Valley Motel**—24 rooms on the Madison River, pool, coin laundry. Off-season rates. 1

mile W on US 287. 406/682-4264. $$

⊞ **Riverside Motel**—12 rooms/cabins, pets, refrigerators, playground, fishing. Off-season rates. Open May-Nov. 346 E. Main. 406/682-4240, 800/535-4139. $$$ K6

⊗ **Ennis Cafe**—Small town charm and hearty servings, kids' menu. ♿. BLD daily. Main St. 406/682-4442. $

Gallatin Gateway, Montana

⊞ **Gallatin Gateway Inn**—35 rooms in a railroad-era grand hotel, pool, bike rentals, continental breakfast, ⊗ restaurant. Off-season rates. 76405 Gallatin Rd. 406/763-4672, 800/676-3522. $$$ K12

Gardiner, Montana

Gardiner Chamber of Commerce, 233 Main, Suite A. 406/848-7971.

▲ **Eagle Creek**—10 sites; free; water; primitive; open all year; grills/fire rings; tables; 30' trailer limit. 3.5 miles NE on Jardine Rd. 406/848-7375.

⊞ **Absaroka Lodge**—41 rooms, pets, white water rafting. Suites have refrigerators, microwaves and rates are about the same as doubles. Off-season rates. US 89. 406/848-7414, 800/755-7414. $$$ K12

⊞ **Wilson's Yellowstone River Motel**—38 rooms, pets, fishing, picnic area. Off-season rates. Open Apr-Oct. 2 blocks from the arch. 406/848-7322. $$

⊞ **Yellowstone Village Motel**—43 rooms/suites/condos, pool, basketball, coin laundry. Off-season rates. US 89. 406/484-7417, 800/228-8158. $$ K6

Livingston, Montana

Livingston Chamber of Commerce, 208 W. Park. 406/222-0850.

International Fly Fishing Center—History of the sport and artifacts. Aquariums and research material. Mon-Sat 10 to 6 (June-Sept); admission fee. I-90 exit 333. 406/222-9369.

Yellowstone Gateway Museum of Park County—Railroads, pioneer and Indian culture, natural resources. Daily noon to 5, 7 to 9 (June-Labor Day); admission fee. 118 W. Chinook St. 406/222-4184.

▲ **Paradise Valley KOA**—78 sites (54 w/hookups); fee; water; modern; showers; open May-Oct; grills/fire rings; tables. Pool; playground; ⊞ cabins; groceries; fishing; bike rentals; dump station. 10 miles S on US 89, follow signs 2 miles E. 406/222-0992.

▲ **Pine Creek**—24 primitive sites; fee; water; primitive; open Memorial Day-Sept; grills/fire rings; tables; 15-day limit. Nature trails; fishing; trailhead to Absaroka-Beartooth Wilderness. 9 miles S on US 89, 2 miles W on Co 540, 2.5 miles W on FR 202. 406/222-1892.

▲ **Snow Bank**—12 primitive sites; fee; water; primitive; open Memorial Day-Sept; grills/fire rings; tables; 15-day limit. Nature trails; fishing. 21 miles S on US 89, 14 miles SE on Co 486. 406/222-1892.

▲ **Yellowstone's Edge RV Park**—95 sites (81 w/hookups); fee; water; modern; showers; open May-Nov; grills/fire rings; tables; firewood. Fishing; groceries; coin laundry. 18 miles S on US 89. 406/333-4036.

⊞ **Murray Hotel**—32 large rooms in historic building, pets, hot tub, ⊗ restaurant. Efficiencies are same price as doubles. Off-season rates. 201 W. Park. 406/222-1350. $$

⊞ **Paradise Inn**—43 rooms, pool; pets, ⊗ restaurant. I-90 & US 89. 406/222-6320. $$

⊩ **The Centennial**—Spend the night in one of Montana's Centennial Train cars. 406/222-5456, 800/590-5456.

⊗ **Livingston Bar & Grill**—Continental cuisine with a touch of the old west by owner/artist Russell Chatham; kids' menu. D daily. 130 N. Main. 406/222-7909. $$

Logan, Montana

Madison Buffalo Jump State Park—Tipi rings can be found atop the bluff, at the base of the cliff and across the ravine to the north. Rock walls and stone piles exist centuries after the jump (pishkun) served its purpose for horse-less hunting. Interpretive exhibits educate visitors about the bison's importance in the lives of plains Indians and detail the process of luring the bison to their deaths. Daily, dawn to dusk (May-Sept); free. I-90 exit 283, 7 miles S on Buffalo Jump Road. 406/994-4042.

Norris, Montana

⚠ Red Mountain—11 sites; free; water; primitive; open all year; grills/fire rings; tables; 32' trailer limit. Fishing; hiking; access to Lee Metcalf Wilderness. 9 miles NE on MT 289. 406/683-2337.

Pioneer Mountains
National Scenic Byway

Gravel/paved road through spectacular scenery from MT 278, west of Dillon to Wise River. Hiking trails, campgrounds, fishing and hot springs along the way.

Blue Creek Trail #425—7-mile trail, good summer hike for families and casual hikers, kids will enjoy the creek crossings. 1 mile S of Elkhorn Hot Springs.

Browns Lake Trail #2—6-mile trail to several high mountain lakes, begins at Mono Creek Campground. Only for the most hearty hikers, 4 miles of extremely steep climbs. 13 miles N of MT 278. 406/832-3178.

Crystal Park—Ready for a change of pace? With nothing more than a few gardening tools and a piece of screen you can spend several hours hunting for crystals and garnets at this forest service site 3 miles north of Elkhorn Hot Springs. Pack a picnic and make a day of it. ⚿ trails and facilities; open 5/15 to 9/30, depending upon weather conditions; free. North of Polaris on MT 278, along the Pioneer Mountains National Scenic Byway. 406/683-3900.

⚠ Boulder Creek—12 sites; fee; water; primitive; open June-Sept; grills/fire rings; tables; 24' trailer limit. Fishing, hiking. 24 miles N of MT 278. 406/832-3178.

⚠ Fourth of July—6 sites; fee; water; primitive; open June-Sept; grills/fire rings; tables; 24' trailer limit. Fishing. 25 miles N of MT 278. 406/832-3178.

⚠ Grasshopper—24 sites; free; water; primitive; open June-Sept; grills/fire rings; tables; 16' trailer limit; group picnic area. Fishing; boat ramp; hiking. 11.5 miles N of MT 278. 406/683-3900.

⚠ Little Joe—4 tent sites/⚿; free; water; primitive; open May-Sept; grills/fire rings; tables. Fishing;

hiking. 16 miles N of MT 278. 406/832-3178.

⚠ Lodgepole—11 sites/⚿; fee; water; primitive; open June-Sept; grills/fire rings; tables; 16' trailer limit. Fishing; hiking. 23 miles N of MT 278. 406/832-3178.

⚠ Mono Creek—5 sites, free, water; primitive; open June-Sept; grills/fire rings; tables; 16' trailer limit. Fishing; hiking. 13 miles N of Hwy 278. 406/832-3178.

Pony, Montana

⚠ Potosi—15 sites; free; water; vault toilets; open Memorial Day-Sept; grills/fire rings; tables; 32' maximum length. Fishing; hiking; soak in nearby Potosi Hot Springs. 3 miles SE on CR 1601, 5 miles SW on FR 1501. 406/682-4253.

West Yellowstone, Montana

West Yellowstone Chamber of Commerce, 30 Yellowstone Ave. 406/646-7701.

Grizzly Discovery Center—See bears and wolves in natural habitats. Educational exhibits and movies. Daily 9 to dusk; admission fee. 2 blocks from park entrance. 406/646-7001, 800/257-2570.

Madison River Canyon Earthquake Area—Interpretive center at Hebgen and Earthquake lakes documents devastation of the 1959 earthquake that created Quake Lake by blocking the river, and killed at least 26 campers. Memorial to those who died and viewpoints of still-visible damage. Always open, visitor center daily 8 to 6 (Memorial Day-Labor Day); donations. 17 miles NW of US 191 on US 287. 406/646-7369.

Museum of the Yellowstone—History of mountain men, cowboys, Indians and the cavalry. Videos and exhibits about trains and Yellowstone Park. Daily 8am to 10pm (Mother's Day to Columbus Day); admission fee. Union Pacific RR depot, 124 Yellowstone Ave. 406/646-7814.

Yellowstone IMAX—Spectacular presentation about Yellowstone: original movie on history and geology of the park. Photography and geology exhibits. Shows hourly. Daily 9 to 9. 101 S. Canyon. 406/646-4100.

⚠ Bakershole—72 sites; fee; water;

primitive; open Memorial Day-Sept; grills/fire rings; tables; 32' trailer limit. Hard-sided units only, no tents. Canoeing; fishing. 3 miles N of US 20 on US 287/191. 406/646-7369.

⚠ Beavercreek—64 sites; fee; water; primitive; open June-Sept; grills/fire rings; tables; 32' trailer limit. Canoeing; fishing; hiking trails. 8 miles N of US 20 on US 191, 17 miles W on US 287. 406/646-7369.

⚠ Lonesomehurst—26 sites; fee; water; primitive; open Memorial Day-Sept; grills/fire rings; tables; 32' trailer limit. Swimming; boating; fishing; hiking. 8 miles W of US 191 on US 20, 4 miles N on Hebgen Lake Rd. 406/646-7369.

⚠ Rainbow Paint—85 sites; fee; water; primitive; open Memorial Day-Sept; grills/fire rings; tables; 32' trailer limit. Swimming; boating; fishing; hiking. 5 miles N of US 20 on US 191, 5.25 miles W on FR. 406/646-7369.

⚠ Yellowstone Grizzly RV Park—152 sites (all w/hookups); fee; water; modern; showers; open May-Oct; grills/fire rings; tables. Recreation area; groceries; coin laundry; dump station. 4 blocks W of park entrance. 406/646-4466.

⊞ Best Western Weston Inn—65 rooms, pets, pool, hot tub. Smoke-free. Off-season rates. 103 Gibbon. 406/464-7373, 800/528-1234. $$ K12

⊞ Hibernation Station—30 cabins, pets, continental breakfast, hot tub. Off-season rates. 212 Gray Wolf. 406/646-4200. $$$ K12

⊞ Holiday Inn Sunspree Resort—123 rooms, family suites, pool, microwaves, daycare center, coin laundry, ⊗ restaurant. Off-season rates. 315 Yellowstone Ave. 406/646-7365, 800/646-7365. $$$+ K18.

⊞ Stage Coach Inn—88 lodge-style rooms, hot tub, ⊗ restaurant, coin laundry. Off-season rates. 209 Madison Ave. 406/646-7381, 800/842-2882. $$$ K12

⊗ Rustler's Roost—Buffalo & home-made baked goods; kids' menu. B L D daily. US 191 & 20. 406/646-7622. $$

Wisdom, Montana

⚠ May Creek—21 sites; fee; water; primitive; open Jul-Aug; grills/fire rings; tables; 32' maximum limit. Fishing; hiking. 17 miles W on Hwy. 43. 406/689-2431.

Wise River, Montana

▲ East Bank—5 sites; free; **no** water; primitive; open all year; grills/fire rings; tables; 24' trailer limit. Fishing; boat ramp. 8 miles W of Wise River on Hwy. 43. 406/494-5059.

▲ Seymour Creek—17 sites; free; water; primitive; open June-Sept; grills/fire rings; tables; 16' trailer limit. Fishing; boat ramp; hiking. 11 miles W of Wise River on MT 43, 4 miles N on MT 274, 8 miles NW on FR 934. 406/832-3178.

⌘ Foolhen Forest Service Cabin—Available December through August, sleeps 4. Winter access by snowmobile only, summer access by 2.5 mile trail. 12 miles W. 406/832-3178.

Yellowstone National Park

Former Corps member John Colter was the first white man known to view this area, not long after the expedition. The geysers and geological wonders were permanently protected in 1872 when over 2 million acres became the world's first national park. There is so much to see: the Grand Canyon of the Yellowstone and Inspiration Point, Norris Geyser Basin, Tower Falls, the Paint Pots, the terraces at Mammoth Hot Springs, Mount Washburn and Old Faithful. Elk, bears, moose, deer, bison and antelope are plentiful, but sighting the elusive wolves is rare. Hiking trails exist for all abilities; be sure to get out of the car and explore. Although the figure 8 driving loop is only 142 miles, it could take 12 hours or more to cover. Plan on taking your time; you won't have any choice during July and August. Traffic crawls, stopping suddenly when animals are spotted. Bison and elk are plentiful on the road, especially in the evening. Reserve a day for the **Beartooth Highway**, a 64-mile, spectacular drive between the northeast entrance and Cooke City, MT. The highway rises from 5,600' to 11,000' at Beartooth Pass, where one of many overlooks provides unparalleled views. Accommodations range from rustic cabins with central bathhouses to the elegant Lake Yellowstone Hotel. If you're selective or on a budget, make reservations *very* early. 307/344-7311 or 307/344-7901. Reservations are accepted for some campgrounds (307/344-7311) and dates are subject to change due to weather/snow conditions.

▲ Bridge Bay—420 sites; fee; water; modern; open Memorial Day-Sept; grills/fire rings; tables; firewood. Boating/rentals; fishing; hiking. 3 miles S of Lake Village.

▲ Canyon Village—271 sites; fee; water; modern; showers; open June-Aug; grills/fire rings; tables; firewood. Fishing; hiking; coin laundry; groceries; dump station. 0.25 mile E of Canyon Village.

▲ Fishing Bridge—358 sites (all w/hookups); fee; water; modern; showers; open May-Sept; grills/fire rings; tables; firewood. Hard-sided units only, no tents. Fishing; coin laundry; groceries; dump station. 1 mile E of Loop Rd on Lake Jct. Rd.

▲ Grant Village—425 sites; fee; water; modern; showers; open June-Oct; grills/fire rings; tables; firewood. Boating; fishing; hiking; groceries; coin laundry; dump station. 2 miles S of West Thumb Junction on Rockefeller Pkwy, 1 mile E on access road.

▲ Indian Creek—75 sites; fee; water; primitive; open June-Sept; grills/fire rings; tables; firewood; 24' trailer length. No reservations. Fishing. 7.5 miles S of Mammoth Hot Springs on Grand Loop Rd.

▲ Lewis Lake—85 sites; fee; water; primitive; open June-Oct; grills/fire rings; tables; firewood. No reservations. Boating; fishing. 10 miles S of West Thumb Junction on US 89.

▲ Madison Junction—292 sites; fee; water; modern; open May-Oct; grills/fire rings; tables; firewood. Fishing; hiking; dump station. 0.25 mile W on US 20.

▲ Mammoth—85 sites; fee; water; modern; open all year; grills/fire rings; tables; firewood. No reservations. Fishing; hiking. 5 miles N of Mammoth Hot Springs on US 89.

▲ Norris—116 sites; fee; water; modern; open May-Sept; grills/fire rings; tables; firewood. No reservations. 1 mile N of Norris Junction on Grand Loop Rd.

▲ Pebble Creek—36 sites; fee; water; primitive; open June-Sept; grills/fire rings; tables; firewood. No reservations. Fishing. 7 miles SW of Tower Junction.

▲ Slough Creek—29 sites; fee; water; primitive; open Memorial Day-Oct; grills/fire rings; tables; firewood. No reservations. 5 miles E of Tower Junction on US 212, 2.5 miles N on Slough Creek Rd.

▲ Tower Falls—32 sites; fee; water; primitive; open Memorial Day-Sept; grills/fire rings; tables; firewood. No reservations. 3 miles S of Tower Junction on Grand Loop Rd.

⌘ Canyon Lodge—609 rooms and cabins, pets, ⊗ restaurants, outdoor recreation. Closed Sept-May. 307/344-7901. $ to $$$ K11

⌘ Grant Village—300 rooms, outdoor recreation, ⊗ restaurants. Grant Village. 307/344-7311. $$ K11

⌘ Lake Lodge—186 rooms and cabins, pets, outdoor recreation, ⊗ restaurant, coin laundry. Closed Oct-June. Lake Village. 307/344-7311. $$ K11

⌘ Lake Yellowstone Hotel—194 rooms and 102 cabins, ⊗ restaurant, outdoor recreation. Closed Oct-May. Lake Village. 307/344-7311. Hotel $$$+. Cabins $$ K11

⌘ Mammoth Hot Springs Hotel—96 rooms and 126 cabins, rooms vary a great deal in price and amenities, outdoor recreation, ⊗ restaurant. Closed Mar/Apr/Oct/Nov. Mammoth Hot Springs. 307/344-7901. Hotel $ to $$$. Cabins $ K11

⌘ Old Faithful Inn—359 rooms in enormous log hotel, outdoor recreation, ⊗ restaurant. Closed Oct-Apr. At Old Faithful. 307/344-7901. $ to $$$ K11

⌘ Old Faithful Snow Lodge and Cabins—100 units in new post and beam building, outdoor recreation, ⊗ restaurant. Closed late fall and late spring. At Old Faithful. 307/344-7901. $ to $$$ K11

CHAPTER 26

July 15 to August 12, 1806

CLARK ON THE YELLOWSTONE

As Captain William Clark's return party moved down the Yellowstone River to the Missouri, riding along its banks or floating its waters, they enjoyed a river that still attracts floaters. The Yellowstone is the longest free flowing river (no dams except for small irrigation diversions) in the United States today.

The land was filled with ripe berries, bison, pronghorns, elk, deer, and grizzly bears, and the river with fish. Later, on July 24, near today's Billings, Clark would write "for me to...give an estimate of the different Spcies of

Wild animals on this river...would be incredibitable. I shall therefore be silent on the Subject." But stony ground also had hurt the horses' hooves, and Clark ordered "Mockersons made of green Buffalow Skin...which Seams to releve them very much."

On July 18, they camped on an island west of Columbus, where the Stillwater River flows into the Yellowstone. During the day, Private George Gibson had fallen off his horse onto a snag that pierced two inches into his thigh. By the next morning, his pain extended from knee to hip. Clark had planned to build canoes

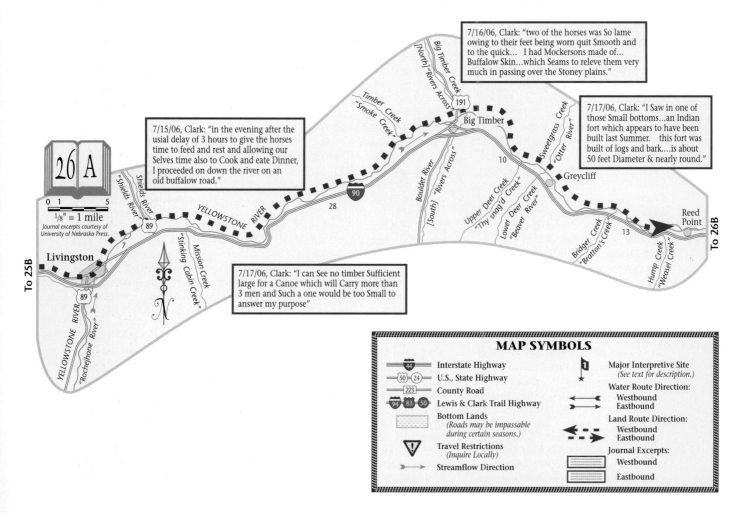

7/16/06, Clark: "two of the horses was So lame owing to their feet being worn quit Smooth and to the quick... I had Mockersons made of... Buffalow Skin...which Seams to releve them very much in passing over the Stoney plains."

7/15/06, Clark: "in the evening after the usial delay of 3 hours to give the horses time to feed and rest and allowing our Selves time also to Cook and eate Dinner, I proceeded on down the river on an old buffalow road."

7/17/06, Clark: "I Saw in one of those Small bottoms...an Indian fort which appears to have been built last Summer. this fort was built of logs and bark....is about 50 feet Diameter & nearly round."

7/17/06, Clark: "I can See no timber Sufficient large for a Canoe which will Carry more than 3 men and Such a one would be too Small to answer my purpose"

MAP SYMBOLS

Interstate Highway	Major Interpretive Site *(See text for description.)*
U.S., State Highway	Water Route Direction:
County Road	Westbound
Lewis & Clark Trail Highway	Eastbound
Bottom Lands *(Roads may be impassable during certain seasons.)*	Land Route Direction: Westbound Eastbound
Travel Restrictions *(Inquire Locally)*	Journal Excerpts: Westbound
Streamflow Direction	Eastbound

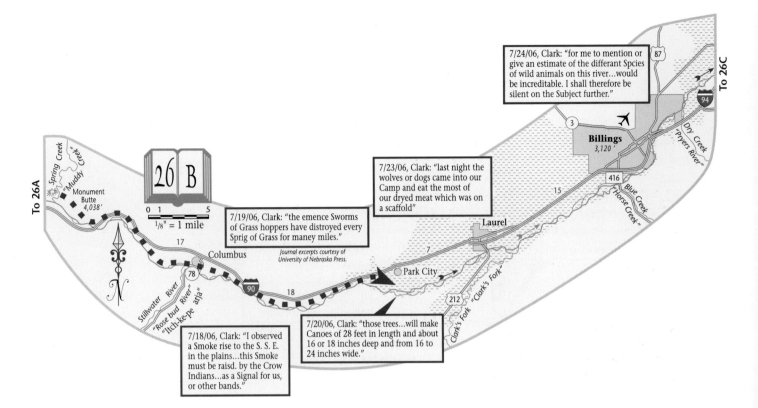

To 26A

To 26C

7/24/06, Clark: "for me to mention or give an estimate of the differant Spcies of wild animals on this river...would be incredidable. I shall therefore be silent on the Subject further."

7/23/06, Clark: "last night the wolves or dogs came into our Camp and eat the most of our dryed meat which was on a scaffold"

7/19/06, Clark: "the emence Sworms of Grass hoppers have distroyed every Sprig of Grass for maney miles."

Journal excerpts courtesy of University of Nebraska Press.

7/18/06, Clark: "I observed a Smoke rise to the S. S. E. in the plains...this Smoke must be raisd. by the Crow Indians...as a Signal for us, or other bands."

7/20/06, Clark: "those trees...will make Canoes of 28 feet in length and about 16 or 18 inches deep and from 16 to 24 inches wide."

$1/8" = 1$ mile

Billings 3,120'

Laurel

Park City

Columbus

Monument Butte 4,038'

soon, but now needed one to carry Gibson. The captain also hoped to apply a poultice of wild ginger to the wound, but neither trees large enough nor ginger could be found. Clark put Gibson on their gentlest horse and piled skins and blankets for him to lie back against. Still, the private could ride only a couple of hours. The party went on and camped on the 19th south of today's Park City, where they found canoe timber.

They stayed here until July 24, and built two canoes, which were lashed together for stability. During this time, others dried bison meat, most of which either wolves or coyotes ate on the night of the 22nd.

Clark didn't mention Gibson's injury again until July 30, when he said Gibson could walk and had killed a bison.

On July 21, half the horses were gone in the morning and Clark feared Indian theft. When men of the Corps found the horses and approached them, the animals escaped into the woods. Clark thought the twenty-four missing horses would return to eat the rich riverbank grass, and when they didn't he again believed they'd been stolen. On the 23rd, he sent another search party out. Private Francois Labiche returned saying he saw tracks of horses running very fast downriver, apparently being driven.

On July 24, Clark's party set off in their twin-hulled boat. They passed a river that Clark at first mistook for the Bighorn River that Indians had told him of. He later renamed this river the Clarks Fork of the Yellowstone; the name remains today, sometimes confused with the Clark Fork River in western Montana. Before the day was over, Sergeant Nathaniel Pryor learned that his horses, trained to chase bison by their original owners, would be hard to handle. He sent one man ahead to scatter any "gangue of buffalow" they met. After driving these horses south across the Yellowstone, Pryor—with privates Hugh Hall, George Shannon and Richard Windsor—left for the Mandan villages.

July 25 brought Clark's group to the sandstone landmark he named [1] Pompy's Tower from the nickname for Sacagawea's little boy; today it is called Pompeys Pillar. Clark carved his name and the date on it, which still can be seen, and climbed to its top for the view. The next day they reached the true Bighorn River, and Clark explored seven miles up it—unaware that Francois LaRocque, a trader they had met at Fort Mandan in the winter of 1804-1805, had explored the Bighorn in 1805. Clark

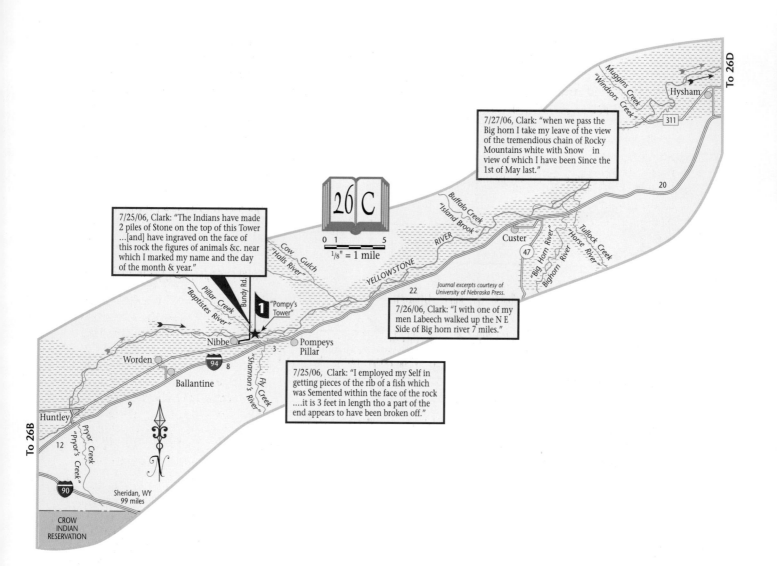

7/25/06, Clark: "The Indians have made 2 piles of Stone on the top of this Tower …[and] have ingraved on the face of this rock the figures of animals &c. near which I marked my name and the day of the month & year."

7/27/06, Clark: "when we pass the Big horn I take my leave of the view of the tremendious chain of Rocky Mountains white with Snow in view of which I have been Since the 1st of May last."

7/26/06, Clark: "I with one of my men Labeech walked up the N E Side of Big horn river 7 miles."

7/25/06, Clark: "I employed my Self in getting pieces of the rib of a fish which was Semented within the face of the rock ….it is 3 feet in length tho a part of the end appears to have been broken off."

Journal excerpts courtesy of University of Nebraska Press.

$^1/_8$" = 1 mile

returned to camp utterly worn out, and went to bed without eating.

They camped on the 29th on an island opposite the mouth of the Tongue River (an Indian name that stayed)—then about a mile upstream from its position at Miles City today. Clark said the Tongue River's water was very muddy and warm, too disagreeable to drink. He noticed that surrounding hills contained "Coal in great quantities."

He named the Buffalo Shoals of the Yellowstone the next day, calling them "by far the wo[r]st place which I have seen on this river." The men had to "let the Canoes down by hand" so the rocks wouldn't split them.

The country around today's town of Terry was "entirely bar of timber…great quantities of Coal…in every Bluff and in the high hills at a distance."

Rain slowed them and muddied the river on August 1, but when the next day was clear, mosquitoes returned to trouble them. So did bears. One "of the large vicious Species… plunged in the water and Swam towards us," probably smelling fresh meat in the canoes. The men wounded it, and the grizzly turned back. Later another swam downstream toward them. Clark pulled ashore, and shot and skinned "Much the largest feemale bear I ever Saw."

They almost had to wait while numbers of bison crossed the river, but "we got through the line between 2 gangues." Clark estimated they traveled eighty-six miles on August 2; it was actually about sixty miles, but still the most in a single day on the Yellowstone, and one of the highest single-day totals of the whole trip.

When Clark tried shooting a bighorn the next day, "the Musquetors were So noumerous that I could not Shute with any certainty and therefore Soon returned to the Canoes." Later, they saw more bighorns, and Private Francois Labiche killed one. Now Clark had the hides and skeletons of a male, a female, and a yearling of this "new" animal to take home.

They reached the **[2]** Missouri River in just a few more miles, in today's North Dakota. The mosquitoes were horrible (Pompy's face was "much puffed & Swelled" from bites), and bison not in sight, so after one night and most of a day, Clark left a note for Lewis telling him they had headed down the Missouri.

Troubled by mosquitoes and grizzlies, the party moved daily until August 7, when "the air was exceedingly Clear and Cold and not a misquetor to be Seen, which is a joyfull circumstance." They stayed at this spot, now under Lake Sakakawea in the area of Tobacco Creek, for two nights.

On the second night here, Pryor and his three men arrived via the Missouri in two bullboats. The very night after they had crossed the Yellowstone, the horse herd had been stolen from a camp on Fly Creek (Clark's Shannon Creek) near today's Hardin. The men followed footprints but couldn't catch up. This

was the territory of the Crow Indians, who excelled in the Plains Indian war-skill of horse-capturing. Although the Crows never warred against whites, Crow people to this day tell of stealing these horses from the Corps. So the foursome hoisted their baggage on their backs and walked back to the Yellowstone at Pompy's Tower, killed a bison, and built two bowl-shaped skin boats as they'd learned from the Mandans. They began to float down the Yellowstone and then the Missouri, with no idea whether they'd catch up with the rest of the Corps of Discovery, but knowing the river would take them to St. Louis.

Now, the enlarged group kept moving downstream. On August 11, they met trappers Joseph Dickson and Forrest Hancock, headed up to the Yellowstone River. On their way up the Missouri the year before, these men had met the Corps' keelboat heading downriver to St. Louis (see Chapter 11). Now Clark knew that their first reports and specimens had, at least, gotten safely as far as the Kansas River.

At noon the next day, "Capt Lewis hove in Sight" and the Corps of Discovery was reunited. Now their main goal was to get back to St. Louis before ice closed the Missouri.

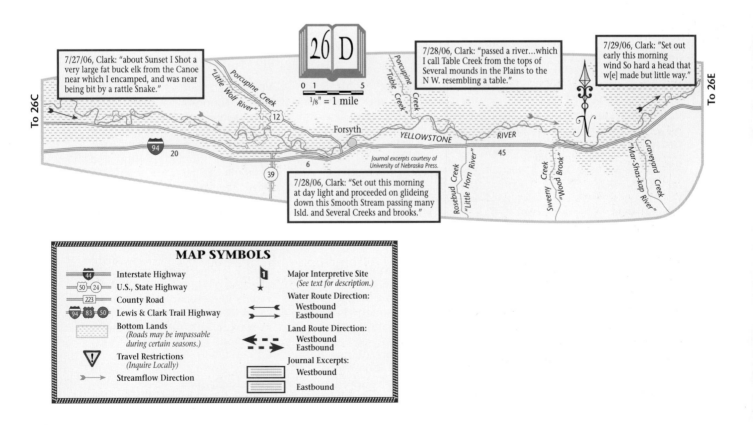

7/27/06, Clark: "about Sunset I Shot a very large fat buck elk from the Canoe near which I encamped, and was near being bit by a rattle Snake."

26 D

0 1 5
1/8" = 1 mile

7/28/06, Clark: "passed a river...which I call Table Creek from the tops of Several mounds in the Plains to the N W. resembling a table."

7/29/06, Clark: "Set out early this morning wind So hard a head that w[e] made but little way."

To 26C

To 26E

"Little Wolf River"

Porcupine Creek

Porcupine "Table Creek"

Forsyth

YELLOWSTONE RIVER

94 20

39

6

Journal excerpts courtesy of University of Nebraska Press.

7/28/06, Clark: "Set out this morning at day light and proceeded on glideing down this Smooth Stream passing many Isld. and Several Creeks and brooks."

Rosebud Creek

"Little Horn River"

45

Sweeny Creek

"Wood Brook"

"Mar-Shas-kop River"

"Graveyard Creek"

N

MAP SYMBOLS

44 — Interstate Highway	Major Interpretive Site (See text for description.)
50 — 24 — U.S., State Highway	
223 — County Road	Water Route Direction:
94 — 83 — 50 — Lewis & Clark Trail Highway	Westbound / Eastbound
Bottom Lands (Roads may be impassable during certain seasons.)	Land Route Direction: Westbound / Eastbound
Travel Restrictions (Inquire Locally)	Journal Excerpts: Westbound
Streamflow Direction	Eastbound

TOURING TODAY

∾ CLARK ON THE YELLOWSTONE ∾

Bridges across the Yellowstone River in this area are in Big Timber, MT (US 191); Columbus, MT (MT 306); Laurel, MT (US 212); Billings, MT (US 87); Pompeys Pillar access road; Forsyth, MT (US 12); Cartersville, MT (MT 447); Miles City, MT (MT 59); Terry, MT (MT 253); Glendive, MT (I-94); Sidney, MT (MT 23, MT 220).

ALONG THE EXPEDITION'S PATH

July 19, 1806
● **Itch-Ke-Pe Park** (Columbus, MT)—City park with river access for fishing, swimming and boating. ▲ 30 sites; fee; water; modern; showers; open Apr-Oct; grills/fire rings; tables. S on MT 78. 406/322-5313.

July 19-24, 1806
Buffalo Mirage Access (Park City, MT)—The Corps carved 2 dugout canoes near here. Undeveloped fishing access site. I-90 exit 426, 7 miles E on frontage road, 6 miles on county road.

July 24, 1806
Two Moon Park (Billings, MT)—All of the trails in this county park along the Yellowstone River are unmarked, except for the nature trail. Expect to see lots of birds, especially in spring and fall. Daily sunrise to sunset; free. On Bench Blvd, off Main St (US 87). 406/245-5843.
Riverside Park (Billings, MT)—Primitive camping area along the river. Fishing, boating access. ♿. I-90 exit 434.

July 25, 1806
[1] ★ Pompeys Pillar National Historic Landmark (Billings, MT)—Only site along the Lewis and Clark trail where physical evidence of the expedition may be viewed by the public. A boardwalk stairway leads to a 200' high rock bearing Clark's carved signature and the date. Visitor center and interpretive programs. Picnic areas. Daily 8 to 8 (May-Sept); admission fee. I-94 exit 23, east of Billings. 406/875-2233.

July 26, 1806
Howrey Island (Billings, MT)—Trails crisscross this 560-acre Yellowstone River island. Bald eagles can be seen, even in the summer, with high concentrations of waterfowl throughout the year. Exit I-94 E of Billings at Hysham, 7 miles W on Sec 311 to just past Myers Bridge. 406/232-7000.

July 27, 1806
West Rosebud Recreation Area (Forsyth, MT)—Boating and fishing access, ▲ primitive camping. W on US 12 at S end of bridge. 406/232-0900.
East Rosebud Recreation Area (Forsyth, MT)—Boating and fishing access, ▲ primitive camping. I-94 Forsyth E exit, N to river. 406/232-0900.

July 28, 1806
Pirogue Island State Park (Miles City, MT)—Hiking on Yellowstone River island with dense forests. Whitetail deer, songbirds, waterfowl and shorebirds. Rockhounds can hunt for moss agates, particularly near the water. 1 mile N on MT 5, 1.5 miles E on Kinsey Rd; 1.5 miles S on gravel road. 406/232-0900.

August 1, 1806
Intake Fishing Access Site (Glendive, MT)—The place to go for paddlefish in May and June. ▲ Undesignated sites; fee; water; primitive; open all year/full operation May-Sept; grills/fire rings; tables. 16 miles NE on MT 16. 406/232-0900.

August 12, 1806
For information on the area where the Corps of Discovery reunited, see April 14, 1805, in Chapter 12, "To the Yellowstone River."

AROUND THE AREA

TOWNS LISTED ALPHABETICALLY

Big Timber, Montana
Big Timber Chamber of Commerce, 219 McLeod, P.O. Box 1012, Big Timber, MT 59011, 406/932-5131.
Crazy Mountain Museum—Take a "Walk in Time" through the museum's exhibit of archaeological treasures and few exhibits from the Young Montana Artists and Montana Reflections competitions. Tue-Sun 1 to 4:30 (summer); free. I-90 at exit 367. 406/932-5126.
Greycliff Prairie Dog Town State Park—An entire community is protected here and watching them is entertaining. Interpretive signs and picnic tables. Restrooms, water and more picnic facilities are available at the rest area a few miles east. Daily sunrise to sunset; admission fee. I-90 exit 377. 406/247-2940.
Natural Bridge—Trail/♿ through gorge to dramatic 100-foot waterfall with scenic overlooks and in-

terpretive signs. Pictographs are to be seen in caves behind the ranger station down the road. Daily sunrise to sunset; free. 25 miles S of Big Timber on MT 298. 406/932-5131.

C. Sharp Arms Company/Montana Armory—Replica Sharp and Winchester rifles along with other firearms. Mon-Fri 8 to 5; free. 100 Centennial Dr. 406/932-4443.

Yellowstone River Fish Hatchery—Over a million Yellowstone cutthroat trout eggs are harvested annually. Outdoor raceways hold 2,500 fish in the summer. Daily 8 to 4:30, tours available; free. Take McLeod St. N from town for 0.5 mile. 406/932-4434.

⛢ Aspen Grove—11 sites; free; water; primitive; open all year; grills/fire rings; tables; 32' trailer limit. Fishing. 25 miles S on MT 298, 9 miles S on Co 212. 406/932-5155.

⛢ Big Beaver—5 sites; free; **no** water; primitive; open all year; grills/fire rings; tables; 32' trailer limit. Fishing. 25 miles S on MT 298, 8 miles S on Co 212. 406/932-5155.

⛢ Chippy Park—8 sites/♿; free; water; primitive; open all year; grills/fire rings; tables; 32' trailer limit. Fishing. 25 miles S on MT 298, 10 miles S on Co 212. 406/932-5155.

⛢ Falls Creek—11 tent sites; free; water; primitive; open all year; grills/fire rings; tables. Fishing; access to Absaroka-Beartooth Wilderness. 30 miles S on MT 298, 5 miles S on Co 212. 406/932-5155.

⛢ Hells Canyon—11 sites; free; no water; primitive; open all year; grills/fire rings; tables; 16' trailer limit. Fishing; hiking; access to Absaroka-Beartooth Wilderness Area. 25 miles S on MT 298, 15 miles S on Co 212. 406/932-5155.

⛢ Hicks Park—16 sites; free; water; primitive; open all year; grills/fire rings; tables; 32' trailer limit. Fishing; hiking; access to Absaroka-Beartooth Wilderness Area. 25 miles S on MT 298,

20 miles S on Co 212. 406/932-5155.

⛢ KOA—75 sites (66 w/hookups); fee; water; modern; showers; open Apr-Sept; grills/fire rings; tables. Pool; hot tub; ⊞ cabins; groceries; coin laundry; dump station. I-90 exit 377, S on Frontage Rd. 406/932-6569.

⛢ West Boulder—10 sites; free; water; primitive; open all year; grills/fire rings; tables; 20' trailer limit. Fishing; access to Absaroka-Beartooth Wilderness. 15 miles S on MT 298, 13 miles W on Co 35/West Boulder Rd. 406/932-5155.

⊞ Deer Creek Forest Service Cabin—Available all year; 4 beds. Last 4 miles by foot or horseback,

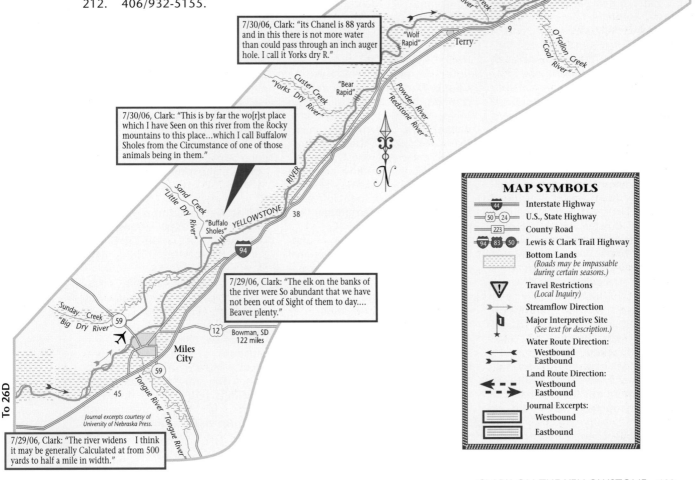

7/30/06, Clark: "its Chanel is 88 yards and in this there is not more water than could pass through an inch auger hole. I call it Yorks dry R."

7/30/06, Clark: "This is by far the wo[r]st place which I have Seen on this river from the Rocky mountains to this place...which I call Buffalow Sholes from the Circumstance of one of those animals being in them."

7/29/06, Clark: "The elk on the banks of the river were So abundant that we have not been out of Sight of them to day.... Beaver plenty."

7/29/06, Clark: "The river widens   I think it may be generally Calculated at from 500 yards to half a mile in width."

Journal excerpts courtesy of University of Nebraska Press.

MAP SYMBOLS

	Interstate Highway
	U.S., State Highway
	County Road
	Lewis & Clark Trail Highway
	Bottom Lands (Roads may be impassable during certain seasons.)
	Travel Restrictions (Local Inquiry)
	Streamflow Direction
	Major Interpretive Site (See text for description.)
	Water Route Direction: Westbound Eastbound
	Land Route Direction: Westbound Eastbound
	Journal Excerpts: Westbound Eastbound

hikers must ford creek several times. Corrals available. 32 miles S of Big Timber. 406/932-5155.

⊞ **West Bridger Forest Service Cabin**—Available June-December; 4 beds. 0.25 mile driveway slick when wet, winter access varies with snow conditions. 27 miles SE of Big Timber on W. Bridger Rd. 406/932-5155.

⊞ **Lewis and Clark Cabin**—Restored log cabin on the Yellowstone River, fishing. 406/252-4066

⊞ **C.M. Russell Lodge**—42 rooms, ⊗ restaurant, coin laundry. Smoke-free. I-90 exit 367. 406/932-5242. $$ K10

⊞ **Super 8**—39 rooms, pets, continental breakfast. Off-season rates. I-90 exit 367. 406/932-8888. $$ K12

Billings, Montana

Billings Chamber of Commerce—Daily 8:30-7:30 (May-Sept), Mon-Fri 8:30 to 5 (rest of year). 815 S. 27th St. (I-90 exit 450) 406/252-4016, 800/735-2635.

Branding Wall—Livestock brands of ranches that participated in the Great Montana Centennial Cattle Drive in 1989. 2nd Ave. N and N 27th.

Chief Otter Trail/Rimrocks—A drive along this ridge to one of its scenic pullouts puts Billings at your feet, literally. The view at night is striking. Take N. 27th St. toward the airport and head E or W on Rimrock Rd.

Lake Elmo State Park—Windsurfing, sailing and the beach/♿ draw crowds during the summer. Concessions, boat rentals; outdoor shower. The south side of the lake is a bit quieter with 0.75-mile woodchip trail and fishing pier/♿. On weekdays, view the wildlife mounts inside the headquarters building. Weekdays 11 to 8, weekends 10 to 9 (June-Aug), sunrise to sunset (rest of year); admission fee. US 87 N to Pemberton Lane, then 1 mile W. 406/247-2940.

Moss Mansion—1903 mansion was originally owned by Preston B. Moss, one of Montana's wealthiest men. Furnishings are original and evoke the opulence of the turn of the 20th century. Tours and special exhibits scheduled year round.

Call for current schedule; admission fee. 914 Division St. 406/256-5100.

Pictograph Cave State Park—Paved, 0.25-mile interpretive trail leads to three caves containing pictographs; guidebook available at trailhead. The trail is steep in sections, providing challenging accessibility. Wooded picnic area and primitive/♿ restrooms. Daily sunrise to sunset; admission fee. Lockwood exit S off I-90, 7 miles S on county road. 406/245-0227 (summer), 406/247-2940 (winter).

Sacrifice Cliff—Legend has it that a group of Crow Indians returned from a hunting trip to find many of their family and friends dead from smallpox. In their despair, they blinded their horses and rode them off a 60-foot cliff. 1 mile W of Billings on the Yellowstone River.

Western Heritage Center—Outstanding museum dedicated to interpretation and preservation of the region's history. Permanent, interactive exhibit combining oral history, videos, photographs and other objects to define life in the Yellowstone Valley from 1880 to 1940. Tues-Sat 10 to 5, Sunday 1 to 5; donations. 2822 Montana Ave. 406/256-6809.

Peter Yegen Jr. Yellowstone County Museum—The nooks and crannies of this log cabin, built in 1893, are filled with artifacts, memorabilia, dioramas and paintings which depict the "glamour" of life in the early west. New exhibits include a trading post and Lewis & Clark displays. Mon-Fri 10:30 to 5, Sat 10:30 to 3; free. At Billings Logan International Airport. 406/256-6811.

Yellowstone Art Center—Rotating exhibits by regional, national and international artists. Permanent gallery of contemporary Western works. Tues-Sat, 11 to 5, until 8 on Thurs, Sun noon to 5; admission fee. 401 N. 27th St. 406/256-6804.

ZooMontana—This park provides natural habitat for its residents and unusual viewing opportunities for visitors. Watch river otters from underwater or tour the Montana Homestead, an early 1900s ranch. Spend some time in the botanical

display that includes a ♿ Sensory Garden set up for the visually impaired to touch, smell and taste the plants. Daily 10 to 8 (May-Sept), 10 to 4 (rest of year); admission fee. 2100 S. Shiloh Rd. 406/652-8100.

▲ **Cooney State Park**—75 sites; fee; water; modern; showers; open all year/full operation May-Sept; grills/fire rings; tables. Swimming; boating; beach; concessions. From I-90 at Laurel, 22 miles SW on U.S. 212 to Boyd; 5 miles W on county road. 406/455-2326 (summer), 406/247-2940 (winter).

▲ **KOA**—192 sites (152 w/ hookups); fee; water; modern; showers; open Apr-Oct; grills/fire rings; tables. Fishing; store; minigolf; playground; dump station. I-90 exit 450, 1 block S on MT 3, 0.75 miles SE on Garden. 406/252-3104.

⊞ **The Billings Inn**—60 rooms, pets, continental breakfast. Suites and efficiencies are reasonable. 880 N. 29th St. 406/252-6800, 800/231-7782. $ K12

⊞ **Comfort Inn**—60 rooms; pool, pets, hot tub; continental breakfast. Suites are about the same as a double. Off-season rates. 2030 Overland Ave. 406/652-5200, 800/221-2222. $$ K18

⊞ **Ponderosa**—130 rooms, pool, pets, ⊗ restaurant, coin laundry, weight room. Off-season rates. 2511 1st Ave N. 406/259-5511, 800/628-9081. $$ K18

⊞ **Rimrock Inn**—83 rooms, pets, continental breakfast, ⊗ restaurant, weight room. 1203 N. 27th St. 406/252-7107, 800/624-9770. $

⊗ **The Cattle Company**—Hearty food in Old West atmosphere, kids' menu. L & D Mon-Sat, D only Sun. In Rimrock Mall, 300 S. 24th St. 406/656-9090. $$

⊗ **Le Croissant**—Bagels, croissants, salads. B & L Mon-Sat. 2711 1st Ave N. 406/245-8885.

Columbus, Montana

Museum of the Beartooths—County history, vehicles and machines. Tue-Sun 1 to 5 (June-Sept); donations. I-90 exit 408. 406/322-4588.

⊞ **Super 8/Townhouse Inn**—72 rooms, pets, weight room, hot

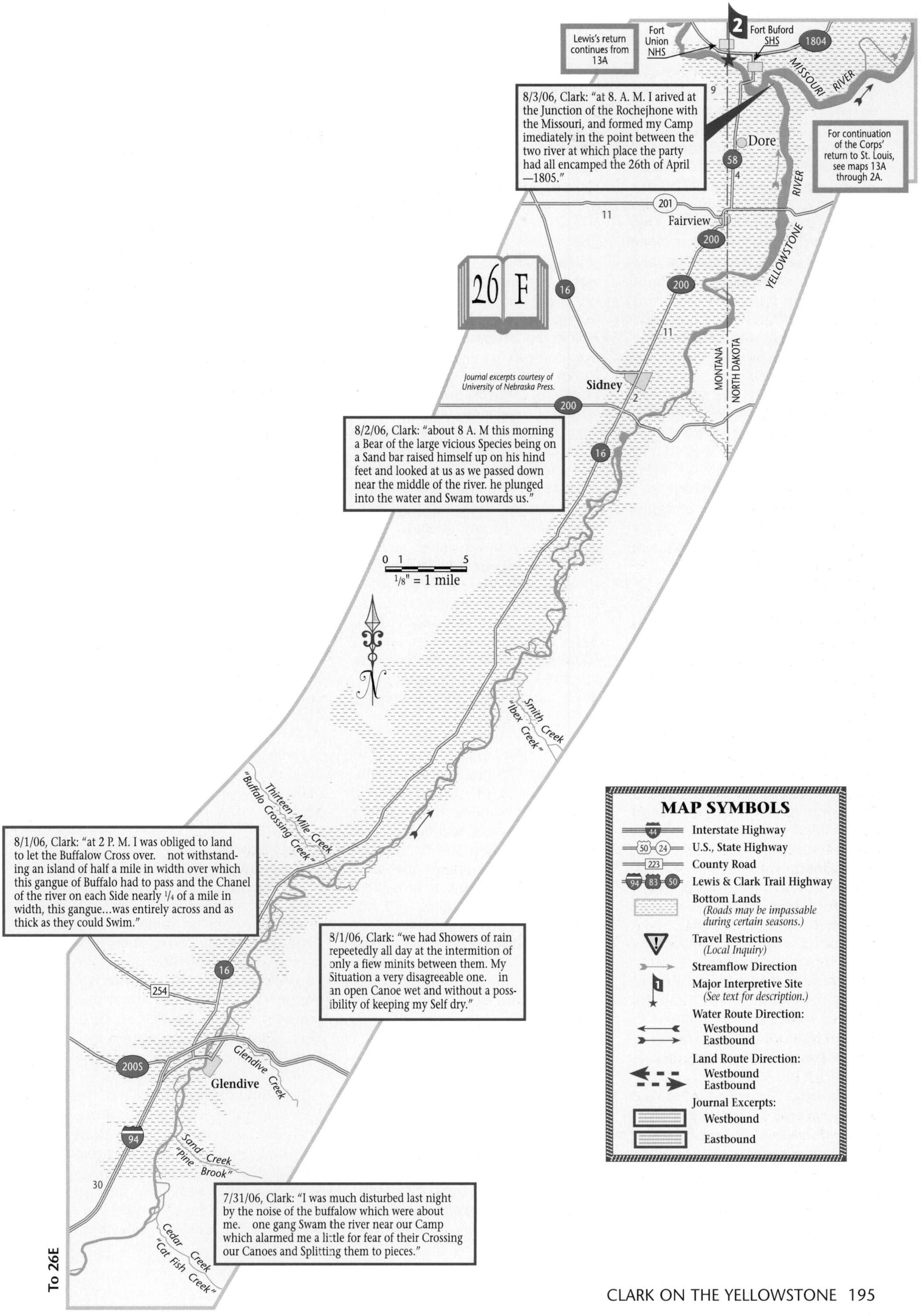
To 12C
Lewis's return continues from 13A
Fort Union NHS
2
Fort Buford SHS
1804
MISSOURI RIVER
8/3/06, Clark: "at 8. A. M. I arived at the Junction of the Rochejhone with the Missouri, and formed my Camp imediately in the point between the two river at which place the party had all encamped the 26th of April —1805."
9
Dore
58
4
For continuation of the Corps' return to St. Louis, see maps 13A through 2A.
RIVER
201
11
Fairview
200
YELLOWSTONE
26 F
16
200
11
MONTANA
NORTH DAKOTA
Journal excerpts courtesy of University of Nebraska Press.
Sidney
2
200
8/2/06, Clark: "about 8 A. M this morning a Bear of the large vicious Species being on a Sand bar raised himself up on his hind feet and looked at us as we passed down near the middle of the river. he plunged into the water and Swam towards us."
16
0 1 5
1/8" = 1 mile
N
Smith Creek
"Ibex Creek"
Thirteen Mile Creek
"Buffalo Crossing Creek"
8/1/06, Clark: "at 2 P. M. I was obliged to land to let the Buffalow Cross over. not withstanding an island of half a mile in width over which this gangue of Buffalo had to pass and the Chanel of the river on each Side nearly 1/4 of a mile in width, this gangue...was entirely across and as thick as they could Swim."
8/1/06, Clark: "we had Showers of rain repeetedly all day at the intermition of only a fiew minits between them. My Situation a very disagreeable one. in an open Canoe wet and without a possibility of keeping my Self dry."
16
254
200S
Glendive
Glendive Creek
94
Sand Creek
"Pine Brook"
30
7/31/06, Clark: "I was much disturbed last night by the noise of the buffalow which were about me. one gang Swam the river near our Camp which alarmed me a litle for fear of their Crossing our Canoes and Splitting them to pieces."
Cedar Creek
"Cat Fish Creek"
To 26E
MAP SYMBOLS
44 Interstate Highway
50 24 U.S., State Highway
223 County Road
94 83 50 Lewis & Clark Trail Highway
Bottom Lands (Roads may be impassable during certain seasons.)
! Travel Restrictions (Local Inquiry)
Streamflow Direction
Major Interpretive Site (See text for description.)
Water Route Direction: Westbound Eastbound
Land Route Direction: Westbound Eastbound
Journal Excerpts: Westbound Eastbound

tub. Rooms with a kitchen are only $5 more. I-90 exit 408. 406/322-4101. $$ K12

Crow Agency, Montana
Little Bighorn Battlefield National Monument—In a climactic confrontation, the Sioux and Cheyenne combined to annihilate U.S. Army troops led by Lieutenant Colonel George Custer. Interpretive programs, a museum, guided bus tours and a driving tour of the battlefield bring the desperation of both sides to life. Originally dedicated as a memorial to the soldiers, the site now recognizes the courage and conviction exhibited by the warriors as well. The museum and programs are entertaining and informative, even for preschoolers. Shaded lawn bordering the cemetery is a pleasant spot to spread a blanket for a picnic. Open all year with programs in the summer only; admission fee. I-90, exit 510 at Crow Agency, E on U.S. 212. 406/638-2621.

Forsyth, Montana
⊞ **Sundowner Inn**—40 rooms, pets, coin laundry, refrigerators. I-94 exit 95. 406/356-2115. $$ K12

Glendive, Montana
Glendive Chamber of Commerce, 313 N. Merrill. 406/365-5601, 800/859-0824.
Frontier Gateway Museum—Seven historical buildings and antique fire engines. Stroll through early Glendive, visit the one-room schoolhouse and see the murder trial exhibit. Mon-Sat 9 to 12 & 1 to 5, Sun 1 to 5 (summer); free. 1 mile E of I-94, exit 215 on Belle Prairie Rd. 406/365-8168.
Klapmeier Agate Collection—A distinctive collection of moss agates. It's hard to believe the intricate landscape scenes on the smooth rock slices are painted by Mother Nature. In the lobby of Best Western Jordan Inn, 222 N. Kendrick 406/365-5655.
• **Makoshika State Park**—Fossils of many species of dinosaurs have been discovered here, including tyrannosaurus rex and triceratops. Visitor center with trail guides, interpretive exhibits, interactive exhibits and videos. Picnic areas, scenic overlooks and hiking trails. The

roads here are steep and not all of them are paved. As in other areas of eastern Montana, the clay roads and trails of Makoshika become treacherous and impassable when wet. Take threatening weather seriously and return to the paved roads and campground before you are stranded. Look out for rattlesnakes and always carry water (whether driving or hiking). ▲ 16 sites; fee; water; primitive; open all year/full operation May-Sept; grills/fire rings; tables. 0.25 mile SE on Snyder Ave. Follow the dinosaur footprint signs. 406/365-6256.
Paddlefish—If you've never seen a paddlefish, check out the Chamber of Commerce office. For an even better look, it's worth a trip to Intake FAS, 16 miles N on Hwy. 16 during the snagging season (mid-May to June 30) to watch anglers pursue these unusual fish. Also one of the best places around to search for moss agates.
⊞ **Best Western Jordan Inn**—95 rooms, pool, pets, ⊗ restaurants, coin laundry. Off-season rates. 223 N. Merrill. 406/365-5655, 800/528-1234. $$ K12
⊞ **Days Inn**—59 rooms, continental breakfast. Off-season rates. 2000 N. Merrill. 406/365-6011, 800/329-7466. $ K12

Hardin, Montana
Big Horn County Historical Museum—Take a picnic and settle in on the grounds of this outdoor museum. Various buildings have been moved here and restored to tell the story of life in the area. Daily 8 to 8, (summer), Tues-Sat 9 to 5 (rest of year); free. I-90 exit 497. 406/665-1671.
▲ **Grandview**—80 sites (60 w/hookups); fee; water; modern; showers; open all year; grills/fire rings; tables. Coin laundry. I-90 exit 495, 3/4 miles S on MT 313. 406/665-2489.
▲ **KOA**—73 sites (30 w/hookups); fee; water; modern; showers; open Apr-Sept; grills/fire rings; tables. Pool; ⊞ cabins; playground; hot tub; coin laundry; dump station. I-90 exit 495, 1 mile N on MT 47. 406/665-1635.
⊞ **The American Inn**—42 rooms, pool/&, continental breakfast, playground, hot tub, exercise

room, coin laundry. Off-season rates. 1324 N. Crawford. 406/665-1870. $$ K12

Miles City, Montana
Miles City Chamber of Commerce, 901 Main. 406/232-2890.
Custer County Art Center—Rotating exhibits of local and regional artists. Overlooks the Yellowstone River. Tue-Sun 1 to 5; free. Water Plant Rd. 406/232-0635.
Range Riders Museum—"Miles Town" replica, hat and gun collections, dioramas, and a gallery of 200 Charles M. Russell prints. Daily 8 to 8 (Apr-Oct); admission fee. West end of Main Street 406/232-4483.
▲ **Miles City KOA**—90 sites (60 w/hookups); fee; water; modern; showers; open Apr-Oct; grills/fire rings; tables. Fishing; pool; ⊞ cabins; playground; groceries; coin laundry; dump station. I-94 exit 135, follow signs. 406/232-3991.
⊞ **Best Western War Bonnet Inn**—54 rooms, pool, pets, hot tub. Off-season rates. 1015 S. Haynes. 406/232-4560, 800/528-1234. $$ K12
⊞ **Comfort Inn**—49 rooms, pool, hot tub, continental breakfast, coin laundry. 1615 S. Haynes. 406/232-3141, 800/228-5150. $$ K15
⊗ **Hole in the Wall**—Beef and great desserts; kids' menu. B L & D daily. 602 Main St. 406/232-9887. $$

Pryor, Montana
Chief Plenty Coups State Park—Plenty Coups, chief of the Crow Tribe, was selected in 1921 to represent all American Indians at the dedication of the Tomb of the Unknown Soldier at Arlington National Cemetery. He laid his war bonnet and coup stick there and prayed for "peace to all men hereafter." His home is preserved as a Crow Tribe interpretive site along with a museum that contains exhibits on his life and the role of the Crows in the Lewis and Clark Expedition, and the confrontations at Little Bighorn and Rosebud battlefields. Picnic area. Daily sunrise to sunset (May-Sept), museum 9 to 5; admission fee. 12 miles E of Billings on MT 384, 23 miles S on

county road to Pryor, 1 mile W on county road. 406/252-1289 (summer), 406/247-2940 (winter).

Shepherd, Montana

Shepherd Ah-Nei—Nature trail loop and several other trails at environmental education center. Daily sunrise to sunset; free. 2 miles N on Shepherd Rd., 2.5 miles E on Scandia Rd., 6 miles N on C.A. Road. 406/657-6262.

Sidney, Montana

Mon-Dak Heritage Center—17 buildings recreate a pioneer street scene. Extensive exhibits. Daily 10 to noon, 1 to 5 (June-Labor Day); admission fee. 120 Third Ave SE. 406/482-3500.

Terry, Montana

Prairie County Museum—Thousands of photographs on display including the touching collection of prints by Evelyn Cameron, who came with her husband to Montana from England in the 1880s. She traveled across the open ranges on horseback with her large-format Graflex camera to photograph the life and culture of early Montanans. Mon, Wed-Fri, 9 to 3, Sat-Sun 1 to 4 (Memorial Day-Labor Day); donations. 105 Logan. 406/637-5442.

Wibaux, Montana

Wibaux Chamber of Commerce, P.O. Box 159, Wibaux, MT 406/795-2412.

Centennial Car Museum—Used to exhibit promotional materials about Montana's territorial centennial during the 1964 New York World's Fair, this railroad car now shelters some out-of-the-ordinary homesteader and Indian memorabilia. Daily 9:30 to 5:30 (Memorial Day to Labor Day); free. Just E of the County Museum. 406/795-2289.

Gateway Museum—Heidt home is a private museum containing fossils and Indian artifacts and a delightful garden. Daily 10 to 4; free. 310 Beaver St. 406/795-8207.

Pierre Wibaux Museum Complex—Formerly an office and town house for rancher Pierre Wibaux, this building has been restored to its original condition and decorated to reflect life in the 1890s. Daily 9 to 5 (summer). On Wibaux St. 406/796-9969.

⊞ **Super 8**—35 rooms, pets, playground. I-94 exit 241W/242E. 406/795-2666. $

CHAPTER 27

August 13 to September 26, 1806
BACK TO THE U' STATES

Joined by trappers Joseph Dickson and Forrest Hancock (who had changed their minds and turned back downstream), the Corps of Discovery traveled, by their estimate, eighty-six miles down the Missouri River on August 13, and the next day reached the Mandan villages in today's North Dakota for a happy reunion. They stayed until the 17th. After much persuading by Captains Meriwether Lewis and William Clark, Mandan Chief Sheheke agreed to accompany them to Washington, D.C.—provided they took his wife and son, and also interpreter René Jusseaume's wife and son.

Private John Colter requested an early discharge, to stay in the Rockies and trap with Dickson and Hancock. The captains agreed, as long as all the other men promised to return to St. Louis. They did, wished Colter every success, and gave him "usefull" gifts. The Corps no longer needed Toussaint Charbonneau and Sacagawea as interpreters, and paid them the agreed-upon $500.33⅓ for Toussaint's work. Clark offered to raise their son Jean Baptiste—"Pompy"—"a butifull promising Child" now nineteen months old. The parents said that in another year he could leave his mother, and then they would send him to Clark.

When the Corps set off on August 17, they paused for a few moments at "the old works"—Fort Mandan—most of which had burned in the interim. Unfortunately, no one wrote what he was thinking—about all they had seen and done since leaving here.

Traveling downstream was fast, except when they were stopped by high winds or the need to hunt. Most days the party moved between forty and eighty miles.

Clark didn't write about Lewis's recovery from his gunshot (see Chapter 24) until he walked for the first time, on August 22. Then "recovering fast," five days later Lewis overdid and was worse for a week. By September 9, though, he could run almost as well as before the wound.

Entering what they considered hostile country—in today's South Dakota—on August 20, the men were especially alert. Besides the Corps' own troubles with the Sioux on the way upriver (see Chapter 9), the Sioux now were at war with the Mandans. And, they had gotten the Arikaras to join with them, despite the treaty the captains arranged in 1804 (see Chapter 11).

Reaching the Arikara villages above the Grand River, the Corps held councils. All was friendly, but Chief Sheheke stuck close to Clark's side. After two days, the Mandans and the Arikaras agreed to peace again, blaming the Sioux for starting it all.

On August 25, after passing the mouth of the Cheyenne River, Clark noted signs of the "Troubleson Tetons" (see Chapter 9). But they turned their attention to unfinished scientific duties. They had no specimens of the mule deer, pronghorn, or prairie dog. Hunters had to go out looking for these, separate from the food hunters.

The desired specimen animals were hard to find, but this was still bison country and so food was plentiful. On August 29, below today's Chamberlain and Oacoma, South Dakota, Clark ascended a small hill and saw "near 20,000 of those animals feeding on this plain." It was "a greater number of buffalow than I had ever Seen before at one time."

The next day, Private Joseph Field was hunting ashore when the Corps moved on, so the captains left privates Reubin Field and George Shannon with a canoe to await him. When the main group stopped for the three to catch up "at the place appointed," Clark was concerned to see men on horseback in the distance. Still, he sent two men to a prairie dog town to kill specimens.

On the opposite bank, Clark saw twenty

more Indians and then "80 or 90 Indian men all armed...Came out of a wood."

But they fired their guns in a friendly salute, which Clark returned. Still suspicious, he and three Frenchmen canoed to a sandbar, where they were met by three young Teton men of Black Buffalo's band, which had harassed the Corps two years before. Clark told them how angry he was that they had been "deef to our councils and ill treated us...two years past" and didn't want to join them in council.

The Corps had to wait for the three hunters coming downriver, and when they arrived at 6 p.m.—Joseph Field having gotten three mule deer—the expedition set off and traveled six more miles, the Tetons taunting them as they left.

They covered seventy miles the next day, but wind and rain made for a restless night. On September 1, with the Field brothers and Shannon left behind to hunt on Pawnee Island between South Dakota and Nebraska, the Corps passed Indians who failed to answer their greeting.

Clark pulled the canoes over, waiting for the three hunters. Then they heard gunshots. Lewis and some men formed a defensive group at the canoes, while Clark and the others ran back to rescue the hunters. But the Indians turned out to be friendly Yanktons, simply target-shooting at an empty keg someone had pitched out of one of the canoes!

Two days later the Corps met two trading boats headed upriver, and camped with their crews below the mouth of the Vermillion River. Scotsman James Aird shared news from the U' States.

our first enquirey was after the President...and then our friends and the State of the politics...and the State [of] Indian affairs...[he] gave us as Satisfactory information as he had it in his power to have Collected...which was not a great deel.

Not when you've been away two years. During a thunderstorm that night, Clark stayed up with Aird and learned more news, including that Vice President Aaron Burr had killed former Secretary of the Treasury Alexander Hamilton in a duel more than two years before.

At noon the next day, September 4, the Corps stopped to pay respects at Sergeant Charles Floyd's grave near today's Sioux City, Iowa (see Chapter 7), found it partially opened, and reclosed it.

They would meet several other boats headed upriver for a winter of fur trading or trapping. All these traders shared their food, and some of the Corps exchanged their leather shirts for linen ones. On the 6th, at today's Little Sioux Delta Park, Harrison County, Iowa, they met a boat owned by René Auguste Chouteau, one of their suppliers two years before. The captains obtained "the first Spiritious liccor which has been tasted...Since the 4 of July 1805," promising to pay Chouteau when they reached St. Louis. (Chouteau would refuse their money.) On September 10, French traders told them that two months earlier Zebulon Pike had set out up the Arkansas River with plans to return down the Red River. He'd name Pike's Peak along the way. On the 12th, near St. Joseph, Missouri, the Corps met interpreters Joseph Gravelines and Pierre Dorion, Sr., who had helped them during the winter at Fort Mandan.

In camp on Leavenworth Island at today's Leavenworth, Kansas, on September 14, "our party received a dram [of the recently purchased liquor] and Sung Songs untill 11 oClock at night in the greatest harmoney."

On the 15th, in what would now be northside Kansas City, Missouri, the captains climbed a hill "which appeared to have a Commanding Situation for a fort."

Twice, the Corps of Discovery heard they had been given up for dead. In the party with Gravelines and Dorion was Robert McClellan, whom both captains knew from the army. Sergeant John Ordway's journal noted that McClellan said "the people in general in the united States were concerned about us as they had heard that we were all killed" or captured and enslaved by the Spanish.

On the 17th, they met a former army captain, John McClallen, who knew Lewis. Clark wrote:

...this gentleman...was Somewhat astonished to See us return and appeared rejoiced to meet us....we had been long Since given out by the people of the U S Generally and almost forgotton, the President of the U. States had yet hopes of us.

But some cows grazing along the Missouri shore on September 20 found out these men were very much alive. Seeing these humble creatures after so long "Caused a Shout to be raised for joy."

And, in a short while, when they arrived at

the village of La Charette, the men asked permission to fire their guns "which was alowed & they discharged 3 rounds with a harty Cheer, which was returned."

They were welcomed cordially, but of course with astonishment at their survival. The next day, when St. Charles came into view, the men rowed furiously downstream toward it. The day was Sunday, so residents were strolling on the riverbank. They, too, received a gun salute from the Corps. That night, citizens invited the men to sleep in their homes, where they happily waited out a morning rainstorm before setting out on the 22nd.

This day brought them to Fort Bellefontaine, the first U.S. military fort west of the Mississippi, built since the Corps had passed the spot in May of 1804. Its artillery company honored their returning army comrades with a salute of seventeen cannon rounds.

The next day, September 23, Clark could write these welcome words: ...*descended to the Mississippi and down that river to St. Louis at which place we arived about 12 oClock. we Suffered the party to fire off their pieces as a Salute to the Town.*

Whatever excitement he may have felt on a safe return, the laconic Clark began his journal of the 24th: "I sleped but little last night..."

The next day they dried out animal skins and stored them in a Chouteau fur company warehouse, and attended a ball in the evening.

The complete final entry in Clark's journal—in his usual understatement—for Friday, September 26, 1806, is:

a fine morning   we commenced wrighting &c.

These "wrightings" were to President Jefferson, family, friends, and newspapers, to spread the word of the expedition's successful return. (And, Clark sent his still-offensive lieutenant's commission to Secretary of War Henry Dearborn, with the briefest possible note that it had "answered the purpose for which it was intended.") Traveling via horse and boat, Lewis's first report to Jefferson reached the President's House in Washington in a month. Along with a summary of the trip after Fort Mandan, native nations met, and trading possibilities, it tantalizingly mentioned animal specimens he was bringing. Even in this first report, Lewis urged that Clark be named captain in rank and pay.

The captains sold leftover gear—from rifles to tomahawks to the surviving "kittles"—at auction, collecting a bit over $400 towards the trip's costs. Good for the federal treasury, but sad for historians and museum-goers ever since.

Resting and attending events in their honor, the captains stayed in St. Louis six weeks before continuing homeward. Sergeants Patrick Gass and John Ordway, and privates Francoise Labiche and Robert Frazer, turned east as escorts for Sheheke and his party. Each settlement they passed had to honor the heroes; Louisville across the Ohio River from Clark's home held a banquet and ball. From Frankfort, Kentucky, Clark headed to Fincastle, Virginia, to visit friends and to court Julia Hancock, for whom he had named a western river. Lewis, with the Sheheke group, reached his own home at Locust Hill in mid-December.

Only two weeks later, Lewis was back in Washington, where he personally but fruitlessly lobbied Secretary Dearborn for Clark's captaincy. Lewis asked for extra pay to the most valued men: gunsmith John Shields, Joseph and Reubin Field, Labiche, and civilian George Drouillard. Congress promptly passed a bill doubling the army pay for the men, and granting them all—including Corporal Richard Warfington and once-mutinous Private John Newman of the return party, and civilians Drouillard and Charbonneau—free land in the West. Clark was given as much land as Lewis, but his pay remained a lieutenant's.

Clark did not reach the capital until late January, after the welcoming ball was over. The following month, Jefferson made appointments that further rewarded the two, naming Lewis governor of Louisiana Territory and Clark its superintendent of Indian affairs—and *general* of its militia. Clark collected the enlisted men's land papers and headed west, to be married on the way to St. Louis.

Lewis spent the summer of 1807 in Philadelphia arranging for scientists to help prepare the journals for publication, and enjoying his fame. Finally, in August, President Jefferson wrote to remind Lewis that he must go to St. Louis and assume his post.

Lewis arrived to share the house that Clark rented according to an agreement the men had made before Clark's wedding, but the arrangement did not last for long. Still the co-captain in spirit, Lewis also announced that Clark would be in charge of government if he himself had to be absent. Besides ignoring the law, this further insulted Territorial Secretary Frederick Bates, whose position equalled that of lieutenant governor. Bates held different views from Lewis's on all sorts of procedures and policies, and now this! As Clark wrote, there was never "an honester man in Louisiana" than Lewis. A good take-charge army officer, Lewis lacked political savvy.

Also in 1807, Sergeant, now Ensign Nathaniel Pryor led the first attempt to return Sheheke, Jussaume, and their group home to the Mandan villages. It ended in a battle with Arikaras that killed three army men and wounded eight. Among the latter was Private George Shannon, who lost a leg from his injury.

Meanwhile, Lewis and Clark partnered with some St. Louis fur men hoping to create a profitable Upper Missouri fur company. In 1808, it seemed practical to send their well equipped first group of traders upriver as part of the second army escort home for Sheheke. Mixing government and private business was not unusual for the time and the place. But the offended Secretary Bates tried to make political hay from Lewis's move. As historian Donald Jackson has written about Lewis as governor "made some doubtful decisions, encountered opposition, and found a bitter and influential enemy in Frederick Bates."

Back in the nation's capital, by spring 1809 Thomas Jefferson was no longer president. The new government was looking into how an expedition with a budget of $2,500 ended up costing $40,000 (including that land and extra pay Congress had voted).

Lewis decided to take all the papers, including the journals, to show Congress just where the money went. As Lewis set out, Clark was concerned about whether the "weight of his [Lewis's] mind" would overcome his partner. Lewis was in bad shape from illnesses, heavy drinking, and possibly his lifelong tendency towards depression. Along the Natchez Trace, on October 11, Lewis apparently took his own life. He died, as his mentor Thomas Jefferson would fourteen years later, heavily in debt.

Clark lived nearly another three decades. He served as Missouri's last territorial governor from 1813 to 1820, but failed to win election as first state governor.

Lewis's trunk of papers was delivered to Monticello, where Clark retrieved the journals in 1810 to take to Philadelphia. Clark and George Shannon worked on them, but the main editor was a rich young lawyer named Nicholas Biddle. With one interruption after another—including the War of 1812—the journals took longer to get into print than the expedition itself had taken. Finally released in 1814, they were a commercial failure.

But the expedition "exploring the interior of the continent of North America, or that part of it bordering on the Missourie & Columbia Rivers," as Lewis wrote in 1803 when inviting Clark along, had not been.

Touring information for this section is included in Chapters 2 through 11.

CHAPTER 28

1806-1870

AFTER THE JOURNEY

Congress voted that enlisted veterans of the expedition be granted 320 acres of land. Privates were paid $5 per month; interpreters $25 a month, (lieutenant) Clark $30 and (captain) Lewis $40.

Most members of the Corps led average lives after their great journey. William Clark kept in touch with some, and in the 1820s recorded what he knew of them. About one fifth of the men returned to the Upper Missouri, working in the fur trade and living about as they had during the expedition.

Following are summaries of their later lives, based on information in various volumes of *The Journals of the Lewis and Clark Expedition*, edited by Gary E. Moulton (University of Nebraska Press); see For Further Exploration section. Death dates are given where known.

Bratton, William. Private. Lived in the settled "West" of his time: Kentucky, Missouri, Ohio, and Indiana. He served in the War of 1812, and died in 1841.

Charbonneau, Jean Baptiste. Twenty-nine months old when his family returned home to the Mandan-Hidatsa villages. His parents accepted Clark's offer to educate him (and his sister Lizette), and he moved into Clark's St. Louis home when he was six. At eighteen, he went to Europe for six years with Prince Paul of Wurttemburg, an early tourist of the American West. Returning to the U.S., Jean Baptiste became a mountain man and fur trader, and a guide whose clients included John C. Frémont. He later settled in California, and died in Oregon, en route to Montana, in 1866.

Charbonneau, Toussaint. Civilian interpreter. About forty-seve in 1805, he was the oldest person on the expedition. A French Canadian, he had lived among the Hidatsas for years before the Corps hired him as interpreter. He worked for trader Manuel Lisa, and Clark—as Superintendent of Indian Affairs—

employed him as an interpreter until Clark's own death. He may have lived to the 1830s.

Clark, William. Co-captain (officially, second lieutenant until posthumously promoted to captain, by Congress, in November 2000). Governor of Missouri Territory 1813-1820, he failed to be elected the first Missouri state governor in 1820. From 1813 to his death in 1838, he was in charge of Indian affairs west of the Mississippi, and was based in St. Louis. Because of the red-haired Clark's importance to them, many Indian people called that city "The Red Head's Town." As an Indian agent, he was compassionate and fair.

Collins, John. Private. Became a trapper for William Ashley, and was one of more than 12 of Ashley's men killed by Arikaras in 1823.

Colter, John. Private. Stayed in the Rockies as a trapper for four years. He became the first white to report on the geysers and bubbling mudpots of what became Yellowstone National Park—but people thought his descriptions mere tall tales. Colter married and settled in Missouri; illness claimed him in 1813.

Cruzatte, Pierre. Private. Enlisted interpreter. Clark thought the one-eyed fiddle player was dead by 1825-1828.

Drouillard, George. Civilian interpreter. Partnered with fur trader Manuel Lisa, and helped build a trading post at the Three Forks, where he was killed by Blackfeet in 1810.

Field, Joseph. Private. Brother of Reubin. Clark thought him killed in 1807.

Field, Reubin. Private. Lived in Kentucky until his death in 1823.

Frazer, Robert. Private. Settled in Missouri and died in 1837.

Gass, Patrick. Sergeant. A career soldier who had enlisted in 1799, he lost an eye in the War of 1812 and was discharged from the army. He settled in West Virginia and lived until 1870, the Corps of Discovery's last survivor.

Gibson, George. Private. Died in St. Louis in 1809.

Goodrich, Silas. Private. Stayed in the army after the expedition.

Hall, Hugh. Private. Known to be in St. Louis in 1809, when Lewis lent him money.

Howard, Thomas Proctor. Private. In trouble at Camp Dubois for "never drink[ing] water" (Clark), he was court-martialled at Fort Mandan for climbing the fence after hours. He had been AWOL, and had shown neighbors and visitors how to breach fort security. But the sentence of fifty lashes was cancelled, and he stayed with the permanent party.

Labiche, Francois. Private. Enlisted interpreter. Settled in the St. Louis area.

Lepage, Jean Baptiste. Private. Enlisted at Fort Mandan and replaced John Newman in the permanent party, but never stood out.

Lewis, Meriwether. Captain. Named governor of Louisiana Territory, the Louisiana Purchase lands beyond the northern border of today's state of Louisiana. Buried near Hohenwald, Tennessee, sixty miles south of Nashville along the Natchez Trace.

McNeal, Hugh. Private. May have been in the army until 1811. Clark thought him dead by 1825-1828.

Ordway, John. Sergeant. After visiting his home state of New Hampshire, settled in Missouri. Was dead by 1817.

Potts, John. Private. Became a fur trapper, and was killed by Blackfeet at the Three Forks in 1808, when partner John Colter escaped.

Pryor, Nathaniel. Sergeant. Continued in the army as an officer, resigning in 1810 and rejoining in 1813. After the War of 1812 (where he was in the Battle of New Orleans), Pryor traded on the Arkansas River and married an Osage woman. He lived with the Osages until his death in 1831. Montana's Pryor Mountains and the towns of Pryor, Montana, and Pryor, Oklahoma, are named for him.

Sacagawea (also Sacajawea, Sakakawea). Civilian interpreter. Little is known about this Shoshone woman who was born around 1788. She was about twelve when Hidatsa raiders captured her at the Three Forks and took her to their North Dakota villages. Charbonneau made her his second wife around 1804. She probably died in 1812 at Fort Manuel near today's Mobridge, South Dakota.

Shannon, George. Private. The youngest enlisted member of the Corps, just eighteen in 1803. Congress voted him a pension after he lost a leg while escorting Shekehe home. He became a lawyer in Kentucky, and later was active in Missouri politics. He died in 1836.

Shields, John. Private. Born in 1769, Shields was the oldest enlisted member of the Corps. Joined relative Daniel Boone trapping in Missouri, then settled in Indiana. Died in 1809.

Thompson, John B. Private. Clark thought him "killed" by 1825-1828.

Weiser, Peter M. Private. Became a trader for Manuel Lisa on the Yellowstone and Missouri. Clark thought him killed by 1825-1828; maybe by the Blackfeet at Three Forks post in 1810, with Drouillard and others.

Werner, William. Private. Clark thought he settled in Virginia.

Whitehouse, Joseph. Private. Often the Corps' tailor. He rejoined the army, served in the War of 1812, and deserted five years later.

Willard, Alexander Hamilton. Private. Worked as a government blacksmith for the Sauk and Fox Indians (hired by Lewis) and later the Delawares and Shawnees. He, his wife, and 12 children, emigrated to California in 1852. Died near Sacramento in 1865.

Windsor, Richard. Private. Later lived in Missouri and Illinois.

York. Civilian. No other name appears for this man, William Clark's slave who was raised with him. A big man and good hunter, he carried a rifle and often went out alone during the trip—not legal privileges for a slave back in Virginia. He was freed by 1811 and ran a wagon freight company in Tennessee and Kentucky that failed by 1832. On his way to Clark in St. Louis, he died of cholera.

Corporal Richard Warfington agreed to winter at Fort Mandan to command the keelboat's return party, spring 1805, even though his army enlistment ended in August 1804. Nothing further is known of him.

The return party included privates **John Dame, John Boley** (who joined the Zebulon Pike expedition in 1806, heading west just as the Corps of Discovery was returning home), **Ebenezer Tuttle,** and **Isaac White.** Former privates **Moses B. Reed,** expelled for desertion, and **John Newman,** drummed out for mutinous talk, traveled back with them.

FOR FURTHER EXPLORATION

Thousands of titles are available in bookstores and libraries for those who want to learn more about the Corps of Discovery, the Indian nations they met, and what the Corps' journals taught other European-Americans. To begin your own exploration, consider these sources.

General Interest

Stephen E. Ambrose, *Undaunted Courage: Meriwether Lewis, Thomas Jefferson, and the Opening of the American West.* (New York: Simon & Schuster, 1996; paper, 1997).

Roy E. Appleman, *Lewis and Clark: Historic Places Associated with their Transcontinental Exploration. (1804-06).* (Washington, D.C.: United States Department of the Interior, National Park Service, 1993).

Gunther Barth, ed., *The Lewis and Clark Expedition: Selections from the Journals Arranged by Topic.* (Boston: Bedford/St. Martin's, 1998)

Frank Bergon, ed., *The Journals of Lewis and Clark.* (New York: Penguin Books, 1989).

Robert B. Betts, *In Search of York: The Slave Who Went to the Pacific with Lewis and Clark.* (Revised Edition, Boulder: Colorado Associated University Press, 2000)

Seamus Cavan, *Lewis and Clark and the Route to the Pacific.* (New York: Chelsea House, 1991).

Paul Russell Cutright, *A History of the Lewis and Clark Journals.* Reprint, Norman: University of Oklahoma Press, 1976.

Bernard DeVoto, *The Journals of Lewis and Clark.* (Boston: Houghton Mifflin Company, 1953).

Albert Furtwangler, *Acts of Discovery: Visions of America in the Lewis and Clark Journals.* Urbana: University of Illinois Press, 1993.

Donald Jackson, *Thomas Jefferson & the Stony Mountains: Exploring the West from Monticello.* (Reprint; Norman: University of Oklahoma Press, 1993).

Landon Y. Jones, ed., *The Essential Lewis and Clark.* New York: Ecco Press, 2000.

David Lavender, *The Way to the Western Sea: Lewis and Clark Across the Continent.* (New York: Doubleday, 1988).

Gary E. Moulton, editor, and Thomas W. Dunlay, Assistant Editor. *The Journals of the Lewis & Clark Expedition.* 12 volumes. University of Nebraska Press, 1986-2000.

James P. Ronda, *Lewis and Clark Among the Indians.* (Lincoln: University of Nebraska Press, 1984).

James P. Ronda, ed., *Voyages of Discovery: Essays on the Lewis and Clark Expedition.* (Helena: Montana Historical Society Press, 1998).

Emory and Ruth Strong, *Seekimg Western Waters: The Lewis and Clark Trail from the Rockies to the Pacific.* Herbert K. Beals, ed.; Portland: Oregon Historical Society Press, 1995.

American Indians

Jan Halliday and Gail Chehak, *Native Peoples of the Northwest.* (Seattle: Sasquatch Books, 1996).

Duane Champagne, *Native America: Portrait of the Peoples.* (Detroit: Visible Ink Press, 1994).

Kate McBeth, *The Nez Perces Since Lewis and Clark.* (1908. Reprint, Moscow, Idaho: University of Idaho Press, 1993).

John C. Ewers, *Indian Life on the Upper Missouri.* (Norman: University of Oklahoma Press, 1968).

Natural History

Paul Russell Cutright, *Lewis and Clark, Pioneering Naturalists.* (1969. Reprint, Lincoln, Nebraska: Bison Books, 1989).

Raymond Darwin Burroughs, ed., *The Natural History of the Lewis and Clark Expedition.* 1961; Reprint, East Lansing: Michigan State University, 1995).

Personalities

Robert B. Betts, *In Search of York: The Slave Who Went to the Pacific with Lewis and Clark.* Revised edition, with a new epilogue by James J. Holmberg. Boulder: Colorado Associated University Press, 2000.

L. R. Colter-Frick, *Courageous Colter and Companions.* Washington, MO (1585 West 5th Street, 63090-1215), 1997.

Richard Dillon, *Meriwether Lewis: A Biography.* (New York: Coward-McCann, 1965).

Donald Jackson, *Thomas Jefferson & the Stony Mountains: Exploring the West from Monticello.* Reprint, with a foreword by James Ronda; Norman: University of Oklahoma Press, 1993.

Donna J. Kessler, *The Making of Sacagawea: A Euro-American Legend.* (Tuscaloosa: University of Alabama Press, 1996).

Carol Lynn MacGregor, *The Journals of Patrick Gass: Member of the Lewis and Clark Expedition.* Missoula, MT: Mountain Press Publishing Company, 1997.

Brigham D. Madsen, *The Lemhi: Sacajawea's People.* (Caldwell, Idaho: Caxton Printers, 1990)

French-Language Titles

La Piste de L'Ouest: Journal de la première traversée du continent nord-américain, I, 1804-1806. Édition préparée et présentée par Michel Le Bris; traduit de l'anglais par Jean (Lambert. Paris: Phébus, 1993).

Le Grand Retour: Journal de la prermière traversée du

continent nord-américain, II, 1804–1806. Édition préparé et présentée par Michel Le Bris; traduit de l'anglais par Jean Lambert. (Paris: Phébus, 1993).

World Wide Web Sites

Sites relating to Lewis and Clark continue to multiply as the expedition bicentennial approaches. Following are some of the best sites open at the time this book went to press. To supplement it, readers are referred to "Lewis and Clark on the Information Superhighway," at www.lcarchive.org

Discovering Lewis and Clark: Issues, Values and Visions. Over 1,000 pages in length, it includes an episode about Jefferson's other expedition, presented in both English and Spanish. www.lewis-clark.org

The Ethnography of Lewis and Clark: Native American Objects and the American Quest for Commerce and Science, by Rubie S. Watson and Castle McLaughlin. www.peabody.harvard.edu/Lewis&Clark/

Exploring the West from Monticello. Chapter 4: www.lib.virginia.edu/exhibits/ lewis_clark/home.html

Firearms of the Lewis & Clark Expedition. www.education.wsu.edu/vpds/lcexpedition/ resources/firearms

"The Journey of the Corps of Discovery." www.pbs.org/lewisandclark

Jefferson National Expansion Memorial. www.nps.gov/jeff/

Lewis and Clark: The Journey of the Corps of Discovery. www.pbs.org/lewisandclark

Lewis and Clark National Historic Trail home page. www.nps.gov/lecl/

Lewis and Clark Trail Heritage Foundation: www.lewisandclark.org/

"The National Lewis and Clark Bicentennial Council" www.lewisandclark200.org

Monticello, Home of Thomas Jefferson. www.monticello.org

Organizations

Lewis and Clark Trail Heritage Foundation, P.O. Box 3434, Great Falls, MT 59403. E-mail: discovery@lewisandclark.org. National headquarters of organization for those interested in ongoing discussions and discoveries, welcoming aficionados and professional historians. Annual meetings at expedition sites. Membership includes quarterly periodical, We Proceeded On. Inquire about regional chapters, nationwide.

National Lewis and Clark Bicentennial Council, Lewis and Clark College, 0615 SW Palatine Hill Rd., Portland, OR 97219. 888-999-1803. bicentennial@lewisand clark200.org. Nonprofit group planning and coordinating events for the expedition's bicentennial, 2003-2006.

National Trail Information

Lewis and Clark National Historic Trail, 1709 Jackson St., Omaha, NE 68102-2571. Administered by the National Park Service in cooperation with federal, state, and local agencies, nonprofit organizations, and private landowners.

State-by-State Trail Information

Idaho Division of Tourism, 700 W. State St., Boise, ID 83720. www.visitid.org

Illinois Department of Commerce & Community, Bureau of Tourism, 110 W. Randolph St., Suite 3-400, Chicago, IL 60601. www.enjoyillinois.com

Indiana Tourism, 1 N. Capitol Ave., Suite 700, Indianapolis, IN 46204-2288. www.indianatourism.com

Iowa Division of Tourism, 200 E. Grand Ave., Des Moines, IA 50309. www.state.ia.us/tourism

Kansas Division of Tourism, 120 W. 10th St., Topeka, KS 66612. www.kansas-travel.com

Kentucky Department of Travel, Box 2011, Frankfort, KY 40602. www.kentuckytourism.com

Missouri Division of Tourism, 301 W. High St., Jefferson City City, MO 65101. www.missouritourism.org

Montana Department of Tourism, P.O. Box 200533, Helena, MT 59620-0533. www.travelmontana.state.mt.us

Nebraska Division of Tourism, P.O. Box 94666, Lincoln, NE 68509-4666. visitnebraska.org

North Dakota Tourism Department, 604 E. Boulevard Ave., Bismarck, ND 58505. www.ndtourism.com

Ohio Division of Travel & Tourism, P.O. Box 1001, Columbus, OH 43216-1001. www.ohiotourism.com

Oregon Tourism and Travel Information, 775 Summer St. NE, Salem, OR 97310. www.traveloregon.com

Pennsylvania Office of Travel & Tourism, Forum Bldg., Room 404, Harrisburg, PA 17120. www.state.pa.us/visit

South Dakota Department of Tourism, 711 E. Wells Ave., Pierre, SD 57501. www.travelsd.com

Virginia Tourism Corporation, 901 E. Byrd St., Richmond, VA 23192. www.virginia.org

Washington Department of Tourism, 101 General Administration Bldg., AX-13, Olympia, WA 98504. www.tourism.wa.gov

Washington, DC CVA, 1212 New York Ave. NW, #600, Washington, DC 20005. www.washington.org

West Virginia Division of Tourism, 2101 Washington St. E., Charleston, WV 25305. www.state.wv.us/tourism

INDEX

St. Albans, MO 34, 36
St. Charles, MO 33, 35, 200; lodging 39; restaurants 39; RV sites 39; today 27, 36, 39
St. Charles Chamber of Commerce 39
St. Deroin, NE 53
St. Francis Xavier Church 132
St. Helena Cathedral 117
St. Joseph Museum 56
St. Joseph, MO 56; lodging 56; RV sites 56
St. Louis, MO 9-10, 21, 27, 33-34, 198; and return party 10, 33; capital of Upper Louisiana 8, 25; Clark at 26, 202; Lewis at 12, 21, 25-26, 27, 33; lodging 30-31; permanent party returns 11, 199, 200; restaurants 31; RV sites 30; today 27-28, 29-31
St. Louis Ambush 30
St. Louis Art Museum 29
St. Louis Blues 30
St. Louis Cardinals 30
St. Louis Children's Aquarium 37
St. Louis Convention and Visitors Bureau 29
St. Louis County, MO 31, 36
St. Louis Rams 30
St. Louis Science Center 29
St. Louis Walk of Fame 30
St. Louis Zoo 30
St. Mary's Mission 132
St. Mary, MT 180; restaurants 180; RV sites 180
St. Mary's, WV 17
St. Matthews, KY 22
St. Paul, OR 160; RV sites 160
St. Stanislaus Conservation Area 36
Ste. Genevieve Museum 24
Ste. Genevieve, MO 21, 23, 24
Sakakawea Monument 82
Salem Sue 85
Saline County, MO 43
Salish Indians 116, 128, 131, 171, 176, 182
Salix, IA 64, 65; RV sites 65
Salmon 169, 170; autumn run 139, 148, 153; Corps' fear of fresh 147; first-salmon ceremony 170
Salmon River 126, 128, 139
Salmon Scenic Byway 130
Salmon, ID 130, 132; lodging 132; restaurants 132; RV sites 132
Salt 162, 165, 171; making 43, 164
Salt Works 164, 165
Salt Works memorial 166-167
Sandy Creek Covered Bridge State Historic Site 38
Sandy River 157, 164
Santa Fe, NM 57
Sarpy County, NE 52
Sauvie Island Wildlife Area 157
Savannah, MO 53, 56
Scenic Park 64
Schilling Wildlife Area 53
Schram Park State Recreation Area 59
Schuylkill Arsenal 12
Sciotoville, OH 18; RV sites 18
Scott, Dred 28, 29
Seals, harbor 154
Seaman 9, 16, 50, 91, 170; injured 98; protects camp 98; stolen 169
Seaquest State Park 160
Seaside Aquarium 168
Seaside Museum and Historical Society 168
Seaside Visitors Bureau 168
Seaside, OR 164, 166-167, 168; lodging 168; restaurants 168
Seaview, WA 168; lodging 168
Sedalia, MO 42
Seeley Lake Chamber of Commerce 180
Seeley Lake, MT 180; restaurants 180; RV sites 180
Sehner-Ellicott-von Hess House 13
Seidensticker Wildlife Collection 124
Sergeant Bluff, IA 63
Sergeant Floyd Monument 64
Sergeant Floyd Riverboat Museum 64
Sergeants 9
Serviceberries 120
Shake Hand (Yankton Sioux) 67
Shannon Creek: See Fly Creek.

Shannon, George 16, 66, 118, 162, 189, 198-199; after expedition 201, 203; creek named for 191; lost in Montana 118; lost in South Dakota 67-68
C. Sharp Arms Company/Montana Armory 193
Shaw Arboretum 38
Shawnee Area Chamber of Commerce 48
Shawnee Mission Park 48
Shawnee Mission State Historic Site 44
Shawnee, KS 48
Sheep, bighorn 96, 98, 191; Indian uses of 98
Sheepshead Trail System 124
Shehekee, Chief 82, 86, 198, 200, 201
Shelby Chamber of Commerce 180
Shelby, MT 178, 180; lodging 180; RV sites 180
Shelter Insurance Gardens 37-38
Shep (statue) 105
Shepherd Ah-Nei 197
Shepherd, MT 197
Shepperd's Dell State Park 169
Sheridan, MT 125
Sherman Peak 136
Shields River 183
Shields River Valley 183
Shields, John; after expedition 200, 203; as blacksmith 27, 109; as gunsmith 26, 166; builds sauna 171; enlists 20; injured 118; kills jackrabbit 68-69; river named for 183; seeks Shannon 67; with Lewis advance party 119, 120
Ship Rock: See Monumental Rock.
Shoal Creek Missouri 46
Short Narrows of Columbia River 149
Shoshone Camp 123
Shoshone Indians 86, 118, 126, 176; and Three Forks area 115; expedition searches for 112, 114, 118, 119-120; horses from 120
Shoshoni Trail Segment 130
SHRA Railroad Museum 65
Shrine to Music Museum 74
Shubert, NE 53; RV sites 53
General Sibley Park 83
Sibley, George C. 42
Sibley, MO 41, 48
Sidney, IA 56
Sidney, MT 192, 197
Silver Lake, WA 160; RV sites 160
Sinque Hole Camp 138
Sioux City Public Museum 65
Sioux City Riverfront Trail 64
Sioux City Visitor Bureau 65
Sioux City, IA 64, 65, 199; Charles Floyd grave 63; lodging 65; restaurants 65; RV sites 65
Sioux County, ND 82
Sioux Falls Convention and Visitors Bureau 73
Sioux Falls Recreation Trail and Greenway 74
Sioux Falls, SD 73-74; lodging 74; restaurants 74; RV sites 74
Sioux Indians 50, 164, 182, 198; Teton 67, 75-77, 198, 199; Yankton 40, 66-67, 199
Sioux Passage County Park 36
Siparyann 104
Sistersville, WV 17
Sitting Bull 71, 85, 93
Sitting Bull Burial Site 85
Six Flags Kentucky Kingdom 24
Six Flags St. Louis 38
Skamokawa, WA 168; RV sites 168
Slaughter River 104
Sleeping Child Creek 128
Slippery Ann 104
Sluice Boxes State Park 110-111
Smith River 112; naming 112
Smith, Robert 112
Smith, Silas B. 166
Smithville, MO 48; RV sites 48
Smokejumper Visitor Center and Aerial Fire Depot 132
Snake River 139-141, 146, 170; today 142
Snakes 50, 72; bull 61; rattlesnakes 119, 122
Snow Creek 98
Snowy Mountains 106
Snyder Bend County Park 64
Society of Memories Doll Museum 56

Soukup and Thomas International Balloon and Airship Museum 73
South Dakota Capitol 79
South Dakota Cultural Heritage Center 78
South Dakota Discovery Center & Aquarium 79
South Dakota National Guard Museum 79
South Dakota Scenic Byway 72
South Pass 136
South Sioux City, NE 64, 65; lodging 65
Southern Indiana Chamber of Commerce 24
Southern Ohio Museum Center 20
Spain 8, 25, 27, 199
Spalding Site, Nez Perce NHP 142
Spalding, ID 139, 142
Spencer Museum of Art 47
Spirit Mound 66; today 70
Spokane Creek 112
Spring Gulch 130
Spring Meadow Lake 117
Square Butte 112
Squaw Creek National Wildlife Refuge 55, 56
Squirrel Cage Jail 59
Stafford Ferry 104
Standing Bear, Chief 60
Standing Rock 85
Standing Rock Indian Reservation 83
Stanton, MO 31; lodging 31; restaurants 31; RV sites 31
Stanton, ND 87
Star City Visitor Center 55
Starbuck, WA 142; RV sites 142
Starlight Theatre 46
Starvation Creek State Park 156
State Historical Society of Missouri 37
Steamboat Hill 22
Steckel Boat Landing 83
Steedman, MO 35
Steubenville, OH 16-17
Stevens, Isaac 131
Stevenson, WA 156, 160-161; lodging 161
Stevensville, MT 128, 130, 132-133
Stillwater River 188-189
Stoddard, Amos 33
Stone State Park 64, 65
Stonehenge 151
Harriett Beecher Stowe House 18
Strategic Air Command Museum 58
Strawberry Island 141
Strehly House 38
Stump Island Park 43
Sturgeon 165
Sugar Lake 52
Sugar Loaf Bottoms 83
Sula, MT 128, 130, 133-133; lodging 133; RV sites 133-133
Sullivan, MO 31; lodging 31; restaurants 31; RV sites 31
Sun River 107-109, 172, 173, 174
Sunset Hills, MO 31
Super Museum 24
Sutton Bay 82
Switzerland County Museum 20, 24
Swooping Eagle: See Toby.
Swope Park 46
Tableau, Pierre-Antoine 80
William Howard Taft National Historic Site 19
Taille de Noyer 30
Guy W. Talbot State Park 157
Tamastslikt Cultural Institute 151
Tavern Cave 34; today 36
Tavern Rock 34
Taylors Landing 37
Tebbetts, MO 35
Teepee Hills Natural Area 105
Tekamah, NE 63
Tendoy (ID) Store 123
Tendoy, ID 126, 128; today 130
Terry, MT 190, 192, 197
Tetoharsky, Chief 139, 141, 146, 148, 149
Teton Sioux: See Sioux Indians.
Teton Trail Village and Old Trail Museum 178
The Dalles Chamber of Commerce 152
The Dalles Dam 149, 150

About the Authors

Barbara Fifer, author of the history overviews, is Special Projects Editor for *Montana Magazine* and editor for Farcountry Press, was Associate Editor for Montana Historical Society Press, and is the author of *Going Along with Lewis and Clark*, and *Everyday U.S. Geography*.

Vicky Soderberg, author of Touring Today sections, was a newspaper sportswriter in Indiana and Illinois before turning to travel writing 10 years ago. Since then she has covered 42 states and 11 foreign countries. Her book, *Montana Family Outdoor Guide*, was published by *Montana Magazine*, and her current travel book project is the *Roadside History of Indiana*. When not traveling with her husband and three children, she also writes mysteries and teaches.

Joseph Mussulman, creator of the maps, is the producer and principal writer for a progressive Web site, Discovering Lewis and Clark, at http://www.lewis-clark.org. He has written several articles about the Lewis and Clark expedition, and is co-publisher of *Montana Afloat*, a series of interpretive maps for 16 of Montana's major floatable rivers, including the Missouri, Jefferson, Beaverhead, and Yellowstone. He has also been a musician, teacher, author, and wilderness ranger.